Using Norton Desktop for DOS

THE NORTON DESKTOP™ FOR DOS

NORTON DESKTOP FOR DOS

The software described in this book is furnished under a license agreement and may be used only in accordance with the terms of the agreement.

Copyright Notice

Copyright © 1992 Symantec Corporation.

All Rights Reserved.

Contains licensed program materials of Metagraphics Software Corporation. Copyright © 1986-1992 Metagraphics Software Corporation, Scotts Valley, CA 95066

Copyright © 1989-1992 SLR Systems Inc. All rights Reserved.

No part of this publication may be copied without the express written permission of Symantec Corporation, Peter Norton Group, 10201 Torre Avenue, Cupertino, CA 95014

Trademarks

Norton Disk Doctor, Norton Commander, Norton Utilities and UnErase are registered trademarks; and Norton Desktop, Norton AntiVirus, Norton Backup, Norton Cache, Norton Mail, Norton Menu, Diskreet, Scheduler, Sleeper, SmartCan, Speed Disk and SuperFind are trademarks of Symantec Corporation.

MCI Mail is a registered service mark of MCI Communications Corporation.

Other product names mentioned in this manual may be trademarks or registered trademarks of their respective companies and are hereby acknowledged.

Printed in the United States of America.

10 9 8 7 6 5 4 3 2 1

Credits

Development Team

Henri Isenberg, Mark Kennedy, Ed Carlin, Torsten Hoff, Doug Watkins, Kevin Flick, Basil Gabriel, Greg Hardyman, Peter Dickinson, David Hertel, John McNamee, Joe Pasquarello, Jim Frantz, Louie Tague, Barry Lulas, Jim Streater, Craig Dickson, Mani M. Manivannan and Keith Mund.

External acquisitions by Bryan Brandenburg.

Graphics provided by Dean Terry.

Product Management Team

Kraig Lane, Alicia Thompson and Lisa Gilmour.

Quality Assurance Team

Felix Rabinovich, Kader Fazlul, Bahram Navi, Dmitry Rapoport, Ken Spreitzer, Alex Beyk, George Chlentzos, Tom Burgess, Julian Rozentur, Meijen Huang, John Fawcett, Ian Colquhoun and Michel Roter.

Documentation Team

Jessica Sutton, Vickie VonBergen, Robert Hoffman, Joan Isenbarger, Karen Artan, Noel Brown, Diane Vader, Kathleen Paquette, Tom Bergantino, Lawrence Lindsey, David Walske, Renée Gentry and Mickey Reilly.

Editing and production provided by Denise Weatherwax, Mark Holcomb, Denise Link, Allen Reed, and Laura Weatherford.

Online help by Robert Hoffman and Dan Rollins.

Layout by Modern Design, Los Angeles.

Additional Acknowledgments

Kim Johnston, John Eusebi, Bob Kirwin, Augusto Polo, Brian Foster, Hector Estrada, Cameron Cotrill and Mike Heilemann.

Special thanks to the individual beta testers, whose input was invaluable. Norton Desktop for DOS would not be the same without all of their suggestions and comments.

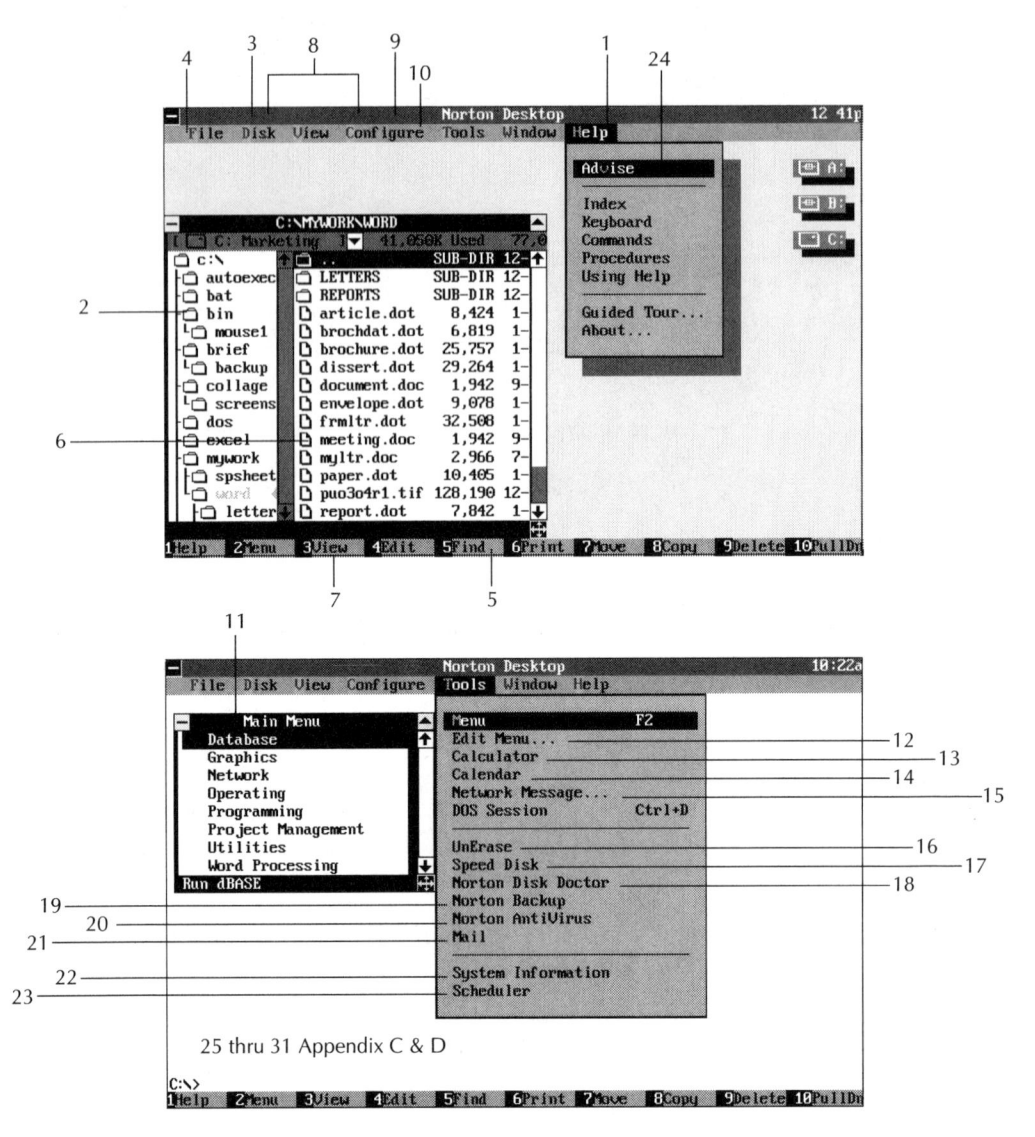

1   Ch 1—Getting Started
2   Ch 2—Using Drive Windows
3   Ch 3—Managing Disks
4   Ch 4—Managing Directories and Files
5   Ch 5—Finding Files with SuperFind
6   Ch 6—Launching Files
7   Ch 7—Viewing Files
8   Ch 8—Linking PCs
9   Ch 9—Configuring Norton Desktop
10 Ch 10—Using the Screen Saver
11 Ch 11—Using the Menu
12 Ch 12—Editing the Menu
13 Ch 13—Using the Calculator
14 Ch 14—Using the Calendar
15 Ch 15—Sending Network Messages
16 Ch 16—Using UnErase
17 Ch 17—Using Speed Disk

18 Ch 18—Using Norton Disk Doctor
19 Ch 19—Using Norton Backup
20 Ch 20—Using Norton AntiVirus
21 Ch 21—Using Norton Mail
22 Ch 22—Using System Information
23 Ch 23—Using Scheduler
24 Ch 24—Using Advise
25 Ch 25—Using Image
26 Ch 26—Using UnFormat
27 Ch 27—Using SmartCan
28 Ch 28—Using Disk Tools
29 Ch 29—Using Norton Cache
30 Ch 30—Creating Corporate Menus
31 Ch 31—Administering Corporate Menus
    App C—Command-Line Reference
    App D—Batch Enhancer Reference

iv

Contents

PART I—BEFORE YOU BEGIN
About this Manual xix

Chapter 1—Getting Started
Norton Desktop for DOS 1-3
    Starting Norton Desktop 1-3
    Exiting Norton Desktop 1-3
The Desktop at a Glance 1-4
Getting Around on the Norton Desktop 1-6
    Using the Button Bar 1-6
    Menus 1-7
    Windows 1-12
    Dialog Boxes 1-20
Before Problems Arise 1-27
    Protecting and Recovering Your Files 1-27
    Enhancing Speed and Performance 1-30
    Using Advise 1-30
Getting Help 1-30
    The Help Menu 1-31
    The Help Window 1-32

PART II—USING THE DESKTOP

Chapter 2—Using Drive Windows
Opening a Drive Window 2-3
Parts of a Drive Window 2-5
Selecting a Drive 2-6
Disk Information 2-7
Finding Directories and Files 2-7
Drive Window Panes 2-9
    Controlling the Panes 2-9

Tree Pane 2-10
File Pane 2-10
View Pane 2-11
Modifying the File Pane 2-11
    Filtering the File Listing 2-12
    Displaying File Details 2-13
    Sorting Files 2-14
    Displaying Files from the Entire Drive 2-16
Updating the Drive Window 2-17
Modifying the Drive Window 2-17
    Resizing the Drive Window 2-17
    Moving the Drive Window 2-18
Working with Multiple Drive Windows 2-18
    Selecting a Drive Window 2-19
    Cascading Open Drive Windows 2-19
    Tiling Open Drive Windows 2-20
    Hiding Drive Windows 2-21
Closing the Drive Window 2-21

Chapter 3—Managing Disks

Copying a Floppy Disk 3-3
Formatting a Floppy Disk 3-4
    Hard Disk Formatting 3-8
    Selecting Floppy Disk Types 3-9
Labeling a Disk 3-9
Making a Disk Bootable 3-10

Chapter 4—Managing Directories and Files

Directory Structures 4-3
    Making Directories 4-3
    Naming Directories and Files 4-4
Selecting Directories or Files 4-4
Using the SELECT Command 4-6
Deselecting Files 4-8
    Using the DESELECT Command 4-9

Moving and Copying Directories and Files 4-10
    Moving Directories and Files 4-10
    Using the PRUNE & GRAFT Command 4-13
    Copying Directories and Files 4-14
Deleting Directories and Files 4-17
    Using the DELETE... Command 4-17
Renaming Directories and Files 4-18
Comparing Directories 4-19
Changing File Attributes 4-20
Compressing Files 4-22
    Viewing the Contents of a Compressed File 4-24
Editing Text Files 4-25
    The Norton Desktop Editor 4-25
    Windows 4-26
    Managing Files You Edit 4-27
    Navigating in the Norton Desktop Editor 4-30
    Selecting Text 4-32
    Inserting and Deleting Text 4-33
    Searching For and Replacing Text 4-35
    Word Wrap 4-38
    Reformatting a File 4-39
    Printing Files in the Norton Desktop Editor 4-40
Printing Files from Norton Desktop 4-40

Chapter 5—Finding Files with SuperFind

Finding Files 5-3
Defining Your Search 5-3
    Searching for Multiple Files 5-6
    Creating Customized File Sets 5-7
Defining Where to Search 5-9
    Searching in Multiple Locations 5-9
    Creating Customized Location Sets 5-10
Making Searches Case-Sensitive 5-13
Creating a Batch File from Matching Files 5-14

Chapter 6—Launching Files

Associating a File 6-3
    Changing an Association 6-4
    Deleting an Association 6-4
    Adding an Association 6-5
    Specifying a Custom Startup Command 6-6
Launching a File 6-7
    Launching From the File Pane 6-7
    Launching Using the RUN... Command 6-8
    Launching From the DOS Command Line 6-9
    Launching From a DOS Session 6-10

Chapter 7—Viewing Files

Viewing a File in the View Pane 7-3
Viewing a File in Norton Viewer 7-5
    Selecting a File within Norton Viewer 7-7
    Exiting Norton Viewer 7-7
    Viewing a Single Record in a Database File 7-7
Word Wrapping Text 7-9
Changing Viewers 7-9
Searching Files 7-11
Viewing Graphic Files 7-13
Changing the Graphic Image 7-13
    Scrolling a Graphic Image 7-13
    Flipping the Graphic Image Horizontally
      or Vertically 7-14
    Zooming the Graphic Image 7-15
    Rotating the Graphic Image 7-15
    Refreshing the Screen 7-15
    Inverting the Graphic Image 7-15

Chapter 8—Linking PCs

Network Link 8-3
    Setting Up the Server 8-3
    Connecting the Client to the Server 8-5

Desktop Link 8-7
    Setting Up the Server 8-8
    Connecting the Client to the Server 8-8
Cloning Norton Desktop 8-10
Port and Cable Options 8-13

PART III—CONFIGURING THE DESKTOP

Chapter 9—Configuring Norton Desktop

Customizing Menus 9-4
    Choosing Long or Short Menus 9-4
    Customizing and Creating Pull-down Menus 9-5
    Establishing a Password 9-18
Configuring Desktop Preferences 9-20
    Configuring a Shutdown Routine 9-21
    Tagging Files in a Drive Window 9-24
    Adding Shadows to the Desktop Windows 9-24
    Scanning Floppy Drives with Norton AntiVirus 9-24
    Previewing Files During Speed Search 9-25
    Including Subdirectories in a Drag-and-Drop
        Procedure 9-25
    Selecting the Desktop Mode 9-26
    Keystroke Preference Selection 9-26
    Displaying Drive Icons on the Desktop 9-27
Configuring the Button Bar 9-28
Setting Confirmation Options 9-31
Setting the Clock 9-31
Setting Video and Mouse Options 9-32
    Selecting Screen Colors 9-33
    Configuring the Display 9-35
    Confirming Selections 9-36
    Selecting Mouse Options 9-36
Selecting the Default Editor 9-38
Configuring the Screen Saver 9-39
Configuring Network Options 9-39

Using Norton Desktop for DOS

Selecting Printer Options 9-40
Selecting File Compression Options 9-44
Configuring Desktop Link 9-46
    Choosing the Desktop Link Options 9-46
Saving Your Changes 9-49

PART IV—USING DESKTOP TOOLS

Chapter 10—Using the Screen Saver

Configuring Sleeper 10-3
    Selecting the Screen Saver Image 10-4
    Selecting Sleeper Options 10-5
    Setting Up a Password 10-8
Using Norton Utilities with Sleeper 10-8
Using Sleeper with Two Monitors 10-9

Chapter 11—Using the Menu

Why Use a Menu? 11-3
    Selecting the Menu 11-3
Creating the Menu Automatically 11-4
Creating the Menu Manually 11-4
    Customizing a DOS Program 11-8
Importing Other Menu Formats 11-8
    Testing the Menu 11-9
Using the Menu 11-9
    Selecting a Menu Item 11-10
    Moving from One Submenu to Another 11-10

Chapter 12—Editing the Menu

Adding a Menu Item 12-3
Modifying a Menu Item 12-3
Adding a Similar Menu Item 12-4
Deleting a Menu Item 12-4
Moving a Menu Item 12-4
Changing the Menu Title 12-5

Updating the Menu Automatically 12-5
Importing Other Menu Formats 12-6
Exiting Norton Menu 12-6

Chapter 13—Using the Calculator
Starting the Calculator 13-3
The Calculator Display 13-3
The Calculator Functions 13-4
Entering Calculations 13-4
Exiting the Calculator 13-5

Chapter 14—Using the Calendar
Accessing the Calendar 14-3
Changing the Displayed Date 14-3
Keeping Notes on Your Calendar 14-4
Exiting from the Calendar 14-5

Chapter 15—Sending Network Messages
Sending a Message to Network Users 15-3
Replying to a Network Message 15-5

Chapter 16—Using UnErase
How UnErase Works 16-3
Starting UnErase 16-4
Recovering Erased Files 16-4
Manual UnErase 16-7
UnErase and DOS 5.0 16-10

Chapter 17—Using Speed Disk
How Speed Disk Works 17-4
Before You Use Speed Disk 17-5
    Memory-Resident Programs 17-5
    Copy-Protected Files 17-5
Using Speed Disk 17-6
Generating Reports 17-7
    Comparing Speed Disk to CHKDSK 17-8

Using the Walk Map 17-9
Customizing Speed Disk 17-10
    Choosing an Optimization Method 17-10
    Configuring Speed Disk 17-11

Chapter 18—Using Norton Disk Doctor

The Six Disk Doctor Tests 18-3
    Partition Table Test 18-3
    Boot Record Test 18-4
    FAT Test 18-4
    Directory Structure Test 18-4
    File Structure Test 18-4
    Lost Cluster Test 18-4
    Surface Test 18-4
Using Norton Disk Doctor 18-5
    A Quick Test 18-7
Configuring Norton Disk Doctor 18-7
    Surface Test Options 18-8
    Custom Message 18-9
    Tests to Skip 18-9
Undoing Changes 18-9
Generating a Report 18-9

Chapter 19—Using Norton Backup

Quick Start 19-3
    Performing a Backup 19-3
    Backup Assistant 19-4
    The Next Step 19-5

Chapter 20—Using Norton AntiVirus

What Is a Virus? 20-3
Norton AntiVirus at a Glance 20-4
    About Virus Intercept 20-5
    About Virus Clinic 20-5
Loading Virus Intercept 20-5
    Versions of Virus Intercept 20-7

Contents **xiii**

Responding to Virus Intercept Messages 20-8
    Virus Infection Alert Box 20-8
    Boot-sector Alert Box 20-9
    Reinoculating Files 20-10
How Virus Intercept Protects Itself 20-11
How Virus Intercept Works with Other Applications 20-11
    Copying Floppy Disks and Files 20-12
    File-compression Programs 20-12
    Communications Programs 20-12
    Backup Programs 20-13
    DOS Format 20-13
    Other Types of Programs 20-13
Using Virus Clinic 20-14
    Scanning Memory 20-14
    Scanning and Inoculating Drives, Directories
        and Files 20-15
    Working with Scan Results 20-17
    Canceling a Scan 20-18
    Understanding Scan Messages 20-18
    Repairing Infected Files 20-20
    Exiting Virus Clinic 20-28
Working with Virus Definitions 20-28
    Viewing and Printing Virus Definitions 20-28
    Updating Virus Definitions 20-30
Configuring Virus Clinic 20-36
    Setting Global Options 20-37
    Setting Passwords 20-39
Configuring Virus Intercept 20-41
    Enabling and Disabling Virus Intercept
        Command Buttons 20-41
    Controlling Alert Boxes 20-42
    Logging Intercept Messages 20-42
Network Scanning 20-44
    Setting the Inoculation Directory 20-44

Chapter 21—Using Norton Mail

Starting and Exiting Norton Mail 21-3
The Folder System 21-5
Processing Mail 21-6
    Creating a Message 21-6
    Lists of Addressees 21-8
    Sending Attachments 21-12
    Adding Message and Addressee Handling 21-14
    Sending and Receiving Messages 21-16
    Reading a Message 21-19
    Replying to a Message 21-20
    Forwarding a Message 21-21
    Editing a Message 21-21
    Copying or Moving a Message Between Folders 21-22
    Printing a Message 21-23
    Deleting a Message 21-23
More About Folders 21-24
    Creating a Folder 21-24
    Opening a Folder 21-25
    Sorting Messages in a Folder 21-26
    Renaming a Folder 21-26
    Deleting a Folder 21-26
Address Book and Mail List Maintenance 21-27
    The Address Book 21-27
    Mail Lists 21-33
    Synchronizing Your Address Book and Mail Lists 21-36
Changing Folder or Mail List Locations 21-37
MCI Accounts 21-37
MCI Telephone Settings 21-41
Modem Settings 21-42
Other Setup Options 21-43
Other Types of Mail 21-45
    Fax 21-45
    Telex 21-46

| Paper Mail 21-46
| Other Electronic Mail Systems 21-46

Chapter 22—Using System Information
| Starting System Information 22-3
| System Information Reports 22-3
| System 22-3
| Disks 22-5
| Memory 22-7
| Benchmarks 22-10
| Report 22-11
| Printing Reports 22-11

Chapter 23—Using Scheduler
| Starting Scheduler 23-3
| How Scheduler Works 23-4
| Organizing Your Schedule 23-5
| Viewing Scheduled Events 23-5
| Adding Scheduled Events 23-6
| Editing Scheduled Events 23-10
| Deleting Scheduled Events 23-11
| Using Norton Utilities with Scheduler 23-12
| Closing Scheduler 23-12

PART V—STANDALONE UTILITIES

Chapter 24—Using Advise
| Types of Problems 24-3
| Getting Advice 24-3
| Understanding a Problem 24-5
| Taking Action 24-6

Chapter 25—Using Image
| How Image Works 25-3
| Taking A Snapshot 25-4

Chapter 26—Using UnFormat

How UnFormat Works 26-3
　　The Image File 26-4
Using UnFormat 26-5
　　Recovering a Disk without the Image File 26-8
　　DOS 5.0 Mirror Program 26-9

Chapter 27—Using SmartCan

How SmartCan Works 27-3
Configuring SmartCan 27-3
　　Enabling or Disabling SmartCan 27-4
　　Protecting Other Drives 27-4
　　Files to Protect 27-5
　　Archived Files 27-6
　　Storage Limits 27-6
Purging Files 27-7
Turning SmartCan On and Off 27-8

Chapter 28—Using Disk Tools

Making a Disk Bootable 28-3
Recovering from DOS's Recover 28-4
Reviving a Defective Diskette 28-5
Creating a Rescue Diskette 28-6
Restoring from a Rescue Diskette 28-7

Chapter 29—Using Norton Cache

Requirements for the Norton Cache 29-3
Using the Norton Cache 29-4
　　Cache Reports 29-4
　　Resetting the Cache 29-6
　　Deactivating the Cache 29-6
　　Removing the Cache from Memory 29-7
Configuring the Norton Cache 29-8
　　Configuration Options 29-9
　　Advanced Options 29-15

Additional Notes 29-18
    DOS BUFFERS 29-18
    DOS FASTOPEN 29-18
    Compatibility with Storage Devices 29-18
    Norton Cache and Windows 29-19
    SMARTDrive 29-19

PART VI—CORPORATE MENUS

Chapter 30—Creating Corporate Menus

Designing a Custom Work Environment 30-3
    Features 30-3
Launching Norton Menu 30-4
    Using Command-Line Options 30-4
    Switching Between Edit and Run Mode 30-4
Selecting a Menu 30-5
Exiting Norton Menu 30-5
Creating a Basic Menu 30-6
    Testing a Menu 30-9
Creating an Advanced Menu 30-9
    Creating a Program Menu 30-9
    Customizing a DOS Program 30-11
    Creating a Submenu 30-12
    Creating a Batch Menu Item 30-12
Editing Menus 30-13
    Adding a Menu Item 30-13
    Modifying a Menu Item 30-13
    Adding a Similar Menu Item 30-14
    Deleting a Menu Item 30-14
    Moving a Menu Item 30-15
    Changing the Menu Title 30-15
    Updating a Menu Automatically 30-15
    Deleting a Menu 30-16
Using Menus 30-17
    Choosing a Menu Item 30-17

Moving from One Submenu to Another 30-17
Closing a Menu 30-18

Chapter 31—Administering Corporate Menus

Setting a Password for a Menu Item 31-3
Customizing Norton Menu 31-3
   Confirm Before Deleting 31-4
   Saving Your Menus Automatically 31-4
   Securing Edit and Exit Privileges 31-5
   Assigning Hotkeys Automatically 31-6
   Sounding a Security Alert 31-7
Enabling a Screen Saver 31-7
Distributing and Maintaining Menus 31-7
   Installing for Several Users 31-8
   Using Menus on Different Computers 31-8
   Exporting a Menu 31-10
   Customizing a Menu for Another Computer 31-11
   Importing Other Menu Formats 31-11
   Updating a Menu Automatically 31-12

PART VII—REFERENCE

Appendix A—Questions and Answers A-1

Appendix B—System Messages B-1

Appendix C—Command-Line Reference C-1

Appendix D—Batch Enhancer Reference D-1

Appendix E—Norton Commander Reference E-1

Appendix F—Menu Maps F-1

Glossary G-1

Index I-1

PART I
BEFORE YOU BEGIN

ABOUT THIS MANUAL

Welcome to Norton Desktop for DOS.

This manual is intended for use both as an instructional manual and a reference manual. You can use it now to learn the basics of Norton Desktop for DOS and later as a reference for performing specific tasks. Below are brief descriptions of each section to give you a flavor of what each section contains. Consult the Table of Contents for an outline of the tasks covered in each chapter.

This manual is divided into seven parts:

- Part I, "Before You Begin," explains the basics of Norton Desktop, such as the desktop components, how to start and quit, how to navigate within Norton Desktop and how to get help.
- Part II, "Using the Desktop," introduces the disk, file and directory management capabilities of Norton Desktop.
- Part III, "Configuring the Desktop," describes how to customize Norton Desktop to suit your needs.
- Part IV, "Using Desktop Tools," describes each of the tools you'll find in Norton Desktop, such as Norton Backup, Norton AntiVirus and Norton Mail.
- Part V, "Standalone Utilities," describes how to use the standalone utilities that come with Norton Desktop, such as SmartCan and Norton Cache.
- Part VI, "Corporate Menus," explains how to create a custom menu system that runs as a DOS shell on each computer in your organization.
- Part VII, "Reference," contains appendices that include commonly asked questions and answers, system messages, menu maps and a glossary.

The Norton Desktop product comes with long and short menus. When you install the product, the short menus are displayed. However, you can change to long menus quickly. It is assumed you are using the full-featured long menus. Commands not available on the short menus are identified with a reference to the long menu, for example, select MAIL from the (long) Tools menu.

xx   *Using Norton Desktop for DOS*

Assumptions

This manual, as well as the other manuals in the Norton Desktop for DOS documentation set, assumes that you are using the keyboard. If you use a mouse you will also find mouse procedures within the chapters where appropriate. Mouse procedures have a mouse icon next to them.

If you do use a mouse, this manual assumes that you are using a right-handed mouse, so the left button is the primary button, clicked with your right index finger. Whenever you are told to "click the button" or "double-click" an item, you should use the left button. In cases when you should use the right button, the documentation will indicate so. Don't feel left out if you prefer to use the mouse with your left hand. You can make your mouse left-handed, so the right button is the primary button. (See the section "Selecting Mouse Options" in Chapter 9, "Configuring Norton Desktop," for directions on how to do this.)

Conventions

To help you find information, the Norton Desktop documentation set adheres to the following conventions:

Symbols

Symbol	Meaning
■	Indicates an item in a list or the step in a single-step procedure.
1	Indicates a step in a multiple-step procedure.
🖱	Indicates instructions for mouse users that differ from the instructions for keyboard users.
ⓘ	Indicates a note of interest.
☞	Indicates a tip or helpful hint.
❗	Indicates a caution or note to which you should pay attention.
🛑	Indicates a warning; read it carefully.

About This Manual **xxi**

Type Styles	**Style**	**Meaning**
	Italic	Indicates a glossary term or emphasizes a given word.
	SMALL CAPS	Indicates the name of a menu command, such as EXIT.
	Initial Caps	Indicates the name of an object, such as a menu, a command button, a dialog box, or a dialog-box component. For example, the File menu or the Cancel button.
	ALL CAPS	Indicates the name of a path, a directory, a file or a DOS command.
	`monospace`	Indicates something you should enter with the keyboard. For example, "Type `*.DOC` to search for all documents."
Keyboard Combinations	**Style**	**Meaning**
	Key+Key	The plus sign indicates that you should press and hold the first key while pressing the second key. Then release both keys. For example, "Alt+Tab" means press Alt and hold it while you press Tab. Then release both keys.
	Key+Key, Key	The plus sign and comma combination indicates that you should press and hold the first key while pressing the second, release them, then press the third key and release it. For example, "Alt+F, C" means press Alt and hold it while pressing F, release both keys, then press C.

Getting Started

This chapter introduces the Norton Desktop for DOS and shows you how to start and quit the program. It tells you how to navigate through the icons, windows, menus and dialog boxes you'll see on your desktop. It also describes the online Help system and tells you how to secure and recover your files should a problem occur.

Contents

Norton Desktop for DOS 1-3
    Starting Norton Desktop 1-3
    Exiting Norton Desktop 1-3
The Desktop at a Glance 1-4
Getting Around on the Norton Desktop 1-6
    Using the Button Bar 1-6
    Menus 1-7
    Windows 1-12
    Dialog Boxes 1-20
Before Problems Arise 1-27
    Protecting and Recovering Your Files 1-27
    Enhancing Speed and Performance 1-30
    Using Advise 1-30
Getting Help 1-30
    The Help Menu 1-31
    The Help Window 1-32

NORTON DESKTOP FOR DOS

This chapter gives you a basic look at working in Norton Desktop for DOS. To practice working with the items you'll see on your desktop, you should install Norton Desktop. If you have not yet installed Norton Desktop, please refer to *Installing Norton Desktop for DOS*.

Norton Desktop for DOS is a graphical computing environment that makes handling files and documents efficient and easy. Norton Desktop lets you perform your day-to-day work without worrying about the technical details of your computer.

Technology shouldn't intimidate you or prevent you from accomplishing great things. Therefore, Norton Desktop for DOS lets you manage data and documents in a familiar environment—a desktop.

Norton Desktop provides almost everything you need to do your work: tools like the Scheduler, Calendar and Calculator, and easy access to your reports, databases and spreadsheets. Norton Desktop also lets you back up your work, scan for viruses and use its comprehensive online Help system.

Starting Norton Desktop

After installation, Norton Desktop becomes the *shell*—the layer between you and DOS that makes managing your work easier.

To start Norton Desktop for DOS:

- Type nd at the DOS prompt (C:>) and press Enter.

   The desktop appears on your screen.

Exiting Norton Desktop

To exit Norton Desktop for DOS:

1. Choose EXIT from the File menu.

   The Exit dialog box appears.

2. Select Exit to exit Norton Desktop and return to DOS.

   Or,

   Select Cancel to return to Norton Desktop.

   Or,

   Select Shutdown.

TIP: Shutdown is dimmed unless you specified a special shutdown sequence using the PREFERENCES... command from the (long) Configure menu.

Or,

- Double-click the close box (the small square box that appears in the upper-left corner of the desktop within the Norton Desktop title bar).

NOTE: By default, you must confirm your exit before returning to DOS. However, you can skip this confirmation by choosing the CONFIRMATION... command from the (long) Configure menu. Then, deselect the Confirm on Exit check box.

THE DESKTOP AT A GLANCE

The *desktop* occupies the entire area of your screen. It contains many components, including windows, icons, menus, dialog boxes and the button bar (Figure 1-1). The screens in Figure 1-1 show a drive window, the open Help menu and a dialog box to illustrate these desktop components.

A *window* is a framed area in which you can view a file listing or contents of a file or perform a task.

An *icon* is a small, pictorial representation of a system component, such as the small pictures that represent your computer's disk drives.

A *pull-down menu* is a list of related *commands*. A menu lets you issue instructions such as getting help about Norton Desktop commands.

A *dialog box* is a special type of window that either prompts you for more information, or issues a message that acts as a warning or confirmation.

The *button bar* appears at the bottom of your desktop. It lets you access the operations you use most often.

Getting Started   1-5

Figure 1-1

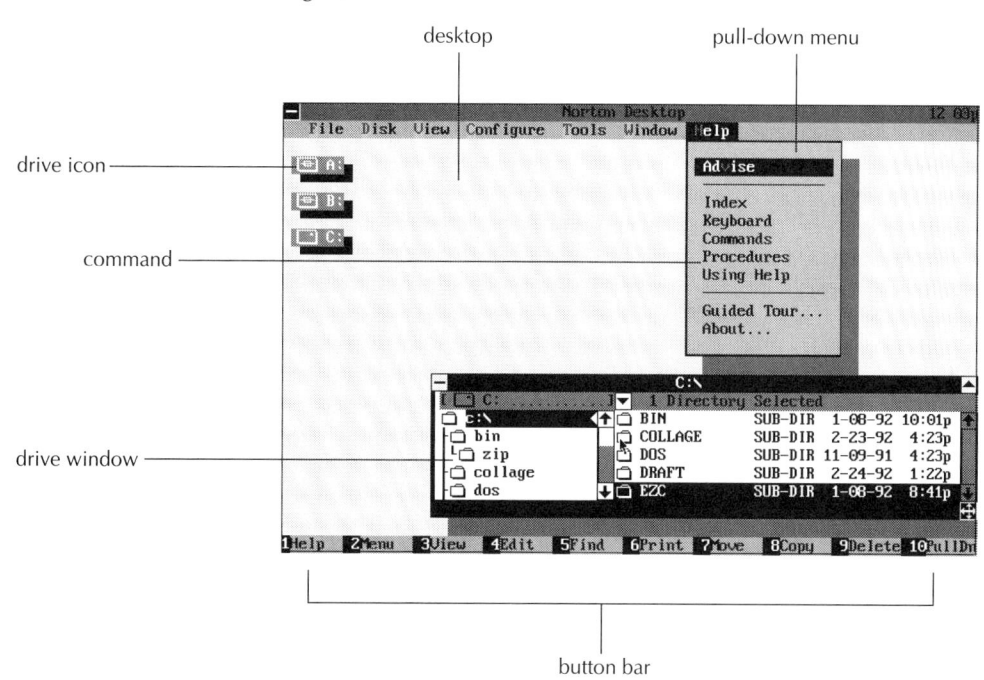

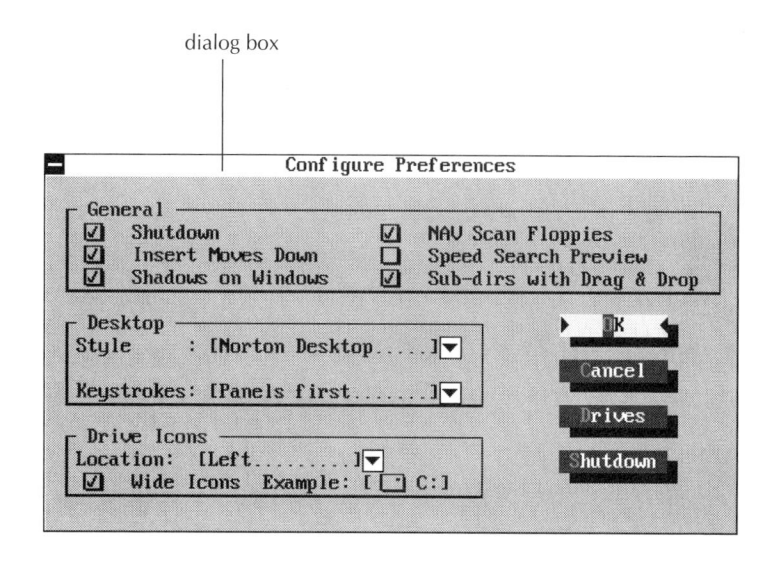

GETTING AROUND ON THE NORTON DESKTOP

The objects you'll see on your desktop include windows, icons, menus and dialog boxes. You can easily select and manipulate these items with the keyboard or a mouse. For help, press F1.

TIP: You can use hotkeys and shortcut keys to select a command from a menu or an option from a dialog box quickly:

- A *hotkey* is a letter that appears in contrasting color in a command's name (on a monochrome display, hotkeys are highlighted). Press Alt+hotkey to select a menu, a command in a menu or a dialog box option. Press a command's hotkey to select that command from an open menu.
- A *shortcut key* appears to the right of a command. For example, you can press Alt+F4 to exit Norton Desktop.

The sections that follow tell you about using the button bar, menus, windows and dialog boxes.

Using the Button Bar

Norton Desktop's button bar, which appears at the bottom of your desktop, lets you easily access the operations that you might use most often, like finding, moving and copying files.

Figure 1-2 shows the default button bar. You can configure the button bar to include those operations you use most often. To do so, choose BUTTON BAR... from the long version of the Configure menu (see the section "Short Menus and Long Menus" later in this chapter). For details about personalizing the button bar, see Chapter 9, "Configuring Norton Desktop."

Figure 1-2

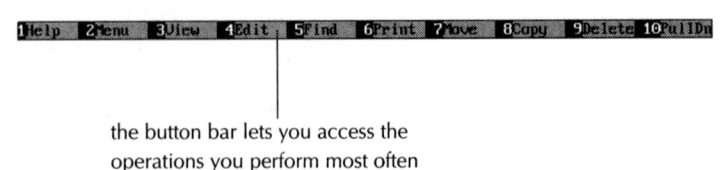

1Help 2Menu 3View 4Edit 5Find 6Print 7Move 8Copy 9Delete 10PulDn

the button bar lets you access the
operations you perform most often

Getting Started 1-7

Table 1-1 shows you the operations you can perform using the button bar.

To access an operation using the button bar, simply press the shortcut key displayed to the left of the button. For example, press F1 for Help. Mouse users, click the button.

Table 1-1

BUTTON	SHORTCUT KEY	DESCRIPTION
Help	F1	Accesses the Help system's index
Menu	F2	Accesses Norton Desktop Menu, where you can create and edit personalized menus
View	F3	Accesses Norton Viewer, which lets you search for and look at your files
Edit	F4	Lets you browse edit your files
Find	F5	Lets you quickly and easily find files with SuperFind
Print	F6	Lets you browse for and print files
Move	F7	Lets you browse for and move files
Copy	F8	Lets you browse for and copy files
Delete	F9	Lets you browse for and delete files
PullDn	F10	Selects the menu bar and highlights the File menu title

Button bar operations

Menus

A command is an instruction, such as Copy or Print, that is carried out by an application. In Norton Desktop, commands are organized into related groups to form menus. Menus are placed together on a menu bar.

Figure 1-3 shows the menus you'll see in the Norton Desktop menu bar.

1-8   Using Norton Desktop for DOS

Figure 1-3

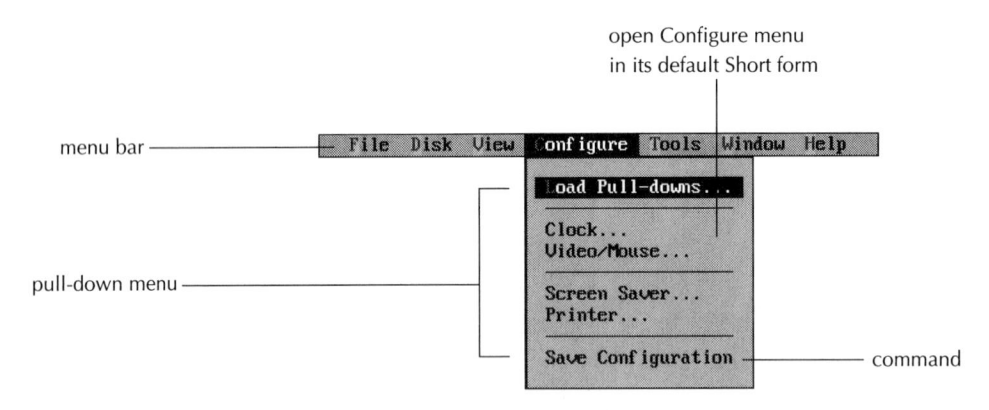

- menu bar — File Disk View **Configure** Tools Window Help
- open Configure menu in its default Short form
- pull-down menu — Load Pull-downs... / Clock... / Video/Mouse... / Screen Saver... / Printer... / Save Configuration — command

Selecting a Menu

To select (or open) a menu:

1   Press F10 to select the menu bar (see Figure 1-3).
2   Use the right and left arrow keys to move to the menu you want to open.
3   Press Enter or DownArrow to open the menu.

TIP: To open a menu in one step, hold Alt while pressing the hotkey, the first letter in the name of the menu you want to open. For example, to open the File menu, press Alt+F.

Or,

- Point to the menu you want to select and click it (see Figure 1-3).

Choosing a Command

To choose a command from an open menu:

1   Use UpArrow and DownArrow to highlight the command (see Figure 1-3).

   Or,

   Press the hotkey. (For example, to choose COPY... from the File menu, press C.)

2   Press Enter.

Getting Started   1-9

TIP: To choose a command in one step, remember to use shortcut keys (the keys that appear to the right of a command) or the button bar, if the command is available there.

Or,
- Point to the command and click it.

TIP: You can open a menu and choose a command from it in one step by pointing to the menu, immediately dragging the mouse pointer to the command you want, then releasing the mouse button. The command is executed when you release the mouse button. If you open the wrong menu, drag the pointer off the menu and onto the desktop, release the mouse button, and start again.

Closing a Menu

To close a menu:

- Press Alt, F10 or Esc.

    Note that the menu bar remains active so that you can select another item.

Or,
- Click anywhere outside the menu.

Short Menus and Long Menus

Norton Desktop menus come in two varieties: Short and Long.

Short menus contain only the most frequently used commands. This streamlines the menus. *Long menus* are expanded menus that list every available command, giving you access to all the power Norton Desktop offers.

Figure 1-4 shows the File menu in its Short and Long versions. As you compare the Short and Long menu sets, you can decide which set you prefer to use. By default, Norton Desktop is set to display Short menus.

Using Norton Desktop for DOS

Figure 1-4

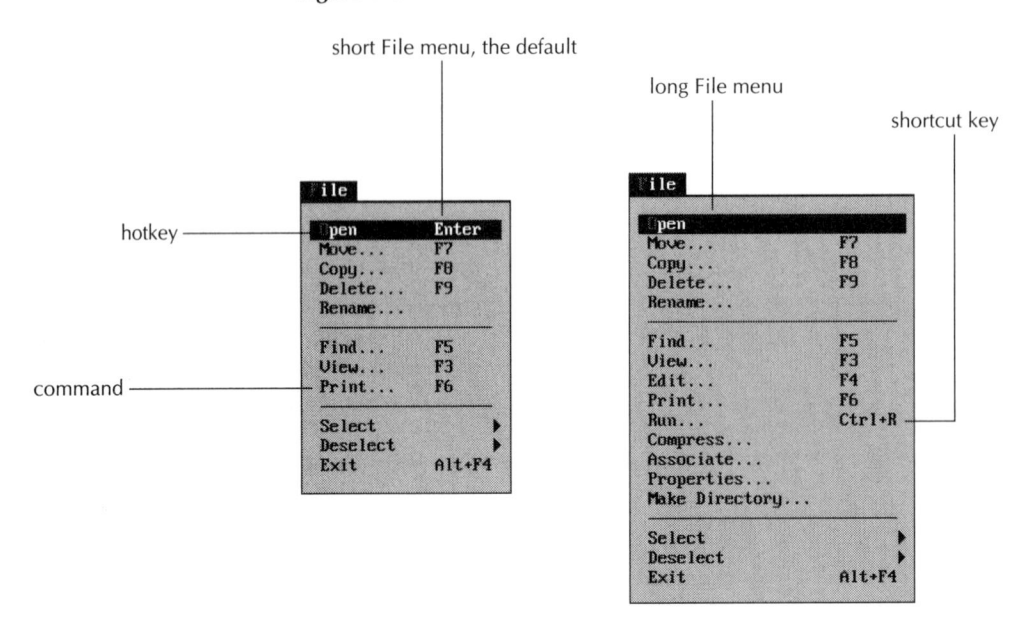

```
                short File menu, the default
                            │
                            │        long File menu
                            │              │
                                                    shortcut key
                                                         │
     ┌─────────────────────┐       ┌─────────────────────┐
     │ File                │       │ File                │
     ├─────────────────────┤       ├─────────────────────┤
hotkey── Open        Enter │       │ Open                │
     │ Move...        F7   │       │ Move...        F7   │
     │ Copy...        F8   │       │ Copy...        F8   │
     │ Delete...      F9   │       │ Delete...      F9   │
     │ Rename...           │       │ Rename...           │
     │                     │       │                     │
     │ Find...        F5   │       │ Find...        F5   │
     │ View...        F3   │       │ View...        F3   │
command─ Print...       F6 │       │ Edit...        F4   │
     │                     │       │ Print...       F6   │
     │ Select           ▶  │       │ Run...         Ctrl+R
     │ Deselect         ▶  │       │ Compress...         │
     │ Exit         Alt+F4 │       │ Associate...        │
     └─────────────────────┘       │ Properties...       │
                                   │ Make Directory...   │
                                   │                     │
                                   │ Select           ▶  │
                                   │ Deselect         ▶  │
                                   │ Exit         Alt+F4 │
                                   └─────────────────────┘
```

Norton Desktop pull-down menus come in two varieties, Short and Long

To select Short or Long menus:

1. Choose LOAD PULL-DOWNS... from the Configure menu.

    The Select Pull-down to Load dialog box appears.

2. Select the SHORT.NDM file for Short menus or the LONG.NDM file for Long menus.

3. Select OK.

    The menu configuration you selected takes effect immediately.

In this manual, menu commands that are available only on the Long menus are identified by the word "long" in parentheses before the menu name. For example, the statement, "Choose LABEL DISK... from the (long) Disk menu," means that the LABEL DISK... command is only found in the long version of the Disk menu. If you see "Choose OPEN... from the File menu," it means that the OPEN... command is available on both the Long and Short versions of the File menu.

When you customize Long menus, you can change both the menu content and the order of the commands on the menu. Thus, in rare circumstances, your Long menus may actually be shorter than Short menus. See Chapter 9, "Configuring Norton Desktop," for more details.

Navigating in a Menu

Table 1-2 summarizes how to navigate within Norton Desktop's pull-down menus.

For more information about creating and personalizing custom menus, see Chapters 11 and 12.

Table 1-2

ACTION	KEYBOARD	MOUSE
Close a menu	Press F10 or Esc	Click anywhere outside of the menu
Load long menus	Press Alt+C, L, select LONG.NDM, press Enter	Click the Configure menu and drag to LOAD PULL-DOWNS..., then release. Select LONG.NDM, select OK.
Load short menus	Press Alt+C, L, select SHORT.NDM, press Enter	Click the Configure menu and drag to LOAD PULL-DOWNS..., then release. Select SHORT.NDM, select OK.
Open a menu	Press Alt+hotkey	Click the menu name
Select a command	From an open menu, press Alt+hotkey or the hotkey From a closed menu, press the shortcut key	Click the menu, drag the mouse to the command, then release
Select the menu bar	Press F10 or Alt	Click the PullDn button on the button bar

Navigating in Norton Desktop's menus

Windows

Drive windows let you access and manage your disks, directories and files. A window displays the contents of a selected disk drive, showing a directory tree, a file listing or a view of a particular file's contents. Refer to Chapter 2, "Using Drive Windows," for complete details about drive windows.

You can display up to eight drive windows on your desktop at one time. You can open more than one drive window for each drive, which makes moving directories and files within the same disk easier. Only one drive window can be active at a time, and you can perform operations only on an active window.

Figure 1-5 shows the desktop with an open drive window.

Figure 1-5

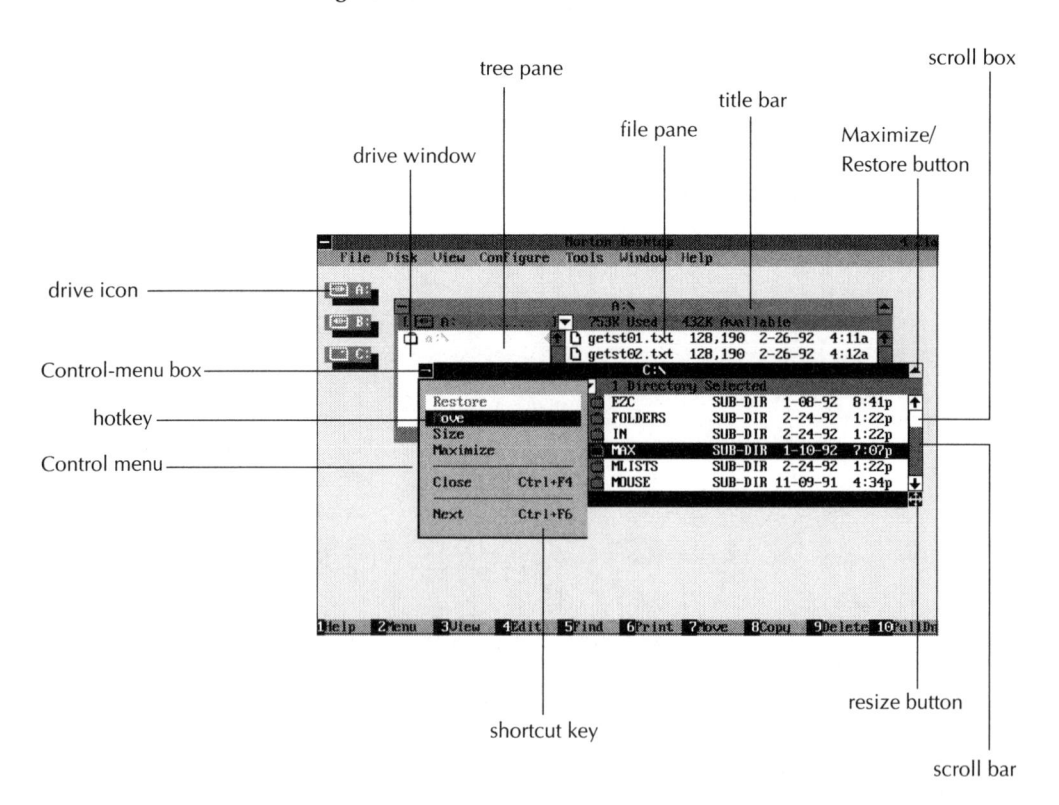

The desktop displays a *drive icon* for each drive available to your computer. You can double-click a drive icon to open the corresponding drive window.

Open the *Control menu* by pressing Alt+Hyphen (-) or Esc. Mouse users can click the *Control-menu box*. The commands in this menu let you move a window, resize it, maximize it to full-screen size, restore a maximized window to its former size, make another window active and close the window. To close the Control menu, press Esc or click the Control-menu box.

To move an active window, use the MOVE command from the Control menu. Mouse users can drag the window's *title bar* with the mouse cursor; when the window is where you want it, release the mouse button. You can move an *inactive* window by holding down the *right* mouse button while dragging the window to a new location on the desktop.

To select a new drive for the active drive window, type the new drive letter in the drive selector combination box or press Ctrl+DownArrow in the *drive selector* (mouse users, click the prompt button as described in the "Dialog Boxes" section later in this chapter) and select a drive from the list of available drives.

The *status bar* displays information about the disk in the current drive window.

The *panes* let you choose how to display information. The tree pane displays a listing of the selected disk's directories. The file pane shows a file listing for the selected directory. The view pane displays the contents of a selected file. For more information, see Chapter 2, "Using Drive Windows."

To select one *file* in an active drive window, press Tab to move to the file pane and use UpArrow and DownArrow to highlight a file or subdirectory. Mouse users can click the file or subdirectory.

To select one or more files in a sequence, use UpArrow and DownArrow to highlight the first file, then press Insert to select the next file. Mouse users can click the first file with the right mouse button and drag the mouse cursor to the last file you want to select.

1-14   *Using Norton Desktop for DOS*

To select all items in a list box, press Ctrl+Slash (/). For details, see Chapter 4, "Managing Directories and Files."

TIP: To find a file or directory quickly, start typing the name you want to find in the active pane. The Speed Search box appears, and the first filename beginning with the letter you typed is selected. Keep typing subsequent letters in the filename until the file for which you are searching is selected.

When a window is not large enough to display its entire contents, it provides a *scroll bar* along the right side of the window to help you move around inside the window. The scroll bar provides a graphical representation of your location within the entire listing and lets you easily move to the item you're trying to find.

NOTE: Drive windows always have scroll bars, even if the entire contents fit within the window.

The *scroll box*, the small box that moves up and down the scroll bar, indicates your location within a file. The scroll box located at the top of the scroll bar indicates that the window is displaying the beginning of the file. Likewise, the scroll box positioned in the middle of the scroll bar indicates that the window is displaying the middle of the file.

To enlarge a window, use the RESTORE command from the Control menu. Once a window is enlarged, the Maximize button is replaced with the Restore button. Mouse users, click the *Maximize/Restore button*. To shrink (or restore) the window again, click the Restore button.

The *resize button* lets mouse users resize the active window.

Drive Icons

Note that the desktop shown in Figure 1-5 contains three drive icons. The desktop displays one drive icon for each drive available to your computer. You may see only two drive icons, for example, A: and C:—usually your computer's floppy and hard drive, respectively. If you are already logged

Getting Started 1-15

on to a network when you start Norton Desktop, you may see many more drive icons. These drive icons represent all local drives plus any network drives that are available to your computer.

You can choose to display only certain types of drive icons. For example, to keep your desktop free of clutter, you may want to keep drive icons down to a minimum by displaying only the icons for your local drives and the network drives you use most often. See Chapter 9, "Configuring Norton Desktop," for more information.

Once you have access to all the drives you want, you're ready to manage your disks and directories and view files. Or you can launch other applications from Norton Desktop. Managing disks is discussed in Chapter 3, using Norton Desktop to manage your directories and files is explained in Chapter 4, and launching files from the desktop is explained in Chapter 6.

Opening a Drive Window

To open a drive window:

1   Choose OPEN DRIVE WINDOW... from the Window menu (Ctrl+W). (See Figure 1-5.)

    The Open Drive Window dialog box appears.

2   Select the drive you want from the Drive drop-down list box.

    Or,

    Type the letter of the drive to select in the Drive list box.

3   Select OK.

    Or,

    ▪ Double-click the drive icon you want to open.

Selecting a Drive Window

There are several ways to organize multiple drive windows on your desktop. In addition to resizing and moving windows, you can cascade, tile or hide them. Cascading windows stacks all open windows so their titles are visible and the currently active window is on top. Tiling windows arranges all open windows side-by-side on the desktop. See Chapter 2, "Using Drive Windows," for details about arranging multiple windows on your desktop.

Before you can move, reshape, shrink, enlarge or restore a window, you must first select it to make it active.

To select a drive window:

- Press Ctrl+Tab until you select the drive window you want to make active.

Or,

- Choose the drive window from the Window menu (Alt+W, #, where # is the number assigned to the drive window).

Or,

- Click the drive window you want.

Closing a Drive Window

You can close open drive windows one at a time, or close all open drive windows in a single step.

To close a single drive window:

- Choose CLOSE from the Control menu.

Or,

- Double-click the Control-menu box.

To close all open drive windows at one time:

- Choose CLOSE ALL from the Window menu.

Navigating in a Window

Table 1-3 summarizes how to navigate in a window.

Table 1-3

ACTION	KEYBOARD	MOUSE
Apply command to selected file	Select file in drive window and then select command from menu	Click file in drive window and then click command from menu
Cascade all open drive windows	Choose CASCADE from the Window menu (Alt+W, C) or press Shift+F5	Click CASCADE from the Window menu
Change the size of a drive window	Choose SIZE from the Control menu, use the arrow keys to resize the window, then press Enter	Drag the resize button (the four-headed arrow in the lower-right corner of the window) until the drive window is the size you want
Close a drive window	Choose CLOSE from the Control menu or press Ctrl+F4	Double-click the Control-menu box
Close all drive windows	Open the Window menu, then choose CLOSE ALL (Alt+W, A)	Click CLOSE ALL from the Window menu
Close the Control menu	Press Esc	Click the Control-menu box
Deselect a file	Tab to file pane and use UpArrow and DownArrow to highlight the file	Click the file
Deselect all files	Press Ctrl+Backslash (\)	
Enlarge a drive window to full-screen size	Choose MAXIMIZE from the Control menu	Click the Maximize button
Hide all open drive windows (without closing them)	Choose HIDE ALL from the Window menu (Alt+W, H) or press Ctrl+F6	Click HIDE ALL from the Window menu
Make an open drive window active	Press Ctrl+Tab until the drive window you want is activated	Click the drive window you want to activate

(continued)

Table 1-3

(continued)

ACTION	KEYBOARD	MOUSE
Move an active drive window	Choose MOVE from the Control menu, use the arrow keys to move the window left, right, up or down, then press Enter	Click the title bar, hold down the mouse button and drag the window to the location you want
Move an inactive drive window		Click the title bar, hold down the right mouse button and drag the window to the location you want
Move down one line in a drive window	Move the cursor to the bottom of the window, then press DownArrow once	Click the down arrow control at the bottom of the scroll bar
Move list items down, one full screen at a time	Press PgDn	Click in scroll bar anywhere below the scroll box
Move list items up one full screen at a time	Press PgUp	Click in scroll bar anywhere above the scroll box
Move to the first item in a list	Press Home	Drag the scroll box to the top of the scroll bar
Move to the last item in a list	Press End	Drag the scroll box to the bottom of the scroll bar
Move up one line in a drive window	Move the cursor to the top of the window, then press UpArrow	Click the up arrow control at the top of the scroll bar
Open a drive window	Choose OPEN DRIVE WINDOW... from the Window menu (Ctrl+W). Type the letter of the drive in the drive selector box or press Ctrl+DownArrow to display a drop-down list of available drives. Select a drive, then select OK.	Double-click the drive icon for the drive you want to open

(continued)

Table 1-3

(continued)

ACTION	KEYBOARD	MOUSE
Open the Control menu	While the drive window is active, press Alt+Hyphen or Esc	Click the Control-menu box
Restore a maximized (enlarged) drive window to its original size	Choose RESTORE from the Control menu	Click the Restore button. (When the window is enlarged to its maximum size, the Maximize button is replaced by the Restore button.)
Scroll continuously through a drive window	Press and hold the appropriate arrow key	Click and hold the appropriate arrow control or drag the scroll box to the location you want to view
Select a file	Tab to file pane and use UpArrow and DownArrow to highlight the file	Click the file
Select all files	Press Ctrl+Slash (/)	
Select more than one file	Tab to the file pane, use UpArrow and DownArrow to highlight the file, press Insert. Repeat for each file you want.	Click on files with right mouse button
Select sequence of files		Click on the first file with the right mouse button and drag the mouse to the last file
Start program	Highlight name of program in the file pane and press Enter	Double-click name of program in file pane
Start program with an associated file	Highlight the file in the file pane with an extension associated with a program and press Enter	Double-click name of the file (in the file pane) that ends in the extension associated with a program
Tile all open drive windows	Choose TILE from the Window menu (Alt+W, T)	Click TILE from the Window menu

Navigating in windows

Dialog Boxes

A dialog box is a special kind of window that either requests or provides information. When you choose a command followed by an ellipsis (...), like COPY DISKETTE..., a dialog box appears.

Each dialog box looks a little different. For details about the dialog boxes you'll see for a specific operation, refer to that chapter. For example, to learn how the dialog boxes work in Norton AntiVirus, you would refer to Chapter 20, "Using Norton AntiVirus."

Figure 1-6 shows the Filter dialog box and the Format dialog box. Not every dialog box component is shown here.

Figure 1-6

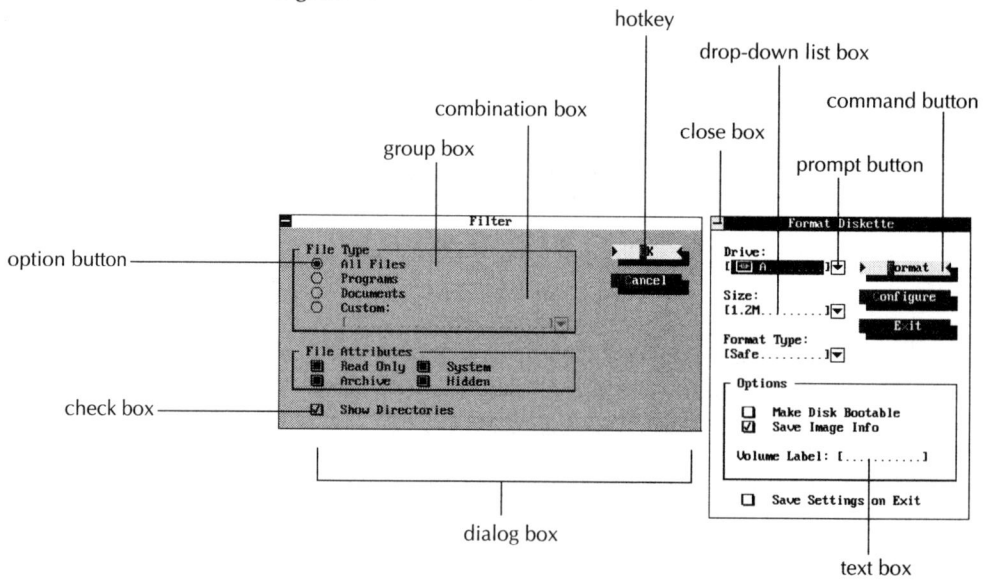

To move to a specific *dialog box component*, press Alt+hotkey or press Tab; press Shift+Tab to move to the previous component. If you are using a mouse, you can click the component you want to change.

The *hotkey* is the highlighted letter of a menu command or a button in a dialog box. Press the hotkey to select a command from an open menu. Press Alt+hotkey to select a command or dialog box option.

Getting Started   1-21

Press Alt +hotkey or press Esc to exit the dialog box. Or, double-click the *close box*.

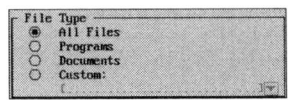

A *group box* helps organize related choices in a dialog box. Each one contains a title that describes how the choices are related. A group box may contain several types of dialog box components. Most often, they contain option buttons and check boxes.

The *check box* acts like a switch, representing an option you can turn on or off. When you select a check box, a checkmark appears in the box, indicating that the option is turned on. To select or deselect a check box, press Alt+hotkey or Tab to the check box and press Spacebar to check or uncheck it. Mouse users can click the check box.

Some check boxes have three possible markings: on, off, and filled. When a square fills the check box, the status of the check box is unimportant. For example, if a check box was labeled "Read-only files," a check mark means you want to search for read-only files. No check mark means you want to search for files that are not read-only. A filled check box means you don't want to check files for this condition.

TIP: You don't have to have good aim to select a check box. Just click anywhere on the descriptive text next to the check box.

Option buttons, sometimes called *radio buttons,* represent a set of choices that are mutually exclusive. This means that you may select only one option at any one time. By default, one of the option buttons is preset—it's the one with the small black dot in the middle. To select an option button, press Alt+hotkey or click the option button.

TIP: You don't have to have good aim. To select an option button, press Spacebar or click the option button itself, or click anywhere on the descriptive text next to the option button.

Every dialog box has at least one *command button*, a rectangular button that carries out the action described by the text on the button. The two most common command buttons are OK and Cancel. OK accepts the information in the dialog box, closes it then performs the action you specified. The OK command button may also ask you to acknowledge that you have paid close attention to a message or warning displayed in a dialog box. When you select Cancel, the dialog box is closed without any of the actions you may have chosen being carried out. Some command buttons open another dialog box.

Most often, one command button is highlighted. This means that the command is the preset (default) choice for that dialog box. Just press Enter or click the button to select the default or highlighted button. To select another command button, press Alt+hotkey or click the button.

NOTE: Pressing Enter is the equivalent of clicking the preselected command button (usually OK). Pressing Esc is the equivalent of selecting Cancel.

A *text box* is the rectangular area into which you type the information needed to complete an action. For example, when you choose MOVE... from the File menu, the Move dialog box appears. You must enter the old and new filenames in the text boxes then select OK. To change information in a text box, move the cursor to the appropriate place in the text box and type the new information.

A *list box* contains a roster of available choices. If all the choices won't fit in the box, the list box contains a scroll bar. (Refer to the "Navigating in a Window" section in this chapter if you are not familiar with scroll bars.) To select an item from a list box, use the arrow keys to highlight it and press Enter, or click the item. To select a different item, use the arrow keys again or click that item name.

TIP: To quickly move to an item in a list box, press the first letter of the item.

Getting Started   1-23

There's also a special type of list box called a *drop-down list box,* which looks like a text box. On closer inspection, you'll notice a *prompt button,* a small button labeled with a down arrow located to the right of the rectangular field. The prompt button indicates that more choices are available. To display a list of choices from a drop-down list box, press Ctrl+DownArrow or click the prompt button. You may now choose from this list just as you would choose from an ordinary list box.

Pull-down menus let you display commands and access other functions like online Help and macros.

A *combination box* combines a text box and a list box. You can enter information into the text box, or you can choose from the items on the list. Many combination boxes have drop-down list boxes or prompt buttons.

Often in a dialog box, you'll need to specify a file or group of files. To specify a particular file, you can take advantage of a special dialog box component—the Browse command button. You can specify a particular group of files. See the "Browsing for Files" section.

Navigating in a Dialog Box

Navigating in a dialog box is easy with either the keyboard or a mouse.

To move to another area in a dialog box:

- Press Alt plus the hotkey.

Or,

- Press Tab to move to the next item; press Shift+Tab to move to the previous item.

Or,

- Click the component you want to change or select.

Table 1-4 shows you how to move around and select items in a dialog box using the keyboard or your mouse.

Table 1-4

ACTION	KEYBOARD	MOUSE
Close a dialog box and cancel the changes made to it	Highlight the Cancel button and press Enter, press Alt+hotkey for the Cancel button, or press Esc	Click the close box, the small square box that appears in the upper-left corner of the dialog box
Close a dialog box and continue processing	Press Alt+hotkey for the desired command button	Click desired command button
Close a drop-down list box	Press Ctrl+UpArrow	Click the prompt button
Deselect a check box	Press Alt+hotkey or tab to the check box and press the Spacebar	Click the check box
Deselect an option button	Select a new option button	Click a new option button
Enter text in a text box	Move to the text box and type in text	Click the text box and type in text
Move cursor left or right in text box	Press LeftArrow or RightArrow	Click the mouse cursor at the desired position
Move to dialog box component with highlighted letter (hotkey) in title	Press Alt+hotkey	Click the component
Move to first item in a list box	Press Home	Drag the scroll box to the top of the scroll bar
Move to last item in a list box	Press End	Drag the scroll box to the bottom of the scroll bar
Move to next component in a dialog box	Press Tab	Click the component
Move to previous component in a dialog box	Press Shift+Tab	Click the component
Move up and down in a list box	Press UpArrow or DownArrow	Click list item

(continued)

Getting Started **1-25**

Table 1-4

(continued)

ACTION	KEYBOARD	MOUSE
Open a drop-down list box	Press Ctrl+DownArrow	Click prompt button
Select a check box	Press Alt+hotkey or tab to the check box and press the Spacebar	Click the check box
Select a command button	Press Alt+hotkey in command button	Click the command button
Select an option button	Press Alt+hotkey or tab to the group box for the buttons, use the arrow keys to reach the correct button, and press the Spacebar	Click the option button
Select default or highlighted command button	Press Enter	Click the command button
Use a combination box	Type into the text box portion or select an item from the list box portion. See text box and list box entries for details.	Type into the text box portion or select an item from the list box portion. See text box and list box entries for details.

Navigation and selection techniques

Browsing for Files

Many dialog boxes contain a Browse command button. When you select this button, a browse dialog box is displayed on the desktop. This dialog box differs slightly with each command. However, it always contains list boxes showing a file list, a directory list and a drive list. The browse dialog box shown in Figure 1-7 appears when you select Browse in the Delete dialog box.

1-26   *Using Norton Desktop for DOS*

Figure 1-7

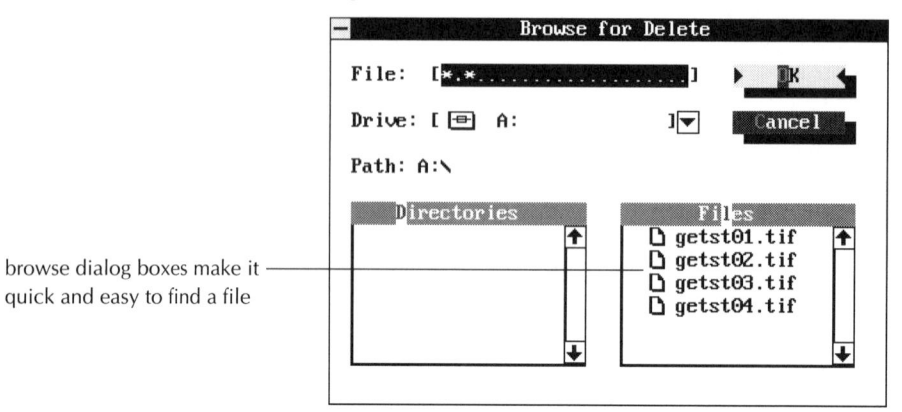

```
┌─ ─────────── Browse for Delete ───────────┐
│  File:  [*.*................]   ► OK ◄   │
│  Drive: [ ▣  A:        ]▼    Cancel       │
│  Path: A:\                                │
│        ┌─ Directories ──┐  ┌─── Files ───┐│
│        │              ▲ │  │ □ getst01.tif▲│
│        │                │  │ □ getst02.tif │
│        │                │  │ □ getst03.tif │
│        │                │  │ □ getst04.tif │
│        │              ▼ │  │             ▼ │
│        └────────────────┘  └───────────────┘│
└────────────────────────────────────────────┘
```

browse dialog boxes make it quick and easy to find a file

To locate a specific file and enter its filename in the appropriate text box in the dialog box:

1 Select a drive from the Drives list box.

The Directories and Files list boxes change to reflect your selection.

2 Select a directory from the Directories list box.

The Files list box changes to reflect your selection.

3 Select a file from the Files list box.

The filename is automatically entered into the appropriate text box within the dialog box.

Using Wildcards

DOS wildcards (? and *) make it easy to specify a file or group of files. They are most useful in text boxes when you want to select files of a similar type (for example, all .DOC files) or files with similar names (for example, MEMO1.DOC and MEMO2.DOC).

A question mark (?) is a variable that represents a single character. To select a group of similarly named files or a group of similar file types, you may want to use the question mark. For example, MEMO?.DOC. In this example, ? takes the place of a single character, so files like MEMO1.DOC and MEMO2.DOC are selected.

An asterisk (*) represents a series of up to eight question marks (for example, QTR*.*). Remember that filenames must be from one to eight characters long, and can optionally have an extension of up to three characters. For example, in QTR*.*, the first asterisk represents from zero to five alphanumeric characters, and the second asterisk represents from zero to three alphanumeric characters. Files such as QTR1.EXE and QTRRLM.C would be selected using QTR*.*.

Alert Boxes

In addition to the dialog boxes associated with commands, you may also see other types of dialog boxes from time to time. When Norton Desktop needs to warn you or simply give you helpful information, an *alert box* appears. You must acknowledge the message by selecting the command button in an alert box before you can continue.

BEFORE PROBLEMS ARISE

Norton Desktop includes numerous tools to help you protect your work, recover data, repair disks and speed up your computer. This section briefly describes each feature and tells you where you can find details about each one.

Before you read on, you should take the time to create a Rescue Diskette. This procedure saves important information about your computer's hard disk to a floppy disk. Then, if your computer ever loses this information, you can use the Rescue Diskette to restore the information on your hard drive. For details about creating the Rescue Diskette, see Chapter 28, "Using Disk Tools."

Protecting and Recovering Your Files

The work you prepare using your computer is important to you. For this reason you should take steps to protect your work from problems that may occur; for example, you might find that you have a defective diskette, or you might accidentally delete a file.

Table 1-5 shows the utilities Norton Desktop provides to help you protect and recover data, and repair disks. This table briefly describes each utility, how to access it and where to look for details about each one.

Table 1-5

FEATURE	DESCRIPTION	HOW TO ACCESS	FOR DETAILS
Norton AntiVirus	Scans for viruses and safeguards your computer from viruses.	Choose NORTON ANTIVIRUS from the (long) Tools menu.	Chapter 20, "Using Norton AntiVirus."
Norton Backup	A complete backup system that provides many powerful tools for protecting your data.	Choose NORTON BACKUP from the Tools menu.	Chapter 19, "Using Norton Backup."
Disk Tools	Performs various data protection and data recovery operations such as making a bootable disk, reviving a defective diskette, creating a Rescue Diskette and restoring a Rescue Diskette.	Type `disktools` at the DOS prompt and press Enter.	Chapter 28, "Using Disk Tools."
Norton Disk Doctor (NDD)	Diagnoses and repairs damaged disks.	Choose NORTON DISK DOCTOR from the Tools menu.	Chapter 18, "Using Norton Disk Doctor."
UnErase	Searches for and recovers erased (deleted) files.	Choose UNERASE from the Tools menu.	Chapter 16, "Using UnErase."
Unformat	Recovers a hard disk that has been formatted, damaged by a virus or corrupted due to a power failure.	Type `unformat` at the DOS prompt and press Enter.	Chapter 26, "Using Unformat."

(continued)

Table 1-5

(continued)

FEATURE	DESCRIPTION	HOW TO ACCESS	FOR DETAILS
SmartCan	Moves deleted files to another, less-used part of your disk to protect them from being overwritten. This helps ensure that your erased files can be recovered.	Type `smartcan` at the DOS prompt and press Enter.	Chapter 27, "Using Smartcan."
Image	Records information about your disk to make it easy to recover deleted files or data from a formatted disk.	Type `image` at the DOS prompt and press Enter.	Chapter 25, "Using Image."

Summary of Norton Desktop's utilities

You can access some of these utilities from Norton Desktop's Tools menu. For example, to access Norton Backup, choose NORTON BACKUP from the Tools menu. Other utilities are command-line utilities.

To access a command-line utility:

1 Choose RUN... from the (long) File menu.

   The Run dialog box appears.

2 Type the command-line feature you want to access in the DOS Command text box.

   To access Disk Tools, for example, type `disktools`

3 Select OK.

For details about command-line utilities, see Appendix C, "Command-Line Reference."

For details about RUN..., see Chapter 6, "Launching Files."

Enhancing Speed and Performance

Norton Desktop provides two features that help your computer work more efficiently: Speed Disk and Norton Cache.

Speed Disk reorganizes the physical layout of all files and directories on your disk to minimize movement of the read-write head of the disk drive. This makes it faster for the computer to read data from your hard disk.

To access Speed Disk, choose SPEED DISK from the (long) Tools menu.

For details, see Chapter 17, "Using Speed Disk."

Norton Cache helps your computer actually work faster. It does this by using some of your computer's RAM (random-access or internal memory) to serve as a buffer or temporary holding area. This speeds operations and often dramatically improves performance.

You can install the Norton Cache when you run the Norton Desktop installation program. Or, you can use the Norton Desktop configuration program to install and change the setup of the cache after you install Norton Desktop.

For details, see Chapter 29, "Using Norton Cache."

Using Advise

Advise helps you diagnose, understand and solve a variety of computer problems. Specifically, Advise addresses common disk problems, DOS error messages and CHKDSK error messages. For each type of problem, Advise lists problems or messages from which you can choose. After you select one, Advise explains what is happening, recommends a course of action and, if indicated, automatically runs a corrective program for you.

To access Advise, choose ADVISE from the Help menu.

For details, see Chapter 24, "Using Advise."

GETTING HELP

Norton Desktop provides an easy way to get help quickly with its context-sensitive online Help system.

To access the online Help system:

- Press F1 to display the Help window, then choose a topic.

Or,

- Select a command for which you want help, then press F1 for context-sensitive help.

Or,

- Open the Help menu and choose a command.

Or,

- Select the Help button on the button bar.

TIP: For more information about using the Help system, choose USING HELP from the Help menu.

The Help Menu

the Help menu lets you get help about many aspects of Norton Desktop

The Help menu is the last item on the Norton Desktop menu bar. Figure 1-8 shows the Help menu.

Figure 1-8

```
Help
  Advise
  Index
  Keyboard
  Commands
  Procedures
  Using Help
  
  Guided Tour...
  About...
```

To get help from the Help menu:

1. Open the Help menu (see Figure 1-8).
2. Choose the command that represents the topic for which you want help.
   - ADVISE provides the information you need to handle various system messages and problems you might encounter and helps you take action to quickly correct the problem.

1-32   Using Norton Desktop for DOS

- INDEX provides an alphabetical listing of all of the available Help topics. When you choose one of the topics, the Help window appears on the desktop.
- KEYBOARD displays specific information about keyboard combinations.
- COMMANDS gives a short description of the commands used in Norton Desktop.
- PROCEDURES provides a brief explanation of how to use Norton Desktop's features.
- USING HELP serves as a guide to using the Help system.
- GUIDED TOUR… introduces you to Norton Desktop.
- ABOUT… provides information about Norton Desktop, including the version and copyright information. Also, information about your system is included.

The Help Window

Figure 1-9 shows the Help window.

When you choose a topic such as COMMANDS from the Help menu, the Help window appears. See Table 1-6 for ways to find out more about any topic.

Figure 1-9

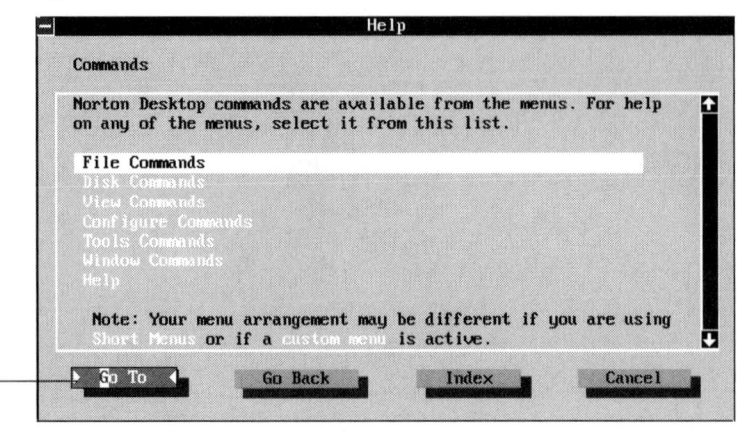

use the command buttons on the Help window to find the information you need

Table 1-6

ACTION	KEYBOARD	MOUSE
Highlight a topic	Use UpArrow and DownArrow	Click the topic
Select a topic	Use UpArrow and DownArrow to highlight the topic, then press Enter or Alt+G	Double-click the topic or select the Go To button
Return to the previous topic you selected	Press Alt+B	Click the Go Back button
View the index, starting with the currently highlighted topic	Press Alt+I	Click the Index Button
Find out more information from a highlighted index topic	Press Alt+H	Click the Help button
Exit the Help system	Press Alt+C or Esc	Click the Cancel button or double-click the close box, the small square box that appears in the upper-left corner of the window

Norton Desktop's Help system

PART II
USING THE DESKTOP

CHAPTER 2

Using Drive Windows

This chapter explains how to change, move, size, organize and customize drive windows. This chapter describes the parts of a drive window and takes an in-depth look at the drive window panes and the commands that relate to them.

Contents

Opening a Drive Window	2-3
Parts of a Drive Window	2-5
Selecting a Drive	2-6
Disk Information	2-7
Finding Directories and Files	2-7
Drive Window Panes	2-9
Controlling the Panes	2-9
Tree Pane	2-10
File Pane	2-10
View Pane	2-11
Modifying the File Pane	2-11
Filtering the File Listing	2-12
Displaying File Details	2-13
Sorting Files	2-14
Displaying Files from the Entire Drive	2-16

Updating the Drive Window 2-17
Modifying the Drive Window 2-17
    Resizing the Drive Window 2-17
    Moving the Drive Window 2-18
Working with Multiple Drive Windows 2-18
    Selecting a Drive Window 2-19
    Cascading Open Drive Windows 2-19
    Tiling Open Drive Windows 2-20
    Hiding Drive Windows 2-21
Closing the Drive Window 2-21

OPENING A DRIVE WINDOW

The *drive window* lets you access and manage your disks, directories and files. It displays the contents of a selected disk drive, showing a directory tree, a file listing, and/or a view of a particular file's contents. You can display multiple drive windows on the desktop—up to eight windows. You can also open more than one drive window for each drive—to make moving directories and files within the same disk easier, for example.

You can use drive windows to easily access and manage your disks, directories and files. A drive window can have up to three kinds of *panes*:

- The *tree pane* displays a directory listing for a selected disk.
- The *file pane* displays a file listing for a selected directory.
- The *view pane* displays the contents of a selected file.

You will learn more about panes in the next section, "Parts of a Drive Window."

To open a drive window:

1 Choose OPEN DRIVE WINDOW... from the Window menu (Ctrl+W).

   The Open Drive Window dialog box opens on the desktop (Figure 2-1).

   Figure 2-1

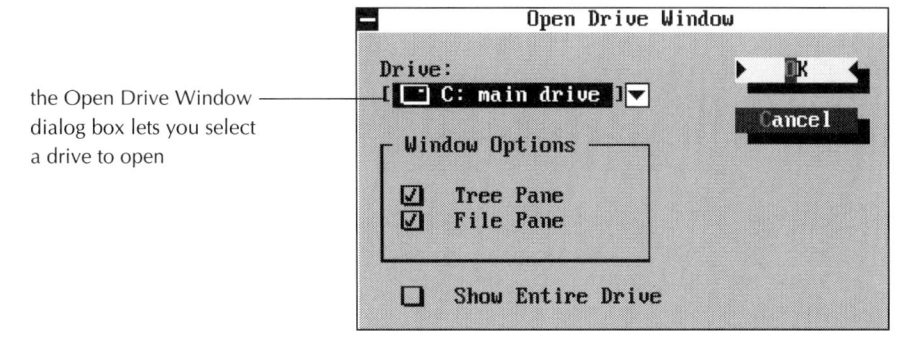

the Open Drive Window dialog box lets you select a drive to open

The Drive combination box defaults to the current drive. If you want to select a different drive:

- Type the letter of the drive in the Drive combination box.

Or,

- Press Ctrl+DownArrow (or click the prompt button) to display a drop-down list of available drives from which you can select another drive.

The Window Options allow you to select the type of panes to display in the drive window. The options that are checked indicate which panes will display when you open the drive window.

If Show Entire Drive is checked, the tree pane is disabled, and the file pane displays all of the files on the selected drive. This feature is explained in detail in the section "Displaying Files from the Entire Drive" later in this chapter.

2 Select OK.

Or,

1 Choose OPEN WINDOW... from the (long) Window menu.

The Open Window dialog box displays (Figure 2-2).

Figure 2-2

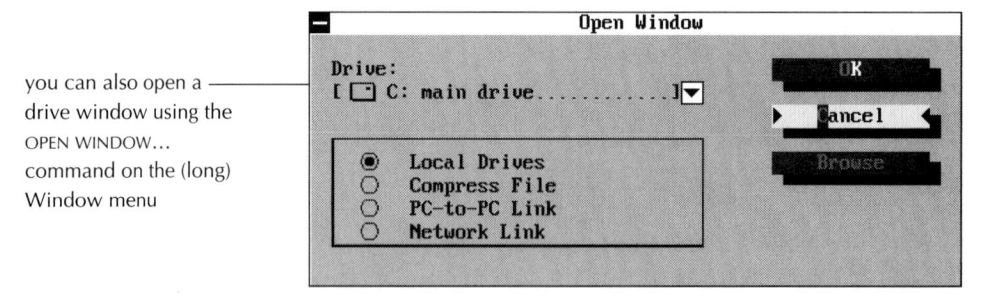

you can also open a drive window using the OPEN WINDOW... command on the (long) Window menu

The Local Drives option button is selected by default.

The Drive combination box defaults to the current drive. If you want to select a different drive:

- Type the letter of the drive in the Drive combination box.

Or,

Using Drive Windows **2-5**

- Press Ctrl+DownArrow (or click the prompt button) to display a drop-down list of available drives from which you can select another drive.

2   Select OK.

Or,

- Double-click the drive icon corresponding to the drive you wish to view.

NOTE: Drive icons are opened using a mouse. If your computer doesn't have a mouse, the drive icons won't automatically display on the screen.

A drive window opens with the same panes it had the last time you opened a window for that drive. The exception is the view pane, which is not opened automatically. For example, if you had just the file pane showing that last time you opened a window for that drive, only the file pane displays the next time you open a window for that drive.

If there are no previous settings for the drive (that is, a window has never been opened for the drive), then the drive window opens with the settings from the currently active window. If there is no active window the settings are determined by the most recently active window.

You can open multiple drive windows on your desktop— for the same drive (to copy or move files between directories, for example) or for other drives by choosing OPEN DRIVE WINDOW… again.

NOTE: If you open a second drive window for the same drive, the drive windows will look the same.

PARTS OF A DRIVE WINDOW

A drive window contains four unique components, as shown in Figure 2-3. In addition, drive windows contain three elements that are common to other windows: a Control-menu box, title bar and a Maximize button.

- The *drive selector* lets you change drives.
- The *status bar* shows information about the current drive.

2-6 Using Norton Desktop for DOS

- You can choose to display from one to three panes:

  The tree pane displays a listing of directories from the selected drive.

  The file pane shows a file listing for the selected directory.

  The view pane displays the contents of the selected file.

- The *Speed Search box* allows you to quickly move through a tree or a file pane directly to a particular directory or file. You won't see the Speed Search box until you start typing the name of a directory or file to search for. If the DOS command line is showing (DOS BACKGROUND from the long View menu is on), you must press Alt+F1 to display the Speed Search box.

Figure 2-3

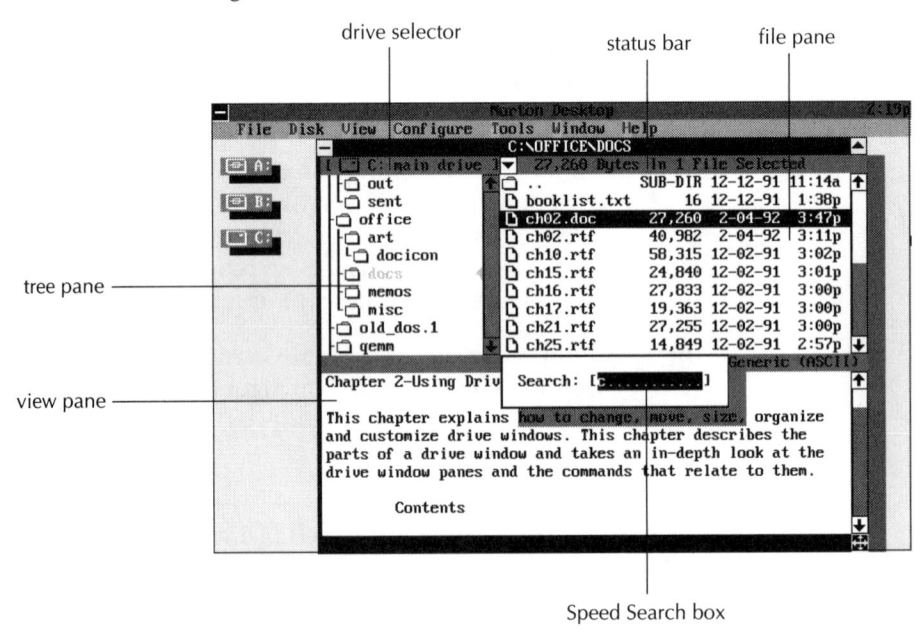

(Screenshot of Norton Desktop showing drive selector, status bar, file pane, tree pane, view pane, and Speed Search box)

SELECTING A DRIVE

The drive selector shows the drive identifier and volume label of the current drive whose contents are displayed in drive window panes. (Note that not all drives have volume labels.) You can quickly display the contents of a different drive by using the drive selector. You don't need to open a new drive window.

To select a new drive for the active drive window:

- Type the new drive letter in the drive selector combination box.

Or,

- Press Ctrl+DownArrow (or click the prompt button) to display a drop-down list of available drives from which you can select another drive.

DISK INFORMATION

The status bar displays information about the disk displayed in the current drive window.

- When nothing is selected, the status bar displays the current disk space used and the space available.
- If you select one or more directories, the status bar shows the number of selected directories.
- If you select one or more files, it displays the number of selected files and the total size of those files.

This information is helpful if you're trying to figure out how many files will fit on a single floppy disk, for example.

FINDING DIRECTORIES AND FILES

The Speed Search feature lets you quickly move to a directory in the tree pane or a file (or subdirectory) in the file pane, depending on which is active.

> **NOTE:** If you want to do a global search for files within a specified directory and its subdirectories, or search for files across one or more drives, see Chapter 5, "Finding Files with SuperFind."

To find a directory or file:

1. Activate the appropriate pane (tree or file) by pressing Tab or Shift+Tab to highlight it, or click the pane.
2. Start typing the name of the file or directory you want to find. The Speed Search box appears (Figure 2-4). For example, type Q to find QTR1.DOC in the active file pane.

    If the DOS command line is on the screen—that is, if DOS BACKGROUND from the (long) View menu is on—press Alt+F1 to display the Speed Search box.

2-8 Using Norton Desktop for DOS

As soon as you start typing in the Speed Search box, the first filename beginning with the letter you typed—"Q" in this example—is selected. (If a match does not exist, the highlight bar doesn't move.)

Figure 2-4

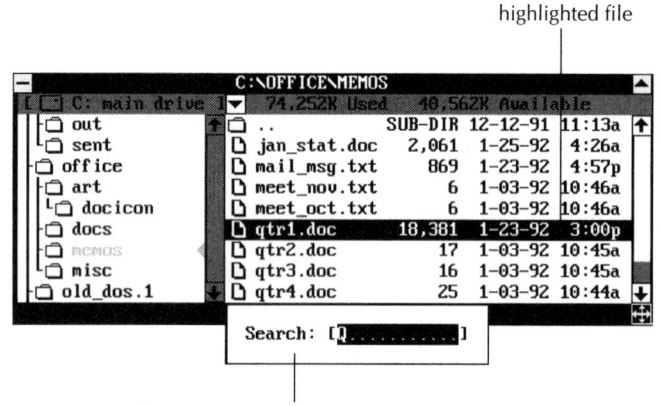

                                                    highlighted file

```
┌─────────────── C:\OFFICE\MEMOS ───────────────┐
│ C: main drive  ▼  74,252K Used   40,562K Available │
│─□ out           │□ ..            SUB-DIR 12-12-91 11:13a│
│ □ sent          │□ jan_stat.doc   2,061  1-25-92  4:26a│
│─□ office        │□ mail_msg.txt     869  1-23-92  4:57p│
│ □ art           │□ meet_nov.txt       6  1-03-92 10:46a│
│  □ docicon      │□ meet_oct.txt       6  1-03-92 10:46a│
│─□ docs          │□ qtr1.doc      18,381  1-23-92  3:00p│
│ □ memos         │□ qtr2.doc          17  1-03-92 10:45a│
│ □ misc          │□ qtr3.doc          16  1-03-92 10:45a│
│─□ old_dos.1     │□ qtr4.doc          25  1-03-92 10:44a│
│          Search: [Q..........]                         │
└────────────────────────────────────────────────────────┘
```

start typing a filename or directory name (press Alt+F1 first if the DOS command line is showing) to reveal the Speed Search box for the active pane and to find the matching file or directory

3 Keep typing the consecutive characters in the file's name until Speed Search highlights the file for which you are searching.

Speed Search selects the first occurrence of a file that matches the text in the Speed Search box. When you backspace over a letter, the file selection changes to reflect what is in the text box.

☞ **TIP:** To find the next directory or file that exactly matches the letters in the Speed Search box, press DownArrow. To go back to the previous match, press UpArrow. This is especially useful when you have many files or directories with similar names on different parts of your disk.

---

4 Press Enter to accept the selection and close the Speed Search box.

Or,

Press Esc to close the Speed Search box without accepting the selection.

DRIVE WINDOW PANES

Note that the matching directory or file is highlighted to distinguish it from other directories or files (see Figure 2-4). But because this may not be the directory or file you actually want, it is not selected until you press Enter.

You can easily change which panes appear in a drive window to fit your particular needs. For example, you may want to display a view pane in addition to the tree and file panes. Or, if you have multiple drive windows on your desktop, you may want to turn off the tree pane and display only the file pane.

NOTE: The changes you make to the drive window are saved when you close the window. So, if you display only the file pane and then close the drive window, only the file pane will display the next time you open a drive window for that drive.

Controlling the Panes

Each pane is controlled by a command on the View menu; the command bears the name of the pane it controls. For example, choose VIEW PANE from the View menu to display the view pane. Choose VIEW PANE again to turn off the view pane. Note that each of these menu commands is a toggle that turns a pane on and off. When a pane is displayed in the drive window, a checkmark appears next to the command. Figure 2-5 indicates that the tree and file panes are on—that is, they are displayed in the current drive window.

NOTE: The menu commands for each pane control the *active window* only.

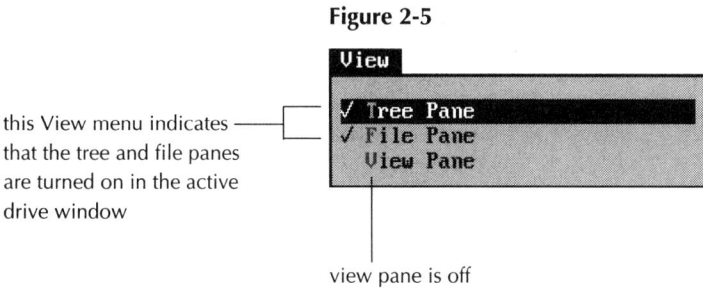

Figure 2-5

this View menu indicates that the tree and file panes are turned on in the active drive window

view pane is off

Tree Pane

The tree pane displays a directory tree, which makes it easy to organize directories. You can easily select directories for directory and file operations, such as moving or copying a file or subdirectory from one location to another.

For information on how to move and copy files, see the section "Moving and Copying Directories and Files" in Chapter 4, "Managing Directories and Files."

The tree pane appears in the drive window by default. If the pane does not appear in the window, simply turn it on.

To display the tree pane in the drive window:

- Choose TREE PANE from the View menu.

NOTE: The TREE PANE command is dimmed whenever you choose SHOW ENTIRE DRIVE from the (long) View menu. This is because SHOW ENTIRE DRIVE lists all of the files on the selected drive, not just those in a specific directory. Therefore, you cannot choose TREE PANE when the SHOW ENTIRE DRIVE command is toggled on.

File Pane

The file pane appears in the drive window by default. It displays a list of files within a selected directory, allowing you to select files for file operations such as copying or deleting. You can also move or copy files by dragging them from one file pane to another file pane in a different drive window. See the section "Moving and Copying Directories and Files" in Chapter 4, "Managing Directories and Files."

To display the file pane in the drive window:

- Choose FILE PANE from the View menu.

By default, the file pane lists all of the files in the selected directory by filename and file icon. You can modify this listing by using the following commands on the View menu:

- FILTER... lists only those directories and files you specify. You can choose to display certain types of files or groups of files with similar filenames or file extensions.

Using Drive Windows **2-11**

- FILE DETAILS… (on the long View menu) displays the filename along with any other information you specify, including file icon, size, date, time attributes and the file's full path. The file's full path is useful when SHOW ENTIRE DRIVE is on.
- SORT BY (on the long View menu) arranges the file listing in the order you specify. You can list files by filename, extension, size, or date and time in ascending or descending order.
- SHOW ENTIRE DRIVE (on the long View menu) displays all of the files on the selected drive. It disables the tree pane, since a tree pane is meaningless when the files of the entire disk are shown.

Each of these commands is discussed later in this chapter.

View Pane

You can view the contents of files that are in your local drives or network drives by using the view pane. The view pane displays the contents of the currently selected file—a WordPerfect, Lotus 1-2-3 or dBASE file, for example—without launching the application that created it. Thus, you can quickly view a file to determine its content and decide whether to use the file, ignore it or delete it.

To display the view pane in the drive window:

- Choose VIEW PANE from the View menu.

For detailed information about viewing files, see Chapter 7, "Viewing Files."

MODIFYING THE FILE PANE

Initially, the file pane lists all of the files in the selected directory by filename and file icon only. This is convenient for quickly seeing all of the files in the directory.

However, you may want to limit the list to specific types of files, see additional details about the files, or sort them in a different order. You can easily modify the listing in the file pane using the FILTER…, FILE DETAILS…, SORT BY and SHOW ENTIRE DRIVE commands.

Filtering the File Listing

By default, the file pane lists all files in the selected directory.

To list only certain file types or specific file groups:

- Choose FILTER... from the (long) View menu.

  The Filter dialog box appears on the desktop (Figure 2-6). You can use the options in this dialog box to display files by type or attribute, or by the custom specification you choose.

Figure 2-6

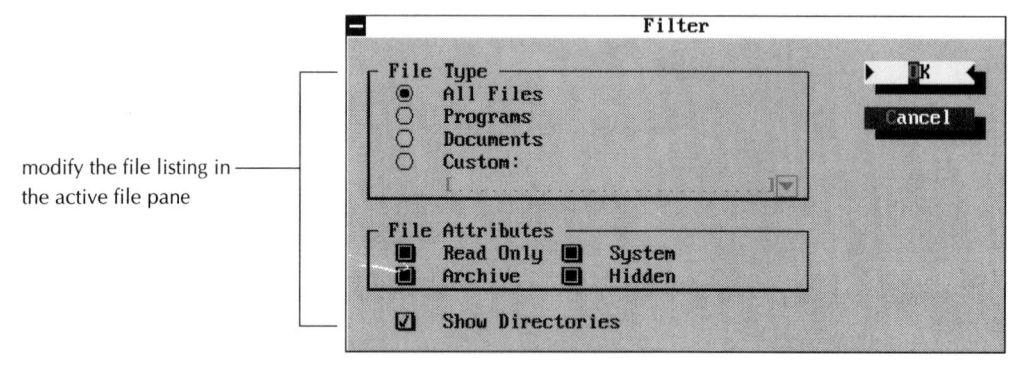

```
┌─                        Filter                        ─┐
│  ┌─ File Type ─────────────────────┐   ► ▓OK▓ ◄        │
│  │  ◉  All Files                   │                   │
│  │  ○  Programs                    │    ▓Cancel▓       │
│  │  ○  Documents                   │                   │
│  │  ○  Custom:                     │                   │
│  │     [              ]▼           │                   │
│  └─────────────────────────────────┘                   │
│  ┌─ File Attributes ──────────────────────────────┐    │
│  │  ▣ Read Only   ▣ System                        │    │
│  │  ▣ Archive     ▣ Hidden                        │    │
│  └────────────────────────────────────────────────┘    │
│     ☑ Show Directories                                 │
└────────────────────────────────────────────────────────┘
```

modify the file listing in the active file pane

Filtering Files by Type

You can display files by file type using the following options:

- **All Files:** displays all files in a selected directory. This is the default.
- **Programs:** displays all files with .BAT, .COM, .EXE and .BTM file extensions. Batch programs typically have a .BAT extension. Application files, such as WordPerfect, Lotus 1-2-3 and dBASE, typically have an .EXE extension or a .COM extension. NDOS batch files have .BTM extensions.
- **Documents:** displays files having .DOC and .TXT extensions. Documents associated with Word usually have .DOC extensions, and several types of editors create files with .TXT extensions.

Using Drive Windows **2-13**

- Custom: displays files with the file extensions you specify.

  You can specify single or multiple file extensions in the Custom combination box (wildcards are allowed). For example, type Q*.* to display all files with a filename that begins with Q. (For information about the ? and * wildcards, refer to Chapter 1, "Getting Started.") Multiple file extensions must be separated with a space. Press Ctrl+DownArrow (or click the prompt button) to display a history of the last 10 custom filters you entered.

Filtering Files by Attribute

Files can have up to four properties, commonly called file *attributes*. (A file does not need to have any attributes.) By default, the check boxes in the Filter dialog box are set to "Ignore" (indicated by the fill). Thus, files are displayed regardless of their attributes. To display only those files with a given attribute or attributes, check the appropriate check boxes:

- Read Only: displays files marked as read-only, which protects them from being modified or deleted.
- Archive: displays files marked as archived. A file marked as archived indicates that the file has not been backed up since it was last modified.
- System: displays DOS or system-related files.
- Hidden: displays files with a "hidden" attribute, which is assigned to critical files to make them harder to access and more difficult to delete than other files.

For detailed information about file attributes, see the section "Changing File Attributes" in Chapter 4, "Managing Directories and Files."

The Show Directories check box, checked by default, displays all subdirectories in a selected directory. If it is not checked, subdirectories do not appear in the file pane.

Displaying File Details

You can control the amount of detail you wish to display for each file listed in the file pane with the FILE DETAILS... command.

All file listings must contain the filename. However, you can optionally include any combination of these items: the file icon, size, date, time and attributes.

In addition, when SHOW ENTIRE DRIVE is active you can optionally display the name of the subdirectory where a file resides.

To specify how files should be listed in the file pane:

1   Choose FILE DETAILS... from the (long) View menu.

    The File Details dialog box appears (Figure 2-7).

2   Check the check boxes for the items you wish to display, including icons, size, date, time, attributes, and directory (the file's full path). The Directory check box is available when SHOW ENTIRE DRIVE is on.

    Note that the dialog box shows a sample file listing. Experiment with checking and unchecking options in the group box until the sample matches the way you want to see your files listed.

3   Select OK.

Figure 2-7

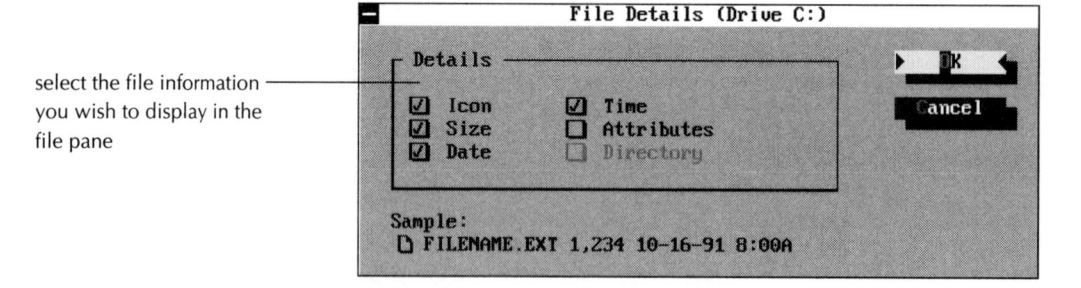

select the file information you wish to display in the file pane

Note that when you display only the filename, the file pane lists files in multiple columns. When you choose to add a detail to the file listing, the file pane displays the filenames in a single column, with selected details in columns to the right of the filenames.

Sorting Files

By default, files are listed alphanumerically by name, in ascending order (from A to Z). You can change this sort order with the SORT BY command.

Using Drive Windows **2-15**

> **NOTE:** If you are using short menus, instead of seeing the SORT BY command, you will see two commands on the (short) View menu: SORT BY EXTENSION and SORT BY NAME.

Selecting the SORT BY command from the (long) View menu causes a cascading menu to appear with the following additional menu commands:

- NAME sorts filenames in alphanumeric order.
- EXTENSION sorts file extensions in alphanumeric order.
- SIZE sorts by file size in descending order (largest files first), by default.
- DATE & TIME sorts by date and time in descending order (most recently modified files first).
- UNSORTED lists directories first and lists files in the same order you would see if you typed DIR from the DOS prompt.

Choose one of these commands to select the primary sort order (Figure 2-8). The secondary sort order is by filename. Thus, when you sort by extension, files are sorted first by file extension, then by filename.

Figure 2-8

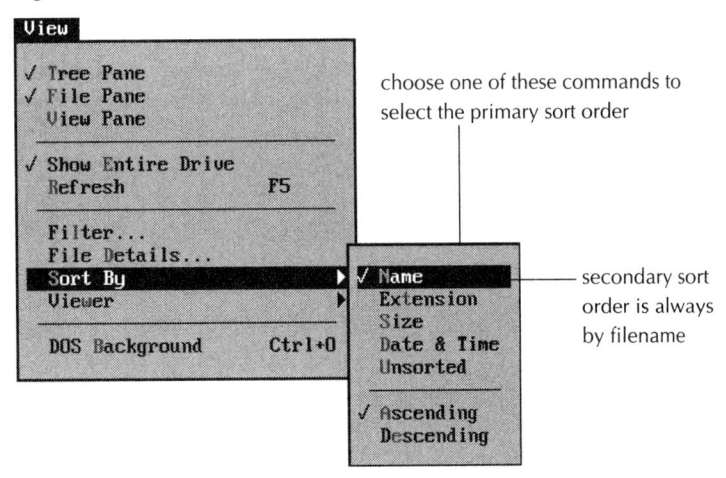

```
View
 √ Tree Pane
 √ File Pane
   View Pane

 √ Show Entire Drive
   Refresh          F5

   Filter...
   File Details...
   Sort By        ▶  √ Name
   Viewer            Extension
                     Size
   DOS Background  Ctrl+O  Date & Time
                     Unsorted

                   √ Ascending
                     Descending
```

choose one of these commands to select the primary sort order

secondary sort order is always by filename

To arrange the file listing in order by filename, extension, size, or date:

1 Choose SORT BY from the (long) View menu.
2 Choose the criterion by which you wish to sort. When you choose a sort criterion, a checkmark appears next to the given menu command. By default, a checkmark appears next to NAME, because the preset sort order is by filename.

To sort by ascending or descending order:

- Choose either ASCENDING or DESCENDING from the View:Sort By menu.

  When you choose one of these sort criteria, a checkmark appears next to the given menu command. ASCENDING is the preset sort order.

NOTE: If UNSORTED is checked, the ASCENDING and DESCENDING options are not available.

NOTE: If you are using the short menus, you can arrange your file listing in ascending order by file extension or filename by choosing the SORT BY EXTENSION or SORT BY NAME command from the (short) View menu.

Displaying Files from the Entire Drive

In addition to displaying the files for a selected directory, the drive window can also show a listing of all the files for a selected disk.

To display all of the files on the selected disk:

- Choose SHOW ENTIRE DRIVE from the (long) View menu.

  Don't be surprised when the tree pane disappears: SHOW ENTIRE DRIVE disables the tree pane, because you cannot display a directory tree when you've chosen to display all the files on a disk. (Note that the TREE PANE menu command is dimmed, and that SHOW ENTIRE DRIVE is checked to indicate that it is on.) When you toggle SHOW ENTIRE DRIVE off, the tree pane returns to the drive window.

> **NOTE:** SHOW ENTIRE DRIVE only controls the file display in the active window.

UPDATING THE DRIVE WINDOW

From time to time, you'll want to update the display in the drive window. For example, when the drive window shows the contents of a floppy disk, you'll want to refresh the drive window if you change floppy disks. You should also refresh the drive window whenever you create a directory or file using another application or from the DOS prompt.

To update the panes displayed in the current drive window:

- Choose REFRESH from the View menu.

MODIFYING THE DRIVE WINDOW

In addition to toggling drive window panes on and off, you can also resize or move the drive window.

> **NOTE:** Any changes you make to the drive window are saved when you close the window. The next time you open a drive window for that drive it will appear as it was the last time it was opened—including its position on the screen, its size and the types of panes that display.

Resizing the Drive Window

Like any other type of window, you can resize an active drive window so that it takes up more or less of your desktop. You cannot, however, change the size of the individual panes.

To change the size of a drive window:

1. Choose SIZE from the Control menu.

   The title bar disappears and the drive window border changes.

2. Use the arrow keys to resize the window.
3. When the window is the size you want, press Enter.

Or,

- Drag the resize button (the four-headed arrow in the lower-right corner of the window) until the drive window is the size you want.

To enlarge a drive window to full-screen:

- Choose MAXIMIZE from the Control menu.

Or,

- Click the Maximize button

The drive window expands to fill the screen. Note that when the window is enlarged to its maximum size, the Maximize button is replaced by the Restore button.

To restore a maximized drive window:

- Choose RESTORE from the Control menu.

Or,

- Click the Restore button.

Moving the Drive Window

You can easily move any active drive window to a new location on the screen.

To move a drive window:

1. Choose MOVE from the Control menu.

   The title bar disappears and the drive window border changes.

2. Use the arrow keys to move the window left, right, up or down.

3. When the window is placed where you want it, press Enter.

Or,

- Move the window to a new location by clicking and holding down the mouse button on the title bar and dragging the window to the location you want.

TIP: To cancel a move or a resize, press Esc *instead of* pressing Enter.

WORKING WITH MULTIPLE DRIVE WINDOWS

There are several ways to organize multiple drive windows on the desktop. In addition to resizing and moving drive windows, you can also cascade, tile or hide them.

Selecting a Drive Window

When there are several drive windows open on your desktop, you can select a drive window using one of several methods.

To select a drive window:

- Press Ctrl+Tab until you activate the given drive window.

Or,

- Choose the drive window from the Window menu (Alt+W, #; where # is the number assigned to the given drive window on the Window menu).

    For example, suppose your Window menu looks like the one shown in Figure 2-9. Press 3 to select the C:\OFFICE\MEMOS drive window. This is especially useful when the drive window you want to select is hidden behind something else.

Or,

- Click the appropriate drive window.

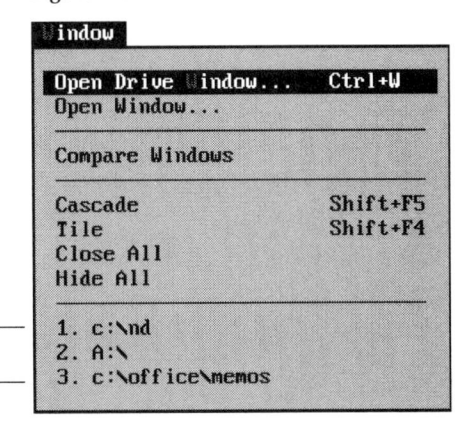

Figure 2-9

```
Window
┌─────────────────────────────────────┐
│ Open Drive Window...     Ctrl+W     │
│ Open Window...                      │
│ ─────────────────────────────────── │
│ Compare Windows                     │
│ ─────────────────────────────────── │
│ Cascade                  Shift+F5   │
│ Tile                     Shift+F4   │
│ Close All                           │
│ Hide All                            │
│ ─────────────────────────────────── │
│ 1. c:\nd                            │
│ 2. A:\                              │
│ 3. c:\office\memos                  │
└─────────────────────────────────────┘
```

one of the ways to select an open drive window is to choose the number assigned to that drive window on the Window menu

Cascading Open Drive Windows

You can arrange all open drive windows on your desktop in a cascading sequence using the CASCADE command on the Window menu.

2-20   Using Norton Desktop for DOS

To cascade all open drive windows:

- Choose CASCADE from the Window menu.

  The title of the active window appears highlighted (Figure 2-10).

Figure 2-10

CASCADE arranges all open drive windows in a cascading sequence

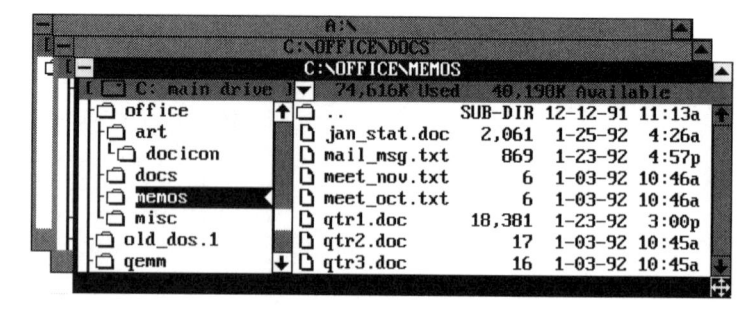

Tiling Open Drive Windows

You can also arrange all open drive windows on your desktop side-by-side using the TILE command on the Window menu.

To tile all open drive windows:

- Choose TILE from the Window menu.

  The active window appears with the title bar highlighted (Figure 2-11).

Figure 2-11

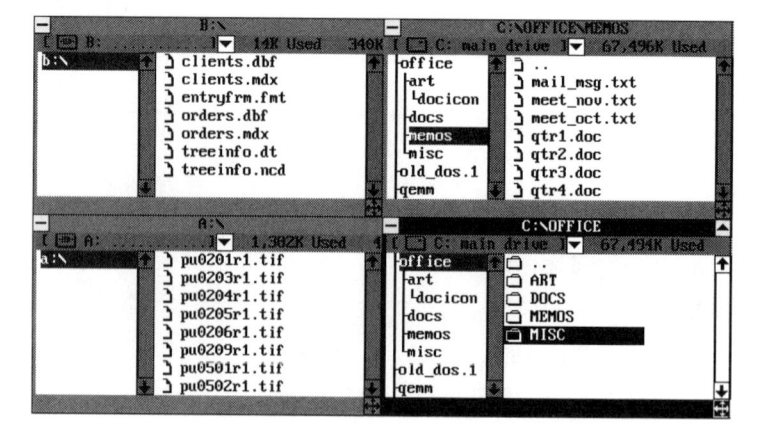

TILE arranges all open drive windows side-by-side

Hiding Drive Windows

You can temporarily clean up your desktop by hiding all open drive windows. Note, however, that hiding the drive windows is *not* a substitute for closing them.

To hide all open drive windows without closing them:

- Choose HIDE ALL from the Window menu.

   This menu command is a toggle; after you choose HIDE ALL, the menu command changes to UNHIDE ALL so you can reveal all of your hidden windows.

CLOSING THE DRIVE WINDOW

You can close drive windows one at a time, or close all drive windows in a single step.

To close a single drive window:

- Choose CLOSE from the Control menu.

Or,

- Press Ctrl+F4.

Or,

- Double-click the Control-menu box

To close all drive windows at one time:

- Choose CLOSE ALL from the Window menu.

Managing Disks

This chapter explains how to perform disk-management tasks using Norton Desktop. You can quickly copy, format and label disks.

Contents

Copying a Floppy Disk 3-3
Formatting a Floppy Disk 3-4
    Hard Disk Formatting 3-8
    Selecting Floppy Disk Types 3-9
Labeling a Disk 3-9
Making a Disk Bootable 3-10

Many of the tasks you perform at your computer are repetitive tasks such as formatting or making multiple copies of floppy disks. With Norton Desktop you can perform these tasks without knowing the DOS commands—you can use pull-down menus instead.

COPYING A FLOPPY DISK

When you copy a floppy disk using the COPY DISKETTE... command, the *source floppy disk* (the floppy disk you are copying *from*) and the *target floppy disk* (the floppy disk you are copying *to*) must have the same disk capacity. You cannot, for instance, perform a disk copy from a 720K floppy disk to a 360K floppy disk.

If your computer has two floppy disk drives and both drives have the same capacity, you can use one drive for the source and the other drive for the target. If your computer has only one floppy disk drive or if it has two drives that are different (for example, one 3½-inch drive and one 5¼-inch drive) you must use the same drive for both the source and the target floppy disk.

TIP: To copy all files from one disk to another when the source floppy disk and target floppy disk have different disk capacities, you can use the COPY... command from the File menu. See Chapter 4, "Managing Directories and Files," for more information about the COPY... command.

To copy the contents of one floppy disk onto another floppy disk:

1   Choose COPY DISKETTE... from the Disk menu.

    The Copy Diskette dialog box appears (Figure 3-1).

2   Select the source drive from the From drop-down list box.

3   If your computer has two floppy disk drives with the same capacity, select the target drive from the To drop-down list box.

    If your computer has two floppy disk drives that have different capacities or your computer has only one floppy disk drive, Norton Desktop automatically makes the target drive the same drive that you selected for the source drive.

Figure 3-1

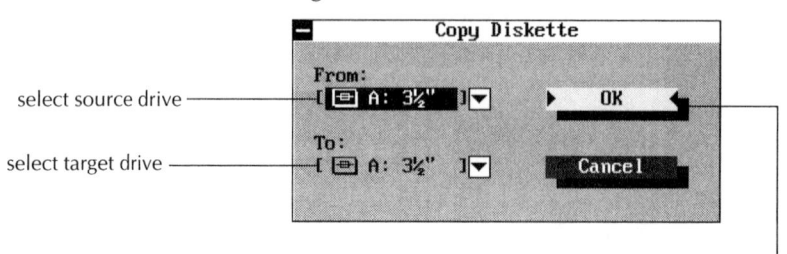

```
┌─────── Copy Diskette ───────┐
│  From:                       │
│  [ 🖴 A: 3½" ]▼    ▶  OK  ◀  │
│  To:                         │
│  [ 🖴 A: 3½" ]▼    Cancel    │
└──────────────────────────────┘
```

select source drive → (From field)
select target drive → (To field)

...then select OK to copy the contents of one floppy disk to another

4 Select OK.

A prompt box appears asking you to insert the source floppy disk into the designated floppy drive.

5 Insert the source floppy disk and select OK.

If you have a dual-floppy computer and both floppy drives have the same disk capacity, insert the target floppy disk into the other floppy disk drive.

If you have a single-floppy computer, Norton Desktop reads the source floppy disk, then a prompt box appears asking you to insert the target floppy disk.

A message box reports the status of the copying.

6 Insert the target floppy disk and select OK.

A message box again appears to update the status of the copying.

When copying is complete, you are asked if you want to make another copy of the same floppy disk. If you want to make another copy, select Yes.

If you elect to make another copy of the source floppy disk, you are prompted to insert another target floppy disk.

FORMATTING A FLOPPY DISK

Formatting a floppy disk prepares the disk to store data. Data is stored on a formatted floppy disk in two areas: the system area and the data area. The system area is an index of the information found on your disk. The data area contains the actual data of your files. Low-level formats physically reformat the *tracks* on your disk and destroy the data stored there. High-level formats simply clear out system information about where all of your data is kept; the actual data is not touched.

You can recover data from your floppy disks even after an accidental—or intentional—format if the system information was saved before the format. You can tell Norton Desktop to save a "snapshot" of this information in a file called IMAGE.DAT. The IMAGE.DAT file stays in the root directory of your hard disk and can then be used later by UnFormat and UnErase to recover data. (Refer to Chapters 26, 16 and 25 if you want more information about UnFormat, UnErase or Image.)

Norton Desktop offers three different ways to format your disk: Safe Format, Quick Format, and DOS Format.

Safe Format:

- Checks the surface of the disk
- Marks any bad sectors
- Reformats tracks that need to be reformatted

Because it doesn't reformat every track, Safe Format is faster than DOS Format. If you tell Norton Desktop to save the system information (this option is selected by default), it creates an IMAGE.DAT file which you can then use to recover data if necessary.

Quick Format is even faster than Safe Format. Quick Format does no physical formatting on your disk at all—it just erases the system information from your disk so the data index is clear and ready to be used again. Again, you can tell Norton Desktop to save the system information in the IMAGE.DAT file. You can use Quick Format only on a disk that has already been formatted.

DOS Format physically reformats all tracks on your disk. The system information is not saved, and any data that was stored on the disk is lost.

To format a floppy disk:

1   Choose FORMAT DISKETTE... from the Disk menu.

    The Format Diskette dialog box appears (Figure 3-2).

3-6 *Using Norton Desktop for DOS*

Figure 3-2

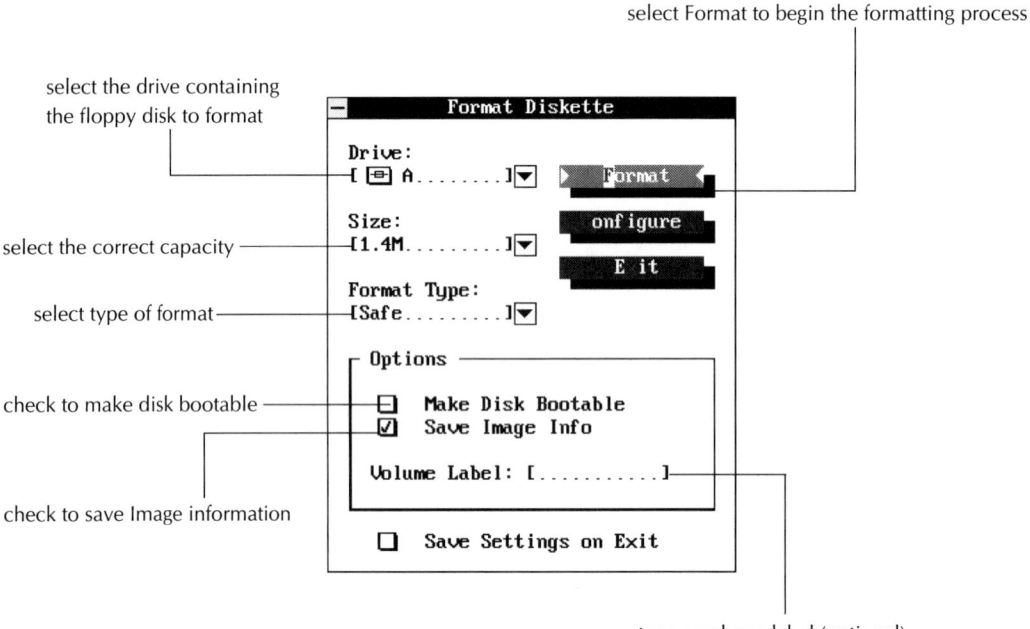

```
                        ┌─── Format Diskette ───┐
                        │                        │
   select the drive     │  Drive:                │   select Format to begin the formatting process
   containing the       │  [▣ A........]▼   ▶ Format
   floppy disk to format│                        │
                        │  Size:            Configure
   select the correct   │  [1.4M.......]▼        │
   capacity             │                    E it │
                        │  Format Type:          │
   select type of format│  [Safe.......]▼        │
                        │  ┌─ Options ─────────┐ │
                        │  │ ☐ Make Disk Bootable│
   check to make disk   │  │ ☑ Save Image Info  │
   bootable             │  │                    │ │
                        │  │ Volume Label: [........] │
   check to save Image  │  └────────────────────┘ │
   information          │     ☐ Save Settings on Exit
                        └────────────────────────┘
                                          │
                                          type a volume label (optional)
```

2 Select the drive containing the floppy disk to be formatted from the Drive drop-down list box.

☞ **TIP:** By default, Safe Format is preset to allow formatting of floppy disks only—this prevents someone from accidentally, or intentionally, reformatting your hard disk. Notice that only floppy drives are listed in the Drive drop-down list box. To enable hard disk formatting, see the "Hard Disk Formatting" section in this chapter.

3 Select the correct floppy disk capacity from the Size drop-down list box.

4 Select the type of format you wish to use from the Format Type drop-down list box.

5 Check the appropriate check boxes in the Options group box to make the disk *bootable* and to save the Image information.

   Make Disk Bootable copies the DOS system files onto your disk.

   Save Image Info saves the system area information to a file called IMAGE.DAT. This check box is dimmed if you've checked the Make Disk Bootable check box or if you've chosen to format your floppy disk with the DOS format.

6 Type up to 11 characters in the Volume Label text box to attach a volume label to your floppy disk. This is optional.

NOTE: A *volume label* is the name of your floppy disk and can help you identify a disk or distinguish one floppy disk from another. The volume label appears whenever you display the contents of the floppy disk.

7 Insert a floppy disk into the appropriate disk drive.
8 Select the Format command button.

   Norton Desktop begins analyzing the floppy disk, and a confirmation box appears, displaying any directories and files found on the floppy disk. You are asked to confirm that you want to format the floppy disk.

9 Select Yes to continue with the format.

   As the format proceeds, Norton Desktop provides a set of statistics: format options chosen, total disk space available, size of system area, bad-sector space and unused disk space.

   When the format finishes, a message box informs you the format was successfully completed.

10 Select OK.
11 To exit from Format Diskette, select Exit.

   Or,

   To format another disk, repeat steps 2 through 10.

Hard Disk Formatting

By default, Norton Desktop protects you from accidentally formatting your hard disk by allowing formatting of floppy disks only. You can override this setting with the Allow Hard Disk Formatting check box in the Configuration dialog box, shown in Figure 3-3.

> **STOP**
>
> **WARNING:** Think twice before formatting your hard disk. Norton Desktop performs a high-level format on your hard disk which clears out all of the system information regarding where your data is stored.

To allow hard disk formatting:

1 Select the Configure command button from the Format Diskette dialog box (see Figure 3-2).

The Configuration dialog box appears on the desktop (Figure 3-3).

Figure 3-3

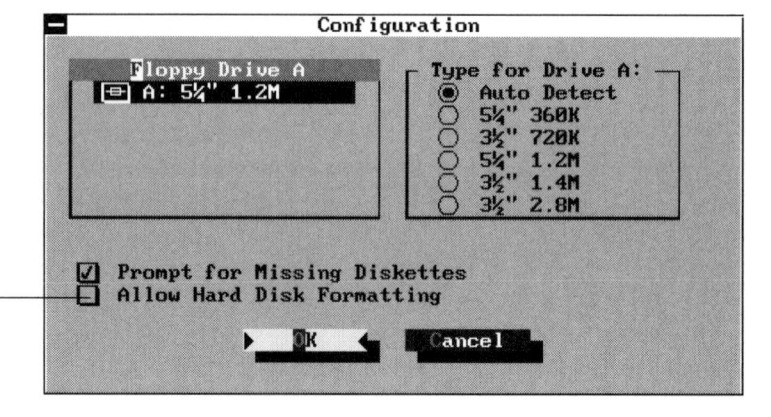

```
┌─────────────────────── Configuration ───────────────────────┐
│  ┌─ Floppy Drive A ──────────┐  ┌─ Type for Drive A: ─────┐ │
│  │ [≡] A: 5¼" 1.2M           │  │ ● Auto Detect           │ │
│  │                           │  │ ○ 5¼"  360K             │ │
│  │                           │  │ ○ 3½"  720K             │ │
│  │                           │  │ ○ 5¼"  1.2M             │ │
│  │                           │  │ ○ 3½"  1.4M             │ │
│  │                           │  │ ○ 3½"  2.8M             │ │
│  └───────────────────────────┘  └─────────────────────────┘ │
│                                                             │
│  [✓] Prompt for Missing Diskettes                           │
│  [ ] Allow Hard Disk Formatting ──── check if you want to   │
│                                       override the safety   │
│           ▶  OK  ◀      Cancel        feature of not        │
│                                       allowing hard disk    │
└─────────────────────────────────────  formats ──────────────┘
```

2 Check the Allow Hard Disk Formatting check box.

3 Select OK.

Notice that your hard disk identifier now appears in the Drive combination box.

Selecting Floppy Disk Types

Norton Desktop automatically detects the number and kind of floppy drives attached to your computer. When you select a floppy drive, Norton Desktop then sets itself to that drive's highest physical capacity. You can, however, format a 720K floppy diskette in a 1.4M floppy drive, for example, by selecting the correct disk capacity from the Configuration dialog box.

To select a different disk capacity:

1 Select the Configure command button from the Format Diskette dialog box (see Figure 3-2).

   The Configuration dialog box appears on the desktop, (see Figure 3-3).

2 Select your computer's type of floppy drive from the Floppy Drive list box.

3 Select one of the Type for Drive option buttons. Auto Detect is preset.

4 Check the Prompt for Missing Diskettes check box if you want to be prompted when a floppy disk drive needs to have a disk inserted.

   Sometimes trying to format an unformatted floppy disk on a laptop computer causes Norton Desktop to report that there is no floppy disk in the disk drive. If you encounter this problem, uncheck this check box. The box is checked by default.

5 Select OK.

LABELING A DISK

A volume label is part of a disk's directory information—it is the disk's name. For example, the volume label of a disk appears in the drive window (Figure 3-4). A volume has no label (it's blank) until you create one for it.

Figure 3-4

disk's volume label is displayed when you use the drive window to view the contents of a disk

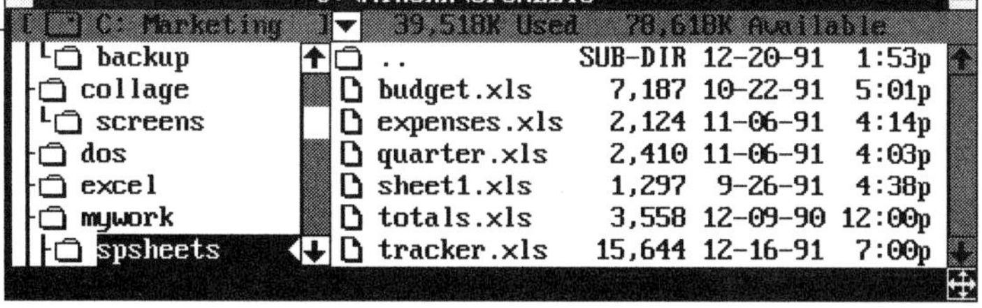

To add or change a volume label:

1 Choose LABEL DISK... from the (long) Disk menu.

The Label Disk dialog box appears on the desktop (Figure 3-5). The current disk drive and its volume label are displayed by default.

Figure 3-5

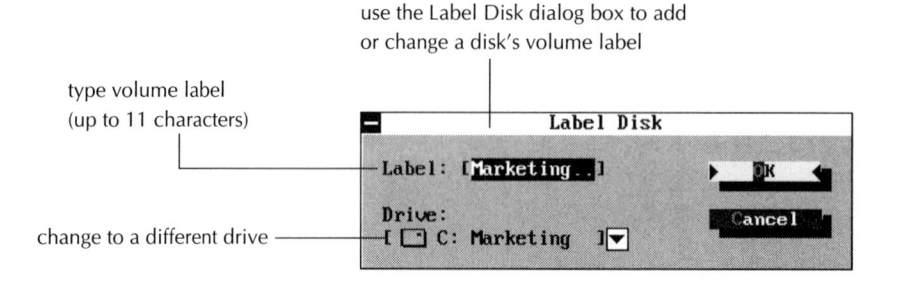

use the Label Disk dialog box to add or change a disk's volume label

type volume label (up to 11 characters)

change to a different drive

```
┌─────────────── Label Disk ───────────────┐
│  Label: [Marketing..]        ► OK ◄      │
│  Drive:                                  │
│  [ ▢ C: Marketing  ]▼        Cancel      │
└──────────────────────────────────────────┘
```

2 To change to a different disk drive, select it from the Drive drop-down list.

3 Type the volume label (using up to 11 characters) in the Label text box.

4 Select OK.

MAKING A DISK BOOTABLE

A disk that contains all of the files and the portion of the operating system necessary to start your computer is called a bootable disk. One way to make a floppy disk bootable is to copy the system files to the disk at the time you format it. Using Norton Desktop, however, you can make a bootable disk at any time—even if the disk already has files on it.

To make a disk bootable:

1 Choose MAKE DISK BOOTABLE... from the (long) Disk menu.

The Make Disk Bootable dialog box appears on the desktop (Figure 3-6).

2 Select the drive that contains the disk you wish to make bootable from the scrollable list.

Managing Disks 3-11

Figure 3-6

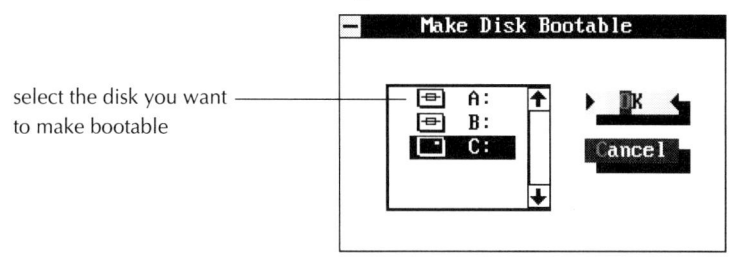

```
┌─ Make Disk Bootable ──────┐
│                            │
│   ┌─ A:    ▶ OK           │
│   ├─ B:                   │
│   └─ C:    Cancel         │
│                            │
└────────────────────────────┘
```

select the disk you want to make bootable

3 Select OK.

If you chose a floppy disk drive, a prompt box appears on the desktop prompting you to insert a floppy disk into the drive.

If you chose a hard disk drive, a prompt box appears on the desktop informing you that the procedure will place new system files on the drive. You should only use this procedure to make a hard disk bootable if it has trouble starting up on its own. Use a bootable floppy containing the same version of DOS as your computer's hard disk.

4 Select OK to copy the system files to the disk.

A message box appears on the desktop when the transfer of files is complete.

5 Select OK to close the message box.

Managing Directories and Files

This chapter explains how to manage your directories and files, including: making directories; copying, moving and deleting directories and files; renaming directories and files; comparing directories; changing file attributes and compressing, editing and printing files.

Contents

Directory Structures 4-3
    Making Directories 4-3
    Naming Directories and Files 4-4
Selecting Directories or Files 4-4
Using the SELECT Command 4-6
Deselecting Files 4-8
    Using the DESELECT Command 4-9
Moving and Copying Directories and Files 4-10
    Moving Directories and Files 4-10
    Using the PRUNE & GRAFT Command 4-13
    Copying Directories and Files 4-14
Deleting Directories and Files 4-17
    Using the DELETE... Command 4-17
Renaming Directories and Files 4-18
Comparing Directories 4-19
Changing File Attributes 4-20

4-1

Compressing Files 4-22
    Viewing the Contents of a Compressed File 4-24
Editing Text Files 4-25
    The Norton Desktop Editor 4-25
    Windows 4-26
    Managing Files You Edit 4-27
    Navigating in the Norton Desktop Editor 4-30
    Selecting Text 4-32
    Inserting and Deleting Text 4-33
    Searching For and Replacing Text 4-35
    Word Wrap 4-38
    Reformatting a File 4-39
    Printing Files in the Norton Desktop Editor 4-40
Printing Files from Norton Desktop 4-40

Managing Directories and Files   4-3

DIRECTORY STRUCTURES

It's important to create and maintain an organized directory structure if you plan to manage your directories and files efficiently. Of course, the fine details relating to how you organize your files ultimately depends on your preferences. Regardless of the little details, however, it's a good idea to maintain a separate directory for each application (such as Harvard Graphics and Microsoft Word, for example). It's wise to keep your data in separate directories as well.

Take some time to decide how you would ideally like to organize your files. Don't worry that you have to come up with the definitive organizational plan right this moment—you can alter your plan later, if necessary. Even if you have been using your current structure for a long time, you can change it easily.

Making Directories

You can make a directory anywhere on any drive with the MAKE DIRECTORY... command. Norton Desktop creates a new subdirectory in the current directory by default.

To make a directory:

1   Choose MAKE DIRECTORY... from the (long) File menu.

    The Make Directory dialog box appears on the desktop (Figure 4-1).

Figure 4-1

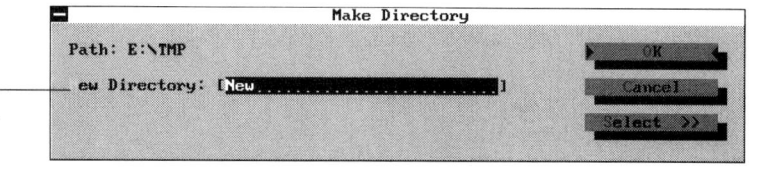

type the name of your new directory in the New Directory text box

```
┌─────────────── Make Directory ───────────────┐
│  Path: E:\TMP                          ┌──OK──┐
│  ew Directory: [New              ]    │Cancel│
│                                        │Select >>│
└──────────────────────────────────────────────┘
```

2   Type the name of your new directory in the New Directory text box.

    Your new directory is created as a subdirectory to the current directory. To select a parent directory other than the current directory, type the new pathname in the New Directory text box along with the directory name or select the Select command button and highlight a new parent directory in the tree pane.

3   Select OK to make your new directory.

Naming Directories and Files

Because DOS only allows you to use up to eight *alphanumeric* characters (characters you can type from the keyboard) when naming your directories and files, it is important that you select names that are concise and meaningful. This section is not intended to be a lesson in creating meaningful names. Rather, it is meant to remind you about DOS naming conventions.

When naming directories and files you need to follow certain DOS rules. Directory names and filenames can range from one to eight alphanumeric characters. The following symbols cannot be used because DOS has reserved them for other purposes:

- a blank or a space
- . " / \ [ ] : | < > = + ; , * ?

In addition, you can add a file extension of up to three alphanumeric characters, with a period (.) before it, when naming files and directories. See your DOS manual for additional information on file naming conventions.

SELECTING DIRECTORIES OR FILES

The Norton Desktop directory and file operations allow you to select the directory or file either before or after you've chosen the operation. For instance, you can choose the MOVE... command before you've indicated what file you'd like to move. It is often easier and more efficient, however, if you select a directory or file from the drive window before choosing the operation.

Selecting a directory is like selecting a file with one exception—in the tree pane, you can select only directories; in the file pane, you can select subdirectories or files. The following section uses the file pane to illustrate selection methods. You can also use these methods to select directories in the tree pane.

To make a selection in the file pane, the pane must be active. Press Tab or Shift+Tab until the file pane has a highlighted border, or click the pane with the mouse.

If you are selecting directories and files with your mouse, you'll notice the left and right mouse buttons have different functions.

- Clicking a filename with the right mouse button selects a file. If the file is already selected, clicking the file again with the right mouse button deselects it.
- Clicking a filename with the left mouse button deselects all files except the file that was just clicked.

To select directories or files:

1. Use UpArrow, DownArrow, PgUp, PgDn, Home or End to highlight the first file you wish to select. (See Chapter 1, "Getting Started," for additional information on navigating within window panes.)
2. Press Insert to select the file.
3. Repeat steps 1 and 2 until you have highlighted all files you wish to select (Figure 4-2).

TIP: To select several files in sequence, check the Insert Moves Down check box in the Configure Preferences dialog box. With this option enabled, the Insert key tags the current file and moves down to the next file, eliminating the need to use the arrow keys. See Chapter 9, "Configuring Norton Desktop," for additional information on configuring your desktop preferences.

Or,

1. Click the first file you wish to select with the right mouse button.
2. Release the mouse button.
3. Repeat steps 1 and 2 until you've highlighted all the files you wish to select.

TIP: To select several files in sequence, click on the first file in the sequence with the right mouse button, then drag the mouse to the last file you wish to select.

4-6   *Using Norton Desktop for DOS*

> **TIP:** To quickly locate a file within the file pane, use Norton Desktop's convenient Speed Search feature: type the first letter of the file you're trying to locate. The highlight bar moves to the first file beginning with the letter you typed. Continue typing the consecutive characters in the file's name until your file is highlighted.
>
> If the DOS command line is on the screen (DOS BACKGROUND from the long View menu is on), press Alt+F1 to display the Speed Search box, then type the first letter of the file you want to highlight.

Figure 4-2

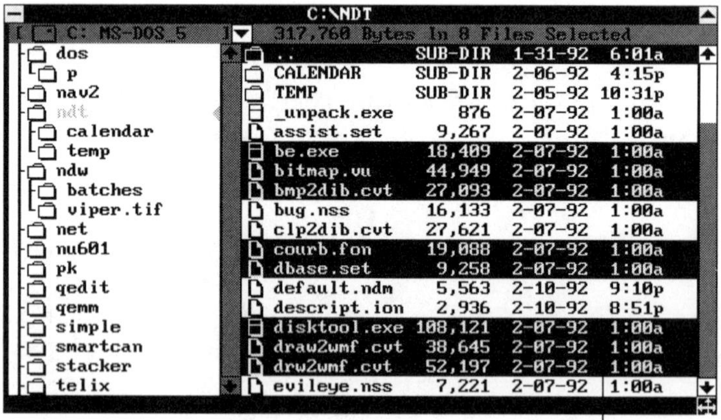

use Insert or the right mouse button to select single or multiple files in the drive window

USING THE SELECT COMMAND

The SELECT command lets you select all or some of the files in a file pane. It also lets you invert the selection. Choose SELECT from the File menu to reveal a cascading submenu containing three menu items: ALL, SOME... and INVERT (Figure 4-3).

Figure 4-3

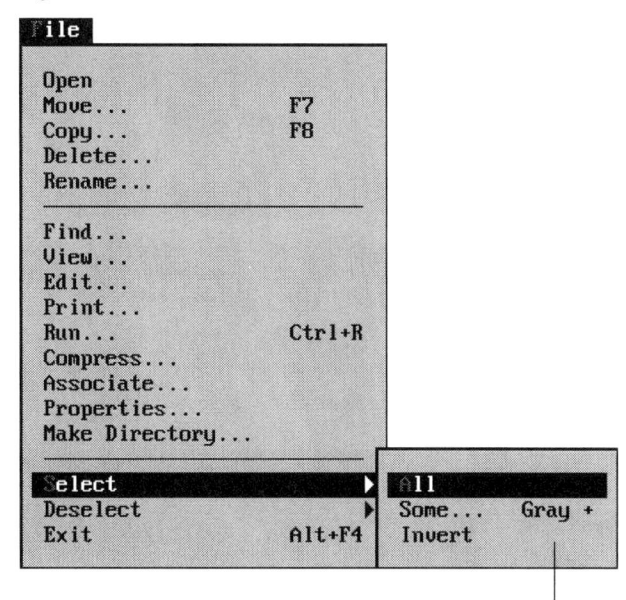

```
File
Open
Move...          F7
Copy...          F8
Delete...
Rename...

Find...
View...
Edit...
Print...
Run...           Ctrl+R
Compress...
Associate...
Properties...
Make Directory...

Select        ▶   All
Deselect      ▶   Some...   Gray +
Exit         Alt+F4   Invert
```

when you choose SELECT from the File menu, a cascading submenu appears revealing three more file selection commands

To select files with the SELECT command:

1 Choose SELECT from the File menu.

The SELECT cascading submenu appears on the desktop.

2 Choose one of the three file selection commands from the cascading submenu.

ALL: selects all the files in the file pane.

SOME... : selects only those files you specify in the Select Some dialog box (Figure 4-4).

a Type the names of the files you wish to select in the File combination box.

You can type wildcards into this text box. For example, type *.DOC *.CDR to select all Microsoft Word documents and CorelDraw files.

You can enter multiple filenames in the combination box, but you must leave a space, comma (,), semicolon (;) or plus sign (+) between each filename.

4-8   Using Norton Desktop for DOS

You can also select filenames from the drop-down *history list*. The File history list displays your last 10 entries in the File combination box. Press Ctrl+DownArrow or click the prompt button to view the list.

b   Select OK to save your file specifications.

Figure 4-4

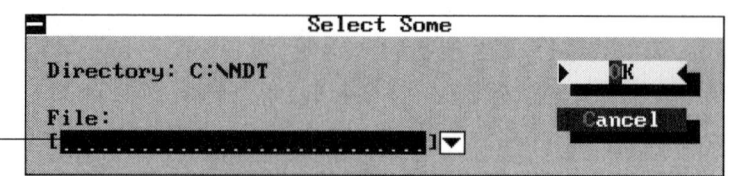

```
┌─────────────────── Select Some ───────────────────┐
│                                                    │
│  Directory: C:\NDT                       ▶  OK  ◀  │
│                                                    │
│  File:                                   Cancel    │
│  [                              ]▼                 │
└────────────────────────────────────────────────────┘
```

type the filenames you wish to select or select them from the drop-down history list

INVERT: selects those files not currently selected, and deselects the currently selected files, all in one step. It is useful when you need to separate a selected group of files. For example, choose SELECT and type *.DOC in the text box. Copy all of the selected files to a new directory. Choose INVERT to deselect all *.DOC files and select all the remaining files. Copy the newly selected files to another directory. You've now separated your .DOC files from the other files in the directory.

> **TIP:** If you want to select from among certain types of files, use the FILTER... command in conjunction with the SELECT command. See Chapter 2, "Using Drive Windows," for more details.

> **NOTE:** To add files to those currently selected in the drive window, simply choose the SELECT command again.

DESELECTING FILES

You can deselect files in much the same way that you select files—by using the Insert key or the right mouse button.

To deselect a file in a group of selected files:

1   Use UpArrow, DownArrow, PgUp, PgDn, Home and End to highlight the file you wish to deselect.

Using the DESELECT Command

2   Press Insert to deselect the file.

Or,

- Click the selected file with the right mouse button to deselect it.

The DESELECT command allows you to deselect all or some of the files in a file pane, or invert your deselected files (thus selecting the deselected files and deselecting all others). Choose DESELECT from the File menu to reveal a cascading submenu containing three menu items: ALL, SOME... and INVERT.

To deselect selected files in the file pane:

1   Choose DESELECT from the File menu.

    The DESELECT cascading submenu appears on the desktop.

2   Choose one of the three file selection commands from the cascading submenu.

    ALL: deselects all the files in the file pane.

    SOME... : deselects only those files you specify in the Deselect Some dialog box.

    a   Type the names of the files you wish to deselect in the File combination box.

        You can type wildcards into this combination box. For example, type `*.XLS` to deselect all Microsoft Excel files.

        You can enter multiple filenames in the combination box, but you must leave a space, comma (,), semicolon (;) or plus sign (+) between each filename.

        You can also deselect filenames from the drop-down history list. The File history list displays your last 10 entries in the File text box. Press Ctrl+DownArrow or click the prompt button to view the list.

    b   Select OK to save your file specifications.

    INVERT: deselects those files that are currently selected, and selects the files that are currently unselected.

TIP: If you want to select from among certain types of files, use the FILTER... command in conjunction with the DESELECT command. See Chapter 2, "Using Drive Windows," for more details.

MOVING AND COPYING DIRECTORIES AND FILES

You can move or copy single files and groups of files (including entire directories and subdirectories) by using the MOVE... and COPY... commands from the File menu.

NOTE: If the Replace option in the Configure Confirmation dialog box is checked, Norton Desktop displays a dialog box if one of the files you are moving or copying is about to overwrite an existing file with the same name. (Refer to "Setting Confirmation Options" in Chapter 9, "Configuring Norton Desktop," if you would like more information.) The Warning dialog box gives you the option of overwriting the existing file or canceling the operation. If you choose not to overwrite the existing file, you can use the RENAME... command from the File menu to rename one of the files.

Moving Directories and Files

Norton Desktop makes moving directories and files quite easy—much easier than using DOS commands. You can move the directories and files within a drive or between drives.

To move directories or files with the MOVE... command:

1 Choose MOVE... from the File menu.

   Or,

   Select the Move button on the button bar (F7).

   The Move dialog box appears on the desktop (Figure 4-5).

2 Type the name of the file you want to move in the Move text box.

   If you selected a file from a drive window before choosing MOVE..., that file's name is already displayed in the Move text box. If you selected multiple files, the

Move text box is replaced with an information line that displays the number of selected files. If you did not select files before choosing MOVE... and want to move multiple files, you can use the * and ? wildcards. (See Chapter 1, "Getting Started," for more information on wildcards.)

3   Check the Include Subdirectories check box to move a directory and all of its subdirectories.

Figure 4-5

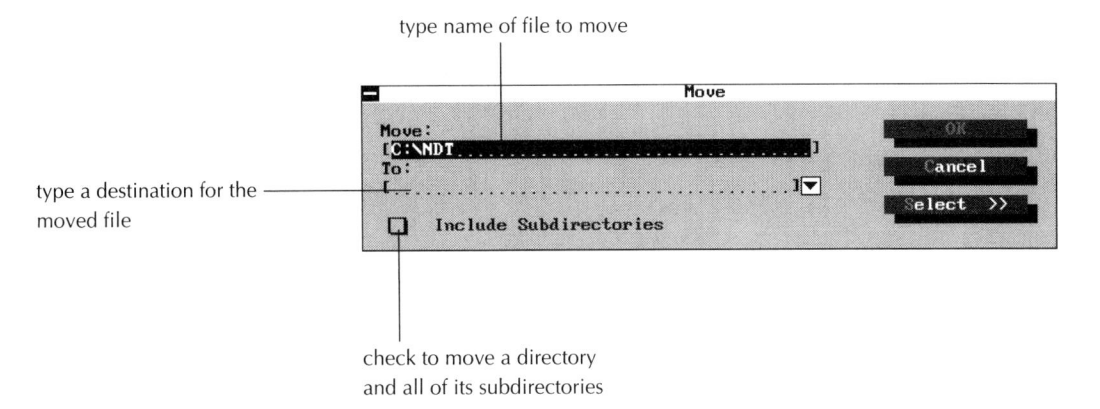

type name of file to move

type a destination for the moved file

check to move a directory and all of its subdirectories

4   Type the destination pathname in the To combination box, or select the destination from the drop-down history list.

The history list displays your last 10 selected destinations and/or the names of the other open windows. This is helpful when you're frequently moving files to the same destinations.

You can also select the Select command button and select the destination from the Drive drop-down list and tree pane that appear at the bottom of the Move dialog box (shown in Figure 4-6).

5   Select OK to move your directory or file.

4-12 *Using Norton Desktop for DOS*

Figure 4-6

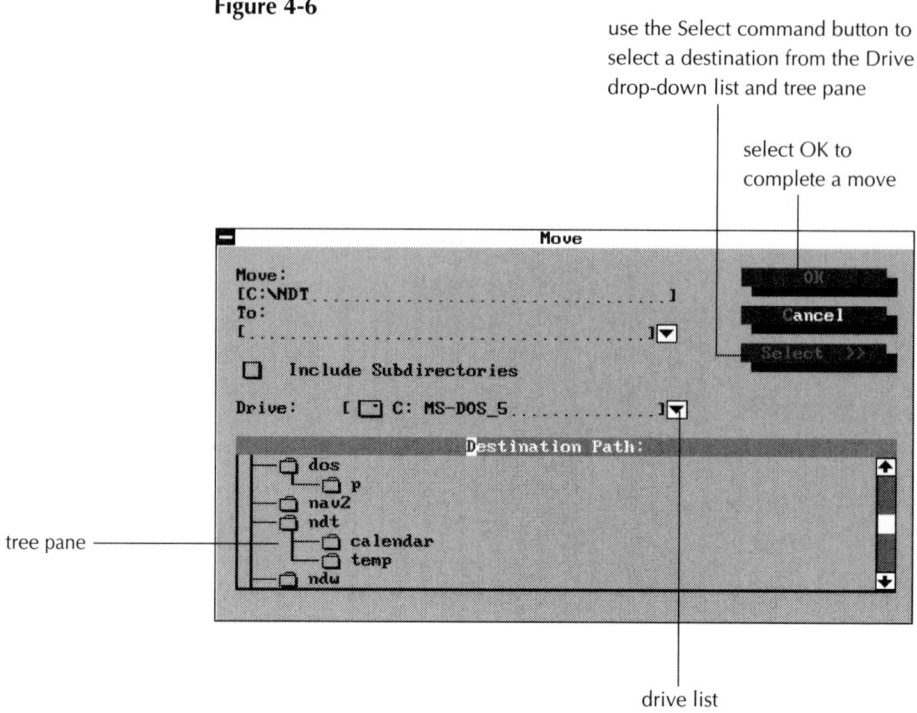

use the Select command button to select a destination from the Drive drop-down list and tree pane

select OK to complete a move

```
┌─────────────────────── Move ───────────────────────┐
│ Move:                                              │
│ [C:\NDT..............................]    ┌─OK──┐ │
│ To:                                        │     │ │
│ [..............................]▼          │Cancel│ │
│                                            │     │ │
│  □  Include Subdirectories                 │Select>>│
│                                            └─────┘ │
│  Drive:  [ □ C: MS-DOS_5..............]▼           │
│          ┌─── Destination Path: ───┐               │
│          │ ─□ dos                  │▲              │
│          │   └─□ p                 │               │
│          │ ─□ nav2                 │               │
│          │ ─□ ndt                  │               │
│          │   ├─□ calendar          │               │
│          │   └─□ temp              │               │
│          │ ─□ ndw                  │▼              │
│          └─────────────────────────┘               │
└────────────────────────────────────────────────────┘
```

tree pane

drive list

🖱 If you are using a mouse, you can move files or directories by dragging them from one location and "dropping" them (releasing the mouse button) at another location.

To move files with the mouse:

1   Click the directories or files in the drive window that you want to move.

    If you select a directory, all of its subdirectories and the files within those subdirectories are also selected by default.

    If you select a directory and then select some of its subdirectories (but not all), the subdirectories you did not specifically select are not moved.

2   Start dragging the directories or files and then press the Alt key and hold it down while you drag the directories or files to their new destination.

    The highlight bar indicates the number of files and/or directories that were selected.

3 Release the mouse button and the Alt key.

If you did not press Alt, the files are copied instead of moved. (See "Copying Directories and Files" later in this chapter for details.)

> **NOTE:** If you want to move only the directory and its files (excluding the subdirectories), hold the Shift key down (as well as the Alt key) after you've started to drag the files or directories, and then release the Shift key when you release the mouse button and the Alt key.
>
> You can change this preference to always exclude subdirectories when a directory is selected using the Configure Preferences dialog box (see Chapter 9, "Configuring Norton Desktop").

Or,

1 Click the directories or files you want to move.

2 Drag the directories or files to the Move button on the Button Bar.

The Move dialog box appears (see Figure 4-5).

3 See steps 2 through 5 in the procedure "To move directories or files with the MOVE... command" for instructions on how to use the Move dialog box.

Using the PRUNE & GRAFT Command

Another method of moving directories and their associated subdirectories and files is to use the PRUNE & GRAFT command from the (long) Disk menu. As the name implies, "prune and graft" means you prune a directory (or remove it) from one area of your *tree structure*, and you graft it (or move it) onto another area of the tree structure. This method has the added benefit of providing a visual illustration of the changes you are making to the tree structure when you move directories.

To move directories with the PRUNE & GRAFT command:

1 Choose OPEN DRIVE WINDOW... from the Window menu (Ctrl+W).

Open a drive window for the drive containing the directory or directories you wish to move.

NOTE: Unlike the MOVE... command, you cannot move directories from one drive to another using the PRUNE & GRAFT command; directory moves must be made within the same drive.

2   Highlight the directory you wish to move.

Use UpArrow, DownArrow, PgUp, PgDn, Home or End to highlight the directory.

Or,

Click the directory name to highlight the directory.

3   Choose PRUNE & GRAFT from the Disk menu.

An instruction box appears on the desktop telling you how to move the directory using arrow keys.

4   Move the directory to its new position.

  a Use the UpArrow or DownArrow key to move the directory.

     Watch the highlighted directory move up and down the tree structure as you press the UpArrow or DownArrow key.

  b Press Enter to confirm the directory's new position.

Or,

  a Click the directory you want to become the new parent directory.

  b Press Enter to confirm the directory's new position.

Copying Directories and Files

Copying directories and files is just like moving directories and files—except you use the COPY... command.

To copy directories and files with the COPY... command:

1   Choose COPY... from the File menu.

Or,

Select the Copy button on the button bar (F8).

The Copy dialog box appears (Figure 4-7).

Managing Directories and Files **4-15**

Figure 4-7

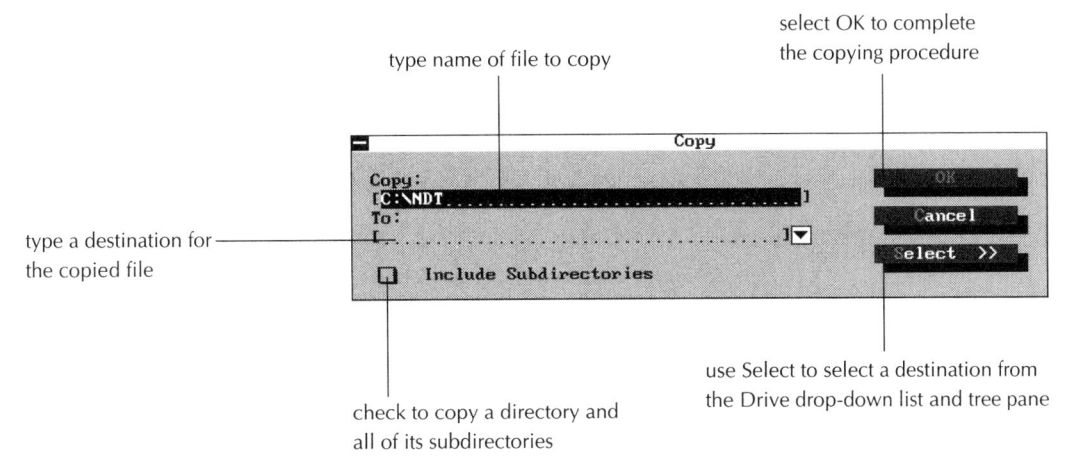

type a destination for the copied file

type name of file to copy

select OK to complete the copying procedure

check to copy a directory and all of its subdirectories

use Select to select a destination from the Drive drop-down list and tree pane

2   Type the name of the file(s) you want to copy in the Copy text box.

If you selected a file before choosing COPY..., that file's name already appears in the text box. If you selected multiple files, the Copy text box is replaced with an information line that displays the number of selected files. If you did not select files before choosing COPY..., and you want to copy multiple files, you can use the * and ? wildcards. (See Chapter 1, "Getting Started," for more information on wildcards.)

3   Check the Include Subdirectories check box to copy a directory and all of its subdirectories.

4   Enter the destination pathname in one of the following three ways:

Type the destination pathname in the To combination box.

Or,

Select the destination from the drop-down history list.

The history list displays your last 10 selected destinations and/or the names of the other open windows. This is helpful if you frequently copy files to the same destinations.

Or,

4-16 *Using Norton Desktop for DOS*

Select the Select command button and select the destination from the Drive drop-down list and tree pane that appear at the bottom of the Copy dialog box.

5   Select OK to copy your directory or files.

If you are using a mouse, you can copy files or directories by dragging them from one location and "dropping" them (releasing the mouse button) at another location.

To copy files with the mouse:

1   Click on the directories or files you want to copy.

   If you select a directory, all of its subdirectories and the files within those subdirectories are also selected by default.

   If you select a directory and then select *some* of its subdirectories (but not all), the subdirectories you did not specifically select are not copied.

2   Drag the directories or files to their new destination.

3   Release the mouse button.

NOTE: If you want to copy only the directory and its files (excluding the subdirectories), hold the Shift key down after you've started to drag the files or directories, and then release the Shift key when you release the mouse button.

You can change this preference to always exclude subdirectories when a directory is selected using the Configure Preferences dialog box (see Chapter 9, "Configuring Norton Desktop").

Or,

1   Select the directories or files you want to copy.

2   Drag the directories or files to the Copy button on the button bar.

   The Copy dialog box appears (see Figure 4-7).

3   See steps 2 through 5 in the procedure "To copy directories and files with the COPY... command" for instructions on how to use the Copy dialog box.

DELETING DIRECTORIES AND FILES

Just as you can copy and move multiple files and whole directories, Norton Desktop also allows you to delete multiple files and directories. When you delete a file in Norton Desktop, the file is marked so that it no longer appears in a directory of your files. It can actually be retrieved later, however, *if you were running SmartCan before the file was deleted*. You can learn more about the recovery of deleted files by reading Chapter 16, "Using UnErase," and Chapter 27, "Using SmartCan."

Using the DELETE... Command

Using the DELETE... command is a good way to remove documents you feel are no longer needed. If you find out later they are needed, you can still recover the information as long as SmartCan was running prior to the file deletion. Generally, you'll select the files for deletion from a drive window before choosing the DELETE... command.

TIP: Compress files or directories you aren't currently using, but don't wish to delete. See the section "Compressing Files" in this chapter for additional information.

To delete a file:

1 Choose DELETE... from the File menu.

   Or,

   Select the Delete button on the Button Bar (F9).

   Or,

   a Select the directories or files you want to delete.

   b Drag the directories or files to the Delete button on the Button Bar.

   The Delete dialog box appears (Figure 4-8).

Figure 4-8
use the Delete dialog box to quickly delete files and directories

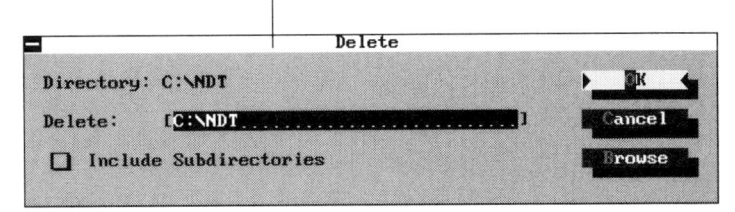

Using Norton Desktop for DOS

2   Type the name of the file(s) you want to delete in the Delete text box.

Or,

Select files for deletion by using the Browse command button and selecting files from the Browse for Delete dialog box.

If you selected a file before choosing the DELETE... command, that file's name already appears in the text box. If you selected multiple files, the Delete text box is replaced with an information line that displays the number of selected files. If you did not select files before choosing the DELETE... command and want to delete multiple files, you can use the * and ? wildcards. (See Chapter 1, "Getting Started," for more information on wildcards.)

3   Check the Include Subdirectories check box to delete a directory and all of its subdirectories.

4   Select OK to delete your directory or files.

RENAMING DIRECTORIES AND FILES

Use the RENAME... command to rename a directory or file. You're probably saying, "You can't rename directories!" If you're using DOS, you're right, you can't rename directories—but using Norton Desktop, you can!

To rename a directory or file:

1   Choose RENAME... from the File menu.

The Rename dialog box appears (Figure 4-9).

Figure 4-9

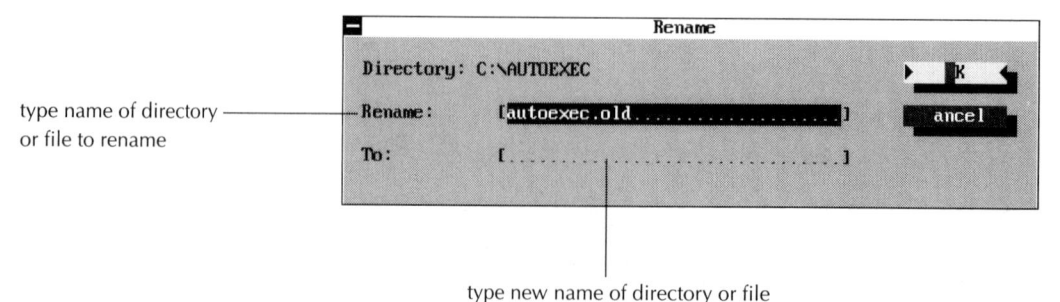

```
┌─────────────────────── Rename ───────────────────────┐
│ Directory: C:\AUTOEXEC                                │
│                                               ► OK   │
│ Rename:    [autoexec.old.................]           │
│                                                 ancel│
│ To:        [.............................]           │
└───────────────────────────────────────────────────────┘
```

type name of directory or file to rename

type new name of directory or file

Managing Directories and Files 4-19

2   Type the name of the directory or file you want to rename in the Rename text box.

   If you selected a directory or file from a drive window before choosing RENAME..., that directory's or file's name already appears in the text box.

3   Type the new name of your directory or file in the To text box.

4   Select OK to rename your directory or file.

COMPARING DIRECTORIES

If you've ever kept copies of files on two different computers or in two different directories, you know how difficult it is to manage the two sets of files. You update a file in one directory, but forget to update it in the other directory. Or you add files to one directory and not to the other directory. Before long, your version-control is out-of-control. Because groups of files are generally organized into directories and subdirectories, a quick way to sort out what-files-are-where is to compare the contents of the two directories or subdirectories.

To compare two directories:

1   Open a separate drive window for the two directories you wish to compare.

2   Select the first directory you wish to compare from one tree pane and the second directory you wish to compare from the second tree pane. The files of the two directories are displayed in the file panes of the two drive windows.

3   Choose COMPARE WINDOWS from the Window menu.

   If more than two drive windows are open, select the directory to compare with the active file pane from the Compare Windows dialog box and then select OK.

   The files of the two directories are compared for files that appear in one directory and not the other, or for files which have the same name but which have a different date, time or size. All files that are different are selected in both file panes.

Once you have established which files are different, you can use the COPY... command to copy files from one directory to the other to make the two directories identical.

CHANGING FILE ATTRIBUTES

When a file is created, DOS creates a directory entry that contains various facts about the file, including the file size, the date and time it was created, and a list of properties that have been assigned to the file.

A file may have up to four properties assigned to it (or it may not have any properties). These properties are known as the read-only, archive, system and hidden *attributes*.

The *read-only attribute* protects a file from being changed or deleted; it is used to guard a file from accidental erasure or modification. However, this protection only goes so far. Norton Desktop can delete read-only files very easily with your permission.

The *archive attribute* indicates that a file needs to be backed up. DOS sets the archive bit (turns it on) whenever it creates or modifies a file. Backup applications, such as Norton Backup (included with Norton Desktop) and the DOS BACKUP command, clear the archive attribute.

The *system attribute* indicates a DOS or system-related file. Files with the system attribute do not appear in the standard DOS directory listing. This attribute is not commonly used.

The *hidden attribute* is assigned to critical files to protect them. Hidden files do not appear in the standard DOS directory listing. Hidden files cannot be deleted, and hidden data files cannot be used by most programs. Two of DOS's own files, IBMBIO.COM and IBMDOS.COM (or MSDOS.SYS and IO.SYS, depending on which version of DOS you use), are hidden, which is why they do not show up in directory listings. Microsoft assigns both the system and hidden attributes to all DOS internal files. For all practical purposes, the hidden and system attributes have the same effect, although this could change in future versions of DOS.

NOTE: The file pane in a drive window displays an icon and the filename for each file by default. You can change the file information displayed in the file pane by using the FILE DETAILS... command from the (long) View menu. See Chapter 2, "Using Drive Windows," for more information.

To assign attributes to files:

1 Choose PROPERTIES... from the (long) File menu.

   The Properties dialog box appears (Figure 4-10).

   If you have selected a file from the drive window, this dialog box displays the file's filename, network owner, size, assigned attributes and the date and time when the file was last modified. To assign attributes to multiple files you can use the * and ? wildcards. (See Chapter 1, "Getting Started," for more information on wildcards.)

   If you have not selected a filename from the drive window, the Properties dialog box looks slightly different. The File text box prompts you for a filename. You can also use the Browse command button to select your file.

Figure 4-10

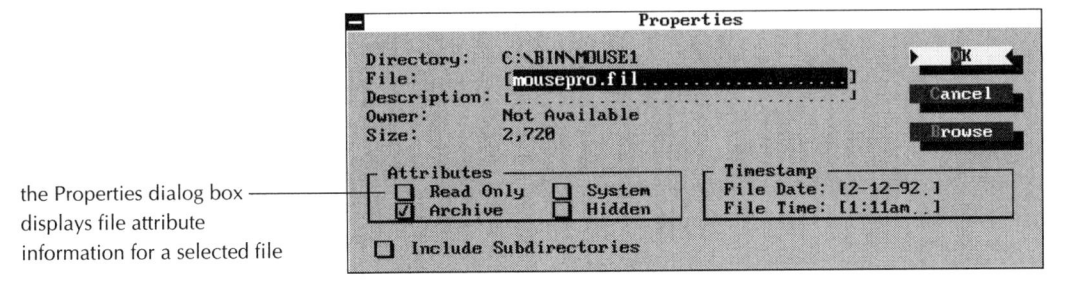

the Properties dialog box displays file attribute information for a selected file

   If you are running NDOS.COM (from Norton Utilities), you can display a short description (40 characters or less) with each of your files. This description appears when you list a directory of your files.

2 Type a short description of the file (40 characters or less) into the Description text box. Attaching a description to the file is optional.

3 Check the check box of each file attribute you wish to assign in the Attributes group box.

4 Check the File Date check box to change the file date; then type a new date in the File Date text box.

5   Check the File Time check box to change the file timestamp; then type a new time in the File Time text box. Include AM or PM as part of your time entry.

6   Check the Include Subdirectories check box to assign attributes to files within the subdirectories.

7   Select OK to assign the file attributes.

NOTE: You can assign attributes to multiple files. Select the files as described earlier in this chapter in "Selecting Directories and Files." The File Properties dialog box will not display any information about the files other than the number of files you have selected. Use the attribute check boxes to assign one or more attributes to these files.

COMPRESSING FILES

Compressing files allows you to keep files on your disk in a format that takes up much less disk space than files that are not compressed. The files are still easy to access—you just decompress them before using them.

To compress files:

1   Choose COMPRESS... from the (long) File menu.

    The Compress dialog box appears (Figure 4-11). The name of the current file or directory appears in the Compress text box by default. If a directory is selected, all files within the current directory are compressed.

Figure 4-11

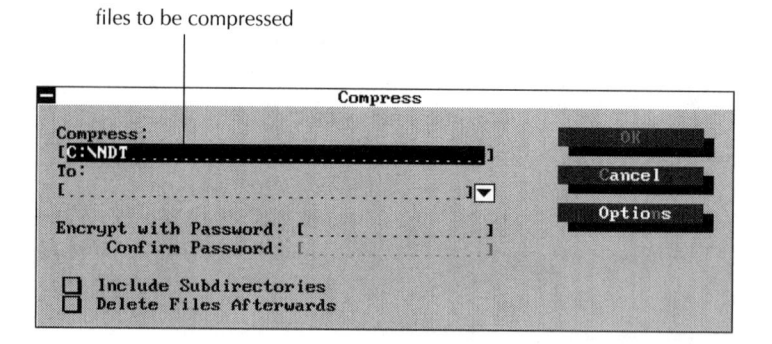

2   To compress files from a directory other than the current directory, delete the current directory name from the Compress text box and type in the directory containing the files you wish to compress.

   If you wish to compress only some of the files from the directory, type the specific filenames separated by a space, comma (,), semicolon (;) or plus sign (+) or use the * and ? wildcards. (See Chapter 1, "Getting Started," for more information on wildcards.)

3   Type the full path and filename for your compressed file in the To text box.

   Or,

   Select the path and filename from the drop-down history list.

   The history list displays the filenames of the last 10 compressed files you've created. This allows you to quickly add new files to an existing compressed file.

   Including an extension on the compressed filename is optional. If you do not specify an extension, the extension .ZIP is used by default.

4   Type a password (up to 15 characters) in the Encrypt with Password text box to require that a password be entered before your compressed file can be decompressed.

   Requiring a password adds a measure of security to your compressed file. Now the file cannot be decompressed unless the person knows the password.

5   Verify your password by typing it again in the Confirm Password text box.

6   Check the Include Subdirectories check box to compress the selected files in all subdirectories of the directory entered in the Compress text box.

7   Check the Delete Files Afterwards check box to delete all the individual files which were compressed after the compressed file has been made.

8   Select OK to create your compressed file.

> **NOTE:** You can also select the options button to access the Configure Compression dialog box where you can set additional file compression options. This dialog box is discussed in detail in the section "Selecting File Compression Options" in Chapter 9, "Configuring Norton Desktop."

Viewing the Contents of a Compressed File

Once you've created a compressed file, it's easy to forget what files it contains. You can easily view the contents of a compressed file by opening a Compress File window.

To view the contents of a compressed file:

1 Choose OPEN WINDOW... from the (long) Window menu.

   The Open Window dialog box appears on the desktop.

2 Select the Compressed File option button.

3 Type the name of the compressed file in the Drive text box.

   Or,

   Select the Browse command button.

   The Browse for Compressed File dialog box appears on the desktop.

   a Select the compressed file you wish to view by using the Drive drop-down list and the Directories and Files list boxes.

   b Select OK to save your selection.

   The filename of the file you wish to view appears in the Drive text box of the Open Window dialog box.

4 Select OK to open a Compressed File window.

   A drive window appears on the desktop displaying a listing of all the files that make up your compressed file.

> **NOTE:** You can use drive windows for compressed files much in the same way as you use normal drive windows—to move or copy files to and from the compressed file drive window. The files you move or copy are compressed or decompressed as needed. You can also delete files from the compressed files drive window. You cannot, however, view the contents of a compressed file.

EDITING TEXT FILES

Norton Desktop lets you edit files from your favorite text editor without having to leave the desktop. If you have not set up a different editor, when you choose EDITOR... from the (long) Configure menu, you access the Norton Desktop Editor. To make another text editor the default editor, see Chapter 9, "Configuring Norton Desktop," for information on selecting or changing the default editor.

To enter the editor with a file selected from a drive window:

1 Select a file to edit from the current drive window. See Chapter 2, "Using Drive Windows," for details.
2 Choose EDIT... from Norton Desktop's (long) File menu.
   Or,
   Select the Edit button on the Button Bar (F4).
   Or,
   Drag your selected file to the Edit button on the Button Bar.
   You enter the editor.

To enter the editor with a file selected by browsing:

1 Choose EDIT... from Norton Desktop's (long) File menu.
   The Browse for Edit dialog box appears on the desktop.
2 Select a file from the list box. See Chapter 1, "Getting Started," for details about using a browse dialog box.
3 Select OK.
   You enter the editor.

The Norton Desktop Editor

Figure 4-12 shows the Norton Desktop Editor with one window open. This is similar to what you see when you first enter this editor.

NOTE: Norton Desktop's editor is an ASCII text editor. Most word processing packages insert special characters (which you cannot see) to control document formatting, such as tabs, bold text, and italics. You can edit only ASCII files in the Norton Desktop default editor.

4-26   *Using Norton Desktop for DOS*

Figure 4-12

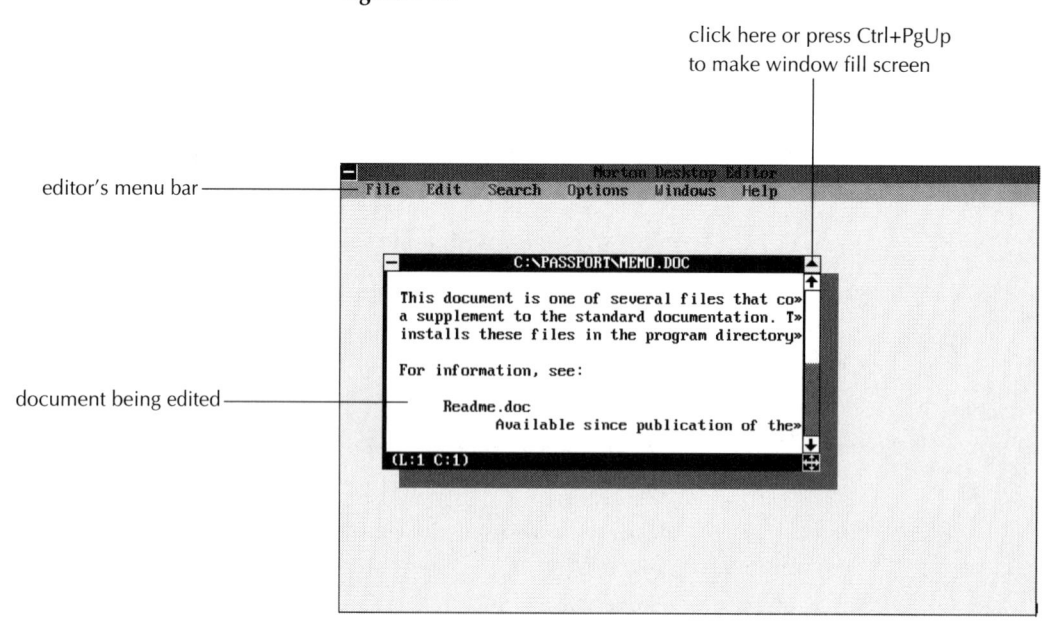

editor's menu bar

document being edited

click here or press Ctrl+PgUp to make window fill screen

Windows

Inside the editor, you can open as many as eight windows. You can have a different window for each file you create or work with, but you cannot use more than one window for the same file.

The name of each open file appears on the Windows menu and on the title bar for the window in which it appears. Windows containing files you are creating are UNTITLED.1, UNTITLED.2, etc., until you save the files.

All the windows, other than the currently selected window, have grayed title bars.

To open a file:

- Choose NEW from the editor's File menu to create a new text file.

    Or,

Managing Directories and Files **4-27**

1 Choose OPEN... from the editor's File menu (Ctrl+O) to open an existing file.

The Open File dialog box appears.

2 Type the pathname for the file.

Or,

Select the filename of the file to open from the list box.

3 Select OK.

To switch from window to window:

- Choose the name of the file you want from the editor's Windows menu.

Or,

- Click the window of the file that you want to make current.

The selected file moves in front of the other windows.

To zoom a window to full-screen:

- Press Ctrl+PgUp or Ctrl+PgDn.

Or,

- Click the prompt button in the upper-right corner of the window.

The window zooms to fill the screen.

To restore a zoomed window to its original size, follow the same procedure.

Managing Files You Edit

From within the Norton Desktop Editor, you can:

- Create new files
- Open existing files
- Close files
- Save files with their current or new names

Table 4-1 briefly explains how to perform each of these functions. Detailed procedures follow the table.

Table 4-1

Function	Explanation	Keystrokes and menu command
Create a new file	Opens a new empty window called UNTITLED.1 (until you save it and change its name).	▪ Choose NEW from the File menu (Ctrl+N).
Open an existing file	Opens a new window containing the specified file.	▪ Choose OPEN... from the File menu (Ctrl+O). See the procedure "To open an existing file."
Close a file	Closes the file in the current window and removes the window from the desktop. If you have made recent changes to the file, you are asked if you want to save them.	▪ Choose CLOSE from the File menu.
Save a file	Saves the current file with all the changes made since it was opened or since the last time it was saved. The file remains in the window.	▪ Choose SAVE from the File menu (Ctrl+S).
Save a file with a new name	Saves the file in the current window as a new file with a different name. The new file appears in the window and contains all the changes made since it was opened or last saved. The former file still exists; it does not contain the latest changes.	▪ Choose SAVE AS... from the File menu. See the procedure "To save a file with a new name."

File management

To save a file with a new name:

1. Choose SAVE AS... from the editor's File menu.

   The Save As dialog box appears.

2. Type the name for the new file. You can use the browse dialog box to select the path for the new filename or to make sure you are not entering an existing filename and pathname.

3. Select OK.

4. If a file exists with that same filename and pathname, a confirmation dialog box appears.

   Select Overwrite to replace the existing file with the current file.

   Or,

   Select Append to append the current file to the existing file.

   Or,

   Select Cancel to return to the file without saving it. You can then repeat the procedure using a different filename and pathname.

To close a file:

1. Choose CLOSE from the editor's File menu.

   If you have not saved your latest changes, a confirmation dialog box appears.

2. Select Yes to save the changes.

   Or,

   Select No to close the file anyway and ignore the changes.

   Or,

   Select Cancel to return to the editor.

3. If you select Yes and the file has not been named, the Save As dialog box appears. Refer to the previous procedure, "To save a file with a new name," for instructions.

Navigating in the Norton Desktop Editor

Scrolling Text in a Window

Often the text of an entire file does not fit in the window at the same time—even if you alter the size of the window. To view all of the text, you can scroll from line to line, page to page, or side to side.

Chapter 1, "Getting Started," explains how to scroll and how to resize windows. This section explains the additional ways to scroll provided by the Norton Desktop Editor.

When the page width of any given line exceeds the width of the window, you see double angle brackets (<< or >>) on the right and/or left sides of the window. If you see >>, this means that you are at the left margin of the file, and there is more text to the right. If you see <<, this means there is text to the left.

Tables 4-2 and 4-3 explain how to scroll text in a window using the keyboard or a mouse.

Table 4-2

To scroll...	Press...
One page upward	PgUp
One page downward	PgDn
12 characters to the right	Ctrl+RightArrow
12 characters to the left	Ctrl+LeftArrow
To center the line marked by cursor in the window	5 (on number pad when NumLock is off)

Scrolling from the keyboard

Table 4-3

To scroll...	Click...
One page upward	Above the scroll box
Continuously upward	And hold above the scroll box
One page downward	Below the scroll box

(continued)

Managing Directories and Files 4-31

Table 4-3 *(continued)*

To scroll...	Click...
Continuously downward	And hold below the scroll box
To the right	On >>
Continuously to the right	And hold on >>
To the left	On <<
Continuously to the left	And hold on <<
To a specific location	Move the scroll box with the mouse

Scrolling with a mouse

Moving the Cursor

You can control the cursor's location from the keyboard or with a mouse. See Tables 4-4 and 4-5.

Table 4-4

To move the cursor...	Press...
To the first character of the current line	Home
To the first character of the top line of your screen	Home, Home
To the first character of the file	Ctrl+Home
	Or,
	Home, Home, Home
	(If the cursor is already at the beginning of the line or the top of your screen, press Home only two times.)
Up one line	UpArrow
Down one line	DownArrow

(continued)

Table 4-4 *(continued)*

To move the cursor...	Press...
Right one character	RightArrow
Left one character	LeftArrow
To the last character of the current line	End
To the last character of the bottom line of your screen	End, End
To the last character of the file	Ctrl+End
	Or,
	End, End, End
	(If the cursor is already at the end of the line or the bottom of your screen, press End only two times.)

Moving the cursor with the keyboard

Table 4-5

To move the cursor...	Click...
To a particular location in the file	The character where you want to position the cursor

Moving the cursor with a mouse

Selecting Text

Editing functions such as Cut and Copy require that you first select the text you want to cut or copy. A section of selected text is generally referred to as a *block*. As you select text, it becomes highlighted.

To select a block of text:

1. Position the cursor at the beginning of the text you wish to select.
2. Press and hold the Shift key while using the editor's navigation keys to move the cursor to the end of the block to select (see Table 4-4).

Or,

1. Click the first or last character of the block.
2. Drag the mouse over the text you wish to include.

To select all of the text:

- Choose SELECT ALL from the Edit menu.

Inserting and Deleting Text

As you edit a file, you may often wish to move text around in your file, insert text from another file, delete text, or replace existing text with new text.

There are several ways to insert text into a file:

- Type the characters to insert at the current cursor location. See the section "Insert and Typeover Modes."
- Insert an entire file at the current cursor location. See the section "Inserting the Contents of One File into Another."
- Move or copy text from one location to another with cut and paste operations. See the section "Cutting, Copying and Pasting."

To delete text:

- To delete the character at the cursor position, highlight the character to delete and press Delete.

Or,

- To delete the character before the cursor position, press Backspace.

Or,

1   Select the character or block of characters to delete.

2   Choose CLEAR from the Edit menu.

Or,

Press Backspace.

Or,

Start typing new text over the selected block.

Insert and Typeover Modes

Most editors have two modes for entering text: insert and typeover. In *Insert mode* the characters you type are inserted before the current cursor position. Insert mode is the default. In *Typeover mode* each character you type replaces the character at the current cursor position.

To switch from one mode to the other in the Norton Desktop Editor, press the Insert key.

Inserting the Contents of One File into Another

To insert the contents of one file into another file:

1   Position the cursor at the location where you want to insert the new text. (Remember, the text will be inserted in front of the cursor.)

    To replace an entire block of text at once, you can highlight the block of text to be replaced.

2   Choose INSERT... (Ctrl+E) from the editor's File menu.

    The File to Insert dialog box appears.

3   Type the filename (including the full pathname if the file is not in the current directory) of the file to be inserted.

    Or,

    Select a file from the Files list box.

4   Select OK

    The text from the inserted file appears in its new location in your file.

Cutting, Copying and Pasting

You can cut or copy text from one file and paste it into other files. Use the text selection methods described earlier in this chapter to select the text.

Managing Directories and Files   **4-35**

To cut or copy text:

1   Highlight the text you wish to cut or copy.
2   Choose CUT from the Edit menu (Ctrl+X). Cut text is removed from your file and is stored in the *clipboard*.
    Or,
    Choose COPY from the Edit menu (Ctrl+C). Copied text remains in its present location in your file, and a second copy is stored in the clipboard.

Cut or copied text can be *pasted* from the clipboard into a new location within the same file or in a different file.

To paste text:

1   Cut or copy the text you wish to paste.
2   Position the cursor at the location where you want to insert the new text.
    Or,
    To replace a block of text with cut or copied text, highlight the block to be replaced.
3   Choose PASTE from the Edit menu (Ctrl+V).
    The text from the clipboard is inserted at the specified position in your file.

NOTE: The following keystrokes allow you to quickly cut, copy and paste text:

Function	Keystroke
Cut	Shift+Delete
Copy	Ctrl+Insert
Paste	Shift+Insert

Searching For and Replacing Text

The search commands allow you to quickly locate text within your file. Once you find the text you want, you can easily replace it with other text.

To search for text:

1 Choose FIND... from the editor's Search menu (Ctrl+F).

The Find dialog box appears on the desktop (Figure 4-13).

Figure 4-13

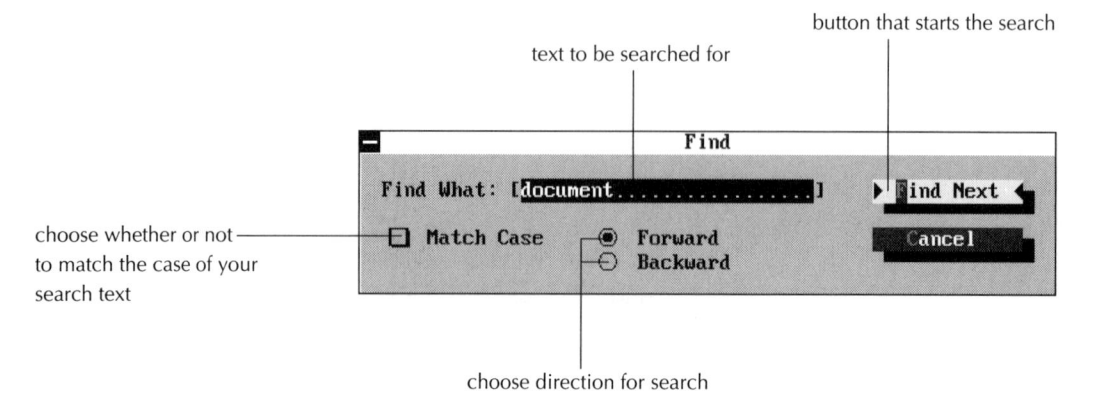

```
                                              button that starts the search
                                                          |
                      text to be searched for             |
                                  |                       |
    ┌─────────────────────────── Find ──────────────────────────┐
    │                                                            │
    │  Find What: [document................]    ▶ Find Next     │
choose whether or not ──── □ Match Case    ⦿ Forward     Cancel │
to match the case of your                  ⊖ Backward            │
search text                                     |                │
                                                |
                                    choose direction for search
```

2 Type the text you want to find in the Find What text box. You can enter up to 64 characters.

> **TIP:** To save some typing, you can highlight text in a file (up to 64 characters) before you choose FIND.... Then, when the Find dialog box opens, the text you highlighted is already entered in the Find What text box.

3 Check the Match Case check box if you want the editor to match the case of the characters in the search text. If this box is checked, "business" does not find a match with "Business" or "BUSINESS," for example. If Match Case is unchecked (the default), then the editor matches the characters regardless of case.

4 Select Forward or Backward.

Forward starts the search at the current cursor position and goes toward the end of the document.

Backward starts the search at the current cursor position and goes toward the beginning of the document.

Managing Directories and Files 4-37

5 Select Find Next to start the search.

If your search text is not found, you hear a beep. Otherwise, the next occurrence of text matching your search text is highlighted. You may repeat this step any number of times.

6 Select Cancel to remove the Find dialog box from the screen.

You can search for a block of text and replace some or all of its occurrences with another block of text. For example, suppose you've typed up a memo detailing the schedule and agenda of Monday's meeting. Just as you are about to distribute the memo, the meeting is changed from Monday to Tuesday. You can use the REPLACE command to quickly replace all references to "Monday" with "Tuesday."

To replace text:

1 Choose REPLACE... from the Search menu (Ctrl+R).

The Replace dialog box appears (Figure 4-14).

Figure 4-14

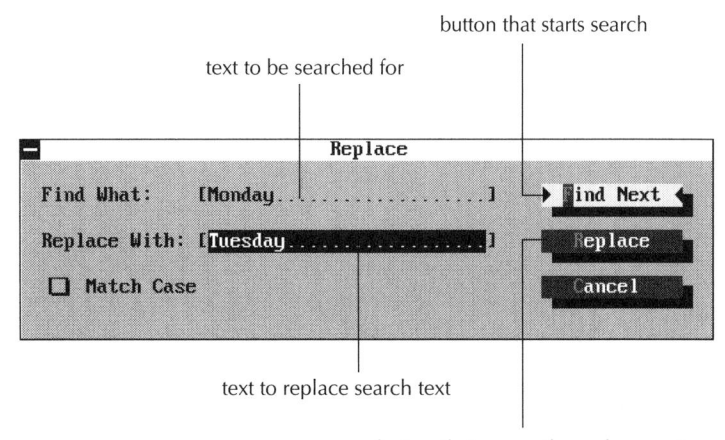

button that starts search

text to be searched for

```
┌─────────────────────── Replace ───────────────────────┐
│                                                        │
│  Find What:     [Monday.................]  → Find Next │
│                                                        │
│  Replace With:  [Tuesday................]    Replace   │
│                                                        │
│  ☐ Match Case                                 Cancel   │
│                                                        │
└────────────────────────────────────────────────────────┘
```

text to replace search text

button that causes the replacement

2 Type the text you want to find (up to 64 characters) in the Find What text box.

> **TIP:** To save some typing, you can highlight text in a file (up to 64 characters) before you choose REPLACE.... Then, when the Replace dialog box opens, the text you highlighted is already entered in the Find What text box.

3   Type the replacement text (up to 64 characters) in the Replace With text box.

4   Check the Match Case check box if you want the editor to match the case of the characters in the search text.

5   Select Find Next to begin the search.

    The first occurrence of your search text is highlighted.

    If your search text is not found you hear a beep.

6   Select Replace to replace your search text with the replacement text.

7   Repeat steps 5 and 6 until you have finished replacing all occurrences of the search text with your replacement text.

Word Wrap

When Word Wrap is on, you don't need to press Enter to end each line as you type text—the Norton Desktop Editor ends the line automatically and continues on to the next line according to the page width you specify. Word Wrap is on by default. When the file is saved to disk, a carriage return/linefeed is inserted at the end of each line created using Word Wrap. If you edit this file at a later date, you may need to use the REFORMAT command. (See the section "Reformatting a File" for details.) When Word Wrap is off, you control the length of each line by pressing Enter, as you would if you were using a standard typewriter.

To turn Word Wrap on or off:

- Choose WORD WRAP from the Options menu (Ctrl+W) to toggle word wrapping on and off.

  When WORD WRAP is on, a checkmark appears on the Options menu in front of the command.

To specify a page width:

1   Choose PAGE WIDTH... from the Options menu.

    The Page Width dialog box appears.

2 Type the desired number of characters per line in the Page Width text box.

3 Select OK.

Page width is ignored when Word Wrap is turned off.

Reformatting a File

When an ASCII file is saved to disk, each line ends in a carriage return/linefeed. The editor treats all the text between carriage return/linefeeds as one unit. In other words, as you edit a file, each line is treated as though it were a separate paragraph. You may need to highlight sections of edited text and use the REFORMAT command to make the lines wrap correctly.

Suppose you are editing a file containing the following text:

```
Let's meet at the Cramer Building on
Sunday, Oct. 4th.
```

Carriage return/linefeeds occur at the end of each line. If you edit this file, replacing "Cramer Building" with "Kalamazoo Bird Sanctuary," you would see:

```
Let's meet at the Kalamazoo Bird
Sanctuary
on Sunday, Oct. 4th.
```

The editor wraps only the text between carriage return/linefeeds. You can manually delete the carriage return after "on," but with large paragraphs, it is easier to use the REFORMAT command.

To reformat a paragraph:

1 Highlight the block of text that you want to reformat as one paragraph. (If you don't highlight text, the editor automatically reformats from the cursor position to the first blank or indented line.)

2 Select REFORMAT from the Edit menu.

The highlighted text is reformatted as a single paragraph.

Printing Files in the Norton Desktop Editor

When you have finished editing a file with the Norton Desktop Editor, you may want to print it. To print a file, you must have a print configuration defined, and your computer must be connected to a printer.

To create or edit a print configuration:

- Select PRINT SETUP... from the editor's File menu.

  The Configure Printer dialog box appears. For more details, see Chapter 9, "Configuring Norton Desktop."

To print a file in Norton Desktop's editor:

- Choose PRINT from the editor's File menu (Ctrl+P) to print the currently active file.

  If no files are open, the PRINT command is dimmed.

  The Print Status dialog box appears, showing you the status of your print job and when the file has finished printing.

  The file is printed.

PRINTING FILES FROM NORTON DESKTOP

Norton Desktop allows you to print any ASCII text file. Simply select the file you wish to print from an open drive window or from the Browse for Print dialog box. To establish what printer your files are printed to and how files are printed, see "Selecting Printer Options" in Chapter 9, "Configuring Norton Desktop."

To print a file from Norton Desktop:

1. Choose PRINT... from the File menu.

   If you selected a file from a drive window before you chose PRINT..., the file immediately begins printing. Skip steps 2 and 3.

   If you did not first select a file from a drive window, the Browse for Print dialog box appears on the screen.

2. Select the file you wish to print using the Directories and Files list boxes.

   Or,

   Type the name of the file to print in the File text box.

3 Select OK to start printing your file.

The Print Status dialog box lets you know when the file has finished printing.

Or,

- Select a file to print and select the Print button on the Button Bar (F6).

Or,

- Drag the file to the Print button on the Button Bar.

Finding Files with SuperFind

This chapter shows you how to use SuperFind to search your computer's drives and directories for files. In addition, you learn how to include the files you find in simple batch commands.

Contents

Finding Files	5-3
Defining Your Search	5-3
Searching for Multiple Files	5-6
Creating Customized File Sets	5-7
Defining Where to Search	5-9
Searching in Multiple Locations	5-9
Creating Customized Location Sets	5-10
Making Searches Case-Sensitive	5-13
Creating a Batch File from Matching Files	5-14

There's nothing more aggravating than misplacing a file. You know it's on your hard disk somewhere, but you can't remember where. Or even worse, you've forgotten where it is *and* what you named it. Fortunately, SuperFind is designed to eliminate such stress. SuperFind searches can be as specific as looking for Excel files you created on January 9, 1992, after 7:30 P.M., or as general as looking for any batch files on any drive and in any directory.

Once SuperFind has located the files you requested, it displays them in a drive window. You can then perform any number of file management operations on them: you can copy all of the files into one subdirectory; you can print them; you can view all of the files; you can include them all in a batch command.

FINDING FILES

The SuperFind dialog box allows you to enter all of the information needed to search for any type of file, anywhere on your computer.

To start SuperFind:

- Choose FIND... from the File menu.

Or,

- Select the Find button on the Button Bar (F5).

    The SuperFind dialog box appears (Figure 5-1). Here you can indicate the files you want to search for and where you want to search for them.

Figure 5-1

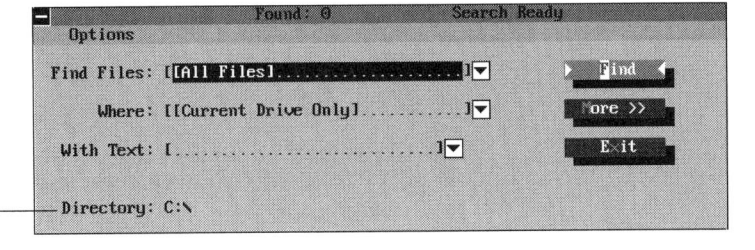

current directory

DEFINING YOUR SEARCH

A file search with SuperFind can be as general or as specific as you want. You can search for a generic category of files such as all spreadsheets, or you can search for one particular file which was created on a specified date, at a specified time, by a specified person.

Norton Desktop comes with a set of predefined file sets. These are groupings of files that allow you to direct or narrow the scope of your search. Some of the general definitions, such as All Files (*.*), let you make a broad search of a particular location. More specific definitions, such as Database Files, allow you to locate certain types of files.

You can also enter your own custom-tailored file specification. Suppose, for example, that you use a .Q1 extension for all Quarter 1 reports. To find those files, just type the file specification `*.Q1`.

To specify what files to search for:

1   Select one of the predefined file sets from the Find Files combination box, or type one or more filenames, or one or more file specifications. See the "Searching for Multiple Files" section later in this chapter for more information.

2   Type a text string to search for in the With Text combination box if you want to search for a file or files that contain a particular text string.

    The With Text combination box contains a history list of the last four search strings you entered. This can save you some time if you frequently search for the same text strings.

3   Select the More>> command button to view additional search criteria options, including date, time, size, and owner (if searching network drives), as well as file attributes.

TIP: To hide the Date, Time, Size and Owner drop-down list boxes and the attributes check boxes again, select the <<Less command button.

---

4   To search for files with a specific date, select a date specifier from the Date drop-down list box.

    Depending on the specifier you select, one or two text boxes are activated next to the Date drop-down list box. Enter the date or dates requested to define the scope of the date used in your search.

If you select Between as your date specifier, the date you are searching for must fall between the two dates you enter (inclusive). For example, if you select "between" and enter the dates 1/14/92 and 2/15/92, SuperFind searches for files created on 1/14/92 and 2/15/92, plus all files created between those dates.

If you select "not between" as your date specifier, the date you are searching for cannot fall between the two dates you enter. For example, if you select Not Between and enter the dates 9/13/91 and 2/18/92, SuperFind searches for all files created *before* 9/13/91 and *after* 2/18/92.

5   To search for files with a specific time, select a time specifier from the Time drop-down list box.

    Depending on the specifier you select, one or two text boxes appear next to the Time drop-down list box. Enter the time or times requested to define the scope of the time used in your search.

    The time specifiers Between and Not Between work exactly as they do in the Date drop-down list box described in step 4.

6   To search for files with a specific size, select a size specifier from the Size drop-down list box.

    Depending on the specifier you select, one or two text boxes appear next to the Size drop-down list box. Enter the file size or sizes in kilobytes. Valid file sizes are from 0 to 65535 kilobytes.

    The size specifiers Between and Not Between work exactly as they do in the Date drop-down list box described in step 4.

7   To search for files created by a particular user, select a user name from the list of network users in the Owner drop-down list. This option is available only if you are connected to a network.

8   To search for files containing the Archive, Read Only, System, Hidden and Directory file attributes, check the appropriate check boxes. There are three possible settings for these attributes:

Checked: SuperFind searches for files where this attribute is set.

Blank: SuperFind searches for files where this attribute is not set.

Gray-filled: SuperFind ignores the setting of this attribute during the search.

9   Select Find to begin the search.

Searching for Multiple Files

SuperFind supports the wildcards * (asterisk), ? (question mark) and | (pipe—a special SuperFind character different from the DOS pipe). The asterisk represents any number of characters; the question mark represents any one character; the pipe represents any one or no characters.

Table 5-1

Wildcard	Will Find...
MEMO.*	MEMO.DOC
	MEMO.BAK
	MEMO.C
MEMO?.DOC	MEMO1.DOC
	MEMO2.DOC
	MEMO9.DOC
MEMO|||.DOC	MEMORPT.DOC
	MEMO12.DOC
	MEMO.DOC

Wildcard examples

Multiple filenames or file specifications must be separated by one of the following delimiters or separators in the File Find combination box:

- space
- (,) comma
- (+) plus sign
- (;) semicolon
- (-) minus sign

The space, comma, plus sign and semicolon all mean "and." The minus sign means "except." (Note that a hyphen may also be part of a filename. If you want to exclude filenames that begin with a hyphen, use two hyphens.)

For example, to find all .BAK, .COM and .ARC files, enter:

    *.BAK *.COM *.ARC

Likewise, to find all files except .EXE and .OVL files, enter:

    . -*.EXE -*.OVL

Creating Customized File Sets

The predefined file sets are very convenient, but there will be times when they don't quite suit your file-searching needs; using a predefined file set might produce more files than you were looking for, or it might overlook files you need. If you know you'll only be needing a customized file set once, you can just type it into the Find Files combination box. If, on the other hand, you frequently need to search for a unique group of files, you might want to create and save your own file set, specially defined to search for exactly the files you need. In addition, you can modify existing file sets to suit your file-searching needs.

To create and save a customized file set:

1. Choose SEARCH SETS... from the SuperFind Options menu.

   The Search Sets dialog box appears (Figure 5-2).

2. Select the File Sets option button at the bottom of the Search Sets dialog box.

   The predefined file set names and definitions appear in the Name and Definition list box.

3. Select the Add command button.

   The Add File Set dialog box appears.

4. Type a name for your new file set in the Name text box. The filename you enter can be up to 30 characters long.

5. Type one or more filenames, or one or more file specifications (up to 30 characters long) in the Definition text box.

6. Select OK to save your new file set.

Figure 5-2

```
                                          select to create a custom
                                          file or location set
           predefined file set name
    ┌─────────────────── Search Sets ───────────────────┐
    │  Name and Definition:                      ▶ OK   │
    │  ┌─────────────────────────────────┐              │
    │  │ [All Files]                   ▲ │    Cancel    │
    │  │   *.*                           │              │
    │  │ [All Files Except Programs]     │     Add      │
    │  │   *.* -*.EXE -*.COM -*.BAT      │              │
    │  │ [Database Files]                │     Edit     │
    │  │   *.DB! *.DTF                   │              │
    │  │ [Documents]                     │    Delete    │
    │  │   *.DOC *.TXT *.WRI           ▼ │              │
    │  └─────────────────────────────────┘              │
    │                                                   │
    │     ● File Sets    ○ Location Sets                │
    └───────────────────────────────────────────────────┘
```
predefined file set definition ──┘

select to view file or location sets

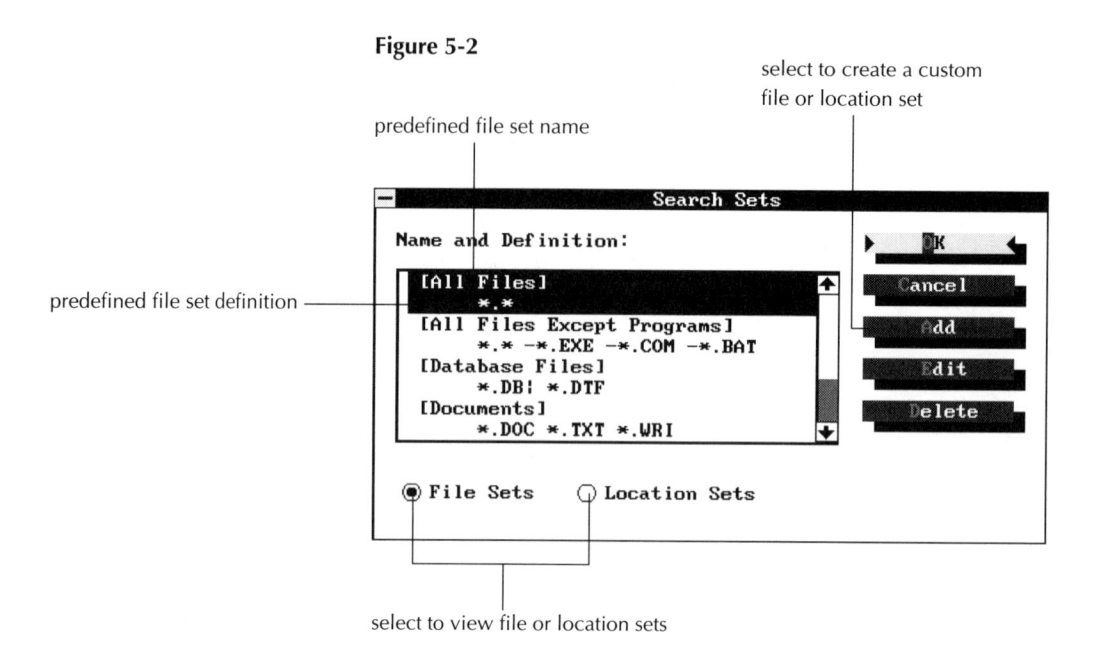

Your new file set is added to the Name and Definition list box in the Search Sets dialog box and in the Find Files drop-down combination box. You can save up to 16 file sets, including the predefined sets. If you have already saved 16 file sets and want to save another one, you must first delete an existing file set.

Editing File Sets

You can edit any of the file sets listed in the Find Files combination box, regardless of whether it's a predefined file set or one you've created.

To edit a file set:

1 Choose SEARCH SETS... from the SuperFind Options menu.

   The Search Sets dialog box appears (see Figure 5-2).

2 Select the file set you want to edit in the Name and Definition list box.

3 Select the Edit command button.

   The Edit File Set dialog box appears. The name and file specifications of the selected file set are already entered in the Name and Definition text boxes, respectively.

4 Edit the name and definition of the file set.

Deleting File Sets

5   Select OK to save your file set edits.

6   Select OK again to close the Search Sets dialog box.

As your file-searching needs change, you'll want to continually add and edit file sets. Once you've saved 16 file sets, you need to delete an existing file set before saving another one.

To delete a file set:

1   Choose SEARCH SETS... from the SuperFind Options menu.

    The Search Sets dialog box appears (see Figure 5-2).

2   Highlight the file set you want to delete in the Name and Definition list box.

3   Select the Delete command button.

    Your highlighted file set is immediately deleted.

4   Select OK to close the Search Sets dialog box.

DEFINING WHERE TO SEARCH

In addition to establishing what to search for, you can also narrow and speed up your file search by establishing where to search. Here again, you can be as general or as specific as you like.

Like file sets, Norton Desktop comes with a set of predefined location sets. These are locations which tell SuperFind where to search for your files. If the predefined location sets are not specific enough for you, you can create a customized location set.

To specify where to search:

1   Select one of the predefined location sets from the Where drop-down combination box (see Figure 5-1), or type a specific drive or a specific directory. See "Searching in Multiple Locations" for more information.

2   Select the Find command button to begin your search.

Searching in Multiple Locations

SuperFind can search for files in more than one location at a time.

- To search a single drive enter the drive letter followed by a colon. For example: C:
- To search all drives enter the wildcard specification: *:

- To search several nonconsecutive drives enter the drive letters (with a colon), separated by a space or semicolon. For example: `C: F: M:`
- To search several consecutive drives, enter the first drive and the last drive (with colons) separated by a hyphen. For example: `F: - K:`
- To search all floppy, hard and/or network drives enter one or more of the following separated by a space or semicolon:
  ```
  floppy:
  hard:
  net:
  ```

Creating Customized Location Sets

You can also create and save your own location sets so that SuperFind searches in the exact locations you specify. The location sets you create appear in the Where combination box along with the predefined location sets. Like the file sets, you can save up to 16 location sets. To save additional sets, you must first delete an existing set.

When you create a customized location set you can specify a list of drives or a single directory (but not more than one directory) for SuperFind to search. If you choose to search a directory, you can also include all of its subdirectories in the search.

To create a customized location set:

1 Choose SEARCH SETS... from the SuperFind Options menu.

   The Search Sets dialog box appears (see Figure 5-2). Notice that the File Sets option button is selected by default.

2 Select the Location Sets option button.

   The predefined location set names and definitions appear in the Name and Definition list box.

3 Select the Add command button.

   The Add Location Set dialog box appears.

4 Type a name (up to 30 characters long) for your new location set in the Name text box.

To select drives for your location set:

1. Select the Drive command button.

   The Select Drives to Search dialog box appears (Figure 5-3).

Figure 5-3

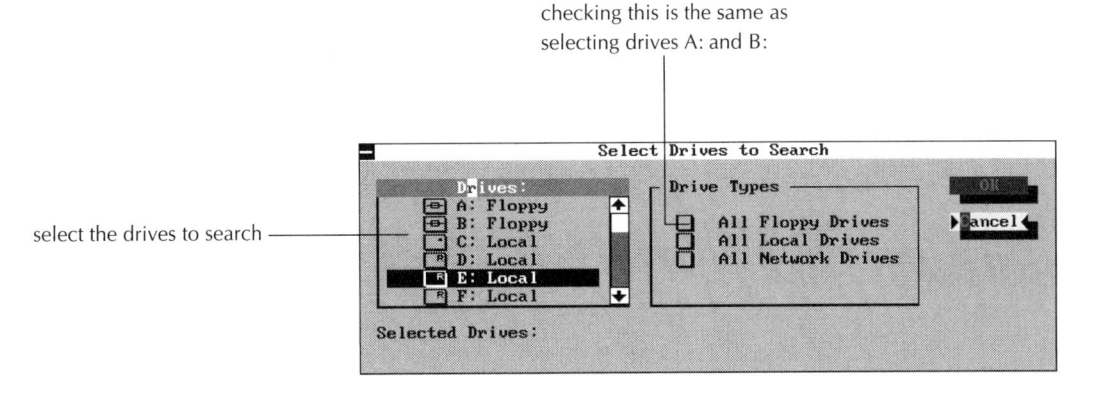

checking this is the same as selecting drives A: and B:

select the drives to search

2. Select the individual drives in the drive list you want to search.

   A list of the drives you've selected appears at the bottom of the dialog box. The number of characters in your drive list cannot exceed 30 characters. If your list extends beyond 30 characters, it will be truncated.

3. Check any check boxes in the Drive Types group to search all drives of a particular type.

4. Select OK.

   The drives you've chosen appear in the Definition text box of the Add Location Set dialog box.

To select a directory for your location set:

1. Select the Directory command button.

   The Select Directory to Search dialog box appears (Figure 5-4).

2. Select the drive containing the directory you want to search from the Drive drop-down list.

3. Select the directory you want to search from the directory list box.

5-12   Using Norton Desktop for DOS

Figure 5-4

select the drive your directory resides on

select the directory you want to search

select to add the directory to your location set

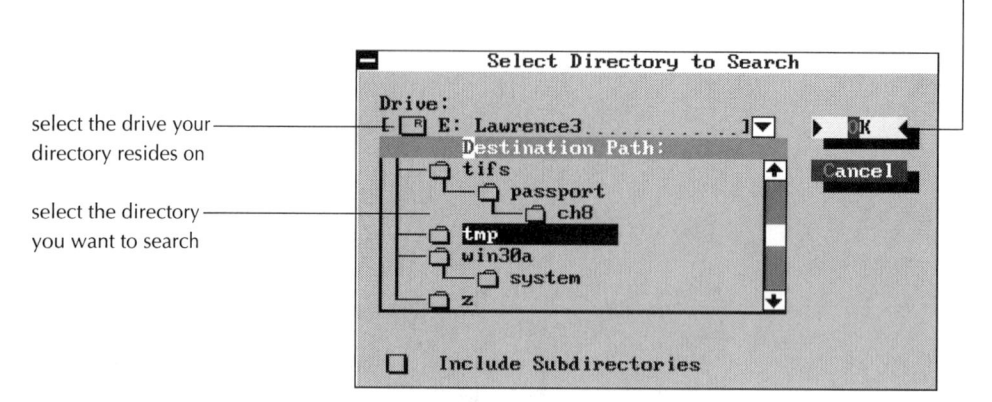

[Select Directory to Search dialog box shown]

4   Check the Include Subdirectories check box to also search all subdirectories of your chosen directory.

5   Select OK.

To save your customized location set:

1   Select OK to save your new location set and to close the Add Location Set dialog box.

The name of your new location set now appears in the Name and Definition list box of the Search Sets dialog box.

2   Select OK to close the Search Sets dialog box.

Editing Location Sets   You can edit any location set listed in the Name and Definition list box, whether it's a location set you created or one that was predefined.

To edit a location set:

1   Choose SEARCH SETS... from the SuperFind Options menu.

The Search Sets dialog box appears (see Figure 5-2).

2   Highlight the location set you want to edit in the Name and Definition list box.

3   Select the Edit command button.

    The Edit Location Set dialog box appears. The name and drive or directory specifications of your location set are already entered in the Name and Definition text boxes, respectively.

4   Edit the entries in the Name and Definition text boxes.

5   Select OK to save your location set edits.

6   Select OK again to close the Search Sets dialog box.

Deleting Location Sets

Deleting location sets allows you to remove location sets you no longer need, or to remove an existing location set to make room for a new one if you already have 16 location sets saved.

To delete a location set:

1   Choose SEARCH SETS... from the SuperFind Options menu.

    The Search Sets dialog box appears (see Figure 5-2).

2   Highlight the location set you want to delete in the Name and Definition list box.

3   Select the Delete command button.

    Your highlighted location set is immediately deleted.

4   Select OK to close the Search Sets dialog box.

MAKING SEARCHES CASE-SENSITIVE

By default SuperFind ignores whether letters are uppercase or lowercase when it searches for text strings. This means that "oh, happy day" is assumed to be the same as "Oh, Happy Day." If you want SuperFind to distinguish between uppercase and lowercase letters when it performs a text search, use the Match Upper/Lowercase command.

To make text searches case-sensitive:

- Choose MATCH UPPER/LOWERCASE from the SuperFind Options menu. Choosing the command again toggles the command off.

    A checkmark appears next to the command name when the command has been selected.

CREATING A BATCH FILE FROM MATCHING FILES

SuperFind has a feature that allows you to write small batch files to perform a specific operation on all matching files found by SuperFind. For example, suppose you are writing a book and you have your chapters saved as CHAP1.DOC, CHAP2.DOC, and so on. To find all of your chapters, tell SuperFind to search for CHAP*.DOC. A drive window is opened listing all the chapters of your book.

CREATE BATCH... allows you to enter text (usually a DOS command or program name) before each of the matching filenames and, optionally, text after each matching filename. Now, you can use the CREATE BATCH... command from the SuperFind Options menu to print these chapters without typing in the same command over and over each time. To do this, just type the command COPY before each filename and the text PRN after each filename. Now just run your DOS batch file to print each chapter. In addition, the list of files and their attached batch command is saved in a single batch file.

To create a DOS batch file from a matching-files list:

1 Perform a search in SuperFind.

2 Choose CREATE BATCH... from the SuperFind Options menu.

   The Create Batch dialog box appears (Figure 5-5).

3 Type a name for your batch file in the Save As text box if you want to save your batch file to use again.

   You can leave this text box blank if you decide not to save your batch file.

4 Type the text you want to appear before each filename in the Insert Before Filename text box.

5 Type the text you want to appear after each filename in the Append After Filename text box.

   The Sample text box lets you preview how your batch command looks.

6 To have each file's full drive, path and filename inserted between the "Before" and "After" text, check the Full Path check box.

   This check box is unchecked by default, which means that only the filename and extension are used.

Figure 5-5

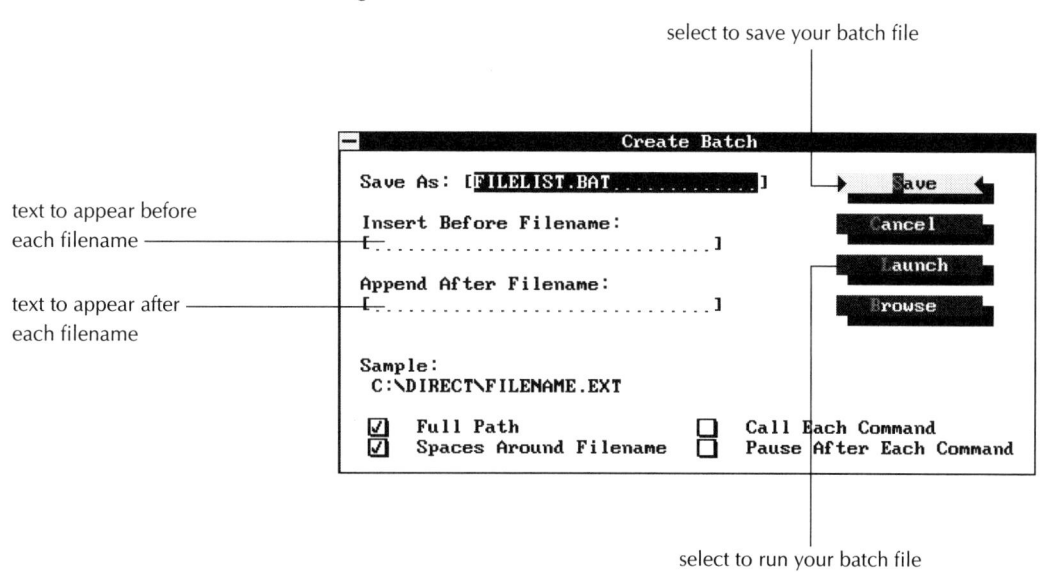

select to save your batch file

```
┌─────────────────── Create Batch ───────────────────┐
│  Save As: [FILELIST.BAT............]    ▶ Save ◀   │
│                                                    │
│  Insert Before Filename:                  Cancel   │
│  [...........................]                     │
│                                           Launch   │
│  Append After Filename:                            │
│  [...........................]            Browse   │
│                                                    │
│  Sample:                                           │
│  C:\DIRECT\FILENAME.EXT                            │
│                                                    │
│  ☑ Full Path              ☐ Call Each Command      │
│  ☑ Spaces Around Filename ☐ Pause After Each Command│
└────────────────────────────────────────────────────┘
```

text to appear before each filename — (points to "Insert Before Filename")

text to appear after each filename — (points to "Append After Filename")

select to run your batch file

7 To add a space character before and after each filename, check the Spaces Around Filename check box.

If you want the text to be positioned right next to the filename, such as when you use quotation marks, uncheck this check box.

8 To insert the word "Call" at the beginning of each line of your batch file, check the Call Each Command check box.

If the text entered before each filename is another batch file, be sure this box is checked. This allows control to return to your batch file after the first batch file is run.

9 To insert a line containing the DOS PAUSE command between each line in your batch file, check the Pause After Each Command check box.

The program will then pause and display the message, "Press any key when ready…" after executing each line.

10 Select Launch to run your batch file.

11 Select Save to save your batch file without running it.

To load or edit existing SuperFind batch files:

1   Select the Browse command button from the Create Batch dialog box (see Figure 5-5).
2   Browse the directories and the files until the desired batch file is located.
3   Select the batch file you want to load or edit.
4   Select OK.

Launching Files

This chapter describes the various ways you can launch a file from Norton Desktop (that is, to start an application with or without a related document). This chapter also shows you how to customize the way files launch—for example, by changing command lines or file associations.

Contents

Associating a File 6-3
    Changing an Association 6-4
    Deleting an Association 6-4
    Adding an Association 6-5
    Specifying a Custom Startup Command 6-6
Launching a File 6-7
    Launching From the File Pane 6-7
    Launching Using the RUN... Command 6-8
    Launching From the DOS Command Line 6-9
    Launching From a DOS Session 6-10

With Norton Desktop you can easily launch a file (run an application with or without a related document) in several ways:

- From a drive window file pane.
- With the RUN... command from the (long) File menu.
- From the DOS command line (DOS BACKGROUND toggled on in the long View menu).
- From a DOS session (using the DOS SESSION command from the long Tools menu).

ASSOCIATING A FILE

In order to launch documents with the application that created them, an association must exist between a file extension and an application. Norton Desktop provides some associations for you. For example, .DOC files are associated with Microsoft Word. The association between the file extension and the application makes it possible to launch the application automatically when you open a document file. For example, because Microsoft Word is associated with files that have .DOC file extensions, selecting a file with a .DOC extension automatically launches Word and opens the .DOC file for you.

Norton Desktop lets you make changes to the associations quickly and easily. With Norton Desktop you can change the default associations, delete associations, add new associations or specify custom startup commands for applications.

To quickly view a list of file associations:

1 Choose ASSOCIATE... from the (long) File menu.

   The Associate dialog box appears on your desktop (Figure 6-1), displaying each file extension that is associated with an application.

2 To view the list by application name, select the Program Name option in the Sort By group box.

   To view the list by file extension, select the File Extension option.

Figure 6-1

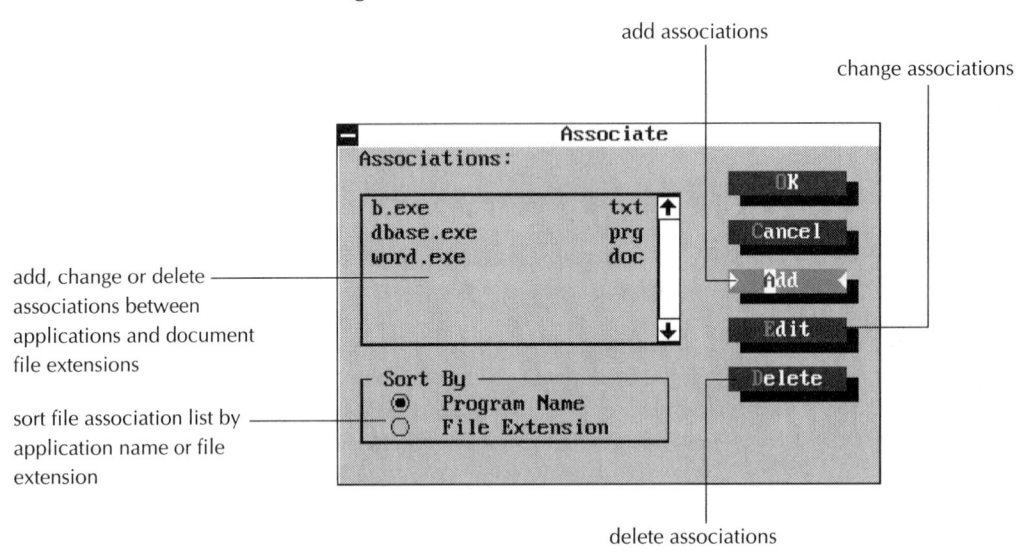

add, change or delete associations between applications and document file extensions

sort file association list by application name or file extension

add associations

change associations

delete associations

Changing an Association

There may be times when you want to change an association. For example, you may want an application to be associated with a file extension other than the one already established.

To associate a different file extension with an application:

1 Select the extension with which the application is currently associated from the Associations list box.
2 Select the Edit button.
   The Edit Association dialog box appears.
3 Type the new file extension over the old file extension in the Extension text box.
4 Select OK.

Deleting an Association

You might want to delete an association if a file extension is currently associated with the wrong application or you have removed the application from your system.

To delete an association:

1 Select the association in the Associations list box.
2 Select the Delete button.
   The association is deleted.

Adding an Association

From time to time, you may want to associate a new file extension with an application. For example, if you frequently type business letters for several people in your office, you might want to use their initials as part of your file-naming convention. Thus, memos typed for Alicia Thompson could have an .AT extension, while those typed for Mark Kennedy could have an .MK extension.

NOTE: You cannot associate an extension with more than one application. For example, you cannot associate the .DOC file extension with both Word and WordPerfect. However, an application can have several file extensions associated with it, as long as the file extensions are unique.

To add a new association between a file extension and an application:

1 Select the Add button from the Associate dialog box.

The Add Association dialog box appears (Figure 6-2).

Figure 6-2

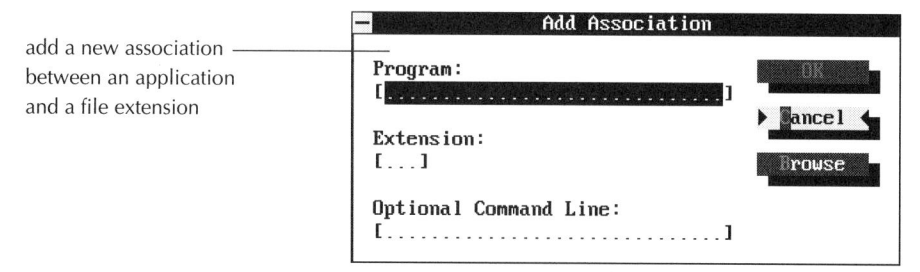

add a new association between an application and a file extension

```
┌─────────────── Add Association ───────────────┐
│                                                │
│  Program:                              ┌─OK──┐ │
│  [............................]       └─────┘ │
│                                      ▶ Cancel ◀│
│  Extension:                                    │
│  [...]                                 ┌Browse┐│
│                                        └──────┘│
│  Optional Command Line:                        │
│  [............................]               │
│                                                │
└────────────────────────────────────────────────┘
```

2 In the Program text box, type the filename and extension for the application to which you want to associate a file extension.

You must include the complete path for the application if one of the following conditions exist:

- You are not planning to launch the application from the directory it resides in.

- The directory name where the application resides is not in the DOS PATH statement (usually part of your AUTOEXEC.BAT file).

3 In the Extension text box, type the file extension that you want to associate with this application. An extension can be one, two or three characters in length. (Do not type the dot that precedes the extension.)

4 Select OK.

Note that the Optional Command Line text box displays the same extension as that displayed in the Extension text box, preceded by a dot and a caret (^) symbol. The caret is a substitution character. When you select a document file to launch, the caret (^) symbol is replaced with the currently selected filename.

Specifying a Custom Startup Command

The Optional Command Line text box is, indeed, optional. You can modify this information if you want to customize the command used to launch a file—perhaps to launch Word with a macro.

If you consistently run Word with a macro (adding the "/macro name" switch to the startup command), you may want to consider modifying the Optional Command Line. The default Optional Command Line is ^.DOC. To have Word run a macro at startup, modify the command line so it looks like this:

```
/macro name ^.doc
```

where "macro name" represents the name of the macro you want to run. This is illustrated in Figure 6-3.

Figure 6-3

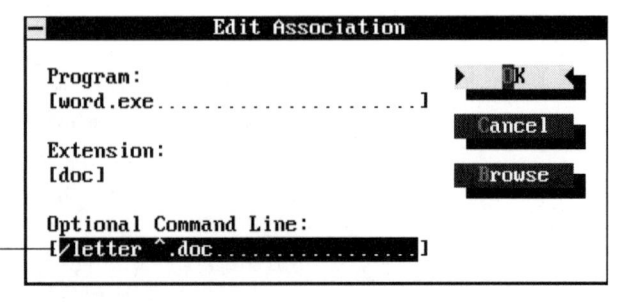

specify a custom startup command

Launching Files **6-7**

> **NOTE:** The Optional Command Line value is an ordinary DOS command that is invoked when you launch a file with a particular association. The DOS command begins with an application filename followed by the document filename. When you select a document file to launch, the caret (^) symbol in the Optional Command Line text box is replaced with the currently selected filename.

LAUNCHING A FILE

Once associations exist between file extensions and applications, you can easily launch files from within Norton Desktop.

If you need information on how to establish associations, see the section "Associating a File" in this chapter.

> **NOTE:** When an application is running, it takes over the entire screen. After you exit the application, the Norton Desktop reappears.

Launching From the File Pane

The file pane in a drive window displays a listing of files. You can open a drive window by choosing OPEN DRIVE WINDOW… from the Window menu (Ctrl+W) or by double-clicking the drive icon. If the file pane is not visible, choose FILE PANE from the View menu.

To launch a file from the file pane:

1   Use the arrow keys to highlight the filename in an open drive window.

2   Press Enter to launch the file and its associated application.

    Or,

    Choose OPEN from the File menu.

Or,

Using Norton Desktop for DOS

- Double-click the filename.

   If the file you selected is an application, the application is launched.

   If the file you selected is a document file and an association exists between the document's file extension and an application, the application is launched and the document file is automatically opened.

   If an association does not exist, a message displays asking if you want to establish an association.

Launching Using the RUN... Command

If you prefer to enter the DOS command that launches your application, you can do this with the RUN... command. (You can also use the RUN... command to execute any DOS command. If you have questions about using DOS commands, refer to your DOS manual.)

The DOS command to launch your application may be as simple as the .EXE filename for an application, or the executable file's name followed by the filename for a document (`WORD MEMO.DOC`, for example).

You must include the complete path for the application if one of the following conditions exist:

- The application you are launching is not in the current directory.
- The directory name where the application resides is not in the DOS PATH statement (usually part of your AUTOEXEC.BAT file).

If the document file you wish to edit (in this example, MEMO.DOC) is not in the current directory, include the complete path.

To launch a file with the RUN... command:

1. Choose RUN... from the (long) File menu (Ctrl+R).

   The Run dialog box appears on the desktop (Figure 6-4).

2. Type the DOS command in the DOS Command combination box to start the application, with a related document if applicable.

   To quickly enter a command you've recently used in the DOS Command combination box, select the command from the command history drop-down list box.

Launching Files **6-9**

Figure 6-4

choose RUN... from the (long)
File menu to launch a file

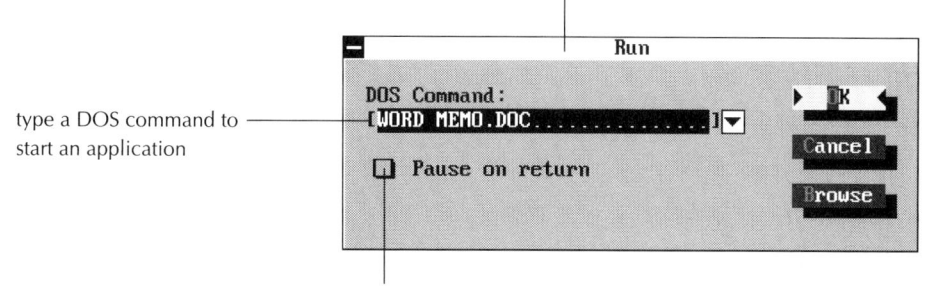

type a DOS command to start an application

```
Run
DOS Command:
[WORD MEMO.DOC        ]  ▶ OK
                         Cancel
□ Pause on return        Browse
```

check to have Norton Desktop pause
before returning to the desktop

TIP: If an association already exists, simply type the filename and extension of the document you wish to edit in the DOS Command combination box. If the file is not in the current directory, include the complete path (C:\ORDERS\MEMO.DOC, for example).

3   Check the Pause on Return check box if you want Norton Desktop to pause before returning to the desktop once the application terminates.

4   Select OK.

Launching From the DOS Command Line

You can also launch files or enter DOS commands from the *DOS command line*.

The DOS command line is a DOS prompt that displays at the bottom of the screen when DOS BACKGROUND in the (long) View menu is toggled on. The DOS command line allows you to enter DOS commands while the Norton Desktop menus and drive windows are still on the screen.

To display the DOS command line:

- Choose DOS BACKGROUND from the (long) View menu (Ctrl+O).

    The drive icons and desktop background disappear but the desktop menus and drive windows remain on the screen. The DOS command line appears.

6-10   *Using Norton Desktop for DOS*

To launch a file from the DOS command line:

- Type the DOS command to start the application, with a related document if applicable.

  You must include the complete path for the application if one of the following conditions exist:

  - The application you are launching is not in the current directory.
  - The directory name where the application resides is not in the DOS PATH statement (usually part of your AUTOEXEC.BAT file).

  If the document file you wish to edit is not in the current directory, include the complete path.

  If an association exists, simply type the filename and extension of the document you wish to edit. If the document file is not in the current directory, include the complete path (`C:\ORDERS\MEMO.DOC`, for example).

To remove the DOS command line:

- Choose DOS BACKGROUND again from the View menu (Ctrl+O).

  The drive icons and desktop background reappear and the DOS command line disappears from the screen.

Launching From a DOS Session

From time to time, you may want to run a program or issue a DOS command from DOS. You do not need to exit Norton Desktop to run a DOS session; you can get to DOS from within Norton Desktop.

To run a DOS session:

- Choose DOS SESSION from the (long) Tools menu (Ctrl+D).

  The desktop clears from the screen and a full-screen DOS prompt appears for you to type DOS commands and start applications.

NOTE: Associations are not honored when you are in a DOS session. To run an application from DOS, you must enter the DOS command that executes that application.

To exit from a DOS session:

- Type EXIT at the DOS prompt and press Enter.

    You are returned to Norton Desktop.

> **CAUTION:** When you are in a DOS session, remember you must exit from DOS to return to Norton Desktop. Do not try to return by typing ND; this starts Norton Desktop again and your computer may run out of memory.

Viewing Files

This chapter describes the Norton Desktop viewing features that let you quickly display the contents of various files without opening the applications that created them.

Contents

Viewing a File in the View Pane 7-3
Viewing a File in Norton Viewer 7-5
    Selecting a File within Norton Viewer 7-7
    Exiting Norton Viewer 7-7
    Viewing a Single Record in a Database File 7-7
Word Wrapping Text 7-9
Changing Viewers 7-9
Searching Files 7-11
Viewing Graphic Files 7-13
Changing the Graphic Image 7-13
    Scrolling a Graphic Image 7-13
    Flipping the Graphic Image Horizontally
      or Vertically 7-14
    Zooming the Graphic Image 7-15
    Rotating the Graphic Image 7-15
    Refreshing the Screen 7-15
    Inverting the Graphic Image 7-15

Norton Desktop makes managing your files easier by letting you view word processor, spreadsheet, graphic, database and *executable* files without having to open the applications that created them. This lets you quickly view a file whose contents you may have forgotten before opening, moving or deleting it.

TIP: You can use the viewing features to read the README.TXT file found in the Norton Desktop directory for the most up-to-date information about the different formats you can view a file in. See the sections "Viewing a File in the View Pane" and "Viewing a File in Norton Viewer" for instructions on how to view a file.

NOTE: In Norton Desktop, you can view files in local drives (drives that are physically attached to your computer—drives A:, B: and C:, for example) and any network drives to which your computer is connected.

You cannot, however, view the contents of compressed files or files on another computer that your computer is linked to (using the Compressed File, Desktop Link or Network Link options of the OPEN WINDOW... command in the Window menu).

There are two ways to view the contents of a file. One way is to view the file in the view pane of the drive window. The other way is to view the file in full-screen mode using Norton Viewer.

VIEWING A FILE IN THE VIEW PANE

The fastest and simplest way to view a file is in the view pane in a drive window.

To view a file using the view pane:

1   Open a drive window for the drive containing the file you want to view (Ctrl+W).

7-4   *Using Norton Desktop for DOS*

2   Choose VIEW PANE from the View menu.

Figure 7-1 shows a drive window with the tree, file and view panes turned on. See Chapter 2, "Using Drive Windows," for more information on drive windows and window panes.

Figure 7-1

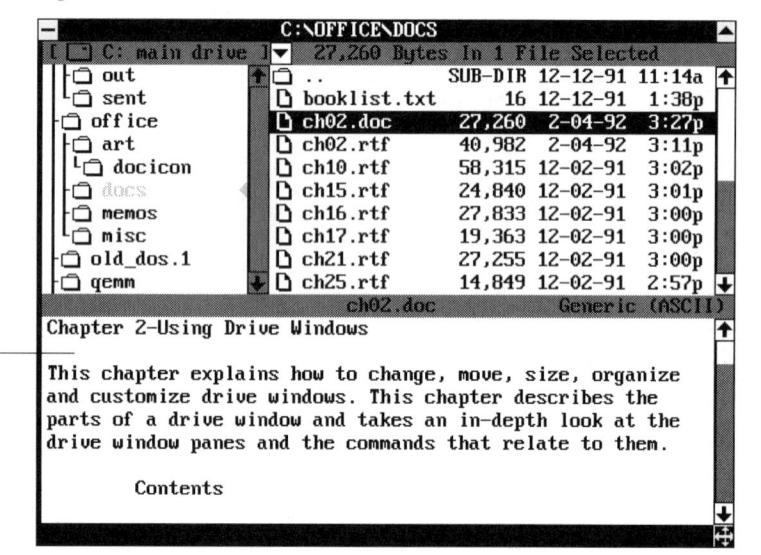

```
┌─────────────────── C:\OFFICE\DOCS ───────────────────┐
│ [ ▭ C: main drive ]▼  27,260 Bytes In 1 File Selected │
│  ▭ out            ↑ ▭ ..           SUB-DIR 12-12-91 11:14a ↑
│  ▭ sent             ▭ booklist.txt      16 12-12-91  1:38p
│ ┤▭ office           ▭ ch02.doc      27,260  2-04-92  3:27p
│ ├▭ art              ▭ ch02.rtf      40,982  2-04-92  3:11p
│ └▭ docicon          ▭ ch10.rtf      58,315 12-02-91  3:02p
│  ▭ docs             ▭ ch15.rtf      24,840 12-02-91  3:01p
│ ┤▭ memos            ▭ ch16.rtf      27,833 12-02-91  3:00p
│ └▭ misc             ▭ ch17.rtf      19,363 12-02-91  3:00p
│ ┤▭ old_dos.1        ▭ ch21.rtf      27,255 12-02-91  3:00p
│ ┤▭ qemm           ↓ ▭ ch25.rtf      14,849 12-02-91  2:57p ↓
│                 ch02.doc                   Generic (ASCII)
│ Chapter 2-Using Drive Windows                              ↑
│
│ This chapter explains how to change, move, size, organize
│ and customize drive windows. This chapter describes the
│ parts of a drive window and takes an in-depth look at the
│ drive window panes and the commands that relate to them.
│
│     Contents
│                                                            ↓
└──────────────────────────────────────────────────────┘
```

choose VIEW PANE from the View menu to display the contents of a selected file in the view pane in a drive window

3   Select the correct directory and file from the tree and file panes, respectively.

The view pane displays the last file selected, so each time you select a new file it replaces the currently displayed file.

☞   **TIP:** If you want to see the file in full-screen mode, choose VIEW... from the File menu. This displays the file using Norton Viewer, discussed later in this chapter.

For more information on viewing graphic files, see the section "Viewing Graphic Files" in this chapter.

Viewing Files 7-5

Whether you are viewing the file in the view pane or in full-screen mode, you can scroll through the file vertically by pressing PgUp and PgDn, and you can scroll horizontally by pressing RightArrow or LeftArrow.

If you are using a mouse, you can scroll vertically through the file using the vertical scroll bar. You can also scroll vertically or horizontally through the file by clicking and holding either mouse button in the left, right, upper, or lower portion of the screen. For example, if you want to scroll left, click and hold the mouse button in the left portion of the screen.

To close the view pane:

- Choose VIEW PANE again from the View menu to toggle it off.

Norton Viewer is useful when you want to view a screenful of information at a time.

VIEWING A FILE IN NORTON VIEWER

To view a file using Norton Viewer:

1 Choose VIEW... from the File menu.

   If you selected a file from a drive window before invoking Norton Viewer, Norton Viewer appears with that file displayed. If you didn't select a file before invoking Norton Viewer, the Browse for a File to View dialog box appears (Figure 7-2).

NOTE: If Norton Viewer appears with the contents of a file displayed, skip steps 2 and 3.

2 Select a file from the Browse for a File to View dialog box.

   Use the Directories, Files, and Drive list boxes to select the file you want to view. You can also choose a file by typing the filename and its path into the File text box.

7-6   *Using Norton Desktop for DOS*

Figure 7-2

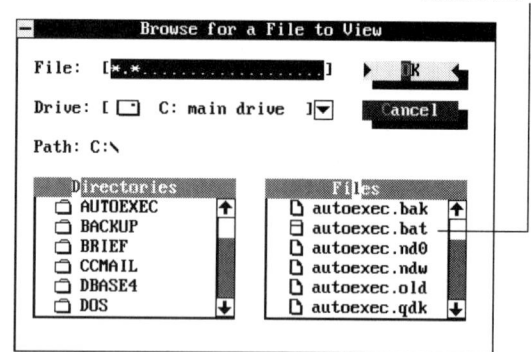

select a file to view

```
┌─ Browse for a File to View ─────────────┐
│ File: [*.*................]  ▶ ▇OK▇     │
│                                         │
│ Drive: [ ☐  C: main drive ]▼  ▇Cancel▇  │
│                                         │
│ Path: C:\                               │
│  ┌─ Directories ──┐  ┌─ Files ──────┐   │
│  │ ☐ AUTOEXEC   ↑ │  │ ▫ autoexec.bak ↑│
│  │ ☐ BACKUP       │  │ ▤ autoexec.bat  │
│  │ ☐ BRIEF        │  │ ▫ autoexec.nd0  │
│  │ ☐ CCMAIL       │  │ ▫ autoexec.ndw  │
│  │ ☐ DBASE4       │  │ ▫ autoexec.old  │
│  │ ☐ DOS        ↓ │  │ ▫ autoexec.qdk ↓│
│  └────────────────┘  └─────────────────┘│
└─────────────────────────────────────────┘
```

3   Select OK.

The file appears on the screen inside Norton Viewer (Figure 7-3).

> **NOTE:** Selecting Cancel from the Browse for a File to View dialog box exits Norton Viewer and returns you to the Norton Desktop.

Or,

1   Select the file you want to view.

2   Drag the file to the View button on the Button Bar.

The file appears on the screen inside Norton Viewer (Figure 7-3).

Figure 7-3

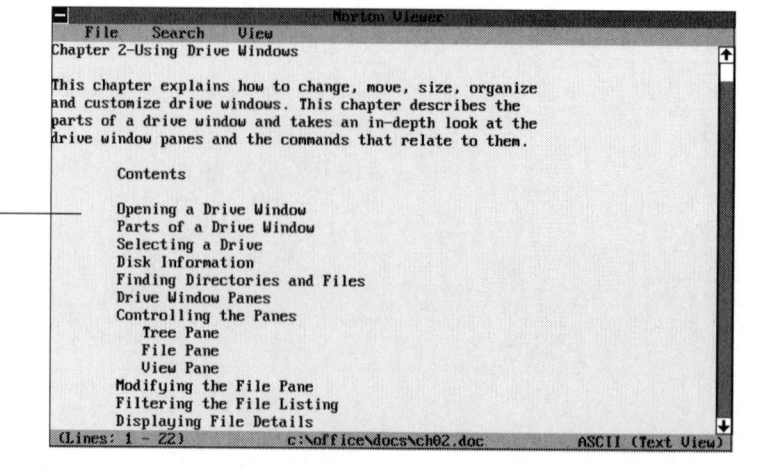

the contents of your selected file appear on the screen inside the Norton Viewer

```
┌──────────────────── Norton Viewer ─────────────────────┐
│  File    Search    View                                │
│ Chapter 2-Using Drive Windows                         ↑│
│                                                        │
│ This chapter explains how to change, move, size, organize│
│ and customize drive windows. This chapter describes the│
│ parts of a drive window and takes an in-depth look at the│
│ drive window panes and the commands that relate to them.│
│                                                        │
│        Contents                                        │
│                                                        │
│        Opening a Drive Window                          │
│        Parts of a Drive Window                         │
│        Selecting a Drive                               │
│        Disk Information                                │
│        Finding Directories and Files                   │
│        Drive Window Panes                              │
│        Controlling the Panes                           │
│           Tree Pane                                    │
│           File Pane                                    │
│           View Pane                                    │
│        Modifying the File Pane                         │
│        Filtering the File Listing                      │
│        Displaying File Details                        ↓│
│ (Lines: 1 - 22)      c:\office\docs\ch02.doc  ASCII (Text View)│
└────────────────────────────────────────────────────────┘
```

Selecting a File within Norton Viewer

Once you are in Norton Viewer, you can select a different file to view.

To view a different file within Norton Viewer:

1 Choose OPEN... from the File menu.

   The Browse for a File to View dialog box appears on your desktop (see Figure 7-2).

2 Select a file from the Browse for a File to View dialog box.

   Use the Directories, Files, and Drive list boxes to select the file you want to view. You can also choose a file by typing the filename and its path into the File text box.

3 Select OK.

   The file appears on the screen inside Norton Viewer (see Figure 7-3).

NOTE: Selecting Cancel from the Browse for a File to View dialog box returns you to the file currently being viewed.

Exiting Norton Viewer

To exit Norton Viewer:

- Choose EXIT from the File menu.

   Norton Viewer closes the open file, exits and returns you to the desktop.

Viewing a Single Record in a Database File

When you are viewing a database file, by default, the records are displayed in a table format—each column is a field in the database and each row is a record. This format allows you to see many records on the screen at a time.

When viewing a database file in Norton Viewer, you can display an individual record with each field shown on a separate line. This format is useful when you want to focus your attention on one record at a time.

To view an individual record in a database file:

1 Select the record you want to view by highlighting it.

7-8   *Using Norton Desktop for DOS*

> **TIP:** Use the FIND... command in the Norton Viewer Search menu to find the record if it is not in view. The FIND... command is discussed later in this chapter.

2. Choose the VIEW RECORD option from the View menu in Norton Viewer.

   Or,

   Press Enter to toggle the view mode.

   The selected record displays with each field shown on a separate line, as shown in Figure 7-4.

Figure 7-4

choose VIEW RECORD from the View menu in Norton Viewer to display a selected database record

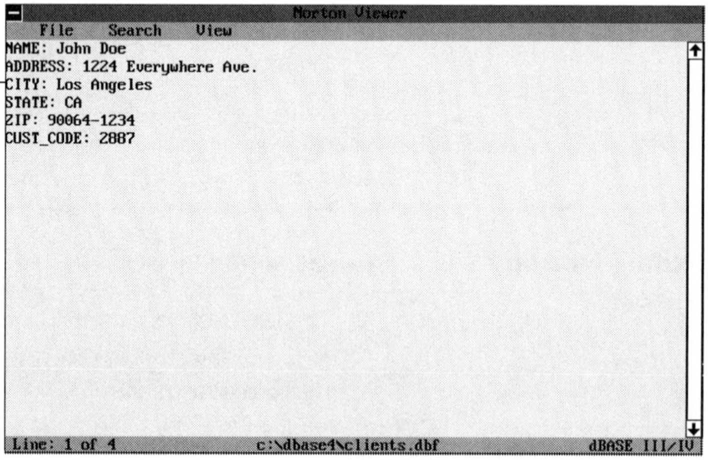

```
┌─────────────────────── Norton Viewer ───────────────────────┐
│   File    Search    View                                    │
│ NAME: John Doe                                              │
│ ADDRESS: 1224 Everywhere Ave.                               │
│ CITY: Los Angeles                                           │
│ STATE: CA                                                   │
│ ZIP: 90064-1234                                             │
│ CUST_CODE: 2887                                             │
│                                                             │
│ Line: 1 of 4           c:\dbase4\clients.dbf    dBASE III/IV│
└─────────────────────────────────────────────────────────────┘
```

You can easily switch between the table view and the individual record view.

To return to the table format:

- Select VIEW RECORD again from the View menu.

  Or,

  Press Enter to return to the table view.

WORD WRAPPING TEXT

To make word processing documents easier to view, you can have the text wrap to fit within the size of the view pane or within the size of the Norton Viewer screen.

To wrap text :

- If you are in Norton Desktop, choose VIEWER from the (long) View menu, then choose WORD WRAP from the cascading menu that appears.

Or,

- If you are in Norton Viewer, choose WORD WRAP from the View menu.

  The text wraps to fit the size of the current view pane or the Norton Viewer screen.

TIP: If you change the size of the view pane, the text does not automatically wrap to the new size. To rewrap the text, choose REFRESH from the View menu in Norton Desktop.

If you decide you don't like the way the text looks wrapped, you can return the text to the original format.

To unwrap the text:

- If you are in Norton Desktop, choose VIEWER from the (long) View menu, then choose WORD WRAP again from the cascading menu that appears.

Or,

- If you are in Norton Viewer, choose WORD WRAP again from the View menu.

  The text returns to its original format.

CHANGING VIEWERS

Viewers are automatically assigned to a file when you view it. If the file type can't be determined, the file displays in either ASCII text file format or hexadecimal format depending on the type of characters in the file. You also have the option of changing the viewer being used to display your file.

TIP: You can view any file type in the ASCII text file format or the hexadecimal format.

7-10 *Using Norton Desktop for DOS*

> **NOTE:** The status bar shows which viewer is being used to display the file.

To change the viewing mode of the current file:

1 If you are in Norton Desktop, choose VIEWER from the (long) View menu, then choose CHANGE VIEWER... from the cascading menu that appears.

   Or,

   If you are in Norton Viewer, choose CHANGE VIEWER... from the View menu.

   The Change Viewer dialog box appears (Figure 7-5).

Figure 7-5

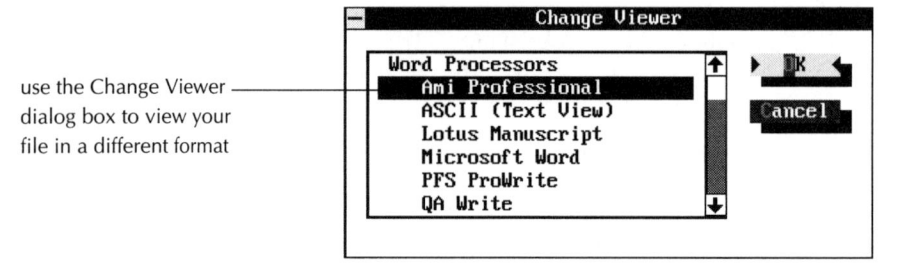

use the Change Viewer dialog box to view your file in a different format

```
┌─────────── Change Viewer ───────────┐
│  Word Processors              ↑     │    ► OK
│  Ami Professional                   │
│  ASCII (Text View)                  │    Cancel
│  Lotus Manuscript                   │
│  Microsoft Word                     │
│  PFS ProWrite                       │
│  QA Write                     ↓     │
└─────────────────────────────────────┘
```

2 Select a different viewer from the list box.
3 Select OK.

   This changes the viewing format of the currently selected file only.

> **NOTE:** If the file cannot be viewed using the viewer you chose, an error message displays telling you so. If this happens, you can choose CHANGE VIEWER... again from the View menu to select another format.
>
> However, you can view any type of file in the ASCII text format or hexadecimal format.

Viewing Files 7-11

SEARCHING FILES

You can quickly search for data in the file you're viewing to help determine a file's contents.

To search for data in a file:

1   If you are in Norton Desktop, choose VIEWER from the (long) View menu, then choose FIND... from the cascading menu that appears.

    Or,

    If you are in Norton Viewer, choose FIND... from the Search menu.

    The Find Text dialog box displays (Figure 7-6).

Figure 7-6

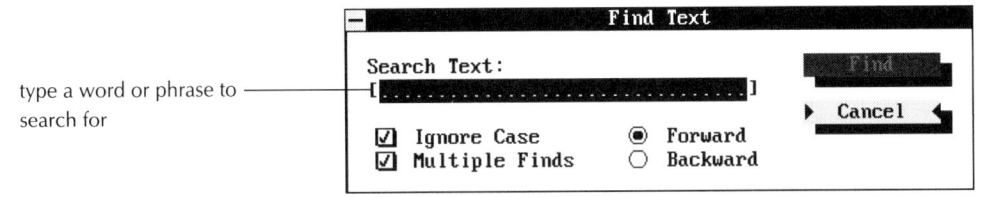

type a word or phrase to search for

```
┌─────────────────── Find Text ───────────────────┐
│ Search Text:                       ┌─ Find ─┐   │
│ [..............................]   └────────┘   │
│                                    ▶ Cancel ◀   │
│   ☑ Ignore Case      ● Forward                  │
│   ☑ Multiple Finds   ○ Backward                 │
└─────────────────────────────────────────────────┘
```

2   Type the word or phrase to search for in the Search Text text box.

3   Select the search options that you want.

    Ignore Case: ignores capitalization when searching.

    Multiple Finds: allows you to search for multiple occurrences of a word or phrase.

    Forward: begins search from the current position forward.

    Backward: begins search from the current position backward.

> **NOTE:** The status bar shows the current position of the file.

4   Select Find to begin the search.

If you've already searched for a word or phrase and now you want to find another occurrence, you can easily do this with the FIND NEXT or FIND PREVIOUS menu commands.

To search for the next occurrence of a word or phrase:

- If you are in Norton Desktop, choose VIEWER from the (long) View menu, then choose FIND NEXT from the cascading menu that appears.

Or,

- If you are in Norton Viewer, choose FIND NEXT from the Search menu.

The search is suspended when a match is found and the matching text is highlighted. If no text is found a message displays telling you so.

NOTE: FIND NEXT and FIND PREVIOUS are dimmed until text has been entered in the Find Text dialog box of the FIND... command.

To search for the previous occurrence of a word or phrase:

- If you are in Norton Desktop, choose VIEWER from the (long) View menu, then choose FIND PREVIOUS from the cascading menu that appears.

Or,

- If you are in Norton Viewer, choose FIND PREVIOUS from the Search menu.

The search is suspended when a match is found and the matching text is highlighted. If no text is found a message displays telling you so.

To go to a specific location in a file:

1 If you are in Norton Desktop, choose VIEWER from the (long) View menu, then choose GO TO... from the cascading menu that appears.

   Or,

   If you are in Norton Viewer, choose GO TO... from the Search menu.

   The Go To dialog box appears.

2 Type the location you wish to go to. The location you specify depends on the type of file you are viewing:

Database: type the record number.

Spreadsheet: type the cell number in the format col/row (D12, C25, etc.).

Hexadecimal format: type the hex offset number.

Other file types: type the line number.

The highlight moves to the location you specified.

VIEWING GRAPHIC FILES

Norton Desktop has greatly simplified viewing *bitmap* and *vector* graphic files in many different ways. For example, you can flip horizontally, flip vertically, rotate, zoom or invert your graphic images with just a few simple keystrokes.

CHANGING THE GRAPHIC IMAGE

Norton Desktop offers many ways for you to change the way your graphic image appears on the screen. The changes you make always affect the entire image. For example, zooming the graphic image changes the size of the whole image.

> **NOTE:** Changing a graphic image while you are viewing it only affects the way the image looks on the screen. It does not affect the actual graphic file on disk.

Regardless of what changes you make, you can always restore the image to its original shape and size by pressing the Home key.

Table 7-1 is a summary of the keystrokes that you can use to alter the graphic image you are viewing. Press F1 to see this keystroke table on your screen.

Scrolling a Graphic Image

Some graphic images take up more than one screenful of space. You can use the scrolling keys to view parts of the image that don't appear on the screen. See Table 7-1 for information about the keys you can use to scroll.

Using Norton Desktop for DOS

Table 7-1

Keystroke	Result
Home	Return to original position and size.
UpArrow	Scroll up five pixels.
DownArrow	Scroll down five pixels.
LeftArrow	Scroll left five pixels.
RightArrow	Scroll right five pixels.
PgUp	Scroll up one screen.
PgDn	Scroll down one screen.
Shift+Tab, Ctrl+LeftArrow	Scroll left one screen.
Tab, Ctrl+RightArrow	Scroll right one screen.
H	Flip horizontally.
V	Flip vertically.
+ (plus key)	Zoom in (increase size of image).
- (minus key)	Zoom out (shrink size of image).
]	Rotate clockwise.
[	Rotate counter-clockwise.
C	Enable/disable screen refresh.
I	Invert colors of graphic image.

Use these keystrokes to change the way your graphic image appears on the screen.

Flipping the Graphic Image Horizontally or Vertically

Flipping an image means "looking at the other side." Pressing H flips the image horizontally from side to side, resulting in a mirror image. Pressing V flips the image vertically from top to bottom, so the image looks like it's upside down.

Zooming the Graphic Image

You can change the size of the graphic image by zooming it. Pressing the + (plus) key increases the size of the graphic image twofold, both horizontally and vertically. The result is an image that is four times as large as the one you started with. Pressing the - (minus) key shrinks the size of the graphic image by half, both horizontally and vertically, resulting in an image that is one-fourth the original size.

Rotating the Graphic Image

You can rotate the graphic image in 90-degree increments in a clockwise or counter-clockwise direction. Pressing the] (right bracket) key rotates the graphic image in a clockwise direction. Pressing the [(left bracket) key rotates the graphic image in a counter-clockwise direction.

Refreshing the Screen

You can control whether the screen clears before the image is redrawn (when rotated, for example) by enabling or disabling the refresh mode. The screen refresh mode is enabled by default (that is, the screen clears before the image is redrawn). Pressing C disables the refresh mode. Pressing C again enables it. If the graphic image fills the entire screen, disabling refresh has no effect.

Inverting the Graphic Image

You can invert the colors of the graphic image by pressing I. In a black-and-white drawing, black becomes white and white becomes black. In a color drawing, a color changes to its complementary color.

Linking PCs

This chapter describes Norton Desktop's PC-linking features. Using Norton Desktop, you can transfer files directly between PCs that are linked by a network or cable. This can be much faster and easier than copying or backing up files onto diskettes and carrying those diskettes to another PC for more copying or restoring.

Contents

Network Link 8-3
   Setting Up the Server 8-3
   Connecting the Client to the Server 8-5
Desktop Link 8-7
   Setting Up the Server 8-8
   Connecting the Client to the Server 8-8
Cloning Norton Desktop 8-10
Port and Cable Options 8-13

Linking PCs **8-3**

Here's how linking PCs works. One PC acts as a *server* for one or more PCs, called *clients*, which may be:

- On the same *local area network* (LAN)
- Linked by a cable

The server starts and ends the client-server session, but it is unavailable for any other tasks during the session. The client accesses the server's files and can transfer data from one machine to the other, etc.

This chapter explains the use of Network Link and Desktop Link and cloning Norton Desktop. To use Network Link or Desktop Link, both the server and its client must have Norton Desktop. When only one of the two PCs has Norton Desktop, you can "clone" the needed files from one to the other before using Network Link or Desktop Link.

Table 8-1

Feature	Requirements
Network Link	The network must support the NetBIOS interface, such as Novell, Lantastic, 3COM, LAN Manager and Banyan Vines.
Desktop Link	The two PCs must be cabled together via serial ports or via parallel ports. See the section "Port and Cable Options" for details about the cables.
Cloning Norton Desktop	The two PCs must be joined with a serial cable. See the section "Port and Cable Options" for details about serial cables.

Summary of requirements for linking PCs

NETWORK LINK

To share files that are on your hard drive, you set up your PC as a server and select the user or group of users that can access your files. Any PC on a LAN that supports the NetBIOS interface can act as a server. The users you select can copy, delete or rename any file on your hard drive.

Setting Up the Server

Set up the server first and then connect the client to the server.

To set up the server:

1. Log on to the network.
2. Start Norton Desktop.
3. Choose SERVE REMOTE LINK from the (long) Disk menu.
4. Select NETWORK LINK. The Network Link dialog box appears (Figure 8-1).

Figure 8-1

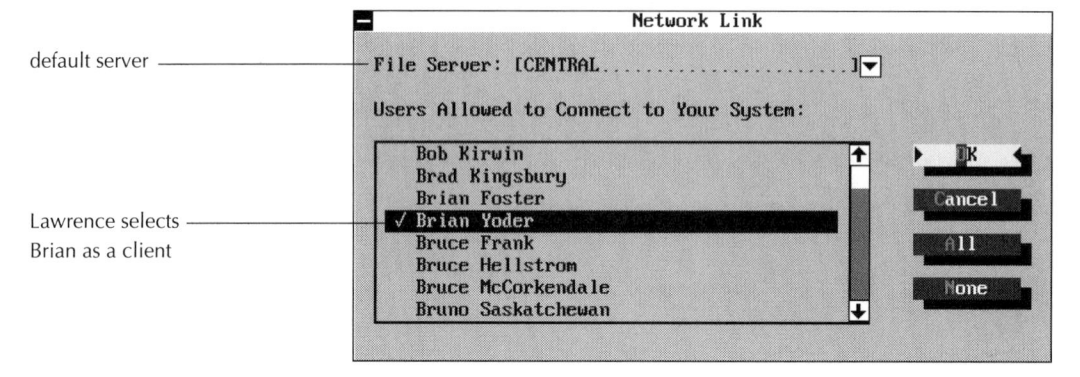

```
┌─────────────────────── Network Link ───────────────────────┐
│                                                             │
│  File Server: [CENTRAL.....................]▼              │
│                                                             │
│  Users Allowed to Connect to Your System:                  │
│                                                             │
│     ┌─────────────────────────────────┬─┐    ┌────────┐    │
│     │ Bob Kirwin                      │↑│    │   OK   │    │
│     │ Brad Kingsbury                  │ │    └────────┘    │
│     │ Brian Foster                    │ │    ┌────────┐    │
│     │ √ Brian Yoder                   │ │    │ Cancel │    │
│     │ Bruce Frank                     │ │    └────────┘    │
│     │ Bruce Hellstrom                 │ │    ┌────────┐    │
│     │ Bruce McCorkendale              │ │    │  All   │    │
│     │ Bruno Saskatchewan              │↓│    └────────┘    │
│     └─────────────────────────────────┴─┘    ┌────────┐    │
│                                              │  None  │    │
│                                              └────────┘    │
└─────────────────────────────────────────────────────────────┘
```

default server — points to File Server: [CENTRAL]

Lawrence selects Brian as a client — points to √ Brian Yoder

5. The name of the default file server appears in the server text box. Use the prompt button to change servers if necessary.
6. Select the names of the people you want to use your files from the list box.

    To select all users, choose All.

    To deselect everyone, choose None.

7. Once you have finished selecting names, choose OK.

    The Connection Status dialog box appears saying "Attempting to establish connection. Please wait...".

Any selected user can now access the server by using the steps in the section "Connecting the Client to the Server."

Ending the Connection   Here is how to end the client/server connection.

To end the client/server connection:

1   Check the Connection Status dialog box to make sure no one is accessing the server.

    If another user is accessing the server, the message in the dialog box reads "Acting as a server for <*user name*>."

2   Select Cancel from the dialog box to end the connection.

Connecting the Client to the Server

Once you have set up a PC as a server, you are ready to connect the client to the server.

To connect the client to the server:

1   Log on to the network.
2   Start Norton Desktop.
3   Choose OPEN WINDOW... from the (long) Window menu.

    The Open Window dialog box appears (Figure 8-2).

Figure 8-2

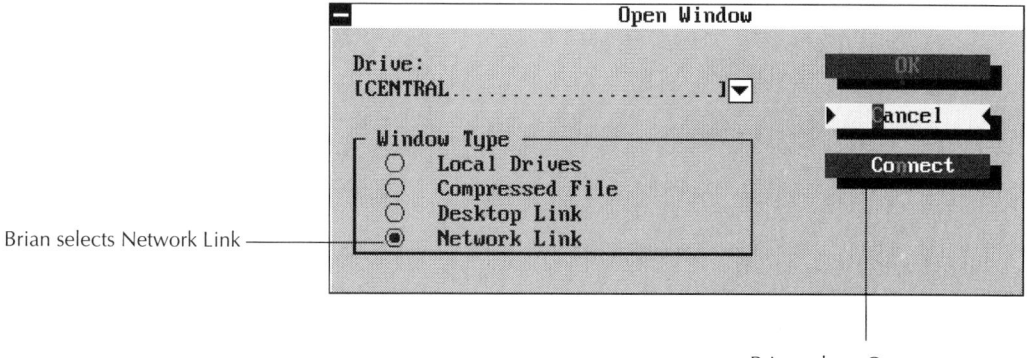

Brian selects Network Link

Brian selects Connect

4   Check Network Link.
5   Select Connect.

    The Network Link Servers dialog box (Figure 8-3) lists all of the PCs that have been set up as servers.

Figure 8-3

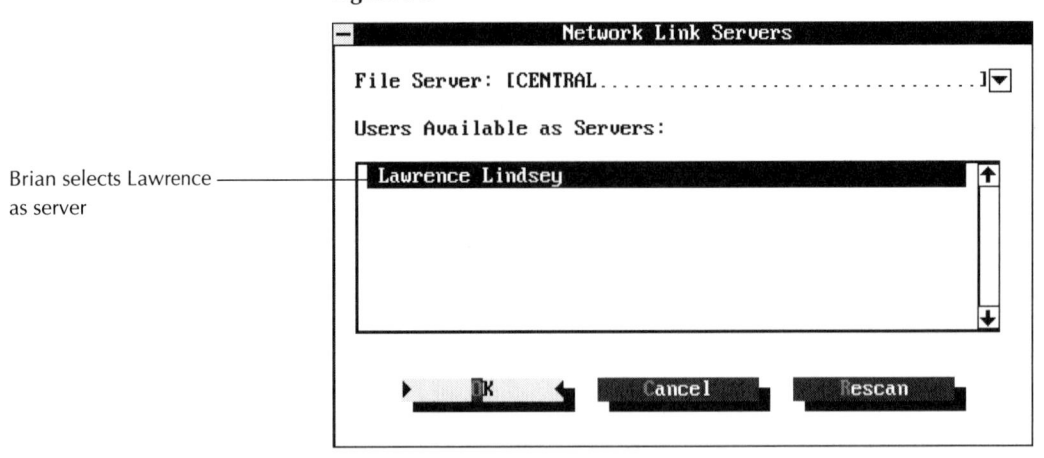

```
┌─ Network Link Servers ─────────────────────┐
│ File Server: [CENTRAL....................]▼│
│                                             │
│ Users Available as Servers:                 │
│ ┌─────────────────────────────────────────┐▲│
│ │ Lawrence Lindsey                        │ │
│ │                                         │ │
│ │                                         │ │
│ │                                         │ │
│ └─────────────────────────────────────────┘▼│
│                                             │
│      ► OK ◄      Cancel       Rescan        │
└─────────────────────────────────────────────┘
```

Brian selects Lawrence as server

6   Choose the name of the user you want to access, then select OK.

    The Connection Status dialog box appears saying "Attempting to connect to *<user name>*."

    If the server becomes unavailable, a message appears: "Unable to connect to *<user name>*."

    Select OK to clear this dialog box. If the connection is successful, you see the Open Window dialog box again.

7   If the name of the drive you want is displayed in the text area of the Drive combination box, select OK (Figure 8-4).

Figure 8-4

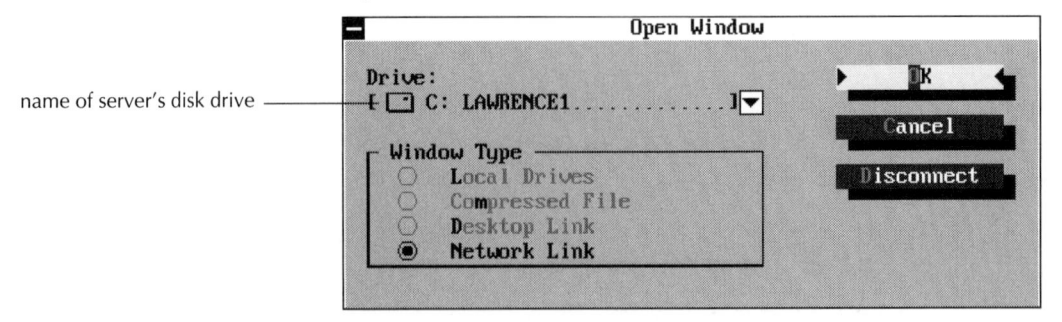

```
┌─ Open Window ──────────────────────────────┐
│ Drive:                        ► OK ◄        │
│ ┼☐ C: LAWRENCE1............]▼               │
│                                Cancel       │
│ ┌─ Window Type ──────────────┐              │
│ │ ○  Local Drives            │ Disconnect   │
│ │ ○  Compressed File         │              │
│ │ ○  Desktop Link            │              │
│ │ ●  Network Link            │              │
│ └────────────────────────────┘              │
└─────────────────────────────────────────────┘
```

name of server's disk drive

You may select any of the drives associated with the server, including network drives, from the drop-down list box. If you want to end the connection, select Cancel or Disconnect.

You now see a drive window showing the contents of the server's drive, such as the one shown in Figure 8-5.

8 You may now copy, delete or rename files on the remote drive.

NOTE: You cannot launch any applications. If an application starts, the communications link is severed.

Figure 8-5

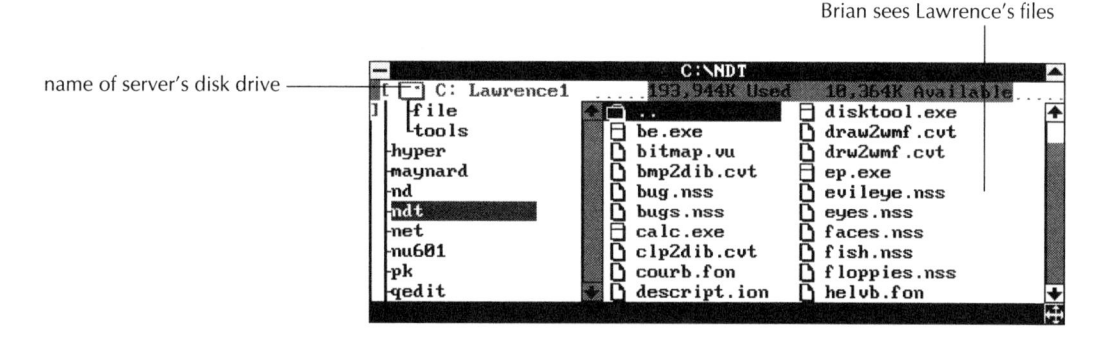

```
name of server's disk drive ─────┐                          Brian sees Lawrence's files
                                 │                                       │
                    ┌──────────────────── C:\NDT ────────────────────┐
                    │ [ ] C: Lawrence1    193,944K Used   10,364K Available │
                    │  ┌file                ...            disktool.exe     │
                    │  └tools               be.exe         draw2wmf.cvt     │
                    │  ├hyper               bitmap.vu      drw2wmf.cvt      │
                    │  ├maynard             bmp2dib.cvt    ep.exe           │
                    │  ├nd                  bug.nss        evileye.nss      │
                    │  ├ndt                 bugs.nss       eyes.nss         │
                    │  ├net                 calc.exe       faces.nss        │
                    │  ├nu601               clp2dib.cvt    fish.nss         │
                    │  ├pk                  courb.fon      floppies.nss     │
                    │  └qedit               descript.ion   helvb.fon        │
                    └─────────────────────────────────────────────────────┘
```

9 When you have finished, select CLOSE from the Control menu (Ctrl+F4) to close the window.

DESKTOP LINK

If you want to transfer files between two PCs, you can use the Desktop Link feature. Desktop Link lets you physically connect two PCs by means of a serial or parallel cable. See the section "Port and Cable Options" for details.

Norton Desktop automatically searches each of the PC's serial and parallel ports until it finds the correct port. It checks parallel ports first because they transfer data faster. If you are using serial cables, Norton Desktop determines the fastest baud rate you have available. You can specify the port and

8-8   Using Norton Desktop for DOS

baud rate using the DESKTOP LINK... menu item on the (long) Configure menu. Both PCs should have the same type of port and the same baud rate (if it applies). See the section "Configuring Desktop Link" in Chapter 9, "Configuring Norton Desktop," for more details.

Setting Up the Server

Set up the server first and then connect the client to the server.

To set up the server:

1   Start Norton Desktop.
2   Choose SERVE REMOTE LINK from the (long) Disk menu.
3   Select DESKTOP LINK.

    The message appears: "Attempting to establish connection. Please wait...".

You can now go to the client PC and follow the steps in the section "Connecting the Client to the Server."

Ending the Connection

At some point, you end the client/server connection using the following steps.

To end the client/server connection:

1   Check the Connection Status dialog box to make sure no one is accessing the server.

    When the connection has completed, the message in the dialog box changes to: "Acting as a server on <*port #*>."
2   Select Cancel from the dialog box.

Connecting the Client to the Server

Once you have set up a PC as a server, you are ready to connect the client to the server.

To connect the client to the server:

1   Start Norton Desktop.
2   Choose OPEN WINDOW... from the (long) Window menu.

    The Open Window dialog box appears (Figure 8-6).

Linking PCs **8-9**

Figure 8-6

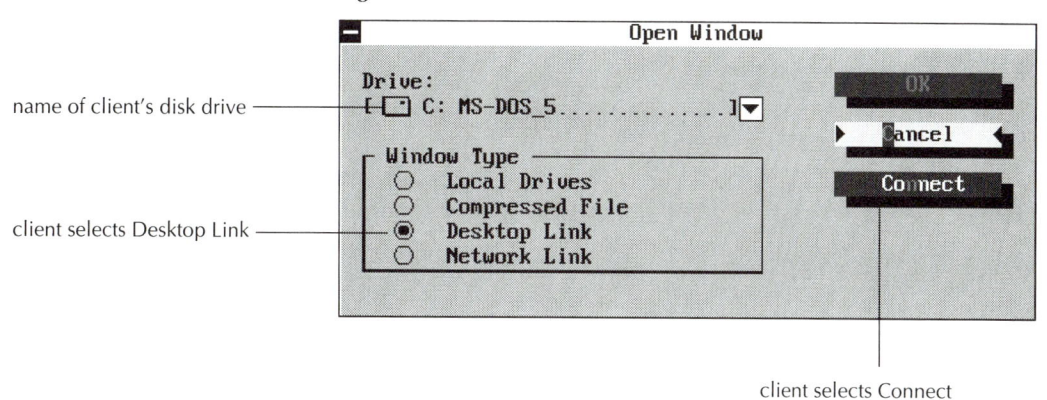

name of client's disk drive → [Open Window dialog: Drive: C: MS-DOS_5; Window Type options: Local Drives, Compressed File, ● Desktop Link, Network Link; buttons: OK, Cancel, Connect]

client selects Desktop Link

client selects Connect

3 Check Desktop Link.

4 Select Connect.

5 If the connection is successful, the Open Window dialog box appears again (Figure 8-7). The names of the server's disk drives appear in the text area of the drive combination box. You may select any of the drives associated with the server, including floppy or hard drives.

6 Select OK to complete the connection.

Or,

Select Cancel or Disconnect to end the connection.

Figure 8-7

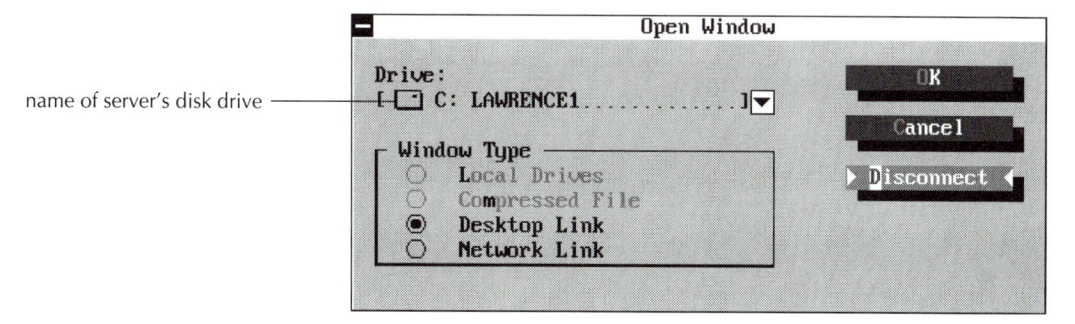

name of server's disk drive → [Open Window dialog: Drive: C: LAWRENCE1; Window Type options: Local Drives, Compressed File, ● Desktop Link, Network Link; buttons: OK, Cancel, Disconnect]

7   You now see a drive window showing the contents of the server's drive, like the one in Figure 8-8. The port name appears in the label box along with the path name of the highlighted directory.

You may copy, delete or rename files on the remote drive; however, you cannot launch any applications. When an application starts, the communications link is severed.

Figure 8-8

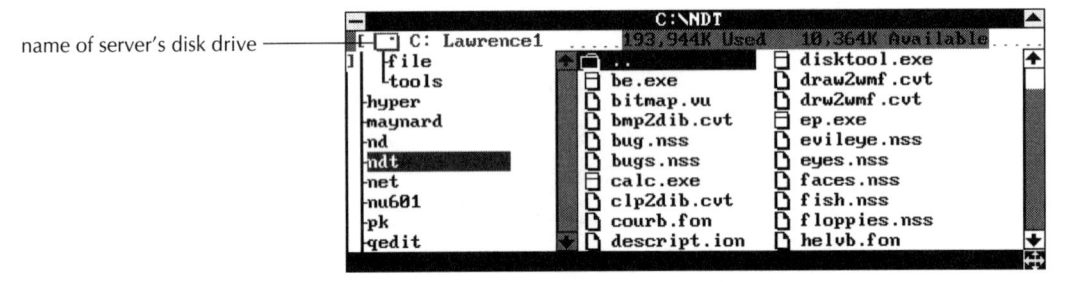

name of server's disk drive ─── C: Lawrence1   193,944K Used   10,364K Available

```
  file                    ..                disktool.exe
  tools                   be.exe            draw2wmf.cvt
 -hyper                   bitmap.vu         drw2wmf.cvt
 -maynard                 bmp2dib.cvt       ep.exe
 -nd                      bug.nss           evileye.nss
 -ndt                     bugs.nss          eyes.nss
 -net                     calc.exe          faces.nss
 -nu601                   clp2dib.cvt       fish.nss
 -pk                      courb.fon         floppies.nss
 -qedit                   descript.ion      helvb.fon
```

8   When you have finished, select CLOSE from the Control menu (Ctrl+F4) to close the window.

CLONING NORTON DESKTOP

You can use Norton Desktop to transfer files between two PCs as long as one of the PCs has Norton Desktop installed. First you "clone" Norton Desktop to the PC that doesn't have it. Cloning Norton Desktop transfers the files you need to use Network Link or Desktop Link from the PC that has Norton Desktop to the one that does not. Cloning does not transfer all the Norton Desktop files.

To clone Norton Desktop, you need a serial cable and a minimum of 1MB of free space on your computer's hard disk. You must use either the COM1 or COM2 serial port. For more details, see the section "Port and Cable Options" later in this chapter.

When you finish cloning the Norton Desktop files, use the procedures described in the sections "Network Link" or "Desktop Link" to transfer files between the two PCs.

To clone Norton Desktop from one PC to another:

1. Join the PCs using a serial cable.

   Steps 2 through 4 are for the PC from which Norton Desktop is being cloned.

2. Choose DESKTOP LINK... from the (long) Configure menu. The Configure Desktop Link dialog box appears.

3. Select Clone....

   The Clone dialog box appears (Figure 8-9).

4. Select the option button for the port being used on the receiving (or remote) PC. Norton Desktop uses that information to modify the bootstrap file, a small program that implements file-transfer protocol and checks for data-transmission errors.

Figure 8-9

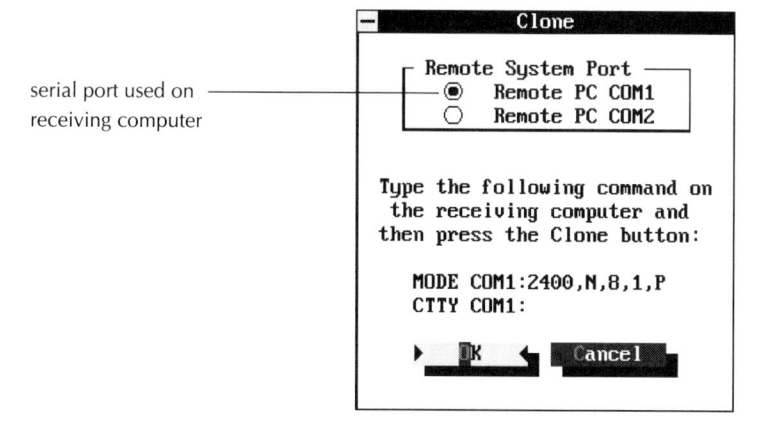

serial port used on receiving computer

```
┌─────────── Clone ───────────┐
│  ┌─ Remote System Port ─┐   │
│  │  ◉  Remote PC COM1   │   │
│  │  ○  Remote PC COM2   │   │
│  └──────────────────────┘   │
│                             │
│  Type the following command on
│  the receiving computer and
│  then press the Clone button:
│
│    MODE COM1:2400,N,8,1,P
│    CTTY COM1:
│
│    ▶ [ OK ]    [ Cancel ]
└─────────────────────────────┘
```

Steps 5 and 6 are for the receiving PC.

5. From the DOS prompt, change to the directory where you want the copy of Norton Desktop to go. For example, if you type:

   MD ND
   CD ND

   you would create a directory named ND in the root directory of your computer's hard drive and change to that directory.

Using Norton Desktop for DOS

6. If the receiving PC is using the COM1 serial port, type the following on the receiving PC:

   MODE COM1:2400,N,8,1,P

   You then see a message that says: "Resident portion of mode loaded."

7. Type CTTY COM1:

   (If the receiving PC is using the COM2 serial port, substitute COM2 for COM1 in the preceding steps.)

   Steps 8 and 9 are for the PC from which Norton Desktop is being cloned.

8. Select OK.

   The Cloning Status dialog box appears (Figure 8-10). A progress bar shows the percentage of the transfer that has been completed.

Figure 8-10

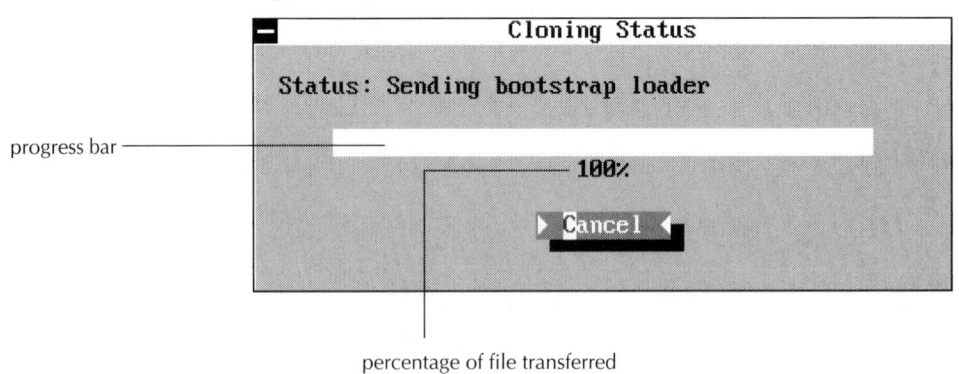

```
┌─────────────── Cloning Status ───────────────┐
│  Status: Sending bootstrap loader            │
│                                              │
│  ┌────────────────────────────────────────┐  │
│  │                                        │  │
│  └────────────────────────────────────────┘  │
│                              100%            │
│                                              │
│              ► Cancel ◄                      │
│                                              │
└──────────────────────────────────────────────┘
```

progress bar ─────────

percentage of file transferred

The receiving PC's monitor displays "Loading bootstrap." After the bootstrap is loaded, the necessary Norton Desktop files are transferred. For each file, a message appears telling the kind of file, its size in bytes, and the percentage of the file that has been transferred. The following is similar to what you see at the time Norton Desktop is six percent transferred.

Linking PCs **8-13**

```
C:\ND>mode com1:2400,n,8,1,p
Resident portion of MODE loaded
COM1: 2400,n,8,1,p
C:\ND>ctty com1:
Loading bootstrap
Receiving Norton Desktop (xxx,xxx) bytes 6%
```

9 When the cloning process is complete, select Cancel to exit the Clone dialog box.

10 Select Cancel to exit the Configure Desktop Link dialog box.

Steps 11 and 12 are for the receiving PC.

11 Type ND and press Enter. The Norton Desktop appears.

12 Use the Configure menu to set up the cloned version of Norton Desktop.

Once you have completed the installation on the receiving PC, you can transfer files between the two machines using the method described in the section "Desktop Link."

PORT AND CABLE OPTIONS

You must know something about ports and cables to use the Desktop Link and cloning features.

Serial ports (also called RS-232 or communications ports) are named COM1 through COM4. In serial communications, information is transferred between computers one bit at a time over a single line. Both sender and receiver must use the same baud rate.

Parallel ports are named LPT1 through LPT3. In parallel communications, multiple bits of data are sent simultaneously over wires connected in parallel.

Parallel communications are faster, but serial cables can communicate over longer distances. Parallel cables are 10 feet or shorter, while serial cables are often 30 to 40 feet.

With Desktop Link, the PCs can be joined together in one of the following ways:

- Serial (DB-9) to serial (DB-9)
- Serial (DB-9) to serial (DB-25)
- Serial (DB-25) to serial (DB-25)
- Parallel (DB-25) to parallel (DB-25)

When cloning Norton Desktop, you must use a serial cable and either COM1 or COM2.

For serial connections you can use a null modem cable, a Laplink cable or a Fastlynx cable. You may wish to purchase a cable, or you can build your own by following one of the pinout diagrams in Figure 8-11.

For parallel connections you can use a standard PC printer cable with an adapter. The adapter converts the end for the printer into a second end (DB-25) for a PC. The pinouts for this cable and adapter also are shown in Figure 8-11. Check the inserts in the product box for information about ordering the cable or adapter.

Figure 8-11 Pinout diagrams

Serial (DB-9) to serial (DB-9)

2 ⟷ 3
3 ⟷ 2
4 ⟷ 6
5 ⟷ 5
6 ⟷ 4
7 ⟷ 8
8 ⟷ 7

Serial (DB-9) to serial (DB-25)

5 ⟷ 7
2 ⟷ 2
3 ⟷ 3
8 ⟷ 4
7 ⟷ 5
4 ⟷ 6
6 ⟷ 20

(continued)

Figure 8-11 *(continued)*

Serial (DB-25) to serial (DB-25)

2 ⟷ 3
3 ⟷ 2
4 ⟷ 5
5 ⟷ 4
7 ⟷ 7
6 ⟷ 20
20 ⟷ 6

Parallel (Centronics) to parallel (DB-25)

1 ⟷ 1
2 ⟷ 2
3 ⟷ 3
4 ⟷ 4
5 ⟷ 5
6 ⟷ 6
7 ⟷ 7
8 ⟷ 8
9 ⟷ 9
10 ⟷ 10
11 ⟷ 11
12 ⟷ 12
13 ⟷ 13
14 ⟷ 14
15 ⟷ 15
16 ⟷ 16
17 ⟷ 17
18-25 ⟷ 25

(continued)

Figure 8-11 *(continued)*

Parallel adapter (Centronics to DB-25)

1 ⟷ 7
14 ⟷ 8
31 ⟷ 9
7 ⟷ 1
8 ⟷ 14
9 ⟷ 16
36 ⟷ 17

2 → 15
3 → 13
4 → 12
5 → 10
6 → 11
10 → 5
11 → 6
12 → 4
13 → 3
32 → 2
33 → 18
19 → 19
21 → 20
23 → 21
25 → 22
27 → 23
29 → 24
30 → 25

PART III
CONFIGURING
THE DESKTOP

Configuring Norton Desktop

This chapter explains how to set up Norton Desktop so that it suits your needs and level of expertise. You can choose the Norton Desktop options to be as simple or as powerful as you'd like.

Contents

Customizing Menus 9-4
    Choosing Long or Short Menus 9-4
    Customizing and Creating Pull-down Menus 9-5
    Establishing a Password 9-18
Configuring Desktop Preferences 9-20
    Configuring a Shutdown Routine 9-21
    Tagging Files in a Drive Window 9-24
    Adding Shadows to the Desktop Windows 9-24
    Scanning Floppy Drives with Norton AntiVirus 9-24
    Previewing Files During Speed Search 9-25
    Including Subdirectories in a Drag-and-Drop
        Procedure 9-25
    Selecting the Desktop Mode 9-26
    Keystroke Preference Selection 9-26
    Displaying Drive Icons on the Desktop 9-27
Configuring the Button Bar 9-28
Setting Confirmation Options 9-31

Using Norton Desktop for DOS

Setting the Clock 9-31
Setting Video and Mouse Options 9-32
    Selecting Screen Colors 9-33
    Configuring the Display 9-35
    Confirming Selections 9-36
    Selecting Mouse Options 9-36
Selecting the Default Editor 9-38
Configuring the Screen Saver 9-39
Configuring Network Options 9-39
Selecting Printer Options 9-40
Selecting File Compression Options 9-44
Configuring Desktop Link 9-46
    Choosing the Desktop Link Options 9-46
Saving Your Changes 9-49

The Configure menu commands, shown in Figure 9-1, make it easy for you to arrange Norton Desktop to fit your style of working. Using this group of commands you can:

- Choose between predefined sets of Short or Long menus.
- Create and edit customized pull-down menus.
- Require a password to protect your set of menus.
- Construct a personalized shutdown routine.
- Adjust the appearance and arrangement of your desktop.
- Configure the Button Bar to suit your needs.
- Require final confirmation before continuing with operations that are difficult to reverse.
- Display a clock on your desktop.
- Control the workings of your mouse.
- Select a default editor.
- Select and configure network settings.
- Select printer options.
- Select file compression options.
- Save your configuration preferences for subsequent Norton Desktop sessions.

Each item is discussed in the order it appears on the Configure menu.

Figure 9-1

the Configure menu provides commands to make setting up Norton Desktop for DOS a simple task

```
Configure
────────────────────
Load Pull-downs...
Edit Pull-downs...
Password...
────────────────────
Preferences...
Button Bar...
Confirmation...
Clock...
Video/Mouse...
────────────────────
Editor...
Screen Saver...
Network...
Printer...
Compression...
Desktop Link...
────────────────────
Save Configuration
```

CUSTOMIZING MENUS

Having the tools you need—when and where you need them—can make a significant difference when it comes to actually using a product. Is the product really set up to suit your style of working, or is it what someone else thinks you should be using?

With the EDIT PULL-DOWNS... command on the (long) Configure menu you can customize the menus so that the tools and commands you need are easily accessible. You can delete any tools and commands you don't use, or you can add new tools and commands so they are quickly available from the desktop.

Choosing Long or Short Menus

Norton Desktop comes with two predefined menu sets called Long and Short menus. Short menus, which display by default, contain a limited set of the most commonly used Norton Desktop commands. Long menus contain all Norton Desktop commands. You can easily toggle back and forth between the two menu styles by using the LOAD PULL-DOWNS... command.

> **NOTE:** A menu set refers to a specific group of menus that is represented by a file with the extension .NDM. The Norton Desktop Long and Short menus are examples of menu sets. Information about the menus and commands are contained in files called LONG.NDM and SHORT.NDM. When you load one of these files, you tell Norton Desktop which set of menus to use.

To display Short or Long menu sets:

1 Choose LOAD PULL-DOWNS... from the Configure menu.

   The Select Pull-down to Load dialog box appears (Figure 9-2).

2 In the Pull-down Menu Files list box, select the filename corresponding to the style of menu you wish to display. Selecting LONG.NDM displays the long menu set; SHORT.NDM displays the short menu set.

3 Select OK.

   The menus corresponding to your selected menu set are now displayed.

Figure 9-2

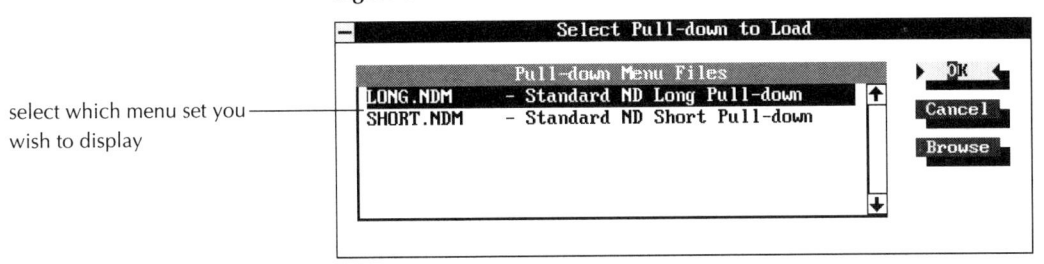

```
┌─────────────── Select Pull-down to Load ───────────────┐
│         ╔═══════ Pull-down Menu Files ═══════╗   ► OK ◄ │
│         ║ LONG.NDM  - Standard ND Long Pull-down ↑║         │
│         ║ SHORT.NDM - Standard ND Short Pull-down ║  Cancel │
│         ║                                         ║         │
│         ║                                         ║  Browse │
│         ║                                       ↓ ║         │
│         ╚═════════════════════════════════════════╝         │
└─────────────────────────────────────────────────────────────┘
```

select which menu set you wish to display

NOTE: If other menu sets are available, they can also be loaded. In addition, if the menu files are located in other drives or directories, use the Browse command button within the Select Pull-down to Load dialog box to locate them. To learn about creating new menu sets, refer to the section "Customizing and Creating Pull-down Menus" in this chapter.

Customizing and Creating Pull-down Menus

In addition to the standard Long and Short menus provided by Norton Desktop, you also have the option of either customizing menus or creating new menu sets using the EDIT PULL-DOWNS... command found on the long Configure menu. Using the Edit Pull-down Menu dialog box, you can:

- Create new menu sets.
- Add menus or commands.
- Remove menus or commands.
- Rearrange the order of menus or commands.
- Change the titles and hotkeys of menus or commands.
- Add your own applications or programs to a menu.

TIP: To create and edit personalized menus using the MENU and EDIT MENU... commands of the Norton Desktop Tools menu, refer to Chapters 11 and 12, "Using the Menu" and "Editing the Menu." If you want to create a comprehensive menuing system complete with multiple cascading submenus and password protection on individual menu commands, see Chapters 30 and 31, "Creating Corporate Menus" and "Administering Corporate Menus."

To open the Edit Pull-down Menu dialog box:

- Choose EDIT PULL-DOWNS... from the (long) Configure menu.

  The Edit Pull-down Menu dialog box appears (Figure 9-3).

Figure 9-3

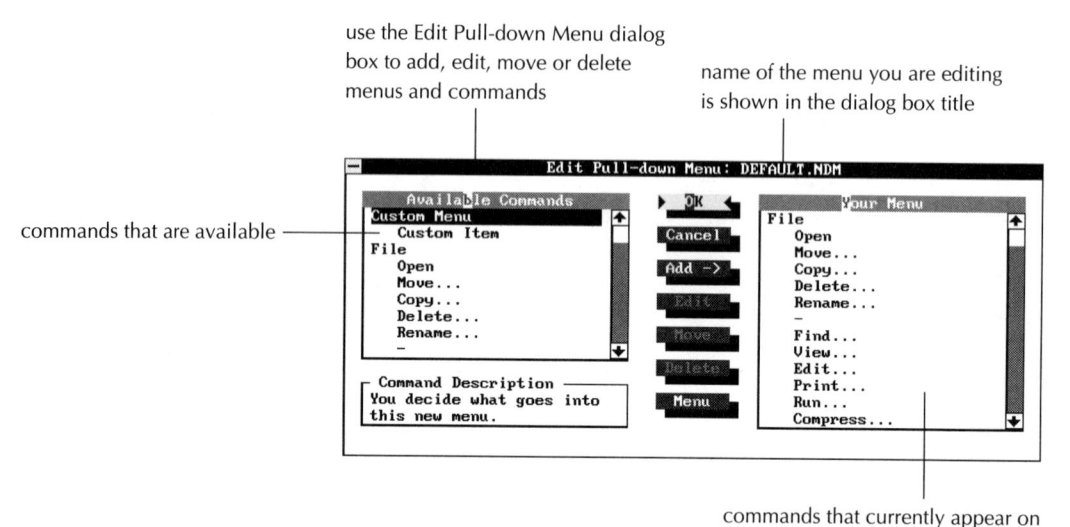

use the Edit Pull-down Menu dialog box to add, edit, move or delete menus and commands

name of the menu you are editing is shown in the dialog box title

commands that are available

commands that currently appear on your Norton Desktop menus

The dialog box contains two list boxes, Available Commands and Your Menu, that allow you to select the menus or commands you wish to work with. The command buttons let you create, edit, move or delete menus or commands, and add external programs or standard menu commands. You can also reset the menus back to the original Norton Desktop configuration.

> **NOTE:** When customizing the pull-down menus you can select menus or menu commands from the Available Commands or Your Menu list boxes or from the Norton Desktop menu bar. If you choose menus or commands from the menu bar, the same item is immediately highlighted in either the Available Commands or Your Menu list box, depending on which list box is currently active.

> **NOTE:** The procedures in the following sections for adding, editing, deleting and moving menu commands assume that you want to change the currently active menu set.
>
> If you do not want to change the current menus but you want to make changes to a different menu set, see the section "Editing Existing Menu Sets" in this chapter.

Adding a New Menu

Norton Desktop comes with seven menus containing commands to help you with a variety of tasks. But wouldn't it be nice to be able to add another menu that contains the applications you use throughout the day to get your work done? For example, instead of using the RUN... command or opening a drive window to start Lotus 1-2-3, you can simply choose the application from a customized menu you've created. Norton Desktop gives you that capability.

To add a new menu to the menu bar:

1   In the Your Menu list box (see Figure 9-2), highlight the menu or command *after* which you want to position your new menu.

    If you highlight a menu name, your new menu is positioned after the highlighted menu. If you highlight a command name, your new menu becomes a submenu of the highlighted command. A submenu is a list of lower-level commands that you access by choosing a higher-level command. For example, when you choose SORT BY from the (long) View menu a submenu appears (Figure 9-4).

2   Highlight Custom Menu from the Available Commands list box in the Edit Pull-down Menu dialog box (see Figure 9-3).

3   Select the Add command button.

    A menu labelled "Custom Menu" is added to the menu bar after the menu you highlighted in step 1. You can see this addition in the Your Menu list box and in the Norton Desktop menu bar. You can change the "Custom Menu" name by selecting it in the Your Menu list box and selecting the Edit command button.

To change the name of this new menu, see the section "Editing Menus and Commands" in this chapter.

To add commands to this menu, see the sections "Adding Standard Menu Commands" and "Adding a Customized Command" in this chapter.

Figure 9-4

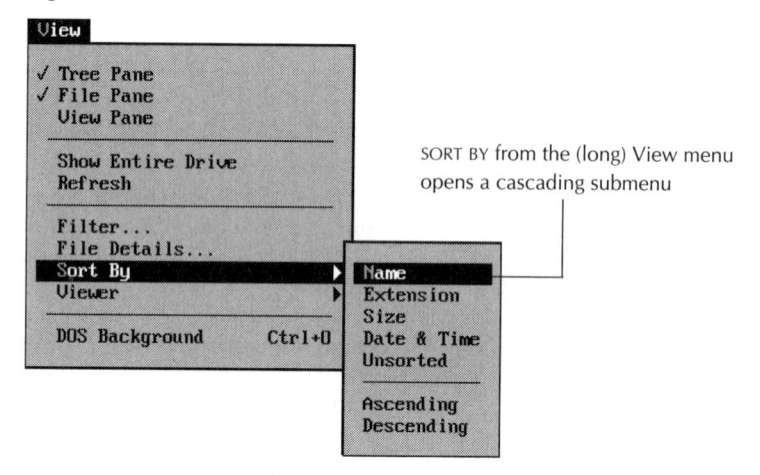

SORT BY from the (long) View menu opens a cascading submenu

NOTE: Adding a menu that you want to appear on the far left of the menu bar (so it's the first menu) is a two-step process. Menus are always added after the menu you've highlighted, so place your new menu *after* whatever menu is currently first, then move the new menu to the position you want. For instructions on how to move a menu, see the section "Moving Menus and Commands" in this chapter.

Adding Standard Menu Commands

You can add any command that appears in the Available Commands list box to one of your menus. This is a great help if you deleted a command earlier and would now like to add it to a menu again or if you want to put the same command on more than one menu.

To add a command or separator line:

1 Highlight the item in the Your Menu list box that is directly above where you want the command or separator added.

If you highlight a menu name, the new command or separator line is added as the first item in that menu.

If you highlight a command or separator line, the new item is added after the item you highlighted.

2   Highlight the command or separator line in the Available Commands list box.

3   Select the Add command button.

The new command or separator line appears directly below the item you highlighted.

4   Select OK to save your changes.

Adding a Customized Command

When you add a standardized command to one of your menus (such as COPY... or MOVE...), you are adding a command that has been defined by Norton Desktop. You also have the option of adding a command that you've defined. You can add up to 10 commands that run other programs, such as Excel or Word, or you can add commands that run batch files you've written. These custom commands can be added to any of the menus in your menu set. You cannot, however, add internal DOS commands such as DIR or RENAME.

To add a customized command:

1   Highlight the item in the Your Menu list box that is directly above where you want to add the new command.

2   Highlight Custom Item in the Available Commands list box.

3   Select the Add command button.

The Edit Custom Item dialog box appears (Figure 9-5).

4   Select the ShortCut button if you want to assign your new command a shortcut key combination.

A shortcut key is a function key or key combination that selects a command without opening the menu. So, although it's not necessary to use your customized menu command, it's a fast way of selecting a command from a menu.

If you decide not to assign a shortcut key, you can skip ahead to step 6.

9-10 Using Norton Desktop for DOS

Figure 9-5

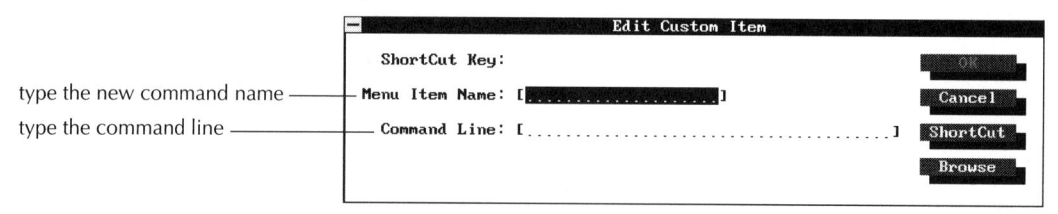

```
┌─────────────── Edit Custom Item ───────────────┐
│   ShortCut Key:                                 │    [ OK ]
│   Menu Item Name: [████████████████████]        │    [ Cancel ]
│   Command Line:   [..........................]  │    [ ShortCut ]
│                                                 │    [ Browse ]
└─────────────────────────────────────────────────┘
```

type the new command name → Menu Item Name
type the command line → Command Line

5 Press the shortcut key combination you want.

You can use any of the following keystrokes as a shortcut key:

- Any function key except F1 (reserved for Help) and F10 (reserved for accessing the pull-down menus from the keyboard)
- A combination of the Shift key plus any function key
- A combination of the Ctrl key and any function key, letter or number
- A combination of the Ctrl and Shift keys plus any function key, letter or number, except Ctrl+M (which is equivalent to pressing Enter)
- A combination of the Alt key with either the Ctrl or Shift key plus a function key, letter or number

The shortcut key combination you enter appears in the dialog box on the line labeled ShortCut Key.

CAUTION: Do not use Ctrl+Alt+Del—that combination is reserved for rebooting your computer.

NOTE: If you enter a shortcut key combination that is already being used by Norton Desktop, the Duplicate Shortcut Keys dialog box appears on the Desktop. You now have the option to use your original entry, press an alternate combination or cancel out of the shortcut key procedure.

If you choose to use a shortcut key combination that is already used by Norton Desktop, the program uses the shortcut key to activate the command that appears first within the menu system (starting from the top of the File menu and moving to the bottom of the Help menu).

Configuring Norton Desktop **9-11**

6   Type the name of the new command in the Menu Item Name text box.

Type a caret (^) immediately in front of the letter you want highlighted in the command name. The highlighted letter will then become the *hotkey* and can be pressed when the menu is open to execute the command.

For example, to add a new command called Account Info with the "I" highlighted, type `Account ^Info` in the Command Name text box.

> **NOTE:** Adding a command name is optional. If you don't enter a name in the Menu Item Name text box Norton Desktop automatically uses the program name as the command name.

7   In the Command Line text box, type the path and filename of the program you want your new command to run. You can also include command line switches and options after the program name.

Suppose you frequently work with a Microsoft Word document titled BUDGET.DOC. If Word is in a directory called WORD, you can add a command that causes Microsoft Word to open BUDGET.DOC by typing `C:\WORD\WORD.EXE BUDGET.DOC` in the Command Line text box. When you choose this command from the menu, BUDGET.DOC automatically opens in Word, ready for you to edit.

You can also select the program name by using the Browse command button and selecting your program from the Browse dialog box.

8   Select OK to add your new command to the menu.

Editing Menus and Commands

The editing features in Norton Desktop allow you to change the name of a menu or command, assign or reassign a shortcut key to a menu or command, or alter the command line of any new command you've added to the menus.

To edit a menu:

1   Highlight the menu you want to edit in the Your Menu list box of the Edit Pull-down Menu dialog box (see Figure 9-3).

2   Select the Edit command button.

    Or,

- Double-click the menu you want to edit in the Your Menu list box.

    The Edit Menu dialog box appears on the desktop, as shown in Figure 9-6.

Figure 9-6

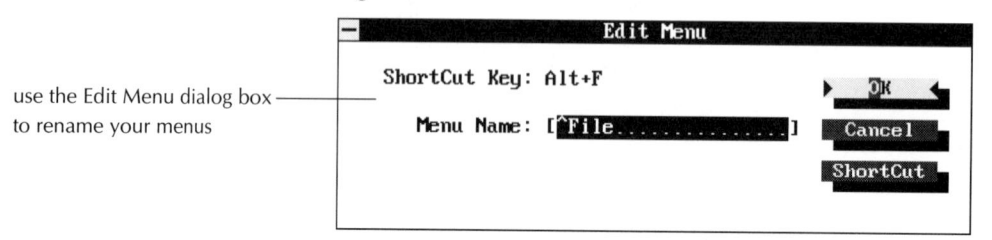

use the Edit Menu dialog box to rename your menus

```
┌─────────────────── Edit Menu ───────────────────┐
│                                                 │
│   ShortCut Key: Alt+F                  ▶ OK ◀   │
│                                                 │
│   Menu Name: [^File............]       Cancel   │
│                                                 │
│                                       ShortCut  │
│                                                 │
└─────────────────────────────────────────────────┘
```

3   Type the new name you want assigned to the menu in the Menu Name text box. Type a caret (^) immediately in front of the letter you want highlighted in the menu name.

    The highlighted letter is used to open the menu from the keyboard (by pressing the Alt key plus the highlighted letter). For example, If you type ^Applications in the Menu Name text box, pressing Alt+A will open the menu.

4   Select the ShortCut command button if you want to assign a different shortcut key combination.

    See the section "Adding a Customized Command" in this chapter for a list of valid shortcut key combinations.

5   Press the shortcut key combination that you want to assign to this menu.

    The shortcut key combination you enter appears on the ShortCut Key line.

6   Select OK to save the new menu name.

To edit a command:

1. Highlight the command you wish to change in the Your Menu list box of the Edit Pull-down Menu dialog box (see Figure 9-3).

2. Select the Edit command button.

    The Edit Menu Item dialog box appears on the desktop, as shown in Figure 9-7.

    Or,

    If you are editing a custom command, the Edit Custom Item dialog box appears (see Figure 9-5).

Figure 9-7

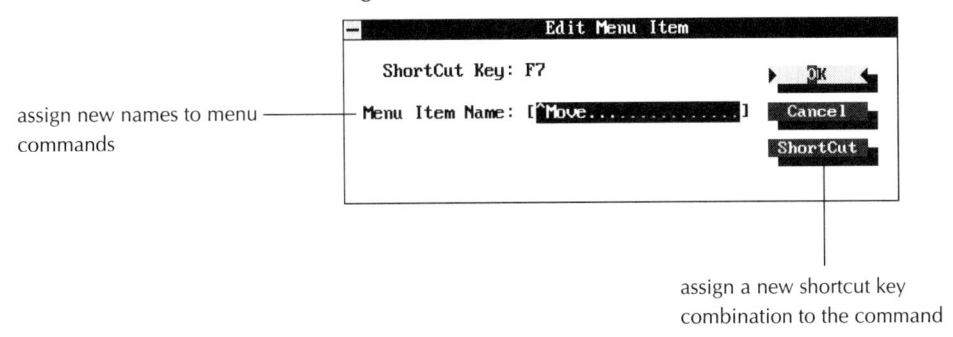

```
┌─────────────── Edit Menu Item ───────────────┐
│                                               │
│   ShortCut Key: F7                  ▶ OK ◀   │
│                                               │
│   Menu Item Name: [^Move..........]  Cancel  │
│                                      ShortCut│
└───────────────────────────────────────────────┘
```

assign new names to menu commands

assign a new shortcut key combination to the command

3. Type the new name you want assigned to the command in the Menu Item Name text box. Type a caret (^) in front of the letter you want highlighted in the name. The highlighted letter will then become the hotkey and can be pressed when the menu is open to execute the command.

4. Select the ShortCut command button if you want to assign a new shortcut key combination to the command.

    A shortcut key is a function key or key combination that selects a command without opening the menu—it's a fast way of selecting commands. See the section "Adding a Customized Command" in this chapter for a list of valid shortcut key combinations.

5   Press the shortcut key combination that you want to assign to this command.

    The shortcut key combination you enter appears on the Shortcut Key line.

NOTE: If you enter a shortcut key combination that is already being used by Norton Desktop, the Duplicate Shortcut Keys dialog box appears on the desktop. You now have the option to use your original entry, type in an alternate combination or cancel out of the shortcut key procedure.

If you decide to use a shortcut key combination that is already used by Norton Desktop, the program uses the shortcut key to activate the command that appears first within the menu system (starting from the top of the File menu and moving to the bottom of the Help menu).

6   To edit the command line of a customized command, type any changes in the Command Line text box.

    If you are editing a Norton Desktop menu command, you will not see the Command Line text box.

7   Select OK to save your changes.

Moving Menus and Commands

Sometimes all it takes to make something easier to use is to move things around a bit. With the EDIT PULL-DOWNS... command you can arrange menus and commands in whatever order works best for you. You can move menus to different positions on the menu bar or move commands to different positions within a menu.

To move a menu's position on the menu bar:

1   Highlight the menu you wish to move in the Your Menu list box of the Edit Pull-down Menu dialog box (see Figure 9-3).

2   Select the Move command button.

    A message box appears on the desktop giving instructions on moving a menu.

3   Press LeftArrow or UpArrow to move the menu's position to the left on the menu bar.

    Or,

Press RightArrow or DownArrow to move a menu's position to the right on the menu bar.

As you press the arrow keys you can see the menu position change on the Norton Desktop menu bar. The menu position also changes in the Your Menu list box.

4   Press Enter to save the menu's new position.

Or,

Press Esc if you want to restore the menu to its original position.

5   Select OK to save your changes.

To move a command's position within a menu:

1   Highlight the command you wish to move in the Your Menu list box of the Edit Pull-down Menu dialog box (see Figure 9-3).

2   Select the Move command button.

A message box appears on the desktop giving instructions on moving a command.

3   Use the UpArrow or DownArrow to move a command up or down, respectively, within the menu.

4   Press Enter to save the command's new position.

Or,

Press Esc if you want to restore the menu to its original position.

5   Select OK to save your changes.

TIP: Commands can change position within the same menu only. To move a command from one menu to another, first add the command to the new menu, then delete the same command from the original menu.

Deleting Menus and Commands

If there are commands or menus that you never use, you may want to delete them from the menu bar to simplify Norton Desktop. If you later change your mind, you can always add them to the menu again.

To delete a menu or command:

1   Highlight the menu or command you wish to delete in the Your Menu list box of the Edit Pull-down Menu dialog box (see Figure 9-3).

2   Select the Delete command button.

    The menu or command is immediately deleted.

3   Select OK to save your changes.

> **NOTE:** When you delete a menu, you also delete all commands appearing on that menu.

Editing Existing Menu Sets

You can also edit existing menu sets without changing the menu you are currently using.

To change an existing menu set:

1   Choose EDIT PULL-DOWNS... from the (long) Configure menu.

    The Edit Pull-down Menu dialog box appears (see Figure 9-3).

2   Select the Menu command button.

    The Menu Operations dialog box appears.

3   Select the Load command button.

    The Select Pull-down to Load dialog box appears.

4   Select the menu set file (.NDM file) you want to change from the Pull-down Menu Files list box.

5   Select OK.

6   Make the changes you wish to your new menu set.

    For instructions on how to add, delete, move or edit menus and menu commands, see the appropriate procedures in the "Customizing Menus" section of this chapter.

> **NOTE:** When making changes to the menu set, don't select OK until you have finished making *all* of the changes you want; selecting OK saves your changes and closes the menu set file.

Creating New Menu Sets You can create a new menu set by altering an existing menu set.

To create a new menu set:

1. Make sure the menu set that you wish to modify is loaded and select EDIT PULL-DOWNS... from the Configure menu.

   For instructions on how to load a different menu, see the section "Choosing Long or Short Menus" in this chapter.

   The Edit Pull-down Menu dialog box appears (see Figure 9-3).

2. Select the Menu command button from the Edit Pull-down Menu dialog box.

   The Menu Operations dialog box appears.

3. Type a title in the Desktop Title text box if you want your menu set to have a different title.

4. Type a description for your customized menu set in the Description text box to serve as a reminder of what the menu system contains.

5. Select the Save As command button.

   The Browse for Menu File to Create dialog box appears.

6. Enter the filename for the new menu set in the File text box.

   Or,

   If you want to save this menu set to an existing menu set file, use the Directories and Files list boxes to select the file.

7. Select OK in the Browse for Menu File to Create dialog box to save your menu set file.

   Your new menu set file is loaded and ready for you to change.

8. Make the changes you wish to your new menu set.

   For instructions on how to add, delete, move or edit menus and menu commands, see the appropriate procedures in the "Customizing Menus" section of this chapter.

9. After you have finished changing the menus, select OK in the Menu Operations dialog box to save your changes.

Now you can load your new menu set using the LOAD PULL-DOWNS... command.

Restoring the Original Menus and Commands

If at any time you decide that you would like to revert to the original Long or Short menu sets of Norton Desktop menus, you can make the change very quickly with the Reset command button located in the Menu Operations dialog box. This is handy if you have added or deleted commands and menus and then changed your mind and decided the original menu system was better after all.

To restore the original menus and commands:

1   Select the Menu command button in the Edit Pull-down Menus dialog box.

    The Menu Operations dialog box appears.

2   Select either the Long Menu option button or the Short Menu option button from the Reset Mode group box.

3   Select the Reset command button.

    A dialog box appears with a message to confirm the reset.

4   Select OK to reset the menu system to either the Default Long Menu or the Default Short Menu, depending on which option button you chose in step 2.

Establishing a Password

You can restrict access to any menu set by requiring a password. This prevents people who do not know your password from editing or using the menus. You can change the password or turn password protection off at any time.

To establish a password:

1   Choose PASSWORD... from the (long) Configure menu.

    The Password dialog box appears (Figure 9-8).

    If you are establishing a password for the first time, the Old Password text box is dimmed.

2   Type a password containing up to 15 characters in the New Password text box.

3   Type the new password again in the Confirm New Password text box.

4   Select OK to save your password.

Figure 9-8

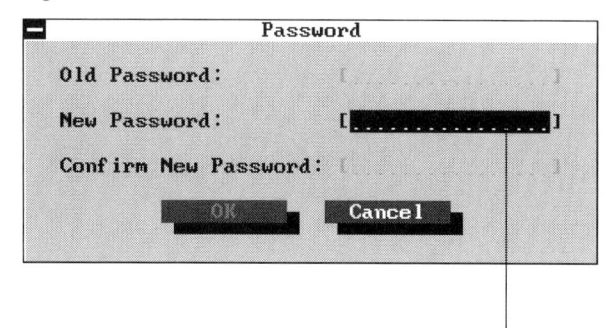

```
┌─────────────── Password ───────────────┐
│  Old Password:      [              ]   │
│  New Password:      [..............]   │
│  Confirm New Password: [           ]   │
│           [ OK ]    [ Cancel ]          │
└─────────────────────────────────────────┘
```

enter a password of up to 15 characters

To change your password:

1   Choose PASSWORD... from the (long) Configure menu.

    The Password dialog box appears.

2   Type your current password in the Old Password text box.

3   Type your new password in the New Password text box.

4   Type the new password again in the Confirm New Password text box.

5   Select OK to save your password.

To disable your password:

1   Choose PASSWORD... from the (long) Configure menu.

    The Password dialog box appears.

2   Type your old password in the Old Password text box.

3   Select the New Password text box and press Enter.

4   Select the Confirm New Password text box and press Enter.

5   Select OK to disable your password.

CONFIGURING DESKTOP PREFERENCES

The Configure Preferences dialog box contains a group of options that allow you to design Norton Desktop to best suit your style of working. Look over the various options, then select those that you feel will make Norton Desktop more efficient for you.

To open the Configure Preferences dialog box:

- Choose PREFERENCES... from the (long) Configure menu.

    The Configure Preferences dialog box appears (Figure 9-9).

Figure 9-9

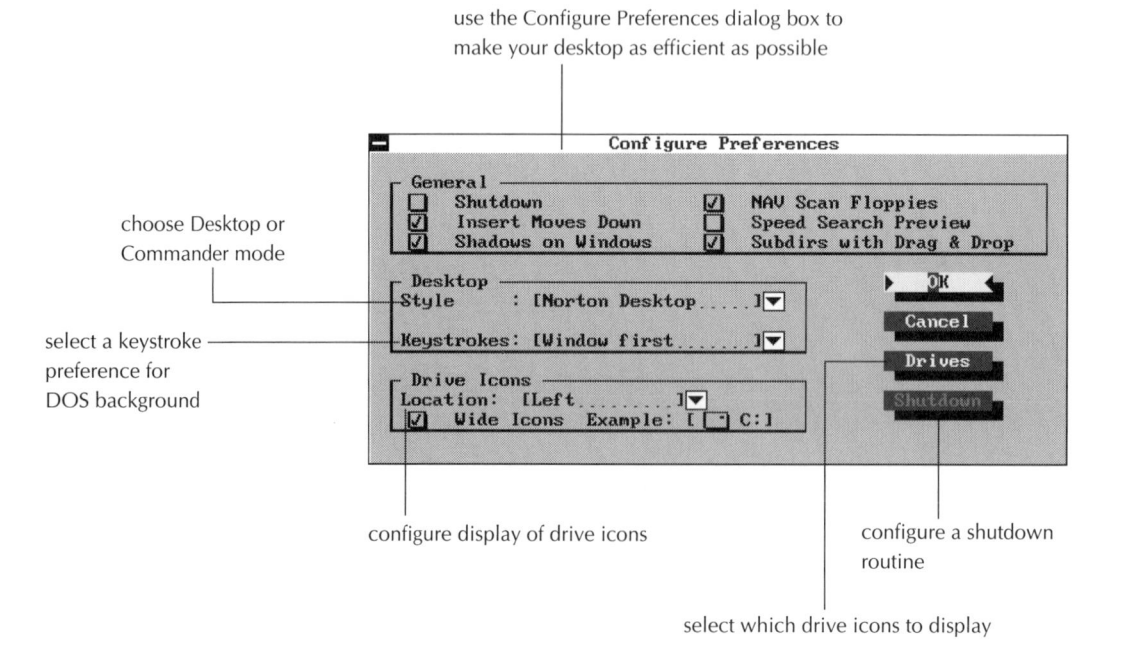

use the Configure Preferences dialog box to make your desktop as efficient as possible

choose Desktop or Commander mode

select a keystroke preference for DOS background

configure display of drive icons

configure a shutdown routine

select which drive icons to display

To save your configuration preferences:

- Select OK to save your configuration preferences.

To exit the Configure Preferences dialog box without saving your changes:

- Select Cancel to exit without saving your changes.

Configuring a Shutdown Routine

Establish your own customized shutdown routine (to be used prior to exiting Norton Desktop) by using the Shutdown check box and the Shutdown command button in the Configure Preferences dialog box.

Your shutdown routine defines the procedures your computer follows immediately prior to and immediately after leaving Norton Desktop and returning to DOS. You can configure your shutdown routine to perform tasks such as sending mail messages, scanning your disk for viruses, optimizing your disk or logging out from your network.

To configure a shutdown routine:

1 Check the Shutdown check box in the Configure Preferences dialog box.

2 Select the Shutdown command button.

   Notice that the Shutdown command button remains dimmed until the Shutdown check box is checked.

   The Shutdown dialog box appears (Figure 9-10).

Figure 9-10

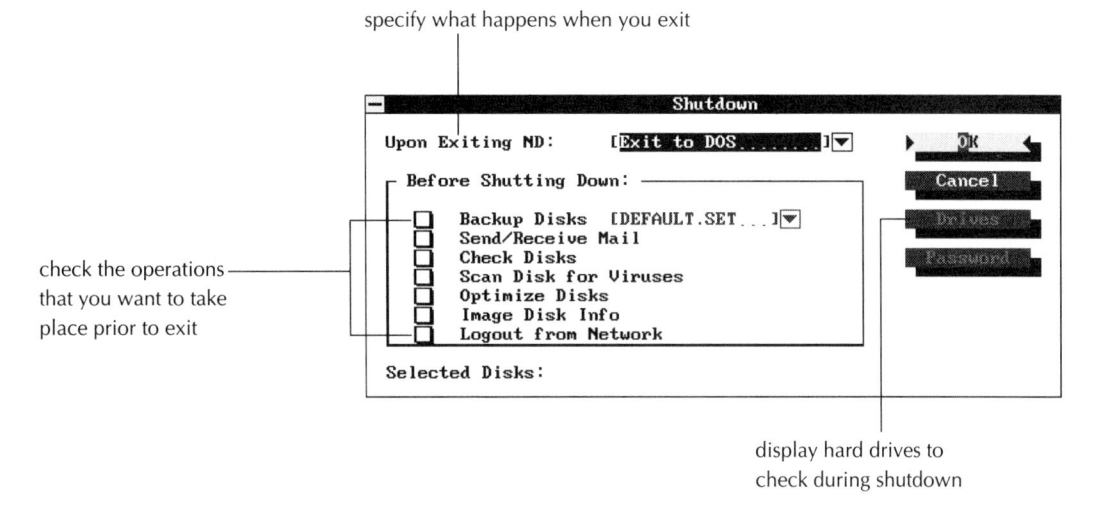

specify what happens when you exit

check the operations that you want to take place prior to exit

display hard drives to check during shutdown

3 Specify what occurs upon exiting Norton Desktop by selecting one of the following from the Upon Exiting ND drop-down list:

   Exit to DOS: returns you to DOS.

Secure Computer: locks the computer and waits for you to enter a password.

Reboot: restarts your computer so memory is cleared and the operating system is reloaded.

4 If you selected Secure Computer in step 3, select the Password command button to establish a password.

If you selected Exit to DOS or Reboot in step 3, skip to step 9.

5 Type your password, up to 15 characters, in the Enter Password text box of the Set Password dialog box.

6 Select OK to save your password.

7 Type your password again in the Verify Password dialog box.

8 Select OK to verify your password.

9 Check the check boxes of those operations you want to take place prior to exiting from Norton Desktop.

Backup Disks: Norton Backup is run.

You can customize your backup routines by creating different SET files in Norton Backup. These SET files are saved to the directory where Norton Desktop is installed and that's where the Shutdown routine searches for them. To customize a backup routine, select your SET file from the drop-down list.

For more information on Norton Backup options, see Chapter 19, "Using Norton Backup," or the *Using Norton Backup for DOS* manual.

Send/Receive Mail: a connection is made to MCI Mail, sending the messages in your Out folder and copying new messages to your In folder. For more information about Norton Mail, see Chapter 21, "Using Norton Mail."

Check Disks: Norton Disk Doctor checks your *partition table*, *boot record*, *root directory* and *lost clusters*. See Chapter 18, "Using Norton Disk Doctor," for more information.

Scan Disks for Viruses: Norton AntiVirus is run. See Chapter 20, "Using Norton AntiVirus," for more information.

Optimize Disks: Speed Disk is run to consolidate the unused space on your disk. For more information on Speed Disk, see Chapter 17, "Using Speed Disk."

Image Disk Info: an updated Image file is created for each drive you've chosen. Refer to Chapter 25, "Using Image," for more information on Image.

Logout from Network: your computer is disconnected from your local area network.

> **TIP:** Norton Desktop keeps a record of the programs you've chosen to include in your shutdown routine in a file called SHUTDOWN.BAT. If you notice that one or more of your selected programs do not run when you exit Norton Desktop, use the editor to view the contents of SHUTDOWN.BAT—a message is recorded there for any program that could not be found.

10 Select the Drives command button to display the Select Local Drives dialog box (Figure 9-11).

Figure 9-11

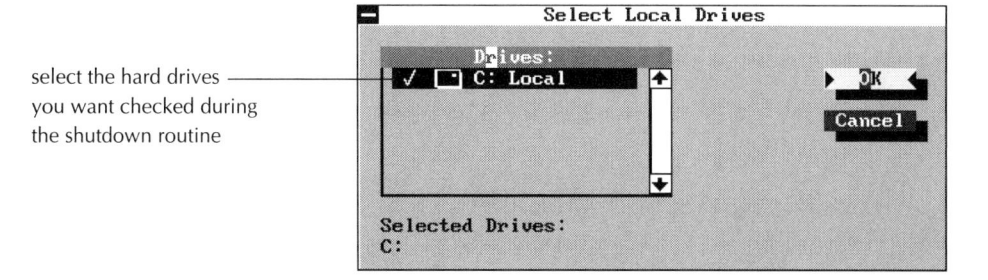

select the hard drives you want checked during the shutdown routine

11 Select the hard drives to which the shutdown routine should apply by selecting the drives from the list box (press the Insert key or click the drives with the right mouse button). All hard drives are selected by default.

The drives you select display at the bottom of the dialog box.

12 Select OK to close the Select Drives dialog box.

13 Select OK to save the shutdown routine selections and close the Shutdown dialog box.

Tagging Files in a Drive Window

The first step in many file operations is to tag the files in the drive window—this is true whether you are copying, moving, compressing or deleting files. From the keyboard, first use the arrow keys to highlight a file, then use the Insert key to tag the file. By checking the Insert Moves Down check box, you can simplify the procedure by expanding the function of Insert so the key tags the current file and then moves down to highlight the next file. Once you've highlighted the first file you want to tag, you can use the Insert key to quickly tag a whole string of consecutive files.

To configure the Insert key to tag the current file, then move down to highlight the next file:

- Check the Insert Moves Down check box in the Configure Preferences dialog box.

  Instead of simply tagging the current file, Insert now tags the current file and moves down to highlight the next file.

Adding Shadows to the Desktop Windows

Displaying shadows on the desktop windows adds a three-dimensional look to your desktop. If this appeals to you, use the Shadows on Windows check box.

To display shadows on the desktop windows:

- Check the Shadows on Windows check box in the Configure Preferences dialog box.

Scanning Floppy Drives with Norton AntiVirus

One hazard of copying files from a floppy disk onto your computer is that it's possible to introduce a virus on your computer system. In all likelihood, the person who gave you the files is probably unaware that the virus exists. You can protect your computer against this situation by automatically scanning a disk (or removable drive) before you use it. If the NAV Scan Floppies check box is checked, Norton AntiVirus scans the disk or removable drive when you open a drive window for it.

Configuring Norton Desktop 9-25

> **NOTE:** If you access a floppy disk or removable drive using a DOS command (from a DOS session or from the DOS command line when DOS BACKGROUND is on), a computer virus can still infect your system because Norton AntiVirus only scans floppy disks that are accessed using the drive windows. You can, however, scan your hard disk once the files have been copied to it.

To automatically scan floppy disks and removable drives with Norton AntiVirus:

- Check the NAV Scan Floppies check box in the Configure Preferences dialog box. This check box is unchecked by default.

Previewing Files During Speed Search

By default, when you use Speed Search to find a directory in the tree pane, the file listing in the file pane does not display the contents of the highlighted directory until you select the directory. Likewise, when using Speed Search to find a file in the file pane, the contents of a file are not displayed in the view pane until you select the file.

To immediately update the file and view panes during Speed Search:

- Check the Speed Search Preview check box to immediately update the file pane as Speed Search moves from one directory to another in the tree pane, and to update the view pane as Speed Search moves from one file to another in the file pane.

Including Subdirectories in a Drag-and-Drop Procedure

If you are using a mouse, you can copy and move files and directories by dragging them from one location and "dropping" them (releasing the mouse button) at another location.

When you use the drag-and-drop method to move or copy a directory, the directory and the files within that directory are automatically selected. If Subdirs with Drag & Drop is checked, subdirectories and the files within those subdirectories are also included when you select a directory to drag-and-drop. If Subdirs with Drag & Drop is unchecked, subdirectories are not automatically included when you select a directory.

To Include Subdirectories in a drag-and-drop procedure:

- Check the Subdirs with Drag & Drop check box in the Configure Preferences dialog box. This check box is checked by default.

Selecting the Desktop Mode

Norton Desktop offers two different methods of accessing the commands: Norton Desktop mode and Norton Commander mode.

Norton Desktop mode offers you maximum functionality of the Norton Desktop for DOS features, while Norton Commander mode provides compatibility with Norton Commander 3.0. Norton Desktop mode is the default, but you can use the Style drop-down list to switch to the Norton Commander mode.

For more information on using the Norton Commander mode, see Appendix E, "Norton Commander Reference."

To switch to Norton Commander mode:

- Select the Norton Commander option from the Style drop-down list in the Configure Preferences dialog box.

To switch to Norton Desktop mode:

1. Choose CONFIGURATION… from the Commander mode Options menu.
2. Select the Norton Desktop option.
3. Select OK to switch back to the Norton Desktop.

Keystroke Preference Selection

Normally, the navigation keys (UpArrow, DownArrow, LeftArrow, RightArrow, Home and End) affect the currently active drive window. But suppose you prefer to type DOS commands on the DOS command line (DOS BACKGROUND on) and would like these navigation keys to affect the DOS command line instead of affecting Norton Desktop's drive window panels.

Whether you prefer to have these navigation keystrokes affect drive window panels or the DOS command line, Norton Desktop can be configured to accommodate either preference.

To change navigation keystroke selection:

- From the Keystrokes drop-down list in the Desktop group box, select Command Line First to have the navigation keys affect the DOS command line when DOS BACKGROUND is on.

Or,

- Select Window First to have the navigation keys affect the currently active drive window when DOS BACKGROUND is on.

NOTE: Regardless of the option you select, you can always navigate in both the drive window and the DOS command line.

If you chose Command Line First, you can navigate through a drive window by pressing Shift plus the navigation key. For example, you can press Shift+UpArrow to move the highlight up one file in the file pane.

Likewise, if you chose Window First, you can use the navigation keys on the DOS command line by pressing Shift plus the navigation key.

Displaying Drive Icons on the Desktop

The drive icons can be a big convenience if you are a mouse user. They allow you to open drive windows by double-clicking on the icons, rather than using the menu commands. If you are using a mouse, your desktop displays drive icons for all floppy drives, hard drives and network drives that are available when Norton Desktop is started. These icons appear down the left side of the desktop. You can choose, however, which drive icons you wish to display (if any) and where you wish to display them.

To display drive icons on your desktop:

1 Select the position of your drive icons from the Location drop-down list.

   Off: turns the drive icons off so they are not displayed.

   Left: displays the drive icons vertically on the left side of your screen.

9-28   Using Norton Desktop for DOS

   Right: displays the drive icons vertically on the right side of your screen.

   Bottom: displays the drive icons horizontally on the bottom of your screen.

2 Check the Wide Icons check box to display drive icons labeled with the drive letter and a graphics image indicating whether the drive is a floppy, hard or network drive.

   If this check box is left unchecked, the icons are labeled with the drive letter only.

3 Select the Drives command button to display the Drives dialog box (Figure 9-12).

Figure 9-12

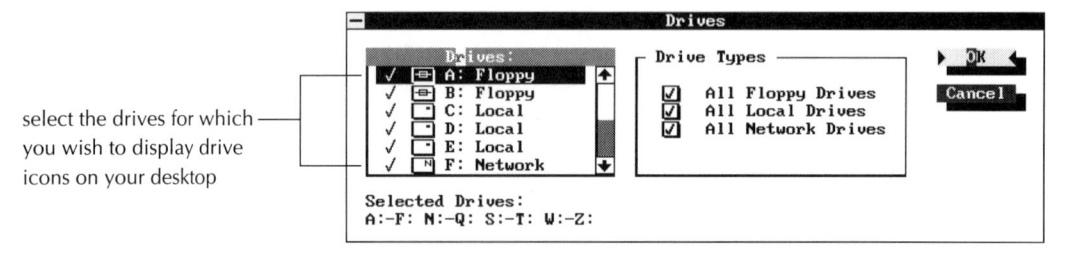

select the drives for which you wish to display drive icons on your desktop

```
┌─────────────────────────── Drives ───────────────────────────┐
│   Drives:                    ┌─ Drive Types ─┐     ► OK ◄    │
│ √ 🖴 A: Floppy          ▲    │ ☑ All Floppy Drives │  Cancel │
│ √ 🖴 B: Floppy               │ ☑ All Local Drives  │         │
│ √ 🗀 C: Local                │ ☑ All Network Drives│         │
│ √ 🗀 D: Local                                                │
│ √ 🗀 E: Local                                                │
│ √ 🖳 F: Network         ▼                                    │
│                                                              │
│ Selected Drives:                                             │
│ A:-F: N:-Q: S:-T: W:-Z:                                      │
└──────────────────────────────────────────────────────────────┘
```

4 Select the drives for which you wish to display drive icons.

   a Use the arrow keys to highlight the drive name.

   b Press Insert to select the drive.

   Or,

   - Click the drive name with the right mouse button.

5 To display all floppy, local and/or network drives, check the appropriate check boxes in the Drive Types group box.

6 Select OK to save your drive selections.

CONFIGURING THE BUTTON BAR

By default, Norton Desktop displays a button bar at the bottom of the screen so that you can execute commands without accessing the menus. The BUTTON BAR... command allows you to change the button bar to suit your needs—you can even turn it off if you don't want the button bar displayed on your screen. You can also configure the Button Bar so that it contains exactly the commands you want.

To turn the button bar off or on:

1   Select BUTTON BAR... from the (long) Configure menu.

    The Configure Button Bar dialog box appears (Figure 9-13).

2   Check the Display Button Bar check box to display the button bar on the screen. The box is checked by default.

    Or,

    Uncheck the Display Button Bar check box to remove the button bar from the screen.

3   Select OK.

Figure 9-13

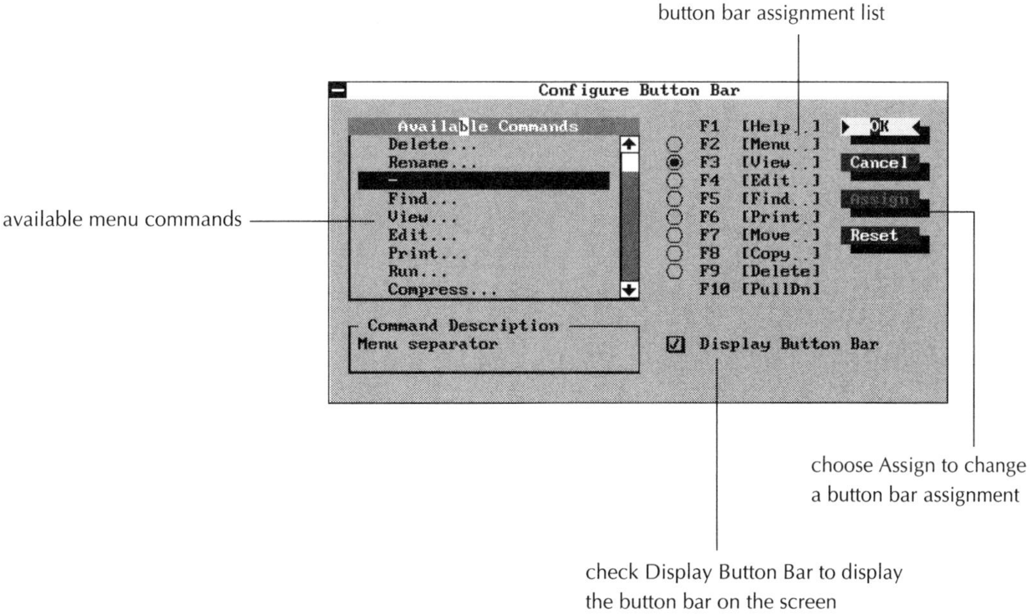

button bar assignment list

available menu commands

choose Assign to change a button bar assignment

check Display Button Bar to display the button bar on the screen

In addition to turning the button bar on and off, you can also change the button bar assignments so that the button bar contains the commands that you use most. The only key assignments that can't be changed are F1 (Help) and F10 (accesses the pull-down menus).

To change a button bar assignment:

1   Select the button bar command that you wish to change from the button bar assignment list on the right side of the Configure Button Bar dialog box.

    When you select a button bar command, its current assignment is highlighted in the Available Commands list box.

2   In the Available Command list box, highlight the menu command that you wish assign to the selected button bar and select Assign.

    Or,

    Double-click with the left mouse button on the command to assign in the Available Commands list box.

    The command you selected is now assigned to the button bar. The cursor moves to the text box automatically so you can change the name that will appear on the button.

3   If you want to change the name that will appear on the button bar, type it in the text box. Only the first six letters of the command name appear in the text box.

4   Repeat steps 1 through 3 until you have made all of the assignments you want.

5   Select OK to save your changes.

You can easily revert back to the default button bar assignments at any time.

To reset the button bar to its default state:

1   Select BUTTON BAR... from the (long) Configure menu.

    The Configure Button Bar dialog box appears (see Figure 9-13).

2   Select the Reset command button.

    A dialog box displays asking you to confirm that you want to reset the button bar to the default settings.

3   Select OK from the confirmation dialog box.

    The button bar assignments in the Configure Button Bar dialog box revert to their default settings.

4   Select OK from the Configure Button Bar dialog box to save these changes.

Configuring Norton Desktop **9-31**

SETTING CONFIRMATION OPTIONS

Norton Desktop lets you decide whether you'd like to be prompted for a final confirmation before performing certain operations such as deleting or dragging and dropping files. Sometimes getting a second chance to consider an operation before implementing it provides a feeling of security; other times it simply slows you down.

You can toggle confirmation boxes on and off by using the Configure Confirmation dialog box.

To set confirmation options:

1. Choose CONFIRMATION... from the (long) Configure menu.

   The Configure Confirmation dialog box appears. All check boxes within this dialog box are checked by default.

2. Check the check box of any operation for which you'd like a confirmation box to appear before performing the operation.

3. Uncheck the check box of any operation for which you don't want a confirmation box to appear.

4. Select OK to save your changes.

SETTING THE CLOCK

Norton Desktop conveniently displays a digital clock in the upper-right corner of the menu bar. You can use the CLOCK... command to turn the clock on and off, or to change it to a 24-hour display.

To change the clock settings:

1. Choose CLOCK... from the Configure menu.

   The Configure Clock dialog box appears (Figure 9-14).

   The current time and date display in the dialog box. You can change your computer's system time and date by changing these settings.

2. To change the time setting, type the correct time into the Current Time text box.

3. To change the date setting, type the correct date into the Current Date text box.

4. To turn off the clock, uncheck the Display Time check box. To turn the clock back on, check this check box. The Display Time check box is checked by default.

9-32   Using Norton Desktop for DOS

Figure 9-14

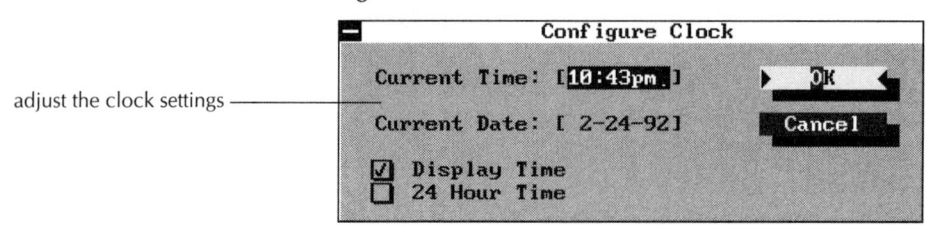

adjust the clock settings ──

```
┌─ Configure Clock ──────────────────────┐
│  Current Time: [10:43pm]      ► OK ◄   │
│  Current Date: [ 2-24-92]     Cancel   │
│  ☑ Display Time                        │
│  ☐ 24 Hour Time                        │
└────────────────────────────────────────┘
```

5   If you want the clock to display 24-hour, or military time, check the 24 Hour Time check box. To return the clock to a 12-hour time display, uncheck this check box.

6   Select OK to save your clock settings.

SETTING VIDEO AND MOUSE OPTIONS

The VIDEO/MOUSE... command gives you control over the appearance and colors of your desktop, as well as the sensitivity, speed, and configuration of your mouse. The various parts of the Configure Video/Mouse dialog box (Figure 9-15) are explained in the sections that follow.

Figure 9-15

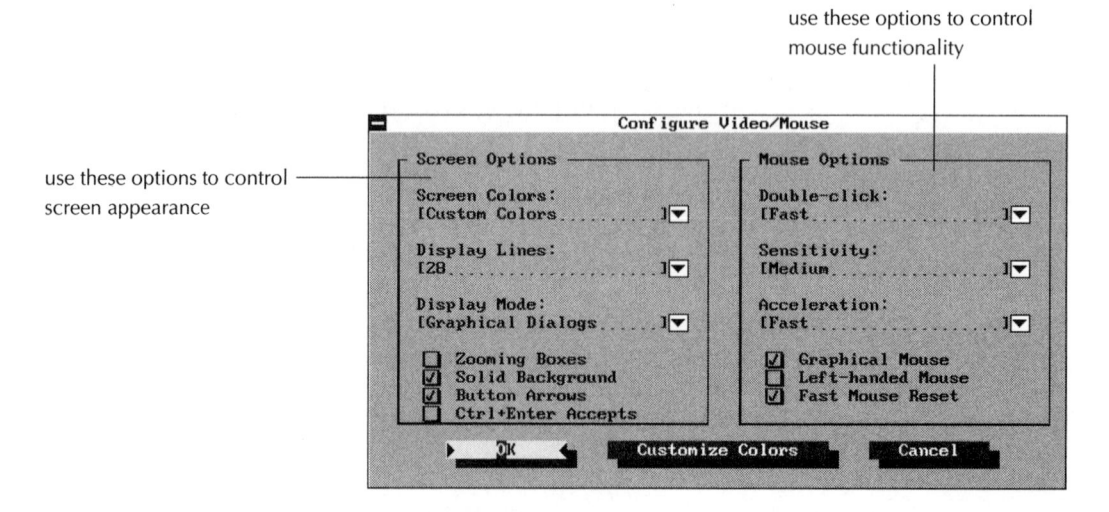

use these options to control mouse functionality

use these options to control screen appearance

```
┌─ Configure Video/Mouse ─────────────────────────────────┐
│ ┌─ Screen Options ──────────┐ ┌─ Mouse Options ───────┐ │
│ │ Screen Colors:            │ │ Double-click:         │ │
│ │ [Custom Colors........]▼  │ │ [Fast.............]▼  │ │
│ │                           │ │                       │ │
│ │ Display Lines:            │ │ Sensitivity:          │ │
│ │ [28...................]▼  │ │ [Medium...........]▼  │ │
│ │                           │ │                       │ │
│ │ Display Mode:             │ │ Acceleration:         │ │
│ │ [Graphical Dialogs....]▼  │ │ [Fast.............]▼  │ │
│ │                           │ │                       │ │
│ │ ☐ Zooming Boxes           │ │ ☑ Graphical Mouse     │ │
│ │ ☑ Solid Background        │ │ ☐ Left-handed Mouse   │ │
│ │ ☑ Button Arrows           │ │ ☑ Fast Mouse Reset    │ │
│ │ ☐ Ctrl+Enter Accepts      │ │                       │ │
│ └───────────────────────────┘ └───────────────────────┘ │
│        ► OK ◄     Customize Colors       Cancel         │
└─────────────────────────────────────────────────────────┘
```

Selecting Screen Colors

To display the Configure Video/Mouse dialog box:

- Choose VIDEO/MOUSE... from the Configure menu.

  The Configure Video/Mouse dialog box appears on the desktop.

Whether you work with a laptop, a black and white, monochrome, CGA, EGA or VGA monitor, you can optimize your screen display using the options on the Screen Colors drop-down list (Figure 9-16) from the Configure Video/Mouse dialog box.

When you install Norton Desktop, the installation program scans your computer to assess what hardware is currently being used and then automatically chooses the default color set for your computer and monitor. To change the default color set, use the Screen Colors option.

Figure 9-16

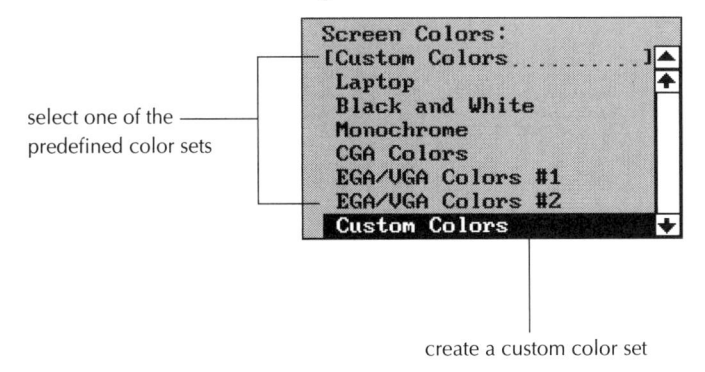

```
Screen Colors:
[Custom Colors.........]
 Laptop
 Black and White
 Monochrome
 CGA Colors
 EGA/VGA Colors #1
 EGA/VGA Colors #2
 Custom Colors
```

select one of the predefined color sets

create a custom color set

To select screen colors:

- Select one of the predefined screen color options from the Screen Colors drop-down list of the Configure Video/Mouse dialog box (see Figure 9-15).

  You also have the option of choosing Custom Colors to create your own color combination.

Customizing Your Color Set

Use the Customize Colors command button to select colors for virtually every element of the screen display.

To select a customized color set:

1. Select Custom Colors from the Screen Colors drop-down list in the Configure Video/Mouse dialog box (see Figure 9-15).

2. Select the Customize Colors command button.

   The Customize Colors dialog box appears (Figure 9-17). On the left is a list of the screen display areas for which you can choose customized colors. On the right is a sample window that previews how your chosen colors will look on the screen.

Figure 9-17

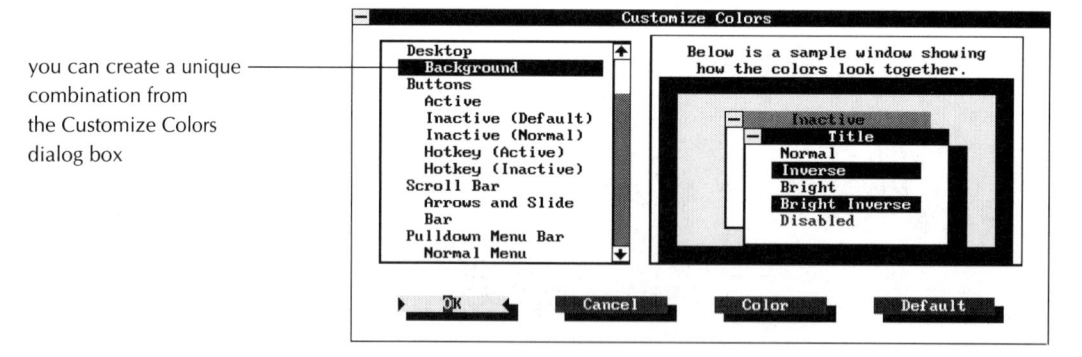

you can create a unique combination from the Customize Colors dialog box

3. Highlight the screen element you want to color-customize from the list shown on the left.

4. Select the Color command button.

   The Color dialog box appears on the desktop.

5. Highlight your color selection.

6. Select OK.

   To reset to the color used by the originally installed program, select the Default button from the Color dialog box (this only resets the screen element you highlighted in step 3 to the default color).

7. Repeat steps 3 through 6 for each screen element you wish to assign a customized color.

8 Select OK to save your color selections.

9 Select OK to close the Customize Colors dialog box.

TIP: To reset all screen elements to their default colors, select Default from the Customize Colors dialog box.

Configuring the Display

Use the display settings to determine how items appear on the desktop.

To select display options:

1 Select the number of lines of data to display on your screen from the Display Lines drop-down list of the Configure Video/Mouse dialog box (Figure 9-15).

Norton Desktop automatically detects the number of lines your screen is currently set to display, and that same number is used, by default, if no changes are made. This option is only available if you have an EGA or VGA monitor.

2 Select your graphics preference from the Display Mode drop-down list. These options determine how the mouse cursor, check boxes and option buttons are displayed on the screen. This option is only available if you have an EGA or VGA monitor.

Standard: displays a square mouse cursor and uses square brackets and parentheses to define check boxes and option buttons, respectively.

Graphical Controls: displays a square mouse cursor with graphically drawn round option buttons and square check boxes.

Graphical Dialogs: displays graphical icons (dialog box and menu borders, file and drive icons, list and combination boxes, and scroll bars) on the desktop.

3 If you want windows and dialog boxes to zoom onto the screen, check the Zooming Boxes check box. Zooming Boxes causes the boxes to zoom open (rather like an explosion—the box first appears very small and then zooms to full size) instead of simply popping up (where the box pops onto the screen full size).

If you prefer pop-up boxes, uncheck the check box. This check box is checked by default.

4   To display the desktop as a solid color rather than as a textured pattern, check the Solid Background check box. This check box is checked by default.

The solid background looks better with some color selections than with others. Notice, for instance, that if you choose Monochrome as your screen color, the Solid Background check box is automatically unchecked. If you decide you prefer a solid monochrome background, simply check the Solid Background check box again.

5   To display triangular arrowheads on the active command button, check the Button Arrows check box. This check box is checked by default.

If you are using the Laptop, Black and White or Monochrome video settings, arrowheads always appear on the active command button, regardless of the Button Arrows setting.

If you are using a color video setting, the active command button displays in a different color so button arrows can be turned off.

6   Select OK to save your selections.

Confirming Selections

From the keyboard, the default method for confirming selections is to press Enter. Normally you use the Tab key to move to the next item in a window or dialog box, and press Enter to confirm the selections made. You can easily change that to have Ctrl+Enter confirm selections.

To use Ctrl+Enter to confirm selections:

- Check the Ctrl+Enter Accepts check box from the Configure Video/Mouse dialog box.

NOTE: This option is particularly helpful to those of you who press Enter expecting to move down to the next line.

Selecting Mouse Options

Use the mouse options to set the speed and sensitivity of your mouse, as well as to configure the mouse for a left-handed user.

To set your mouse options:

1. Select the double-clicking speed (Slow, Medium, or Fast) of your mouse from the Double-Click drop-down list from the Configure Video/Mouse dialog box.

   The speed controls how quickly you must double-click your mouse to initiate responses on your screen. If you are new to using a mouse, you may want to start with the Slow speed and increase the speed as your proficiency increases.

2. Select the mouse sensitivity (Default, Low, Medium, or High) from the Sensitivity drop-down list. Default leaves the current Sensitivity setting without changes.

   Mouse sensitivity determines how far the mouse cursor moves on the screen when the mouse is moved on the surface of your desk. The mouse cursor moves the smallest distance with a low sensitivity setting and the greatest distance with a high sensitivity setting. You may want to select a Medium sensitivity if you are new to using a mouse.

3. Select the mouse acceleration rate (Default, None, Medium or Fast) from the Acceleration drop-down list. Default leaves the current Acceleration setting without changes.

   The acceleration setting determines the acceleration rate of the mouse cursor on the screen as your mouse moves across the surface of your desk. The farther you move the mouse, the faster the mouse cursor moves.

   If you have only recently started using a mouse, an acceleration setting of None gives you the greatest control.

4. Check the Graphical Mouse check box to display the mouse cursor as a small arrow.

5. Check the Left-handed Mouse check box to configure the mouse as a left-handed mouse, making the right mouse button the primary button. This check box is unchecked by default.

6 Check the Fast Mouse Reset check box to cause your mouse to quickly reset (become active again) following the execution of a command that may have affected the mouse driver. A slow mouse reset causes a noticeable pause, while a fast mouse reset takes a fraction of a second.

> **TIP:** Slow mouse reset works on all computers; fast mouse reset works on most computers. The easiest way to test the option on your computer is to check the Fast Mouse Reset check box and see if it works. If your mouse cursor refuses to move from its initial position, return to the slow reset setting.

7 Select OK to retain your configuration choices for subsequent Norton Desktop sessions.

SELECTING THE DEFAULT EDITOR

When you select a document file in a drive window and then choose the EDIT... command (or when you press F4), Norton Desktop launches the default Norton Desktop editor, which allows you to edit your text files and perform copying, pasting and *block operations.* For more information about the default Norton Desktop editor, see Chapter 4, "Managing Directories and Files."

If you prefer to use a text editor other than the default editor, use the EDITOR... command to specify another editor.

To change the default editor:

1 Choose EDITOR... from the (long) Configure menu.

The Configure Editor dialog box appears (Figure 9-18).

2 Select the External option button. (The Built In option button is selected by default.)

3 In the text box, type the filename and extension of the editor you want to use.

If the editor's directory is not in the DOS PATH statement (usually in your AUTOEXEC.BAT file) or in the Norton Desktop directory (that is the directory where Norton Desktop is installed), you must include the editor's full pathname.

You can also use the Browse button to select an editor from the Browse for Editor dialog box.

4 Select OK.

Figure 9-18

choose the EDITOR... command from the (long) Configure menu and use this dialog box to change Norton Desktop's editor

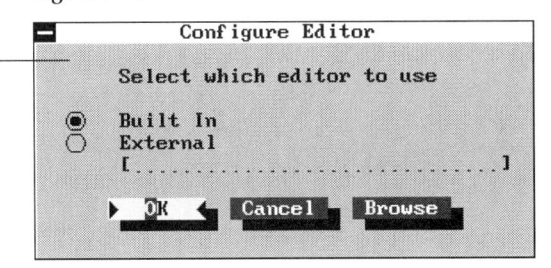

CONFIGURING THE SCREEN SAVER

Norton Desktop includes a screen saver called Sleeper. For information on how to configure and use this command, see Chapter 10, "Using the Screen Saver."

CONFIGURING NETWORK OPTIONS

By default, Norton Desktop will automatically detect the type of network you are using and configure itself correctly. Thus, when you use any feature of Norton Desktop that communicates over a network, such as Network Link, you do not need to confirm network options manually.

In certain situations, however, you may want to manually configure Norton Desktop for a specific type of network. For instance, you may have both Novell and Lantastic networks installed on your computer. Since Norton Desktop will default to Novell even when it detects other networks are present, you will have to manually configure Norton Desktop for the Lantastic network.

To configure your network:

1 Choose NETWORK... from the (long) Configure menu.

The Configure Network dialog box appears.

2 Select the appropriate network type from the Network Type drop-down list.

3   Type a new name for your workstation in the Workstation Name text box if you want to uniquely identify your workstation.

    This will allow other users to easily identify your workstation for sending network messages, for example. This is optional.

    If your computer is connected to a Novell network, the Workstation Name text box is grayed.

4   Type a new timeout period in seconds in the Network Timeout text box if you want to change the amount of time that Norton Desktop will take to attempt to establish a communications link with another computer on the network.

    The longer the timeout period, the longer Norton Desktop attempts to establish a connection. If your network is heavily used, you may want to increase the Network Timeout period by a few seconds.

5   Check the Trap Network Messages check box if you want network messages to display in a dialog box.

    Or,

    Uncheck the Trap Network Messages check box if you want the network to handle the display of network messages.

6   Select OK to save your configuration settings.

SELECTING PRINTER OPTIONS

Norton Desktop's installation program automatically sets the printer options to the most commonly used settings for your printer. To change any of these default settings, use the PRINTER... command from the Configure menu. All printing options are conveniently displayed in the Configure Printer dialog box.

If you sometimes use different printers or printing formats requiring different settings, Norton Desktop allows you to create a printer configuration file for each printer or format—that way when you switch printers or formats, all you have to do is select the correct configuration file, instead of going through the entire configuration procedure each time.

You can add, change, delete or rename these printer configuration files in the Configure Printer dialog box.

Configuring Norton Desktop **9-41**

To display the Configure Printer dialog box:

- Choose PRINTER... from the Configure menu.

    The Configure Printer dialog box appears on the desktop, (Figure 9-19).

Figure 9-19

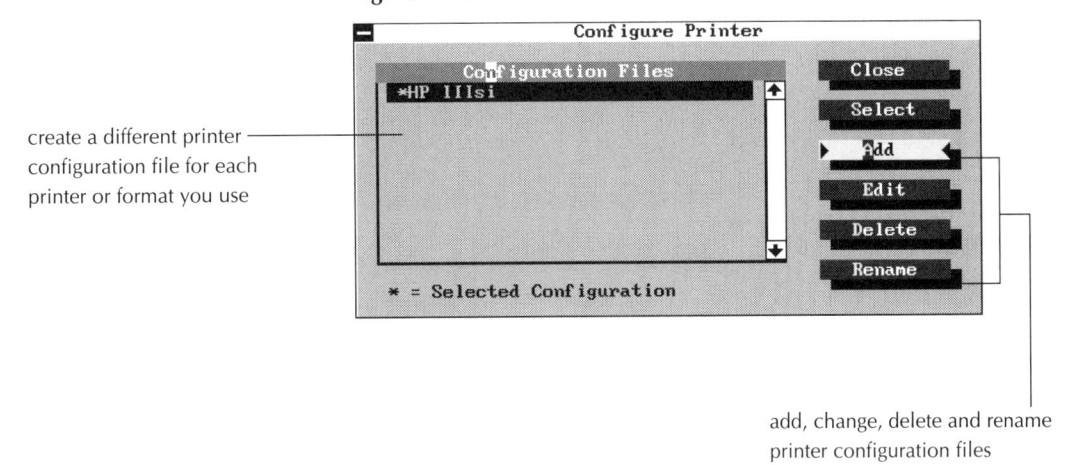

create a different printer configuration file for each printer or format you use

add, change, delete and rename printer configuration files

To quickly create a customized printer configuration file, use the Add command button in the Configure Printer dialog box.

To create a new printer configuration file:

1. Select the Add command button in the Configure Printer dialog box.

    The Configuration Name dialog box appears on the desktop, as shown in Figure 9-20.

Figure 9-20

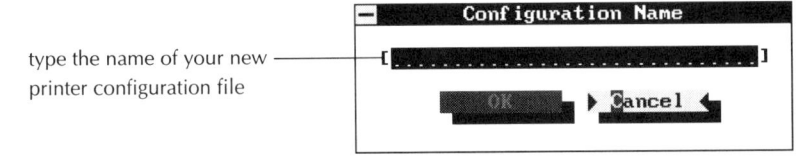

type the name of your new printer configuration file

9-42 *Using Norton Desktop for DOS*

2   Type the filename of your configuration file in the text box.

   Use a descriptive name so that selecting the correct configuration file later is easy. If you are creating a special configuration file to be used with your PostScript printer, you might name your configuration file "Postscript."

3   Select OK.

   The Printer Settings dialog box appears on the desktop, as shown in Figure 9-21.

Figure 9-21

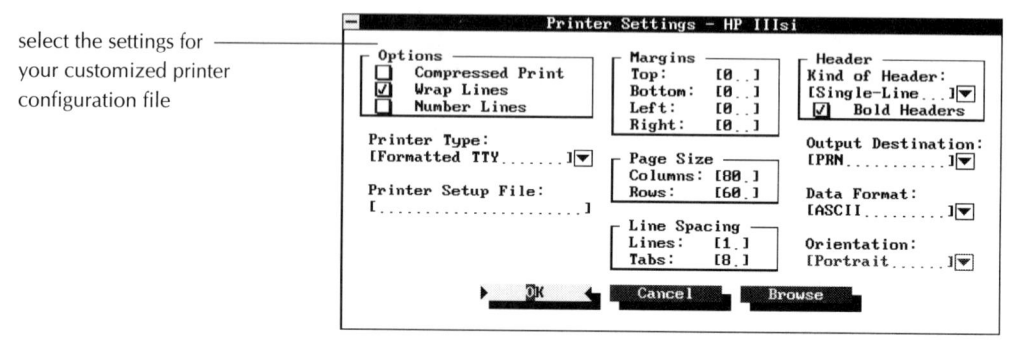

select the settings for your customized printer configuration file

```
┌─────────────── Printer Settings - HP IIIsi ───────────────┐
│ ┌─ Options ──────────┐  ┌─ Margins ──────┐  ┌─ Header ──────────────┐
│ │ □ Compressed Print │  │ Top:    [0..]  │  │ Kind of Header:       │
│ │ ☑ Wrap Lines       │  │ Bottom: [0..]  │  │ [Single-Line...]▼     │
│ │ □ Number Lines     │  │ Left:   [0..]  │  │ ☑ Bold Headers        │
│ └────────────────────┘  │ Right:  [0..]  │  └───────────────────────┘
│ Printer Type:           └────────────────┘   Output Destination:
│ [Formatted TTY.......]▼  ┌─ Page Size ───┐   [PRN..........]▼
│                          │ Columns: [80.]│
│ Printer Setup File:      │ Rows:    [60.]│   Data Format:
│ [....................]   └───────────────┘   [ASCII.........]▼
│                          ┌─ Line Spacing ┐
│                          │ Lines: [1.]   │   Orientation:
│                          │ Tabs:  [8.]   │   [Portrait......]▼
│                          └───────────────┘
│        ► OK ◄           Cancel          Browse
└───────────────────────────────────────────────────────────┘
```

4   Check the check box of each item you wish to select from the Options group box.

   Compressed Print: prints your data in compressed mode. Compressed Print is unchecked by default.

   Wrap Lines: automatically wraps your text. If Wrap Lines is turned off, you must place a carriage return at the end of each line of text to force a line break. Wrap Lines is checked by default.

   Number Lines: sequentially numbers each line of your output in the left margin. Number Lines is unchecked by default.

5   Select the type of printer you are using from the Printer Type drop-down list.

6   To use a setup file to send control codes to your printer, type the filename in the Printer Setup File text box.

   Or,

   Select the Browse button to select the setup file from the Printer Setup File dialog box.

If the setup file is not stored in the Norton Desktop directory, be sure to include the complete path with the filename.

Using a printer setup file is optional.

7   Enter the top, bottom, left and right margins in the appropriate Margins text boxes.

Top and bottom margin settings are measured in rows. Left and right margin settings are measured in columns. All margins are preset to zero.

8   Enter the page size in the Columns and Rows text boxes in the Page Size group box.

Page width is measured in columns, where an 80-column width is the default. Page height is measured in rows, where a 60-row height is the default.

9   Enter a number to indicate the line spacing in the Lines text box of the Line Spacing group box. Thus, 1 indicates single spacing (the default), 2 indicates double spacing, and so on. Norton Desktop allows values between 1 and 10, inclusive, in this text box.

10 Enter the number of columns to be used between tab settings in the Tabs text box of the Line Spacing group box (8 is the default).

11 Select the header style you want to appear on your printed output from the Kind of Header drop-down list.

None: suppresses the header information so no header appears on your output.

Single-Line: prints the filename, current date and time, and page number at the top of each page. Single-Line is the default.

Two-Line: prints the filename, current date and time, page number, and the file's creation or last modification date at the top of each page.

12 Check the Bold Headers check box if you want the headers printed in bold text. Bold Headers is checked by default.

13 Select where your output should be directed from the Output Destination drop-down list.

14 Select the format of your data from the Data Format drop-down list.

ASCII: uses eight *bits* to define each character. Most of the time, data is in the ASCII format. This format is selected by default.

WordStar: uses the first seven bits to define the character and the eighth bit for control information. This is an accepted format that has assumed the WordStar name.

EBCDIC: used only by mainframe computers and IBM's Display Write. Select EBCDIC to print files that have been downloaded from a mainframe computer to a PC.

15 Select the page orientation you wish to use from the Orientation drop-down list. This option is dimmed unless you have specified a PostScript or HP LaserJet printer as your printer type. A portrait orientation is the default.

Portrait prints your data so the page orientation is taller than it is wide.

Landscape prints your data so the page orientation is wider than it is tall.

16 Select OK to save your printer settings.

SELECTING FILE COMPRESSION OPTIONS

Compressing files is like packing away your winter clothes in a cedar chest. They're still around in case you need them, but they take up much less space than they do when hanging in your closet. When you compress files they stay on your hard or floppy disk until you need them, but they take up much less space. The COMPRESS... command from the (long) File menu lets you choose the files you want to compress or decompress. To select *how* you would like the files compressed, use the COMPRESSION... command from the (long) Configure menu.

To set up the file compression procedure:

1 Choose COMPRESSION... from the (long) Configure menu.

The Configure Compression dialog box, shown in Figure 9-22, appears on the desktop.

2 Select one of the storage options from the Storage Method group box.

Configuring Norton Desktop 9-45

There are two basic methods of storing or compressing files: implode and shrink. Imploding files offers greater file compression at a slower pace; shrinking offers less compression at a faster pace.

You can specifically tell Norton Desktop to implode or shrink files, or you can allow the program to automatically select the best method of storing your files.

3 To store the full path in addition to the filename, check the Store Full Pathnames check box.

When files are compressed a temporary storage area is created—this is where the compressing procedure actually takes place. When the compression procedure is finished, the temporary storage area is deleted. This means that you need to have more disk space available than your final compressed file will actually consume. If this is a problem (because you're short on disk space), use the Use Temporary Work Directory check box.

Figure 9-22

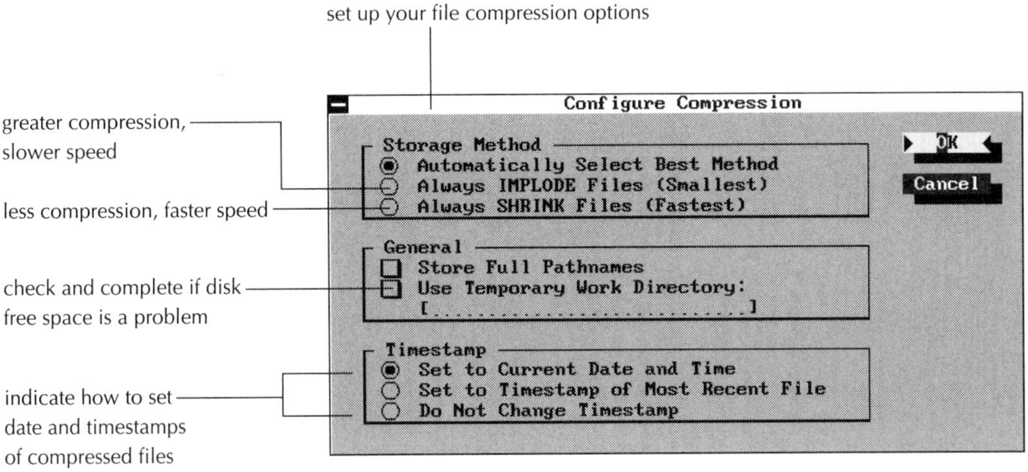

set up your file compression options

greater compression, slower speed

less compression, faster speed

check and complete if disk free space is a problem

indicate how to set date and timestamps of compressed files

4 To create the compressed file on a disk drive other than the one on which it will finally be stored, check the Use Temporary Work Directory check box and type the drive and directory where the compressed file is to be created in the text box.

5   Indicate how a date and time, or timestamp, should be assigned to the compressed file by selecting one of the option buttons from the Timestamp group box.

Set to Current Date and Time: assigns the date and time that the compressed file is created.

Set to Timestamp of Most Recent File: assigns the date and time of the most recent file to the entire file. For example, if your compressed file is made up of BUDGET.XLS, which has a timestamp of 9-20-91, 4:30 P.M., and SALES.XLS, which has a timestamp of 10-3-91, 2:47 P.M., the program will assign your compressed file the same timestamp as SALES.XLS because it is the most recent file.

Do Not Change Timestamp: retains the original timestamp of the compressed file when the file is updated.

By default, the compressed file is given the current date and time when it is updated.

6   Select OK to save your selections.

CONFIGURING DESKTOP LINK

Copying and moving files from one computer to another when you're not hooked up to a network used to mean you had to copy the files from one computer onto floppy disks, then copy the files from the disks onto the other computer. Now you can link two computers with a cable and perform file management operations such as copying, moving, deleting and renaming files from one computer to another without carrying disks back and forth.

Choosing the Desktop Link Options

You can use the Configure Desktop Link dialog box to specify the ports being used by the computers you want to link, or for the computer you are cloning from. You can also specify how fast the computers should transmit the data and how to check the data to be certain it has been sent correctly. The ports on the two computers you want to link can be different, but they must be the same type (serial or parallel). The speed and error checking information should be the same for both machines.

> **NOTE:** Be careful when you are choosing connection ports so that you don't accidentally disable another piece of equipment that is connected to your computer.

To open the Configure Desktop Link dialog box:

1   Choose DESKTOP LINK... from the (long) Configure menu.

    The Configure Desktop Link dialog box appears, as shown in Figure 9-23.

Figure 9-23

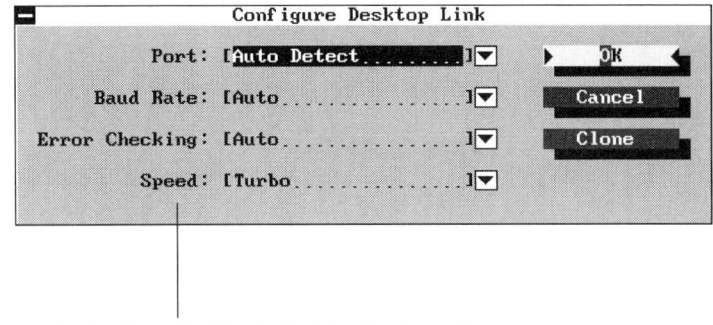

```
┌─────────────────── Configure Desktop Link ───────────────────┐
│         Port: [Auto Detect........]▼      ▶  OK              │
│    Baud Rate: [Auto...............]▼         Cancel          │
│ Error Checking: [Auto..............]▼         Clone           │
│        Speed: [Turbo..............]▼                         │
└──────────────────────────────────────────────────────────────┘
```

use the Configure Desktop Link dialog box to configure your system for linking to another computer—this allows you to copy, move, delete and rename files without having to transfer files to floppy disks

2   Select the communication port your computer is using to send or receive data from the Port drop-down list.

    Select Auto Detect if you want Norton Desktop to automatically detect the correct port.

3   Select the rate at which your computer will transmit data from the Baud Rate drop-down list.

    Select Auto if you want Norton Desktop to automatically determine the highest baud rate at which your computer can transmit data.

If you select a baud rate higher than your computer can actually transmit the data, Norton Desktop automatically drops the baud rate to the highest rate at which your computer can successfully transmit data.

> **TIP:** Using a 7-wire cable to connect your two computers will speed up the transmission of your data. You'll notice that each baud rate appears on the Baud Rate drop-down list twice—once with the "7-wire" notation, and once without the notation. If you are using a 7-wire cable, select the baud rate followed by the "7-wire" notation.

When sending data from one computer to another, Norton Desktop checks the data once it has been received; if errors are discovered, the data is sent again.

4   Select the error-checking method from the Error Checking drop-down list.

Auto: Norton Desktop automatically selects the best method of error checking. This is generally the recommended setting.

Use Checksum Only: the ASCII character values of all data sent are added together and the total is transferred along with the block of data; when the data arrives the ASCII character values are added together again to check that the number sent is the same as the number received. If the numbers do not match, the data is sent again. Checksum error checking is slightly faster than CRC error checking.

Use CRC Only: a more sophisticated equation is used that catches transposition errors not caught by the Checksum method. CRC error checking is more accurate than Checksum error checking.

5   Select the transmission speed from the Speed drop-down list.

Turbo: Sends large blocks of data (4K at a time).

Normal: Sends regular-sized blocks of data (2K at a time).

Slow: Sends smaller blocks of data (512-bytes at a time).

If you are unsure which transmission speed to select, leave the speed set to Turbo. Norton Desktop will try sending larger blocks of data. If errors occur, Norton Desktop will automatically drop the speed down.

6   Select OK to save your configuration settings.

> **NOTE:** In order to use the Desktop Link feature, both computers must have Norton Desktop on them. The Clone button allows you to "clone" Norton Desktop on to the computer that doesn't have Norton Desktop on it. This procedure is explained in the section "Cloning Norton Desktop" in Chapter 8, "Linking PCs."

For more information about linking computers and transferring files between them, see Chapter 8, "Linking PCs."

SAVING YOUR CHANGES

The SAVE CONFIGURATION command saves your current configuration settings so they are used in subsequent Norton Desktop sessions (versus being used for this session only).

To save your current configuration settings:

1   First be certain the desktop's appearance and configuration is the way you want it for future Norton Desktop sessions.

2   Choose SAVE CONFIGURATION from the Configure menu.

PART IV
USING DESKTOP TOOLS

Chapter 10: Using the Screen Saver

This chapter describes how to use the Norton Desktop screen saver, Sleeper, to protect your screen and hide its contents when you're not working at your computer.

Contents

Configuring Sleeper 10-3
    Selecting the Screen Saver Image 10-4
    Selecting Sleeper Options 10-5
    Setting Up a Password 10-7
Using Norton Utilities with Sleeper 10-8
Using Sleeper with Two Monitors 10-9

When the same fixed image is constantly displayed on your screen, it can "burn in," leaving a permanent ghost image. Sleeper, the Norton Desktop screen saver, protects your screen by blanking it or by displaying constantly moving graphical images when you're not using your computer.

You can also use the screen saver to hide the contents of your screen when you're working on confidential projects. If an unauthorized person walks into your office or if you need to leave your desk while working on a sensitive project, you can activate Sleeper to hide the screen contents rather than exiting from the file you're working on.

NOTE: Be aware that Sleeper does not work with Windows applications.

CONFIGURING SLEEPER

Before using Sleeper the *terminate-and-stay-resident (TSR)* program, NSCHED.EXE, must first be installed—this is normally done automatically when you install Norton Desktop. If you chose not to install NSCHED.EXE when you installed Norton Desktop, see *Installing Norton Desktop for DOS* for instructions on installing the program manually.

Norton Desktop's automated installation program configures Sleeper to display the Starless Night Sleeper image (your screen is totally blank so that it looks like your monitor is turned off) after an absence of activity from your computer disk, keyboard or mouse for three minutes. You can change Sleeper to suit your preference by changing the configuration of Sleeper using the Configure Screen Saver/Sleeper dialog box.

TIP: You can immediately activate Sleeper from the keyboard by using the hotkey combination Ctrl+Alt+Z.

To display the Configure Screen Saver/Sleeper dialog box:

- Choose SCREEN SAVER... from the Configure menu.

    The Configure Screen Saver/Sleeper dialog box appears (Figure 10-1).

Figure 10-1

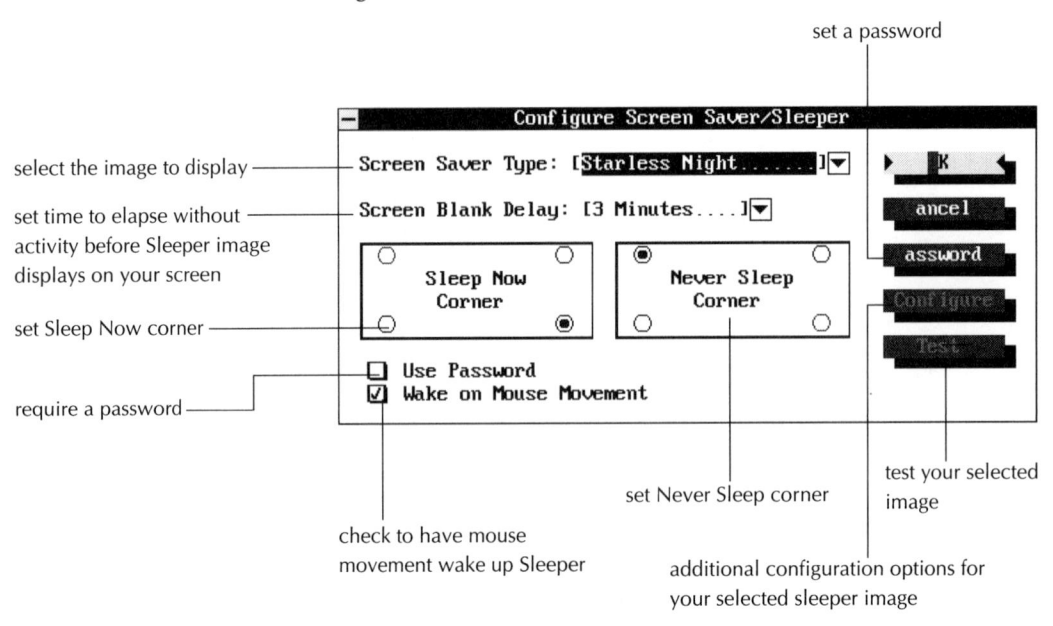

```
                                                    set a password
                                                          |
        ┌─────────── Configure Screen Saver/Sleeper ───────────┐
select the image to display ──── Screen Saver Type: [Starless Night....]▼   ► OK ◄
set time to elapse without ──── Screen Blank Delay: [3 Minutes....]▼        Cancel
activity before Sleeper image
displays on your screen           ○          ○    ●          ○             Password
                                    Sleep Now        Never Sleep
set Sleep Now corner ────           Corner             Corner              Configure
                                  ○          ●    ○          ○
                                                                             Test
                                  ☐ Use Password
require a password ─────          ☑ Wake on Mouse Movement
                                                                    test your selected
                               |                  |                 image
                               |        set Never Sleep corner
                       check to have mouse
                       movement wake up Sleeper   additional configuration options for
                                                  your selected sleeper image
```

Selecting the Screen Saver Image

Sleeper protects and hides the contents of your screen by either completely blanking the screen so it looks like the monitor has been turned off or by displaying constantly moving graphical images. You can select the image you want to display from the Screen Saver Type drop-down list box in the Configure Screen Saver/Sleeper dialog box. Starless Night is displayed by default.

To select the screen saver image:

1   Select the image you want to display from the Screen Saver Type list box in the Configure Screen Saver/Sleeper dialog box (see Figure 10-1).

    Images that are not supported by your computer's video card are dimmed.

    Some of the screen images require you to specify additional information, such as what message you want to display or the .PCX path and filename. If the particular image you've selected requires additional information, the Configure command button is active. If the Configure command button is not active, skip to step 5.

Using the Screen Saver **10-5**

2   Select the Configure command button.

3   Enter the requested information in the text or browse box.

4   Select OK to save your configuration information.

5   Select the Test command button to quickly preview your chosen Sleeper image (NSCHED.EXE must be loaded). This gives you the chance to see what the image will look like before closing the Sleeper configuration box. The test continues until you press any key or move the mouse.

6   Select OK to save your selection.

If Sleeper can't find the graphics file for the image you've chosen, it displays a message saying it can't find the file and displays Starless Night instead.

Displaying a .PCX File

Suppose you have a great .PCX graphics file that you'd like to use as your Sleeper image. You can simply tell Sleeper to use your 16-color .PCX file instead of one of the provided Sleeper images.

To display a .PCX file:

1   Select PCX File from the drop-down list of screen saver images in the Screen Saver Type list box.

2   Select the Configure command button.

The Browse for PCX File dialog box appears on the desktop.

3   Type the .PCX path and filename in the File text box.

Or,

Select the .PCX file from the Directories and Files list boxes.

4   Select OK to load the .PCX file as your screen saver image.

Selecting Sleeper Options

The Screen Blank Delay defines the length of time that must elapse without any activity from the keyboard, mouse or disk before Sleeper displays a graphics image on your screen.

To set the time that must elapse before Sleeper displays an image:

- Select a time from the Screen Blank Delay drop-down list box.

If you select Off, the delay feature is disabled. You can still activate Sleeper by using the Sleep Now Corner or pressing the hotkey combination Ctrl+Alt+Z.

> **WARNING:** Turn the screen saver off before running any program, such as communications applications, that you do not want interrupted.

The Sleep Now Corner defines where to position the mouse cursor so that Sleeper immediately displays your graphics image. By default, the Sleep Now Corner is in the lower-right corner of your screen.

To set the Sleep Now Corner:

- Select one of the Sleep Now Corner option buttons from the Configure Screen Saver/Sleeper dialog box (see Figure 10-1).

The Never Sleep Corner defines where to position the mouse cursor to disable Sleeper temporarily—this means the Sleeper image does not appear, even in the absence of any activity from the keyboard, mouse or disk. By default, the Never Sleep Corner is in the upper-left corner of your screen.

To set the Never Sleep Corner:

- Select one of the Never Sleep Corner option buttons from the Configure Screen Saver/Sleeper dialog box.

To prevent accidental mouse movements from waking up Sleeper you can configure Sleeper so that touching the keyboard is required to wake up the screen saver.

To prevent the mouse from waking Sleeper:

- Uncheck Wake on Mouse Movement in the Configure Screen Saver/Sleeper dialog box.

Setting Up a Password

If you are using Sleeper to hide your screen from unauthorized eyes, you don't want anyone to come into your office and awaken your screen simply by moving the mouse or touching the keyboard. You can further protect any confidential information by requiring a password to awaken the screen.

Normally when Sleeper is active, any activity from the mouse, keyboard or disk immediately turns off the Sleeper image. If you establish a password to be used with Sleeper, any activity from your computer produces a dialog box prompting you for your password. You must then enter the correct password before the Sleeper image is turned off. The dialog box gives you 30 seconds to enter your password to awaken the screen; otherwise the dialog box disappears and the Sleeper image remains active.

To set a Sleeper password:

1   Check the Use Password check box in the Configure Screen Saver/Sleeper dialog box.

2   Select the Password command button.

    The Password dialog box appears (Figure 10-2).

    The first time you enter a password, the Old Password text box is dimmed and the New Password text box is highlighted by default.

3   Type the password you want to use (up to 15 characters) in the New Password text box.

4   Press Enter to save your new password.

5   Verify your new password by typing it again in the Confirm New Password text box.

6   Select OK to close the Password dialog box and save your new password.

    Now a password must be entered before the screen can be awakened.

To change your password:

1   Select the Password command button.

    The Password dialog box appears on the desktop.

2   Type your current password in the Old Password text box.

Figure 10-2

you use the Password dialog box to set a password that must be entered to awaken the screen

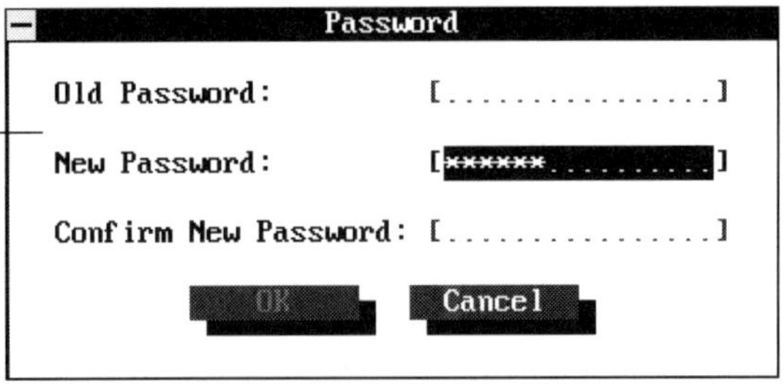

```
┌─ ─────────── Password ───────────┐
│  Old Password:      [................]  │
│  New Password:      [******..........]  │
│  Confirm New Password: [................] │
│            OK           Cancel           │
└──────────────────────────────────────────┘
```

3   Press Enter to enter the old password.
4   Type your new password in the New Password text box.
5   Press Enter to enter your new password.
6   Verify your new password by typing it again in the Confirm New Password text box.
7   Select OK to close the Password dialog box.

NOTE: Sleeper does not prevent others from rebooting your computer to access your files. It will, however, prevent anyone from seeing the screen you were working on when Sleeper was activated.

USING NORTON UTILITIES WITH SLEEPER

To avoid the loss or corruption of data, it is critical that certain utilities not be interrupted in the middle of a procedure. The utilities have been designed to automatically disable Sleeper until they have finished processing data whenever this could present a problem. The utilities that turn off Sleeper while they are active are:

- Disk Tools
- Image
- Norton Disk Doctor
- SFORMAT
- Speed Disk
- UnErase
- UnFormat

USING SLEEPER WITH TWO MONITORS

When the above utilities have finished processing data, they automatically turn Sleeper back on again.

Believe it or not, you can use Sleeper even if you have two monitors connected to your computer. Norton Desktop automatically checks to see what computer hardware you are using when it is installed. If you have two monitors connected to your computer, Norton Desktop detects the two monitors at that time. You can activate Sleeper and choose a Sleeper image by following the instructions in the "Configuring Sleeper" and "Selecting the Screen Saver Image" sections of this chapter. Sleeper displays your chosen image on the primary monitor and displays Starless Night on the secondary monitor.

If you have installed a monochrome monitor as your primary monitor and a CGA or VGA monitor as your secondary monitor, Norton Desktop does not detect the presence of your CGA or VGA card. This means you are able to select only those Sleeper images that do not require CGA or VGA support.

Using the Menu

This chapter explains how to create, personalize, and use the menu that you can access from the Tools menu. Launching applications from this menu will save you time and keystrokes.

Contents

Why Use a Menu? 11-3
    Selecting the Menu 11-3
Creating the Menu Automatically 11-4
Creating the Menu Manually 11-4
    Customizing a DOS Program 11-8
Importing Other Menu Formats 11-8
Testing the Menu 11-9
Using the Menu 11-9
    Selecting a Menu Item 11-10
    Moving from One Submenu to Another 11-10

WHY USE A MENU?

Suppose that you use a word processing program on your computer to write sales proposals and also an accounting program to do your bookkeeping. To start either program, you might first type a command at the DOS prompt that changes to the directory in which the program resides then type the command that actually starts the program.

If you forget which directory the program is in, you have to search through a list of directories to find it. If you type the wrong command, you may get the message "Bad command or filename." Wouldn't it be easier to have instant access to all of your programs on a menu? Now you can have just such a menu with Norton Desktop for DOS.

With the menu, you can access any program or file on your hard disk or a network to which your computer is connected.

Selecting the Menu

To select (or open) the menu:

- Choose MENU from the Tools menu.

    If the menu has been created, it appears.

The menu will look something like the menu shown in Figure 11-1, except the applications listed will be those on your computer.

Figure 11-1

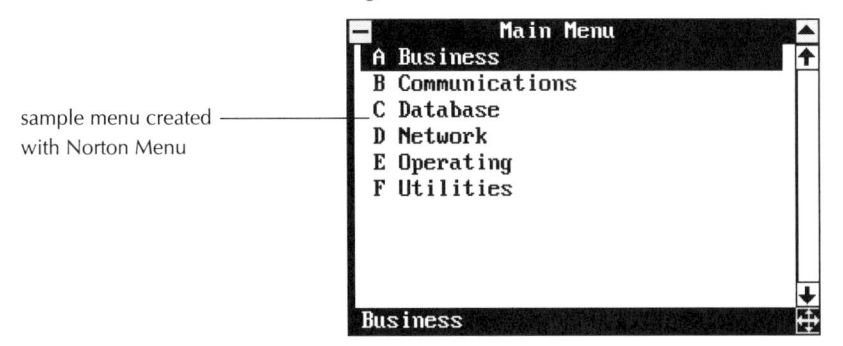

```
┌─────────── Main Menu ───────────┐
│ A Business                      │
│ B Communications                │
│ C Database                      │
│ D Network                       │
│ E Operating                     │
│ F Utilities                     │
│                                 │
│ Business                        │
└─────────────────────────────────┘
```

sample menu created with Norton Menu

If you do not yet have a menu, the Norton Menu dialog box asks whether you want to create one manually or have one built automatically.

- To create the menu automatically, select Autobuild and then follow the steps described in "Creating the Menu Automatically."
- To create the menu manually, select Create and then follow the steps described in "Creating the Menu Manually" later in this chapter.
- To return to the Norton Desktop, select Cancel.
- To import a menu from another product (Norton Commander or Direct Access), select Import and then follow the steps described in "Importing Other Menu Formats" later in this chapter.

For information on how to use the menu, see "Using the Menu" later in this chapter.

CREATING THE MENU AUTOMATICALLY

If you want the program to search your hard disk for applications and add any it finds to your menu, follow this procedure.

To create a menu automatically:

- Select Autobuild from the Norton Menu dialog box.

    The program scans your hard disk(s) for the applications that it can recognize, organizes them by software category, and places them into submenus. For example, it places any games it finds on the "Entertainment" submenu. When it is done, it displays the menu which is named Main Menu.

For information on how to use the menu, see "Using the Menu" later in this chapter.

To make changes to the menu, see Chapter 12, "Editing the Menu."

CREATING THE MENU MANUALLY

If you want to choose exactly which programs your menu will contain, follow this procedure.

To create a menu manually:

1   Select Create from the Norton Menu dialog box.

    You enter the Norton Menu application.

2 Choose NEW... from the File menu (Ctrl+N).

The New Menu dialog box appears.

3 Type in the title for the menu in the New Menu Title text box. A menu title can contain up to 32 alphanumeric characters.

4 A file must be created for that menu. You can name that file or let Norton Menu name it for you.

- If you want to name it, select the File option button from the Menu File Name group box. Then type in the DOS pathname for the file. (Parts of a pathname already appear in the text box in case you want to use them.)

- If you want Norton Menu to create the name, select the Auto option button.

5 Select OK. Your new menu appears, but it has no items on it.

You are now ready to add menu items.

The three types of menu items are:

- Program   Lets you run a DOS program or execute a DOS command from the menu.
- Submenu   Lets you create a submenu. A submenu is a menu contained within a menu.
- Batch   Lets you create or attach an internal batch file and run it from the menu.

This section describes how to add a DOS program or command to the menu. For information on adding the other item types to the menu, see "Creating an Advanced Menu" in Chapter 30, "Creating Corporate Menus."

To add menu items:

1 Choose ADD... from the Edit menu (Ctrl+A).

The Add Menu Item dialog box appears (Figure 11-2).

2 Select the menu item type. For now, select the Program button, which adds a DOS program or command to the menu.

11-6 *Using Norton Desktop for DOS*

Figure 11-2

the Add Menu Item dialog box lets you add DOS programs or commands to your menu

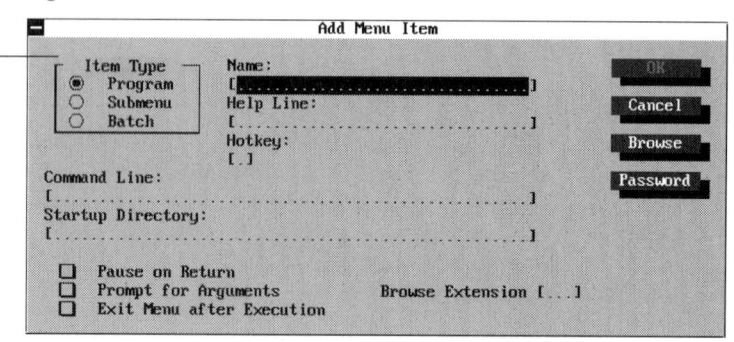

```
┌─────────────────────── Add Menu Item ───────────────────────┐
│  ┌─ Item Type ─┐   Name:                                    │
│  │ ◉ Program   │   [................................]   OK │
│  │ ○ Submenu   │   Help Line:                               │
│  │ ○ Batch     │   [................................] Cancel│
│  └─────────────┘   Hotkey:                                  │
│                    [ ]                               Browse │
│  Command Line:                                              │
│  [........................................]       Password │
│  Startup Directory:                                         │
│  [........................................]                │
│                                                             │
│  ☐ Pause on Return                                          │
│  ☐ Prompt for Arguments         Browse Extension [...]      │
│  ☐ Exit Menu after Execution                                │
└─────────────────────────────────────────────────────────────┘
```

3 Type a descriptive menu item name in the text box. The name you type will appear in alphabetical order on the menu. The item name can be up to 32 alphanumeric characters (letters, numerals or characters).

4 Type the help text for the item in the Help Line text box. The help text can contain up to 32 alphanumeric characters (letters, numerals or characters).

If a hotkey appears to the left of the menu item, you can press that key to select the menu item.

5 Type the program's executable filename, command-line options and pathname, then select any options needed to customize the program you selected in step 2. For example, to run WordPerfect you would type a command similar to the following:

D:\WP\wp.exe

Go to step 6.

> **NOTE:** You don't need to type a full pathname if the directory is included in your DOS path statement.

Or,

To save keystrokes, select the Browse button.

The Browse for Program dialog box appears (Figure 11-3), which lets you browse for and select a program quickly and easily. Using a browse dialog box is explained in Chapter 1, "Getting Started."

Using the Menu 11-7

Figure 11-3

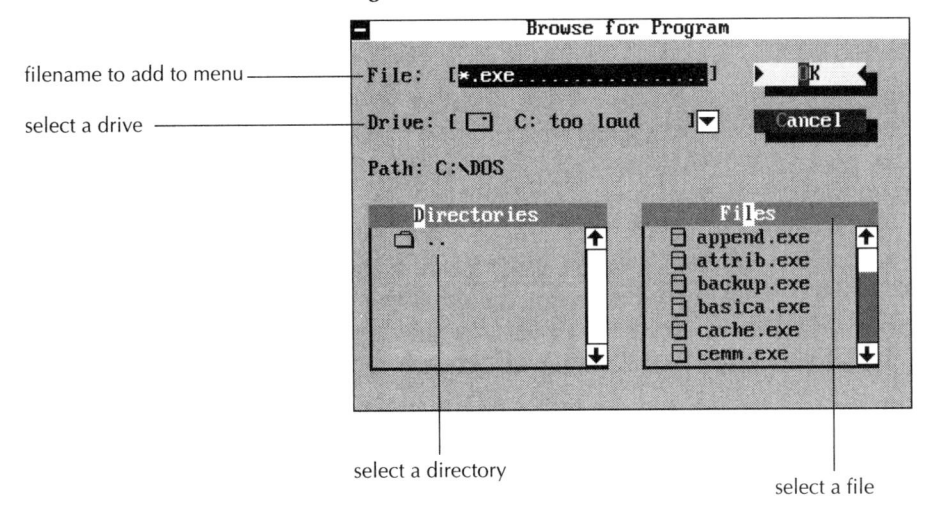

```
                    Browse for Program
File:   [*.exe............]      ▶  OK  ◀
Drive:  [ ▼ ] C: too loud  [▼]    Cancel
Path: C:\DOS

      Directories              Files
   □ ..                    ▲   ▣ append.exe   ▲
                               ▣ attrib.exe
                               ▣ backup.exe
                               ▣ basica.exe
                               ▣ cache.exe
                               ▼ ▣ cemm.exe   ▼
```

- filename to add to menu → File:
- select a drive → Drive:
- select a directory → Directories
- select a file → Files

See the "Customizing a DOS Program" section later in this chapter for more information on the options that customize a program.

Select a file from the Files list box then select OK.

The Edit Program Item dialog box appears.

6 Edit the entries or select OK to accept them as they appear.

Certain applications must launch from a specific directory. When you add an application to a menu that needs to start from a specific directory, the program can automatically change to the application's startup directory before the application launches. To launch an application from a specific directory, type a startup directory in the text box.

7 Place a checkmark in any of the check boxes that apply. See the section "Customizing a DOS Program" for details.

8 Select OK.

The menu item appears on the menu.

9 Repeat steps 1 through 8 for each program you want to create a menu item for.

Customizing a DOS Program

Keeping Messages on the Screen

The Add Menu Item dialog box has three check box options that make your menu items more powerful.

Some applications or DOS commands display messages or other information on your screen. If the information is important, you might want to keep it on your screen so that it can be read before disappearing.

To keep information on your screen:

- Check Pause on Return in the Add Menu Item dialog box. The screen will pause until you press any key.

Prompting for Arguments

You can have a menu item ask for program arguments before it executes.

To prompt for arguments:

- Check Prompt for Arguments in the Add Menu Item dialog box.

    If you would like to pass a filename to the program, you can specify a file extension in the Browse Extension text box.

When the menu item is selected, the Enter Program Arguments dialog box lets you enter any program information the menu item needs before it executes.

Exiting to Norton Desktop

You can instantly leave a menu after a menu item has executed and return to the Norton Desktop.

To exit from a menu after a menu item executes:

- Check Exit Menu after Execution in the Add Menu Item dialog box.

    After the menu item runs, Norton Menu terminates, and the Norton Desktop appears.

IMPORTING OTHER MENU FORMATS

If you have been using a menu created by Direct Access or Norton Commander, you can import it for instant use in Norton Menu.

To import a menu to the Norton Menu format:

1 Choose IMPORT... from the File menu.

   The Menu Import dialog box appears.

2 Select the option button that corresponds to the type of file—Norton Commander or Direct Access—that you want to import.

3 Type the filename in the Filename To Import Autobuild field and then select OK.

   Or,

   Choose the Browse button to browse a list of files, select a filename, and then select OK.

4 Select OK.

   A dialog box asks whether you want to append the new menu to the old one or replace the old menu entirely.

5 Select Replace or Append.

   The new menu appears.

TESTING THE MENU

Before you use your new menu regularly, it's a good idea to test how it will look and work. First, check to make sure that the correct commands are included. Next, test it to make sure that it runs properly.

To test the menu:

- Select the menu items one at a time to determine whether they work correctly.

If you find a menu item that is not working properly, see "Customizing a DOS Program" earlier in this chapter for information on options that might correct the problem.

If you want to make any changes to menu items, see Chapter 12, "Editing the Menu."

USING THE MENU

This section describes how to use the menu to launch your applications.

Selecting a Menu Item

Menu items either run a program or take you to a *submenu*, one level lower.

To select an item from the menu:

- Select the menu item and then press Enter.

Or,

- Double-click the menu item.

TIP: Check the Autoassign Hotkeys check box in the Preferences dialog box to have a hotkey automatically assigned to a menu item. The hotkey appears to the left of the menu item. You can press that key to select the menu item. For more information on hotkeys, see Chapter 31, "Administering Corporate Menus."

Moving from One Submenu to Another

You can display more than one submenu at once.

To move among submenus:

- Choose NEXT from the Control menu.

Or,

- Click the submenu's title bar to make it active.

  The active submenu appears on the top of the menu stack. The title bars of the other submenus are visible, each just layered above the rest.

To return to the main menu:

- Click the main menu's title bar.

Chapter 12: Editing the Menu

This chapter tells you how to make changes to the menu described in the previous chapter. You'll learn how to add, change, copy, move and delete menu items. It also explains how to change the menu title.

Contents

Adding a Menu Item 12-3
Modifying a Menu Item 12-3
Adding a Similar Menu Item 12-4
Deleting a Menu Item 12-4
Moving a Menu Item 12-4
Changing the Menu Title 12-5
Updating the Menu Automatically 12-5
Importing Other Menu Formats 12-6
Exiting Norton Menu 12-6

Now that your favorite applications are organized on a menu, life is easier. What happens when you add a new program to your computer and need to add it to the menu? No problem—changing the menu is easy. You can move, copy, delete or edit any menu item. You can also add new menu items and change the menu title.

To select (or open) the menu for editing:

- Choose EDIT MENU... from the Tools menu.

    The menu appears along with a menu bar at the top your screen. The menu bar includes an Edit menu, which lets you make changes to the menu.

ADDING A MENU ITEM

See "Adding a Menu Item" in Chapter 11, "Using the Menu."

MODIFYING A MENU ITEM

To modify a menu item:

1   Highlight the menu item you want to modify (if the menu item is contained in a submenu, select the main menu item first).

2   Choose MODIFY... from the Edit menu (Ctrl+E).

    The Edit Menu Item dialog box appears (Figure 12-1).

Figure 12-1

the Edit Menu Item dialog box lets you change a menu item and customize a DOS program

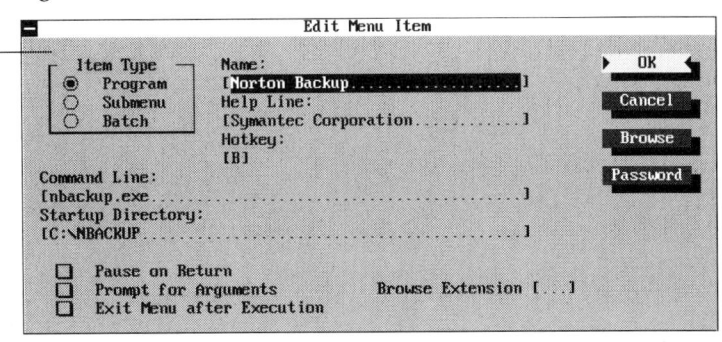

3   Type any changes you want.
4   Select OK.

    The changed menu item appears on the menu.

ADDING A SIMILAR MENU ITEM

Sometimes you might want to add a menu item that is very similar to an item already on a menu. It's easy—just copy the existing menu item and make any changes you want.

To copy a menu item:

1   Select the menu item to copy.
2   Choose COPY from the Edit menu (Ctrl+C).
3   Choose PASTE from the Edit menu (Ctrl+V).

   The copy is inserted into the menu. If hotkeys are automatically assigned to your menu items, they change to reflect the new menu item sequence.

TIP: The COPY command duplicates the menu item and places it in your computer's memory in an area called the paste buffer. Once the menu item is in this paste buffer, you can use the PASTE command (Ctrl+V) to move the menu item to another position on the same menu or to another menu.

DELETING A MENU ITEM

To delete a menu item:

1   Highlight the menu item to delete.
2   Choose CLEAR from the Edit menu (Ctrl+B).

   The item is removed from the menu. If hotkeys are automatically assigned to your menu items, the hotkeys change to reflect the new menu item sequence.

NOTE: You can have the program display a confirmation dialog box before it deletes the item. See the "Confirm Before Deleting" section of Chapter 31, "Administering Corporate Menus."

MOVING A MENU ITEM

To move a menu item to a new location:

1   Highlight the menu item to move.
2   Choose CUT from the Edit menu (Ctrl+X).
3   Highlight the item that you want to be under the one you are moving.

4   Choose PASTE from the Edit menu.

The menu item appears in the new location.

TIP: The CUT command removes the menu item and places it in the computer's memory in an area called the paste buffer. Once the menu item is in this paste buffer, you can use the PASTE command (Ctrl+V) to move the menu item to another position on the menu or to another menu.

CHANGING THE MENU TITLE

To change the menu title:

1   Choose MENU TITLE... from the Edit menu (Ctrl+T).

The Edit Menu Title dialog box appears. This dialog box contains the menu's title.

2   Type the new menu title then select OK.

The menu appears with the new title.

NOTE: This option changes the menu's title only; it does not change the menu or submenu filename.

UPDATING THE MENU AUTOMATICALLY

When you make changes to your computer's disk and path information, the menu will no longer work if the changes affect the programs or DOS commands that are referenced. You could, of course, manually change all the disk and path information. Or you can update the menu automatically, using the Autobuild feature. The Autobuild feature customizes the menu to account for any variations in disk and directory structures.

To update the menu automatically:

1   Select AUTOBUILD... from the File menu.

The Autobuild or Update Menus dialog box appears.

2   Select Update an Existing Menu and then select OK.

The program scans for the new disk and path information and updates the menu.

IMPORTING OTHER MENU FORMATS

If you have been using a menu created by Direct Access or Norton Commander, you can import it for instant use in Norton Menu.

To import a menu for use in Norton Menu:

1 Choose IMPORT... from the Edit menu.

   The Menu Import dialog box appears.

2 Select the option button that corresponds to the type of file—Norton Commander or Direct Access—that you want to import.

3 Type the filename in the Filename to Import field then select OK.

   Or,

   Choose the Browse button to browse through a list of files, select a filename, then select OK.

4 Select OK.

   The new menu appears in place of the old menu.

EXITING NORTON MENU

To exit the menu:

- Choose EXIT from the File menu.

NOTE: If you have the Confirm on Delete option turned on, a dialog box asks whether you would like to exit Norton Menu. When you select Yes, Norton Desktop appears.

Chapter 13: Using the Calculator

This chapter explains how to use the Norton Desktop Calculator to perform basic mathematical operations.

Contents

Starting the Calculator 13-3
The Calculator Display 13-3
The Calculator Functions 13-4
Entering Calculations 13-4
Exiting the Calculator 13-5

Using the Calculator **13-3**

The Norton Desktop Calculator stays neatly tucked away on your computer so you can easily access it when it's needed. You can use the Calculator to quickly perform calculations, such as double-checking sales figures in a report or adding up your third-quarter entertainment expenses.

STARTING THE CALCULATOR

To start the Norton Desktop Calculator:

- Choose CALCULATOR from the Tools menu.

    The Calculator, (Figure 13-1), appears on the desktop.

Figure 13-1

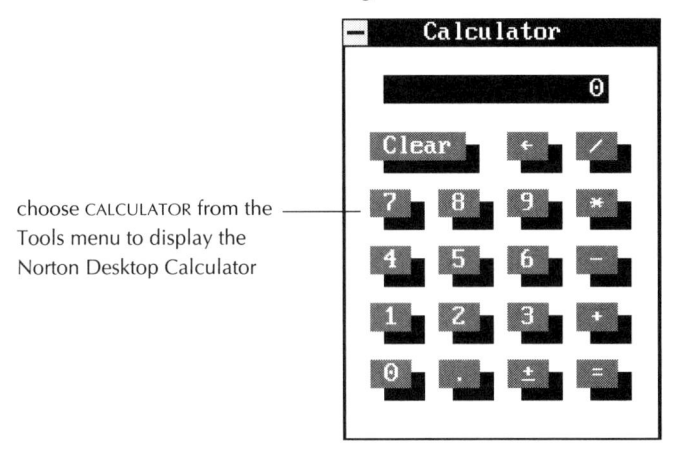

choose CALCULATOR from the Tools menu to display the Norton Desktop Calculator

The numbers and operations of the Calculator can be accessed easily using the keyboard or a mouse.

Keyboard users can use the Enter, =, Backspace, decimal point, +, –, *, /, \ and numbers keys by pressing the corresponding keys on the keyboard or keypad (be certain the Num Lock key on the keypad is activated).

To select any number or operation using a mouse, simply click the appropriate key.

THE CALCULATOR DISPLAY

Your Norton Desktop Calculator allows up to 15 digits in the display area. A decimal point counts as one digit, which means the Calculator can actually display up to 14 significant digits.

THE CALCULATOR FUNCTIONS

The Norton Desktop Calculator performs the four basic mathematical operations of addition, subtraction, multiplication, and division. Table 13-1 lists the operation keys of the Calculator and their functions.

Table 13-1

Operator	Function
+	Addition
–	Subtraction
*	Multiplication
/	Division
=	Compute final result
Clear	Clear the display
+/–	Change the sign
←	Backspace

Use the Norton Desktop Calculator to perform basic mathematical operations.

ENTERING CALCULATIONS

Your numerical entries to the Calculator must be separated by pressing one of the mathematical operator keys (+, –, *, or /); in other words, numbers and operators are entered in normal algebraic order. For instance, to add 12 and 27: enter 12, press the + sign, then enter 27. When you have finished entering your calculations, press the equal sign key to compute the answer.

To enter calculations:

1   Type your first number (up to 15 digits), allowing for a decimal point and/or a minus sign if necessary.

   To enter negative numbers, type the number, then change the sign—press the backslash key (\) from the keyboard or click the change sign key (+/–) with the mouse.

2   Select the appropriate mathematical operator key (+, –, *, or /).

EXITING THE CALCULATOR

3 Type your next number.

4 Repeat steps 2 and 3 until all of your calculations have been entered.

5 Select the equal sign key (=) or press Enter.

When you have completed your calculations, it's easy to put the Calculator away on the desktop until it's needed again.

To exit the Calculator:

- Press Esc.

Or,

- Double-click the Close box.

Using the Calendar

This chapter explains how to use the Norton Desktop Calendar to make notes, to-do lists and appointments.

Contents

Accessing the Calendar 14-3
Changing the Displayed Date 14-3
Keeping Notes on Your Calendar 14-4
Exiting from the Calendar 14-5

The Norton Desktop Calendar allows you to free up desk space and organize your work by keeping a calendar on your computer instead of on top of your desk. You can also make notes and keep track of appointments on your Norton Desktop Calendar, just as you would on a wall or desk calendar.

ACCESSING THE CALENDAR

To access the calendar:

- Choose CALENDAR from the Tools menu.

  The Norton Desktop Calendar appears on the desktop, as shown in Figure 14-1, displaying the current month, with the current day highlighted by default.

Figure 14-1

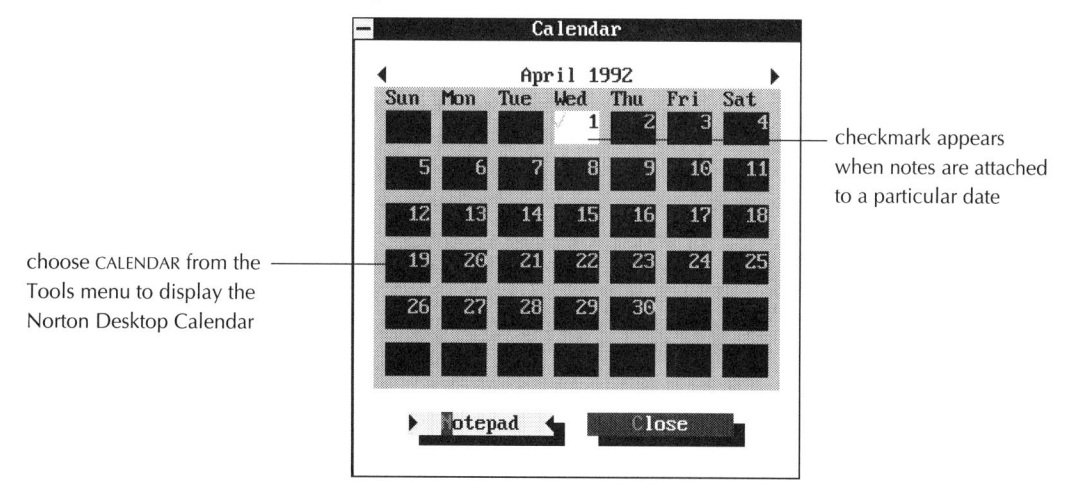

choose CALENDAR from the Tools menu to display the Norton Desktop Calendar

checkmark appears when notes are attached to a particular date

CHANGING THE DISPLAYED DATE

The Norton Desktop Calendar can display any month from January 1980 to December 2107.

Using either the keyboard or a mouse, you can move quickly through the calendar pages.

To change the month display:

- To display a later month, press PgDn or Ctrl+RightArrow.
- To display an earlier month, press PgUp or Ctrl+LeftArrow.

- To quickly display January of the current year, press Ctrl+Home.
- To quickly display December of the current year, press Ctrl+End.

Or,

- To display an earlier month, click with the *left mouse button* on the left arrowhead of the month title bar.
- To display a later month, click with the *left mouse button* on the right arrowhead of the month title bar.

To change the year display:

- To display an earlier year, press Ctrl+PgUp.
- To display a later year, press Ctrl+PgDn.

Or,

- To display an earlier year, click with the *right mouse button* on the left arrowhead of the month title bar.
- To display a later year, click with the *right mouse button* on the right arrowhead of the month title bar.

KEEPING NOTES ON YOUR CALENDAR

One of the main purposes of a calendar is to catalog your daily events. In order to do that, you have to be able to make notes on your calendar to remind yourself of project deadlines, appointments and important tasks.

When you select a specific date from the Norton Desktop Calendar and select Notepad, the Notes dialog box appears on the desktop so you can enter pertinent notes for that date. Then when you see a checkmark on your Calendar, be sure to check the Notepad.

To add notes to the Calendar:

1 Select the date you wish to attach a note to.

TIP: To quickly move to the 1st of the current month, press Home. To move to the last day of the current month, press End. To go to January 1 of the current year, press Ctrl+Home. To go to December 31 of the current year, press Ctrl+End.

Using the Calendar   **14-5**

2 Select the Notepad command button.

The Calendar Notepad appears on the desktop, as shown in Figure 14-2.

Figure 14-2

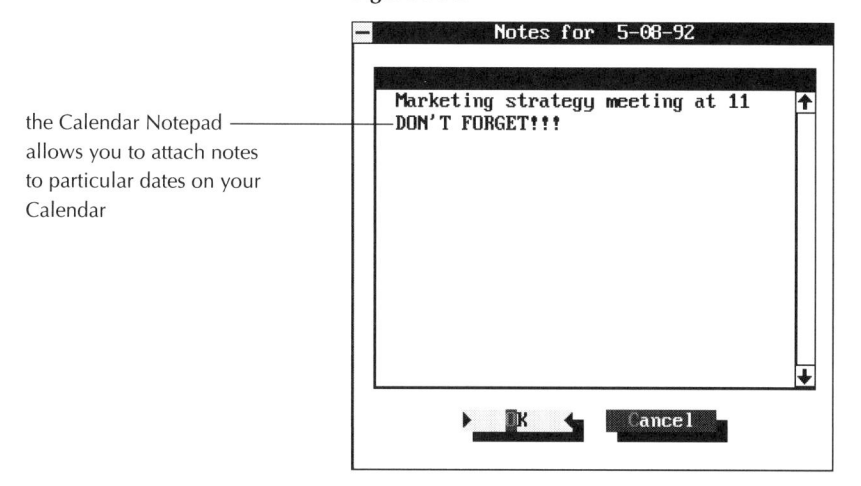

the Calendar Notepad allows you to attach notes to particular dates on your Calendar

```
┌─────────── Notes for  5-08-92 ───────────┐
│                                          │
│  ┌────────────────────────────────────┐  │
│  │ Marketing strategy meeting at 11 ↑ │  │
│  │ DON'T FORGET!!!                    │  │
│  │                                    │  │
│  │                                    │  │
│  │                                    │  │
│  │                                  ↓ │  │
│  └────────────────────────────────────┘  │
│                                          │
│         ▶  OK  ◀      Cancel             │
│                                          │
└──────────────────────────────────────────┘
```

3 Type your notation into the Notepad.

4 Select OK.

Dates with attached notations are now indicated on the Calendar by a checkmark.

EXITING FROM THE CALENDAR

To exit from the Calendar:

- Select the Close command button.

Or,

- Select CLOSE from the Control menu.

Or,

- Double-click the Control-menu box.

Chapter 15: Sending Network Messages

This chapter explains how to send and reply to network messages.

Contents

Sending a Message to Network Users 15-3
Replying to a Network Message 15-5

Have you ever called a last-minute meeting and wished you could send out a quick message to your co-workers on the network? With Norton Desktop you can do just that. You can also receive and reply to urgent messages others send to you.

> **NOTE:** The recipients don't have to be running Norton Desktop to receive your message. The message you send or reply to is seen immediately unless one of the following situations exists:
>
> - The Trap Network Messages option in the Configure Network dialog box is checked and the recipient of your message is in a DOS session or has launched an application from the Norton Desktop. However, once the recipient returns to the desktop, your message appears. For more information about the Trap Network Messages option, see the section, "Configuring Network Options," in Chapter 9, "Configuring Norton Desktop."
> - The receiving computer has blocked network messages from displaying. This is done using a network command, not a Norton Desktop command.

SENDING A MESSAGE TO NETWORK USERS

If your computer is connected to a network, you can use Norton Desktop to send a message to anyone who is logged onto the same *file servers* to which your computer is connected.

To send a message to other users on the network:

1   Choose NETWORK MESSAGE... from the (long) Tools menu.

    The Network Message dialog box appears on the desktop (Figure 15-1). Your user name automatically appears on the From message line.

2   Type the message you wish to send in the Message text box.

    The length of the message you can send varies depending on the length of your login name. The length of your login name plus the length of your message cannot exceed 58 characters.

15-4   *Using Norton Desktop for DOS*

Figure 15-1

send a message to users on the network using the Network Message dialog box

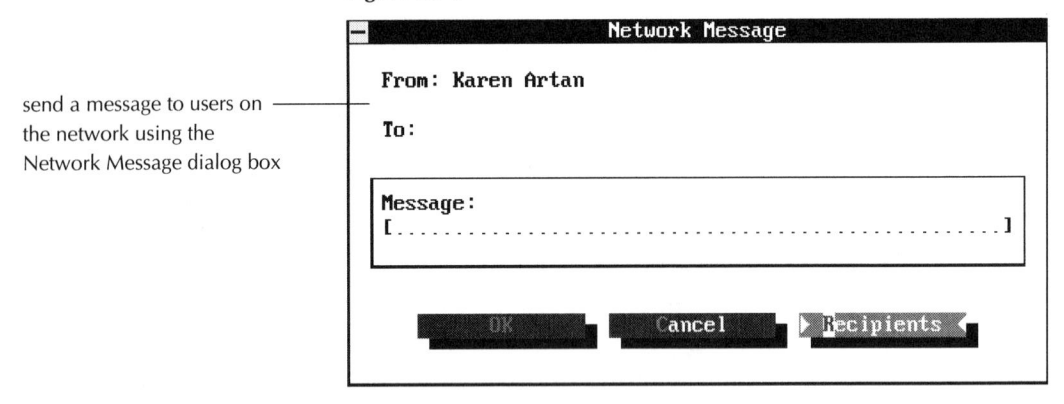

```
┌─────────────────── Network Message ───────────────────┐
│                                                        │
│  From: Karen Artan                                     │
│                                                        │
│  To:                                                   │
│                                                        │
│  ┌──────────────────────────────────────────────────┐  │
│  │ Message:                                         │  │
│  │ [..............................................]│  │
│  │                                                  │  │
│  └──────────────────────────────────────────────────┘  │
│                                                        │
│        [  OK  ]      [ Cancel ]    ▶ Recipients ◀     │
│                                                        │
└────────────────────────────────────────────────────────┘
```

3 Select the Recipients button to display a list of user names.

The Connected Network Users dialog box appears (Figure 15-2). The File Server combination box shows the file server name. The box below it contains the names of all users currently logged onto the file server.

Figure 15-2

file server name

select a recipient from the user names of the people currently connected to the file server

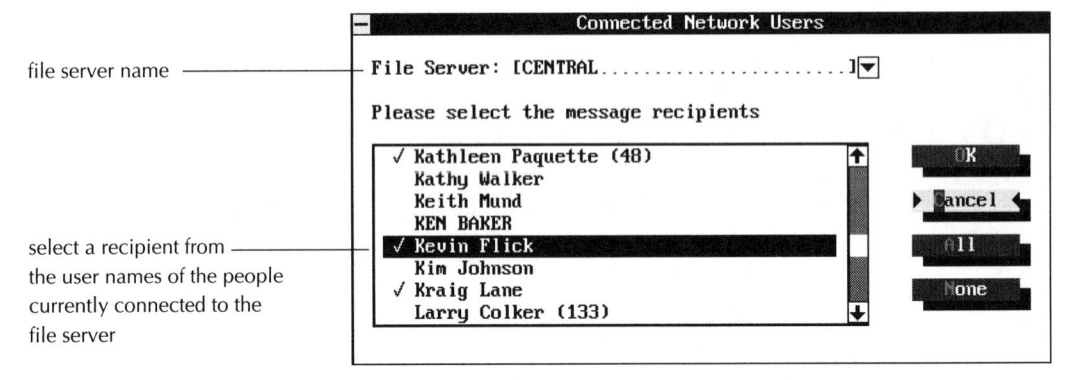

```
┌───────────────── Connected Network Users ─────────────────┐
│                                                            │
│  File Server: [CENTRAL....................]▼               │
│                                                            │
│  Please select the message recipients                      │
│  ┌────────────────────────────────────┐↑    ┌──────┐       │
│  │ √ Kathleen Paquette (48)           │     │  OK  │       │
│  │   Kathy Walker                     │     └──────┘       │
│  │   Keith Mund                       │    ▶ Cancel ◀      │
│  │   KEN BAKER                        │     ┌──────┐       │
│  │ √ Kevin Flick                      │     │ All  │       │
│  │   Kim Johnson                      │     └──────┘       │
│  │ √ Kraig Lane                       │     ┌──────┐       │
│  │   Larry Colker (133)               │↓    │ None │       │
│  └────────────────────────────────────┘     └──────┘       │
└────────────────────────────────────────────────────────────┘
```

4 If you want to choose names from a different file server, select the prompt button (Ctrl+DownArrow) to reveal a list of available file servers and select another server.

5   Select the names of the users to whom you wish to send the message. A checkmark appears next to each name you select.

Choosing the All button selects all of the names in the list.

Choosing the None button deselects any names currently selected.

TIP: If the name you are looking for is not in view, you can use the Speed Search feature by typing the first letter of the name you are looking for (press Alt+F1 first if the DOS command line is showing).

For additional information on using Speed Search, see the section "Finding Directories and Files" in Chapter 2, "Using Drive Windows."

6   Select OK to exit the Connected Network Users dialog box.

7   Select OK again to send the message.

NOTE: If a message can't be sent (because the user logged out just before you sent the message, for example) Norton Desktop displays a message telling you so.

REPLYING TO A NETWORK MESSAGE

Messages can be sent to you by other network users or by the network file server. When a network message is sent to you, the message appears on your screen in the Network Message dialog box (Figure 15-3). The dialog box shows the name of the person who sent the message (or the name of the file server), the day, date and time the message was sent, and the actual message. You can reply to the message if it was sent by another network user; however, if the message is from a file server you cannot reply to it.

Figure 15-3

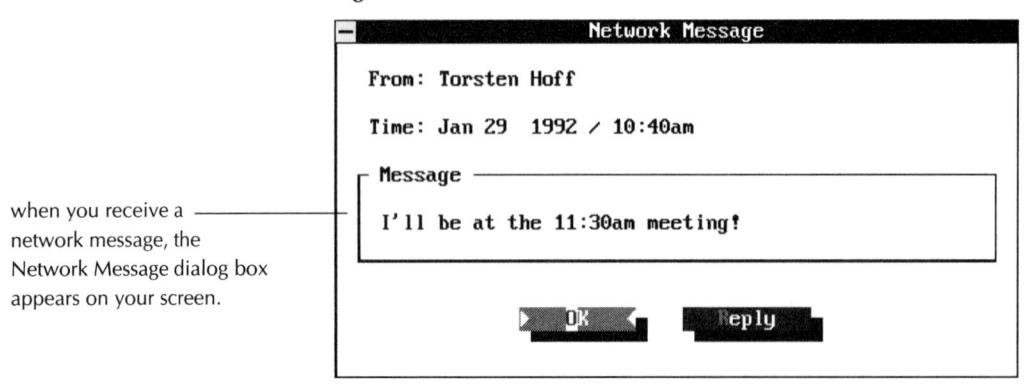

```
┌─────────────────── Network Message ───────────────────┐
│ From: Torsten Hoff                                    │
│                                                       │
│ Time: Jan 29  1992 / 10:40am                          │
│ ┌─ Message ───────────────────────────────────────┐   │
│ │ I'll be at the 11:30am meeting!                 │   │
│ └─────────────────────────────────────────────────┘   │
│                                                       │
│              ▶ OK ◀        Reply                      │
└───────────────────────────────────────────────────────┘
```

when you receive a network message, the Network Message dialog box appears on your screen.

To reply to a network message:

1. Choose the Reply button in the Network Message dialog box.

   The Network Message dialog box appears with your user name on the From message line and the user name of the person who originated the message on the To message line.

2. If you want to send your reply to additional people, choose the Recipients button to select more names from the list of user names (see Figure 15-2).

   The Connected Network Users dialog box appears. The Server combination box shows the file server name. The box below it contains the names of all users currently logged onto the file server.

3. If you want to choose names from a different file server, select the prompt button (Ctrl+DownArrow) to reveal a list of available file servers and select another server.

4. Select the names of those users you wish to receive your message. A checkmark appears next to the selected names.

   Choosing the All button selects all of the names in the list.

   Choosing the None button deselects any names currently selected.

5. Select OK to exit the Connected Network Users dialog box.

6. Select OK again to send your reply.

Using UnErase

This chapter explains how to use UnErase to recover files that were erased or deleted by mistake.

Contents

How UnErase Works	16-3
Starting UnErase	16-4
Recovering Erased Files	16-4
Manual UnErase	16-7
UnErase and DOS 5.0	16-10

When you erase or delete a file, the data doesn't completely disappear. Rather, the file's name is removed from directory listings so you can no longer see it and the precise record of the data's location is blanked out. But the filename (minus the first letter) and the data remain intact on the disk until they are overwritten by new files. UnErase automatically searches for and recovers erased (deleted) files.

TIP: As an additional safety measure, always use Erase Protect to erase-protect your files. UnErase is aware of files that were erase-protected and recovers them with 100 percent reliability because Erase Protect prevents overwriting of the file's data area. See Chapter 27, "Using Erase Protect" for more information.

Although you cannot usually recover erased files over a network, you can recover erased network files if you use Erase Protect. (Some networks, such as Netware 386, provide their own deleted file recovery system.) See your network supervisor for information.

HOW UNERASE WORKS

To illustrate how UnErase works, think of a tape recorder. When you use an audio or video tape recorder, you don't have to buy a new tape every time you wish to record your favorite music or your child's birthday party. You can record new material on a used tape by rewinding it back to a suitable point and recording over the existing material. In the process, of course, you completely destroy whatever used to be on that particular place in the tape. The same is true for data storage on your disks. Anytime you save a new file, DOS overwrites part of the existing data area with a new file. When you use UnErase to recover a file, it looks only for data that does not belong to any currently listed file.

WARNING: If you have an emergency situation and you've not yet installed the Norton Desktop, stop! Do not install the program on your hard disk. Any new files copied to your hard disk might overwrite erased files, preventing full recovery. Refer to the "Emergency Procedures" card that is included with your distribution package.

STARTING UNERASE

There are two ways to start UnErase.

To start UnErase:

- From the Norton Desktop, choose UNERASE from the Tools menu.

Or,

- Type `unerase` at the DOS prompt.

RECOVERING ERASED FILES

Recovering erased files is a straightforward and usually automatic procedure. The following procedures show you how to recover erased files in a variety of different situations.

To recover an erased file when you know its filename and directory:

1   Choose UNERASE from the Tools menu.

    The name, size, date, time and status of each erased file are displayed in a list box (Figure 16-1).

2   If the file to be recovered was on a different drive, choose CHANGE DRIVE from the File menu.

    A list box is displayed with all available drives from which to choose.

3   If the file to be recovered was in a different directory, choose CHANGE DIRECTORY from the File menu.

    A directory tree is displayed. Select the desired directory or use Speed Search (just start typing the directory name).

4   When the proper drive and directory are selected, highlight the file to be recovered in the list box.

5   Select the UnErase button located in the lower-right corner of the screen.

    You are prompted to enter a new first letter for the filename.

    If the file was protected with Erase Protect, the first letter of the filename is preserved. In this case, the file is recovered and UnErase is done.

6   Type a new first letter for the filename.

    After you enter the first letter of the filename, UnErase automatically recovers the erased file. The prognosis in the right column of the list of erased files changes to RECOVERED.

Using UnErase   **16-5**

DOS overwrites the first letter of the filename when it erases a file. The first letter that you enter does not need to be the original letter; any letter will do as long as the renamed file does not have the same name as another existing file. You can rename the file later.

Figure 16-1

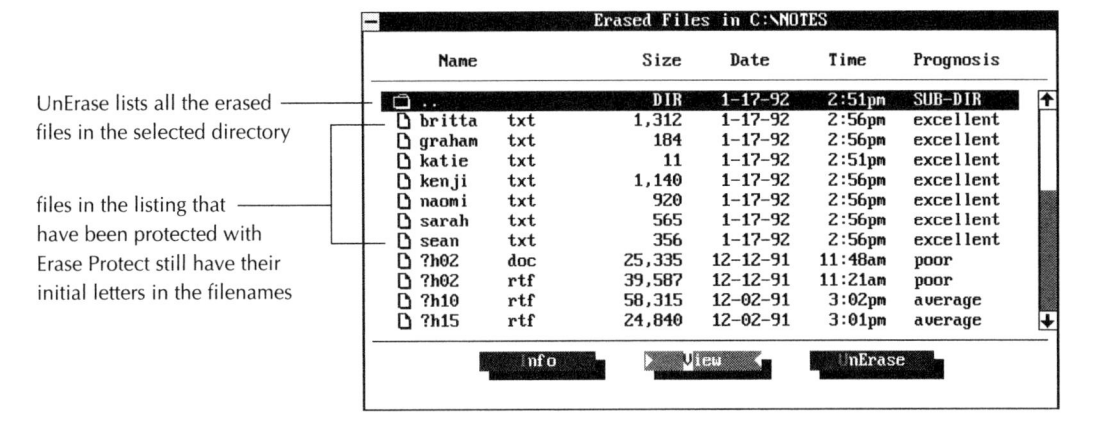

UnErase lists all the erased files in the selected directory

files in the listing that have been protected with Erase Protect still have their initial letters in the filenames

Name		Size	Date	Time	Prognosis
..		DIR	1-17-92	2:51pm	SUB-DIR
britta	txt	1,312	1-17-92	2:56pm	excellent
graham	txt	184	1-17-92	2:56pm	excellent
katie	txt	11	1-17-92	2:51pm	excellent
kenji	txt	1,140	1-17-92	2:56pm	excellent
naomi	txt	920	1-17-92	2:56pm	excellent
sarah	txt	565	1-17-92	2:56pm	excellent
sean	txt	356	1-17-92	2:56pm	excellent
?h02	doc	25,335	12-12-91	11:48am	poor
?h02	rtf	39,587	12-12-91	11:21am	poor
?h10	rtf	58,315	12-02-91	3:02pm	average
?h15	rtf	24,840	12-02-91	3:01pm	average

Info   View   UnErase

To recover an erased file when you don't know its directory:

1   Choose UNERASE from the Tools Menu.

2   Choose VIEW ALL DIRECTORIES from the File menu.

    All erased files on the drive are listed.

3   In the list box, highlight the file to be recovered.

4   Select the UnErase button located in the lower-right corner of the screen.

5   Type the first letter of the filename when prompted.

NOTE: To list "erase-protected" files in deleted directories, you must use the VIEW ALL DIRECTORIES command on the File menu, not the LOST NAMES command on the Search menu (used when the original directory has been deleted and cannot be recovered).

To recover more than one or all the erased files in a directory:

1   Choose UNERASE from the Tools menu.

2   Select individual files by pressing the Spacebar to tag desired files or clicking them with the mouse.

    Or,

    Choose SELECT GROUP from the File menu (Gray +) to enter a DOS wildcard specification (*.* means all files).

3   Select the UnErase button below the list of erased files.

4   Check the "prompt for missing 1st letter" check box if you want to enter the first character for each filename. Alternatively, UnErase will generate an unambiguous first letter automatically.

5   Select the UnErase button in the "prompt for missing 1st letter" dialog box.

CAUTION: Always check any files you've recovered with the application that created them before depending on the files. You may not be able to recover all of the files displayed, because recovering one file can sometimes interfere with the chances of recovering others.

TIP: If you are recovering more than one file, recover the smaller files first and the larger files last.

To recover an erased file when you know the filename, but its directory has been removed:

1   Find the name of the removed directory in the erased files list box and recover the directory using the same steps outlined in the previous examples by highlighting it in the list and selecting the UnErase button. (A directory is actually a special kind of DOS file.)

2   Recover the file or files from the newly restored directory.

To recover an erased file when the directory cannot be recovered:

1. Choose SEARCH FOR LOST NAMES from the Search menu.

   A list of erased files is displayed.

2. In the list box, highlight the desired file to recover.

3. Select the UnErase button.

   The recovered file is placed in the current directory (since the original directory no longer exists).

NOTE: Just as the data area of an erased file may be overwritten by a new file, DOS may overwrite the directory entry of an erased file with a new file entry. This may prevent full or complete recovery.

To recover an erased file when you don't remember the filename:

The Search menu has two other tools to locate erased files:

- SEARCH FOR TEXT from the Search menu lets you enter a piece of distinctive text from the file. (Optionally, check Ignore Case so that capitalization is ignored.)
- SEARCH FOR DATA TYPES from the Search menu lets you narrow the search to text, Lotus or dBASE files.

MANUAL UNERASE

If all the automatic methods for recovering an erased file are unsuccessful, usually due to file fragmentation and partial overwriting of the erased file's space, you can still try to recover the file.

CAUTION: Manual UnErase is a tool for experts and its use is not recommended unless you know what you are doing.

Use Manual UnErase only when:

- You've tried UnErase and it was unsuccessful.
- You're recovering text and you see that all clusters are not in the right order on the screen.

- You know exactly where a file is located. Manual UnErase lets you choose the clusters you want in the file.

Try the automatic method before manually recovering your files. If automatic recovery is unsuccessful, the following procedure may help recover erased files.

To manually recover an erased file:

1 Select the erased file from the erased files list box (Figure 16-1).

2 Choose MANUAL UNERASE... from the File menu.

3 Insert the first character of the erased filename in the dialog box.

After the filename is entered, you can start with the Add Clusters option (which is already highlighted), and use the found clusters as a base you can add to and subtract from. Pressing the Add Clusters button opens the Add Clusters dialog box, (Figure 16-2).

Figure 16-2

the Add Clusters dialog box lets you manually UnErase a file by adding and deleting file clusters

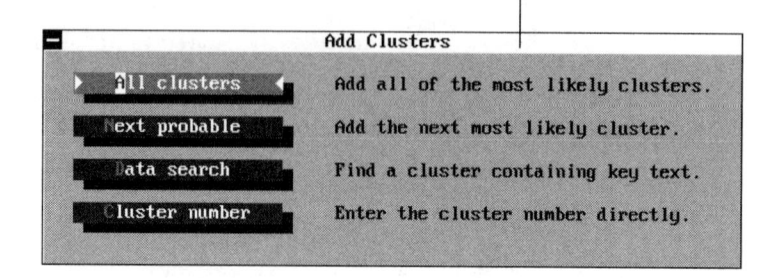

```
┌─ Add Clusters ─────────────────────────────────────┐
│  ▶ All clusters ◀    Add all of the most likely clusters. │
│    Next probable     Add the next most likely cluster.    │
│    Data search       Find a cluster containing key text.  │
│    Cluster number    Enter the cluster number directly.   │
└────────────────────────────────────────────────────┘
```

To add all clusters:

- Select All Clusters.

  This allows you to "tweak" the file by adding and deleting clusters until the file is correct.

To delete a cluster:

1. Position the highlight over the cluster number in the Added Clusters list box.
2. Press Del to remove the cluster.

To add the next probable cluster:

- You can also add clusters one at a time. Select the Next probable button from the Add Cluster... menu.

What if you find all the right pieces (say, all your paragraphs in your letter), but they're in the wrong order?

To change the order of the clusters:

1. Select a cluster in the Added Clusters list box by pressing the Spacebar.
2. Use UpArrow and DownArrow to move the selected cluster to a new location. Press Enter to drop the cluster in the new location.

To search for specific text:

1. Choose the Data Search option.
2. Enter the text in the Data Search text box and select the Find button.

Searches are case-sensitive unless you select the Ignore case check box.

NOTE: A Data search can be quite time-consuming when searching an entire disk or large directory.

Sometimes, you know the physical location of the file (cluster numbers).

To enter the starting and ending cluster numbers of the file:

1. Choose Cluster Number.
2. Insert the starting and ending cluster numbers in the Cluster Number dialog box.

    If the cluster range contains no free clusters, an alert box appears.

NOTE: UnErase will let you add only free, unallocated clusters.

When you save the erased file, the selected clusters are written to the file and you automatically return to the UnErase screen.

To save your work:

- Choose Save.

    If you've selected more data than the erased file originally held and you try to save the file, Manual UnErase asks you to Save Anyway or Resume the procedure.

If you decide to select a new directory or search for another file, you can leave Manual UnErase without saving the file by selecting Cancel. You will be asked if you want to abandon your "work in progress."

UNERASE AND DOS 5.0

UnErase fully supports DOS 5.0's Mirror and Delete Tracking features. Mirror fulfills the same functions as the Norton Image program, saving a copy of the bookkeeping information for the disk. UnErase checks for Image and Mirror data, and if both are found, uses the most recent information.

The DOS 5.0 Mirror program also has a memory-resident module called Delete Tracking, which must be installed prior to use. Delete Tracking fulfills many of the same functions as the Norton Erase Protect program. However, while Erase Protect guarantees a 100-percent recovery, Delete Tracking cannot. Delete Tracking does not protect an erased file's data, nor does it remove old and obsolete entries from its data file. This makes Delete Tracking much less reliable than Erase Protect. Also, Delete Tracking does not work on a network.

Delete Tracking files look very much like Erase Protect files. If Delete Tracking is being used, the files will have their first letters supplied, but their prognosis for recovery can vary based on the current status of the disk.

Using Speed Disk

This chapter explains how to use Speed Disk—a program that speeds up data retrieval by reorganizing the physical layout of all files and directories on your disk.

Contents

How Speed Disk Works	17-4
Before You Use Speed Disk	17-5
Memory-Resident Programs	17-5
Copy-Protected Files	17-5
Using Speed Disk	17-6
Generating Reports	17-7
Comparing Speed Disk to CHKDSK	17-8
Using the Walk Map	17-9
Customizing Speed Disk	17-10
Choosing an Optimization Method	17-10
Configuring Speed Disk	17-11

When you use your computer, there are a lot of things going on behind the scenes. This is especially true of the way your computer stores files on disk. As you work with more and more files—creating, copying, and erasing or deleting them—those files get stored in "bits and pieces" called *clusters* all over your hard disk. Over time, this slows down your work because the computer takes longer and longer to find those pieces.

Speed Disk reorganizes the physical layout of all files and directories on a disk so as to minimize movement of the read-write head of the disk drive. This allows your computer to read data from the disk much faster.

First, Speed Disk consolidates all of the unused data space on your disk and places it at the end of the disk (that is, at the inner tracks of the disk, which are usually farthest from the read-write head); second, it defragments your files by consolidating the pieces that make up the files.

When you start Speed Disk, it analyzes your disk and recommends an optimization method to maximize system performance, including No Optimization Necessary if that is appropriate. The methods are described in the section "Choosing an Optimization Method" later in this chapter.

You can also generate a report indicating the percent of a disk, subdirectory or file that is fragmented. The report can help you decide how often to run Speed Disk.

Use Speed Disk when you:

- Suspect that your applications are taking more time than they used to when reading and writing files.
- Frequently edit and save large files (this increases the likelihood of file fragmentation).
- Want to see a map of the space utilization on your hard disk and find out the extent of file fragmentation.

NOTE: Network drives are not displayed in the drive selection list box, because you cannot use Speed Disk on a network drive.

HOW SPEED DISK WORKS

When you save a file, DOS writes it to disk in physical units called *clusters*. A cluster usually contains between 2 and 8 kilobytes (usually 512 bytes for floppies), depending on the operating system version and disk size.

When you first create and save a file, DOS often, but not always, finds enough contiguous unused clusters to write the complete file. But as you add to the file and save it repeatedly over time, the next contiguous clusters might be occupied by other files created in the meantime. In that case, DOS must split the original file across non-contiguous, unused clusters. Thus, a file becomes *fragmented*. As file fragmentation increases, read-write head movement increases, and it takes longer to read and write data from the disk. Unfragmenting a file consists of putting all fragments of a file in the correct sequential order in contiguous sectors; this is done for every file on the disk.

Speed Disk can perform a number of different optimizations as it rearranges a disk. You have the option of unfragmenting only files or unfragmenting only the free space. Such options can save you time or create large blocks of unused disk space (so you can save a large file without fragmenting it, or create a Windows swap file). Various other options let you fine-tune the specific placement of directories and files for maximum performance. For example, all directories can be placed at the beginning of the disk, which speeds access time as a directory must always be accessed before a file can be accessed. All directories specified in your PATH statement can be placed before all other directories at the beginning of the disk, as these are the directories DOS searches first for programs.

NOTE: Speed Disk can optimize a disk of any size containing up to 1024 directories. The actual maximum capacity depends on available memory and number of files on the disk.

BEFORE YOU USE SPEED DISK

You need to be aware of two types of programs when working with Speed Disk: memory-resident programs (TSRs) and copy-protected programs.

Memory-Resident Programs

Because Speed Disk is physically reordering the organization of your disk, you don't want anything to disturb the procedure before it is completed. Make sure you don't have any memory-resident programs active that might access the disk while Speed Disk is running.

For example, never use Speed Disk with a fax/modem program running in the background waiting for a call. If you get an incoming call, the fax/modem program will try to write the fax data to the drive while Speed Disk is working. Not only will you lose the fax data, but you might scramble your hard drive as well.

Also, disable any scheduling TSRs. They wait to be activated so that data (their own data files or temporary files, for example) can be written at any given time. Disk caches, such as Microsoft's SMARTDrive, also wait to write in the background.

Although Speed Disk detects the presence of DOS's FASTOPEN, we recommend that you not use it—use Norton Cache instead. For more information on Norton Cache, see Chapter 29, "Using Norton Cache."

NOTE: You don't have to worry about any Peter Norton programs. They are all managed automatically by Speed Disk.

Copy-Protected Files

Certain copy-protected programs put one or more files on your hard disk that must not be relocated. These programs make note of where on the disk the files were initially installed; if the files are subsequently moved, the copy-protection scheme assumes an illegal copy has been made and won't let the program run. Most of these protection techniques set the hidden or system attribute (or both) for their immovable files; a few use other methods.

Speed Disk takes special precautions to avoid disturbing such programs. Each file on the disk is examined separately to determine if it can be safely moved.

> **CAUTION:** Because of the plethora of different IBM-compatible computers and strange copy-protection schemes, it is impossible to verify beforehand that Speed Disk is compatible with each and every combination. Therefore, *before* running Speed Disk on your machine the first time, back up your entire hard disk. After you have verified once that Speed Disk is compatible with your machine, this precaution shouldn't be necessary again (unless you add new applications).

USING SPEED DISK

Using Speed Disk is simple and almost completely automatic. Speed Disk tests your system and recommends an appropriate optimization method.

> **CAUTION:** Don't turn off or otherwise disable your machine while Speed Disk is running. This caveat applies any time your computer is writing to the disk, because turning off the power at such a time could damage files. You can safely interrupt Speed Disk before it has finished by pressing Esc. After Speed Disk has finished its work, you should reboot your system.

To optimize a disk:

1   Choose SPEED DISK from the (long) Tools menu.

    Speed Disk tests system memory to make sure that data won't be corrupted during the optimization process.

2   Select the drive you wish to optimize and then select OK.

    Speed Disk reads and analyzes the data on the selected drive. When done, a map of the disk is displayed with the Recommendation dialog box (Figure 17-1). This dialog box reports the percentage of the disk that is not fragmented and recommends an appropriate optimization method.

Using Speed Disk   **17-7**

3   Select Optimize.

    Speed Disk "animates" the disk map as it works. The Legend box in the lower-right corner explains the various symbols that appear on the disk map during the optimization process, while the Status box displays a progress report and the method of optimization that is in use.

Figure 17-1

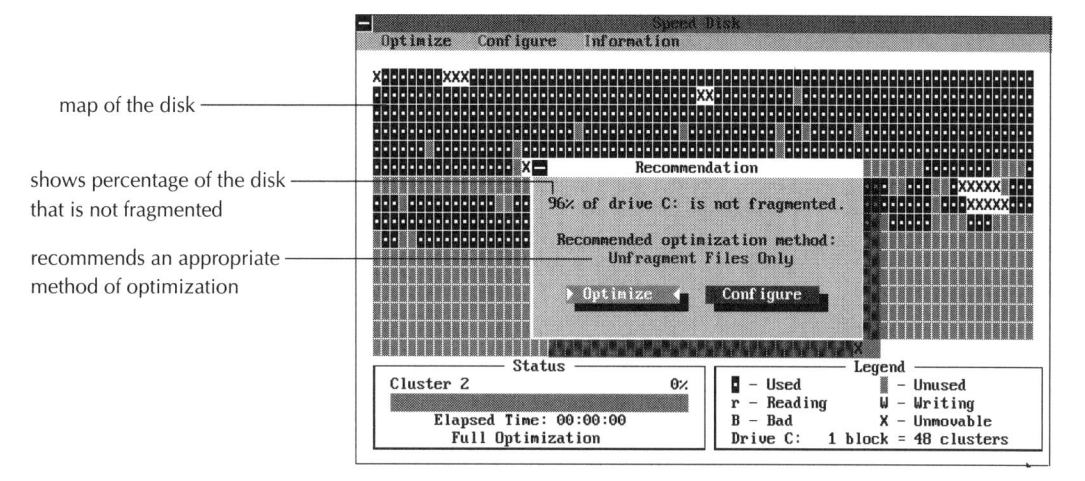

- map of the disk
- shows percentage of the disk that is not fragmented
- recommends an appropriate method of optimization

GENERATING REPORTS

Each time you run Speed Disk, it reports the percentage of the disk that contains fragmented files and recommends an optimization method (if optimization is needed). Sometimes, however, you may just want to see which files are badly fragmented and then make a decision to optimize your disk or not, based on that information.

To generate a File Fragmentation Report:

1   If you have just started Speed Disk, select Configure when an optimization method is recommended.

2   Select FRAGMENTATION REPORT... from the Speed Disk Information menu.

    The File Fragmentation Report displays two scrollable list boxes: a directory tree on the left and the directory contents on the right.

17-8 Using Norton Desktop for DOS

3 Select the desired directory from the left list box (Figure 17-2).

4 Select the name of the file about which you want information from the right list box.

If a file is fragmented, the percentage is indicated in the display. 100% means a file is completely unfragmented. The number of fragments and number of clusters are also shown. Note that subdirectories are listed as files in their parent directories (a directory is actually a special kind of DOS file).

Figure 17-2

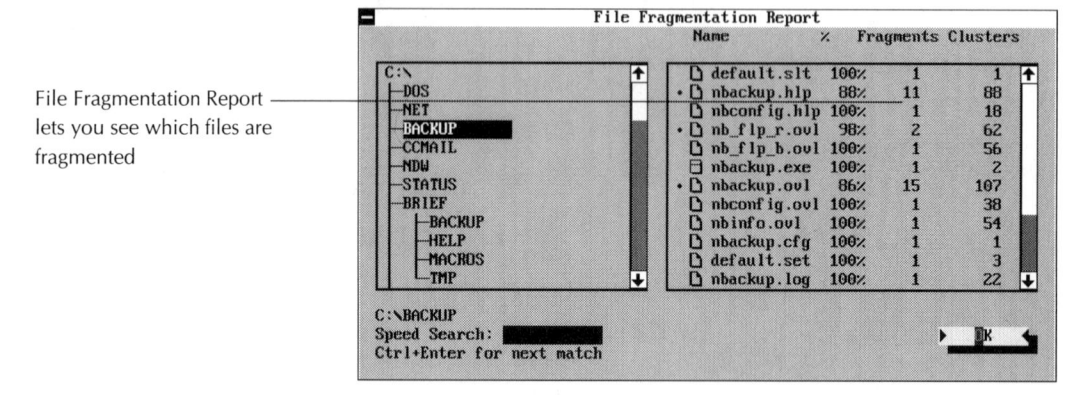

File Fragmentation Report lets you see which files are fragmented

Name	%	Fragments	Clusters
default.slt	100%	1	1
nbackup.hlp	88%	11	88
nbconfig.hlp	100%	1	18
nb_flp_r.ovl	98%	2	62
nb_flp_b.ovl	100%	1	56
nbackup.exe	100%	1	2
nbackup.ovl	86%	15	107
nbconfig.ovl	100%	1	38
nbinfo.ovl	100%	1	54
nbackup.cfg	100%	1	1
default.set	100%	1	3
nbackup.log	100%	1	22

Other information about the selected drive is available through the Information menu's DISK STATISTICS... item. Here you will find a report on the percentage of the disk used, number of files, number of clusters marked as bad, number of clusters allocated to unmovable files, and more.

To generate a Disk Statistics report:

- Choose DISK STATISTICS... from the Speed Disk Information menu.

Comparing Speed Disk to CHKDSK

The DOS CHKDSK report and Speed Disk's Disk Information do not always agree on the number of files and directories on a disk. In fact, both are correct.

- CHKDSK reports the number of hidden files and the number of user files separately. The sum of these will equal the number reported by Speed Disk.

- CHKDSK reports the number of subdirectories on a disk but does not count the root directory. Speed Disk counts the root as a directory and so always reports one more directory than CHKDSK.
- CHKDSK reports the volume label as a hidden file of 0 length. Speed Disk doesn't include the volume label as a file.

USING THE WALK MAP

The Walk Map lets you discover what files occupy any block on the disk. The legend in the lower-right corner helps you interpret the characters on the disk map. The block-to-cluster ratio varies, depending upon the size of the disk and the screen resolution.

To get information about a block:

1 Choose WALK MAP from the Information menu.
2 Use the arrow keys to move the cursor to a block on the map and press Enter.

Or,

- Double-click on a block.

    The Contents of Map Block scrollable list box appears displaying the clusters represented by one character of the disk map. Under File is the name of the file or directory which currently occupies the cluster (or the words "Not Used"). Under Status, you may see the following:

    - **Optimized:** Belongs to an unfragmented file or directory.
    - **Fragmented:** Belongs to a fragmented file or directory.
    - **Unmovable:** Belongs to a hidden or read-only file, a file in a hidden directory, or a file that you have listed as unmovable (see "Unmovable Files" later in this chapter).
    - **Bad Cluster:** Marked in the FAT as being unusable (these are never examined or moved by Speed Disk).

Press Enter or select OK to get back to the map walk and continue until you've finished your stroll.

CUSTOMIZING SPEED DISK

With Speed Disk's ability to automatically recommend and perform the most appropriate method of optimization, you may never need to make use of the options available in Speed Disk's menus. However, you may want more control over file placement on the disk or access to more information about the state of the files on your disks.

Speed Disk lets you customize the layout of files and directories on your disk to provide maximum performance for your particular work style. You can specify:

- The method of optimization.
- The order of directories and files.
- Any files that should not be moved at all (applies to some copy-protected files and some system files).
- Whether or not to verify the data that gets moved around during optimization.

NOTE: You fine-tune the way Speed Disk optimizes your disk by using both the Optimize and Configure menus.

Choosing an Optimization Method

Although Speed Disk automatically makes a recommendation for an optimization method, you may want to choose a particular method of the five different methods available. These range from a complete (but lengthy) full optimization to a quick compression that unfragments free space only.

To choose a specific optimization method:

1. Select Configure from the Speed Disk Recommendation dialog box.
2. Choose OPTIMIZATION METHOD... from the Speed Disk Optimize menu.
3. Select one of the five optimization methods:

   Full Optimization is a fast optimization that fully optimizes your disk by unfragmenting all files. This method does not concern itself with directory placement, only with defragmentation. It does not reorder directories even if you specified them, nor does it place files that go first. When full optimization is done, there are no "holes" or empty spaces between files on your disk.

Full with Directories First offers the best gains in performance. It fully optimizes your disk and moves directories to the front. It does not concern itself with actual file placement, but places files that go first in the front of the disk. It also defragments files so there are no holes in your disk structure.

Full with File Reorder is the most complete method of optimization; however, it takes the most time to run. It fully optimizes your disk, reordering files by directory, with no "holes" in your disk structure. The only real advantage this method has over the first two methods is that files associated with directories that are placed first are also placed closer to the front of the disk.

Unfragment Files Only attempts to unfragment as many files as possible. It won't necessarily fill in all the "holes" in your disk and some large files may not be unfragmented at all. You should run Speed Disk about twice a week with the Unfragment Files Only option selected.

Unfragment Free Space simply moves data forward on the disk to fill in the free space, but does not unfragment files. It is quick, but may or may not result in significant speed improvements. The advantage to this method is that any new files you add will go at the end of the disk and will be unfragmented. This method can also be used to create enough free space so Windows can make a permanent swap file.

4 Choose BEGIN OPTIMIZATION from the Optimize menu.

Configuring Speed Disk

The Configure menu of Speed Disk contains options that give you control over the specific placement of files and directories:

- Directory order
- File sort
- Files to place first
- Unmovable files

17-12   Using Norton Desktop for DOS

> **NOTE:** It's important to remember that these choices affect how fast Speed Disk works. In other words, each option you select here adds to the amount of time Speed Disk takes to run.

Directory Order

The DIRECTORY ORDER... option of the Configure menu lets you specify the sort order of directories on the disk. The "current" directory order appears in the Directory Order list box on the right side of the screen. All directories that appear in this list box are placed in front of the rest of the directories at the beginning of the disk, minimizing their access time. The default order is taken from the DOS path, usually specified in your AUTOEXEC.BAT file.

To add a directory to the Directory Order list:

1   Choose DIRECTORY ORDER... from the Speed Disk Configure menu.

   A directory tree appears in the Directory List on the left side of the screen.

2   Make sure that the Directory List is selected and then highlight the directory to add to the Directory Order.

   Or,

   You can use Speed Search to locate a directory—just start typing the directory name.

3   Select Add.

   The directory you have selected from the Directory List is added to the list in the Directory Order list box. Where the directory appears in the list depends on the last location of the selection bar in the Directory Order list box. The added directory appears immediately above the most recently selected directory.

To delete a directory from the Directory Order list:

1   Choose DIRECTORY ORDER... from the Speed Disk Configure menu.

   A directory tree appears in the Directory List on the left side of the screen.

2   Highlight a directory in the Directory Order list.

3   Select Delete. (Don't worry, you're not actually deleting a directory, just removing it from a list.)

To move a directory within the Directory Order list:

1   Choose DIRECTORY ORDER... from the Speed Disk Configure menu.

    A directory tree appears in the Directory List on the left side of the screen.

2   Highlight the directory to move from the Directory Order list.

3   Select Move. Two arrowheads at the ends of the highlight indicate the selected directory.

4   Position the selected directory in the list with UpArrow and DownArrow or with the mouse.

5   Press Enter to "drop" the directory at the desired location.

File Sort

The FILE SORT... option of the Speed Disk Configure menu allows you to select the sort criteria for files within directories. The default is "unsorted," which is the current order that appears when DOS displays directory listings.

To sort files:

1   Choose FILE SORT... from the Speed Disk Configure menu. The File Sort dialog box opens.

2   Select the order you want from the Sort Criterion choices.

    You can sort in either ascending or descending order by the following criteria:
    - name
    - file extension
    - date and time
    - file size

Files to Place First

The FILES TO PLACE FIRST... option of the Speed Disk Configure menu lets you move the files you specify to the front of the disk, where they will be accessed in the shortest amount of time.

The Files to Place First dialog box lets you add filenames or file specifications with the * and ? wildcard characters. Delete and Move work the same as they do in the other dialog boxes in the Configure menu. Insert adds an empty text box above the current location of the selection bar in the list of file specifications.

TIP: The file specifications *.EXE and *.COM are a good choice for Files to Place First. These files tend to be read frequently, but are never written.

Unmovable Files

By default, all hidden and system files are considered unmovable by Speed Disk. In addition, some copy-protection schemes depend on finding certain files in the same disk location each time the files are accessed. If you determine that you have such files, type their filenames into the scrollable list box of the Unmovable Files dialog box. You can enter up to 10 file specifications. Wildcards are allowed. (If more than 10 unmovable files are on the disk, they will not get moved even though they are not displayed in the dialog box.)

To add files to the Unmovable Files list:

1   Choose UNMOVABLE FILES... from the Speed Disk Configure menu.

    The Unmovable Files dialog box is displayed.

2   Type the file specification in the text entry box.

3   To add more file specifications, press DownArrow to display another text entry box and repeat step 2.

To delete files from the Unmovable Files list:

1   Choose UNMOVABLE FILES... from the Speed Disk Configure menu.

    The Unmovable Files dialog box is displayed.

2   Select the file specification you want to delete.

3   Select Delete.

Other Options...

OTHER OPTIONS... contains three more configuration choices.

- **Read-After-Write** is an extra safety measure. You can choose to have data read back immediately after it is written to verify that it was written correctly. Turn this option off if you want Speed Disk to work faster.

- **Clear Unused Space** is used for data security. It wipes (writes zeros in) all unused clusters of the disk after the optimization process.

- **Beep When Done** is just that. A beep sounds when the optimization is completed.

Save Options to Disk

To save your changes:

- Choose SAVE OPTIONS TO DISK from the Speed Disk Configure menu.

  The configuration changes you've made are saved for future use.

Using Norton Disk Doctor

This chapter shows you how to use Norton Disk Doctor—a preventive maintenance program that examines your disk for technical problems and gives you the option to correct them.

Contents

The Six Disk Doctor Tests	18-3
Partition Table Test	18-3
Boot Record Test	18-4
FAT Test	18-4
Directory Structure Test	18-4
File Structure Test	18-4
Lost Cluster Test	18-4
Surface Test	18-4
Using Norton Disk Doctor	18-5
A Quick Test	18-7
Configuring Norton Disk Doctor	18-7
Surface Test Options	18-8
Custom Message	18-9
Tests to Skip	18-9
Undoing Changes	18-9
Generating a Report	18-9

Norton Disk Doctor runs numerous tests to determine the health of your disk, warns you if it finds problems, and gives you the option to correct them. The tests and corrections are performed automatically, so you need not have any fear even if the way a computer works is a complete mystery to you.

For extra safety, you can even undo any changes Norton Disk Doctor has performed.

Norton Disk Doctor also examines the disk surface for physical defects and generates a report about your disk. If testing is interrupted, you can print the report on what happened so far.

Use Norton Disk Doctor to diagnose your disk for a variety of possible disk problems:

- If you have trouble accessing a disk.
- If you notice problems when you try to run applications.
- If your computer will not start and you suspect problems with the boot disk or partition (see the first "tip" below).
- If files or directories seem to be missing but were never deleted.

NOTE: Practice preventive maintenance by running Norton Disk Doctor daily. For your convenience and maximum protection, you can have the Norton Desktop installation program place the necessary command in your AUTOEXEC.BAT file so that Norton Disk Doctor runs a quick test of your hard disk every time you start your computer.

THE SIX DISK DOCTOR TESTS

Norton Disk Doctor automatically performs six general tests to discover where problems may lie (Figure 18-1).

Partition Table Test

Although a hard disk is usually configured as a single disk drive, it can be partitioned into one or more disks. The partition table shows DOS how to find the DOS drive partitions. If the data in a partition table becomes damaged in any way, DOS may not be able to access the hard disk at all.

18-4   Using Norton Desktop for DOS

Figure 18-1

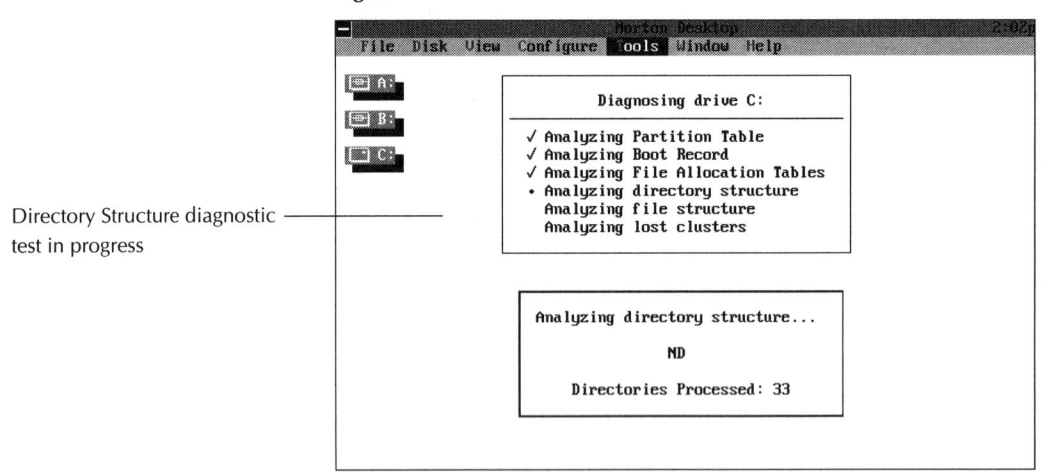

Directory Structure diagnostic test in progress

```
                            Norton Desktop                    2:02p
 File  Disk  View  Configure  Tools  Window  Help

  A:              ┌─────────────────────────────────────┐
                  │         Diagnosing drive C:         │
  B:              │                                     │
                  │  √ Analyzing Partition Table        │
  C:              │  √ Analyzing Boot Record            │
                  │  √ Analyzing File Allocation Tables │
                  │  • Analyzing directory structure    │
                  │    Analyzing file structure         │
                  │    Analyzing lost clusters          │
                  └─────────────────────────────────────┘

                  ┌─────────────────────────────────────┐
                  │    Analyzing directory structure... │
                  │                  ND                 │
                  │       Directories Processed: 33     │
                  └─────────────────────────────────────┘
```

Boot Record Test The boot record sector is a special place on a disk that tells DOS about disk characteristics such as size and other technical information. If the boot record becomes damaged, DOS may not be able to access the disk properly.

FAT Test The File Allocation Table (FAT) is like the index of a book. It enables DOS to find all the data belonging to a file. If the FAT is damaged, DOS may not be able to access one or more files properly.

Directory Structure Test The directory structure is like the table of contents for a book and enables DOS to find files on the disk. If the directory structure becomes damaged, DOS may not be able to access portions of or entire directories on the disk.

File Structure Test The File Structure Test makes sure that each file's directory entry matches its FAT entry. To extend the book analogy, the table of contents (directory structure) and the index (FAT) must find the same things.

Lost Cluster Test Files are written to disk in pieces (usually between 2K and 4K in size on a hard disk) called clusters. The Lost Cluster Test looks for clusters that contain valid data but cannot be linked up with any known file.

Surface Test The Surface Test checks for physical defects on the disk.

Using Norton Disk Doctor **18-5**

> **TIP:** If you use the Surface Test on a regular basis and notice the same problems occurring, your disk could be developing major problems. Be sure to make frequent backups. See Chapter 19, "Using Norton Backup," for more information about backups.

USING NORTON DISK DOCTOR

To start Norton Disk Doctor:

- Choose NORTON DISK DOCTOR from the Tools menu.

To diagnose a disk:

1. Select Diagnose Disk from the Norton Disk Doctor main dialog box.

    Norton Disk Doctor analyzes the partition table of your hard disk and then presents a list box of available drives.

2. Select the drive to diagnose.

    You can select more than one drive by pressing the Spacebar for each desired drive.

3. Select Diagnose to begin the suite of tests.

    If any errors are encountered, don't panic. Norton Disk Doctor displays a screen explaining the problem and asks for your permission to correct it (Figure 18-2). Simply follow the screen prompts to fix them.

    Before making any changes, Norton Disk Doctor will ask if you want to create an UnDo file—just in case the changes made were not exactly what you expected. Have a floppy disk handy for the UnDo file and follow the screen prompts.

4. Next, perform the Surface Test to test the disk surface for physical defects. This step is optional, but should be run weekly. Accept the default settings when the Surface Test options screen is displayed and select Begin Test (see Configuring Disk Doctor below).

    The Norton Disk Doctor screen shows the progress of the surface test (Figure 18-3).

Figure 18-2

Norton Disk Doctor error screen reporting lost clusters found

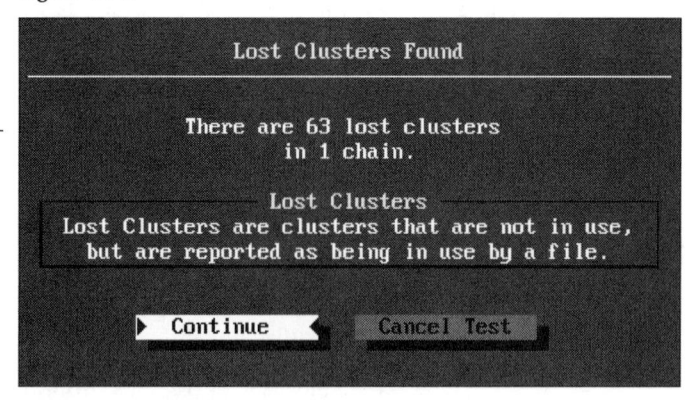

```
┌─────────── Lost Clusters Found ───────────┐
│                                           │
│       There are 63 lost clusters          │
│              in 1 chain.                  │
│                                           │
│   ┌──────────── Lost Clusters ──────────┐ │
│   │ Lost Clusters are clusters that are │ │
│   │ not in use, but are reported as     │ │
│   │ being in use by a file.             │ │
│   └─────────────────────────────────────┘ │
│                                           │
│      ▶ Continue ◀      Cancel Test        │
└───────────────────────────────────────────┘
```

Figure 18-3

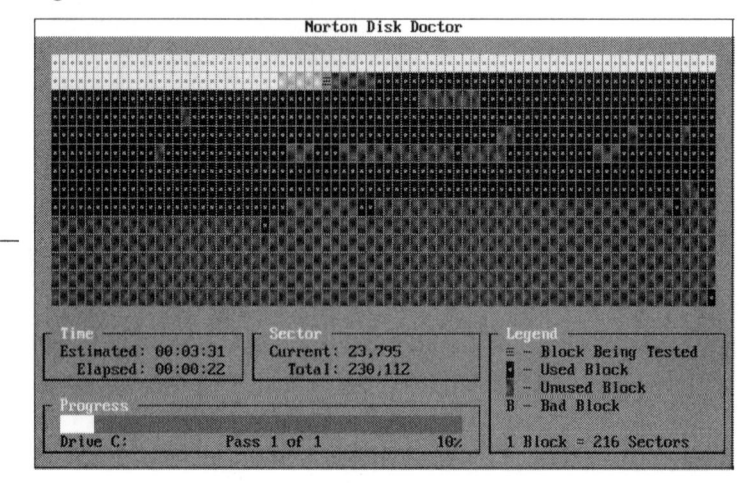

Norton Disk Doctor performing a surface test

```
┌──────────────── Norton Disk Doctor ────────────────┐
│                                                    │
│              [surface test grid display]           │
│                                                    │
│ ┌─Time──────────┐ ┌─Sector────────┐ ┌─Legend─────┐ │
│ │Estimated:     │ │Current: 23,795│ │▓ = Block   │ │
│ │     00:03:31  │ │Total: 230,112 │ │   Being    │ │
│ │Elapsed:       │ │               │ │   Tested   │ │
│ │     00:00:22  │ │               │ │▓ = Used    │ │
│ └───────────────┘ └───────────────┘ │   Block    │ │
│ ┌─Progress────────────────────────┐ │  = Unused  │ │
│ │███░░░░░░░░░░░░░░░░░░░░░░░░░░░░░ │ │   Block    │ │
│ │Drive C:   Pass 1 of 1      10%  │ │B = Bad Blk │ │
│ └─────────────────────────────────┘ │1 Block =   │ │
│                                     │ 216 Sectors│ │
│                                     └────────────┘ │
└────────────────────────────────────────────────────┘
```

5   When the testing is completed, a brief summary screen shows the results of all tests. Select Report to generate and display a report of the test results, which may be printed. This step is optional but highly recommended as it is the only record of what occurred during diagnosis.

> **TIP:** Keep a DOS boot disk with Norton Disk Doctor on it (the program is called NDD.EXE and is located in your Norton Desktop directory). If ever you can't boot from your hard disk, you'll be able to boot from the floppy disk and run Norton Disk Doctor.

> **TIP:** If you're having problems with a floppy diskette, run Norton Disk Doctor. You may be able to save hours of work by reclaiming files from disks that have small, bad areas–especially if you don't have backups.

To perform only the surface test:

1 Select Surface Test from the Norton Disk Doctor main dialog box.

   See "Surface Test Options" later in this chapter for information on the Surface Test configuration.

2 Select the drive to test.

3 Select OK.

   Norton Disk Doctor skips the six general tests and only performs the Surface Test on the selected drive or drives.

A Quick Test

You may wish to perform a quick test of your disk without using the Norton Desktop menus. A special command-line switch is provided to do just that. All the tests except the Surface Test are performed.

To perform a quick test:

- Choose RUN... from the (long) File menu and type `ndd /quick`, or type `ndd /quick` in the DOS command text box.

- If you have more than one drive, for example, C: and D:, type `ndd c: d: /quick`

   You can place this command in your AUTOEXEC.BAT file so that a quick test is executed whenever you start your computer.

CONFIGURING NORTON DISK DOCTOR

Norton Disk Doctor can be configured to reflect your work needs and preferences.

To configure Norton Disk Doctor:

- Select Options from the Norton Disk Doctor main dialog box.

   The Norton Disk Doctor options are described in the following sections.

Surface Test Options

the Surface Test dialog box lets you determine the type of test Norton Disk Doctor performs

Surface Test has the following four options (Figure 18-4):

Figure 18-4

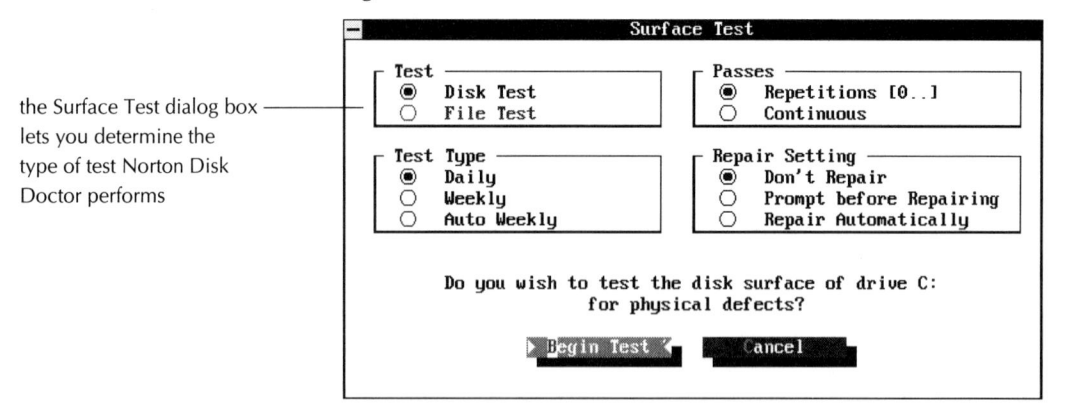

```
┌─ Surface Test ─────────────────────────────────────┐
│  ┌─ Test ─────────────┐  ┌─ Passes ─────────────┐  │
│  │  ● Disk Test       │  │  ● Repetitions [0..] │  │
│  │  ○ File Test       │  │  ○ Continuous        │  │
│  └────────────────────┘  └──────────────────────┘  │
│  ┌─ Test Type ────────┐  ┌─ Repair Setting ─────┐  │
│  │  ● Daily           │  │  ● Don't Repair      │  │
│  │  ○ Weekly          │  │  ○ Prompt before Repairing │
│  │  ○ Auto Weekly     │  │  ○ Repair Automatically │
│  └────────────────────┘  └──────────────────────┘  │
│                                                    │
│        Do you wish to test the disk surface of drive C: │
│                   for physical defects?            │
│                                                    │
│              ▶ Begin Test ◀      Cancel            │
└────────────────────────────────────────────────────┘
```

Test

If you select Disk Test, Norton Disk Doctor tests every section of the disk, searching for bad areas. Selecting this option slows down the diagnosis, but a thorough check is made of your entire disk. File Test is faster; however, it tests only the area currently used by existing files and does not test unused space.

Passes

Select the number of passes Norton Disk Doctor should make over the disk by entering any value up to 999. Testing the disk once is usually sufficient; however, some errors don't show up the first time. Select Continuous to test a disk for hard-to-find or intermittent defects over an extended period of time (for example, overnight). Pressing the Esc key allows you to interrupt the testing.

Test Type

The Daily test type is a quick scan of the disk. The Weekly test type is a full test that requires twice the time but catches harder-to-detect errors. Auto Weekly is the Weekly test type if the day of week is a Friday, and the Daily test type on all other days. Note that if the Weekly test type is selected, a full test is performed regardless of the day.

Repair Setting

Don't Repair diagnoses the disk but doesn't fix any errors encountered.

Prompt before Repairing reports the file in which the error was found and asks if you want to repair the file. If you respond Yes, Norton Disk Doctor moves the bad data to a new, reliable location and marks the bad area so that DOS won't use it for data storage. Repair Automatically repairs the disk without stopping to prompt you.

Always check repaired files before relying on them.

Custom Message

You can use this option if you are configuring Norton Disk Doctor for other users and want them to call you when a problem arises. You can specify a message to display (such as "Call for Philip") if any errors are encountered—but the user can't proceed and is returned to the main menu.

> **NOTE:** Your system administrator may set a custom message when configuring your system.

Tests to Skip

With this option, you can select the tests that you would like Norton Disk Doctor to skip if you have a nonstandard disk system. For example, you might skip the partition tests if you're using security software that encodes partition tables. You can also skip partition testing if you're using non-standard partition software.

UNDOING CHANGES

Norton Disk Doctor saves disk changes in a file called NDDUNDO.DAT. This file is located in the root directory of the drive you select. To undo disk changes that were made the last time you ran Norton Disk Doctor, select the Undo Changes button on the main screen and select the letter of the drive containing the UnDo file. Norton Disk Doctor searches for the NDDUNDO.DAT file and returns the disk to its original condition.

GENERATING A REPORT

After the tests are completed, Norton Disk Doctor displays a summary screen (Figure 18-5). The test results are defined as follows:

Ok	No problems were found
Fixed	The problems found were fixed
Skipped	The test was skipped
Not Fixed	Problems were detected but not corrected
Cancelled	The test was cancelled

18-10 *Using Norton Desktop for DOS*

Figure 18-5

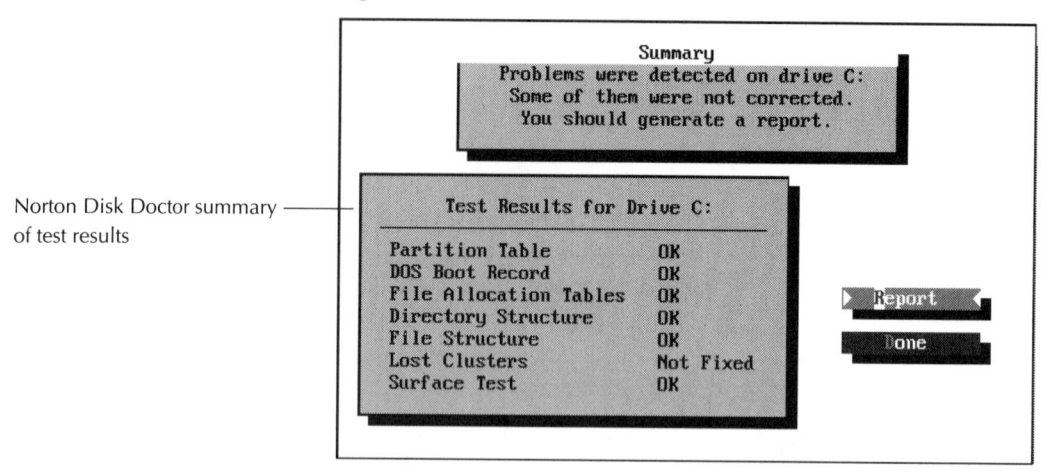

Norton Disk Doctor summary of test results

```
                    Summary
         Problems were detected on drive C:
          Some of them were not corrected.
             You should generate a report.


         Test Results for Drive C:

         Partition Table            OK
         DOS Boot Record            OK
         File Allocation Tables     OK         Report
         Directory Structure        OK
         File Structure             OK         Done
         Lost Clusters              Not Fixed
         Surface Test               OK
```

To generate a report:

- Select REPORT from the Summary Screen.

    Norton Disk Doctor lets you scroll through the report on the screen. You may also print the report or save it to a file.

To save the report as a file:

- Select Save As....

    Enter a filename for the report in the text box (for example, `A:NDD.RPT`).

CAUTION: If any errors were found, you should save the report to a disk other than the one you're testing so that you do not write to a damaged disk.

Using Norton Backup

This chapter introduces Norton Backup for DOS. It contains a Quick Start so you can perform a backup right away, if you prefer. For complete information on Norton Backup, see *Using the Norton Backup for DOS*.

Contents

Quick Start 19-3
    Performing a Backup 19-3
    Backup Assistant 19-4
    The Next Step 19-5

QUICK START

Norton Backup is a complete backup system that provides you with many powerful and easy-to-use tools for protecting your data.

Before reading this chapter, you should first complete the installation procedure.

If you need more information about navigation or using dialog boxes, see Chapter 1, "Getting Started" in *Using the Norton Backup for DOS*.

This section describes how to perform a backup using Norton Backup. It assumes that you have installed and configured Norton Backup, have completed the compatibility tests, and are working at advanced or basic program level.

NOTE: If you have not completed the installation and configuration procedures, you'll see a message directing you to do so when you start Norton Backup. See the *Norton Backup Installation Guide* for complete details.

Performing a Backup

Follow this procedure to perform a full backup of your computer's first hard drive to diskettes. For example, if your computer has drives C:, D:, and E:, this procedure backs up all files on the C: drive.

TIP: You can also use SuperFind to select or deselect files before you launch Norton Backup. And if you can't remember what a file contains, you can use Norton Viewer to preview its contents before you include it in the backup. For more information, see Chapter 5, "Finding Files with SuperFind." For more information about Norton Viewer, see Chapter 7, "Viewing Files."

Before you begin the backup, gather enough labels and diskettes or tapes to hold your backup set. To determine the maximum number of diskettes you will need, look at the Backup dialog box.

To perform a backup:

1. Choose NORTON BACKUP from the Norton Desktop Tools menu.
2. Select Backup.

   The Backup dialog box appears.

   For this backup, Backup To is set to your A: drive.
3. To change the backup destination, choose the Backup To button. Select the medium of your choice and choose OK.
4. Choose Start Backup.
5. Follow the prompts to insert a diskette or tape that appear in the Backup Progress screen.

   Make sure to label and number each diskette of the backup set as you go along or to label the backup tape when you are done.
6. Choose OK in the alert box that appears when the backup is complete.

Backup Assistant

During installation, an alert box asks whether you want to use the Backup Assistant. If you choose OK, Norton Backup schedules automatic backups for you.

> **NOTE:** As explained during installation, you must reboot after completing the installation in order for scheduled backups to run.

At 4:00 P.M. on the day Norton Backup is installed, the Backup Assistant will perform a full backup of your first hard drive, usually C:, to diskettes. Every Friday thereafter, it will perform a full backup at 4:00 P.M. On Monday through Thursday, it will perform an incremental backup at 4:00 P.M.

Before 4:00 P.M. on the day you install Norton Backup, gather enough diskettes and labels to store your backup set. Your computer must be turned on. At 4:00 P.M., a Reminder dialog box asks if you want to start the backup, postpone it, or cancel it. If you choose to start it, your application is saved in its current state and the backup starts.

You'll see a series of Norton Backup screens, and the Backup Progress screen appears. Follow the prompts that appear on the screen. As the backup proceeds, it prompts you to change diskettes in the drive. When the backup is completed, Norton Backup quits and returns you to the application in which you were working before the reminder appeared.

The Next Step　　Now that you have some background information and have performed your first backup, you may be interested in learning more about concepts and terminology used by Norton Backup. See *Using the Norton Backup for DOS* for the information you need to use Norton Backup's tools to create a sound backup routine.

Using Norton AntiVirus

When you installed Norton Desktop for DOS, you scanned your hard disk for viruses using the Virus Clinic feature. As another part of the installation you decided if you wanted to install Virus Intercept to continually monitor for viruses. This chapter explains how to use Norton AntiVirus to most effectively protect your valuable data from being damaged by computer viruses.

Contents

What Is a Virus? 20-3
Norton AntiVirus at a Glance 20-4
    About Virus Intercept 20-5
    About Virus Clinic 20-5
Loading Virus Intercept 20-5
    Versions of Virus Intercept 20-7
Responding to Virus Intercept Messages 20-8
    Virus Infection Alert Box 20-8
    Boot-sector Alert Box 20-9
    Reinoculating Files 20-10
How Virus Intercept Protects Itself 20-11
How Virus Intercept Works with Other Applications 20-11
    Copying Floppy Disks and Files 20-12
    File-compression Programs 20-12
    Communications Programs 20-12
    Backup Programs 20-13

DOS Format 20-13
Other Types of Programs 20-13
Using Virus Clinic 20-14
Scanning Memory 20-14
Scanning and Inoculating Drives, Directories
   and Files 20-15
Working with Scan Results 20-17
Canceling a Scan 20-18
Understanding Scan Messages 20-18
Repairing Infected Files 20-20
Exiting Virus Clinic 20-28
Working with Virus Definitions 20-28
Viewing and Printing Virus Definitions 20-28
Updating Virus Definitions 20-30
Configuring Virus Clinic 20-36
Setting Global Options 20-37
Setting Passwords 20-39
Configuring Virus Intercept 20-41
Enabling and Disabling Virus Intercept
   Command Buttons 20-41
Controlling Alert Boxes 20-42
Logging Intercept Messages 20-42
Network Scanning 20-44
Setting the Inoculation Directory 20-44

WHAT IS A VIRUS?

In a human being, a virus is an infectious disease that spreads by contact with an infected person or touching a contaminated surface. In a computer, a virus is a mischievous program that is spread from one computer to another either by copying an infected file to a hard disk, or by having an infected file transmitted to a computer through a network or over a modem line.

Some viruses do annoying but relatively harmless things, such as displaying unwanted messages on your screen or slowing down your computer's performance. Some viruses do destructive things such as deleting files or reformatting your hard disk.

Viruses attack executable files, also known as program files, including overlay files, drivers, binary files and system files. Data files are generally safe from infection, but they can be damaged by the effects of viruses.

A virus can only become active if you run an infected file or boot your computer from a disk infected with a boot-sector virus. Running an infected program can cause the virus to spread to the computer's memory, to other programs, or to its system files.

To protect your system from viruses, observe the following rules:

- Avoid using pirated copies of programs. Buy legal copies of all software applications that you use, make working back-up copies and write-protect them. If a virus should attack your system, you will be able to delete the infected file and replace it with an uninfected copy.
- Use Norton AntiVirus to scan your hard disk and inoculate all of your files before you have any problems.
- Scan all files that you download from bulletin boards for viruses before using them.
- If your computer is attached to a large network of computers or has multiple users, enable Virus Intercept to guard your system against infected files.

NORTON ANTIVIRUS AT A GLANCE

Norton AntiVirus helps to protect your files in three ways:

- By scanning disks to search for specifically identifiable viruses
- By automatically scanning program files as they are loaded and copied
- By inoculating files in order to detect infections by new, previously unknown viruses (with "Scan for Unknown Viruses" enabled)

Scanning your disk with Norton AntiVirus reveals the presence of all known viruses. How you deal with viruses depends on the types of viruses they are. Viruses fall into the following groups:

- System area viruses

   System area viruses infect by copying themselves to areas on your hard drive and floppies that are usually hidden and not accessed by users, such as the boot sector and partition table.

- File-infecting viruses

   File-infecting viruses parasitically attach themselves to the files that you execute (those that actually contain program instructions). This way they ensure that they are run along with the program.

Norton AntiVirus can remove many viruses from your files, but some viruses cause irreparable harm to the files they infect. In such cases, your only option is to replace the infected file with a clean copy from a backup or from the original program disk.

You may need a Rescue Disk to recover from a virus in the partition table or the boot sector. See Chapter 28, "Using Disk Tools," for instructions on creating a Rescue Disk.

In the event that a virus is discovered in memory, you also need a bootable system disk with the same version of DOS as on your hard disk to recover from system file infectors and to restart your system. If you need to create a bootable disk, you can use the MAKE BOOTABLE DISK... command from the Norton Desktop (long) Disk menu. This must be done on a machine that is free of viruses. If you don't have the same DOS version on a bootable disk, you should make one now and write protect it.

Norton AntiVirus has two parts: Virus Clinic and Virus Intercept.

About Virus Intercept

Virus Intercept is a program that can be loaded into memory automatically every time your computer starts up. It works like a sentry in the background, alerting you when it detects an infected file or suspects that a virus is present. For example, if you attempt to run an infected file, Virus Intercept detects the virus, halts all program activity and a Virus Intercept alert box appears on the screen informing you that the virus was detected. You then decide if you want to go ahead and run the program and risk spreading the infection, or prevent the program from loading. See *Installing Norton Desktop for DOS* for information on activating Virus Intercept and the sections on Virus Intercept in this chapter for more information.

About Virus Clinic

Virus Clinic is used to scan for viruses, delete infected files or attempt to repair files. If a virus is discovered in Virus Clinic, you will see a message in the scan results dialog box telling you the name of the virus. Files that have changed since the last time they were *inoculated* will show up as possibly having an *unknown virus*. (This occurs only if Detect Unknown Viruses is enabled.) See "Scanning and Inoculating Drives, Directories and Files" in this chapter to learn more about unknown viruses and how to deal with unknown viruses discovered by Virus Clinic.

LOADING VIRUS INTERCEPT

For continuous protection of your files, Virus Intercept must be loaded into the computer's memory before any other application whenever your configuration allows. There are several reasons why you might not load it first, such as when installing a high-memory manager or if you are using disk-compression software. If you let the install program modify your CONFIG.SYS file, Virus Intercept will load into memory each time you boot your computer, whether you turn it on from the power switch (a "cold boot") or you press Ctrl+Alt+Delete (a "warm boot").

You can tell whether Virus Intercept has loaded by watching for a message similar to that shown in Figure 20-1.

Figure 20-1

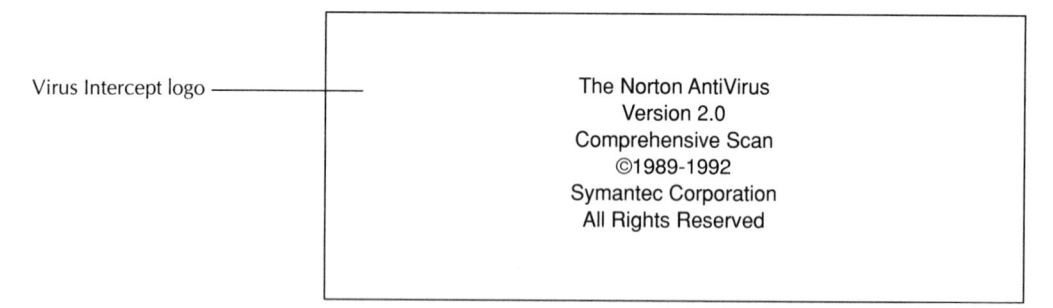

Virus Intercept logo ─────

The Norton AntiVirus
Version 2.0
Comprehensive Scan
©1989-1992
Symantec Corporation
All Rights Reserved

TIP: To stop Virus Intercept from loading when you start your computer, wait for the beep from the BIOS startup that you normally hear when you start your computer. Then immediately press and hold both Shift keys until the message "Norton AntiVirus Not Loaded" appears.

As you use your computer, Virus Intercept scans for viruses when you do any of the following:

- Launch an application or an inoculated file.
- Copy or move files (provided you have the version of Norton AntiVirus called NAV_.SYS loaded). See "How Virus Intercept Works with Other Applications" in this chapter for more information.
- Start or restart your computer either with the power button or by pressing Ctrl+Alt+Delete.

Virus Intercept also scans files to determine if they are inoculated. If a file has already been inoculated—that is, if Norton AntiVirus has assigned data used to verify file integrity—Virus Intercept verifies the inoculation data to see whether it has changed. If you want, Virus Intercept can also tell you whether a file has not been inoculated, but only when you have configured Virus Clinic's settings to inoculate files.

Versions of Virus Intercept

There are three variations of Virus Intercept. You can choose a version based on the amount of available memory your computer has. Norton Desktop's configuration program lets you select the variation you want when you install Virus Intercept. Each version has different scanning capabilities.

Table 20-1

Virus Intercept	Memory Required	Scanning Capabilities
NAV_.SYS	Approximately 38K	Comprehensive. Scans when you launch an application or copy a file, and can detect boot-sector and partition-table viruses.
NAV&.SYS/B	Approximately 4K	Scans when you launch applications and can detect boot-sector viruses on diskettes (in any drive).
NAV&.SYS	Approximately 1K	Scans only when you launch applications.

Virus Intercept version variations

If you decide to add Virus Intercept protection at a later time to your CONFIG.SYS file, you can use the editor that comes with Norton Desktop. Refer to Chapter 4 for information about editing files in the Norton Desktop Editor. Then, add a line like this:

    DEVICE=C:\IND\NAV_.SYS

If you want Virus Intercept to load before any other program, make it the first device statement and load it into high memory with a line like this:

    DEVICEHIGH=C:\IND\NAV_.SYS

20-8 Using Norton Desktop for DOS

> **NOTE:** When Virus Intercept loads, virus definitions are read into memory where they protect your files from viruses. If you add or delete a virus definition and NAV_.SYS is loaded, the changes to the virus definitions take effect only after you restart your computer. If NAV&.SYS or NAV&.SYS/B is loaded, the virus definitions are effective immediately. For details, see the section "Working with Virus Definitions" later in this chapter.

RESPONDING TO VIRUS INTERCEPT MESSAGES

If Virus Intercept detects a virus, it lets you know. Virus Intercept can display an alert box on the screen, play an alarm sound or combine both the alert box and the alarm. You can choose the method you prefer by configuring the options in the Intercept dialog box. See the section "Setting Global Options" for details.

This section discusses the alert boxes that may appear on your screen. Note that Virus Intercept merely detects a problem. If you decide to act on the information, you must use Virus Clinic to repair the infected file.

Virus Infection Alert Box

If the pop-up alert box is enabled, Virus Intercept displays an alert box (Figure 20-2) when it detects a virus. This alert box shows the name of the infected file and the name of the virus in the file.

Figure 20-2

```
                      Virus Intercept Alert!

virus infection alert box ──── WARNING! You MUST respond now! The file:
appears when Virus Intercept   C:\DOS\FORMAT.EXE
detects a known virus          contains a strain of the "Dark Avenger" virus.



        [Proceed] will NOT infect                    [STOP] file access
```

The virus infection alert box gives you two options: Proceed or Stop. If an unknown virus is detected, you also have the option to reinoculate the file. See the section "Scanning and Inoculating Drives, Directories and Files" for more information about inoculating and reinoculating files.

To respond to a virus alert box:

- Select Proceed to close the alert box and launch the application anyway. Select Proceed only when you are certain that the message is a false alarm. The Proceed button can be disabled so that it cannot be selected. See the section "Configuring Virus Intercept."

CAUTION: Beware! False alarms are rare. If you decide to proceed, the virus could infect other files.

Or,

- Select Stop to prevent the application from starting.

    The alert box closes and you are returned to the command line. At this point, you can start Virus Clinic to repair or delete the damaged file. See the section "Repairing Infected Files" for complete instructions.

Boot-sector Alert Box

If Virus Intercept detects a boot-sector/partition-table virus, you will see a Boot Sector alert box (Figure 20-3).

Figure 20-3

Virus Intercept displays this alert box when it detects a boot-sector or partition-table virus

```
                        Virus Intercept Alert!

WARNING! You MUST respond now!
DO NOT BOOT USING THE DISK IN DRIVE A: WHICH
contains a strain of the "Curse" virus.



[Proceed] will NOT infect                                    [STOP]
```

Using Norton Desktop for DOS

If the boot-sector/partition-table infector has infected your hard disk, you should immediately turn to the section "Boot-sector and Partition-table Infectors."

Reinoculating Files

If you have enabled Scan for Unknown Viruses, Norton AntiVirus will go one step further than checking a file for all known viruses. Virus Intercept scans files before they are loaded and compares them to the inoculation data. A change in the file's inoculation data could indicate that an unknown virus has infected the file. If the file has changed in some way since it was inoculated, an alert box appears (Figure 20-4). This particular alert box appears only if the Allow Proceed or Allow Reinoculate check boxes are checked in the Intercept dialog box. You have three choices: Proceed, Reinoculate or Stop.

You should select Proceed only if you are certain the file is not infected.

Reinoculating tells Virus Intercept that the file is free of viruses; this is not recommended unless you are certain that the file is not infected—for example, if you know a file was updated when you installed a new version of the program. (See "Configuring Virus Intercept" later in this chapter for more information about enabling and disabling these command buttons.) The buttons that are actually available are determined by settings in the Intercept dialog box.

Figure 20-4

the Virus Intercept alert box tells you when an inoculated file has changed

```
                    Virus Intercept Alert!

WARNING! You MUST respond now! The file:
C:\DOS\CHKDSK.EXE
has changed since it was inoculated. If this file has been upgraded
then Reinoculation is suggested, otherwise this could be an unknown
virus.

[Proceed] with file access    [Reinoculate] file    [STOP] file access
```

To respond to an unknown virus alert:

- Select the Reinoculate button to create new inoculation data for the file and allow the program to continue execution.

Or,

- Select Proceed to start the application without inoculating the file if you are *certain* that the file is not infected. (You can only select Proceed if the Proceed button has not been disabled.)

Or,

- Select Stop to prevent file access, close the alert box and return to DOS.

    When you return to the command line, you can start Virus Clinic and scan the disk.

HOW VIRUS INTERCEPT PROTECTS ITSELF

To protect itself from viruses, Virus Intercept does not allow any application to read or write to the NAV_.SYS file. Consequently, you cannot view, erase or modify the attributes of this file while Virus Intercept is active. When you back up your files, you should exclude NAV_.SYS from the backup because the backup program will not be able to read this file. Note that this self-protection feature is not available for the smaller versions of Virus Intercept (NAV&.SYS, NAV&.SYS /B). For more information on the .SYS files see *Installing Norton Desktop for DOS*.

HOW VIRUS INTERCEPT WORKS WITH OTHER APPLICATIONS

This section explains how Virus Intercept interacts with other programs, including DOS.

TIP: To stop Virus Intercept from loading when you start your computer, wait for the beep from the BIOS startup that you normally hear when you start your computer. Then immediately press and hold both Shift keys until the message "Norton AntiVirus Not Loaded" appears.

Copying Floppy Disks and Files

Copying a floppy disk, as with the DOS COPY command, is one of the most common ways for a virus to infect files. When you copy files, it is important to check them for viruses. When you use the DOS COPY command, Virus Intercept cannot scan files for viruses. Therefore, you should scan the floppy disk with Virus Clinic before you make a copy of the disk or any of its files.

With NAV_.SYS loaded, Intercept scans files before allowing DOS to copy them. Virus Intercept is always checking that you don't accidentally copy an infected file to or from a floppy or network drive.

However, Virus Intercept cannot check for viruses when you:

- Use the DOS DISKCOPY command to duplicate a diskette
- Copy files using LapLink or similar direct connection software such as Desktop Link or Commander Link
- Download files with a modem

File-compression Programs

Virus Intercept does not detect viruses in files that are compressed, archived or packed, such as those compressed with PKZIP or PKARC. Therefore, you must decompress the files first, then scan those files for viruses.

CAUTION: The specific use of self-extracting compressed files is unique. Norton AntiVirus cannot identify viruses in such files. You should scan immediately after executing these programs to verify that they have not spread a virus.

Communications Programs

When using Virus Intercept with time-sensitive communication applications such as ProComm Plus, Crosstalk and SmartCom, these applications may "crash" (fail to operate properly) or lose data after a Virus Intercept alert box is displayed. This happens because Virus Intercept stops all other activity when a virus infection alert box is displayed. This is most likely to happen if you're multitasking or if you're transferring an infected file to another computer.

Backup Programs

Many backup programs don't recommend using a device driver, such as Virus Intercept, while they are running.

If Virus Intercept is setup to Detect Unknown Viruses but not to Auto Inoculate files when possible unknown viruses are discovered, Virus Intercept may display an alert message when you try to back up an uninoculated file. If this happens, the backup program may stop and wait for you to respond to the alert box, which is fine. However, the backup program may crash because of the unexpected interruption caused by the alert box. Refer to the section "Configuring Virus Intercept" for more information about enabling and disabling Norton AntiVirus global options. Also see Figure 20-5 for a picture of the Global dialog box.

NOTE: Virus Intercept cannot check for viruses when you restore files from compressed backup media, such as tape, or with high-speed, floppy-disk-based backup programs. After restoring files, scan them for viruses before you execute them.

DOS Format

If Virus Intercept is configured with system area write protection (NAV_.SYS /W), Intercept displays a warning during the formatting of a floppy disk. Such warnings are normal and you should choose Proceed (sometimes three or four times) until the disk is successfully formatted. This is perhaps the only instance where you should proceed with such a warning.

Other Types of Programs

Virus Intercept has been tested and certified to work under DesqView and DOS 5.0 task switcher. However, Virus Intercept may be incompatible with some multitasking/TSR managers.

USING VIRUS CLINIC

To scan a drive or directory, you must first start Virus Clinic.

To start Virus Clinic:

- Choose NORTON ANTIVIRUS from the Norton Desktop Tools menu.

Or,

1. Choose RUN... from the Norton Desktop (long) File menu.
2. Type nav in the DOS Command text box.

Or,

- Type nav at the DOS prompt to run Virus Clinic as a standalone program.

The main Virus Clinic screen appears.

Scanning Memory

The first scan in any Virus Clinic session starts with scanning memory for viruses. You cannot cancel a memory scan. Virus Clinic will not scan memory again if you perform another scan during this session.

If Virus Clinic discovers a virus in memory it will stop scanning to prevent spreading the virus to the files on your disk. Virus Clinic cannot eliminate a virus from memory. To do this, restart your computer from a write-protected system disk.

TIP: If you're fortunate you made a Rescue Disk before your computer became infected.

To remove a virus from memory:

1. If a virus is detected in memory, turn off the computer from the power switch.
2. Start the computer from an uninfected, bootable DOS floppy disk that contains the same version of DOS as your hard disk. This guarantees that the virus will not become active during system startup. Do not try to execute any files.
3. Insert the Installation Disk and type nav to launch Virus Clinic. Do not run Virus Clinic from your hard disk because your hard disk may be infected.

Scanning and Inoculating Drives, Directories and Files

4   Scan all drives for viruses and repair or delete all infected files. Read the following sections for more detail on how to do this.

When Detect Unknown Viruses is enabled (checked) in the Global dialog box, information about each executable file is stored in an *inoculation file*. Then, whenever Virus Clinic or Virus Intercept scans one of these files, it validates the file against its inoculation data. This enables Norton AntiVirus to detect infections by new viruses that it is unable to specifically identify. Infections of this type are reported as "unknown" viruses.

Files are inoculated in two ways:

- **Virus Clinic:** If you enable "Auto-inoculate" in the Global dialog box from the Options menu, Virus Clinic automatically creates the inoculation data for all program files which have not previously been inoculated. (Using Virus Clinic is the fastest way to inoculate all files on a drive.)

- **Virus Intercept:** If "Auto-inoculate" is enabled, Virus Intercept automatically creates inoculation data for files that have not previously been inoculated. If "Auto-inoculate" is not enabled, Intercept displays the Virus Intercept alert box where you may choose Inoculate to create inoculation data.

You can scan and inoculate a single file, all files in a directory or all files on a drive with the following procedure:

To scan and inoculate drives, directories and files:

1   Choose GLOBAL... from the Virus Clinic Options menu.
     The Global dialog box appears (Figure 20-5).

2   Check Detect Unknown Viruses and Auto-inoculate if they are not checked already. Auto-inoculate is checked by default, but is not enabled unless Detect Unknown Viruses is also checked.

3   Select OK to save the changes.

4   Choose either DRIVE..., DIRECTORY... or FILE... from the Scan menu.

Figure 20-5

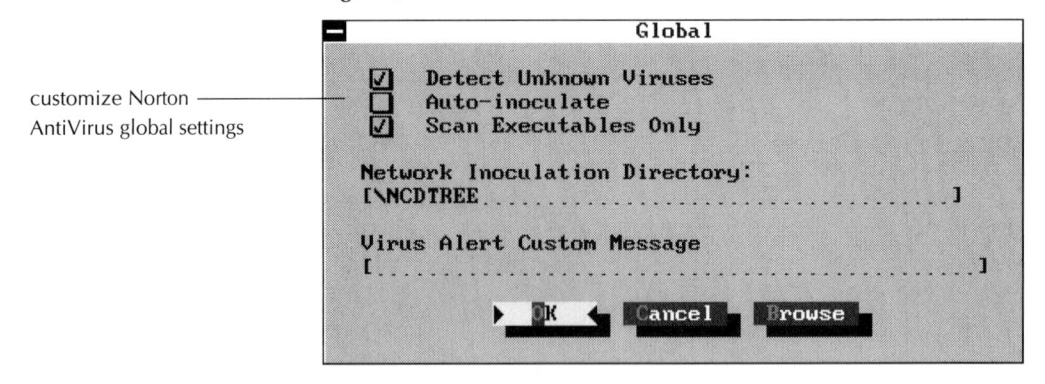

```
┌─────────────────────── Global ───────────────────────┐
│  ☑  Detect Unknown Viruses                           │
│  ☐  Auto-inoculate                                   │
│  ☑  Scan Executables Only                            │
│                                                      │
│  Network Inoculation Directory:                      │
│  [\NCDTREE.........................................] │
│                                                      │
│  Virus Alert Custom Message                          │
│  [.................................................]│
│                                                      │
│         ▶ OK ◀    Cancel    Browse                   │
└──────────────────────────────────────────────────────┘
```

customize Norton AntiVirus global settings

5 Specify the exact item you want to scan from the dialog box that appears next.

- **To scan one or more drives:** specify the drive name and type.
- **To scan specific directories:** specify the path and drive; if you wish to include subdirectories, make sure that check box is checked.
- **To scan individual files:** specify the filename, drive and directory. Filenames and directory names appear in list boxes. You may select the file to scan from the list box or type the filename in the text box.

6 Select OK to begin the scan.

The progress and results of the scan appear in the Scan Results dialog box.

As the files are inoculated, Virus Clinic stores the inoculation data in a file in the root directory on the same drive as the inoculated files. The inoculation file is a hidden system file (NAV._NO). On network drives it is stored in the path you specify in the Global settings.

Removing the Inoculation File

As you reorganize your hard disk, deleting and adding files, your inoculation data file grows. To conserve disk space, you may occasionally want to remove the inoculation file and rescan the drive to reinoculate the files.

To remove the inoculation file:

1   Choose UNINOCULATE... from the Virus Clinic Tools menu.

    The Uninoculate Drives dialog box appears (Figure 20-6).

Figure 20-6

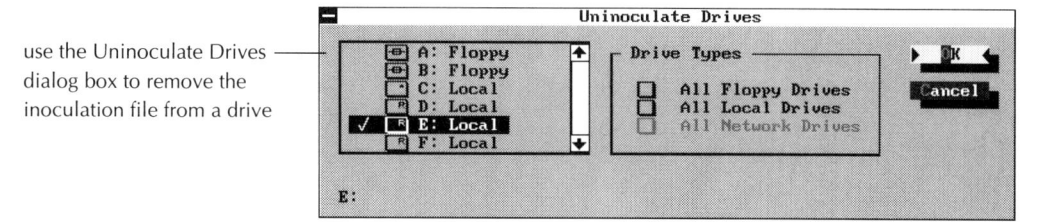

use the Uninoculate Drives dialog box to remove the inoculation file from a drive

2   Select the drive where the inoculation file is stored in the Drives list box.

    Or,

    Check the appropriate Drive Types check box to select all drives of a specific type.

3   Select OK to remove the inoculation data file for all the files on the selected drive(s).

Working with Scan Results

When a file, directory or drive is scanned, the Scan Results dialog box appears (Figure 20-7). The Scan Results dialog box shows information about the scan as it progresses. The progress bar tells you what percentage of the scan has been completed. The command buttons on the right—Scan, Repair, Delete, Reinoc and Print—let you work with the results of the scan.

The list box displays the following:

- The filename and full path of each infected file detected.
- The name of the virus infecting it (if known).
- Summary information indicating the number of files scanned and the total number of viruses detected. If no infected files are found, the Scan Results dialog box displays only the summary information and the total infected files found is 0.

Figure 20-7

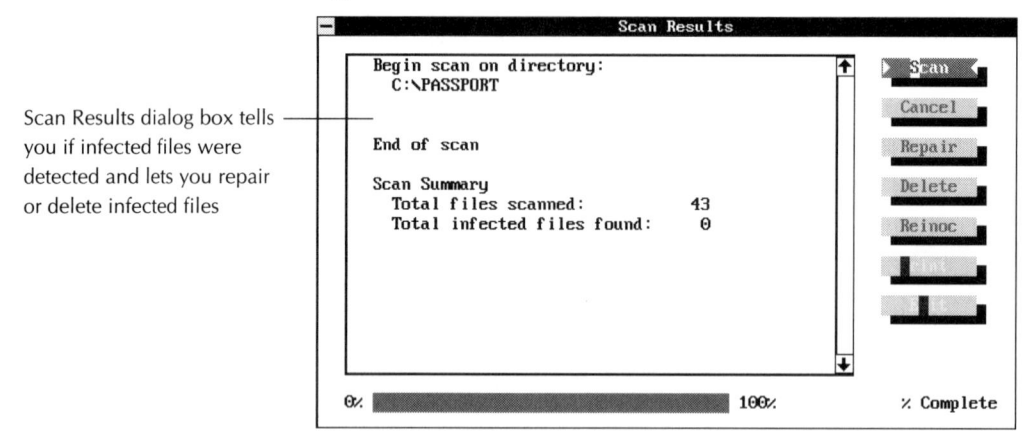

Scan Results dialog box tells you if infected files were detected and lets you repair or delete infected files

Canceling a Scan

The Cancel button is available during the scan but disappears when the scan is complete. Canceling a scan will not harm your files. You cannot cancel a memory scan.

To cancel a scan:

1   Select the Cancel button.

    The message "Are you sure you want to cancel the scan?" appears.

2   Select Yes to confirm cancellation.

    The scan is immediately canceled and cannot be restarted from the cancellation point. The message "Scan canceled" along with the total files scanned and the total infected files found so far appears in the list box. You can still use the available buttons in the Scan Results dialog box to manage any infected files.

Understanding Scan Messages

If a file is infected with a known virus, you'll see this message: "This file contains a strain of <virus name>."

NOTE: Virus Clinic reports only the first virus it finds in a file. The message in the Scan Results dialog box doesn't indicate whether the file is infected with multiple viruses. After you repair or delete an infected file, you should rescan to make sure that all viruses are eliminated.

If Scan for Unknown Viruses is enabled, Virus Clinic displays the message "This file may contain an unknown virus" when it detects a change in a file. This message does not necessarily indicate the presence of a virus; it is displayed in the following circumstances:

- An unknown virus has altered the file.
- The file has been upgraded or otherwise changed (perhaps because the program has been reconfigured).

If you upgraded or changed the file and are sure that no virus exists, you can reinoculate the file (provided the Virus Clinic configuration option Allow Reinoc is checked in the Clinic dialog box). If you did not change the file and there is no reason to believe that a configuration has changed the file, then a virus may exist or the file may have been damaged somehow. You need to eliminate the virus by deleting the file with Virus Clinic and replace the file with an uninfected copy from a write-protected program disk.

To delete and restore the file:

1. Select the filename of the file to delete from the Scan Results dialog box.
2. Select Delete, then select Delete again to delete the selected file.

   Or,

   Select Delete All to delete all infected files shown in the Scan Results dialog box.
3. Select Yes to confirm the deletion.

   The Delete Files dialog box opens. Virus Clinic shows you the filenames as it is deleting the files. You can select Cancel to stop the process.
4. Replace the file with an uninfected copy, preferably from the write-protected program disk.
5. Choose GLOBAL... from the Virus Clinic Options menu and make sure that both the Detect Unknown Viruses and Auto-inoculate options are checked.
6. Scan the file to inoculate this new, uninfected copy.

CAUTION: An infected file that is deleted in Virus Clinic is unrecoverable; it cannot be recovered even with special file recovery utilities, such as Norton Utilities.

Repairing Infected Files

The only time you should attempt to repair a file is when there is no uninfected copy available (the situation is different for infected system areas such a boot sectors and partition tables). But before you try to repair an infected file for which you have no uninfected replacement, you should make a backup copy of it. Making a copy of an infected file with the DOS COPY command will not put the virus into memory, but it will infect the disk the file is copied to, so make sure that you label that disk as having a live virus on it.

Executable Infections

Viruses often attack one or more executable files. If you see a message in the Scan Results dialog box that says "This file contains a strain of <virus name>," you have an infected executable file.

To repair an infected file:

1 Choose EXIT from the Virus Clinic Scan menu to exit Norton AntiVirus.

   Or,

   Double-click the close box to exit Norton AntiVirus.

2 Exit Norton Desktop.

3 Copy the infected file to a floppy disk and label the disk as an infected disk. When you copy the file, Virus Intercept is activated. You may also want to use the DOS RENAME command to change the file's extension to something like .BAD, to prevent the infected file from being run by mistake.

4 Select "Proceed with file access" to complete the copying process.

5 Start Virus Clinic by typing `nav` at the command prompt.

6 Choose DRIVE... from the Scan menu and specify the drive that contains the infected floppy disk.

7 Select the file you want to repair from the Scan Results dialog box.

If the Repair button is unavailable, it means that there are no repairable files in the files list. In this case, you must delete the infected files. Skip the rest of the steps and refer to the section "Understanding Scan Messages" for instructions on deleting a file in Virus Clinic.

If the Repair button can be selected, it means at least one of the files in the list can be repaired. Proceed to step 8.

8 Select Repair.

The Repair Files or Sectors dialog box opens (Figure 20-8).

Figure 20-8

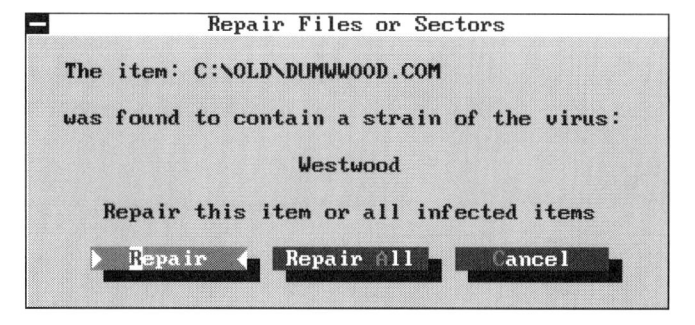

repair the selected infected file or all infected files

```
Repair Files or Sectors

The item: C:\OLD\DUMWWOOD.COM

was found to contain a strain of the virus:

                    Westwood

    Repair this item or all infected items

        Repair    Repair All    Cancel
```

9 Select Repair to repair the highlighted file only.

Or,

Select Repair All to repair all repairable infected files that are listed in the Scan Results dialog box.

10 After you have repaired the files you want, select Scan to rescan those files.

11 Repeat steps 6 through 10 until no more infected files are detected.

When an infected file is repaired, the message "File repaired to remove virus <virus name>" appears below the filename in the Scan Results dialog box.

After you repair an infected file, it is a good idea to verify that the repaired file works properly. Start the application that uses the repaired file, create a file, save it and check it to make sure the application is running properly. If it does not, the file could be damaged. Refer to the next section, "If a File Cannot Be Repaired."

If a File Cannot Be Repaired

Sometimes an infected file cannot be repaired. Virus Clinic cannot repair the following types of files:

- **A file for which Norton AntiVirus does not have a virus definition.** To increase your chances of being able to repair a file, make sure you have downloaded the most current virus definitions (see the section "Updating Virus Definitions").

- **A file that has been attacked by a destructive virus.** Some viruses irreparably damage the files they infect.

- **Infected files that are stored on a write-protected disk or write-protected drive.** Norton AntiVirus appears to repair the infected file, but the file is not repaired and the infection remains on the disk. You must remove the write-protection and start the repair process over.

If an infected file cannot be repaired, the only option is to delete the file and replace it with an uninfected copy. You must remove write-protection to delete a file. See the section "Understanding Scan Messages" for more information about deleting files in Virus Clinic.

Boot-sector and Partition-table Infections

When your computer starts up, a small program in the partition table is launched that indicates where to find the bootable partition of the hard disk. When the bootable partition is found, a small program in the boot sector is launched to load DOS. A *boot-sector virus* is a virus that infects this small program in the boot sector. The boot-sector infector overwrites (replaces) a portion of the boot sector on the infected disk.

The virus loads into memory *before* DOS and Virus Intercept, taking control of your computer or even preventing your computer from starting up at all from the infected media.

Your boot sector can be infected by:

- Booting or even attempting to boot your computer from a floppy disk with an infected boot sector. *Even data disks can infect your computer in this fashion, because all disks have boot sectors whether they are system disks or not.*
- Using an infected file that infects boot sectors or partition tables.

A *partition-table virus* is a virus that infects the small program in the partition table that locates the bootable partition. The virus loads into memory *before* DOS and Virus Intercept, taking control of your computer or preventing your computer from starting up at all from the infected hard disk.

Your partition table can be infected by:

- Booting or even attempting to boot your computer from a floppy disk with an infected boot sector. *Even data disks can infect your computer in this fashion.*
- Using an infected file that infects boot sectors or partition tables.

The partition-table infector overwrites (replaces) a portion of the partition table on the infected disk.

Recovering from a Boot-sector or Partition-table Virus

It is possible to have a boot-sector or partition-table virus on either a hard disk or a floppy disk. If you have a boot-sector or partition-table virus on your computer's hard disk, see the following procedures. If you have a boot-sector or a partition-table virus on a floppy disk, go to the next section, "Restoring the Boot Sector of an Infected Floppy Disk."

To attempt repair of a hard disk's boot sector or partition table:

1. Scan the disk using Virus Clinic.
2. Select the infected item in the Scan Results dialog box and see whether the Repair function is available.

   If the Repair button is dimmed, the boot sector or partition table is not repairable. Skip the remaining steps and proceed to the Rescue Disk procedure explained next.

   If the Repair function is available, continue with step 3.

3   Select the Repair button to see whether the boot sector or partition table can be repaired.

If the Repair button in the next dialog box is dimmed, the boot sector or partition table is not repairable, though at least one file in the list probably can be repaired. Skip the remaining steps and proceed to the Rescue Disk option explained below.

If this Repair function is available, you should be able to repair the boot sector. Continue with step 4.

4   Select Repair to fix the boot sector.

5   Rescan the hard drive to verify.

> **TIP:** You might want to rescan all your floppy disks to try to discover where the boot-sector infector came from.

If you are not able to repair the boot sector or partition table as described above, your Rescue Disk can help. If you created a Rescue Disk you can restore the boot sector from that disk. For more information, see Chapter 28, "Using Disk Tools," for information about creating a Rescue Disk.

To restore the boot sector or partition table from the Rescue Disk:

1   Turn off your computer and restart it from a bootable, uninfected, write-protected floppy disk with the same version of DOS as your hard disk.

2   When you see the A:> prompt, remove this floppy disk from the drive.

3   Insert the Norton Desktop for DOS program disk that contains the program files for Norton AntiVirus.

4   Type nav at the prompt to launch Norton AntiVirus from this disk.

5   Select Cancel from the Scan Drives dialog box to skip scanning a drive.

6   Choose RESTORE FROM RESCUE DISK... from the Virus Clinic Tools menu and have your Rescue Disk ready.

7   Follow the prompts and instructions to restore your hard disk's boot sector from your Rescue Disk.

8   Rescan the hard drive to verify.

> **TIP:** You might want to rescan all your floppy disks to try to discover where the boot-sector infector came from.

To restore the boot sector when no Rescue Disk is available:

1. Turn off your computer and restart it from a bootable, uninfected, write-protected floppy disk with *exactly* the same version of DOS as your hard disk.

2. At the A:> prompt, type the following:

    ```
    C:<pathname>\SYS C:
    ```

    where <pathname> indicates the directory path where the DOS files on your hard disk are located (for example, \DOS).

    You should see the "System transferred" message. You now have a clean boot sector. Continue with step 3.

3. Rescan all your floppy disks to try to discover where the boot-sector infector came from.

To restore the partition table when no Rescue Disk is available:

1. Have available an uninfected, write-protected, DOS system disk with the same version of DOS as your hard disk.

2. Call Technical Support while at your computer for instructions on how to proceed. You will be asked to use special programs from Norton Desktop for DOS.

Restoring the Boot Sector of an Infected Floppy Disk

All floppy disks have a boot sector, even if they are not system (bootable) disks. The small program in the boot sector of a floppy disk can be infected by boot-sector *or* partition-table infectors. The virus overwrites a portion of the boot sector on the floppy disk.

The virus can be transferred to other floppy disks or to hard disks if you start or restart your computer while the infected floppy disk is in a disk drive.

If Virus Intercept is active, start with step 1. If Virus Intercept is not loaded, exit from Virus Clinic and start with step 7.

To restore the boot sector of an infected floppy disk:

1 Remove the infected floppy disk from the disk drive. *Make sure all floppy disks are removed from all drives.*

2 Scan your hard disk using Virus Clinic to be sure it is virus-free. If it is not, repair or delete infected files as necessary.

3 Exit from Virus Clinic.

4 Restart your computer and wait for a beep.

5 After the beep, simultaneously press and hold both Shift keys.

The "Norton AntiVirus Not Loaded" message appears. Virus Intercept is now disabled and won't interfere with the steps to follow. Continue with step 6.

6 Now that you know your hard disk is virus-free, reinsert the infected floppy disk.

7 Copy all files from the floppy disk to another (uninfected) floppy or to your hard disk, using the DOS COPY or XCOPY command. *This does not transfer the boot-sector virus.*

CAUTION: Do not use the DOS DISKCOPY command, as it *will* transfer the virus.

---

8 Reformat the floppy disk. This destroys the virus.

9 Copy the files back to this floppy disk from your hard disk or another floppy disk.

10 Rescan all your floppy disks in case the virus came from a different floppy disk.

System Files and COMMAND.COM Infections

If your COMMAND.COM file or its replacement (such as Norton Utilities' NDOS) is infected, or if a hidden DOS file (such as IO.SYS or MSDOS.SYS, or IBMBIO.SYS or IBMCOM.SYS) is infected, first see whether the file can be repaired.

To attempt repair of an infected system file or the COMMAND.COM file:

1. Select the file in the Scan Results dialog box and see whether the Repair function is available.

    If the Repair button is dimmed, COMMAND.COM is not repairable and must be deleted.

    If the Repair function is available, continue with step 2.

2. Select the Repair button to see whether COMMAND.COM itself can be repaired.

    If the Repair button in the next dialog box is dimmed, COMMAND.COM is not repairable, though at least one file in the list probably can be repaired. You will have to delete COMMAND.COM.

    If this Repair function is available, you should be able to repair COMMAND.COM. Continue with step 3.

3. Select Repair to fix the file.

    Note that you may be forced to delete the file if repair is not possible or is unsuccessful.

To delete and restore COMMAND.COM when repair is not possible or is unsuccessful:

1. You will need a bootable disk to complete this procedure. Delete the system file or COMMAND.COM (or its replacement) in Virus Clinic's Scan Results dialog box by selecting Delete then selecting Delete again when it appears in the next dialog box.

2. Select OK to confirm the deletion.

3. Exit from Virus Clinic. Refer to "Exiting Virus Clinic" in this chapter if you need instructions.

    You may see a message that the COMMAND.COM file or COMMAND.COM replacement is missing. Continue with step 4. For system files skip to step 6.

4. Reboot from your bootable disk.

5. You must restore the deleted file by copying COMMAND.COM from an uninfected, write-protected DOS disk with the same version of DOS as your hard disk.

Using Norton Desktop for DOS

6 At the A:> prompt, type the following:

   C:<pathname>\SYS C:

   where <pathname> indicates the directory path where the DOS files on your hard disk are located (for example, \DOS).

   You should see the "System transferred" message. You have restored your DOS system files.

Exiting Virus Clinic

To exit Virus Clinic:

1 Choose EXIT from the Virus Clinic Scan menu.

   Or,

   Press Escape.

   Or,

   Double-click the close box.

   The Warning! dialog box is displayed with the message, "Would you like to exit The Norton AntiVirus?"

2 Choose Yes to exit Virus Clinic.

   You are returned to Norton Desktop for DOS.

WORKING WITH VIRUS DEFINITIONS

To keep your computer safe from new viruses, you should update Norton AntiVirus's internal virus definitions by:

- Adding new virus definitions when they become available
- Deleting outdated virus definitions

This section shows you how to:

- View the current virus definitions
- Print a list of virus definitions for your reference
- Update virus definitions
- Load a definitions file
- Add virus definitions manually

Viewing and Printing Virus Definitions

You can find out which viruses Norton AntiVirus scans for and eliminates by viewing the list of virus definitions. To see additional virus definition names, scroll through the list. The total number of virus definitions is displayed below the virus list box.

To view the virus list:

- Choose MODIFY LIST… from the Virus Clinic Definitions menu.

    The Modify List dialog box appears (Figure 20-9).

Figure 20-9

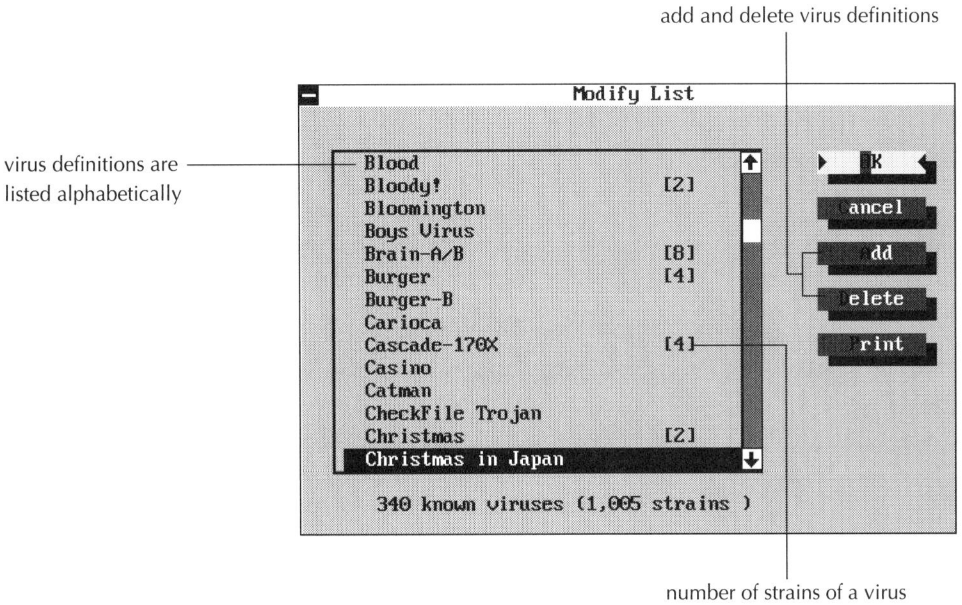

virus definitions are listed alphabetically

add and delete virus definitions

number of strains of a virus

> **NOTE:** Viruses go by many aliases. If you do not see a particular virus name in the list, you may still be protected from it. It may be listed under a more common name.

To keep a list of virus definitions, you can print the contents of the virus list box or save it to a file for future reference.

To create a list of virus definitions:

1 Select Print from the Modify List dialog box (see Figure 20-9).

   The Print Virus List dialog box appears (Figure 20-10).

Figure 20-10

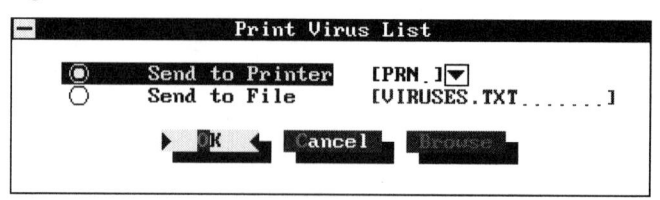

the Print Virus List dialog box lets you print a list of the virus names to a printer or to a file

```
┌─────────────── Print Virus List ───────────────┐
│  ⦿   Send to Printer    [PRN.]▼                │
│  ○   Send to File       [VIRUSES.TXT........]  │
│            ▶ OK ◀   Cancel    Browse           │
└────────────────────────────────────────────────┘
```

2   To print the list select Send to Printer.

Or,

To save the list to a file, select Send to File.

The file is saved to the default filename VIRUSES.TXT in the Norton AntiVirus directory. To save the file to a different directory or filename, type the full pathname and filename in the filename text box.

3   Select OK to begin printing or to save the file.

Updating Virus Definitions

At the time of this writing, Norton AntiVirus provides protection from more than 1,000 computer viruses; however, new viruses are constantly being reported. To protect your computer from new viruses, you should update Norton AntiVirus's virus definitions on your computer as new definitions become available.

You can obtain current virus definitions from:

- Bulletin board services (BBSs), including Symantec's BBS, CompuServe and user group BBSs in your area.
- The Faxline (this is best used for small numbers of virus definitions to save you typing time).
- Symantec's virus definitions update disk service.

Virus Newsline The Virus Newsline is a telephone service that provides round-the-clock news about viruses and how to obtain new virus definitions; you can reach it at (408) 252-3993. Before you call, have paper and a pencil ready to write down any important information.

A recorded message gives the latest virus news and information, but not the actual virus definitions. It provides information about available virus definitions and how you can obtain them.

Bulletin Board Services Updates to the virus definitions file are posted on several bulletin board services, including the Symantec BBS, Patricia Hoffman's EXCALIBUR BBS, National Computer Security Association's BBS and Symantec's NORUTL Forum on CompuServe. Updates may also be available on user-group BBSs in your area. This section explains how to use the Symantec BBS and CompuServe's NORUTL Forum.

Symantec BBS To download the current virus definitions file from the Symantec BBS, you must access the BBS using communications software, a modem and your computer.

Set your communications application to no parity, 8 data bits and 1 stop bit. For information about these settings, see the user's guide that was supplied with your communications software.

Once you've set up your communications software and modem correctly, you can call the Symantec BBS at (408) 973-9598 for 300- to 2400-baud modems or (408) 973-9834 for 9600-baud modems. Once you've successfully connected with the BBS, choose the option to download the latest virus definitions update. Then select the appropriate file-transfer protocol and download the file. Save the file to your hard disk, then disconnect from the BBS.

NOTE: You can download a *complete* set of virus definitions or a file with just the virus definitions published *since the last release* of the virus definitions file.

CompuServe NORUTL Forum	CompuServe is a bulletin board service available only to paid subscribers. You can find the current Norton AntiVirus virus definitions file in the NORUTL Forum, NAV-IBM Library Section.

After you disconnect from the BBS, you'll need to load the virus definitions file into Norton AntiVirus using the LOAD FROM FILE... command in the Definitions menu. See the section "Loading a Definitions File." |
| **Faxline** | If you don't have a modem and communications software, the Faxline provides a fast way to get a new virus definitions using your facsimile machine (fax). The Faxline is available 24 hours a day, 7 days a week. The service is free, but you will have to pay the cost of the telephone call.

You can call the Faxline at (310) 575-5018 from a touch-tone phone or from a fax machine. (For assistance using this service, call (310) 477-2707.) If you call from a touch-tone phone, you must give your fax telephone number so that the definitions can be transmitted there. If you call from a fax, it must be properly set to receive the virus definitions you request. Refer to your facsimile machine's user's guide for settings to use for receiving documents. |
| **Virus Definitions Update Disk Service** | In addition to the free update services described above, Symantec's virus definitions update disk service supplies floppy disks containing the most current virus definitions file available at the time your order is processed; updates are normally available quarterly. You can order by calling (800) 343-4714, extension 756. |

> **NOTE:** Please state which size and capacity (5½-inch/360K or 3½-inch/720K) floppy disks you need when you place your order.

Loading a Definitions File	After you have retrieved the latest virus definition file, you can incorporate the file into your local virus definitions database as follows:

To load a virus definition file:

1. Copy the newest virus definitions file into the NAV directory.
2. Launch Virus Clinic. Refer to "Using Virus Clinic" in this chapter if you need instructions.
3. Choose LOAD FROM FILE... from the Virus Clinic Definitions menu.

   The Load from File dialog box opens (Figure 20-11).

Figure 20-11

use the Load from File dialog box to update virus definitions

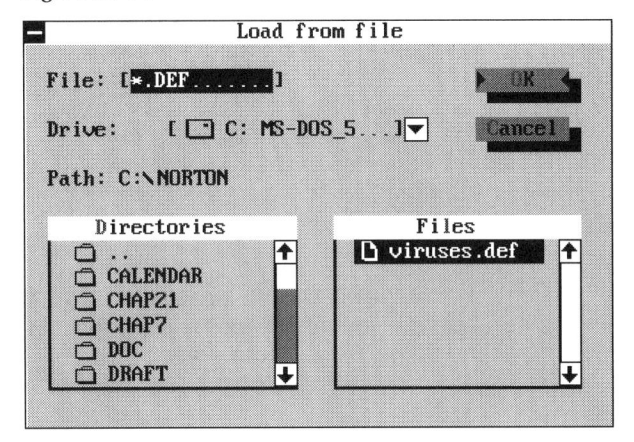

Make sure the directory with the current virus definitions file is the current directory, such as C:\NAV. If it is not, use the Drive or Directories list boxes to change the drive and/or directory.

4. Select the virus definitions filename in the Files list box.

   The filename appears in the File text box.
5. Select OK to load the virus definitions file into Norton AntiVirus and close the Load from File dialog box.

The virus definitions are now updated. By selecting MODIFY LIST... from the Virus Clinic Definitions menu you can view all current virus names in the virus definitions file.

Using Norton Desktop for DOS

Adding Virus Definitions Manually

If you do not have communications software and a modem, you can also obtain new virus definitions using a fax machine. (See the "Faxline" section.) You can then add any new virus definitions manually. Before you type a virus definition, you must have all the definition parameters: virus name, length, checksum and definition string.

To add a virus definition:

1 Select MODIFY LIST... in the Definitions menu.

   The Modify List dialog box appears.

2 Select Add in the Modify List dialog box.

   The Add Virus Definition dialog box opens (Figure 20-12).

Figure 20-12

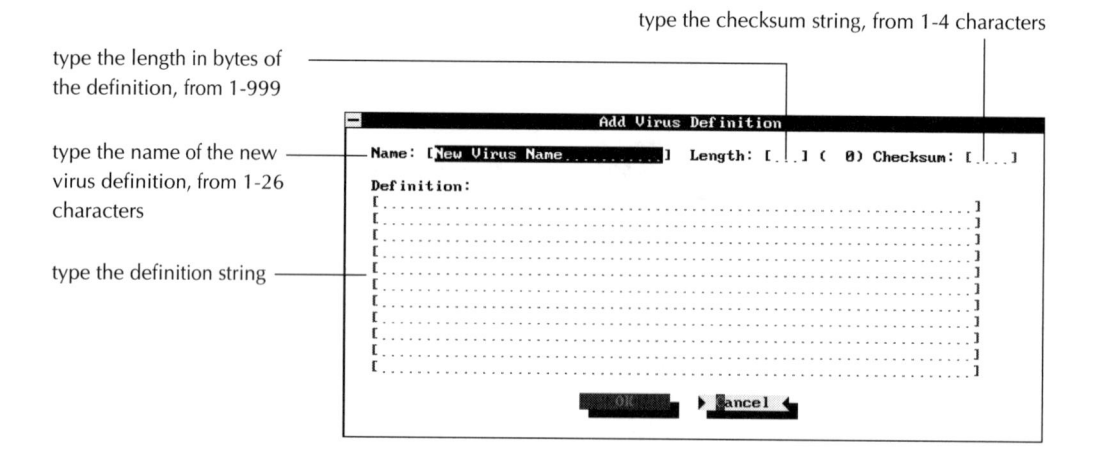

type the length in bytes of the definition, from 1-999

type the name of the new virus definition, from 1-26 characters

type the definition string

type the checksum string, from 1-4 characters

```
┌─────────────────── Add Virus Definition ───────────────────┐
│ Name: [New Virus Name........]  Length: [...] ( 0) Checksum: [...] │
│ Definition:                                                 │
│ [......................................................... ] │
│ [......................................................... ] │
│ [......................................................... ] │
│ [......................................................... ] │
│ [......................................................... ] │
│ [......................................................... ] │
│ [......................................................... ] │
│ [......................................................... ] │
│                    ██OK██   ▶ Cancel ◀                     │
└─────────────────────────────────────────────────────────────┘
```

3 Type the name of the virus definition in the Name text box. The virus definition name can be from 1 to 26 characters long and must be all characters. (You cannot use commas.)

4 Type the length of the virus definition in the Length text box. The entry must be a number from 1 to 999 representing the length in bytes.

5   Type the checksum string in the Checksum text box. The string can be from 1 to 4 characters long.

6   Type the virus definition string in the Definition text box. You may type the entire string without spaces, or to increase readability you can type two characters and a space, two more characters and a space and continue until you complete the definition string. Virus Clinic automatically puts the letters you type in uppercase.

    Compare the entry with the written definition that you received from Symantec and correct any errors before continuing; it must match exactly. As you complete each Definition text box, Virus Clinic checks to see that your entries are correct. If an error is detected, a beep sounds and Virus Clinic moves the cursor to the error.

7   When you have finished typing the definition, select OK.

    If there is an error in the definition, the error message "Unable to add this definition" appears. You cannot save the definition until the error is corrected.

NOTE: The virus definition takes effect immediately in Virus Clinic. However, the version of Virus Intercept that is loaded determines when the virus definition is effective for Virus Intercept. If NAV_.SYS is loaded, the virus definition is not effective in Virus Intercept until you restart the computer. If NAV&.SYS or NAV&.SYS /B is loaded, the virus definition is effective immediately. See *Installing Norton Desktop for DOS* for an explanation of the .SYS files used with Virus Intercept.

Deleting a Definition

Occasionally a virus definition may become out of date. When this happens, you should delete it from the virus definitions list.

To delete a virus definition:

1   Choose MODIFY LIST... from the Definitions menu.

    The Modify List dialog box appears (see Figure 20-9).

2   Select the name of the virus that you wish to delete from the virus name list box.

20-36 *Using Norton Desktop for DOS*

3 Select Delete.

A message "You have selected the virus definition: <virus name>. Do you really wish to delete this definition?" appears.

4 Select Yes to delete this virus definition.

Once a virus definition is erased from the list, files are no longer protected from that virus. The delete function can be password-protected to prevent unauthorized users from deleting virus definitions.

CONFIGURING VIRUS CLINIC

The option buttons in Virus Clinic let you repair, delete or reinoculate infected files and specify whether or not scanning of network drives is allowed. These are powerful features, and if you are sharing a computer or using Norton AntiVirus on a network, you may want to disable some of these command buttons.

- When a virus is found the best way to protect your other files is to delete the infected file and replace it with an uninfected copy from an original program disk. So you may want to disable the Repair or Repair All buttons.
- To prevent accidental deletion of files, you can disable the Delete and the Delete All buttons.
- If you don't want to allow reinoculation of files from a virus alert box or from a scan in Virus Clinic, you may want to disable the Reinoc and the Reinoc All buttons.

To enable or disable Virus Clinic command buttons:

1 Choose CLINIC... from the Virus Clinic Options menu.

The Clinic dialog box appears (Figure 20-13).

2 To disable a button, uncheck the check box for that command.

Or,

To enable a button, check the check box for that command. (All commands are enabled by default.)

3 Select OK to save the changes.

Figure 20-13

use the Clinic dialog box to set different options for scanning in Virus Clinic

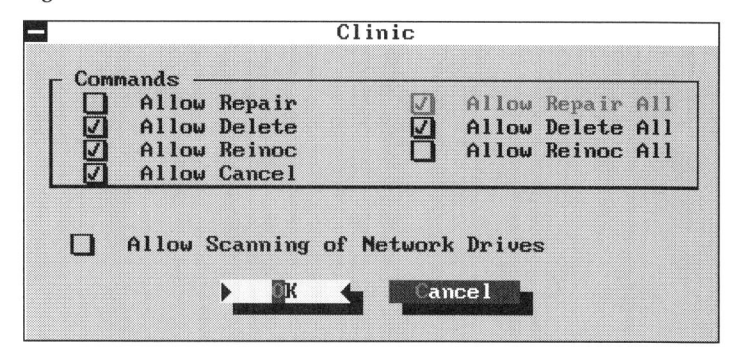

Table 20-2 shows the relationship between the option buttons and the dialog boxes where the commands appear. These features do not affect the options for Virus Intercept. See "Configuring Virus Intercept" later in this chapter for additional information.

Table 20-2

This check box...	Affects this button...	In this dialog box...
Allow Repair	Repair	Scan Results
Allow Repair All	Repair All	Repair Infected Files
Allow Delete	Delete	Scan Results
Allow Delete All	Delete All	Delete Infected Files
Allow Reinoc	Reinoc	Scan Results
Allow Reinoc All	Reinoc All	Reinoc Files
Allow Cancel	Cancel	Scan Results

Relationship between check boxes and option buttons.

Setting Global Options

Configuration options that effect both Virus Clinic and Virus Intercept are accessed using the GLOBAL... command on the Norton AntiVirus Options menu. Use global options to enable or disable the following options:

- Detect unknown viruses
- Auto-inoculate files
- Scan only executable files (to reduce scanning time)

Using the Global dialog box, you can also do the following:

- Specify the network inoculation directory
- Create a custom virus alert message

To set global options:

1   Choose GLOBAL... from the Virus Clinic Options menu.
    The Global dialog box appears (see Figure 20-5).

2   To detect possible virus activity, thus determining if files have changed between scans, check Detect Unknown Viruses.
    If this box is not checked, Norton AntiVirus scans only for viruses that it can specifically identify.
    If this box is checked Norton AntiVirus compares the current file status to the inoculation data previously created.

3   To allow an inoculation file to be created automatically as the disk is being scanned, check Auto-inoculate. This is strictly for files that do not have previous inoculation data.

4   To limit the scan to executable files only (including .COM, .EXE and .SYS files), check Scan Executables Only. Checking this option reduces scanning time.

5   To change the network inoculation directory, type the pathname and directory name in the Network Inoculation Directory text box. This directory must already exist on all network drives. If it does not exist, you must create the directory on each network drive.

6   To customize the alert message, move the cursor to the Virus Alert Custom Message text box and type a new message. A custom message can be up to 76 characters long.

7   Select OK to save the changes.

Setting Passwords

A password can prevent others from changing your configuration of CLINIC..., INTERCEPT... and GLOBAL... commands in the Options menu and UNINOCULATE... in the Virus Clinic Tools menu.

To establish a password:

1 Choose SET PASSWORD... from the Virus Clinic Options menu.

   The New Password dialog box appears (Figure 20-14).

Figure 20-14

New Password becomes Change Password when you already have a password established

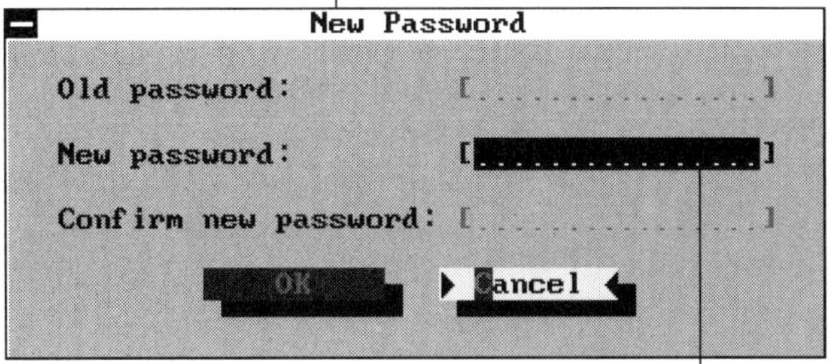

set a new password or change an existing password

2 Type a 4- to 15-character password in the New Password text box. As you type, Norton AntiVirus replaces, or masks, the characters with asterisks (*) for security.

3 Choose OK.

4 Type the password again in the Confirm New Password text box.

5 Choose OK again to save the password.

From now on, any time you try to use the CLINIC..., INTERCEPT... or GLOBAL... commands from the Options menu or choose UNINOCULATE... from the Tools menu, you must enter a password. However, once you have entered the correct password for any password-protected command, Norton AntiVirus will not ask for a password again during the current session, regardless of the menu command chosen.

> **NOTE:** If you forget your password, you're not completely out of luck. You can reinstall Virus Clinic from the original Norton Desktop for DOS installation disk.

If you use a password, you will have additional security if you change your password from time to time.

To change your password:

1. Choose CHANGE PASSWORD... from the Virus Clinic Options menu.

    The Change Password dialog box appears.

2. Type your current password in the Old Password text box.

    If the password you type is valid, Virus Clinic lets you continue. If the password you type is incorrect, the message "Incorrect Password!" appears. Select OK and type your password again.

3. When the password is accepted, select OK.
4. Type your new password in the New Password text box.
5. Select OK.
6. Enter your new password again in the Confirm New Password text box.
7. Choose OK to save the password.

If you decide not to use password-protection after all, you can remove it by deleting your current password.

To delete your password:

1. Choose CHANGE PASSWORD... from the Virus Clinic Options menu.

    The Change Password dialog box appears.

2. Type your current password in the Old Password text box.
3. Select OK.

4   Move the cursor to the New Password text box and select OK. (Do not type anything in the New Password text box.)

A dialog box appears asking you if you want to remove the password.

5   Select Yes.

The password is removed.

CONFIGURING VIRUS INTERCEPT

The Commands buttons in the Intercept dialog box allow you to determine whether the Proceed and Reinoculate buttons in the Virus Intercept alert boxes are enabled or disabled.

Enabling and Disabling Virus Intercept Command Buttons

To enable or disable Virus Intercept command buttons:

1   Choose INTERCEPT... from the Virus Clinic Options menu.

The Intercept dialog box appears

2   Check Allow Proceed to enable the alert box Proceed button.

Uncheck Allow Proceed to disable Proceed and prevent this from happening accidentally. Allow Proceed is unchecked by default.

If Allow Proceed is checked, you can select Proceed to continue when you receive a Virus Infection alert. However, remember that should you decide to proceed, you could launch an application that has a virus and spread that virus to other files.

3   Check Allow Reinoculate to enable the alert box Reinoculate button.

Uncheck Allow Reinoculate to prevent accidental reinoculation of an infected file.

If Allow Reinoculate is checked, when a virus infection alert box appears you can select the Reinoculate button.

Controlling Alert Boxes

The alert options in the Intercept dialog box let you control the alert box display and sound.

To set Virus Intercept alert box options:

1   Choose INTERCEPT... from the Options menu.

    The Intercept dialog box appears

2   To sound an audible alarm when Norton AntiVirus detects a virus, check Enable Beep Alert. The default is on. The beep lasts only a few seconds, but while it is active, the keyboard will not accept anything you type.

3   To display the Virus Intercept alert box when a virus is detected, check Enable Popup Alert. The default is on.

4   To tell Norton AntiVirus how long to display the alert box, type a number from 1 to 60 in the Seconds to Display Alert Box text box. The default is 0.

    Setting the time to display the Virus Intercept alert box is especially important for network users. When an alert box appears, it would normally remain on the screen until a response is recorded, thus tying up the network server. If the Seconds to Display Alert Box option is checked, Virus Intercept selects the default button, clears the alert box and makes the server available for use.

5   Select OK to save the changes.

Logging Intercept Messages

If you have set a short display time or if Norton AntiVirus is running unattended when you are away from your computer or on a network server, it is a good idea to keep a record, or *log*, of all Virus Intercept alert boxes and the responses to them. Later, you can review the log file to see if any viruses were found while your computer was unattended.

To start a log file:

1   Choose INTERCEPT... from the Virus Clinic Options menu.

    The Intercept dialog box appears.

2 To keep a log file, check the Enable Log to File check box.

The log file is saved as an ASCII file under the filename specified in the Filename text box (C:\AUDIT.LOG by default).

Enable Log to File should be checked whenever you enter a time in the Seconds to Display Alert Box. When both options are selected, Norton AntiVirus clears the Virus Intercept alert box from the screen, records the time the alert occurred and records the response in a *log file*.

3 To change the filename and/or pathname, just type the new one in the Filename text box.

Over time, a log file can become quite large. If this happens, you can back up the log file to another drive, save it to a network drive, delete it, print it, or start a new log file.

The Audit Log does not store the scan results for Scan Clinic. The Audit Log records messages from Virus Intercept only. Audit Log will not record Intercept messages about attempts to write to the boot sector if you have enabled system area protection with NAV_.SYS /W.

To start a new log file:

- Open the Intercept dialog box and enter a new log filename in the Filename text box that appears below Enable Log to File. Select OK to save the changes.

Or,

- Delete the existing log file. A new log file is started automatically.

To review the contents of a log file:

- Open the log file as you would open any ASCII file using the word processor of your choice.

Or,

- Print the log file from DOS by typing `COPY AUDIT.LOG PRN:` where AUDIT.LOG represents the name and path of the log file.

NETWORK SCANNING

You can prevent viruses from spreading across a network by obtaining a site license from Symantec to allow you to run Virus Intercept on all of the workstations in your network. Once loaded, Virus Intercept prevents an infected file from being activated or executed from any drive, including network drives. Because Virus Intercept is loaded before network drivers, all workstations will remain secure.

Note that boot-sector and partition-table infectors will not normally "migrate" across a network. One partition-table infector that *will* is a virus called Tequila, because it can also infect executable files.

Your network administrator should use Virus Clinic to scan file servers regularly to detect and eliminate any infected files.

Setting the Inoculation Directory

When scanning and inoculating network drives, you can specify the directory where the inoculation file is stored. The default will be the root directory of the drive being scanned, but you may want to specify a directory with more limited read-and-write access to prevent the file from being tampered with.

To set the inoculation directory:

1 Choose GLOBAL... from the Virus Clinic Options menu.
   The Global dialog box appears (see Figure 20-5).

2 Type the full pathname of the directory in which you want to store the inoculation file in the Network Inoculation Directory text box.
   If Detect Unknown Viruses is checked, the Browse button is activated, allowing you to browse for a file.

3 Select OK.

Any directory specified in the Network Inoculation Directory text box must already exist on all network drives. If it does not already exist, you must create the directory on each network drive.

Using Norton Mail

This chapter explains how to:

- Start and exit Norton Mail
- Manage a system of folders
- Create, send and receive messages
- Create and maintain an address book and mail lists
- Set up your MCI accounts, telephone numbers, modem settings and other options

Contents

Starting and Exiting Norton Mail 21-3
The Folder System 21-5
Processing Mail 21-6
    Creating a Message 21-6
    Lists of Addressees 21-8
    Sending Attachments 21-12
    Adding Message and Addressee Handling 21-14
    Sending and Receiving Messages 21-16
    Reading a Message 21-19
    Replying to a Message 21-20
    Forwarding a Message 21-21
    Editing a Message 21-21
    Copying or Moving a Message Between Folders 21-22

Printing a Message 21-23
Deleting a Message 21-23
More About Folders 21-24
Creating a Folder 21-24
Opening a Folder 21-25
Sorting Messages in a Folder 21-26
Renaming a Folder 21-26
Deleting a Folder 21-26
Address Book and Mail List Maintenance 21-27
The Address Book 21-27
Mail Lists 21-33
Synchronizing Your Address Book and Mail Lists 21-36
Changing Folder or Mail List Locations 21-37
MCI Accounts 21-37
MCI Telephone Settings 21-41
Modem Settings 21-42
Other Setup Options 21-43
Other Types of Mail 21-45
Fax 21-45
Telex 21-46
Paper Mail 21-46
Other Electronic Mail Systems 21-46

Norton Mail is an easy-to-use electronic mail program that allows you to send and receive mail using your MCI account. Your messages can be sent:

- To people with accounts on electronic mail systems associated with MCI.
- Using fax, telex and paper mail through MCI. See the section "Other Types of Mail" for details.

The *Installing Norton Desktop for DOS* guide explains how to install and configure Norton Mail.

STARTING AND EXITING NORTON MAIL

You can choose to start Norton Mail from Norton Desktop, Norton Menu or from DOS.

To start Norton Mail:

- From Norton Desktop, open the (long) Tools menu and choose MAIL.

TIP: If you want to attach a file to your next mail message:
- First select the file(s) from the current drive window; then select MAIL from the (long) Tools menu.

The Message From dialog box appears. See the sections "Creating a Message" and "Sending Attachments" for more information.

Or,

- Open the File menu, choose RUN... and type NMAIL in the DOS Command text box.

Or,

- From Norton Menu, select NMAIL (or whatever name you assigned to NMAIL.EXE).

Or,

- From the DOS prompt, type NMAIL and press Enter.

Or,

- Use a batch file. For example, to have Norton Mail start up every time you turn on your computer, you can include NMAIL in your AUTOEXEC.BAT file.

21-4 *Using Norton Desktop for DOS*

For more details about the command line used when running a DOS command from the Norton Desktop, from the DOS prompt, or from a batch file, see Appendix C, "Command-Line Reference."

When you start Norton Mail, the Norton Mail desktop appears (Figure 21-1).

Figure 21-1

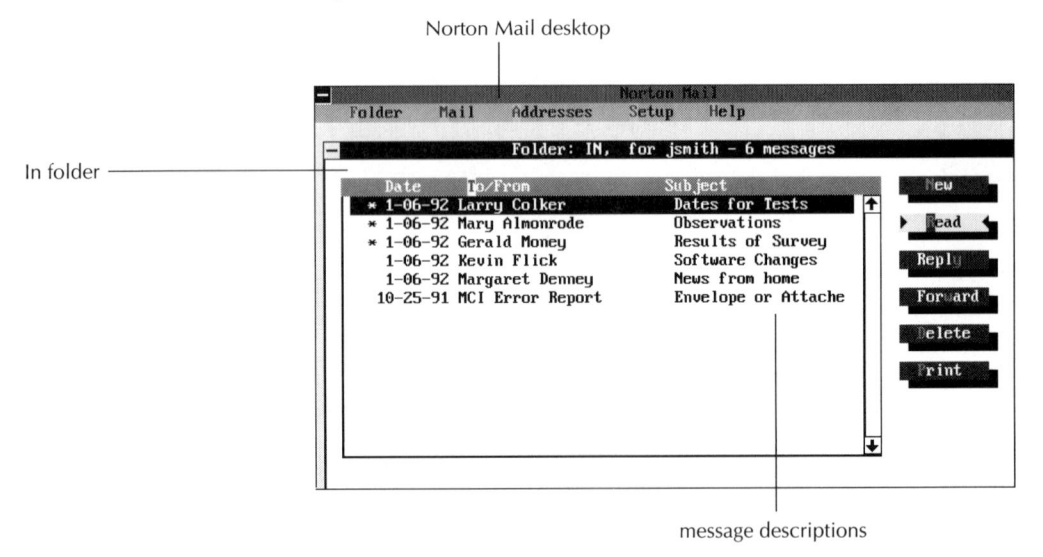

Norton Mail desktop

In folder

message descriptions

The In folder displays descriptions of messages it has for the MCI account currently selected for viewing. The section "MCI Accounts" has details about selecting an account to view.

You see either the short or extended version of the message description depending on whether you have the Extended Message Info option checked or unchecked. See the section "Other Setup Options" for details.

To exit Norton Mail:

- From the Norton Mail desktop, open the Folder menu and choose EXIT.

  A dialog box appears, and you must confirm your exit.

THE FOLDER SYSTEM

If you have unsent messages at the time you exit, Norton Mail displays the Exit dialog box with "REMINDER: Your OUT Folder Has Messages." Most users send the messages in their Out folders prior to ending a Norton Mail session.

You use a system of folders to store mail messages. You need to know something about the folder system to get started with Norton Mail.

The folders are really directories, and the messages are stored in files. Every Norton Mail user has In, Out, Sent and Draft folders. The folders and their uses are explained in Table 21-1.

Table 21-1

Folder Name	Purpose
In	Stores messages you receive through MCI Mail.
Out	Stores messages that are waiting to be sent during the next MCI Mail session.
Sent	Stores messages that were sent by you in previous MCI Mail sessions.
Draft	Stores incomplete messages you are preparing or editing. You move them to the Out folder when you want to send them.

The Norton Mail Folders

You can also create additional folders. For example, if you want to sort mail by topic, you can create folders with topical names, such as Orders or Private, and move messages on those topics to those folders. Each of the folders you create becomes a subdirectory of the FOLDERS directory. See the section "More About Folders" for details about creating, opening, sorting, renaming and deleting folders.

Using Norton Desktop for DOS

When you configure Norton Mail, you specify the location of:

- The In, Out, Sent and Draft folders
- The FOLDERS directory

You can change these locations later. See the section "Changing Folder or Mail List Locations" for details.

PROCESSING MAIL

Norton Mail allows you to:

- Create messages (including addressing them, attaching files to them and specifying special handling for messages or individual addressees)
- Send and receive mail messages
- Reply to messages
- Forward messages
- Read messages
- Edit messages
- Copy or move messages to other folders
- Print messages
- Delete messages

Messages that you create, reply to or forward are placed in the folder designated to receive newly created messages. By default, this is your Out folder. See the section "Other Setup Options" for details about selecting a folder for this purpose.

Creating a Message

Messages you create display the left-arrow symbol (←) in front of their message descriptions. This indicates that they can be sent.

To create a message:

1   From the Norton Mail desktop, select the New button to the right of the current folder (see Figure 21-1).

   Or,

   From the Norton Mail desktop, open the Mail menu and choose NEW MESSAGE... (Ctrl+N).

   The Message From dialog box appears (Figure 21-2).

Using Norton Mail **21-7**

Figure 21-2

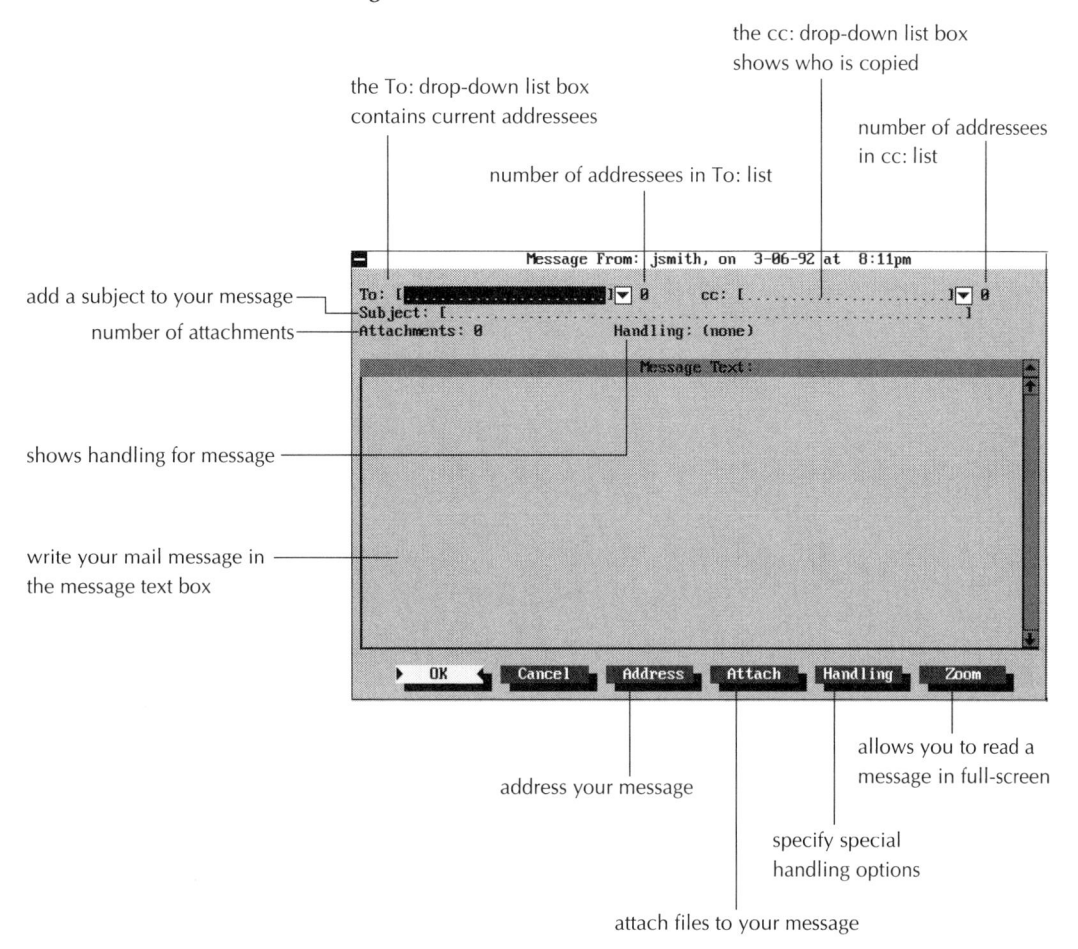

- the cc: drop-down list box shows who is copied
- the To: drop-down list box contains current addressees
- number of addressees in cc: list
- number of addressees in To: list
- add a subject to your message
- number of attachments
- shows handling for message
- write your mail message in the message text box
- address your message
- attach files to your message
- specify special handling options
- allows you to read a message in full-screen

2 To address the message, fill in the To: and cc: drop-down list boxes. You must have at least one recipient in the To: box for a message to be accepted by Norton Mail. Follow the steps in the section "Adding an Addressee to a List" to fill first one and then the other box. You cannot type characters into these boxes.

3 To attach files to the message, see the section "Sending Attachments" for details.

4 To give the message a subject, type the subject of the message in the Subject text box. The subject can be no longer than 59 characters.

5   To create the text of the message, select the message text box just below the Subject text box.

TIP: To switch from a full-screen view of the message text and the Message From dialog box (or vice versa), do one of the following:

- Select the Zoom button.
- Press Ctrl+PgUp or Ctrl+PgDn.

Or,

- Select the prompt button above the vertical scroll bar.

6   Type the text of your message. Refer to the section called "Editing Text Files" in Chapter 4, "Managing Directories and Files," for information about editing your message.

NOTE: Usually addressees or messages do not require any special handling. See the section "Adding Message and Addressee Handling" when any special handling is needed.

7   When you complete the message, select OK to exit the Message From dialog box. If you did not select at least one addressee for the To: list box, the Selected Addressees dialog box appears now and you must enter a recipient in the To: drop-down list box.

The message is stored in the folder designated to receive newly created messages until your next MCI Mail session.

Lists of Addressees

An addressee from your address book can become part of the To: or cc: lists for a message or a mail list. This section explains how to select addressees for lists, change their types and delete them from lists.

The only way to edit information about an addressee in a list is to edit the information about that addressee in the address book itself. See the section "The Address Book" for details.

You start from the Selected Addressees dialog box (Figure 21-3). When this dialog box is not empty, you see the names of the selected addressees, an optional note and the type of address being used for that addressee. The To: List option button at the bottom of the box is selected by default. The numbers of addressees already in the To: and cc: lists appears next to the buttons.

Figure 21-3

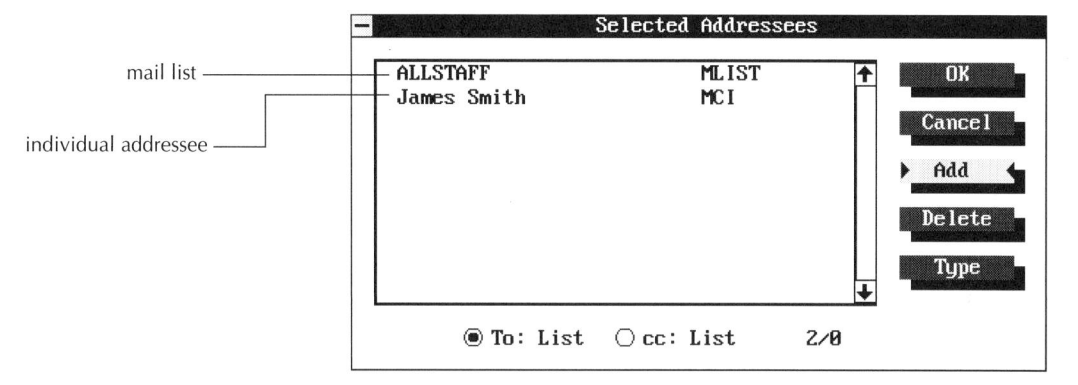

```
┌─────────────────── Selected Addressees ───────────────────┐
│  ALLSTAFF            MLIST              ↑    ┌────────┐   │
│  James Smith         MCI                     │   OK   │   │
│                                              └────────┘   │
│                                              ┌────────┐   │
│                                              │ Cancel │   │
│                                              └────────┘   │
│                                              ┌────────┐   │
│                                            ▶ │  Add   │ ◀ │
│                                              └────────┘   │
│                                              ┌────────┐   │
│                                              │ Delete │   │
│                                              └────────┘   │
│                                              ┌────────┐   │
│                                         ↓    │  Type  │   │
│                                              └────────┘   │
│         ● To: List    ○ cc: List    2/0                   │
└───────────────────────────────────────────────────────────┘
```

mail list — ALLSTAFF
individual addressee — James Smith

Adding an Addressee to a List

You add addressees to the To: and cc: drop-down list boxes and to mail lists using the steps below.

To add addressees to the list:

1 In the Message From dialog box, select Address (see Figure 21-2).

   Or,

   From the Mail Lists dialog box:

   a Select the name of the mail list.
   b Select New.
   c Type the name of the new mail list.
   d Select OK.

   Or,

   ■ Select the name of a mail list. Then select Open.

   Or,

   ■ Double-click the name of a mail list.

   The Selected Addressees dialog box opens (see Figure 21-3).

2   Select either the To: List or cc: List option button at the bottom of the dialog box.

3   Select Add.

    The Address Book dialog box displays the addressees you have in your address book along with a note about each addressee and the type of address currently selected for each addressee.

4   Select one or more addressees. (See the section "The Address Book" if you want more information about using the address book.)

5   Select OK to exit the Address Book dialog box.

6   Select OK to exit the Selected Addressees dialog box.

7   Select OK to exit the Message From dialog box.

    Or,

    Select Close to exit the Mail Lists dialog box.

Changing the Type of an Address

You may have several types of addresses for an individual addressee. For example, if the address type is MCI and you want to send a fax to this person, you need to change the type to FAX. The default type is the one most recently selected in the address book, but you can easily change this.

Table 21-2 shows the available address types.

Table 21-2

Type	Explanation
PAPER	Paper Mail address
TELEX	Telex address
EMS	Electronic Mail System address (for affiliates of MCI Mail)
FAX	Fax address
MCI	MCI Instant address

Address types

To change the type of address for an addressee:

1. Go to the Selected Addressees dialog box as explained in the previous section (see Figure 21-3).
2. Select either the To: List or cc: List option button.
3. Select the addressee. Then select Type.

   Or,

   Double-click the addressee.

   The Address Type dialog box appears (Figure 21-4).

Figure 21-4

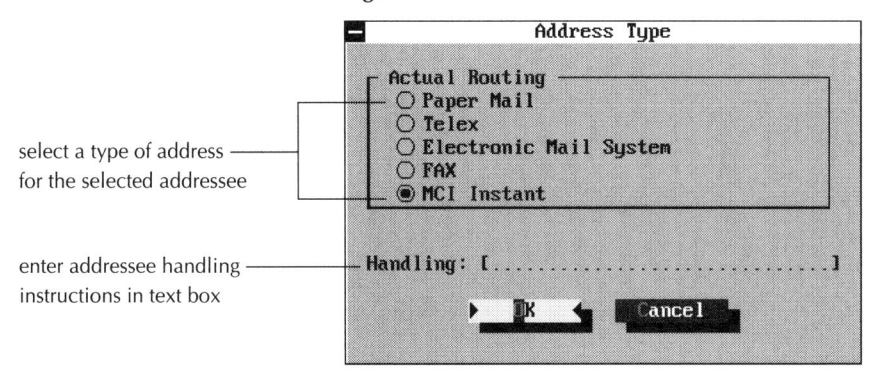

select a type of address for the selected addressee

enter addressee handling instructions in text box

```
┌─ Address Type ─────────────────┐
│ ┌─ Actual Routing ───────────┐ │
│ │  ○ Paper Mail              │ │
│ │  ○ Telex                   │ │
│ │  ○ Electronic Mail System  │ │
│ │  ○ FAX                     │ │
│ │  ● MCI Instant             │ │
│ └────────────────────────────┘ │
│ Handling: [.................]  │
│        [ OK ]    [ Cancel ]    │
└────────────────────────────────┘
```

4. Select the option button for the desired type. Buttons are dimmed when the addressee does not have an address of that type.
5. Select OK to exit the Address Type dialog box.
6. Select OK to exit the Selected Addressees dialog box.
7. Select OK to exit the Message From dialog box.

   Or,

   Select Close to exit the Mail Lists dialog box.

Deleting an Addressee from a List

If you want to update a mailing list, you may sometimes need to delete an addressee from the list.

To delete an addressee from a list:

1. Go to the Selected Addressees dialog box as explained in the section "Lists of Addressees" (see Figure 21-3).
2. Select either the To: List or cc: List option button at the bottom of the dialog box.

3   Select the addressee.
4   Select Delete.

    If the Confirm Deletes option is checked, the Confirm Deletion dialog box displays the name of the addressee, and you select OK to confirm the deletion. See the section "Other Setup Options" for details about this option.

5   Select OK to exit the Selected Addressees dialog box.
6   Select OK to exit the Message From dialog box.

    Or,

    Select Close to exit the Mail Lists dialog box.

Sending Attachments

You may want to attach a file, such as a text file or a program file, and send it along with your message. Before you start Norton Mail from the Norton Desktop, you can select files from the current drive window to attach to your next message and go directly to the Message From dialog box.

Once you are in Norton Mail, you can browse through the directories on available drives for a file to attach to the message using the procedures in this section.

Attaching a File to a Message

Browsing is an easy way to locate the file you want to attach. You can attach only one file per browse. If you know the file's pathname, you can type it directly into the File text box.

To attach a file to a message:

- From Norton Desktop, you can select any files in the current drive window that you wish to attach to your next mail message. Then choose MAIL from the (long) Tools menu to start Norton Mail.

Or,

1   From the Message From dialog box, select Attach (see Figure 21-2).

    The Attach Files dialog box appears (Figure 21-5).

2   Select Browse.

    The Browse for Attachment dialog box appears.

3   Select the filename of the file to attach to your message from the list. (Using a browse dialog box is explained in Chapter 1, "Getting Started.")

Figure 21-5

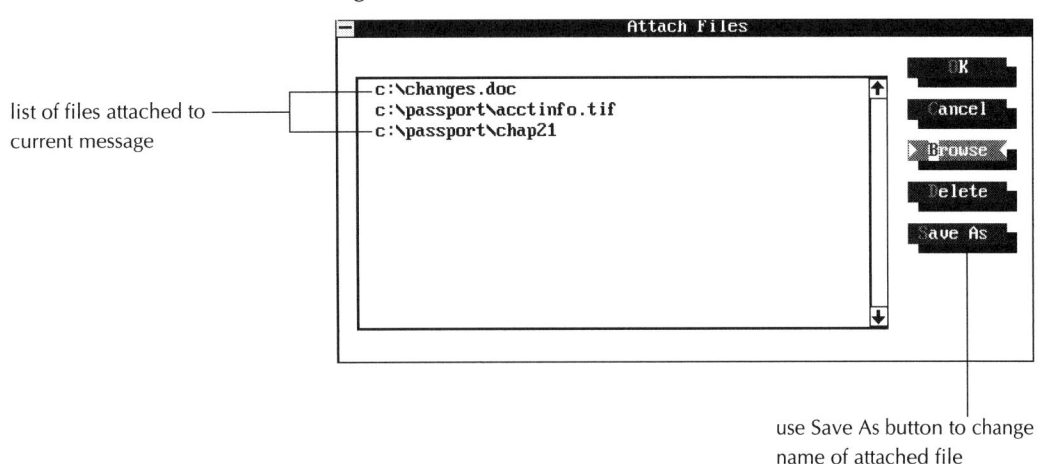

list of files attached to current message

use Save As button to change name of attached file

4   Select OK to exit the Browse for Attachment dialog box.

5   Select OK to exit the Attach Files dialog box.

Deleting a File from the List of Attached Files

Deleting a file from the list of attached files only detaches the file from the message. The file itself is not deleted from the disk or network.

To delete an attached file from the Attach list box:

1   From the Message From dialog box, select Attach (see Figure 21-2).

    The Attach Files dialog box appears (see Figure 21-5).

2   Select the filename of the file that you want to delete from the list.

3   Select Delete.

    If the Confirm Deletes option is checked, the Confirm Deletion dialog box displays the name of the selected file, and you select OK to confirm the deletion. See the section "Other Setup Options" for details about this option.

4   Select OK to exit the Attach Files dialog box.

Changing the Name of an Attached File

You can change the name of an attached file. This actually makes a copy of the file with the pathname you provide. The new file is attached to the message.

To change the name of an attached file:

1. From the Message From dialog box, select Attach (see Figure 21-2).

   The Attach Files dialog box appears (see Figure 21-5).

2. Select the filename to be changed.
3. Select Save As.

   The Save As dialog box appears.

4. In the As text box, edit the existing pathname or type a new pathname for the file.
5. Select OK to exit the Save As dialog box.
6. Select OK to exit the Attach Files dialog box.

Adding Message and Addressee Handling

Sometimes a message, such as one being sent as paper mail, needs some kind of special handling. You may specify message handling by selecting check boxes or by typing customized handling instructions. Handling for an individual addressee is also available. See your MCI Mail manual for more information about available handling options in each case.

To specify how MCI is to handle your message:

1. From the Message From dialog box, select Handling (see Figure 21-2).

   The Message Handling dialog box appears, as shown in Figure 21-6.

2. Check any combination of the following check boxes:
   - RECEIPT
   - ONITE
   - MEMO
   - DOC
   - CHARGE:
   - SIGN:
   - FORM:

Using Norton Mail   21-15

Figure 21-6

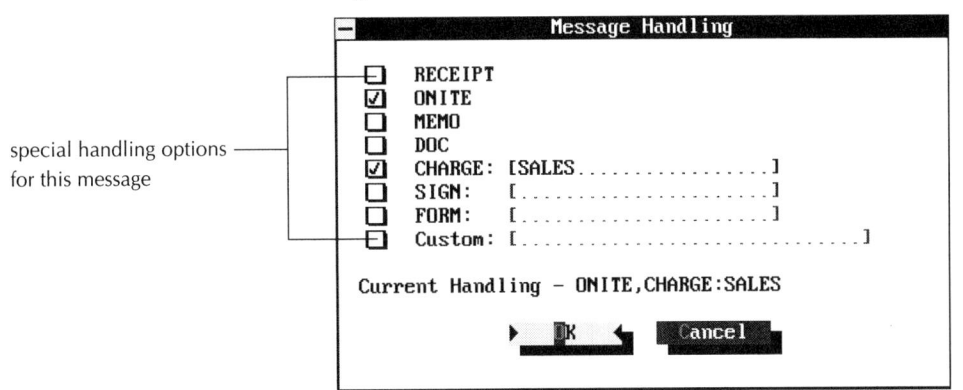

```
┌─ ────────────── Message Handling ──────────────┐
│                                                │
│        ☐   RECEIPT                             │
│        ☑   ONITE                               │
│        ☐   MEMO                                │
│        ☐   DOC                                 │
│        ☑   CHARGE:  [SALES................]    │
│        ☐   SIGN:    [....................]    │
│        ☐   FORM:    [....................]    │
│        ☐   Custom:  [........................]│
│                                                │
│     Current Handling - ONITE,CHARGE:SALES      │
│                                                │
│              ▶  OK  ◀      Cancel              │
│                                                │
└────────────────────────────────────────────────┘
```

special handling options for this message

NOTE: The colon after the check box name indicates that additional MCI information is required.

Your choices are added to the Current Handling text box at the bottom of the dialog box and are separated by commas. The Current Handling text box may contain up to 29 characters; if you try to enter more than 29 characters, the data is truncated.

3 If you select a check box whose label ends with a colon (such as CHARGE:), type the additional information required in the text box next to that check box. See your MCI Mail manual for details about what to type.

4 Select OK to save your selections and exit the Message Handling dialog box.

To specify customized message handling:

1 From the Message From dialog box, select Handling (see Figure 21-2).

The Message Handling dialog box appears (see Figure 21-6).

2 Check Custom.

3 Enter a maximum of 29 characters in the text box. See your MCI Mail manual for details.

4 Select OK to save your selections and exit the Message Handling dialog box.

To specify per addressee handling:

1 From the Message From dialog box, select Address (see Figure 21-2).

The Selected Addressees dialog box appears (see Figure 21-3).

2 Select the To: List or cc: List option button.
3 Select the addressee.
4 Select Type.

The Address Type dialog box appears (see Figure 21-4).

5 Select the Handling text box.
6 Type the handling instructions. See your MCI Mail manual for details.
7 Select OK to exit the Address Type dialog box.
8 Select OK to exit the Selected Addressees dialog box.

Sending and Receiving Messages

An MCI Mail session both sends and receives messages. Norton Mail attempts to send all the messages in your Out folder. All the messages that are sent go into your Sent folder. All the messages that are received go into your In folder. Before attempting to send or receive messages, be sure your modem is turned on and working correctly.

Norton Mail does the following for you:

- Dials the MCI service
- Connects to MCI Mail
- Sends messages from your Out folder and moves them to your Sent folder
- Receives messages and places them in your In folder
- Ends the MCI Mail session
- Disconnects (hangs up)
- Repeats the Send/Receive for each active account in turn

To send and receive messages:

1 From the Norton Mail desktop (see Figure 21-1), open the Mail menu and choose SEND/RECEIVE... (Ctrl+S).

The Send/Receive dialog box appears (Figure 21-7).

Using Norton Mail 21-17

Figure 21-7

```
┌─ ─────────────── Send/Receive for jsmith ───────────────┐
│         Date       To/From         Subject              │
│  ← 1-06-92 To:    Margaret Denney  News from home       │
│  ← 1-06-92 To:    Margaret Denney  Kick-off Information │
│  ← 1-06-92 To:    Kevin Flick      Software Changes     │
│                                                         │
│  ┌ Time ──────────┐ ┌ Message ──────┐ ┌ Modem Activity ┐│
│  │ Elapsed: 00:00:04│ │ Sent:     0/3 │ │ . Transmitting ││
│  │ Estimated: 00:01:30│ │ Received: 0/0 │ │ + Receiving    ││
│  └──────────────────┘ └───────────────┘ └────────────────┘│
│                     Percent Complete: 5%  Status: For: jsmith│
│   ▶ Cancel                                              │
└─────────────────────────────────────────────────────────┘
```

- list of messages to be sent
- estimated time for this account
- percent complete
- number of messages sent/received
- type of current modem activity
- account being processed

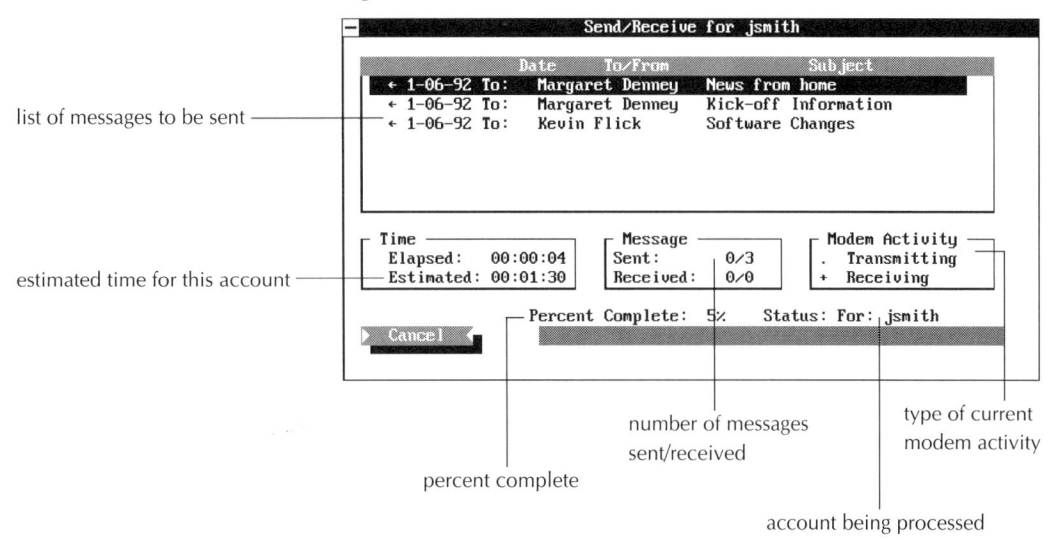

The Send/Receive dialog box lists the messages being sent and received for the account being processed.

The Time group box shows the amount of time taken to send or receive messages for the current account and the amount of time estimated to complete the process.

The Message group box shows the number of messages that have been sent followed by the total number to send for this account. The number of messages received for this account is also shown.

The Modem Activity group box shows whether the modem is transmitting or receiving. The dot (.) in front of the activity changes to a plus (+) when that activity occurs.

This dialog box also shows the percentage of completion and the status of the current message.

If the sound is on, you may hear the dial tone, dialing and connection to MCI Mail. For details about sound, see the section "Modem Settings."

If the connection fails, Norton Mail retries until one of the following occurs:

- A connection is made
- Ten unsuccessful attempts have been made
- You select Cancel

When the session is over, the Mail Session Done message box appears.

2   Select OK to end the session.

After a mail session, Norton Mail makes your In folder the current folder. If you have more than one account, you may need to change which account is viewable. For more information, see the section "MCI Accounts."

To cancel the session:

1   From the Send/Receive dialog box, select Cancel.

A message box appears asking you if you really want to cancel or if you want to resume the session.

2   Select Cancel again and the session ends.

Correcting an Envelope Error

When a message cannot be sent because of an error, such as a wrong address in its header (also called its envelope), MCI disconnects and returns an error message. Norton Mail does the following:

- Beeps you.
- Briefly displays "Envelope Error" on the status line of the Send/Receive dialog box.
- Attaches the MCI error message to the beginning of your mail message.
- Puts the message in your In folder. The description says that the message is from "MCI Error Report" and that its subject is "Envelope Error."
- Redials the MCI service to finish the MCI Mail session.

To correct an Envelope Error:

1   When the mail session is over, select the message that could not be sent. It is now stored in the In folder.

2   Select Read to see the error message.

3   If the message is zoomed, return to the previous dialog box.

4   Select Reply. The error information is automatically deleted.

5   You can correct the address in the address book.

    a   Select Address to see the Selected Addressees dialog box (see Figure 21-3).

    b   Select Add.

        The Address Book dialog box appears.

    c   Select Edit to edit the address. For details, see the section "The Address Book."

    Or,

    You can delete the incorrect address from the message or make other corrections.

Reading a Message

Incoming unread messages have an asterisk (*) in front of them to indicate that they have not yet been read. After you read the message, the asterisk disappears. Incoming messages never display a left-arrow symbol (←) in front of them because they cannot be sent.

To read a message:

1   From the current folder, select the message you want to read.

2   Select the Read button to the right of the current folder.

    Or,

    Open the Mail menu and choose READ....

    Or,

- From the current folder, double-click the description of the message.

    The Message From dialog box appears unless the Full Page Read option is checked. See the section "Other Setup Options" for details about this option.

While you are reading a message, you cannot edit it, make changes to the addressees, and so forth.

After you have read a mail message, you may want to reply to it, forward it to another person, print it for your future reference, move it to another folder or delete it.

Replying to a Message

When you reply to a message, you can have the text of the message included in your reply. See the section "Other Setup Options" for details about the Include Message Text in Replies option.

Messages you create by replying to another message have the left-arrow symbol (←) in front of their message descriptions. This indicates that they can be sent.

To reply to a message:

1   From the current folder, select a message to reply to.
2   Select the Reply button (Figure 21-8).
    Or,
    Open the Mail menu and choose REPLY... (Ctrl+R).

The Message From dialog box appears (see Figure 21-2). The sender's name becomes the addressee. The account being viewed is always the sender of this message. The information from the Subject text box in the old message is transferred to the new message's Subject text box.

Figure 21-8

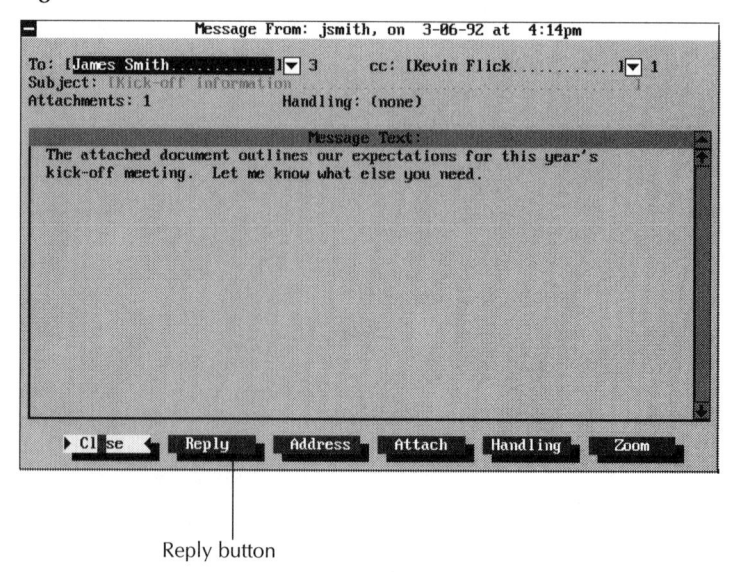

Reply button

3 Write your reply from the Message From dialog box (which is described in detail in the section "Creating a Message," starting with step 2).

4 Select OK to save your message and exit the Message From dialog box.

The new message goes into the folder you specified to receive new messages, or you are prompted for a folder. See the section "Other Setup Options" for details.

Forwarding a Message

Messages you create by forwarding another message have the left-arrow symbol (←) in front of their message descriptions. This indicates that they can be sent.

To forward a message:

1 From the current folder, select a message to forward.

2 Select the Forward button located to the right of the current folder.

Or,

Open the Mail menu and choose FORWARD... (Ctrl+F).

The Message From dialog box appears (see Figure 21-2). The To: and cc: boxes are now empty. The entire text of the message, preceded by information from the MCI Mail envelope, becomes the new message. The information from the Subject text box in the original message is transferred to the new message's Subject text box. The account being viewed is always the sender of this message.

3 You can add some information of your own to the message before you forward it. Use the Message From dialog box to edit the message or add new text to it.

4 Select OK to save your message and exit from the Message From dialog box.

The new message goes into the folder you have specified to receive new messages, or you are prompted for a folder. See the section "Other Setup Options" for details.

Editing a Message

If a message can be sent, indicated by the left-arrow symbol (←) in front of it, you can edit the message. When you edit a message, it is not moved to another folder.

To edit a message:

1 From the current folder, select a message to edit.
2 Open the Mail menu and choose EDIT... (Ctrl+E).
   The Message From dialog box appears (Figure 21-9).

Figure 21-9

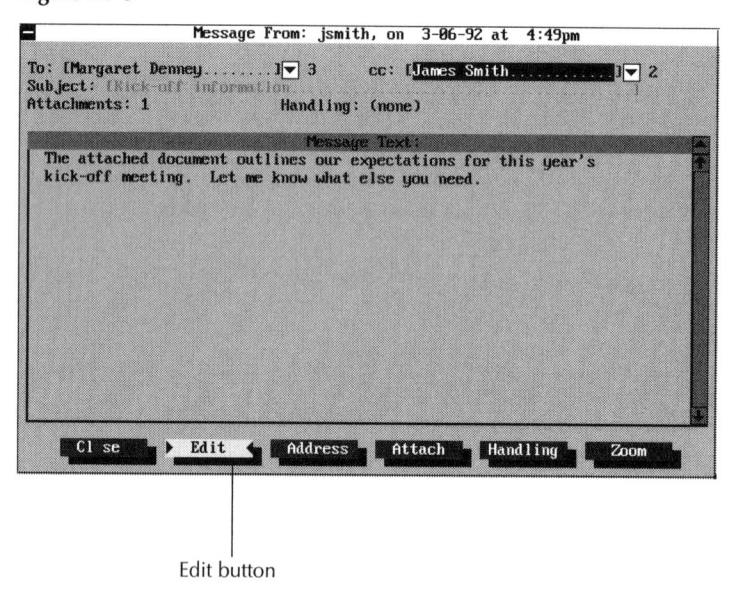

[Screenshot of Message From dialog box with Edit button indicated]

Edit button

3 Edit the selected message. See the section "Editing Text Files" in Chapter 4, "Managing Directories and Files," if you need more information about the Norton Desktop editing feature.
4 Select OK to exit the Message From dialog box.

Copying or Moving a Message Between Folders

Copying a message copies it to the specified folder and leaves it in the current folder as well. Moving a message copies it to the specified folder and deletes it from the current folder.

To copy or move a message between folders:

1 From the current folder, select a message to copy or move.
2 To copy a message, open the Mail menu and choose COPY... (Ctrl+C). The Copy dialog box appears.

Or,

To move a message to another folder, open the Mail menu and choose MOVE... (Ctrl+V). The Move dialog box appears.

The Copy and Move dialog boxes are identical except for their names. You see the number of messages you selected to copy or move and the folders that are available.

3   Select the target folder for the message.
4   Select OK to exit the dialog box.

The selected file is copied or moved to its new location.

Printing a Message

You may wish to keep printed copies of your mail messages. You can print one message at a time or several messages at once.

To print a mail message, you must first have set up a print configuration, and your computer must be connected to a printer. For details, see Chapter 9, "Configuring Norton Desktop." To get to the Configure Printer dialog box, open the Setup menu and choose PRINTER....

To print a message:

1   From the current folder, select the messages you want to print.
2   Select the Print button to the right of the current folder.

Or,

Open the Mail menu and choose PRINT....

A Message dialog box appears showing the pathname of each message being printed. The dialog box disappears when you select OK or when the message has been sent to the printer.

Deleting a Message

When you have finished with a message, you may want to delete it. You may delete one message at a time or several messages at once.

To delete a message:

1   From the current folder, select the message(s) to delete.
2   Select the Delete button to the right of the current folder.

MORE ABOUT FOLDERS

Or,

Open the Mail menu and choose DELETE... (Ctrl+D).

The Delete dialog box displays the number of messages being deleted.

3   Select OK to confirm the deletion.

The section called "The Folder System," earlier in this chapter, explained the four folders—In, Out, Sent and Draft—that Norton Mail creates automatically and uses to store your messages. This section explains how to:

- Create a folder
- Open a folder
- Sort messages in a folder by name, date or subject
- Rename a folder
- Delete a folder

You can open and sort the contents of any folder, but you can only rename and delete folders that you have created.

To change the location (or pathname) of a folder, see the section "Changing Folder or Mail List Locations" later in this chapter.

Creating a Folder

When you create your own folders, their names become subdirectories of the path you specified for the FOLDERS directory. For example, if you specified C:\ND\FOLDERS, creating a folder named Private results in a subdirectory for messages named C:\ND\FOLDERS\PRIVATE.

To create a new folder:

1   From the Norton Mail desktop, open the Folder menu and choose FOLDERS....

The Folders dialog box appears, listing the existing folders in alphabetical order (Figure 21-10).

2   Select New to create a new folder. The New dialog box appears.

3   Type the name for the new folder in the text box. If you type a character that is not appropriate for a filename, you hear a beep, and the character is ignored.

Figure 21-10

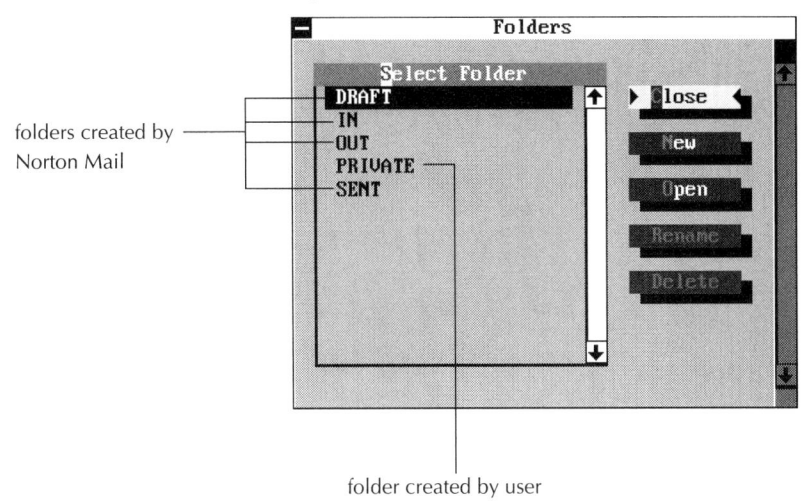

folders created by Norton Mail → DRAFT, IN, OUT, SENT

folder created by user → PRIVATE

4   Select OK to exit the New dialog box. The newly created folder is highlighted in the Folders dialog box.

5   Select Close to exit the Folders dialog box.

Opening a Folder

As you enter Norton Mail, you see the messages in the In folder for the account you are currently viewing.

To open a folder:

- From the Norton Mail desktop (see Figure 21-1), open the Folder menu and choose IN, OUT, SENT or DRAFT—if you want one of those folders. (The shortcut to the In folder is Ctrl+B.)

Or,

1   From the Norton Mail desktop, open the Folder menu and choose FOLDERS....

   The Folders dialog box appears, listing your folders in alphabetical order (see Figure 21-10).

2   Select a folder, then select Open.

   Or,

   Double-click the folder name.

To see the messages in another folder, switch to that folder and open it.

Sorting Messages in a Folder

The messages in a folder can be sorted by name, date or subject.

To sort messages:

1 Open the folder that contains the messages you want to sort.

2 From the Norton Mail desktop (see Figure 21-1), open the Mail menu and choose one of the following:
- SORT BY FROM sorts the messages alphabetically by name of recipient.
- SORT BY DATE sorts the messages by date and time.
- SORT BY SUBJECT sorts the messages by subject.

Renaming a Folder

The In, Out, Sent and Draft folders cannot be renamed. You can rename only folders that you created.

To rename a folder:

1 From the Norton Mail desktop (see Figure 21-1), open the Folder menu and choose FOLDERS....

The Folders dialog box appears (see Figure 21-10).

2 Select a folder to rename.

3 Select Rename.

The Rename dialog box appears.

4 Type the new name for the folder in the text box.

5 Select OK to change the name of the folder and exit the Rename dialog box.

6 Select Close to exit the Folders dialog box.

Deleting a Folder

The In, Out, Sent and Draft folders cannot be deleted. You can delete only folders that you have created.

To delete a folder:

1 From the Norton Mail desktop (see Figure 21-1), open the Folder menu and choose FOLDERS....

The Folders dialog box appears, listing your folders in alphabetical order (see Figure 21-10).

2 Select a folder to delete.

3   Select Delete.

If the Confirm Deletes option is checked, the Confirm Deletion dialog box displays the name of the folder, and you select OK to confirm the deletion. (See the section "Other Setup Options" for details about this option.)

If Confirm Deletes is not checked, the folder is deleted immediately—unless it contains messages. If a folder contains messages, a dialog box appears, listing the filenames for the messages in the folder. Select Yes to continue the deletion or No to return to the Folders dialog box without deleting the folder.

4   Select Close to exit the Folders dialog box.

ADDRESS BOOK AND MAIL LIST MAINTENANCE

The address book contains the addresses of the people to whom you send mail. As in a personal address book, you can add, edit and delete its entries. You can enter addresses, auto-add them from mail you receive, or input them from Norton Commander Mail or Lotus Express. Mail lists allow you to easily send messages to an entire group at once instead of addressing a message to many different recipients individually. Each mail list can be divided into To: and cc: lists. Keeping mail lists up-to-date makes it easier to send mail.

The Address Book

This section explains how to:

- Open the address book
- Add an addressee
- Edit the information for an existing addressee
- Copy an addressee
- Delete an addressee

To open the address book:

- From the Norton Mail desktop, open the Addresses menu and choose ADDRESS BOOK... (Ctrl+A).

Or,

1   From the Message From dialog box, select Address (see Figure 21-2).

The Selected Addressees dialog box appears (see Figure 21-3).

2 Select Add.

Or,

1 From the Mail Lists dialog box, select Open.

The Selected Addressees dialog box appears (see Figure 21-3).

2 Select Add.

The Address Book dialog box appears displaying a list of the addressees. The name of the addressee, an optional note and a type of address appear for each entry, as shown in Figure 21-11.

You may have several types of addresses for an entry, but only one type is the default. You can easily reset the address type when you are addressing a message. See the section "Changing the Type of an Address" earlier in this chapter for more information about address types.

NOTE: If you enter the address book from the Address menu, the Address Book dialog box displays a Close button rather than OK and Cancel buttons. If you enter the address book from the Mail Lists or the Message From dialog boxes, the Address Book dialog box displays OK and Cancel buttons instead of Close. Refer to Figures 21-11 and 21-13. Chapter 1, "Getting Started," explains the difference between a Close button and the OK/Cancel combination.

If you enter the Address Book dialog box from the Address menu, you can select only one addressee at a time. If you enter the Address Book dialog box from the Mail Lists or the Message From dialog boxes, you can select multiple addressees to include in the mail list or the message. Otherwise, you can select only one addressee at a time.

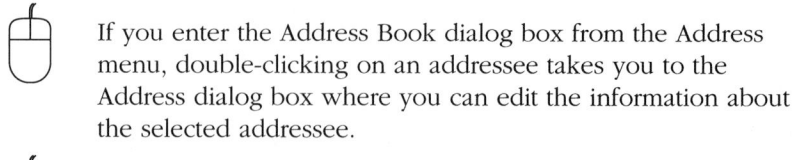

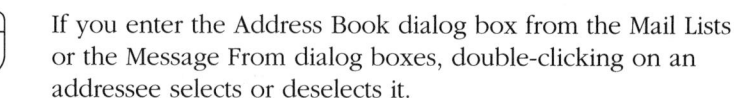

If you enter the Address Book dialog box from the Address menu, double-clicking on an addressee takes you to the Address dialog box where you can edit the information about the selected addressee.

If you enter the Address Book dialog box from the Mail Lists or the Message From dialog boxes, double-clicking on an addressee selects or deselects it.

Figure 21-11

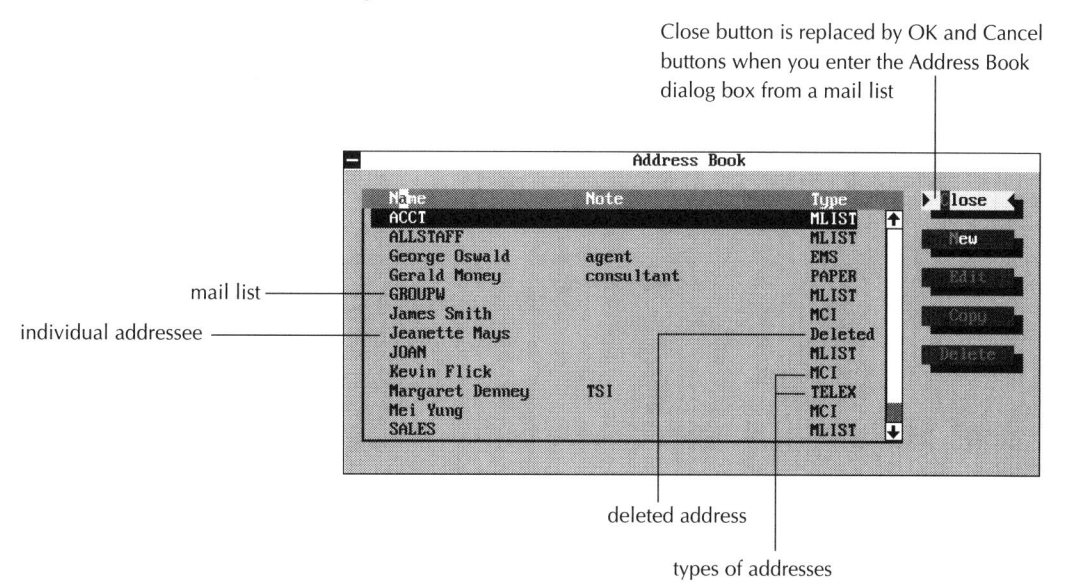

Close button is replaced by OK and Cancel buttons when you enter the Address Book dialog box from a mail list

```
                           Address Book
  Name              Note              Type          Close
  ACCT                                MLIST
  ALLSTAFF                            MLIST         New
  George Oswald    agent              EMS
  Gerald Money     consultant         PAPER         Edit
  GROUPW                              MLIST
  James Smith                         MCI           Copy
  Jeanette Mays                       Deleted
  JOAN                                MLIST         Delete
  Kevin Flick                         MCI
  Margaret Denney  TSI                TELEX
  Mei Yung                            MCI
  SALES                               MLIST
```

mail list → GROUPW
individual addressee → Jeanette Mays
deleted address
types of addresses

Adding an Addressee to the Address Book

Adding addressees to your address book allows you to send messages to more people.

To add an addressee to the address book:

1   From the Address Book dialog box, select New (see Figure 21-11).

    The Address dialog box appears (Figure 21-12).

2   Select the appropriate Address Type option button. The available choices are:

    - Paper Mail
    - Telex
    - EMS
    - FAX
    - MCI Instant (the default type)

    If you do not want an MCI Instant address, select the option button for another type of address. When you select a type, the text boxes associated with that type of address appear in the dialog box. The title of the dialog box changes from MCI Address to Telex Address, FAX Address, and so on.

Figure 21-12

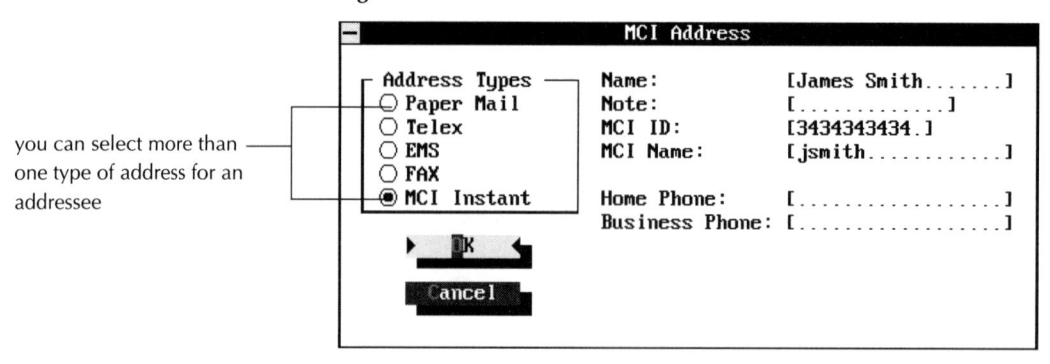

```
┌─                    MCI Address                      ─┐
    ┌─ Address Types ─┐  Name:         [James Smith.......]
    │ ○ Paper Mail    │  Note:         [...............]
    │ ○ Telex         │  MCI ID:       [3434343434.]
    │ ○ EMS           │  MCI Name:     [jsmith............]
    │ ○ FAX           │
    │ ● MCI Instant   │  Home Phone:     [..................]
    └─────────────────┘  Business Phone: [..................]
              ▶ OK ◀
              Cancel
```

you can select more than one type of address for an addressee

3   Type the address information in the appropriate text boxes.

- Name
- MCI ID
- MCI User Name
- Note (whatever you enter in the Note text box appears in the Address Book)

4   When you have finished, select OK and return to the Address Book dialog box.

Or,

If you want other types of addresses, select the option button for that type of address and repeat steps 3 and 4.

5   Exit the Address Book dialog box. Select Close if you entered the address book from the Address menu. Otherwise, you select OK.

Editing an Address in the Address Book

To keep addresses up-to-date, you need to edit your address book.

To edit information about an existing addressee:

1   From the Address Book dialog box (see Figure 21-11), do one of the following:

- Select the desired addressee. Then select Edit.
- Type the name of the desired addressee. This brings up a speed search box. As you type the name, the highlight moves to the first matching addressee.

Using Norton Mail 21-31

- If the Address Book dialog box has the Close button as the first button, double-clicking on the addressee takes you directly to the Address dialog box.

  The Address dialog box appears (see Figure 21-12).

2 Select the appropriate Address Type option button.
3 Type the address information in the appropriate text boxes.
4 Select OK.
5 Exit the Address Book dialog box.

Copying an Address in the Address Book

To add an addressee whose address is similar to one already in your address book, you can copy that existing address and edit it.

To create an addressee that is similar to one you already have:

1 From the Address Book dialog box, select an addressee to copy (see Figure 21-11).
2 Select Copy.

   The Address dialog box appears with the copied address information.

3 Select the appropriate Address Type option button.
4 Type the address information in the appropriate text boxes.
5 Select OK.
6 Exit the Address Book dialog box.

Deleting an Address in the Address Book

When an addressee is deleted, its type becomes "Deleted" in the Selected Addressees dialog box (see Figure 21-3) during the current Norton Mail session. A deleted addressee does not appear in the next mail session.

Use the following procedure to delete addressees from the address book or restore addressees whose type is "Deleted." (See Appendix C, "Command-Line Reference," to learn how to override this with /UNERASE or make it permanent with /PURGE.)

If you delete an addressee from the address book, you should also delete that addressee from any mail lists.

To delete an addressee from the address book:

1 From the Address Book dialog box, select the addressee to delete (see Figure 21-11).

2 Select Delete.

   If the Confirm Deletes option is checked, the Confirm Deletion dialog box displays the name of the addressee, and you select OK to confirm the deletion. See the section "Other Setup Options" for more about this option.

3 Exit the Address Book dialog box. If you entered the address book from the Address menu, you select Close. Otherwise, you select OK.

To restore a deleted addressee to the address book:

1 From the Address Book dialog box, select the addressee to restore (see Figure 21-11).

   The Delete button changes to an Undelete button when a deleted addressee is selected, as shown in Figure 21-13.

Figure 21-13

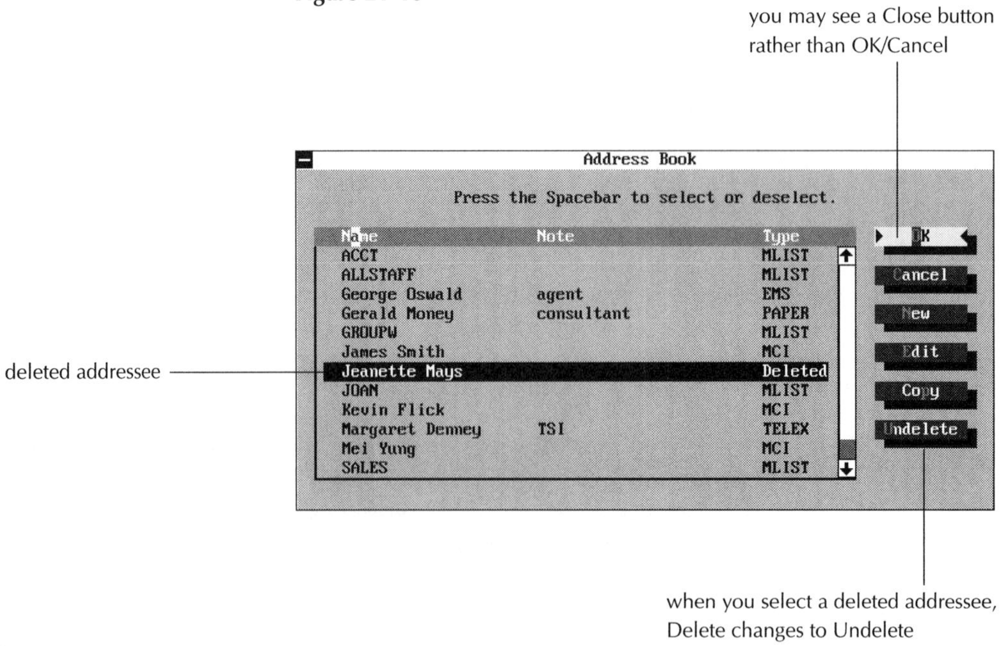

you may see a Close button rather than OK/Cancel

```
┌─ ──────────────── Address Book ────────────────┐
│         Press the Spacebar to select or deselect.          │
│   Name              Note             Type                  │
│   ACCT                               MLIST     ▶ OK ◀      │
│   ALLSTAFF                           MLIST                 │
│   George Oswald    agent             EMS       Cancel      │
│   Gerald Money     consultant        PAPER                 │
│   GROUPW                             MLIST     New         │
│   James Smith                        MCI                   │
│   Jeanette Mays                      Deleted   Edit        │
│   JOAN                               MLIST                 │
│   Kevin Flick                        MCI       Copy        │
│   Margaret Denney  TSI               TELEX                 │
│   Mei Yung                           MCI       Undelete    │
│   SALES                              MLIST                 │
└────────────────────────────────────────────────┘
```

deleted addressee ──── (Jeanette Mays row)

when you select a deleted addressee, Delete changes to Undelete

Automatic MCI Additions to the Address Book

2   Select Undelete.

   If the Confirm Deletes option is checked, you select OK to confirm the undeletion. See the section "Other Setup Options" for details about this option.

3   Exit the Address Book dialog box.

Auto-Add allows you to add addresses from selected mail messages to the address book automatically from:

- Selected messages in the current folder
- Each message you read as you read it

To add addresses from selected messages:

1   From the current folder, select messages whose addresses you want to add to the address book.

2   Open the Addresses menu and choose AUTO-ADD.

   The addresses of the messages you selected are added to the address book.

To add addresses from every message you read:

1   From the Norton Mail desktop (see Figure 21-1), open the Setup menu and choose OPTIONS....

   The Options dialog box appears.

2   Check the Auto-Add Address check box.

3   Select OK to save your changes and exit the dialog box.

   Any new addresses from messages you read are automatically added to the address book.

Mail Lists

Mail lists make sending messages to groups of people easy. When you select a mail list, your message will be sent to all the To: and cc: addressees in the mail list. Each mail list is a file. These files are stored in the MLISTS directory. You specify the location of this directory when you configure Norton Mail. To change the location of the MLISTS directory, see the section "Changing Folder or Mail List Locations."

This section explains how to:

- Create mail lists
- View their contents

21-34 *Using Norton Desktop for DOS*

- Rename mail lists
- Delete mail lists

See the section "Lists of Addressees" for explanations about adding addressees to and deleting them from lists.

To create a mail list:

1   From the Norton Mail desktop (see Figure 21-1), open the Addresses menu and choose MAIL LISTS....

    The Mail Lists dialog box appears (Figure 21-14).

Figure 21-14

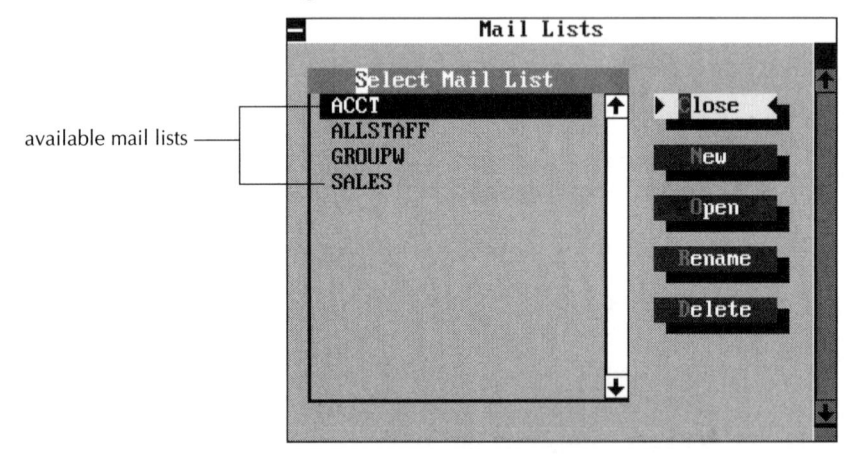

[Mail Lists dialog box showing Select Mail List with entries ACCT, ALLSTAFF, GROUPW, SALES (labeled "available mail lists"), and buttons Close, New, Open, Rename, Delete]

2   Select New to create a new mail list.

    The New dialog box appears and asks you to enter the name of the new mail list.

3   Type a legal DOS filename. If you enter a character that is not appropriate in a filename, you hear a beep and the character is ignored.

4   Select OK.

    The Selected Addressees dialog box appears (see Figure 21-3).

5   Select Add.

    The Address Book dialog box appears (see Figure 21-11).

6 Select addressees. (See the section "The Address Book" for details.)
7 Select OK to exit the Address Book dialog box.
8 Select OK to exit the Selected Addressees dialog box.
9 Select Close to exit the Mail Lists dialog box.

To view the contents of a mail list:

1 From the Norton Mail desktop (see Figure 21-1), open the Addresses menu and choose MAIL LISTS.... The Mail Lists dialog box appears (see Figure 21-14).
2 Select the name of the mail list. Then select Open.
   Or,
   Double-click the name of the mail list.
   The Selected Addressees dialog box (see Figure 21-3) displays the addressees currently in the mail list. When you select a mail list, you are notified about any addressees in it that are no longer in the address book. You may want to delete these addressees.
3 Select OK to exit the Selected Addressees dialog box.
4 Select Close to exit the Mail Lists dialog box.

To rename a mail list:

1 From the Norton Mail desktop (see Figure 21-1), open the Addresses menu and choose MAIL LISTS....
   The Mail Lists dialog box appears (see Figure 21-14).
2 Select Rename to rename an existing mail list.
   The Rename dialog box displays the current name of the mail list and asks you to enter the new name.
3 Type a legal DOS filename. If you enter a character that is not appropriate in a filename, you hear a beep and the character is ignored.
4 Select OK to exit the Rename dialog box.
5 Select Close to exit the Mail Lists dialog box.

To delete a mail list:

1. From the Norton Mail desktop, open the Addresses menu and choose MAIL LISTS....

   The Mail Lists dialog box appears (see Figure 21-14).

2. Select a mail list.

3. Select Delete.

   If the Confirm Deletes option is checked, the Confirm Deletion dialog box displays the name of the mail list, and you must select OK to confirm the deletion. If this option is not checked, the mail list is deleted immediately. See the section "Other Setup Options" for more about this option.

4. Select Close to exit the Mail Lists dialog box.

Synchronizing Your Address Book and Mail Lists

The address book and the mail lists are in separate files. Since mail lists reference information in the address book, the mail lists and the address book must have the same sequence ID. The sequence ID is like a version number. Whenever you update the address book or any mail list, the sequence ID for all of them increases. When you start Norton Mail with the address book or any mail lists out of synchronization, a dialog box lists the sequence IDs for the address book and each mail list. This tells you which items in the list are mismatched.

For example, if you use someone else's address book with your mail lists or an old backup of your address book with your current mail lists, the sequence IDs will be out of synchronization.

The address book is in a file named MCIADDNR.BK in the same directory as your other Norton Desktop files. The mail lists are in the MLISTS directory. See the Directories dialog box for the complete pathname to the MLISTS directory.

NOTE: If you are backing up your address book, be sure to back up your mail lists as well.

CHANGING FOLDER OR MAIL LIST LOCATIONS

You can use the Directories dialog box to change the locations (pathnames) for your folders and mail lists.

To change folder or mail list locations:

1 From the Norton Mail desktop (see Figure 21-1), open the Setup menu and choose DIRECTORIES....

   The Directories dialog box appears (Figure 21-15).

Figure 21-15

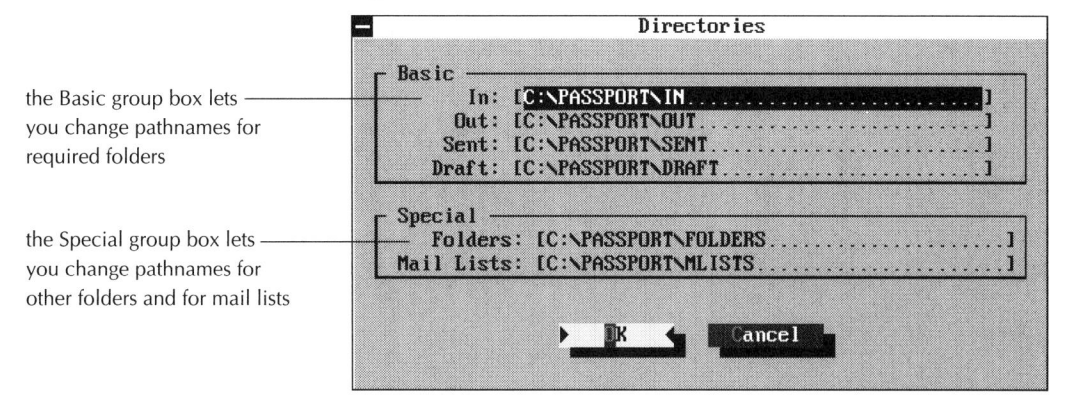

```
┌─                      Directories                      ─┐
│ ┌─ Basic ────────────────────────────────────────────┐ │
│ │       In: [C:\PASSPORT\IN.....................]   │ │
│ │      Out: [C:\PASSPORT\OUT....................]   │ │
│ │     Sent: [C:\PASSPORT\SENT...................]   │ │
│ │    Draft: [C:\PASSPORT\DRAFT..................]   │ │
│ └────────────────────────────────────────────────────┘ │
│ ┌─ Special ──────────────────────────────────────────┐ │
│ │  Folders: [C:\PASSPORT\FOLDERS................]   │ │
│ │Mail Lists: [C:\PASSPORT\MLISTS................]   │ │
│ └────────────────────────────────────────────────────┘ │
│              ▶  OK  ◀      Cancel                      │
└─────────────────────────────────────────────────────────┘
```

- the Basic group box lets you change pathnames for required folders
- the Special group box lets you change pathnames for other folders and for mail lists

2 Type the new pathname for a folder or mail list in the appropriate text box or edit the existing pathname. (This text box cannot be left empty.)

3 Select OK to exit the Directories dialog box.

MCI ACCOUNTS

To use Norton Mail, you must have at least one MCI account. You may have as many as six. If you do not already have an account, contact MCI for information.

Mail can be sent and received only for active accounts. Any number of accounts may be active at one time, but only one account can be viewed at a time.

This section explains how to:

- Add an account
- Select an account for viewing
- Edit account information
- Delete an account

To add an MCI account:

1 From the Norton Mail desktop (see Figure 21-1), open the Setup menu and choose MCI ACCOUNTS....

The MCI Accounts dialog box appears (Figure 21-16). It lists information about your accounts.

Figure 21-16

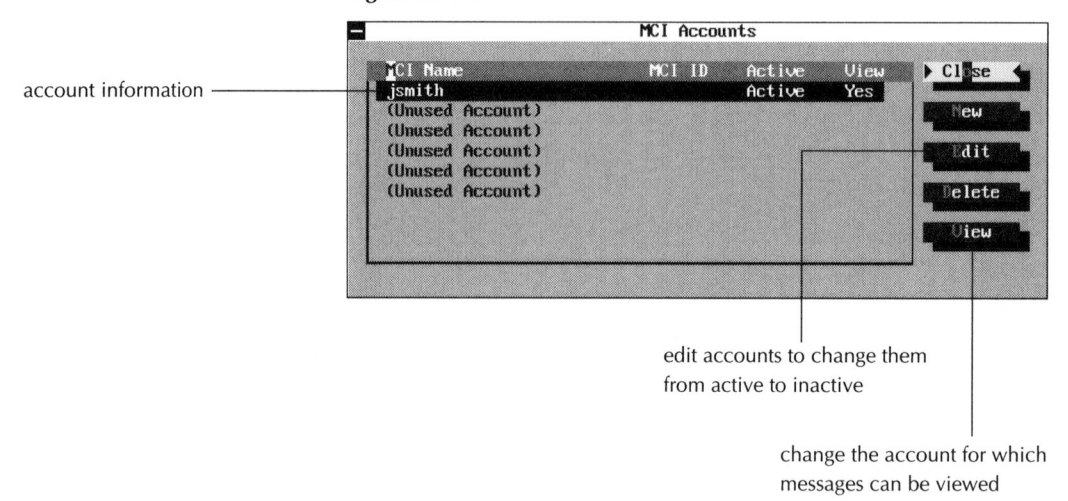

account information

```
┌─────────────────── MCI Accounts ───────────────────┐
│  MCI Name              MCI ID    Active    View   │ ▶ Close ◀
│  jsmith                          Active    Yes    │
│  (Unused Account)                                  │   New
│  (Unused Account)                                  │
│  (Unused Account)                                  │   Edit
│  (Unused Account)                                  │
│  (Unused Account)                                  │   Delete
│                                                    │
│                                                    │   View
└────────────────────────────────────────────────────┘
```

edit accounts to change them from active to inactive

change the account for which messages can be viewed

2 Select New.

The Account Information dialog box appears (Figure 21-17).

3 Select the MCI User Name text box.

4 Type the user name assigned to your account by MCI.

5 Select the MCI Password text box.

6 Type the password assigned to your account by MCI in the MCI Password text box. As you type the characters of your password, asterisks appear in the text box for security purposes. If you think you mistyped your password, enter it again.

7 Select the MCI ID text box.

8 Type the ID assigned to your account. The maximum length for the ID is 12 characters.

9 To make this account active, check Make Account Active - Send/Receive Mail.

Figure 21-17

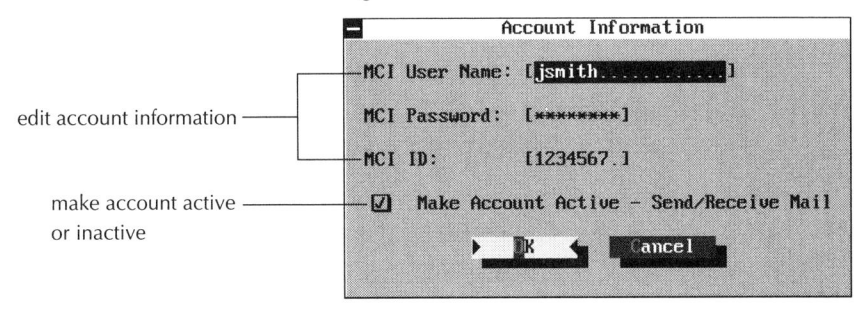

```
┌─ Account Information ─────────┐
│ MCI User Name: [jsmith       ]│
│ MCI Password: [********]      │
│ MCI ID:        [1234567.]     │
│ ☑ Make Account Active - Send/Receive Mail │
│        ▶ OK ◀    Cancel       │
└───────────────────────────────┘
```

- edit account information
- make account active or inactive

10 Select OK to exit the Account Information dialog box.

11 If you want this account to be the one you view, select the account, then select View.

12 Select Close to save the information and exit the MCI Accounts dialog box.

Only one account can be selected for viewing at a time. That account has a Yes in the view column.

Messages from the account chosen for viewing are the only ones that appear in any folder. All created or forwarded messages and all replies are sent from the viewed account.

To view an MCI account:

1 From the Norton Mail desktop (see Figure 21-1), open the Setup menu and choose MCI ACCOUNTS....

The MCI Accounts dialog box appears (see Figure 21-16).

2 Select the account.

3 Select View.

The word Yes appears in the View column for the selected account.

4 Select Close to exit the dialog box.

You can edit an account to:

- Change its status from active to inactive (or vice versa)
- Change its MCI name or number

To edit MCI account information:

1. From the Norton Mail desktop (see Figure 21-1), open the Setup menu and choose MCI ACCOUNTS....

   The MCI Accounts dialog box appears (see Figure 21-16).

2. Select an account. Then select Edit.

   Or,

   Double-click the name of an account.

   The Account Information dialog box appears.

3. Edit the information in the text boxes. You can edit the following:
   - MCI User Name
   - MCI Password
   - MCI ID

4. To change the active status of the account, check or uncheck Make Account Active - Send/Receive Mail.

5. Select OK to exit the Account Information dialog box.

6. Select Close to save the information and exit the MCI Accounts dialog box.

You must have at least one MCI account at all times. You can delete an account only if you have more than one.

To delete an MCI account:

1. From the Norton Mail desktop (see Figure 21-1), open the Setup menu and choose MCI ACCOUNTS....

   The MCI Accounts dialog box appears (see Figure 21-16).

2. Select Delete.

   If the Confirm Deletes option is checked, the Confirm Deletion dialog box displays the name of the account being deleted, and you must select OK to confirm the deletion. If this option is not checked, the account is deleted immediately. See the section "Other Setup Options" for more about this option.

3. Select Close to exit the MCI Accounts dialog box.

MCI TELEPHONE SETTINGS

You use the MCI Telephone dialog box, shown in Figure 21-18, to set up or change your MCI Mail access telephone number.

Entering both a primary and an alternate number allows you to switch back and forth easily between two MCI telephone numbers by changing the selected option button.

Figure 21-18

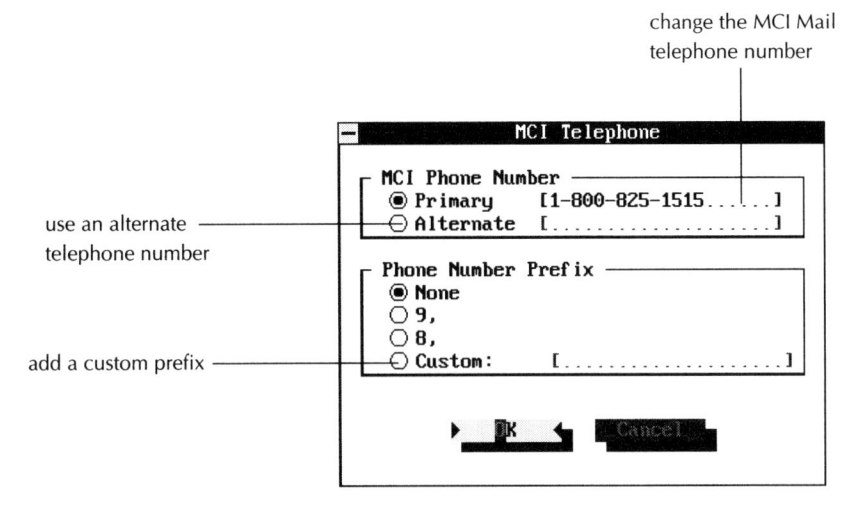

```
                                    change the MCI Mail
                                    telephone number
                  ┌─────────── MCI Telephone ───────────┐
                  │ ┌─ MCI Phone Number ──────────────┐ │
                  │ │ ● Primary   [1-800-825-1515...] │ │
use an alternate ─┼─┤ ○ Alternate [.................] │ │
telephone number  │ └─────────────────────────────────┘ │
                  │ ┌─ Phone Number Prefix ───────────┐ │
                  │ │ ● None                          │ │
                  │ │ ○ 9,                            │ │
                  │ │ ○ 8,                            │ │
add a custom ─────┼─┤ ○ Custom:   [.................] │ │
prefix            │ └─────────────────────────────────┘ │
                  │        ▶  OK  ◀    Cancel           │
                  └─────────────────────────────────────┘
```

To specify a telephone number:

1 From the Norton Mail desktop (see Figure 21-1), open the Setup menu and choose MCI TELEPHONE....

   The MCI Telephone dialog box appears (Figure 21-18).

2 Select Primary.

   Or,

   Select Alternate.

   The telephone number beside the selected option button is used for the current mail session.

   Primary is the default setting; a default MCI 800 number is displayed in the text box beside the button.

3 If necessary, type an MCI telephone number in the text box next to the option button you selected.

4 To provide two telephone numbers, repeat steps 2 and 3.

NOTE: Before continuing, make sure that the selected option button is the one for the telephone number that you want to use next.

5 Select the appropriate option button for your telephone number prefix.

- Select None, the default, if you need no prefix.
- Select 8 or 9 if necessary to access an outside line from your telephone.
- Select Custom if you need to enter a prefix other than 8 or 9. Type the desired prefix (such as *70, which cancels call waiting on most telephone systems) in the text box.

6 Select OK to save the telephone number information and exit the dialog box.

MODEM SETTINGS

You use the Modem Settings dialog box shown in Figure 21-19 to enter information about your modem and telephone.

Figure 21-19

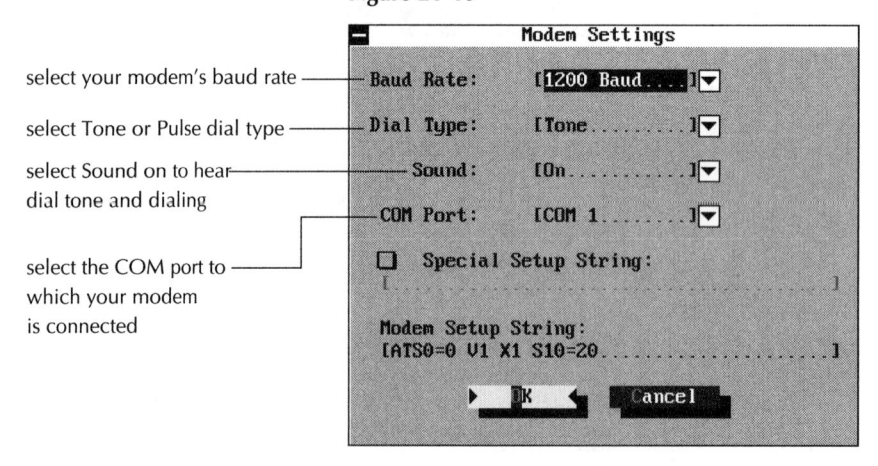

```
                    Modem Settings
    Baud Rate:    [1200 Baud...]▼
    Dial Type:    [Tone........]▼
    Sound:        [On..........]▼
    COM Port:     [COM 1.......]▼

    ☐ Special Setup String:
    [                                        ]

    Modem Setup String:
    [ATS0=0 V1 X1 S10=20.....................]

              ▶  OK  ◀    Cancel
```

select your modem's baud rate — Baud Rate
select Tone or Pulse dial type — Dial Type
select Sound on to hear dial tone and dialing — Sound
select the COM port to which your modem is connected — COM Port

To specify modem and telephone settings:

1 From the Norton Mail desktop (see Figure 21-1), open the Setup menu and choose MODEM....

The Modem Settings dialog box appears (Figure 21-19).

2 Select the baud rate from the Baud Rate drop-down list box.

   You can select 300, 1200, 2400 or 9600 baud, depending on the speed at which your modem can transmit and receive data. Check your modem's manual if you are uncertain about this information. MCI may support 9600 baud in the future.

3 Select the dial type from the Dial Type drop-down list box.

   You can select Tone or Pulse depending on your telephone's dial type.

4 Select the sound setting you desire from the Sound drop-down list box.

   You can select On or Off. On allows you to hear the dial tone and the telephone dialing. Off does not. If you are in a modem pool or are using some internal modems, you may not hear dialing even if On is selected.

5 Select the COM port setting from the COM Port drop-down list box.

   You can select COM 1, COM 2, COM 3 or COM 4, depending on the serial port to which your modem is connected.

6 Select OK to save the modem settings and exit the dialog box.

CAUTION: Unless you are an advanced user, you should not use the Special Setup String text box or change the settings in the Modem Setup String text box. If you need more information refer to the "Configuring Norton Mail" chapter in *Installing Norton Desktop for DOS*.

OTHER SETUP OPTIONS

The Options dialog box (Figure 21-20) allows you to specify the following options:

- Where newly created messages are placed
- Whether you read messages on the full screen or from a text box
- What information about a message appears in a folder
- Whether you confirm deletions

21-44   *Using Norton Desktop for DOS*

- Whether the text of a message appears in the reply to it
- Whether new addresses are automatically added to your address book

Figure 21-20

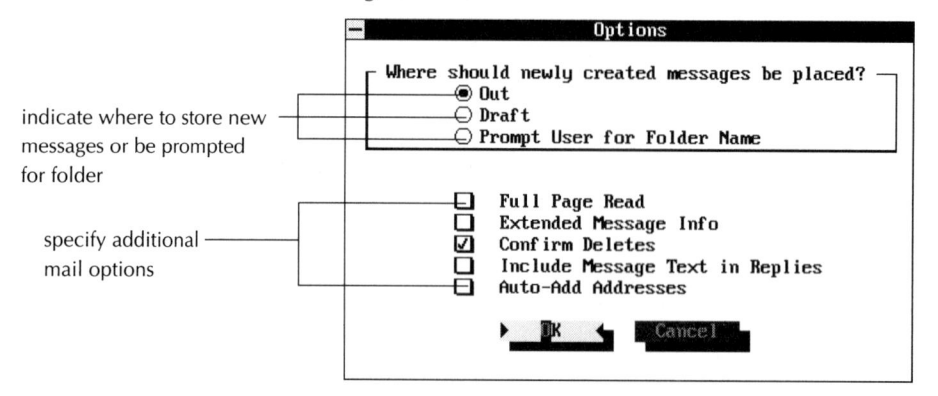

indicate where to store new messages or be prompted for folder

specify additional mail options

```
┌─                         Options                          ─┐
│ ┌─ Where should newly created messages be placed? ─┐       │
│ │        ● Out                                      │       │
│ │        ○ Draft                                    │       │
│ │        ○ Prompt User for Folder Name              │       │
│ └───────────────────────────────────────────────────┘       │
│                                                             │
│              □  Full Page Read                              │
│              □  Extended Message Info                       │
│              ☑  Confirm Deletes                             │
│              □  Include Message Text in Replies             │
│              □  Auto-Add Addresses                          │
│                                                             │
│              ▶  OK  ◀        Cancel                         │
└─────────────────────────────────────────────────────────────┘
```

To specify additional Norton Mail options:

1   From the Norton Mail desktop (see Figure 21-1), open the Setup menu and choose OPTIONS....

The Options dialog box appears (Figure 21-20).

2   To indicate which folder should store messages that you create, select the Out folder or the Draft folder.

Or,

If you want to be prompted about the folder every time you create a message, select Prompt User for Folder Name. When you create a message, the Which Folder dialog box appears with a list of all available folders. At that time, you select the folder you want.

3   To see your messages zoomed to full screen, check Full Page Read. When you select Read and Full Page Read is checked, messages are shown full screen. When you exit from a zoomed message, you return to the current folder.

Or,

To view your messages in a text box showing eight lines at a time, uncheck Full Page Read (the default). When you select Read and Full Page Read is unchecked, the message displays in a text box as part of the Message From dialog box.

4   To see the extended version of information about each message when viewing a folder, check the Extended Message Info check box. The extended version includes information such as the time the message was sent, its size and its filename.

Or,

To see the short version of information about each message, leave the box unchecked. The short version shows only one line displaying the date, the subject, and who sent or received the message.

5   To have the Confirm Deletion dialog box appear every time you delete something, check Confirm Deletes. It allows you to OK (confirm) or Cancel the deletion before it is performed. The Confirm Deletes check box is checked by default.

Or,

Uncheck Confirm Deletes if you want deletions to be performed immediately without confirmation. The only exception is the deletion of messages. You must confirm all message deletions.

6   To have the text of the original message appear in the reply, check the Include Message Text in Replies check box. By default, the original message is not included in replies, so this box is unchecked.

7   To have all new addresses added to your address book automatically, check the Auto-Add Addresses check box. By default, the box is unchecked and addresses are not added automatically.

8   Select OK to save the changes and exit the dialog box.

OTHER TYPES OF MAIL

MCI Mail is not only for MCI electronic mail. You can send a message as a fax, telex, paper mail (using postal services once the message is printed by MCI), or using other electronic mail systems affiliated with MCI Mail.

Fax

You can use Norton Mail to have MCI send a fax to the recipients specified in your message.

Telex

Telex is the international standard for telecommunications. Telex messages transmitted for you by MCI Mail let you access the worldwide telex system without having to acquire, install and maintain special equipment or pay a special monthly line charge. You transmit and receive your messages over your telephone. MCI Mail takes care of the rest. You pay only for the messages it can deliver.

However, be aware that telex machines:

- Cannot display more than 69 characters per line.
- Can only display uppercase letters, numbers, periods, commas, apostrophes, question marks, parentheses, colons, plus and minus signs, forward slashes (/) and equal signs.
- Keyboard characters other than those discussed above are translated. For example, brackets and braces become parentheses, @ becomes the characters "AT," and a variety of other characters become forward slashes.

Paper Mail

Paper Mail is an MCI option that allows you to create and send paper mail via MCI. Your message is printed at whichever MCI Mail Digital Post Office (DPO) site is closest to the message's destination: New York, Los Angeles, Chicago, Washington, D.C., Melbourne or Brussels. It is then routed by that country's postal service. Paper mail sent using MCI can have no more than 80 characters per line. Your message is printed on MCI letterhead unless you have registered your own letterhead with MCI. You may also register your signature. See your MCI Mail manual for more information about paper mail.

Other Electronic Mail Systems

MCI Mail is affiliated with other electronic mail systems (EMS). For a list of those that can be accessed (and how to access them), see your materials from MCI.

Using System Information

This chapter shows you how to use System Information to display and print detailed reports of your hardware and software characteristics, including benchmark tests comparing your system to several common ones.

Contents

Starting System Information 22-3
System Information Reports 22-3
    System 22-3
    Disks 22-5
    Memory 22-7
    Benchmarks 22-10
    Report 22-11
Printing Reports 22-11

System Information reports the operational status of your computer: the hardware, memory usage, network conditions, disk drives, and benchmark comparisons to other computers.

Use System Information to:

- Report your computer's configuration and check on its performance.
- Have detailed system information about your computer available for technical support calls.
- Maintain a history of your system configuration.

Some of the information is quite technical in nature, but don't worry if you don't understand all of it (or even most of it). You can always press F1 for help to get a brief definition of each element.

NOTE: System Information recognizes and reports all the standard PC family members within practical limitations. System Information also recognizes specialty models of the PC family, such as the 3270-PC, and many PC compatibles; but it can't identify all MS-DOS computers in existence. If System Information doesn't recognize your machine, it will attempt to find and show you identifying marks, such as a copyright notice and your computer's ROM-BIOS date.

STARTING SYSTEM INFORMATION

To start System Information:

- Choose SYSTEM INFORMATION from the (long) Tools menu. The System Summary screen appears.

SYSTEM INFORMATION REPORTS

System Information generates a series of screens for each group of reports: System, Disks, Memory, Benchmarks, and Report. You can select the appropriate option from the pull-down menus, or use the Next button to cycle through all the reports.

System

The System menu (Figure 22-1) contains six options to display detailed information about your hardware and software use, as well as a network summary.

Figure 22-1

the System menu contains options to display detailed information about your hardware and software use

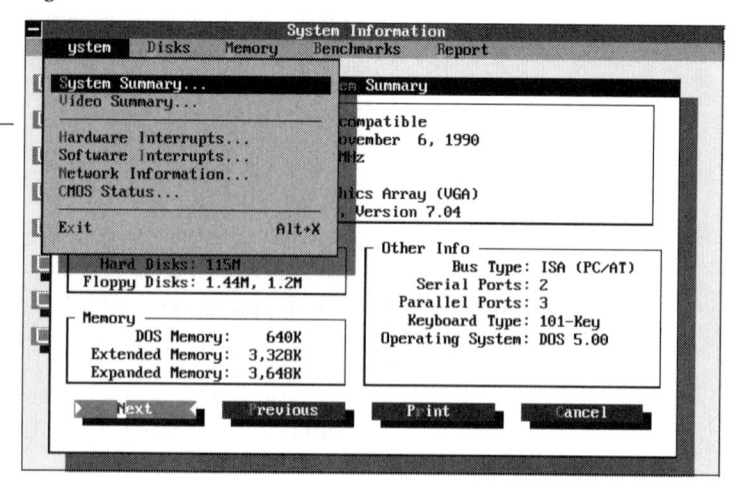

System Summary

The system summary is a complete overview of your system, including the computer type, clock speed, number and types of disk drives, memory capacities, serial and parallel ports, and DOS version.

Video Summary

The video summary reports the type of video display, character size (width and height of characters in pixels), and video memory capacity.

> **NOTE:** If your video card has more than 256K of video memory, SYSINFO will show it as 256K of memory "or more," instead of displaying the actual amount. The reason for this is that IBM defined a standard way to ask a video card how much memory it has available (using a BIOS call), but IBM limited the response to 256K or less. To remain compatible with IBM, cards from other manufacturers will say they have 256K of memory even if they have more.

Hardware Interrupts

The hardware interrupt is a mechanism by which a piece of hardware, such as a keyboard or modem, can interrupt whatever the computer is doing and force it to do something else. This screen displays the Interrupt Request (IRQ) number (or priority), address, usage, and which program uses the interrupt.

Software Interrupts   A software interrupt is a memory address (also called a vector) of a system-level piece of programming or a table of information. DOS and BIOS services are executed through interrupts, and other programs and device drivers can also use interrupts. The Software Interrupt screen displays the interrupt number, address, usage, and which program is using it.

Network Information   This report, which shows user and network information, is available only if your computer is attached to a network.

CMOS Status   ATs and more advanced computers have a special, battery-powered CMOS chip (Complimentary Metal-Oxide Semiconductor) to maintain information about the drives, memory and other data that your system needs when booting. The battery makes sure that this information is retained even when you turn off your computer. Incorrect CMOS values are shown in red or boldface. To correct errors, run your computer's SETUP program or boot your computer from the Diagnostic Disk that came with it. If you continue to have CMOS problems, you may need to replace the battery.

TIP: The last piece of information in the CMOS Status report is the CMOS Checksum. This is a calculation used by the computer to determine if any values in the CMOS chip have changed outside of the setup program. If the Checksum status is not OK, you should run the setup program regardless of the other values.

Disks

The Disks menu contains options to display the number, availability, and type of disk drives; their physical and logical characteristics; and the starting and ending locations of your partitions.

Disk Summary   The Disk Summary screen lists disk drives, types, and sizes (and default directory for hard disks).

Disk Characteristics   The Disk Characteristics screen reports the logical and physical characteristics for each drive (Figure 22-2). Make sure there is a diskette in each floppy drive you wish to check.

The Logical Characteristics determine how much space the smallest file on the disk will take (files are stored on disk in pieces called clusters) and how much space is available for files.

The rest of the Logical Characteristics simply tell you how the disk is organized and how much is allocated to the overhead of keeping track of the data.

The Physical Characteristics of a drive are the number of heads, tracks, and sectors per track. On some systems, especially those with ESDI, IDE, SCSI or RLL drive controllers, the values reported will be different from those of the actual drive. This is because the values are converted by the disk controller to make the drive look like one the computer knows how to use.

Figure 22-2

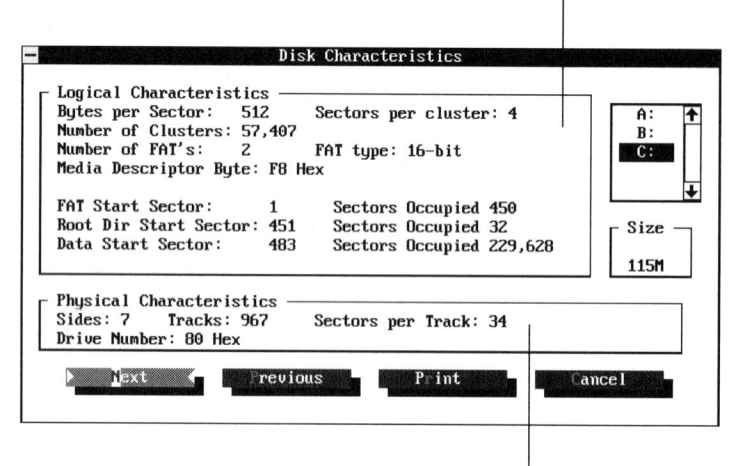

Logical Characteristics of the selected drive

```
┌─────────────────── Disk Characteristics ───────────────────┐
│ ┌─ Logical Characteristics ──────────────────────┐         │
│ │ Bytes per Sector:    512    Sectors per cluster: 4 │  A: │
│ │ Number of Clusters: 57,407                         │  B: │
│ │ Number of FAT's:     2      FAT type: 16-bit       │  C: │
│ │ Media Descriptor Byte: F8 Hex                      │     │
│ │                                                    │     │
│ │ FAT Start Sector:      1    Sectors Occupied 450   │     │
│ │ Root Dir Start Sector: 451  Sectors Occupied 32    │ Size│
│ │ Data Start Sector:     483  Sectors Occupied 229,628│    │
│ └────────────────────────────────────────────────────┘ 115M│
│ ┌─ Physical Characteristics ─────────────────────┐         │
│ │ Sides: 7    Tracks: 967    Sectors per Track: 34 │       │
│ │ Drive Number: 80 Hex                             │       │
│ └──────────────────────────────────────────────────┘       │
│      [ Next ]    [ Previous ]    [ Print ]   [ Cancel ]    │
└────────────────────────────────────────────────────────────┘
```

Physical Characteristics of the selected drive

Partition Tables

Some hard disks are configured as more than one logical drive or with more than one operating system (such as UNIX). This report displays the partition tables on your hard disks, including the operating system (this will usually be DOS), whether the computer will try to boot from it, and the size and location of the partitions. Unused space will not be reported.

Memory

The Memory menu contains six options to report the total amount of memory, the amounts and addresses reserved by DOS and resident programs (such as the Norton Cache or Erase Protect), and the amount available for your application programs. Two of the options report on extended or expanded memory, if available.

Memory Usage Summary

The Memory Usage Summary reports DOS usage of memory, overall memory (used by screen display adapters, expanded and extended memory), and memory used by ROM-BIOS extensions. The amount listed for display memory here may be less than the amount listed for Video Memory on the Video Summary screen, because the video memory is paged in and out of the display memory window.

Expanded Memory

Expanded memory is "paged" memory, which means that it does not appear as one long stream of memory, but rather as multiple pages of memory that are seen by DOS one page at a time. This allows DOS to address a large amount of memory, but only a small portion at a time. Expanded memory was originally developed for XT-class (8088) computers, which could not use extended memory.

The Expanded Memory screen, shown in Figure 22-3, details the current setup of your Expanded Memory Manager (EMM). In order to use expanded memory (and to see this screen) you must have an EMM installed.

Figure 22-3

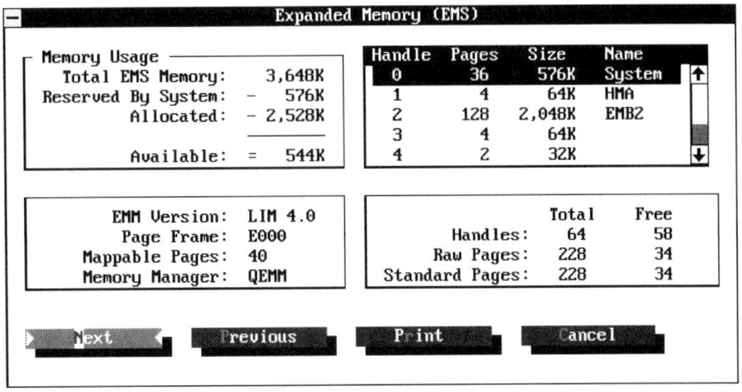

the Expanded Memory screen shows current setup of your EMM

```
┌─ Expanded Memory (EMS) ─────────────────────────────┐
│ ┌─ Memory Usage ──────────────┐ Handle Pages Size  Name    │
│ │  Total EMS Memory:  3,648K  │   0      36   576K  System │
│ │  Reserved By System: - 576K │   1       4    64K  HMA    │
│ │       Allocated:   - 2,528K │   2     128 2,048K  EMB2   │
│ │                             │   3       4    64K         │
│ │       Available:   =   544K │   4       2    32K         │
│ └─────────────────────────────┘                            │
│                                                            │
│ ┌─────────────────────────────┐              Total   Free  │
│ │  EMM Version:    LIM 4.0    │   Handles:    64     58    │
│ │    Page Frame:   E000       │ Raw Pages:   228     34    │
│ │ Mappable Pages:  40         │ Standard Pages: 228  34    │
│ │ Memory Manager:  QEMM       │                            │
│ └─────────────────────────────┘                            │
│                                                            │
│    Next        Previous       Print       Cancel           │
└────────────────────────────────────────────────────────────┘
```

When an expanded memory block is allocated by an application, the application receives a "handle" to the block from the EMM. System Information can find these handles and display information on the memory blocks to which they refer. This includes the number of expanded memory pages "owned" by the handle. If the EMM follows the LIM version 4.0 specification of EMS (Expanded Memory Specification), handles can be associated with names that describe the block, or identify the owner of the block. System Information can display these names, but since it is not a requirement under EMS, not all handles will have names.

System Information can also display information on the expanded memory pages; both standard pages, which are 16K in size, and "raw" pages, which can be any size. If raw pages are not supported on your system, the number of raw pages is the same as the number of standard pages.

Extended Memory

Extended memory is only available on 286 or greater computers. It is memory beyond the 1-megabyte boundary that DOS can address directly (640K conventional memory and 384K high memory).

The Extended Memory screen, shown in Figure 22-4, details the current setup of your eXtended Memory Manager (XMM). In order to use extended memory (and see this screen), you must have an XMS (eXtended Memory Specification) driver installed, such as HIMEM.SYS.

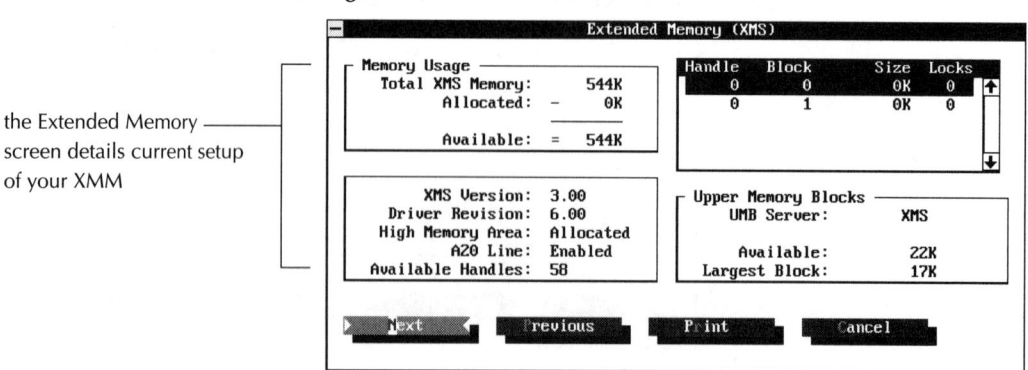

Figure 22-4

the Extended Memory screen details current setup of your XMM

```
┌─────────────────────── Extended Memory (XMS) ───────────────────────┐
│ ┌─ Memory Usage ──────────────────┐  Handle  Block    Size   Locks  │
│ │    Total XMS Memory:    544K    │    0       0       0K      0   │
│ │        Allocated:  -     0K     │    0       1       0K      0   │
│ │                                 │                                 │
│ │        Available:  =   544K     │                                 │
│ └─────────────────────────────────┘                                 │
│                                                                     │
│ ┌─────────────────────────────────┐ ┌─ Upper Memory Blocks ───────┐ │
│ │      XMS Version:  3.00         │ │    UMB Server:      XMS     │ │
│ │   Driver Revision: 6.00         │ │                             │ │
│ │   High Memory Area: Allocated   │ │    Available:       22K     │ │
│ │         A20 Line:  Enabled      │ │    Largest Block:   17K     │ │
│ │   Available Handles: 58         │ │                             │ │
│ └─────────────────────────────────┘ └─────────────────────────────┘ │
│                                                                     │
│      ▶ Next ◀      Previous      Print         Cancel               │
└─────────────────────────────────────────────────────────────────────┘
```

In the most basic terms, allocating a block of extended memory is the same as allocating a block of expanded memory. The application receives a handle to the block from the XMM, which System Information can locate and use to display information. An extended memory block can be "locked" by applications, and System Information can display the "lock count" for each handle. Normally, you won't see any locks (a zero value means the block is "unlocked") unless you are running in a multitasking environment such as Windows or DESQView.

System Information can also display information on the Upper Memory Blocks (UMBs) used on your system. Normally, UMBs are supported only on 386 or higher computers and are managed by 386 memory managers (such as QEMM 386). System Information can also display information on the UMBs managed by DOS 5.0. Look at the UMB Server on System Information's screen to see whether DOS or the XMM is handling the UMBs. If UMBs are not supported on your machine, the UMB Server is set to "None."

NOTE: Some memory managers, such as QEMM 386, are both EMS and XMS drivers. They can mix extended and expanded memory together, supplying whatever kind of memory an application asks for without question. With one of these drivers, you may find blocks named "EMB" followed by a number on the Expanded Memory screen. These are Extended Memory Blocks (EMB), which means that the block is really extended memory. If you then go to the Extended Memory screen, you may not find the same amount of Extended Memory allocated, because extended memory is allocated in blocks of 1K, while expanded memory is allocated in blocks of 16K.

Memory Block List

This report shows DOS memory block usage, including the size of blocks in bytes, the owner or program, and the type (data, program or environment). This can be useful for finding holes in memory, indicating that the memory could be used more efficiently.

TSR Programs The TSR report displays technical information about memory-resident programs (size, owner who loaded it, and hooked interrupt-vectors). As you highlight a TSR, System Information will try to display the location of the program, the command line with which it was loaded, and the number of allocation blocks it takes. Some TSRs strip this information out to save memory, so it may not show for all TSRs.

Due to DOS constraints, the last TSR to grab a particular interrupt will be the only one with that interrupt listed as hooked. The other TSRs are dependent upon this one to pass them the interrupt if they need it.

Device Drivers This report lists device drivers installed with the address, ID name (an 8-byte signature in the device driver, such as CON or PRN), and description if System Information recognizes the ID name.

Benchmarks

The Benchmarks menu contains four options to test your computer's CPU (central processing unit) and hard disk against the performance of several popular PCs. You don't need a Computer Science degree to understand these results. Test results are reported as indexes relative to the original IBM PC-XT.

CPU Speed A graphical display shows how your CPU speed compares to that of other popular computers. The test is dynamic; therefore, mouse movement will decrease the speed. If your computer has a "turbo" switch, try changing speeds to see the graph change.

Hard Disk Speed A graphical display shows how your hard disk speed compares to that of other popular computers. However, it may not be possible to perform this benchmark on all types of disk controllers.

Overall Performance Index The CPU and disk indexes are combined in the Overall Performance Index to give you one number for comparing your system against other popular systems.

Network Performance Speed This option measures throughput for writes and reads on a network. Of course, you must be connected to a network.

Report

The Report menu lets you review the contents of your DOS startup files, CONFIG.SYS and AUTOEXEC.BAT, as well as generate a report containing everything found by System Information.

View CONFIG.SYS

The CONFIG.SYS file determines system configuration and defines which device drivers DOS loads at boot time. This screen displays the contents of your CONFIG.SYS file on the screen. If you do not have a CONFIG.SYS file or did not boot from a disk with a CONFIG.SYS file, this option is not available.

View AUTOEXEC.BAT

The AUTOEXEC.BAT file determines which programs are run at startup. This screen displays the contents of your AUTOEXEC.BAT file. If you do not have an AUTOEXEC.BAT file or did not boot from a disk with an AUTOEXEC.BAT file, this option is not available.

PRINTING REPORTS

The Print Report option of the Report menu lets you generate a report to a disk file or the printer. A screen of options lets you control the level of detail in the report (Figure 22-5). Use the report for archival purposes, debugging systems or comparing systems, or to prepare for a technical support call.

Figure 22-5

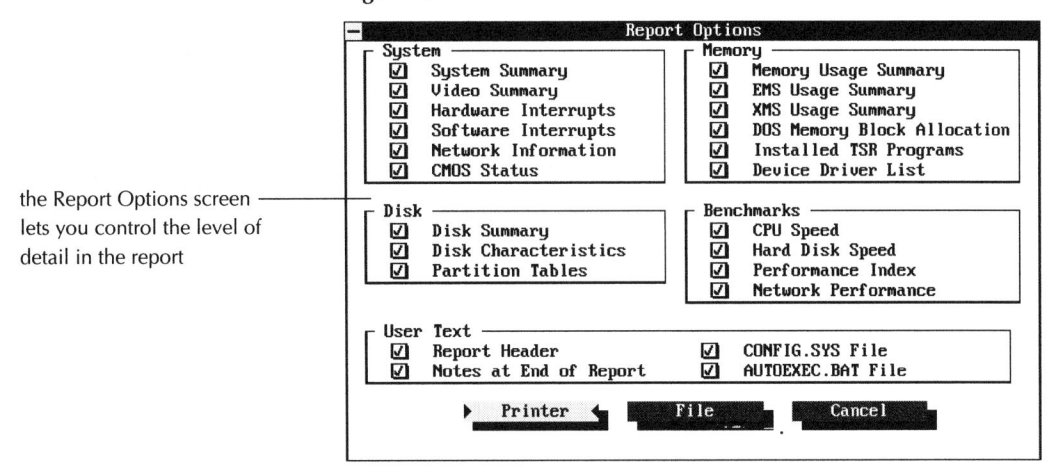

the Report Options screen lets you control the level of detail in the report

To generate a report:

1. Choose PRINT REPORT from the Report menu.
2. Check the reports you want to generate from the Report options dialog boxes.
3. To print the report, select Printer as the report destination.

   Or,

   To save the report to a file, select File as the report destination. You will be prompted to enter a filename in the text box.

Using Scheduler

This chapter explains how to use Scheduler to run applications or batch files automatically or to display messages at specified times.

Contents

Starting Scheduler 23-3
How Scheduler Works 23-4
Organizing Your Schedule 23-5
    Viewing Scheduled Events 23-5
    Adding Scheduled Events 23-6
    Editing Scheduled Events 23-10
    Deleting Scheduled Events 23-11
Using Norton Utilities with Scheduler 23-12
Closing Scheduler 23-12

STARTING SCHEDULER

Scheduler can help you organize your work by automatically running applications and batch files at scheduled times and by displaying messages to remind you of upcoming events. For example, you can schedule a program, such as Norton Backup, to run every day at 4:00 P.M. and then forget about it. When 4:00 P.M. rolls around, your computer displays a message that it is about to run Norton Backup. You simply insert a floppy disk or tape, and your files are automatically backed up. That's all there is to it!

To run scheduled events, the Scheduler terminate-and-stay-resident (TSR) program, NSCHED.COM, must first be installed. This program stays active in the memory of your computer so it can run your scheduled events at the correct time, regardless of what else you happen to be doing (of course, your computer must be turned on). The easiest way to install NSCHED.COM is during Norton Desktop's installation procedure.

You can install NSCHED.COM at any time simply by typing NSCHED at the DOS prompt.

If you choose SCHEDULER from the Tools menu before NSCHED.COM has been installed, an alert box appears telling you that scheduled events do not execute until NSCHED.COM has been installed.

Certain TSRs such as network drivers and print spoolers must be loaded before NSCHED.COM. Norton Desktop automatically adjusts your AUTOEXEC.BAT file to load TSRs in the correct order when you choose the Easy installation option. If you choose Advanced installation, or if you manually adjust your AUTOEXEC.BAT file, be sure to read *Installing Norton Desktop for DOS* for additional information on loading TSRs in the proper order.

To start Scheduler:

- Choose SCHEDULER from the Tools menu.

    The Scheduler dialog box appears (Figure 23-1). The dialog box allows you to view, add, edit or delete scheduled events.

Scheduler lets you add, edit, delete or view scheduled events

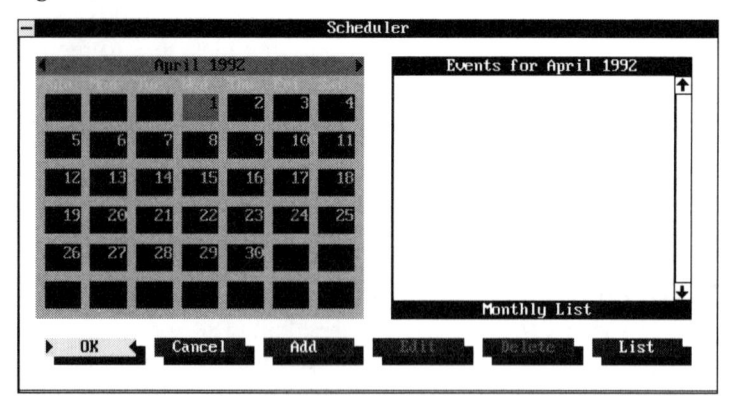

Figure 23-1

HOW SCHEDULER WORKS

The Scheduler dialog box displays a calendar for the current month on the left side and a list of currently scheduled events on the right side. Dates containing scheduled events are indicated on the calendar with a checkmark. Scheduler can actually display any month from January 1980 to December 2107.

To change the month display:

- To display a later month, press PgDn or Ctrl+RightArrow from the keyboard.
- To display an earlier month, press PgUp or Ctrl+LeftArrow from the keyboard.

Or,

- To display a later month, click the right arrowhead of the month title bar.
- To display an earlier month, click the left arrowhead of the month title bar.

Scheduler automatically runs an event at the scheduled time. If your computer is turned off when an event is scheduled to run, the event runs automatically the next time NSCHED.COM is loaded. (By default, Norton Desktop installs NSCHED.COM to load each time you start your computer.)

Using Scheduler **23-5**

Scheduler shares a TSR and data file with Norton Backup (for additional information on Norton Backup, see Chapter 19, "Using Norton Backup"). This means you can schedule your backup through Scheduler or Norton Backup—either way, it will appear on the Scheduler's list of scheduled events.

Scheduler can handle up to 50 scheduled events. Since backups scheduled through Norton Backup also appear in the Scheduler, don't forget to include them in your total number of scheduled events.

ORGANIZING YOUR SCHEDULE

Scheduler gives you the control and flexibility to create a personal schedule of events. A list box displays the programs, batch files, and messages you've chosen to execute. The Event Scheduler dialog box allows you to easily add, edit, view and delete your scheduled events.

Viewing Scheduled Events

The list of events catalogs all currently scheduled events by giving a brief description of each event. Optionally, the listing can show the frequency and scheduled date and time of each event. You can choose to display all scheduled events or to display the events on a daily or monthly basis.

To set the viewing options of scheduled events:

1. Select the List command button from the Scheduler dialog box (Figure 23-1).

   The Event List Options dialog box, shown in Figure 23-2, appears on the desktop.

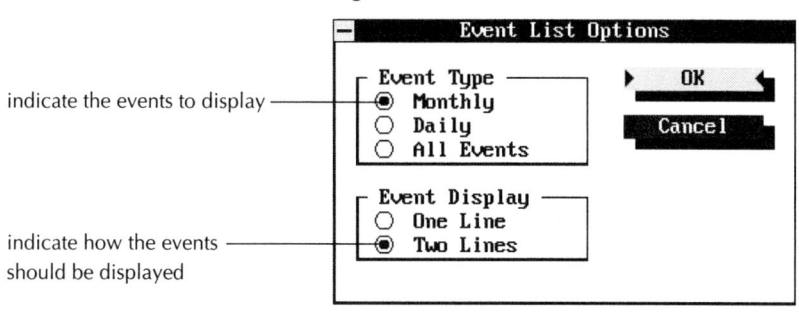

Figure 23-2

```
┌─────────── Event List Options ───────────┐
│                                          │
│  ┌─ Event Type ──────┐   ▶   OK   ◀      │
│  │ ◉ Monthly         │                   │
│  │ ○ Daily           │      Cancel       │
│  │ ○ All Events      │                   │
│  └───────────────────┘                   │
│                                          │
│  ┌─ Event Display ───┐                   │
│  │ ○ One Line        │                   │
│  │ ◉ Two Lines       │                   │
│  └───────────────────┘                   │
└──────────────────────────────────────────┘
```

- indicate the events to display → (Event Type)
- indicate how the events should be displayed → (Event Display)

2   Select one of the Event Type option buttons to indicate which events to display:

    Monthly: displays all events for the chosen month.

    Daily: displays all events for the chosen day.

    All Events: displays all scheduled events.

3   Select one of the Event Display option buttons to indicate how the events should be displayed.

    One Line: displays a brief description of the event.

    Two Lines: displays a brief description, as well as the frequency, date, and time of the event (two-line display is the default).

4   If you've chosen to list events on a monthly or daily basis, select the month you wish to display from the Scheduler calendar.

    Press PgUp or PgDn, Ctrl+LeftArrow or Ctrl+RightArrow, or click the left or right arrowheads on the calendar title bar to cycle backward and forward, respectively, through the months.

5   If you've chosen to list events on a daily basis, select the date you wish to display from the Scheduler calendar (use the arrow keys or click the correct date).

    The list of currently scheduled events appears on the right side of the Scheduler dialog box.

6   Select OK to save your selections.

Adding Scheduled Events

The Add command button displays the Event Editor dialog box, as shown in Figure 23-3, which prompts you for the information needed to schedule a new event.

To add an event to Scheduler:

1   Select the Add command button from the Scheduler dialog box (see Figure 23-1).

    The Event Editor dialog box appears on the desktop (Figure 23-3) containing the preset scheduling information: the currently highlighted calendar date, current time, day of week and a frequency of Once. You can accept these entries or change them to suit your scheduling needs.

Figure 23-3

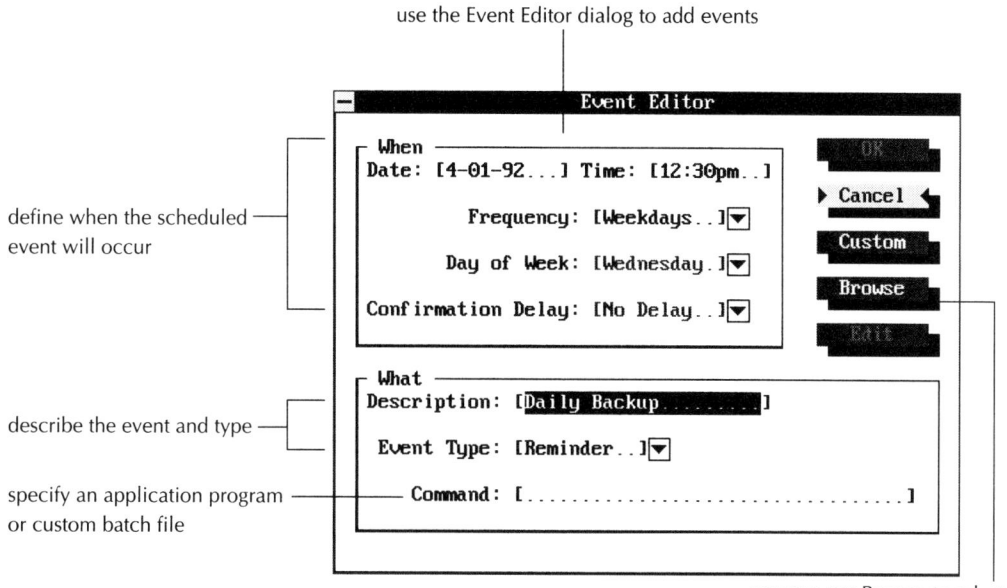

use the Event Editor dialog to add events

```
┌─ Event Editor ─────────────────────────────────┐
│  ┌─ When ──────────────────────────────┐       │
│  │ Date: [4-01-92...]  Time: [12:30pm..] │   OK      │
│  │                                      │   Cancel   │
│  │        Frequency: [Weekdays..]▼      │            │
│  │                                      │   Custom   │
│  │      Day of Week: [Wednesday.]▼      │            │
│  │                                      │   Browse   │
│  │ Confirmation Delay: [No Delay..]▼    │            │
│  └──────────────────────────────────────┘   Edit     │
│                                                      │
│  ┌─ What ──────────────────────────────┐             │
│  │ Description: [Daily Backup........]  │             │
│  │                                      │             │
│  │  Event Type: [Reminder..]▼           │             │
│  │     Command: [.......................] │         │
│  └──────────────────────────────────────┘            │
└──────────────────────────────────────────────────────┘
```

- define when the scheduled event will occur
- describe the event and type
- specify an application program or custom batch file
- you can use Browse to select an application or batch file to run at the scheduled time

2 In the Date and Time text boxes, type the date and time the message, program or batch file is to be run. If the event is to be run more than once, enter only the first date and time it will run.

> **NOTE:** If you don't include A.M. or P.M. in your time entry, Scheduler converts your entry to a military-time format. Times less than 12 (for example, 10:42) are assumed to be A.M. Times 12 or greater (for example, 14:15) are assumed to be P.M.
>
> When entering A.M. and P.M. in the Time text box, A.M. should be entered as AM, and P.M. as PM; don't include the periods. Notice that it doesn't matter whether you type the letters in uppercase or lowercase.

3   To select the frequency and the day of the week (for weekly events) the event is to be run, highlight the Frequency drop-down list and select the frequency with which you want to run the event.

    To run the event more than once a week, select Custom from the Frequency list.

4   Highlight the Day Of Week drop-down list and select the day of the week you want to run the event.

    Again, you can select the day of the week by typing the first letter of the day you've chosen.

5   If you've chosen to run an event more than once a week, select the Custom command button.

    If you are not running an event more than once a week, skip to step 8.

6   Place a checkmark in the check box of each day you wish your event to run.

7   Select OK.

8   Enter a brief description of the event you are scheduling in the Description text box. The description you enter here appears in the event list.

    This is an optional entry. If you don't enter a description, the scheduled message or command line appears in the event list.

9   Select the type of event you want to run from the Event Type drop-down list.

    Reminder: displays any message up to 160 characters long.

    Program: runs any DOS application.

    Batch File: runs any batch file.

10 Type the event you want to run in the Command text box.

    To display a reminder, type the message you want displayed, up to 160 characters.

    To run a program or batch file, type the name of the program or batch file including its full path if it is not in one of the following locations:

    - Your Norton Desktop directory (the directory where Norton Desktop is installed).

- A directory listed in your PATH statement (usually part of the AUTOEXEC.BAT file).
- Your directories that are included in the Novell network MAP statement (if you are a network user).

You can also quickly select your program or batch file by using the Browse command button.

11 Select OK to add the scheduled event.

Confirming Events Before Running

Certain scheduled programs or batch files may take over your computer for extended periods of time. There will certainly be times when you happen to be working on something else and would prefer not to be interrupted when one of these events is scheduled to run. You can control this situation by requiring a confirmation box to appear before a program or batch file is run. This gives you the option of confirming, postponing or cancelling the scheduled event.

A program or batch file confirmation box is configured by the Confirmation Delay combination box in the Event Editor dialog box. Confirmation Delay is set to No Delay by default, which means that there is no delay (and no confirmation box appears) when the program or batch file is scheduled to run. To activate the confirmation box, choose one of the listed times.

The times on the Confirmation Delay list indicate how long the confirmation box remains on the screen before your scheduled event is run. For example, suppose you select 10 Minutes from the Confirmation Delay list. When an event is scheduled to run, a confirmation box appears on your screen. The confirmation box gives you the option to run the scheduled event now, postpone it for the number of minutes you indicate, disable the Scheduler TSR so all events are cancelled, or cancel only this event. If you do nothing, the confirmation box remains on your screen 10 minutes and then your event runs automatically.

Times on the Confirmation Delay list range from 30 seconds (the confirmation box remains on your screen for 30 seconds or until you select OK before running your event) to Forever (the confirmation box stays on your screen until you select OK—however long that takes).

To display a confirmation box prior to running a program or batch file:

1 Select Program or Batch File from the Event Type drop-down list in the Event Editor dialog box (Figure 23-3).

2 From the Confirmation Delay drop-down list, select the length of time the confirmation box should remain on your screen before your scheduled event is run.

Notice that Confirmation Delay is set to No Delay by default—in other words, events are automatically run at their scheduled times, regardless of what you are working on at the time.

Editing Scheduled Events

When your plans change, you can easily edit scheduled events using the Edit command button from the Event Scheduler dialog box.

To edit a scheduled event:

1 Highlight the event you want to edit on the event list found in the Scheduler dialog box (see Figure 23-1).

2 Select the Edit command button.

The Event Editor dialog box appears on the desktop, showing your event's scheduling information (see Figure 23-3).

> **TIP:** You can also invoke the Event Editor dialog box simply by double-clicking the event you wish to edit on the event list.

3 Change any incorrect information. See the section "Adding Scheduled Events" in this chapter for additional information on scheduling events.

4 Select OK to save your edits.

Creating and Editing Batch Files

You can also use the Event Editor dialog box to create a batch file or edit an existing batch file.

To create a batch file:

1 Select Batch File from the Event Type drop-down list in the Event Editor dialog box.

2. Type the name of the batch file in the Command text box including the full pathname.
3. Select Edit.

   A dialog box appears with the message: "Batch file does not exist. Create new file."
4. Select OK.

   The Batch File Editor dialog box is displayed.
5. Type the text of the new batch file in the text area.
6. Select Save to save the new batch file.

   You are returned to the Event Editor dialog box.
7. Select OK to add the new scheduled event.

To edit a batch file:

1. Select Batch File from the Event Type drop-down list in the Event Editor dialog box (Figure 23-3).
2. Type the name of the batch file you want to edit in the Command text box or use the Browse command button to quickly select the name of the batch file to edit.
3. Select Edit.

   The Batch File Editor dialog box appears containing the text of the batch file you selected.
4. Make any editing changes to the text of the batch file.
5. Select Save to save your changes to the batch file.

   You are returned to the Event Editor dialog box.
6. Select OK to save any changes you made to the current scheduled event.

   Or,

   Select Cancel to exit the Scheduler without changing the current event.

Deleting Scheduled Events

To delete a scheduled event:

1. Highlight the you want to delete from the events list found in the Scheduler dialog box (Figure 23-1).
2. Select the Delete command button.

   A confirmation box appears prompting you to verify that you want to delete this event.
3. Select OK to delete the event.

USING NORTON UTILITIES WITH SCHEDULER

To avoid the loss or corruption of data, it is critical that certain utilities not be interrupted in the middle of a procedure. The utilities have been designed to automatically disable Scheduler until they have finished processing data whenever a problem could occur if the utility program were interrupted. The utilities that turn off Scheduler while they are active are:

- Disk Tools
- Image
- Norton Disk Doctor
- Norton Mail communications session
- SFORMAT
- Speed Disk
- UnErase
- Unformat

When the above utilities have finished processing data, they automatically turn Scheduler back on again. If a program or message was scheduled to run while Scheduler was disabled, a dialog box appears on the desktop as soon as Scheduler is enabled again displaying your message or asking if you'd like to run your program now.

CLOSING SCHEDULER

When you have finished adding, editing and deleting your scheduled events, you'll want to close Scheduler while keeping it active (remember that Scheduler cannot run your events if it isn't active).

To close Scheduler:

- Select OK in the Scheduler dialog box.

To exit Scheduler without saving your changes:

- Select Cancel.

PART V
STANDALONE UTILITIES

Using Advise

This chapter explains Advise, which is found on the Norton Desktop Help menu. It can help you diagnose common problems and interpret DOS and CHKDSK error messages. If problems or errors are found, Advise can automatically run the proper program from the Norton Desktop to remedy the situation.

Contents

Types of Problems 24-3
Getting Advice 24-3
    Understanding a Problem 24-5
    Taking Action 24-6

Advise on the Norton Desktop helps you diagnose, understand and remedy many common computer problems ranging from general system malaise to specific symptoms associated with cryptic DOS messages.

The Advise system is divided into three problem groups:

- Common disk problems
- DOS error messages
- CHKDSK error messages

For each group, Advise lists problems or messages for you to choose from. After you make your selection, Advise explains what is happening, recommends a course of action, and, if indicated, automatically runs a corrective program for you.

TYPES OF PROBLEMS

Common disk problems are situations that frequently occur. The examples have been culled from the voluminous files of the Software Support engineers at Peter Norton Computing. You can often avoid a help call by browsing through the listing of Advise topics and finding a case that matches your dilemma.

The DOS error messages result from file and disk operations. If you ever receive a DOS error message that you do not understand, you can find it here. It will be demystified and a course of action suggested.

CHKDSK (check disk) is a program provided by DOS to test the condition of your disks. Before Peter Norton, it was the only diagnostic tool available—but it's limited in function and cryptic in its diagnostic messages. If you use CHKDSK and get an "error found" message, locate the message in the Advise CHKDSK listing and again follow the recommended action. Please note, however, you are almost always better off using Norton Disk Doctor to diagnose problems on your disk rather than CHKDSK.

GETTING ADVICE

Advise is the first option on the Norton Desktop Help menu.

To start Advise:

- Choose ADVISE from the Help menu.
  The Advise main index is displayed.

There are four entries in the Advise main index. The first is on line help for using the Advise system itself. The next three entries are the problem groups.

To choose a problem group:

1   Select an entry in the main index.
2   Select the Help button.

Or,

- Double-click the entry.

    An index of entries for the group is displayed (Figure 24-1).

Figure 24-1

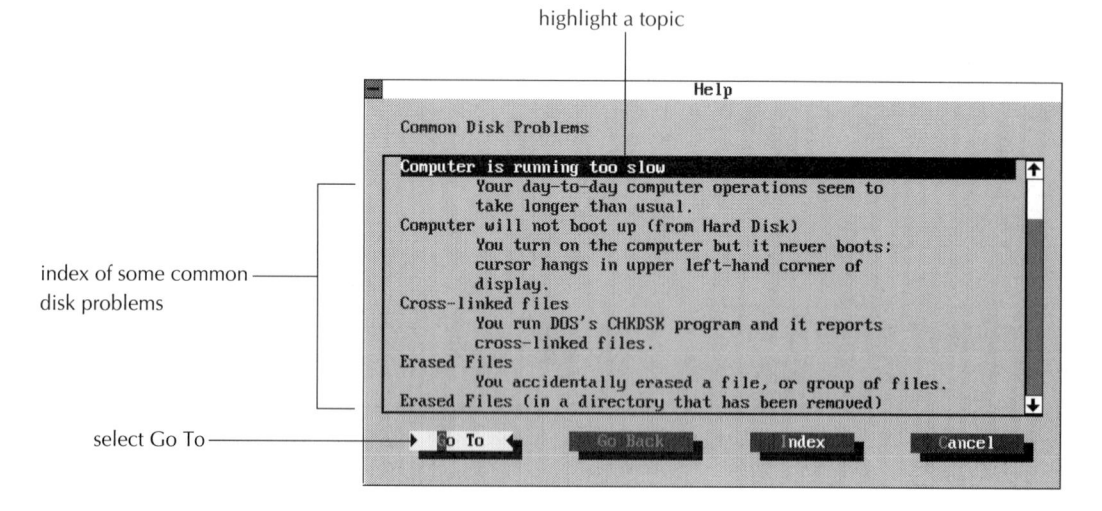

Note the row of buttons at the bottom of the screen: Go To, Go Back, Index, and Cancel. No matter where you are in the Advise system, the Index button takes you to the main index. Cancel exits the Advise system.

To chose an Advise topic:

1   Select the topic or error message in the listing.
2   Select the Go To button.

Or,

- Double-click the topic or error message.

  The topic is expanded to an explanation and course of action (Figure 24-2).

Figure 24-2

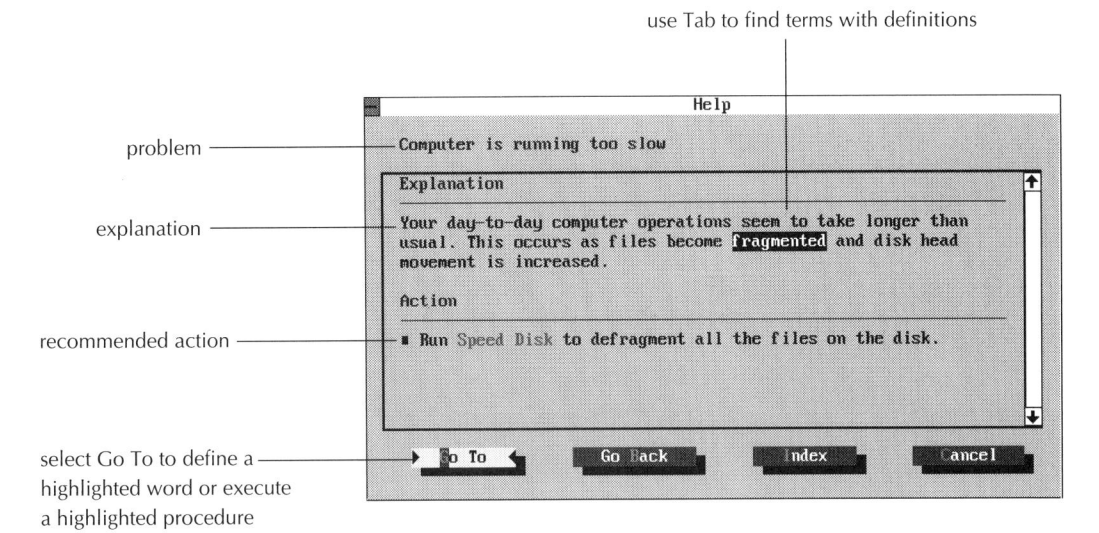

Callouts:
- use Tab to find terms with definitions
- problem
- explanation
- recommended action
- select Go To to define a highlighted word or execute a highlighted procedure

Help window contents:

Computer is running too slow

Explanation

Your day-to-day computer operations seem to take longer than usual. This occurs as files become **fragmented** and disk head movement is increased.

Action

- Run Speed Disk to defragment all the files on the disk.

Buttons: Go To | Go Back | Index | Cancel

Understanding a Problem

Each expanded topic follows a consistent format. The top of the screen shows the title from the index. The body of the topic starts with a simple explanation of the problem or error message. Following that is a recommended course of action with specific steps to take to correct the problem.

Technical terms within the explanation are displayed in a contrasting color or intensity.

To get a definition for a technical term:

1. Select the word you want to define.
2. Select the Go To button.

Or,

- Double-click the word.

  The screen displays a brief definition of the highlighted word.

24-6   *Using Norton Desktop for DOS*

To return to the topic, select the Go Back button.

Some terms may have further definitions within them. Simply select Go To and Go Back as necessary.

Taking Action

After the problem explanation, the proper corrective action is given. In some cases, Advise determines that a diagnostic or remedial program, such as the Norton Disk Doctor, should be run. In other cases, you will have to perform an action, such as closing a drive door.

For your convenience, Advise automatically runs the appropriate corrective program, if indicated. In these cases, note that the Go To button changes to Run when the program name is highlighted (Figure 24-3).

To run a corrective program:

1   Highlight the program name.
2   Select the Run button.

Or,

- Double-click the program name.

    Help is on the way.

Figure 24-3

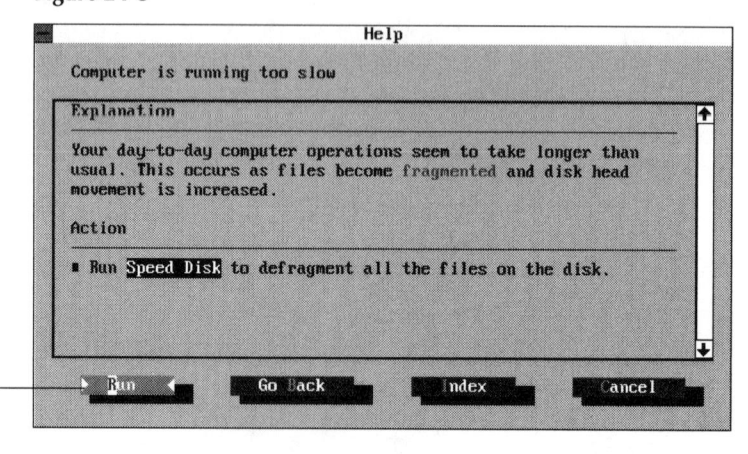

```
┌─────────────────────── Help ───────────────────────┐
│ Computer is running too slow                        │
│ ┌─ Explanation ──────────────────────────────────┐ │
│ │ Your day-to-day computer operations seem to    │ │
│ │ take longer than usual. This occurs as files   │ │
│ │ become fragmented and disk head movement is    │ │
│ │ increased.                                     │ │
│ │                                                │ │
│ │ Action                                         │ │
│ │                                                │ │
│ │ ■ Run Speed Disk to defragment all the files   │ │
│ │   on the disk.                                 │ │
│ └────────────────────────────────────────────────┘ │
│   [ Run ]    [ Go Back ]    [ Index ]   [ Cancel ] │
└────────────────────────────────────────────────────┘
```

select Run to have Advise automatically run a corrective program

NOTE: In a few situations, the problems cannot be corrected without the programs provided by the Norton Utilities, a more powerful toolkit designed to remedy a larger range of disk errors. If you are fortunate enough to also have the Norton Utilities, Advise will run the proper program for you. If not, you will have to seek outside assistance.

Using Image

This chapter explains Image, a program that records information about your disk to make it easy to recover deleted files or data from a formatted disk.

Contents

How Image Works 25-3
Taking A Snapshot 25-4

HOW IMAGE WORKS

Image takes a "snapshot" of the system area of your disk. Then, if you inadvertently format your disk, UnFormat uses the information to recover your data. UnErase also uses the information to help recover deleted files. Image does not eat up any of your computer's precious memory, so there is no penalty for its use.

Image is sure protection against potential disaster. For your convenience and maximum protection, the Norton Desktop installation program can place the necessary command in your AUTOEXEC.BAT file so that Image runs automatically every time you start your computer.

Image records the system area of your disk (Boot Record, File Allocation Table and root directory information) in a special file called IMAGE.DAT. The file is marked "read-only" so that you won't delete it by mistake. A second, very small file called IMAGE.IDX is also created, but this file is hidden so it won't appear in your directory listing. (Use FIND from the File menu if you want to prove that this file really exists.)

When Image runs, usually from your AUTOEXEC.BAT file when you start your computer, the message

```
Updating IMAGE for drive C:...
```

tells you Image is working. Then

```
Finished updating IMAGE for drive C:
```

tells you Image is done and has saved the information.

NOTE: Other features of the Norton Desktop, like Speed Disk and Format Diskette (which may alter disk bookkeeping), also update the IMAGE.DAT file. See Chapter 3, "Managing Disks," and Chapter 17, "Using Speed Disk," for information on these components.

TAKING A SNAPSHOT

Although Image runs automatically whenever you start your computer (provided it is installed as part of Norton Desktop), you may occasionally want to take another snapshot of your disk. For example, if you've made significant changes to your disk during the day, you may want to run Image again at the end of the day. This way, if a problem occurs at your next computer session, you can be sure that the latest information was saved.

To run Image for the C drive:

- Choose RUN... from the (long) File menu and type `image c:`, or type `image c:` at the DOS prompt.

To run Image for more than one drive:

- Type `image c: d:` if you have drives C and D.

NOTE: The IMAGE.DAT file is stored in each disk drive's root directory, where it must reside. You cannot tell the program to store the file elsewhere on your disk. Whenever Image runs, a new IMAGE.DAT file is created, and the old one is renamed IMAGE.BAK for extra safety.

Using UnFormat

This chapter explains how you can use UnFormat to recover your data from disks that have been accidentally reformatted or damaged in some other way.

Contents

How UnFormat Works 26-3
    The Image File 26-4
Using UnFormat 26-5
    Recovering a Disk without the Image File 26-8
    DOS 5.0 Mirror Program 26-9

UnFormat is a program that lets you recover from situations that may appear hopeless: damaged disks or disks that have been reformatted accidentally.

Use UnFormat to:

- Recover a hard disk that has been reformatted, either accidentally or deliberately.
- Rebuild a disk that has been damaged by a virus.
- Rebuild a disk that has been corrupted due to a power failure.
- Recover a floppy disk that has been formatted with Safe Format (FORMAT DISKETTE... from the Disk menu).

For maximum safety, UnFormat automatically prompts you through the program and warns when anything "undoable" is about to occur.

WARNING: If you have an emergency situation and you have not yet installed the Norton Desktop or you cannot access the program from your hard disk, do not attempt to copy UNFORMAT.EXE to your hard disk. Any new files copied to your hard disk might overwrite existing data, preventing complete recovery. Follow the procedure outlined on your Emergency Card, which was included with your copy of the Norton Desktop package.

NOTE: UnFormat can be run from a network, but you cannot UnFormat a network drive.

HOW UNFORMAT WORKS

The information on your disk is stored in two areas: the system area and the data area. The system area contains bookkeeping information that DOS uses to find files on your disk. The data area contains the actual data in your files.

On a hard disk, the DOS FORMAT command reinitializes the system area which contains the Root Directory, Boot Record and the File Allocation Tables but it does not overwrite the data area of the hard disk. Even though the disk appears to be empty (the message "No files found" is displayed), the data that made up your files is still there.

On floppy diskettes, however, the DOS FORMAT program erases everything. If the DOS FORMAT program was interrupted, it may be possible to recover any remaining files from the floppy diskette using UnFormat or UnErase (this may require some manual recovery).

> **TIP:** Always format floppy disks using the Safe Format option of FORMAT DISKETTE... from the Disk menu. Then, UnFormat can be used to recover a diskette if necessary. See Chapter 3, "Managing Disks," for more information.

The Image File

UnFormat searches the disk for the lost bookkeeping information first and reassembles it if it can be found. If the bookkeeping information can't be found, UnFormat tries to reassemble the disk from scratch.

When UnFormat searches the disk for the bookkeeping information, it looks for the file IMAGE.DAT that is created by the Norton Desktop Image program. Image takes a snapshot of the critical system information area of your hard disk. UnFormat also looks for files created by the DOS 5.0 Mirror program (see the section "DOS 5.0 Mirror Program" at the end of this chapter).

The recovery process is faster when the IMAGE.DAT file is used; however, this file is not absolutely necessary for UnFormat to operate. If IMAGE.DAT isn't present, UnFormat can still recover data, but the final result depends on file fragmentation and the number of small files versus large files, as well as other factors. Don't expect a 100-percent recovery—the root directory will be lost—and be aware that you might not get anything that is useful.

> **TIP:** To protect against data loss, make sure the Image program is run every time you start your computer. The easiest way to do this is to let the Norton Desktop install program place the required command in your AUTOEXEC.BAT file. See *Installing Norton Desktop for DOS* and Chapter 25, "Using Image," for more information.

Using UnFormat **26-5**

> **TIP:** To keep your disks in order in case of the need to run UnFormat or UnErase, use SPEED DISK from the (long) Tools menu regularly to eliminate file fragmentation. File fragmentation makes it harder for UnFormat and UnErase to recover files. See Chapter 17, "Using Speed Disk" for more information.

USING UNFORMAT

When you are running UnFormat, numerous prompts help prevent you from doing anything you may later regret. If you change your mind, you can also press Esc at any time before the actual unformatting begins.

To UnFormat a disk:

1. Choose RUN... from the (long) File menu or type `unformat` at the DOS prompt.

2. Read the first message to make sure you are doing the right thing and then select CONTINUE.

   You are presented with a list of available drives.

3. Select the Drive to Unformat from the drive list box and then select OK.

   UnFormat asks if you've used Image or the DOS 5.0 Mirror program to create a copy of the system area of your disk (see the section "DOS 5.0 Mirror Program" at the end of this chapter).

4. Select Yes to accept the default setting if you have used either of these programs, or if you're not certain (Figure 26-1).

Figure 26-1

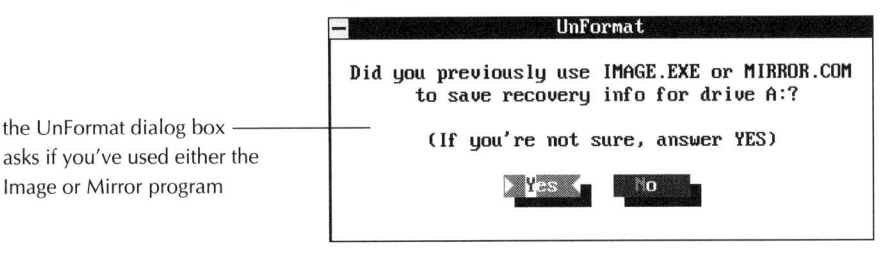

the UnFormat dialog box asks if you've used either the Image or Mirror program

```
┌─────────────── UnFormat ───────────────┐
│  Did you previously use IMAGE.EXE or MIRROR.COM │
│        to save recovery info for drive A:?      │
│                                                 │
│        (If you're not sure, answer YES)         │
│                                                 │
│           [ Yes ]      [ No ]                   │
└─────────────────────────────────────────┘
```

The list of files currently stored on the selected drive is displayed along with the message "Are you sure you want to UnFormat it?" Do not use UnFormat unless you're sure you want to recover your disk.

5   To continue, select Yes (or press Enter).

UnFormat searches for the IMAGE.DAT file. If found, you are told the last time the Image file was updated.

You are given the option of using the most recent version or the previous version. The reason for this is simple: if damage occurs to your disk late in the day, you may not notice it until the next day after you've started your computer. If Image is included in your AUTOEXEC.BAT file (as it should be), when you started your computer Image automatically updated a copy of the damaged system area, thus making the most recent version of IMAGE.DAT unusable. In this case, you would need to select Previous to restore the previous version.

6   Select Recent to restore the most recent version of IMAGE.DAT.

Or,

Select Previous to restore the previous version of IMAGE.DAT.

Restoring the disk at this point overwrites any current data.

7   Select Yes to continue.

UnFormat allows you the option of performing a full or partial restoration.

NOTE: When a disk has been accidentally formatted, there is a strong chance that changes were made to the disk after the IMAGE.DAT file was last updated. Any changes that are not reflected in the Image file will not be recovered.

8   Select Full if you're not sure whether you want a partial restoration or a full restoration of your disk. A full restoration includes recovering the Boot Record, File Allocation Tables and Root Directory.

Or,

Using UnFormat 26-7

Select partial restoration if you know exactly what the problem is; for example, your Boot Record is damaged, and you know how to correct the problem.

Once you choose the recovery method, UnFormat reconstructs the data. A map is used to depict the progress of directory searching and file recovery. The UnFormat Disk panel located in the lower-left corner of the screen displays cluster numbers and the percentage completed of the recovery process as it progresses (Figure 26-2).

The Legend panel located in the lower-right corner of the screen displays the characters used to signify sectors, files, and directories.

Figure 26-2

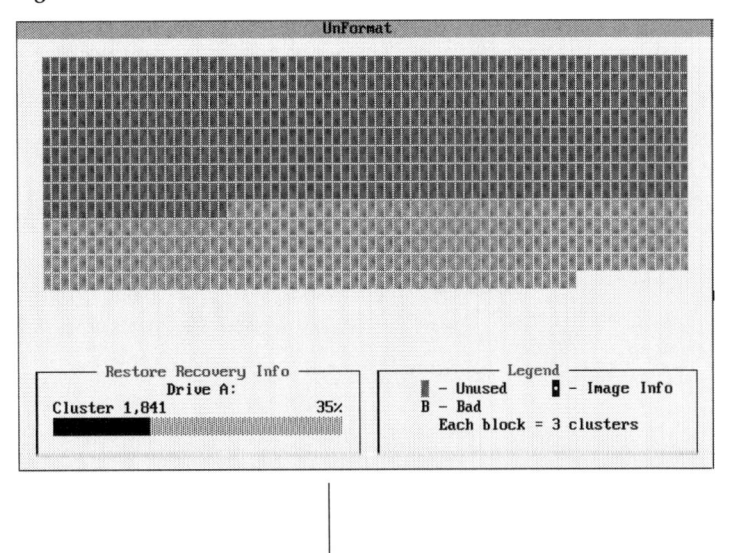

the UnFormat progress screen shows the completed percentage of the recovery as it progresses

The next screen advises you to run Norton Disk Doctor (NDD). This doesn't necessarily mean that you have a problem with the recovered disk. Disk Doctor cleans up any disk problems that might have occurred due to changes made on the disk after the IMAGE.DAT file was created.

To diagnose a drive with Norton Disk Doctor:

- Choose RUN... from the (long) File menu or at the DOS prompt, type `ndd c: /quick` where C: is the drive designation.

  The /quick option simply tells Norton Disk Doctor to skip the surface test. See Chapter 18, "Using Norton Disk Doctor," for more information.

Recovering a Disk without the Image File

If you have accidentally formatted a disk and have not used the IMAGE command to create the IMAGE.DAT file, you may still be able to recover much of your data.

To UnFormat a disk without the Image file:

1. Choose RUN... from the (long) File menu or type `unformat` at the DOS prompt.

2. Select the drive to unformat from the drive list box and then select OK.

3. Accept the default setting Yes when UnFormat asks if you've used the Image or Mirror programs. (They may have been used by another program without your being aware of it.)

   The message "Are you sure you want to UnFormat it?" is displayed. Do not use UnFormat unless you're sure you want to recover your disk.

4. Select Yes to continue.

   When UnFormat has finished, the subdirectories directly under your root directory will be named DIR0, DIR1, and so on. All filenames in your root directory will be lost. Use the Manual UnErase procedure to recover these files. (See Chapter 16, "Using UnErase" for more information.)

   Use the RENAME... command from the File menu to rename the directories. See Chapter 4, "Managing Directories and Files" for details.

> **NOTE:** If the recovered disk is not bootable, choose the Make a Disk Bootable option from the Disk Tools program. See Chapter 28, "Using Disk Tools," for more information.

DOS 5.0 Mirror Program

UnFormat also detects and uses information saved in Mirror files in DOS 5.0. Mirror files are much like the Image files created by the Image program of the Norton Desktop. They both save important information about a drive. UnFormat can use either Image or Mirror information, and, if both are found, the most recent one is used.

Using SmartCan

This chapter shows you how you can ensure that accidentally deleted files can be recovered with 100-percent accuracy.

Contents

How SmartCan Works 27-3
Configuring SmartCan 27-3
    Enabling or Disabling SmartCan 27-4
    Protecting Other Drives 27-4
    Files to Protect 27-5
    Archived Files 27-6
    Storage Limits 27-6
Purging Files 27-7
Turning SmartCan On and Off 27-8

Using SmartCan **27-3**

Using SmartCan is the best protection you can have against accidentally deleted files—a precaution that the wise computer user will always take. When SmartCan is active, deleted files can be recovered with 100-percent accuracy using UNERASE from the Tools menu.

For your convenience and maximum protection, the Norton Desktop installation program can place the necessary command in your AUTOEXEC.BAT file so that SmartCan is working every time you start your computer.

HOW SMARTCAN WORKS

SmartCan is a memory-resident program that uses about 10K of RAM. SmartCan sits quietly in memory, but intercepts any command that deletes or erases a file. SmartCan prevents deleted files from being overwritten by placing the deleted files in a hidden directory called "SMARTCAN." On a network drive, the hidden directory is called NCDTREE/SMARTCAN.

SmartCan automatically purges the protected files after a given number of days (or whenever the space is absolutely needed), freeing up the space and allowing DOS to use it.

NOTE: If you are on a network, your network administrator must create the SMARTCAN directory. But you will probably create your own Erase Protect configuration.

CONFIGURING SMARTCAN

SmartCan comes with a default configuration: all files (except files that have a .TMP, .SWP or .INI file extension) on the C: drive are protected for five days. This configuration is appropriate for most users, but you can change it if your needs are different. You can control the files that are protected by SmartCan as well as the automatic purge criteria.

CAUTION: Because SmartCan is a memory-resident program, it must be loaded before any other applications, including Norton Desktop.

To configure SmartCan:

1. At the DOS prompt, type `smartcan`

   The Configure SmartCan dialog box appears on your desktop. Figure 27-1 shows the default settings that are in effect immediately after Norton Desktop is installed.

2. Select your configuration options (which are explained in more detail in the following sections).

3. Select OK.

Figure 27-1

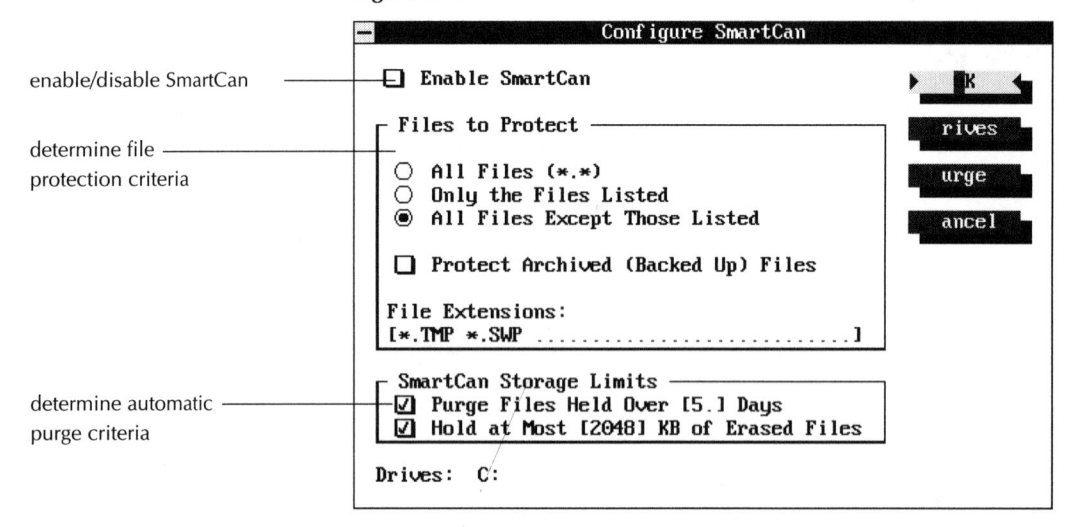

```
┌─────────────────── Configure SmartCan ───────────────────┐
│                                                           │
│   [ ] Enable SmartCan                         ► OK ◄      │
│   ┌─ Files to Protect ──────────────────┐                 │
│                                             rives        │
│     ○ All Files (*.*)                                    │
│     ○ Only the Files Listed                 urge         │
│     ● All Files Except Those Listed                      │
│                                             ancel        │
│     [ ] Protect Archived (Backed Up) Files               │
│                                                           │
│     File Extensions:                                      │
│     [*.TMP *.SWP ..........................]             │
│                                                           │
│   ┌─ SmartCan Storage Limits ──────────────────┐         │
│     [✓] Purge Files Held Over [5.] Days                  │
│     [✓] Hold at Most [2048] KB of Erased Files           │
│                                                           │
│     Drives:  C:                                           │
│                                                           │
└───────────────────────────────────────────────────────────┘
```

Annotations:
- enable/disable SmartCan → Enable SmartCan checkbox
- determine file protection criteria → Files to Protect section
- determine automatic purge criteria → SmartCan Storage Limits section

Enabling or Disabling SmartCan

You can enable SmartCan by checking the Enable SmartCan check box.

Unchecking the check box disables SmartCan. If the box is unchecked, deleted files will *not* be preserved and protected files will not automatically be purged to make room for new data.

Protecting Other Drives

By default, floppy drives are not protected. You can also specify network drives for protection.

To protect another drive:

1 Select the Drives button on the right side of the Configure SmartCan dialog box.

    All available drives are listed.

2 Select which drives you want to protect.

    You can select individual drives or use the Drive Types box on the right side to check All Floppy Drives, All Local Drives and All Network Drives. You can check any combination of the three.

3 Select OK.

NOTE: Any SmartCan options you set apply to all selected drives.

Files to Protect

While SmartCan is enabled, the criteria set up in the Files to Protect group box apply to all deleted files, whether they are deleted individually, in a group, or as part of a directory deletion. The options in the Files to Protect group box let you determine which files you want to protect—either all files or files specified by file extension.

To protect all files:

- Select All Files. Press Spacebar, if necessary, to change your selection.

If you have a small hard disk or disk space is at a premium, you may choose to protect only certain types of files rather than all files. You may choose to protect only data files and not the applications that create them; for example, you can protect your word processor documents but not the word processor itself. This strategy assumes that you can always reinstall the application from its distribution disks or your backups if it is accidentally deleted.

To specify which files to protect:

1 Select the Only the Files Listed button.

2 Enter up to nine different file extensions for files to protect in the File Extensions text box. For example, `*.DBF` and `*.DOC` would protect database and word processor files.

The other way to identify which files to protect is to say all files except certain file types, such as program files.

To specify files by exclusion:

1   Press Spacebar to select All Files Except Those Listed.
2   Enter up to nine different file extensions for files to exclude from protection in the File Extensions text box. For example, `*.EXE`, `*.COM`, and `*.OVL` would protect all files except program files.

> **TIP:** You do not need to use SmartCan to erase protect temporary files that are swapped in and out by applications or backup files created by applications. For example, *.SWP, *.TMP and *.INI file types are excluded by default. If you want to exclude *.BAK files as well, select All Files Except Those Listed and add *.BAK to the list.

Archived Files

A file is marked as archived if it has been backed up with the DOS BACKUP command or the Norton Backup program (accessed from the Tools menu). SmartCan does not automatically include archived files when it saves files, because you should be able to restore these files from your backup disks, if necessary. (See Chapter 4, "Managing Directories and Files," for an explanation of the archive attribute.)

If you prefer, you can protect all files, archived or not.

To protect archived files also:

- Check the Protect Archived (Backed Up) Files check box.

Keep in mind that it's likely that your SMARTCAN directory will fill up a lot faster this way, causing old files to be purged sooner.

Storage Limits

By default, SmartCan purges files from the SmartCan after they have been preserved for five days. It places a 2048K (or 2MB) limitation on the amount of space taken up by the SmartCan. You can change either of these criteria in the SmartCan Storage Limits group box.

To change the number of days that files are protected:

- Type over the default entry of five days to establish a different time limit.

Files are automatically purged with no warning after the specified time limit.

To eliminate the time limit:

- Uncheck the Purge Files check box.

Changing the space limit is usually not necessary because SmartCan automatically purges files as needed to make room for new or expanded files on the disk. However, changing the limit to suit your needs is useful if you plan to run your machine with SmartCan not loaded or disabled. In this case, SmartCan cannot perform its housekeeping chores.

To establish a space limit:

1. Check the Hold at Most check box.
2. Enter a space limit in kilobytes.

   The minimum limit is 16K. Any smaller number will be changed to 16.

When the limit is reached, SmartCan purges the oldest files first.

PURGING FILES

SmartCan automatically purges files after a specified amount of time. The Purge Files window displays a list of files that are being protected by SmartCan. If you want, you can purge these files manually.

To purge files:

1. At the DOS prompt, type `smartcan`
2. Select the Purge button.

   The Purge Deleted Files dialog box is displayed.
3. Select Drive to specify the drive to purge from (including network drives).

   A list of protected files is displayed.

4 Specify which files to purge from the list box (with the Spacebar) or select Tag to enter a wildcard file specification.

5 Select Purge.

TIP: Examine the list of protected files in the Purge Deleted Files dialog box to see if any files are being saved that are not necessary to save. Remove protection for these files in the future. See the section "Files to Protect" earlier in this chapter for details.

CAUTION: On a network, the system administrator will usually purge files, if necessary. However, if you do this yourself, do not remain in the purge window any longer than absolutely required. While the purge window is open, SmartCan is inactive on the selected drive and files deleted by other network users will not be added to the Smartcan.

TURNING SMARTCAN ON AND OFF

After SmartCan is configured to your liking, you can turn it on and off without using the Enable SmartCan check box in the SmartCan dialog box.

To turn SmartCan on:

- At the DOS prompt, type `smartcan /on`

If you are performing a general cleanup of your disk, you may want to temporarily turn off erase protection. Note that any files deleted while SmartCan is disabled won't be protected.

To turn SmartCan off:

- At the DOS prompt, type `smartcan /off`

If you've forgotten whether SmartCan is on or off, which drives are protected, and the other SmartCan settings, you can get a quick status report.

To find out the SmartCan status:

- At the DOS prompt, type `smartcan /status`

  The SmartCan status is displayed (see Figure 27-2).

TIP: You can use the RUN command in the (long) File menu to check the SmartCan status. However, do not use the RUN command to load SmartCan (see the caution at the beginning of this chapter).

Figure 27-2

in case you forget, the SmartCan Status Screen shows you whether SmartCan is on or off, which drives are protected, and other settings

```
c:\ >smartcan /status
SmartCan, Norton Utilities 6.01 with Norton Desktop 1.00
Copyright 1992 by Symantec Corporation

SmartCan Status:      Enabled
Drives Protected:     C: (SmartCan is empty)
Files Protected:      All files except those with these extensions
                      TMP, SWP
Archive Files:        Not Protected
Files Deleted After:  5 days

c:\ >
```

Using Disk Tools

This chapter explains how to use the Disk Tools utilities—a set of programs that perform data protection or data recovery operations, such as making an unbootable disk bootable or reviving a defective disk.

Contents

Making a Disk Bootable 28-3
Recovering from DOS's Recover 28-4
Reviving a Defective Diskette 28-5
Creating a Rescue Diskette 28-6
Restoring from a Rescue Diskette 28-7

Disk Tools is a set of utilities that perform various data protection or data recovery operations. Using Disk Tools, you can:

- Make a Disk Bootable
- Recover from DOS's RECOVER
- Revive a Defective Diskette
- Create a Rescue Diskette
- Restore from a Rescue Disk

These tools are powerful, but easy to use. Most of them are completely automatic with plenty of prompts to make sure that you don't do any inadvertent damage.

TIP: All computer users should create a rescue diskette to permit recovery from unexpected computer failures. This simple procedure can bring the sunshine back to an otherwise grim day. See "Creating a Rescue Diskette" later in this chapter for the procedure.

Figure 28-1

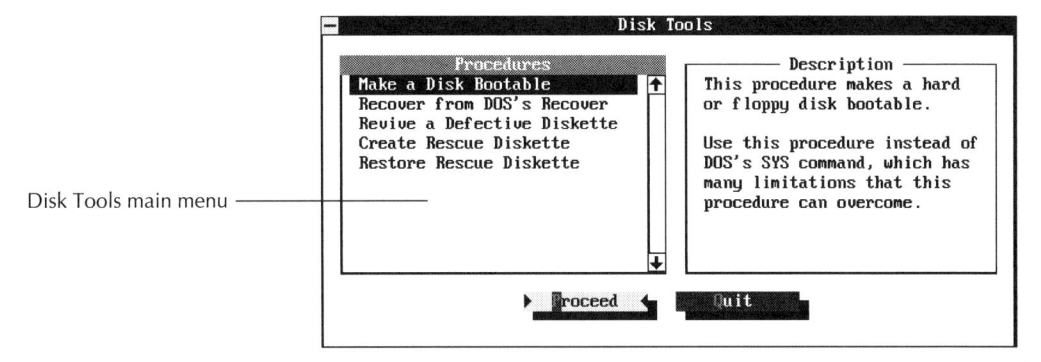

Disk Tools main menu

MAKING A DISK BOOTABLE

The Make a Disk Bootable procedure will take whatever steps are necessary to make any disk bootable, no matter what is currently occupying the system area.

When necessary (on a hard disk with no bootable partition), this option, unlike DOS, will actually modify the partition table to make the specified disk bootable. It will also copy DOS's COMMAND.COM file to the newly bootable disk.

To make a disk bootable:

1. Choose RUN... from the (long) File menu and type `disktool` or type `disktool` at the DOS prompt.

    The Disk Tools menu appears (see Figure 28-1).

2. Choose MAKE A DISK BOOTABLE from the Disk Tools menu.

    A list of available drives is displayed.

3. Select the disk you wish to make bootable from the list of active drives.

> **NOTE:** If you're familiar with DOS's SYS command (with DOS versions earlier than 4.0), you've probably received the error message "No room for system files." Make a Disk Bootable solves this problem.

RECOVERING FROM DOS'S RECOVER

DOS's RECOVER command does not do what most people assume. After using the program on a damaged disk, you will find that all of your files, no matter what their original location, are now in the root directory and have cryptic, machine-generated names. RECOVER does *not* recover erased or deleted files—use UnErase for this purpose (see Chapter 16, "Using UnErase"). Disk Tools undoes the operation performed by RECOVER, restoring your disk to the state it was in before you ran the DOS RECOVER command.

> **TIP:** Never use the DOS RECOVER command! If you are having problems with your disk, always use the NORTON DISK DOCTOR from the Tools menu instead. If you cannot access Norton Disk Doctor on your hard disk, follow the procedures outlined on the "Emergency Card" that was distributed with your copy of Norton Desktop.

To recover after using the DOS RECOVER command:

1. Choose RUN... from the (long) File menu and type `disktool`, or type `disktool` at the DOS prompt.

    The Disk Tools menu appears (see Figure 28-1).

2   Choose RECOVER FROM DOS'S RECOVER from the Disk Tools menu.

    A list of available drives is displayed.

3   Select the disk you wish to recover from DOS's RECOVER from the list of active drives.

    Follow the screen prompts of precautionary messages to begin the recovery process. Disk Tools displays a map depicting the progress of directory search and file recovery. When completed, the directories under your root directory will be named DIR00001, DIR00002 and so on. The files in the root directory will be named FILE000n. Use RENAME from the File menu to rename the files and directories in the root.

REVIVING A DEFECTIVE DISKETTE

If you ever tried to use a floppy disk in your computer and received a "Sector Not Found" error message, it probably means the diskette is defective.

This procedure makes a defective floppy disk usable again, but data will be lost from the defective areas of the disk. You will get back most data, but not all data. The procedure resurrects a defective diskette—either 5¼-inch or 3½-inch, but not a hard disk—by laying down new physical format information. Unlike a DOS format, however, you will still have access to the original data on the disk after formatting.

To revive a defective diskette:

1   Choose RUN... from the (long) File menu and type `disktool`, or type `disktool` at the DOS prompt.

    The Disk Tools menu appears (see Figure 28-1).

2   Choose REVIVE A DEFECTIVE DISKETTE from the Disk Tools menu.

    A list of available floppy drives is displayed (for example, A: and B:).

3   Select the disk drive from the list of active floppy drives.

4   Insert the defective diskette in the drive and select OK.

    The progress of the revival is displayed. When the revival is completed, a message appears advising you of this.

CREATING A RESCUE DISKETTE

The Create Rescue Diskette procedure saves vital system information about your hard disk. If the need should ever arise, you can restore this information with its sister procedure, Restore Rescue Diskette.

The following current system information is saved on the rescue diskette:

- Partition Tables. These record how hard disks are divided into drives (created by FDISK).
- Boot Records. These contain bookkeeping information about the drives necessary to keep track of files and directories (created by FORMAT).
- CMOS values. ATs and more advanced computers have a special, battery-powered CMOS chip (Complimentary Metal-Oxide Semiconductor) to maintain information about the drives, memory and other data that your system needs when it starts up.

To create a Rescue Diskette:

1 Choose RUN... from the (long) File menu and type `disktool`, or type `disktool` at the DOS prompt.

   The Disk Tools menu appears (see Figure 28-1).

2 Choose CREATE RESCUE DISKETTE.

   A list of drives is displayed.

3 Select the disk drive on which you want to store the rescue information.

   If you choose a floppy drive, the rescue files are placed in the root directory of the floppy disk. Make sure a formatted diskette is in the selected drive.

   If you choose another type of drive, a text box appears in which you type the desired directory location to hold the rescue files. The directory must already exist.

CAUTION: You can save the system information either on a floppy disk or in a directory of another type of drive (for example, a network drive). Don't use a local hard disk for the rescue files, use a floppy disk instead. You will have a big problem if you try to restore system information from a disk that is already damaged.

After you've made the drive (or drive and directory) selection, the rescue files are written to the disk.

4   Select OK when Disk Tools is done.

5   If you chose a floppy disk, remove it from the drive, label it "Rescue Disk" and, if you have more than one system, note which computer the rescue disk is for. Then store the rescue diskette in a safe place.

> **TIP:** Use a boot disk (one that will start your computer) for the Rescue Diskette. Copy the Disk Tools program (DISKTOOL.EXE) to the Rescue Diskette so that it, too, will be available, if ever needed. See Chapter 3, "Managing Disks," for information on how to make a boot disk or the first section in this chapter, "Making a Disk Bootable."

> **TIP:** Always write-protect diskettes that contain important data so that you don't accidentally erase or format the disk. If you are using 5 ¼-inch diskettes, affix a write-protect tab over the notch on the right side of the diskette. If you are using 3 ½-inch diskettes, slide the little plastic switch in the top-right corner of the diskette up, so that the hole is open.

RESTORING FROM A RESCUE DISKETTE

The Restore Rescue Diskette procedure allows you to restore your hard disk system information; but this information must have been previously saved using the Create Rescue Diskette procedure.

> **CAUTION:** Only run this procedure if you cannot access partitions on your hard disk and you've already tried running the NORTON DISK DOCTOR from the Tools menu. If you cannot access Norton Disk Doctor on your hard disk, follow the procedures outlined on the "Emergency Card" that was distributed with your copy of the Norton Desktop.

To restore the system from your Rescue Diskette:

1   Choose RUN... from the (long) File menu and type `disktool` or type `disktool` at the DOS prompt.

    The Disk Tools menu is displayed.

2   Choose RESTORE RESCUE DISKETTE from the Disk Tools menu.

    A cautionary screen appears reminding you to try running Disk Doctor first.

3   If you wish to continue, select Yes. Otherwise, select No (or press Esc).

4   Check which information you want to restore (see the previous section for details):
    - Partition Tables
    - Boot Records
    - CMOS Values

5   Select OK to continue.

    A list of available drives is displayed.

6   Select the drive that contains the rescue files. If the selected drive is not a floppy drive, a text box appears for you to enter the directory that contains the rescue files.

    The system is restored from the Rescue Diskette.

Using Norton Cache

This chapter explains how to use the Norton Cache—a program that speeds up computer operations. Configuration options to maximize performance and usage tips are described.

Contents

Requirements for the Norton Cache 29-3
Using the Norton Cache 29-4
    Cache Reports 29-4
    Resetting the Cache 29-6
    Deactivating the Cache 29-6
    Removing the Cache from Memory 29-7
Configuring the Norton Cache 29-8
    Configuration Options 29-9
    Advanced Options 29-15
Additional Notes 29-18
    DOS BUFFERS 29-18
    DOS FASTOPEN 29-18
    Compatibility with Storage Devices 29-18
    Norton Cache and Windows 29-19
    SMARTDrive 29-19

The Norton Cache helps your computer work faster. It does this by using some of your computer's RAM (internal memory) to serve as a *buffer,* or temporary holding area. Whenever your computer reads data from a disk, Norton Cache also puts a copy of that data in the special buffer. Then, if your computer needs to access this same data again, Norton Cache takes the data from that buffer instead of looking for it on the hard disk. Since your computer can work much faster when using its memory than it can when accessing the hard disk, this speeds operations and often dramatically improves performance.

You won't even be aware of the Norton Cache, except that you'll notice an improvement in the speed of your computer. Just how much speed improvement you see depends on the type of computer you own and the kinds of applications you use. For example, disk-intensive applications such as database programs will seem to fly.

NOTE: The Norton Cache, like any disk cache, is designed to be used each time you use your computer. The only times you will want to disable the cache are when you have run out of memory or when you are running a disk optimization or a disk repair program.

For maximum safety, the following programs from the Norton Desktop automatically disable Norton Cache:

- Norton Disk Doctor
- Speed Disk
- Norton AntiVirus
- Norton Backup

REQUIREMENTS FOR THE NORTON CACHE

The minimum system requirements for Norton Cache are:

- DOS 3.0 or higher
- 256K of conventional memory

However, for efficient disk caching you should really have a minimum of 384K of extended and/or expanded memory. For best results, dedicate approximately 20 percent more memory to the cache than the total amount of data your computer accesses at any given time. For instance, if you use your computer to access a 512K file repeatedly, you should allocate about 600K for a disk cache.

> **NOTE:** If you have no extended or expanded memory, you probably should not use a disk cache. While the minimum size for an effective disk cache is 64K (more is better), even this may be too big a chunk of your conventional DOS memory to devote to a cache as many applications require over 500K to run.
>
> Exceptions to this recommendation include the following: if you often perform disk-intensive activities or if you use a laptop computer with an auto-power-down hard disk.

USING THE NORTON CACHE

Once the Norton Cache is up and running, there are a few cache operations that may be valuable from time to time. These are performed with the use of command-line switches that instruct the cache to perform a particular function. For a complete summary of switches, refer to NCACHE in Appendix C, "Command-Line Reference."

If you have not yet installed the Norton Cache or wish to reconfigure it, please refer to the section "Configuring the Norton Cache" later in this chapter.

Cache Reports

If you ever have trouble loading applications or otherwise suspect memory problems, it is valuable to know how much memory is devoted to the cache and which drives are being cached. Norton Cache provides the information in two forms: Status and Report. The first, Status, is a brief summary of memory and drive usage. The second, Report, also includes a detailed breakdown of buffering, drive configuration and cache efficiency.

To find out cache status:

- Type `ncache /status` at the DOS prompt.

Or,

- Choose RUN... from the (long) File menu, type `ncache /status` and check the Pause on Return check box.

You are presented with a summary of memory usage by the cache (Figure 29-1).

Using Norton Cache **29-5**

Figure 29-1

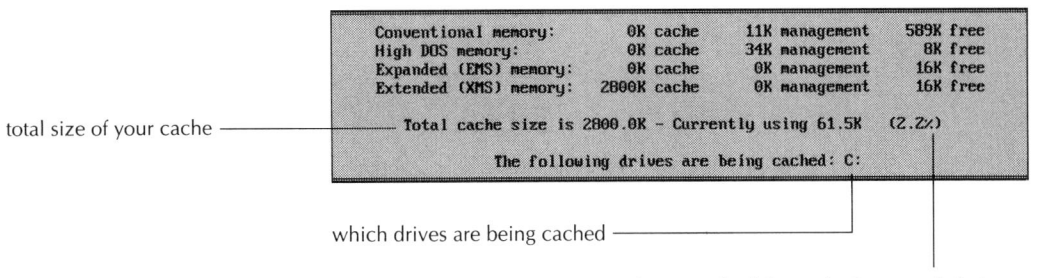

```
Conventional memory:      0K cache    11K management   589K free
High DOS memory:          0K cache    34K management     8K free
Expanded (EMS) memory:    0K cache     0K management    16K free
Extended (XMS) memory: 2800K cache     0K management    16K free

     Total cache size is 2800.0K - Currently using 61.5K  (2.2%)
              The following drives are being cached: C:
```

total size of your cache

which drives are being cached

how much of the cache is currently being used (may be less than the total cache size if you have not read many files yet)

The Norton Cache status screen shows how much memory is used for the cache program, the actual buffer and the cache allocation tables, and lists how much of each type of memory is left. This is broken down into DOS memory (the area from 0 to 640K that programs can load into), expanded memory and extended memory (on 80286 or greater computers only).

To get a detailed report with the buffer and drive configurations:

- Type `ncache /report` at the DOS prompt.

Or,

- Choose RUN... from the (long) File menu, type `ncache /report` and check the Pause on Return check box.

This report is quite detailed (Figure 29-2). For an explanation of any unfamiliar elements please refer to NCACHE in Appendix C, "Command-Line Reference."

In the example illustrated in Figure 29-2, neither drive A: nor drive B: is being cached, while drive C: has IntelliWrites enabled.

This report provides you with a helpful listing of the cache statistics. The cache statistics show how much of the cache is devoted to each drive and how successfully that drive has been cached. The Cache Hits/Disk Reads section of the screen shows how many sectors have been read from the cache versus how many have been read from the disk physically.

Using Norton Desktop for DOS

Note that the number shown here is not the number of files read but, rather, the number of sectors read. The percentage of Hits versus Reads lets you know how efficiently your cache is configured. The higher your percentages, the more effective the cache settings; however, because data must initially be read from the disk, it is impossible to achieve a 100-percent hit ratio.

Figure 29-2

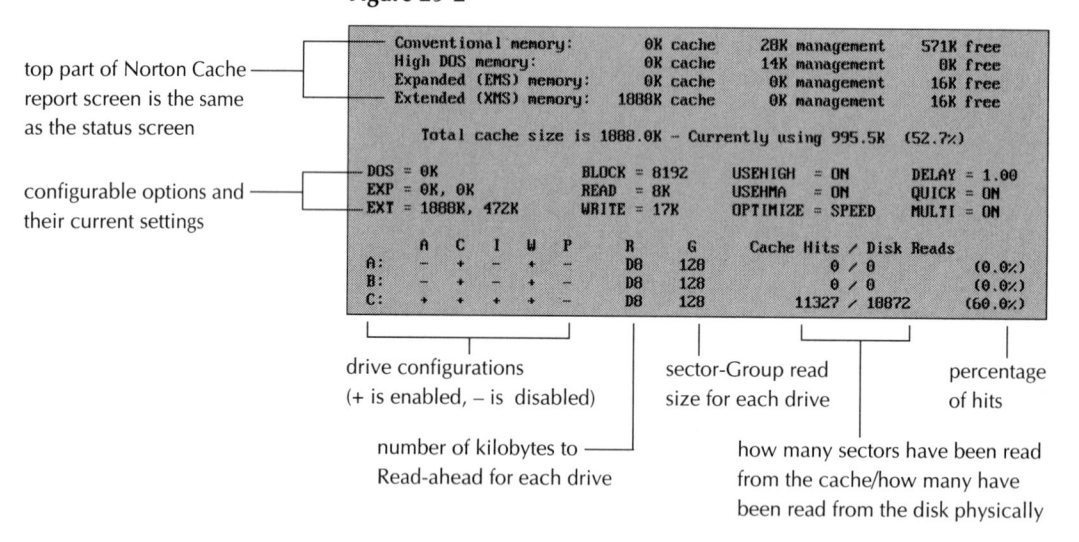

```
┌─ Conventional memory:        0K cache      28K management     571K free
│  High DOS memory:            0K cache      14K management      0K free
│  Expanded (EMS) memory:      0K cache       0K management     16K free
└─ Extended (XMS) memory:   1888K cache       0K management     16K free

      Total cache size is 1888.0K - Currently using 995.5K (52.7%)

┌─ DOS = 0K                BLOCK = 8192      USEHIGH = ON       DELAY = 1.00
│  EXP = 0K, 0K            READ  = 8K        USEHMA  = ON       QUICK = ON
└─ EXT = 1888K, 472K       WRITE = 17K       OPTIMIZE = SPEED   MULTI = ON

       A   C   I   W   P      R     G       Cache Hits / Disk Reads
   A:  -   +   -   +   -      D8   128              0 / 0          (0.0%)
   B:  -   +   -   +   -      D8   128              0 / 0          (0.0%)
   C:  +   +   +   +   -      D8   128          11327 / 18872      (60.0%)
```

- top part of Norton Cache report screen is the same as the status screen
- configurable options and their current settings
- drive configurations (+ is enabled, − is disabled)
- number of kilobytes to Read-ahead for each drive
- sector-Group read size for each drive
- how many sectors have been read from the cache/how many have been read from the disk physically
- percentage of hits

Resetting the Cache

Occasionally you may want to reset the cache and clear the cache of all previously cached data. All deferred disk writes are written to disk before the actual cache reset is made.

To reset the cache:

- Choose RUN... from the (long) File menu and type `ncache /reset` or type `ncache /reset` at the DOS prompt.

Deactivating the Cache

Occasionally, you may want to temporarily deactivate caching.

To deactivate the cache:

- Choose RUN... from the (long) File menu and type `ncache /-A` or type `ncache /-A` at the DOS prompt. This will disable caching for all drives.

To reactivate caching:

- Choose RUN... from the (long) File menu and type `ncache /A` or type `ncache /A` at the DOS prompt.

You can also activate and deactivate caching for specific drives. See NCACHE in Appendix C, "Command-Line Reference," for details.

Removing the Cache from Memory

If you've chosen to have the Norton Cache loaded from your AUTOEXEC.BAT file *and* it is the last TSR loaded, you can also remove the cache from memory. (See the section "Configuring the Norton Cache" later in this chapter, for instructions on how to install or reconfigure the Norton Cache.)

To remove the cache from memory:

- Type `ncache /uninstall` at the DOS prompt.

Remember, this will not work if the cache is loaded from your CONFIG.SYS file.

NOTE: You cannot remove the cache from memory from within the Norton Desktop. First, exit the Norton Desktop, and then type `ncache /uninstall` at the DOS prompt to remove the Norton Cache from memory.

To reload the cache:

- Type `ncache /install` at the DOS prompt.

If the Norton Cache is loaded from CONFIG.SYS, you will have to reboot your computer after removing the command that loads the cache from your CONFIG.SYS file.

To remove the command that loads the cache from CONFIG.SYS:

1 Choose RUN... from the (long) File menu and type `ndconfig` or type `ndconfig` at the DOS prompt.

   This loads the Norton Desktop configuration program.

2. Choose Startup Programs from the Configure Norton Desktop dialog box.

The Startup Programs dialog box appears, displaying a list of Norton Desktop programs.

3. Highlight Cache Disks.
4. Select Configure.

The Norton Cache configuration dialog box is displayed.

5. Select Do Not Load the Norton Cache from the Loading options.
6. Select OK to exit the Norton Cache dialog box and return to Startup Programs.
7. Select Save to save the configuration changes.
8. Select Quit to exit the Norton Desktop configuration program.
9. If you ran NDCONFIG from the RUN... command on the (long) File menu, exit the Norton Desktop and then reboot your computer.

Or,

If you ran NDCONFIG from the DOS prompt, reboot your computer.

CONFIGURING THE NORTON CACHE

The Norton Cache can be installed and configured as part of the Norton Desktop installation program. Alternatively, you can install or reconfigure the cache after the Norton Desktop is installed using the Norton Desktop configuration program (NDCONFIG).

NOTE: The configuration settings for the Norton Cache are saved in a file called NCACHE.INI, which is placed in your Norton Desktop directory. This file is read when the cache is loaded into memory either from your CONFIG.SYS file or your AUTOEXEC.BAT file. When you install or configure the Norton Cache, the settings do not take effect until you reboot your computer and the cache is loaded into memory.

If you are already using the cache, you may want to read this section just to find out what the cache is doing.

Using Norton Cache **29-9**

Configuration Options

The configuration options of the Norton Cache are divided into two dialog boxes. The main dialog box contains options that cover a basic installation, which is probably all you'll ever need. In fact, you can safely accept the preset options and not worry a bit. There is, however, an Advanced Option for those users who are familiar with cache intricacies and wish to fine-tune the cache for specific environments.

> **NOTE:** Technical wizards (you know who you are) may prefer to manually install the cache using the command-line switches described in Appendix C, "Command-Line Reference."

If you did not install the Norton Cache as part of the Norton Desktop installation and want to install it now, or you want to reconfigure an already installed cache, the procedures in the following sections guide you through the steps.

To either install or reconfigure the Norton Cache, after the Norton Desktop is installed:

1. Choose RUN... from the (long) File menu and type `ndconfig` or, at the DOS prompt, type `ndconfig` to load the Norton Desktop configuration program.
2. Choose Startup Programs from the menu.

   The Startup Programs dialog box appears, displaying a list of Norton Desktop programs.
3. Highlight Install Norton Cache.
4. Select Configure.

   The Norton Cache configuration dialog box appears (Figure 29-3).

Each configuration option of the Norton Cache main dialog box is described in the following sections.

Figure 29-3

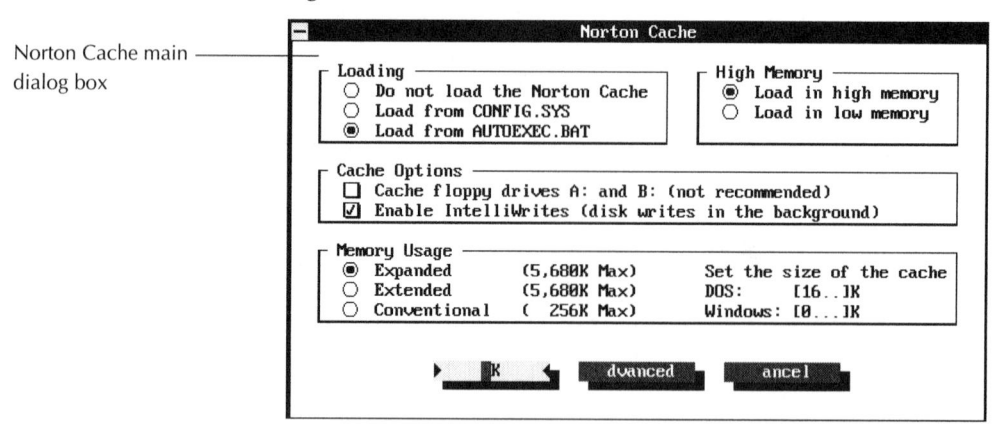

Norton Cache main dialog box

```
┌─ Norton Cache ─────────────────────────────────────────┐
│ ┌─ Loading ──────────────────────┐ ┌─ High Memory ───┐ │
│ │ ○ Do not load the Norton Cache │ │ ◉ Load in high memory │ │
│ │ ○ Load from CONFIG.SYS         │ │ ○ Load in low memory  │ │
│ │ ◉ Load from AUTOEXEC.BAT       │ └─────────────────┘ │
│ └────────────────────────────────┘                     │
│ ┌─ Cache Options ──────────────────────────────────────┐ │
│ │ ☐ Cache floppy drives A: and B: (not recommended)   │ │
│ │ ☑ Enable IntelliWrites (disk writes in the background) │ │
│ └──────────────────────────────────────────────────────┘ │
│ ┌─ Memory Usage ───────────────────────────────────────┐ │
│ │ ◉ Expanded      (5,680K Max)   Set the size of the cache │ │
│ │ ○ Extended      (5,680K Max)   DOS:     [16..]K      │ │
│ │ ○ Conventional  ( 256K Max)    Windows: [0...]K      │ │
│ └──────────────────────────────────────────────────────┘ │
│          ▶ OK ◀    dvanced    ancel                    │
└────────────────────────────────────────────────────────┘
```

Loading

The command to load the Norton Cache can be placed in either your CONFIG.SYS file or your AUTOEXEC.BAT file. The main difference between the two methods is that if the cache is loaded from the AUTOEXEC.BAT file, it can be removed from memory with a command-line switch; however, the Norton Cache must be installed from CONFIG.SYS for compatibility with a few device drivers. (See the warning in the section "Saving the Configuration" later in this chapter.)

If you are not sure which method is appropriate for you, configure the Norton Cache to load from AUTOEXEC.BAT.

To load the Norton Cache from CONFIG.SYS:

- Select Load from CONFIG.SYS in the Loading group box.

To load the Norton Cache from AUTOEXEC.BAT:

- Select Load from AUTOEXEC.BAT in the Loading group box.

High Memory

The Norton Cache can be loaded in either high memory or conventional memory (below 640K). In order to use high memory, you must be using an extended memory manager (XMS) such as EMM386 or QEMM. If you are not sure whether your system supports high memory, choose it anyway. If the cache cannot be successfully loaded in high memory, it will be loaded in conventional memory.

To load the cache in high memory:

- Accept the default, Load in High Memory, from the High Memory group box.

Cache Options

Caching floppy drives can be a dangerous practice: you might remove a disk while data is still being cached and before it is written to disk. You may consider this option if you are using, for example, a laptop computer without a hard disk.

To disable caching of floppy drives:

- Make sure that the Cache Floppy Drives A: and B: check box is *unchecked* (the default) in the Cache Options group box.

IntelliWrites reduce the amount of head movement necessary to complete a requested series of disk writes and increase the amount of data that is written to disk during each rotation of the disk. In addition, IntelliWrites provide simultaneous disk writing and program execution. When IntelliWrites are enabled, Norton Cache actually allows the current running application to continue executing in the foreground while it performs the actual disk writing in the background.

To enable IntelliWrites:

- Check Enable IntelliWrites (the default) in the Cache Options group box.

Memory Usage

The default configuration for the Norton Cache uses all available extended memory (less 16K of extended memory) for the cache. This is appropriate unless you run applications that also require use of this memory. Try to use a minimum of 384K of extended and/or expanded memory for efficient disk caching. Remember, more is better.

CAUTION: If neither expanded nor extended memory is available, Norton Cache uses a default of 128K of DOS memory for the cache. Using conventional DOS memory for disk caching is not recommended.

NOTE: Norton Cache requires an expanded memory manager to be LIM EMS 4.0-compatible.

The Memory Usage group box contains fields in which to enter the amount of memory to use for the Norton Cache under normal circumstances and the amount of memory the cache should use if Windows is running. The total amounts of expanded, extended, and conventional memory available on your system are displayed.

When running Windows 3.x in the enhanced mode on an 80386 or greater computer, you can force the cache to retain a minimum amount of memory for its own use. For example, if you have only two megabytes of memory, you will probably want Windows to be able to grab it all. If you have four megabytes of memory, you should retain one megabyte for the cache.

To specify how much memory to devote to the cache:

- Select the type of memory to use for the cache in the memory usage box and enter the amount of memory to devote to the cache.

  If you don't use any other programs that require expanded or extended memory, accept the defaults, which will be the total amount of each type of memory available.

To specify memory usage when running Windows:

- Enter the minimum amount of memory Norton Cache should retain for its own use when running Windows in enhanced mode in the second field.

  If you don't use Windows, type 0 for this amount.

NOTE: If you are using Windows, you must use XMS memory for the cache.

Saving the Configuration

After specifying the Norton Cache options, you're almost done. Unless, of course, you want to go on to the Advanced Options described in the next section.

The configuration settings for the Norton Cache are saved in a file called NCACHE.INI, which is placed in your Norton Desktop directory.

To save the Norton Cache configuration:

- Select OK from the Norton Cache main dialog box (see Figure 9-3).

    The configuration is saved and you exit the Norton Cache main dialog box and return to the Startup Programs dialog box.

Depending upon which installation you chose, either your AUTOEXEC.BAT file or your CONFIG.SYS file has been modified to contain the cache installation command.

You can verify the placement of the /INSTALL command line in either your AUTOEXEC.BAT or CONFIG.SYS file.

To view your AUTOEXEC.BAT or CONFIG.SYS file:

1 Select Edit at the bottom of the Startup Programs dialog box.

    The Editing Startup Files dialog box appears.

2 Select the file you want to view from the File drop-down list box.

If you chose CONFIG.SYS, the line to load the cache will contain the following words:

    DEVICE = C:\ND\NCACHE.EXE /INSTALL

For maximum compatibility with other device drivers, make sure that the line is the last one in your CONFIG.SYS file.

If you chose AUTOEXEC.BAT, the command line to load the cache will contain the following words:

    NCACHE /INSTALL

Make sure the line is not placed after a line that runs a batch file or menu program that does not return to AUTOEXEC.BAT. For most situations, the line will already be in the right place.

To move the cache installation line within your AUTOEXEC.BAT or CONFIG.SYS file:

1. Select the desired line using the UpArrow and DownArrow keys and select Move.

   Or,

   Click the right mouse button on the desired line.

   Two arrowheads at the ends of the highlight indicate the selected line.

2. Position the selected line with the UpArrow and DownArrow keys.

   Or,

   Hold the left mouse button down and drag the line to its new location.

3. Select Drop to place the line at its new location.

4. When you are satisfied, select Save if you've moved any lines in your AUTOEXEC.BAT or CONFIG.SYS files.

   Or,

   Select Cancel if there are no changes or you feel you've messed things up and want to gracefully back out without making any changes.

   You are returned to the Startup Programs dialog box.

5. Select Save to save the changes you've made for the Norton Desktop startup programs.

6. Select Quit to leave NDCONFIG, the Norton Desktop configuration program.

The next time you start your computer, wear a seat belt.

WARNING: You must be careful when using Norton Cache with device drivers that, in effect, create a disk-within-a-disk (as do some compression and encryption programs). Norton Cache *must* be loaded from the CONFIG.SYS file *before* most disk-within-a-disk drivers. However, this is not necessary if you are using the Norton Utilities Diskreet program or with Stacker; you can safely load Norton Cache from CONFIG.SYS before or after those two programs.

Using Norton Cache **29-15**

Advanced Options

The Advanced Options dialog box lets you precisely configure the buffering method for the cache. As a convenience, you can also select one of three factory-balanced sets of defaults that optimize the cache for either speed, efficiency or memory. If desired, select one of the optimized default settings as a starting point for finer tuning. These settings are described in the section "Optimize," later in this chapter.

To display the Advanced Options dialog box:

- Select the Advanced button from the Norton Cache main dialog box (see Figure 29-3).

  The Advanced Options dialog box opens (Figure 29-4).

  If necessary, refer to the steps earlier in this chapter on how to get to the Norton Cache dialog box in NDCONFIG.

Figure 29-4

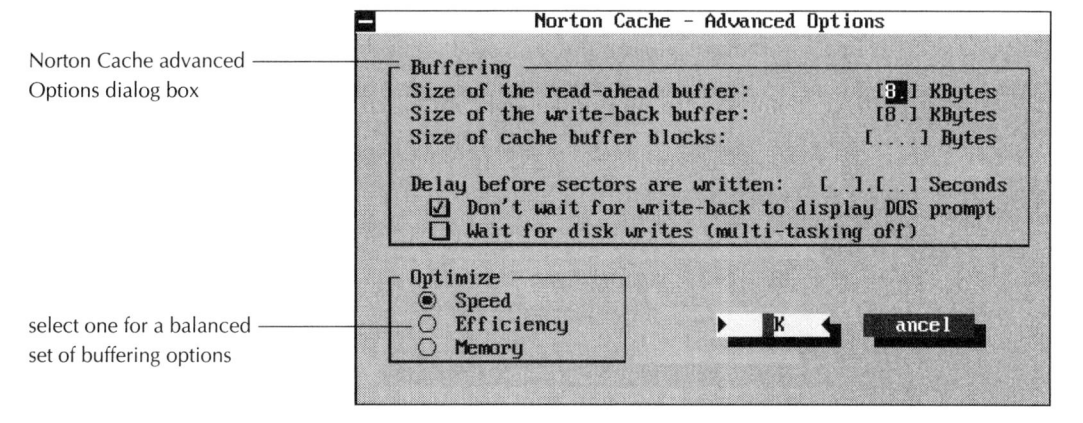

```
┌─ Norton Cache - Advanced Options ──────────────────┐
│  ┌ Buffering ──────────────────────────────────┐   │
│  │ Size of the read-ahead buffer:     [ 8] KBytes│   │
│  │ Size of the write-back buffer:     [ 8] KBytes│   │
│  │ Size of cache buffer blocks:       [....] Bytes│  │
│  │                                              │   │
│  │ Delay before sectors are written: [..].[..] Seconds│
│  │ [X] Don't wait for write-back to display DOS prompt│
│  │ [ ] Wait for disk writes (multi-tasking off) │   │
│  └──────────────────────────────────────────────┘   │
│  ┌ Optimize ─────────────┐                          │
│  │ ● Speed               │   ► OK ◄    Cancel       │
│  │ ○ Efficiency          │                          │
│  │ ○ Memory              │                          │
│  └───────────────────────┘                          │
└─────────────────────────────────────────────────────┘
```

Norton Cache advanced Options dialog box

select one for a balanced set of buffering options

There are two group boxes in the Advanced Options dialog box: Buffering and Optimize. The Buffering group gives you complete control over the behavior of the cache. Unless you have a particular need to fine-tune the cache so precisely, you can safely skip to the Optimize group and select one of the three choices—a balanced set of the buffering options.

Buffering

The first option in the Buffering group is the Size of the Read-Ahead Buffer: the maximum amount of data, in kilobytes, that can be read ahead on a drive being cached. The default size is 8K. Values must be a multiple of 1K, between 8K and 64K inclusive, or 0. A value of 0 disables read-ahead entirely. If files are highly fragmented, a smaller value will improve performance. Conversely, if files are not highly fragmented, a larger value improves performance.

The next option is the Size of the Write-Back Buffer (IntelliWrites). The value specified represents the maximum amount of data, in kilobytes, that will be written to disk in one operation in the background. It must be a multiple of 1K, between 8K and 64K inclusive, or 0. A value of 0 disables IntelliWrite support entirely. For maximum speed, the size should equal the largest track size of your disks.

The third option is the Size of Cache Buffer Blocks. A cache buffer block is a group of contiguous sectors that Norton Cache has cached. Cache blocks are used to reduce the amount of memory required to manage the cache. Valid cache block sizes are 512, 1024, 2048, 4096 or 8192 bytes. Larger cache block sizes require less memory to manage than do smaller cache block sizes. In addition, larger cache block sizes provide faster access to cached data. However, smaller cache block sizes generally provide more efficient use of memory.

The Delay Before Sectors Are Written option is used to instruct Norton Cache to defer disk writes for up to $59^{99}/_{100}$ seconds for each cached drive that also has IntelliWrite support enabled. The format for this option is *ss.hh*, where *ss* is the number of seconds between 0 and 59, and *hh* is the number of hundredths of a second between 0 and 99 to delay the write.

The Don't Wait for Write-Back to Display DOS Prompt option controls how quickly Norton Cache returns to the DOS prompt after exiting an application that had disk writes deferred. When checked (the default), the cache returns to the DOS prompt immediately. When unchecked, the cache makes sure all deferred writes have been written to disk prior to returning to the DOS prompt; this may be useful if you are caching floppy drives.

Optimize

The Wait for Disk Writes (Multi-tasking Off) option is checked by default. This makes sure the Norton Cache does not have problems with multi-tasking products such as Windows.

As an alternative to entering specific values for buffering options, you can choose from a set of balanced defaults for speed, efficiency or memory in the Optimize group box.

NOTE: If you did not choose Advanced Options from the Norton Cache main dialog box, Norton Cache defaults to the Speed setting.

To select a balanced set of default values for the Norton Cache:

- Select Speed, Efficiency or Memory from the Optimize group box.

The configuration values for each option are as follows:

Speed
- Read-Ahead buffer is 8K.
- Write-Back buffer is the same size as the largest track size in kilobytes of all drives being cached.
- Delay before writing is 1.0 seconds.
- Cache buffer block size is 8192 bytes.

Efficiency
- Read-Ahead buffer is 8K.
- Write-Back buffer is 8K.
- Delay before writing is 1.0 seconds.
- Cache buffer block size is the smallest for the specified cache size (usually 512 bytes).

Memory
- Read-Ahead buffer is disabled (0K).
- Write-Back buffer is disabled (0K).
- Delay before writing is 0.0 seconds (no delayed writes).
- Cache buffer block size is 8192 bytes.

ADDITIONAL NOTES

The Norton Cache is a sophisticated program that should function in harmony with your computer's configuration. The following tips will help you get the most out of Norton Cache.

DOS BUFFERS

Your CONFIG.SYS file may have a line that says BUFFERS = *nn* where *nn* represents the number of buffers for your computer. If it has such a line, you should change the number of buffers to between 3 and 10, the optimal amount being determined by your percentage of hits ratio (see the "Cache Reports" section earlier in this chapter). Try starting with BUFFERS = 5.

DOS FASTOPEN

Remove FASTOPEN from your AUTOEXEC.BAT or CONFIG.SYS if it is present. FASTOPEN buffers the FAT (file allocation table) and directory structure of the disk, but is inefficient and causes problems with other programs. Norton Cache buffers the FAT and directory structure more efficiently than FASTOPEN.

Compatibility with Storage Devices

Norton Cache has been designed to provide the highest level of compatibility with virtually any mass storage device that is compatible with DOS. While many other disk-caching utilities perform their caching at the BIOS level of your computer, Norton Cache performs its disk caching at the DOS level. This means that Norton Cache works with any drive of any capacity supported by DOS, as well as removable media drives like Iomega's Bernoulli Box and Syquest's Removable Cartridge Drive.

Norton Cache automatically locks certain drives that support removable media locking, whenever it defers a disk write targeted to such a drive. When the physical disk write is complete, Norton Cache automatically unlocks the drive. This assures that a disk does not get removed accidentally before Norton Cache actually writes the deferred disk writes to disk. Currently, Norton Cache supports automatic drive locking for Iomega's Bernoulli Box and Syquest Removable Cartridge Drives. Please refer to the Norton Desktop READ.ME file to learn about any additional drives for which Norton Cache provides automatic drive-locking support.

> **NOTE:** To prevent drives from being continually locked and unlocked during intensive write operations, Norton Cache will wait approximately 2.5 seconds after the last deferred write has been written to disk before unlocking any drives it has locked automatically.

Norton Cache and Windows

Norton Cache must be loaded prior to running Windows. You will get an error message if you try to install Norton Cache from within Windows.

> **NOTE:** On a few computers if you run Windows 3.x in 386 enhanced mode and have enabled IntelliWrites in Norton Cache, you may need to add the following line to the [386Enh] section of your Windows SYSTEM.INI file:
>
> ```
> VirtualHDIrq=false
> ```
>
> This will ensure that Norton Cache performs as expected when writing data to disk in the background. However, the line should be added to SYSTEM.INI *only* if needed; adding this on a computer that doesn't need it will slow down the system.

SMARTDrive

If you have been using Microsoft's SMARTDrive disk cache with Windows or DOS 5.0, you should replace it with Norton Cache. If you attempt to load Norton Cache while SMARTDrive is loaded, Norton Cache will display a warning message.

PART VI
CORPORATE MENUS

Creating Corporate Menus

This chapter introduces Norton Menu, a menu-building program that organizes frequently used applications on menus. It assumes that you are in charge of creating a menu system for a group of people in an organization.

Contents

Designing a Custom Work Environment	30-3
Features	30-3
Launching Norton Menu	30-4
Using Command-Line Options	30-4
Switching Between Edit and Run Mode	30-4
Selecting a Menu	30-5
Exiting Norton Menu	30-5
Creating a Basic Menu	30-6
Testing a Menu	30-9
Creating an Advanced Menu	30-9
Creating a Program Menu Item	30-9
Customizing a DOS Program	30-11
Creating a Submenu	30-12
Creating a Batch Menu Item	30-12
Editing Menus	30-13
Adding a Menu Item	30-13
Modifying a Menu Item	30-13

Adding a Similar Menu Item 30-14
Deleting a Menu Item 30-14
Moving a Menu Item 30-15
Changing the Menu Title 30-15
Updating a Menu Automatically 30-15
Deleting a Menu 30-16
Using Menus 30-17
Choosing a Menu Item 30-17
Moving from One Submenu to Another 30-17
Closing a Menu 30-18

DESIGNING A CUSTOM WORK ENVIRONMENT

You can use Norton Menu to create a custom menu system for yourself or for your entire workgroup, designed for the way you or the people in your group like to work. You can then run the menu system as a DOS *shell* on each computer in your organization. Doing so has several advantages:

- You can reduce the learning curve for both novice and advanced users, thereby increasing productivity.
- You can limit access to applications and files on each computer's hard disk.
- You can safeguard against serious mistakes by making users select DOS commands from a menu, instead of having them rely on their memories and navigational skills to perform risky tasks, such as formatting a disk. In fact, you can use custom menus to prevent users from ever seeing the DOS prompt at all.
- You can stop users from inadvertently or intentionally interfering with each other's hard disks.
- Norton Menu will give all the computers in your organization a professional look and feel.
- You can easily maintain the menu system as your organization's hardware and software requirements change.

Creating a menu system is easy—no programming experience is needed.

Features

Norton Menu has several features that sets it apart from other menu-building programs. If you are a systems administrator in charge of creating menus for a workgroup, you will find that Norton Menu's automatic menu-building and menu-updating features make it fast and easy for you to create and maintain menus for your workgroup.

You can use Norton Menu to:

- Launch applications from menus
- Create and edit menus
- Build and update menus automatically
- Protect menu items with a password

- Customize menus to suit your or your workgroup's preferences
- Import other menus (Direct Access, Norton Commander) for use in Norton Menu

Now that you have a good idea of the power of Norton Menu, you're ready to get started.

LAUNCHING NORTON MENU

To launch Norton Menu from the DOS prompt:

- Type nmenu then press Enter.

If you prefer, you can add the NMENU command to the last line of the AUTOEXEC.BAT file to launch Norton Menu each time the computer starts.

Using Command-Line Options

This section describes the NMENU command syntax and options. The command syntax is:

    NMENU pathname [/edit] [/run]

Command-line options affect Norton Menu as a whole and stay in effect for the duration of the session. The command-line options are:

/edit   Lets you run and edit menus. This is the recommended mode for single-user menu systems.

/run   Runs menus but removes the menu bar so that users can run menus to launch applications but not edit the menus.

Switching Between Edit and Run Mode

To switch from edit to run mode:

- Choose RUN MODE from the Options menu (Alt+R).

  The program runs the menu but removes the menu bar so that users cannot edit it.

To switch from run to edit mode:

- Press Alt+R.

  The program displays the menu bar so that users can edit the menu.

SELECTING A MENU

A menu is stored in a menu file. To select a menu, open the menu file.

To select (or open) a menu file:

1 Choose OPEN... from the Norton Menu File menu (Ctrl+O).

The Open Menu dialog box appears (Figure 30-1). This dialog box contains a list of menu titles and their corresponding menu filenames. The filename consists of up to the first eight characters of the menu title and the .NMF extension.

Figure 30-1

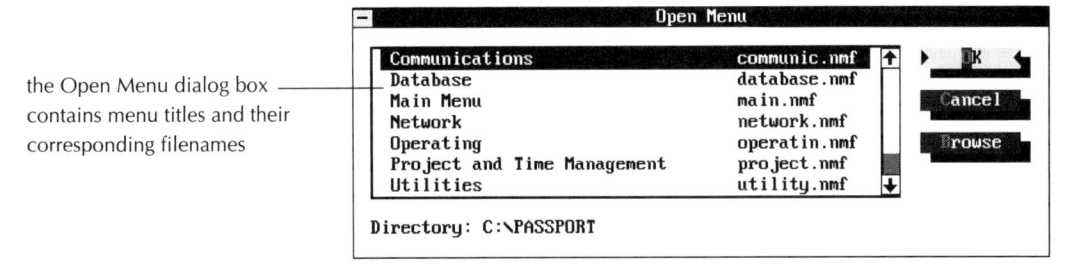

the Open Menu dialog box contains menu titles and their corresponding filenames

Open Menu	
Communications	communic.nmf
Database	database.nmf
Main Menu	main.nmf
Network	network.nmf
Operating	operatin.nmf
Project and Time Management	project.nmf
Utilities	utility.nmf

Directory: C:\PASSPORT

OK / Cancel / Browse

The current directory appears at the bottom of the dialog box. To change the directory:

a Select Directory.

b Type a directory name then select OK.

The new directory appears in the dialog box.

2 Select a file from the list of menu filenames displayed in the list box.

3 Select OK.

The menu you chose in step 2 appears.

EXITING NORTON MENU

To exit Norton Menu:

1 Choose EXIT from the Norton Menu File menu.

If you have the Confirm on Delete option turned on, a dialog box asks whether you would like to exit Norton Menu.

2 Select Yes to exit or No to continue.

When you select Yes the DOS prompt appears.

CREATING A BASIC MENU

This section describes how to create your first menu.

To create a menu:

1. Select NEW... from the Norton Menu File menu (Ctrl+N).

   The New Menu dialog box appears (Figure 30-2).

Figure 30-2

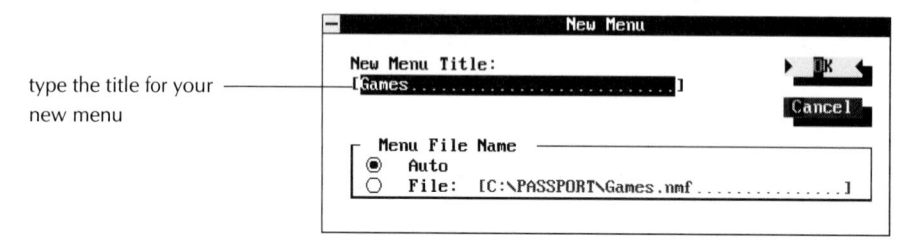

```
┌─────────────────── New Menu ───────────────────┐
│                                                 │
│  New Menu Title:                    ▶ OK ◀     │
│  [Games.......................]                 │
│                                      Cancel     │
│  ┌─ Menu File Name ──────────────────────────┐ │
│  │ ◉  Auto                                   │ │
│  │ ○  File:  [C:\PASSPORT\Games.nmf.......] │ │
│  └───────────────────────────────────────────┘ │
└─────────────────────────────────────────────────┘
```

type the title for your new menu — points to the Games field

2. Type a title for the menu. The title will appear in the center of the menu's title bar. A menu title can contain up to 32 alphanumeric characters.

3. By default, Norton Menu creates a filename that is composed of up to the first eight characters of the menu title and the file extension .NMF. To create a menu file with a different filename, select the File option button and type the new filename in the text box.

4. Select OK.

   The menu appears. Now you are ready to add menu items.

The three types of menu items are:

- Program   Lets you run a DOS program or execute a DOS command from a menu.
- Submenu   Lets you create a submenu. A submenu is a menu contained within a menu.
- Batch   Lets you create or attach an internal batch file and run it from a menu.

This section describes how to add a DOS program or command to a menu. For information on adding the other item types to a menu, see "Creating an Advanced Menu" later in this chapter.

To add menu items:

1. Select ADD... from the Edit menu (Ctrl+A).

   The Add Menu Item dialog box appears (Figure 30-3). This dialog box lets you add a menu item.

Figure 30-3

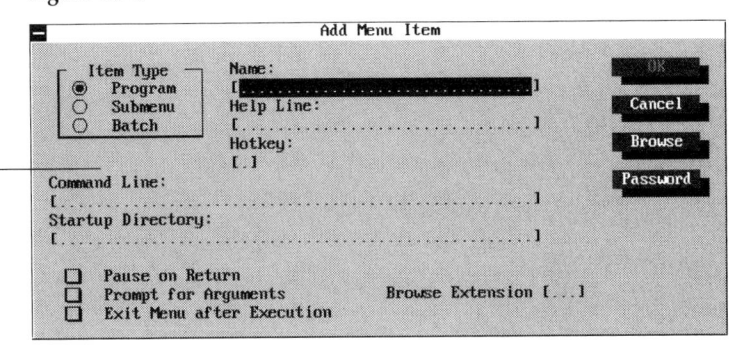

the Add Menu Item dialog box lets you create submenus, and add batch files as menu items

2. Select the menu item type. For now, select the Program button, which adds a DOS program or command to your menu. See "Creating a Submenu" and "Creating a Batch Menu Item" for information about the other types.

TIP: You can select a program using the Browse button. Skip to step 4.

3. Type a descriptive menu item name in the menu item text box. The name you type will appear in alphabetical order on the menu. The item name can be up to 32 alphanumeric characters.

4. Type the help text for the item in the Help Line text box. The help text can contain up to 32 alphanumeric characters.

5. Type the program's executable filename, command-line options, and pathname in the Command Line text box, then select any options needed to customize the program. For example, to run WordPerfect, you would type a command similar to the following:

   ```
   D:\WP\wp.exe
   ```

30-8 *Using Norton Desktop for DOS*

> **NOTE:** You don't need to type a full pathname if the directory is included in your DOS path statement.

Or,

Select the Browse button.

The Browse for Program dialog box appears (Figure 30-4). Using a browse dialog box is explained in Chapter 1, "Getting Started."

Figure 30-4

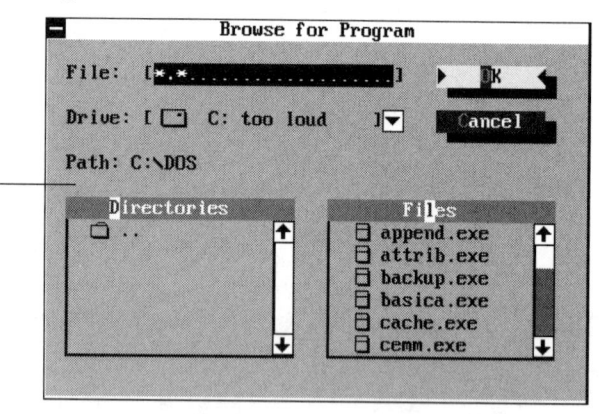

the Browse for Program dialog box lets you browse for and select a file quickly and easily

Select a program file from the Files list box.

6 Select OK.

The Add Menu Item dialog box appears.

7 Edit the entries or select OK to accept them.

8 Select OK.

The menu item appears on the menu.

9 Repeat steps 1 through 8 for each program you want to create a menu item.

Testing a Menu

Before you use or distribute a menu, it's a good idea to test how it will look and work. First, check to make sure that the correct commands are included. Next, test the menu to make sure that it runs properly.

To test a menu:

- Select the menu items one at a time to determine whether they work correctly.

Skip to "Using Menus" for information on how to use the menu you just created.

If you want to make any changes to the menu items, see "Editing Menus."

CREATING AN ADVANCED MENU

Now that you have created a basic menu, this section explains more about the menu item types and describes some of the more advanced features that let you customize a menu.

Before you begin to create menus, or a *menu system*, for other users, you should take a few moments to evaluate your audience. Consider the following questions:

- How experienced are my users?
- Which, if any, DOS programs will they need?
- Should I assign password protection to menu items?
- Should the menu pause after running a program? For example, you might want the program to pause and display a screen of information after a DOS command executes.
- Should the program return to the DOS prompt or to Norton Menu?
- Can I create a single menu for all users or do I need to create submenus? A menu can contain up to 100 items. However, you will probably want to limit the number of menu items so that each menu fits on one screen.

Creating a Program Menu Item

This section describes how to add a DOS program or command to a menu.

To create a program menu item:

1. Choose ADD... from the Edit menu (Ctrl+A).

   The Add Menu Item dialog box appears. This dialog box contains three option buttons that correspond to the three menu item types. (See Figure 30-3.)

2. Select Program as the menu item type.

3. Type the menu item name, help text and hotkey for the item. The menu item name will appear in alphabetical order on the menu and can be up to 32 alphanumeric characters. The help text can contain up to 32 alphanumeric characters and embedded blanks.

4. Type the program's executable filename, command-line options and pathname, then select any options needed to customize the program.

   Or,

   Select the Browse button.

   The Browse for Program dialog box appears (see Figure 30-4). You can use this dialog box to browse for and select a program file. For more information on how to use this dialog box to locate and select a specific file, see Chapter 1, "Getting Started."

   Certain applications must launch from a specific directory. When you add an application to a menu that needs to launch from a specific directory, Norton Menu can automatically change to the application's startup directory before the application launches. To launch an application from a specific directory, type another startup directory in the text box.

5. Edit the entries or select OK to accept them as is.

   The menu items appear on the menu.

6. Repeat steps 1 through 5 for each menu item you want to add.

See the sections "Creating a Submenu" and "Creating a Batch Menu Item" later in this chapter for information about Submenu and Batch Item types.

Customizing a DOS Program

The Add Menu Item dialog box has three check boxes that make your menus more powerful.

Keeping Messages on the Screen

Some applications or DOS commands display messages or other information on the screen. If the information is important, you might want to keep it on the screen so that users can read it before the screen disappears.

To keep information on the screen:

- Check Pause on Return in the Edit Menu Item dialog box.

  The screen pauses until the user presses any key.

Prompting for Arguments

You can have a menu item prompt the user for program arguments before it executes.

To prompt for arguments:

- Check Prompt for Arguments in the Add Menu Item dialog box.

  If you would like to pass a filename to the program, you can specify a file extension in the Browse Extension text box.

When the menu item is selected, the Enter Program Arguments dialog box appears to allow the user to enter any program information the menu item needs before it runs the program.

Exiting to DOS

You can instantly leave a menu after a menu item has been run and return to the DOS prompt.

To exit from a menu after a menu item executes:

- Check Exit Menu after Execution in the Edit Menu Item dialog box.

  After the menu item is run, Norton Menu terminates and the DOS prompt appears.

Creating a Submenu

A submenu is a menu you access, or call, from a main menu or from another submenu. For example, you can have a main menu named Word Processing that contains the menu items WordPerfect, Microsoft Word and JustWrite. When you choose a word processing program, a submenu might display a list of utility programs and printing options for that program. Submenus are a good way to organize programs by application type.

To create a submenu:

1 Choose ADD... from the Edit menu.

    The Add Menu Item dialog box appears (see Figure 30-3).

2 Select the Submenu option button.

3 Type the submenu item name, help text, hotkey and submenu filename.

    Or,

    Select the Browse button and select the submenu file from the list.

4 Select OK.

Creating a Batch Menu Item

A DOS batch file contains several different commands, all of which are executed in sequence. You can create a batch file to execute DOS commands and launch applications from a menu.

Batch files can contain up to 127 characters per line and must have the file extension .BAT.

NOTE: Norton Menu can store your batch file internally if it is about 100 lines or less. Store larger batch files outside the program to avoid memory restrictions.

To create a batch file menu item:

1 Select Batch from the Add Menu Item dialog box.

2 Type the name, help text and hotkey for the menu item.

3 Type your batch file in the Batch File Text box.
4 Select OK.

If you double-click the prompt button for the Batch File Text box, you enter the Norton Desktop Editor where it may be easier to edit your batch file.

For more information about the editing capabilities of the Norton Desktop editor, see "Editing Text Files" in Chapter 4, "Managing Directories and Files."

EDITING MENUS

Now that your favorite applications are organized on a menu, life is easier. What happens when you add a new program to your computer and need to add it to a menu? No problem—changing a menu is easy. The Edit menu lets you move, copy, delete or edit any menu item. You can also add new menu items, change the menu title and delete the menu.

NOTE: You can also use the Autobuild feature to update a menu automatically after changing your software or hardware. See "Updating a Menu Automatically" for information on how to use this feature.

Adding a Menu Item

See the procedure for adding a menu item in "Creating an Advanced Menu."

Modifying a Menu Item

To modify a menu item:

1 Highlight the menu item you want to modify. If the menu item is contained in a submenu, select the main menu item first.

2 Choose MODIFY... from the Edit menu (Ctrl+E).

The Edit Menu Item dialog box appears (Figure 30-5). This dialog box contains the menu item name, hotkey, help line and other options depending on the menu item type.

3 Type any changes.
4 Select OK.

The edited menu item appears on the menu.

Figure 30-5

use the options in the Edit Menu Item dialog box to edit an existing menu item

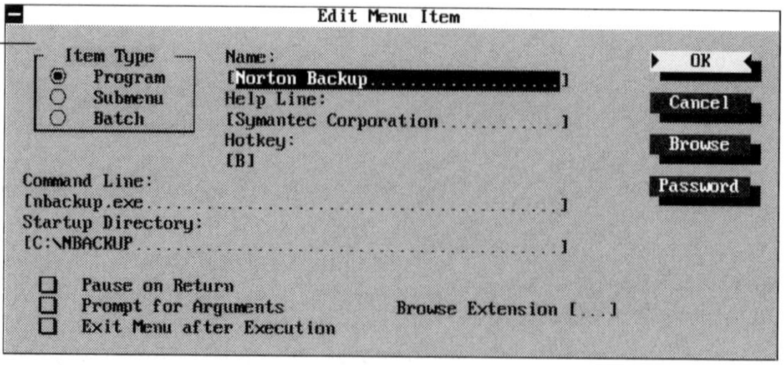

```
┌─────────────────────── Edit Menu Item ───────────────────────┐
│ ┌─ Item Type ─┐  Name:                                        │
│ │ ● Program   │  [Norton Backup...................]    ▶ OK ◀ │
│ │ ○ Submenu   │  Help Line:                                   │
│ │ ○ Batch     │  [Symantec Corporation............]    Cancel │
│ └─────────────┘  Hotkey:                                      │
│                  [B]                                   Browse │
│ Command Line:                                                 │
│ [nbackup.exe.............................................]   │
│                                                     Password  │
│ Startup Directory:                                            │
│ [C:\NBACKUP..............................................]   │
│                                                               │
│   ☐ Pause on Return                                           │
│   ☐ Prompt for Arguments           Browse Extension [...]     │
│   ☐ Exit Menu after Execution                                 │
└───────────────────────────────────────────────────────────────┘
```

Adding a Similar Menu Item

Sometimes you might want to add a menu item that is very similar to an item already on a menu. Easy—just copy the existing menu item and make a few minor changes.

To copy a menu item:

1   Select the menu item you want to copy.
2   Choose COPY from the Edit menu (Ctrl+C).
3   Choose PASTE from the Edit menu (Ctrl+V).

   A copy of the menu item appears on the menu. If the program is automatically assigning hotkeys to your menu items, the hotkeys change to reflect the new menu item sequence.

TIP: The COPY command duplicates the menu item and places it in your computer's memory in an area called the paste buffer. Once the menu item is in the paste buffer, you can use the PASTE command (Ctrl+V) to move the menu item to another position on the same menu or to another menu.

Deleting a Menu Item

To delete a menu item:

1   Highlight the menu item to delete.
2   Choose CLEAR from the Edit menu (Ctrl+B).

   The item is removed from the menu. If the program is automatically assigning hotkeys to your menu items, the hotkeys change to reflect the new menu item sequence.

Moving a Menu Item

NOTE: You can have the program display a confirmation dialog box before it deletes the item. See "Confirm Before Deleting" in Chapter 31, "Administering Corporate Menus."

To move a menu item to a new location:

1. Highlight the menu item you want to move.
2. Choose CUT from the Edit menu (Ctrl+X).
3. Highlight the item that you want to be under the one you are moving.
4. Choose PASTE from the Edit menu (Ctrl+V).

   The menu item appears in the new location.

TIP: The CUT command removes the menu item and places it in your computer's memory in an area called the paste buffer. Once the menu item is in this paste buffer, you can use the PASTE command (Ctrl+V) to move the menu item to another position on the same menu or to another menu.

Changing the Menu Title

To change the menu title:

1. Choose MENU TITLE… from the Edit menu.

   The Edit Menu Title dialog box appears. This dialog box contains the menu's title.
2. Type the new menu title then select OK.

   The menu appears with the new title.

NOTE: This option changes the menu's title only; it does not change the menu's or submenu's filename.

Updating a Menu Automatically

When you make changes to your computer's disk and path information, the menu will no longer work if the changes affect the programs or DOS commands that are referenced. You could, of course, manually change all the disk and path information. Or you can have the program update the menu automatically, using the Autobuild feature. The Autobuild feature customizes the menu to account for any variations in disk and directory structures.

To update a menu automatically:

1   Choose AUTOBUILD... from the File menu.

    The Autobuild or Update Norton Menus dialog box appears.

2   Select Update an Existing Menu then select OK.

    The program scans for the new disk and path information and updates the menu.

For more information on the Autobuild feature, see "Distributing and Maintaining Menus" in Chapter 31, "Administering Corporate Menus."

Deleting a Menu

A menu is stored in a menu file. To delete a menu, delete the menu file.

To delete a menu:

1   Choose DELETE... from the Norton Menu File menu.

    The Delete Menu dialog box appears, which displays a list of menu titles and their corresponding menu filenames. The filename consists of up to the first eight characters of the menu title and the file extension .NMF.

    The current directory appears at the bottom of the dialog box. If you want to change the directory:

    a   Select Directory.

        The Change Directory dialog box appears.

    b   Type a directory name in the Path text box and select OK.

        The menu files in that directory appear in the Delete Menu dialog box.

2   Select a file from the list of menu files.

3   Select Delete.

    The program deletes the menu.

4   Select Close to exit the Delete Menu dialog box.

NOTE: To delete the current menu (the topmost menu that appears on the screen), choose CLOSE... from the Norton Menu File menu and then follow the procedure above to delete it.

USING MENUS

This section describes how to use a menu to launch your applications.

Choosing a Menu Item

Menu items either run a program or take you to a submenu, one level lower.

To choose an item from the menu:

- Highlight the menu item then press Enter.

Or,

- Double-click the menu item.

TIP: You can have Norton Menu assign one key, called the *hotkey*, to a menu item. The hotkey appears to the left of the menu item. Press that key to select the menu item. For more information, see Chapter 31, "Administering Corporate Menus."

Moving from One Submenu to Another

You can display more than one submenu at once. To make it easier to find and move submenus, Norton Menu layers the open menus so that the main menu and each submenu's title bar is visible. The active menu appears in the front of the stack.

To move among submenus:

- Click the submenu's title bar to make it active.

  The active submenu appears in the front of the stack. The title bars of the other submenus are visible, each just above the rest.

Closing a Menu

To return to the main menu:

- Click the main menu's title bar.

To close a menu:

1. Press Esc.
2. Choose CLOSE from the Control menu.

Administering Corporate Menus

This chapter explains how to set menu security, customize Norton Menu, and distribute and maintain a corporate menu system. It assumes you are in charge of administering menus for several users.

Contents

Setting a Password for a Menu Item 31-3
Customizing Norton Menu 31-3
    Confirm Before Deleting 31-4
    Saving Your Menus Automatically 31-4
    Securing Edit and Exit Privileges 31-5
    Assigning Hotkeys Automatically 31-6
    Sounding a Security Alert 31-7
Enabling a Screen Saver 31-7
Distributing and Maintaining Menus 31-7
    Installing for Several Users 31-8
    Using Menus on Different Computers 31-8
    Exporting a Menu 31-10
    Customizing a Menu for Another Computer 31-11
    Importing Other Menu Formats 31-11
    Updating a Menu Automatically 31-12

SETTING A PASSWORD FOR A MENU ITEM

All menus and menu items you create with Norton Menu are normally available to all users. However, you can restrict user access to a particular menu item by protecting it with a password.

Whenever you choose MODIFY... from the Norton Menu Edit menu to add or edit a menu item, the Edit Menu Item dialog box appears. This dialog box contains a Password command button that lets you set a password for the menu item. See Chapter 30, "Creating Corporate Menus," for more information on the Add Menu Item and Edit Menu Item dialog boxes.

To specify a password for a menu item:

1   Select the Password button.

    The Password dialog box appears.

2   Type the new password. Asterisks appear in the box as you type. Press Enter.

3   Type the new password again in the Confirm New Password text box and press Enter.

    Whenever a user tries to access that menu item, they will be prompted to enter the password.

CUSTOMIZING NORTON MENU

The Preferences dialog box (Figure 31-1) appears when you choose PREFERENCES... from the Options menu. This dialog box lets you customize these details:

- Whether you will be prompted to confirm deletions of menu items and files.
- When you will be prompted to save menu files after making changes to them.
- Whether a password will be needed to edit menus.
- Whether hotkeys will be automatically assigned to your menu items.
- Whether a security alert will sound when a user has three unsuccessful login attempts.

31-4   Using Norton Desktop for DOS

Figure 31-1

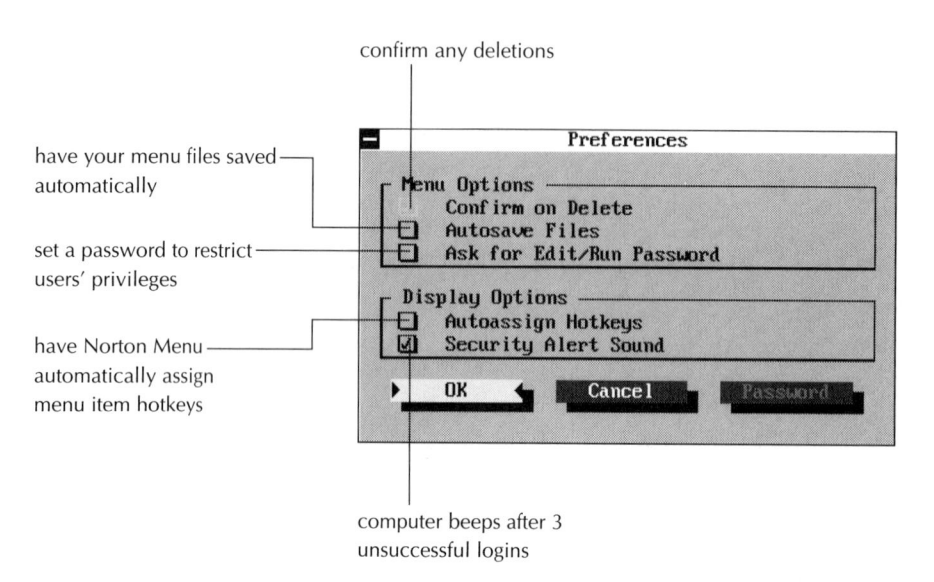

confirm any deletions

have your menu files saved automatically

set a password to restrict users' privileges

have Norton Menu automatically assign menu item hotkeys

```
┌─ Preferences ──────────────────────┐
│ ┌─ Menu Options ──────────────────┐│
│ │    Confirm on Delete            ││
│ │ ☐  Autosave Files               ││
│ │ ☐  Ask for Edit/Run Password    ││
│ └─────────────────────────────────┘│
│ ┌─ Display Options ───────────────┐│
│ │ ☐  Autoassign Hotkeys           ││
│ │ ☑  Security Alert Sound         ││
│ └─────────────────────────────────┘│
│    [  OK  ]   [ Cancel ]  [Password]│
└────────────────────────────────────┘
```

computer beeps after 3 unsuccessful logins

Confirm Before Deleting

Norton Menu normally deletes a menu item or file as soon as you select it and choose the DELETE... command. If you want to be prompted to confirm the deletion, you can turn on the confirm on delete feature.

To display a confirmation dialog box before deleting:

1   Choose PREFERENCES... from the Norton Menu Options menu.

    The Preferences dialog box appears.

2   Check Confirm on Delete.

3   Select OK.

To turn the confirmation dialog boxes off, uncheck the check box.

Saving Your Menus Automatically

Norton Menu automatically saves a menu into a menu file without first asking you whether you want to do so. The menu filename begins with the first eight characters in the menu title and ends with the file extension .NMF. For example, a menu titled "Main" will be stored in a menu file named MAIN.NMF.

Administering Corporate Menus   31-5

To automatically save your menus:

1   Choose PREFERENCES... from the Norton Menu Options menu.

    The Preferences dialog box appears.

2   Check Autosave Files.

3   Select OK.

To turn the autosave feature off, uncheck the check box. When you make changes to a menu, a dialog box will ask if you want to save them instead of saving them automatically.

Securing Edit and Exit Privileges

As the Norton Menu administrator, you might want to set a password to restrict menu editing and exiting privileges. When you set a password, Norton Menu prompts you to type it before you can run the menus without editing privileges or exit the program, as described in Chapter 30, "Creating Corporate Menus." Any user who types the correct password gains access to all features of Norton Menu.

To set an edit/run password:

1   Choose PREFERENCES... from the Norton Menu Options menu.

    The Preferences dialog box appears.

2   Check Ask for Edit/Run Password.

    The Password button becomes active.

3   Select the Password button.

    The Password dialog box appears.

4   Type the new password. Asterisks appear in the box as you type. Press Enter.

5   Type the new password again in the Confirm New Password text box.

To change the edit/run password:

1   Choose PREFERENCES... from the Options menu.

    The Preferences dialog box appears.

2   Check Ask for Edit/Run Password.

    The Password button becomes active.

3   Select the Password button.

    The Password dialog box appears.

4   Type the current password in the Old Password text box and press Enter.

    If you type the incorrect password, the message "Incorrect Password" appears. Select OK, delete the incorrect password then type the password again.

5   Type the new password in the New Password text box and press Enter.

6   Type the new password again in the Confirm New Password text box and press Enter.

To remove the edit/run password:

1   Choose PREFERENCES... from the Options menu.

    The Preferences dialog box appears.

2   Check Ask for Edit/Run Password.

    The Password button becomes active.

3   Select the Password button.

    The Configure Password dialog box appears.

4   Type the current password in the Old Password text box and press Enter.

5   Press Enter again. Do not type a password.

    A dialog box asks whether you want to remove the password.

6   Select Yes.

    Norton Menu removes the password.

To turn the edit/run password feature off without removing the password, uncheck the check box.

Assigning Hotkeys Automatically

You can have Norton Menu automatically assign one key, called the hotkey, to a menu item. The hotkey appears to the left of the menu item. You can press that key to select the menu item. Norton Menu automatically assigns hotkeys in alphabetical order from A through Z, and then in numerical order from 1 through 9.

NOTE: If a menu contains more than 36 items, Norton Menu will not automatically assign a hotkey to item 37 or higher.

To assign hotkeys automatically:

1   Choose PREFERENCES... from the Norton Menu Options menu.

    The Preferences dialog box appears.

2   Check Autoassign Hotkeys then select OK.

To turn the autoassign feature off, uncheck the check box.

Sounding a Security Alert

The security alert sounds an audible alarm when a user makes three unsuccessful login attempts. The alarm lasts only a few seconds.

To sound a security alert after three unauthorized login attempts:

1   Choose PREFERENCES... from the Options menu.

    The Preferences dialog box appears.

2   Check the Security Alert Sound check box then select OK.

To turn the security alert off, uncheck the check box.

ENABLING A SCREEN SAVER

When a fixed, unchanging image is constantly displayed on your screen, it can "burn in," leaving a permanent ghost image. A screen saver protects your screen by "blanking" it or by displaying constantly moving images when you are not using your computer.

To enable a screen saver:

- Choose SCREEN SAVER... from the Options menu.

See Chapter 10, "Using the Screen Saver," for more details on enabling a screen saver.

DISTRIBUTING AND MAINTAINING MENUS

To set up a menu system for several users, follow the same steps that you use to create a menu for one user:

- Install Norton Menu
- Build a menu system
- Distribute the menu system

To implement a menu system, you need to distribute the menu file that contains the menu system for each computer. The menu system can be as simple or as advanced as you want; it is possible that you might only need to distribute a single menu for use on all the computers in your office.

You do not need to create menus on each computer. Instead, you can create them on your own computer, customize them as needed, and copy them to other users' computers. Or you can keep a company-wide menu in a shared directory on a network drive.

Installing for Several Users

You can install Norton Menu on each computer using floppy disks. However, before you do so, you need to specify a Norton Menu directory and menu directory name.

It is a good idea to install Norton Menu in the same directory on each computer. If you want to share common menu files in a shared directory on a network drive, Norton Menu *must* be in the same directory. The default directory for Norton Menu is ND.

If you want to store the menu files in a different directory, use the same directory name for each computer (such as ND\NMENU).

If you must use different directory names, be sure to keep track of the directory name in which you install Norton Menu on each computer.

Using Menus on Different Computers

Most likely, not all the computers in your organization will have the same configuration—some will have one hard disk; others, several. And most likely, their directory structures will differ.

For example, a menu that points to Microsoft Windows in a certain disk and directory will work fine on the computer for which it was created, but if you want to use the same menu on other computers, chances are that the disk and directory structures will differ and the menu will not work. You could, of course, manually change all the disk and path information. Or you can have Norton Menu rebuild the menu system automatically, as shown in Figure 31-2.

Figure 31-2

On your computer

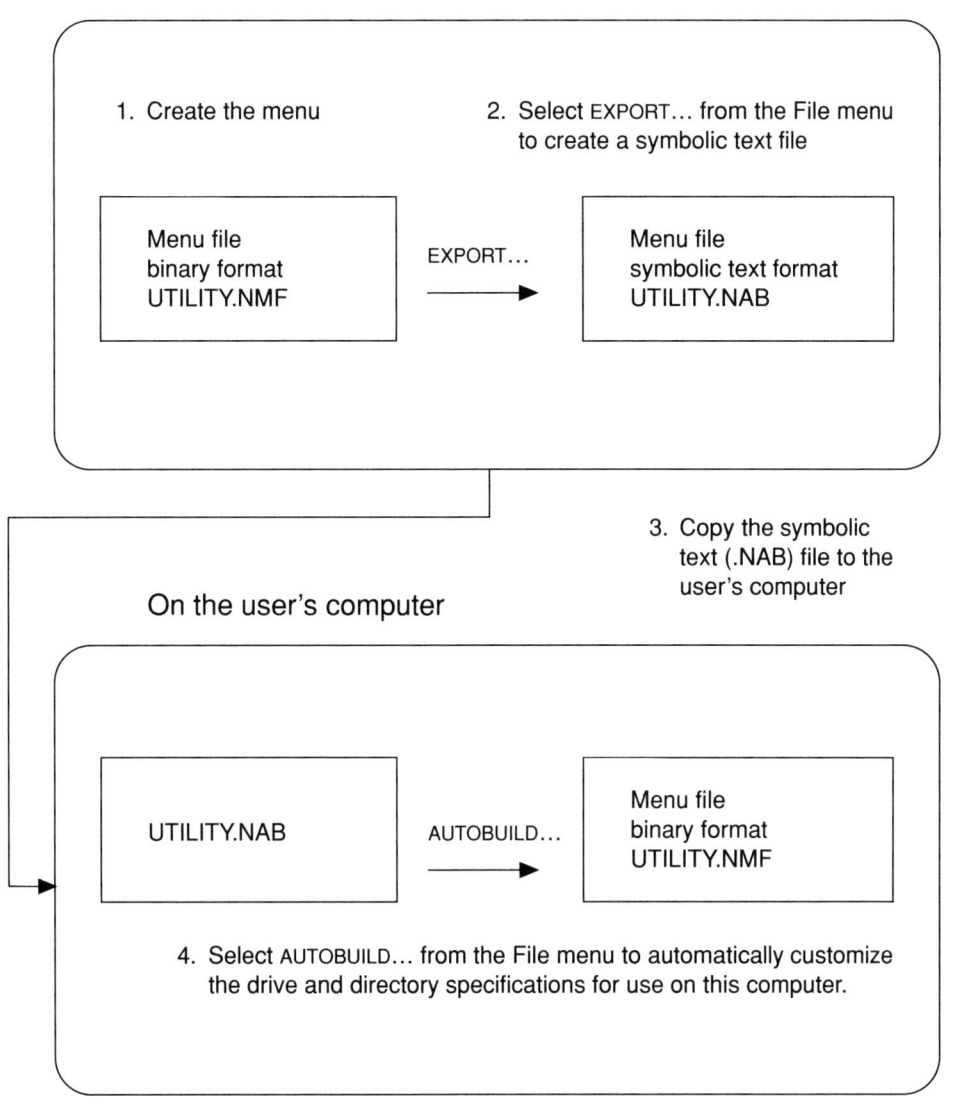

1. Create the menu

2. Select EXPORT... from the File menu to create a symbolic text file

| Menu file binary format UTILITY.NMF | --EXPORT...→ | Menu file symbolic text format UTILITY.NAB |

3. Copy the symbolic text (.NAB) file to the user's computer

On the user's computer

| UTILITY.NAB | --AUTOBUILD...→ | Menu file binary format UTILITY.NMF |

4. Select AUTOBUILD... from the File menu to automatically customize the drive and directory specifications for use on this computer.

31-10   *Using Norton Desktop for DOS*

Exporting a Menu   A menu is stored in a *binary* menu file (code as opposed to human-readable ASCII text). When you have created and tested a menu and do not plan to make any major changes to it, you can export the binary menu file into a *symbolic text* file, as shown in Figure 31-3. Exporting a menu file to a text file is like taking a "snapshot" of the menu. All the menu items, passwords and hotkeys are stored in the file.

Figure 31-3

```
master.nab    ←↑→↓   PgUp PgDn Home End  F→Find N→Next P→Print Esc→Quit
item          "WordPerfect"
type          PROGRAM
command       "wp.exe"
assoc         "wphelp.fil"
help          "WordPerfect Corporation"

item          "WordStar"
type          PROGRAM
command       "ws.exe"
assoc         "wsmsgs.ovr"
help          "WordStar International"

item          "WordStar 2000"
type          PROGRAM
command       "ws2.exe"
assoc         "ws2.cfg"
help          "WordStar International"

item          "XyWrite III Plus"
type          PROGRAM
command       "editor.exe"
assoc         "chkstack.com"
help          "Xyquest, Inc."
```

Exporting a menu system into a symbolic text file has several advantages:

- You can easily transport the file to other computers.
- You can update the file easily when you make any changes to your computer's disk and path information.
- You can edit the file with any text editor, including the Norton Desktop editor.

To export a binary file into a symbolic text file:

1   Select EXPORT... from the Norton Menu File menu.
2   Select a file from the list in the dialog box.
3   Select OK.

   The menu file is converted to a symbolic text file with a .NAB file extension.

You can manually edit the symbolic text file with any text editor. For information about using the Norton Desktop editor, see the "Editing and Creating Files" section of Chapter 4, "Managing Directories and Files."

Copying the Menu File

To use a particular menu system on another computer, copy the symbolic text file into the directory in which you installed Norton Menu.

The next step is to automatically rebuild the symbolic text (.NAB) file into a Norton Menu (.NMF) file that contains the proper disk and directory information.

Customizing a Menu for Another Computer

The Autobuild feature customizes the symbolic text file to account for any variations in disk and directory structures. To do this, it converts the symbolic text file back into a binary file.

To convert a text file into a binary file:

1   Choose AUTOBUILD... from the Norton Menu File menu.

    The Autobuild or Update Norton Menus dialog box appears.

2   Select the Autobuild a Menu Script button.

3   Select a source file. The default source file is MASTER.NAB, which scans for applications on your hard disk(s) and organizes them by category. If you want to use a file you have just exported, select another symbolic text (.NAB) file.

    Or,

    Select Browse and choose a file from the Files dialog box.

    The filename appears in the Autobuild or Update Norton Menus dialog box.

4   Type the new menu's destination in the Path text box.

5   Select OK.

    When the program finishes building the file, the menu appears. A user can now work with the menu exactly as if it had been created on that particular computer.

Importing Other Menu Formats

If you are already using menus created by Direct Access or Norton Commander, you can import them for use in Norton Menu.

To import a menu to the Norton Menu format:

1 Choose IMPORT... from the File menu.

   The Menu Import dialog box appears.

2 Select the option button that corresponds to the type of file—Norton Commander or Direct Access—that you want to import.

3 Type the filename in the Filename to Import field then select OK.

   Or,

   Choose the Browse button to browse a list of files, select a filename, then select OK.

4 Select OK.

   The new menu appears in place of the old menu.

Updating a Menu Automatically

When you make changes to your computer's disk and path information, the menu will no longer work if the changes affect the programs on it. You could, of course, manually change all the disk and path information. Or, you can have the program update the menu automatically, using the Autobuild feature. The Autobuild feature customizes the menu to account for any variations in disk and directory structures.

To update the menu automatically:

1 Select AUTOBUILD... from the Norton Menu File menu.

   The Autobuild or Update Menus dialog box appears.

2 Select Update an Existing Menu then select OK.

   The program scans for the new disk and path information and updates the menu.

PART VII
REFERENCE

Questions and Answers

This appendix contains some common questions about Norton Desktop and the answers to these questions.

Contents

Norton Desktop	A-3
Norton Desktop Tools	A-6
Norton Cache	A-6
SmartCan	A-7
Norton Disk Doctor	A-8
UnErase	A-8
Image	A-9
Speed Disk	A-9
Norton Backup	A-10
Norton AntiVirus	A-16
Viruses	A-16
Virus Intercept	A-20
Virus Clinic	A-21
Virus Definitions	A-23
Configuration	A-24

NORTON DESKTOP

Question Many commands seem to be missing from the Norton Desktop menus. How do I access them?

Answer Only the most common commands are accessible the first time you run Norton Desktop for DOS. Shorter menus often make it easier to select the command—or the menu item—you want. Needless to say, however, a command is not easy to select if it's not there. To access every Norton Desktop command you must change to the full menu set.

To load the Norton Desktop full menu set:

1. Choose LOAD PULL-DOWNS... from the Configure menu.
2. Select LONG.NDM from the Select Pull-down to Load dialog box.
3. Select OK.

Question When I am in graphic mode, moving the mouse causes "ghost" mouse pointers to appear on the screen. Is there something I can do to prevent this?

Answer Change the display mode to Standard by following this procedure:

1. Select VIDEO/MOUSE... from the Configure menu.
2. Choose Standard from the Display Mode drop-down list box in the Screen Options group box.
3. Select OK to accept the change.

Question I can see the mouse pointer but it doesn't move when I move the mouse. What should I do?

Answer Try speeding up the mouse driver initialization. Follow this procedure:

1. Select VIDEO/MOUSE... from the Configure menu to access the Configure Video/Mouse dialog box.
2. Check the Fast Mouse Reset check box in the Mouse Options group box.

Using Norton Desktop for DOS

If the problem persists, contact your mouse's manufacturer and request the latest version of the mouse driver.

Question **How can I select multiple files in drive windows without a mouse?**

Answer Highlight the files and press the Insert key. Continue this procedure until all desired files have been highlighted.

Question **Norton Desktop seems as if it is trying to access drives I don't even have! Why is that?**

Answer If you have any device drivers, such as DISKREET.SYS or SSTOR.SYS, which assign drive letters to non-existing drives, Norton Desktop tries to access these drives. Possible solutions are to remove these device drivers if they are not necessary, or, in the case of Diskreet, to actually provide drives for the reserved drive letters. To create NDISKs for DISKREET.SYS, refer to the Norton Utilities' documentation.

Question **Some drive icons have a small, superscripted "R" on them. What does this mean?**

Answer The "R" signifies a drive that is set up or communicated using a device driver. Examples are STACKER volumes, RAM drives, external hard drives that require device drivers, and so on.

Question **Why can't I label a network drive?**

Answer You must be the system administrator to label network drives. Generally, Norton Desktop cannot label network drives.

Question **Why does Norton Desktop "hang" when I try to run it?**

Answer Try deleting the ND.HST file, which is located in your Norton Desktop directory (probably ND). ND.HST stores history information for Norton Desktop. If this file becomes corrupted, Norton Desktop may freeze when loading.

Question   I have multiple printers connected to my machine. Is there any way I can configure Norton Desktop to print to all of them correctly?

Answer   Yes. You must create printer configuration files for each of your printers. Then simply select the correct printer before you print.

To begin to create printer configuration files, select PRINTER... from the Configure menu to open the Configure Printer dialog box. Refer to Chapter 9, "Configuring Norton Desktop," for more information.

Question   I want to make my D: drive bootable. Even though I ran the Make Disk Bootable procedure, my computer does not boot from the D: drive. What is wrong?

Answer   DOS starts only from the A: or the C: drive. No other drives can be used for booting a DOS-based computer.

Question   How can I list all the files on my C: drive in a drive window?

Answer   Select SHOW ENTIRE DRIVE from the (long) View menu.

Question   Some of the Screen Saver modules do not work on my machine. Can this be fixed?

Answer   Certain Screen Saver modules require VGA (video graphics array) capabilities. Your machine must have a VGA graphics adapter as well as a VGA-capable monitor.

Question   Can I import menus from Direct Access or Norton Commander into Norton Desktop?

Answer   Yes. Select EDIT MENU... from the Tools menu. Within Norton Menu, select IMPORT... from the File menu.

Question   When I compress files with .EXE, .COM and .SYS extensions, the compressed file is not much smaller than the individual .EXE, .COM and .SYS file sizes. Am I doing something wrong?

Answer   No. Compressing .EXE, .COM and .SYS files does not result in high compression ratios since they contain little redundant data. Compressing data files such as files created by word processing, graphics or other data-intensive applications yields much higher compression ratios.

Question Why can't I use my computer when someone else is connected to it via the Network Link?

Answer When you are the server during either Network or Desktop Link, your computer must act as a slave to the other computer that is connected as the client. This is a limitation of DOS, which can only run one program at a time.

Question How can I transfer files using the Desktop Link feature if I don't have Norton Desktop installed on the other machine?

Answer Use the Clone feature of Desktop Link. For more information, see Chapter 8, "Linking PCs."

Question I can't seem to copy any files to one of my network drives using the drive windows. What could be the problem?

Answer If you do not have write access to a network drive, you cannot copy files to or create files on that drive. Ask your network administrator for write access.

Question My computer is connected to two networks, Novell and Lantastic. Norton Desktop always defaults to Novell. Can I set it to support only the Lantastic network?

Answer You can set Norton Desktop to default to any one of the networks it supports. To change network types, select NETWORK... from the (long) Configure menu.

NORTON DESKTOP TOOLS

Norton Cache

Question I have installed Norton Cache, but my computer's Disk Index rating in System Information has not improved. Other caches make the rating higher. Is Norton Cache working?

Answer Norton Cache is disabled during the Disk Index testing performed in System Information. This is to give an accurate Disk Index instead of a cache-inflated rating.

Question	I get a fatal XMS/EMS error after I have loaded Norton Cache. What should I do?
Answer	First, make sure you are not loading any other caches. Then make sure the cache buffers are configured with XMS memory, not EMS memory. Refer to Chapter 29, "Using Norton Cache," for more information.
Question	I have a 286-based computer with 4MB of RAM. Why won't the cache load high?
Answer	Because you don't have an upper-memory block (UMB) server loaded on the system; UMB servers are available only for 386 machines. HIMEM is not a UMB server—it manages only the HMA and XMS memory. You need the UMB server EMM386.EXE for DOS 5.0, QEMM 5.x or 6.x, or 386MAX 5.x.

A note to those of you who use Quarterdeck's QRAM: Because QRAM uses a proprietary technique to provide UMBs on 286-based computers, Norton Cache cannot load itself into high memory. |

SmartCan

Question	Since I loaded SmartCan, the DOS DIR command reports different amounts of free space. What is the problem?
Answer	This is because SmartCan changes the value of available space that DIR reports so that DIR does not include the space occupied by the hidden files in the hidden directory called TRASHCAN. CHKDSK is not modified in this manner.
Question	I am hearing a lot of beeps from my system since I've installed SmartCan. What is wrong?
Answer	Try unchecking the Protect Archived (Backed Up) Files check box in the Configure SmartCan dialog box. Also, you can purge the SMARTCAN directory of all old files, and then add the /SKIPHIGH switch to the SmartCan line in your AUTOEXEC.BAT file.

Using Norton Desktop for DOS

Question	Since I've loaded SmartCan, my system has slowed down. It now takes five minutes to check the SMARTCAN. What can I do?
Answer	Try limiting the size of the SMARTCAN—2048K is usually a good size. Also, use the exclude list to exclude temporary and swap files (files having the extensions .TMP and .SWP) from SMARTCAN. See Chapter 27, "Using SmartCan," for more information.
Question	How much memory does SmartCan take to run?
Answer	SmartCan is an 8K TSR and loads into high DOS (UMB) memory; if high memory is available, SmartCan does not use *any* conventional memory.

Norton Disk Doctor

Question	Norton Disk Doctor stops in the middle of a surface test and tells me my drive door is open. What's going on?
Answer	You probably have SmartDrive loaded. Remove it and Norton Disk Doctor should operate properly. If this does not solve the problem, call Symantec Technical Support for further assistance. See the Symantec Customer Service Plan in the back of this manual for details.
Question	Can I run Norton Disk Doctor on my stacker volumes?
Answer	Yes. Norton Disk Doctor diagnoses, detects, and repairs any problems with stacker volumes as if they were normal drives. However, you should run SCHECK.EXE, the Stacker utility, before you run Norton Disk Doctor, as SCHECK can handle certain problems inherent to stacker volumes that Norton Disk Doctor may not be able to repair.

UnErase

Question	Can I use UnErase to recover deleted files on my network drive?
Answer	Yes. If you had SmartCan loaded on the workstation that deleted the files from the network, UnErase can recover those files. However, if SmartCan was not loaded *prior to deletion*, UnErase cannot recover the deleted files.

Image

Question I noticed a hidden file called IMAGE.IDX in my root directory. Did Norton Desktop create this hidden file?

Answer Yes. The IMAGE.IDX file is created when Image is executed. Do not move or delete this file as it is an integral part of Norton Desktop's data-recovery features. The IMAGE.DAT and IMAGE.BAK files should also be left alone.

Question I have DOS 5.0's MIRROR. Do I need Image?

Answer Both perform the same function. Since the Norton Utilities programs can use either, the use of MIRROR is not required. However, if you are using Safe Format, unless IMAGE.DAT or IMAGE.BAK were on the disk to be unformatted, you cannot save any UNFORMAT information.

Question How can I delete the Image files in my root directory?

Answer Use the File Attributes program, FA.EXE, with the /CLEAR switch and specify IMAGE.* to clear the attributes on the files; then you can delete the files through DOS by typing this command at the prompt: FA IMAGE.* /CLEAR

Speed Disk

Question I'd like to automatically run Speed Disk on Monday and Friday of every week. Can this be done?

Answer Yes. Use the Scheduler to create a custom event frequency that executes Speed Disk on Monday and Friday of every week. See Chapter 23, "Using Scheduler," for more information.

Question I did a full optimization with file reorder and it doesn't look like Speed Disk moved the files. Why?

Answer Speed Disk does not change the directory when it is updating the files, so you can't use the directory to see what order the files are in—it would be like trying to use a card catalog to see what order the books are in. The only way you can see the actual order of the files is to use Speed Disk's Walk Map function.

Question	**What are all those Xs on my screen?**
Answer	Unmovable files, such as system or hidden files, are marked as Xs. In addition, Speed Disk marks lost clusters as unmovable files. Therefore, if the number of Xs has grown since the last time you ran Speed Disk, run Norton Disk Doctor to see if some of the unmovable files are lost clusters. See Chapters 17 and 18 if you need additional information about Speed Disk and Norton Disk Doctor.
Question	**Can I run Speed Disk on my network drive?**
Answer	No. You cannot run Speed Disk on non-DOS drives, which includes most network drives except for DOS FAT file-system-based networks such as Lantastic (you must boot the network drive as a standalone DOS computer).
Question	**Speed Disk runs out of memory when I try to optimize my computer's large hard disk.**
Answer	Unload all TSRs and device drivers; if possible, load DOS into high memory, then run Speed Disk again. If your computer has DOS 5.0, QEMM or 386MAX, you can maximize upper memory blocks (UMBs); Speed Disk can use high memory to optimize a large drive that contains many files.
Question	**Can I run Speed Disk on my stacker volume?**
Answer	No. Speed Disk does not allow itself to run on a stacker volume. Stacker 2.0 and up includes its own disk optimizer called SDEFRAG.

NORTON BACKUP

Question	**When I am restoring my backup set, I sometimes get the message "Catalog file is corrupt." What does this mean?**
Answer	If you get this message during a restore, then try using the rebuild function to rebuild a catalog. If the error persists, there may not be enough memory to restore the whole backup. Try rebuilding only half of the backup disks. By restoring half of the backup set at a time, Norton Backup uses less memory. You may need to delete the catalog file from the hard disk in order to get to the restore menus. The

reason for this is that the Norton Backup tries to load the most current catalog. If that catalog file is corrupt, then you will receive the "Catalog file is corrupt" message.

Question **I get the following message when I'm trying to run a backup: "Maximum number of subdirectories per drive reached." What does this mean?**

Answer Usually this means that you have exceeded the amount of RAM necessary to execute Norton Backup in its entirety or you have exceeded the maximum number of directories per drive allowed. If the total number of directories on your drive (logical) is less than 2,040 then try freeing up more conventional memory.

Question **After inserting the first disk of a new backup, the following message appears: "Diskette in drive A is defective."**

Answer This could be either a software or hardware conflict. Try removing all TSRs and optional device drivers from memory to see if this resolves the problem. If this does not work, set Norton Backup to use low-speed DMA.

Question **"Packed file is corrupt" is the message displayed by DOS when I try to install Norton Backup. What is the problem?**

Answer Try increasing the number of buffers in the CONFIG.SYS file to 30 or so. If your computer has DOS 5.0 installed, use the LOADFIX utility. Refer to your DOS documentation for more information.

Question **The messages "Correcting Bad Disk" and then "Cannot recover data from damaged diskette using Error Correction" appear when I attempt to restore or when Verifying my data from the Restore section.**

Answer Try removing all TSRs and optional device drivers.

Question **The error messages "Files do not match" or "Incorrect checksum for file" are displayed when I restore a backup with error correction enabled.**

Answer Try setting Norton Backup to use low-speed DMA. If this does not resolve the problem, then try removing all TSRs and optional device drivers.

Question **The message "Incompatible setup file" appears when I attempt to initialize Norton Backup from the DOS prompt.**

Answer This indicates that Norton Backup tried to read either a corrupted copy of the DEFAULT.SET setup file or that it was not created with the same version of Norton Backup that is currently being used on the system. You need to delete all files with a filename of DEFAULT.* from the hard drive (these may be either in the current Norton Backup directory or possibly in another subdirectory). After doing this, run Norton Backup and allow it to create a new DEFAULT.SET file.

Question **The message "Backup does not detect a mouse on this system" is displayed during auto-configure when installing Norton Backup for the first time.**

Answer Your mouse is not fully Microsoft-compatible. Usually only the mouse driver needs to be upgraded. Contact the mouse manufacturer for an updated driver or try using a current version of the Microsoft mouse driver.

Question **What does Verify actually do during a restore?**

Answer It reads the selected files for verification from the backup set into RAM and then reads the same files on the hard disk into another area of RAM. Then, Verify compares the files between the two areas of memory.

Question **Does Norton Backup work with SUBSTituted drives?**

Answer Yes.

Question **Should you be able to restore your backed-up files to a floppy?**

Answer No.

Question **What is the maximum number of macros that can be created in Norton Backup?**

Answer You can create one per setup file; however, only one setup file can be loaded at a time.

Questions and Answers	A-13

Question	**Why doesn't Norton Backup allow me to change any of the options in the program?**

Answer	Press Spacebar instead of Enter in order to select any of the options. This places a dot in the selection box next to your selected option.

Question	**Is there an easy way to select or deselect All Files for either Backup or Restore without going into Select Files and doing it manually?**

Answer	With the logical drive highlighted in the Backup From/Restore Files window, press Spacebar or use the mouse (double-click with the left button or single-click with the right) to toggle between All Files and no files.

Question	**I thought I backed up my files to a floppy disk; however, when I look at that floppy disk's directory using DOS DIR, the names of the files that were backed up do not appear on the screen. Where are they?**

Answer	When Norton Backup writes to a floppy, it creates a component file on the disk. The filename of this file is the same as the catalog name, with the extension that corresponds to the number of the floppy in the backup set (for example, CC10415.001 is the first backup disk created on April 15th). The actual files are packed into the data area of the component file. They cannot be retrieved through DOS; this can only be done through the Restore section of Norton Backup. In order to verify that the backup was successful, use the Verify option of Restore, which can be run immediately following the backup.

Question	**What options do you recommend for Backup/Restore?**

Answer	Most of the options (including Data Compression) should really be left up to the individual. Read *Using Norton Backup for DOS* to determine which options would work best. However, we strongly recommend that Data Verification be set to Read and Compare (the highest level of data integrity) during Backup and Restore and that you use Verify to verify your backups whenever you change anything in your system configuration (for example, new TSRs, device drivers, or Norton Backup's format or data compression options).

Question Why did Norton Backup require fewer floppy disks for a backup than what the program indicated it was going to need?

Answer Norton Backup's estimate of how many disks are required for backup is based on the assumption that no data will be compressed. This is because it is rather difficult to estimate how successful data compression will be without knowing the nature of the data being compressed. A good estimate for the number of disks needed would be approximately 60 percent of the number that would be needed if no compression were used.

Question I told the program to back up drive D:, but it keeps backing up C:. What's wrong?

Answer The DEFAULT.SET file is defined initially to back up All Files on the C: drive. You need to *unselect* the files for the C: drive by pressing the Spacebar on the line that reads **[-C-] All files**. Remember that the Backup From list box is a list of which drives you have selected to be backed up. In this case, you will notice that next to the drive letter C: it is either All Files or Some Files. The highlight allows you to edit the list of your drives; it it does not choose the drive to be backed up.

Question Can I run Norton Backup for DOS out of Windows 3.0?

Answer Norton Backup should run fine if Windows is in Real or Standard mode. If in 386/Enhanced mode, you need to set up a Windows PIF (Program Information File) with options Full Screen and Exclusive, or use the Norton Backup for Windows program. Generally, Norton Backup should not be run in Windows in any mode because it works very intimately with your PC's hardware.

Question The Backup program doesn't seem to be accepting my Includes/Excludes. What am I doing wrong?

Answer If the Includes/Excludes don't seem to be taking effect, the problem may be that you have selected some of the files/directories from the Select Files tree which takes highest precedence over anything else. In order to use the Include/Exclude list, you first want to unselect all the files on the drive by highlighting the appropriate drive letter in the

Backup From window using the Spacebar. Another method is to highlight the directory(s) on the Select Files tree and press Alt+Spacebar. Afterwards, you can use Include/Exclude again. Finally make whatever manual selections are necessary (these override the Includes/Excludes if there is a conflict).

Question **Why would Norton Backup indicate that a Restore is complete when it did not restore any files (as shown by no checkmarks next to the filenames in the top-right corner of the Restore screen) and it only took a few seconds for this entire process to finish?**

Answer Norton Backup is probably trying to restore some older files over some newer files (for example, restoring a corrupted database). Configure Norton Backup to the Advanced restore mode and then choose Options followed by Overwrite Files. Change this option to Always Overwrite or delete the unwanted files on the hard drive first.

Question **After I select the files to be backed up or to be restored, why is there a dot to the left of the filenames in the Select Files window instead of a checkmark?**

Answer When choosing Backup, this indicates that you are either performing an Incremental backup and have tried to select a file that has not changed since the last Full or Incremental backup or the file has been deselected from backup or restore because it is either a read-only, hidden or system file. To change this last option, in the Norton Advanced Backup dialog box select Select Files then select Special. Uncheck the Exclude Read-only Files check box, as well as the rest of the other options, to allow you to restore files that have these attributes set.

Question **I'm trying to restore to a different computer than the one on which I performed the backup. Norton Backup says there are no catalogs found or it tells me that the incorrect disk has been inserted into the drive. Why would this happen?**

Answer In this case, Norton Backup does not have the correct catalog loaded for the backup set, or currently there are no catalogs on the hard disk. After performing a backup, a catalog is created both on the hard disk where the backup was performed and on the last disk of the floppy backup set. In order to transfer this catalog to the new hard disk, you can either select Catalog from the Restore dialog box and then select Retrieve, or you can copy this catalog (file with extension .FUL, .INC, .DIF or .CPY) from the original computer. If you have the incorrect catalog loaded, select Catalog, highlight the desired catalog and press Spacebar to select it, and then select Load to make the selected catalog the current catalog.

NORTON ANTIVIRUS

Viruses

Question Virus Clinic stops scanning when a virus is found in memory. Why is that?

Answer Scanning stops to limit the spread of a virus on your disk. A virus in memory can infect any file that Virus Clinic *scans*. Virus Clinic needs to scan files in order to detect viruses that are already infecting them. If scanning continues when a virus is in memory, the virus will probably infect all the files that are scanned! Restarting your computer removes the virus from memory so that files may be safely scanned.

Question I have a boot-sector infector. What should I do?

Answer When your computer starts up, a small program in the partition table is launched that indicates where to find the bootable partition of the hard disk. When the bootable partition is found, a small program in the boot sector is launched to load DOS. A boot-sector infector is a virus that infects this small program in the boot sector. The virus loads into memory before DOS and Virus Intercept, taking control of your computer or even preventing your computer from starting up at all from the infected media.

Your boot sector can be infected by:

- Booting or even attempting to boot your computer from a floppy disk with an infected boot sector. Even data disks can infect your computer in this fashion.
- Using an infected file that infects boot sectors or partition tables.

The boot-sector infector overwrites (replaces) a portion of the boot sector on the infected disk.

See Chapter 20, "Using Norton AntiVirus," for complete instructions on repairing infected system files.

If you are not able to repair the boot sector, your Rescue Diskette can help. If you created a Rescue Diskette when you installed Norton AntiVirus on your hard disk, you can restore the boot sector from that disk. Refer to Chapter 28, "Using Disk Tools," and Chapter 20, "Using Norton AntiVirus," for instructions on creating a Rescue Diskette and using a Rescue Diskette to restore your system files.

Question **I have a partition-table infector. What should I do?**

Answer When your computer starts up, a small program in the partition table is launched that indicates where to find the bootable partition of the hard disk. When the bootable partition is found, a small program in the boot sector is launched to load DOS. A partition-table infector is a virus that infects the small program in the partition table that locates the bootable partition. The virus loads into memory before DOS and Virus Intercept, taking control of your computer or preventing your computer from starting up at all from the infected hard disk.

Your partition table can be infected by:

- Booting or even attempting to boot your computer from a floppy disk with an infected boot sector. Even data disks can infect your computer in this fashion.
- Using an infected file that infects boot sectors or partition tables.

The partition-table infector overwrites (replaces) a portion of the partition table on the infected disk.

See Chapter 20, "Using Norton AntiVirus," for complete instructions on repairing infected system files.

If you are not able to repair the partition table, your Rescue Diskette can help. If you created a Rescue Diskette when you installed Norton AntiVirus on your hard disk, you can restore the boot sector from that disk. Refer to Chapter 28, "Using Disk Tools," and Chapter 20, "Using Norton AntiVirus," for instructions on creating a Rescue Diskette and using a Rescue Diskette to restore your system files.

To proceed when no Rescue Diskette is available:

1 Have available an uninfected, write-protected, DOS system disk with the same version of DOS as your hard disk.
2 Call Technical Support while at your computer for instructions on how to proceed.

Question **I have a virus in the boot sector of a floppy disk. What should I do?**

Answer All floppy disks have a boot sector, even if they are not system (bootable) disks. The small program in the boot sector of a floppy disk can be infected by boot-sector or partition-table infectors. The virus overwrites a portion of the boot sector on the floppy disk.

The virus can be transferred to other floppy disks or to hard disks if you start or restart your computer while the infected floppy disk is in a disk drive.

To restore the boot sector of an infected floppy disk, refer to Chapter 20, "Using Norton AntiVirus," for complete instructions.

Question **Virus Clinic or Virus Intercept reports finding a possible unknown virus. What should I do?**

Answer You do not necessarily have a virus. This message is generated if an unknown virus has altered the file or if the file in question has changed since it was last inoculated (perhaps by upgrading or reconfiguring). If you upgraded or changed the file and are reasonably sure that no virus exists, you can go ahead and reinoculate the file. If you are not certain that the file is free from viruses, you should delete it and replace it with an uninfected copy. See Chapter 20, "Using Norton AntiVirus," for more information.

Keep in mind that viruses typically infect numerous files randomly. If you experience problems with the same file again and again, it is probably a matter of reconfiguration rather than a virus. If you experience problems with many different, unrelated files, you probably have an unknown virus.

Question **What should I do when my COMMAND.COM file or another system file is infected?**

Answer If your COMMAND.COM file or its replacement (such as Norton Utilities NDOS), or another of your computer's system files (such as IO.SYS or MSDOS.SYS, or IBMBIO.SYS or IBMCOM.SYS) is infected, first see whether the file can be repaired. If repair is not possible or is unsuccessful, it may be necessary to delete the file and restore it. See Chapter 20, "Using Norton AntiVirus," for complete instructions.

Question **After repairing or deleting viruses, Norton AntiVirus indicates no additional viruses exist. Why does my computer become reinfected after I run certain programs?**

Answer Most programs use filenames with the following extensions: .EXE, .COM, .SYS, .DRV, or .OV? (where ? means any character). However, some programs use extensions other than these. If you have configured Norton AntiVirus to scan executable files only, programs with these non-standard extensions are not scanned and they may contain a virus.

Question **How do I prevent viruses from spreading across a network?**

Answer Obtain a site license from Symantec to allow you to run Virus Intercept on all of the workstations in your network. Once loaded, Virus Intercept prevents an infected file from being activated or executed from any drive, including network drives. Since Virus Intercept is loaded before network drivers, all workstations will remain secure.

Note that boot-sector and partition-table infectors do not normally migrate across a network. One partition-table infector that does is a virus called Tequila, because it can also infect executable files.

Your network administrator should use Virus Clinic to scan file servers regularly to detect and eliminate any infected files.

Virus Intercept

Question   **Why doesn't Virus Intercept load when I start my computer?**

Answer   If the message "The Norton AntiVirus" (followed by version number and type of scan) does not appear when you start your computer, Virus Intercept is not being loaded. Check your CONFIG.SYS file to make sure that the appropriate device statement for Virus Intercept is present. The DEVICE statement should contain both the drive and directory of Virus Intercept's active file, followed by either NAV_.SYS, NAV&.SYS, or NAV&.SYS /B, depending on which level of virus protection you desire.

Question   **Why does my computer lock up when a Virus Intercept alert box appears?**

Answer   Certain high-memory management software such as QEMM386 and 386MAX normally use video-display memory for other programs. Such behavior creates a conflict with Norton AntiVirus and may result in screen lockup. You must modify your CONFIG.SYS file to exclude the video-display memory from use.

To exclude video-display memory from use:

1. Turn off your computer and restart it again.
2. Use a text editor to modify the QEMM386 device statement in your CONFIG.SYS file (if you have such a statement) by adding `X=B000-B7FF` to the end of the statement that begins with `DEVICE=QEMM386.SYS`

   Or,

   Use a text editor to modify the 386MAX device statement in your CONFIG.SYS file, if you have such a statement, by adding `EXCLUDE=B000-B7FF` to the end of the statement that begins with `DEVICE=386MAX.SYS`
3. Restart your computer for the changes to take effect.

This should clear up the problem when a Virus Intercept alert box appears.

Question Why can't I copy, move, delete, or do anything else to my NAV_.SYS file?

Answer If your CONFIG.SYS file was modified during installation to include a device statement that loads NAV_.SYS at startup, then the NAV_.SYS file is active in memory. You cannot view, edit, delete, move, copy, overwrite, or change the attributes of the file (such as read-only, hidden, system) while it is active in memory.

Question After moving or renaming an executable file or renaming a directory, why does Virus Intercept display an inoculation alert even though the file or directory was already inoculated?

Answer Your computer is probably not infected with a virus. Norton AntiVirus keeps track of the status and location of all your executable files in an inoculation file it creates on your hard disk. When you move or rename an executable file or rename the file's directory, the entry for that file in the inoculation file is no longer valid. Therefore, the Norton AntiVirus acts as if there is no inoculation record for this file and displays the alert box.

Question Why isn't my backup program working properly while Virus Intercept is loaded in memory?

Answer Virus Intercept is compatible with most popular backup programs, including Norton Backup. However, some backup programs may not function properly or may quit unexpectedly when Virus Intercept is active.

The best action is to disable Virus Intercept temporarily before backing up, then reload Virus Intercept into memory afterward. Refer to Chapter 20, "Using Norton AntiVirus," for instructions on disabling Virus Intercept at startup.

Virus Clinic

Question Why doesn't my program work properly even though it was repaired in Virus Clinic?

Answer Some strains of common viruses are not fully repairable because the viruses may have inconsistencies that are extremely difficult for an anti-virus program to resolve.

(Remember that viruses usually do not go through quality-assurance testing!) Repairs, in some cases, may not be 100-percent effective. The best course of action is to reinstall your program from uninfected, write-protected program disks.

Question **Why do I get a message saying no files were scanned after I scan a floppy disk?**

Answer Assuming that files exist on the floppy disk, it is likely that the floppy disk has no executable files, and the Scan Executables Only option is checked (which it is by default). This situation arises when scanning floppy disks used to store only data (such as text). Keep in mind that while data files can be damaged by viruses, they cannot contain viruses or spread viruses to other files. These files cannot be repaired by Norton AntiVirus because there is no actual virus that can be isolated; there is only damaged data.

Question **Why can't I scan my network drives?**

Answer You can obtain access to network drives by checking the Allow Scanning of Network Drives configuration option, but you should do this only if you are your company's network administrator. If more than one person scans network drives simultaneously, performance of the entire network slows down noticeably.

Question **How often should I scan hard disks and floppy disks for viruses?**

Answer Viruses can only come from outside your computer. They can be brought into your computer by using external media such as floppy disks, cartridges, or other hard disks. Or they can infect your computer across unprotected networks, bulletin board services, and through file transfers.

If you never connect to other systems or media through a modem or cable and your computer is virus-free, you do not need to scan it again until you use an outside source of files, such as a floppy disk. Get into the habit of scanning floppy disks before you use them, especially if you suspect that files on those floppy disks may have come from an unprotected source.

If you actively use networks, electronic bulletin boards, or external media, scan after you download files. If this is not possible, be sure to scan the files you copy to your computer before you use them for the first time.

Virus Definitions

Question Where can I obtain definitions for new viruses?

Answer There are several places where you can get virus definitions, including computer bulletin board services (BBSs) and update disks. Refer to the "Updating Virus Definitions" section in Chapter 20, "Using Norton AntiVirus," for more information.

Question I deleted one or more of the virus definitions that came with Norton AntiVirus. How can I retrieve them?

Answer The NAV_.SYS file on the Norton AntiVirus program disk contains the most current virus definitions available at the time of the release. If you delete some of these virus definitions and wish to retrieve them, you have three ways to do so:

- Get the latest ALL file from a bulletin board service which posts virus definition updates for Norton AntiVirus (see "Updating Virus Definitions" in Chapter 20, "Using Norton AntiVirus," for more information on bulletin boards).
- Reinstall the NAV_.SYS file from your original program disk. If you selected Comprehensive Scan when you first installed Norton AntiVirus, then NAV_.SYS is active in memory and must be disabled before you can copy the new file to the appropriate directory. Refer to Chapter 20, "Using Norton AntiVirus," for directions on disabling Virus Intrercept at startup.
- Get the latest virus definitions update disk, available from Symantec (see "Updating Virus Definitions" in Chapter 20, "Using Norton AntiVirus," for more information on obtaining update disks). Follow the instructions provided with the update disk. You can also retrieve any additional virus definitions you've downloaded or obtained yourself since you originally installed Norton AntiVirus.

Configuration

Question   **Why can't I scan or change the configuration, or setup, of Norton AntiVirus from the command line?**

Answer   You must customize Norton AntiVirus, specifying your name and company, before scanning drives or making any setup changes from the command line.

System Messages

This appendix lists the system messages that may appear on your screen from time to time. They are organized by topic, so that all general system messages are grouped together, all the messages you may see while printing are grouped together, and so on. Each message is explained briefly.

Note that anything appearing in angle brackets (< >) within a message in this appendix is replaced by the actual name of a file or location in the alert box on your screen. For example, if you try to copy the file MEMO.DOC and it is too large to fit on the target drive, you would see the system message "The file MEMO.DOC could not be copied: insufficient space."

Contents

General	B-3
Launching Files	B-3
Managing Files	B-3
Managing Disks	B-5
Network	B-8

GENERAL

Can't drop here

An attempt to drop a file or directory onto a restricted area or object of Norton Desktop (such as the desktop itself) will cause the directory or the file icon to turn into this message.

The Secure Computer option requires that a password be set.

You must supply a password in order to use the Secure Computer option. See Chapter 9, "Configuring Norton Desktop," for more information.

This option will not work with the following display type: <display type>

The type of display adapter your computer has could not support the chosen display options.

LAUNCHING FILES

Error executing application. No association exists for <filename>.

An attempt to execute a file which did not have a valid application association was made. Use the ASSOCIATE... command from the (long) File menu to create a valid association for the specified file.

MANAGING FILES

A prior tree exists, use this or the partial tree just scanned?

A drive scan operation was aborted before completion. This will leave the old directory tree and the new partial tree information.

Building Tree

If the file TREEINFO.DT does not exist on a drive Norton Desktop is attempting to open and read, this message will be displayed while the directory structure of the drive is being scanned. The TREEINFO.DT file is similar to Norton Change Directory's (NCD.EXE) TREEINFO.NCD, but is faster and more efficient.

Cannot write file <filename>.

The system cannot write data to the file you specified. Is the file a read-only file? If you are using a floppy disk, is it write-protected? If it is a network file, do you have write privileges? Or is someone else writing to this file at the same time?

Directory <directory name> does not exist. Do you want to refresh the drive window?

When Norton Desktop cannot relocate a directory that once existed on a drive, this message will be displayed.

Directory <drive>:\<directory name> does not exist.

A reference was made to a nonexistent directory.

File <filename> could not be deleted.

The file to be deleted does not exist.

File(s) can't be renamed to new locations.

Files must be renamed to new locations using the MOVE... command in the (long) File menu. Files cannot be renamed to new locations using the RENAME... command in the (long) File menu.

Invalid file specification: <drive>:\<file specification>

The file specifications were not valid or the specified files do not exist.

Not enough memory for desired operation.

Norton Desktop attempted to perform an operation which required more memory than was available. Usually a large application program which requires nearly 640K of RAM to run will trigger this message if you attempt to run it within Norton Desktop.

The file <filename> could not be copied: insufficient space.

The target drive for the copy operation did not contain enough free space to accommodate the new file.

System Messages   B-5

The file <filename> could not be found. The filename or path is invalid.

The system could not find the file you requested. Make sure you entered a valid pathname and/or filename.

The file <filename> is read-only. Do you want to delete it anyway?

Normally, files which are read-only cannot be deleted. Norton Desktop will allow deletion of such files if you request it.

Unable to open the file <filename>.

The system cannot open the file you specified. Check to see whether the file is already open or whether you entered the pathname correctly. Verify that the file actually exists.

Unable to read file.

The system cannot read the file you requested. This message usually signifies an error in your hard disk, floppy disk or network. Make a backup of the affected disk and try to save any data you can. Run Norton Disk Doctor from the Emergency Disk.

MANAGING DISKS

Copy Diskette requires DOS version 3.2 or above.

Norton Desktop cannot perform a disk copy with a version of DOS prior to 3.2.

Drive <drive>: is write-protected.

You cannot write data to the drive you specified. Check to see whether the disk you are using is a read-only or a write-protected disk, or whether you have write privileges for the named drive on your network.

Drive <drive>: does not support the requested format.

An attempt to format a floppy disk with the wrong format type was made. For example, if Norton Desktop attempted to format a 3½-inch 720K double-sided, double-density floppy diskette as a 1.44MB double-sided, high-density diskette, the above message would appear.

Drive <drive>: is empty. Please insert the TARGET diskette.

Norton Desktop determined that the target floppy drive did not contain the target floppy disk.

Error reading drive <drive>:

Norton Desktop could not read the drive. Run Norton Disk Doctor to diagnose the drive in question.

Error reading from temporary file. Unable to finish copying diskette.

Norton Desktop could not properly read the temporary file that contains source diskette data during a disk copy operation. The temporary file may have become corrupted.

Error reading the SOURCE diskette. Try copying files instead of the entire diskette.

Norton Desktop encountered unrecoverable errors during a disk copy operation. The source diskette may be damaged; attempt to copy individual files using the COPY... command from the (long) File menu.

Error writing drive <drive>:

The system cannot write data to the drive you specified. This message usually signifies a hardware error. Check that you specified the correct drive.

No local drives found.

Norton Desktop could not locate any local drives. Local drives refer to hard drives that are physically installed into the computer. Floppy drives are not considered as local drives.

The TARGET diskette does not have the same format as the SOURCE diskette. Do you want to reformat the diskette?

Norton Desktop determined that the target diskette has a format type that is different from the source diskette. In order to make a disk copy, the target disk must have the same format type as the source disk.

The TARGET diskette in drive <drive>: is flawed or is the wrong type. Unable to finish formatting diskette.

Norton Desktop has determined that the target diskette is defective or is not the same type as the source diskette. For instance, attempting to copy a 5 1/4-inch high-density diskette to a 5 1/4-inch low-density diskette may trigger this system message.

The TARGET diskette in drive <drive>: is flawed. Unable to finish copying diskette.

An unrecoverable write error on the target diskette has been encountered. Norton Desktop will not be able to complete the disk copy operation.

The TARGET diskette is not formatted. Do you want to format it?

The target diskette is unformatted.

The TARGET diskette is write-protected. Please remove the write-protect tab or slide the write-protect button over its notch.

Norton Desktop cannot write or format the target diskette because it was write-protected.

The TARGET diskette labeled "<disk name>" is already formatted. Do you want to overwrite data?

A Safe Format was attempted on an already formatted disk.

Unable to modify volume label.

The disk that contains the volume label to be modified is either write-protected, unformatted or damaged.

Writing temporary file to hard drive. Copy Diskette will restart, using only memory for temporary storage.

To perform a high-speed, one-pass disk copy of high-density floppy disks, Norton Desktop stores source disk data on the hard drive in the form of a temporary file.

NETWORK

Attempting to connect to <workstation name>.

When Norton Desktop is attempting to connect to another user (ultimately, another computer or workstation on a network) via the Network Link, this message will be displayed until the connection is established.

Disconnect from <workstation name>?

If the client (the user who is accessing another user's workstation via the Network or Desktop Link) of an established network selects the Disconnect command button from the Open Window dialog box, Norton Desktop will issue this prompt.

Registering NetBIOS name...

For all networks other than Novell, Norton Desktop will register the workstation's name on the network for future reference.

The message was not sent to station <user name>/ <workstation name> because network messages are blocked.

With Novell networks, the NetWare command CASTOFF will block any incoming network messages. When you see this message, the recipient user has issued the CASTOFF command to block all incoming network messages.

The message was not sent to <user name>/<workstation name> because the message buffer is full.

The network's server message buffer was full and therefore unable to store any additional messages until the recipient user clears previous messages.

The message was not sent to <user name>/<workstation name> because the user is no longer logged in.

Users must be logged in to receive messages via the Network Message operation.

Unable to connect to <workstation name>.

Norton Desktop was unable to establish a Network Link to another workstation on the network. There may be network problems; contact your network administrator.

Command-Line Reference

This appendix explains how to run several of the Norton Desktop components as separate utility programs, as well as command-line options for the desktop itself. For example, you can run the Calculator, SmartCan or Speed Disk without loading Norton Desktop first.

This icon indicates information for the technically savvy user.

Contents

Syntax Diagram Conventions C-4
    Conventions C-4
    Definitions C-5
Quick Help C-6
Global Switches C-6
NDCALC (Calculator) C-6
DISKTOOL (Disk Tools) C-7
IMAGE (Image) C-7
NCACHE (Norton Cache) C-7
    Install Switches C-8
    Reconfigure Switches C-11
    Drive Switches C-12
ND (Norton Desktop) C-13
NDD (Norton Disk Doctor) C-14

NMAIL (Norton Mail) C-15
NMENU (Norton Menu) C-15
NSCHED (Norton Scheduler) C-15
SFORMAT (Safe Format) C-16
SMARTCAN (SmartCan) C-17
SPEEDISK (Speed Disk) C-18
VIEW (Norton Viewer) C-19
SYSINFO (System Information) C-19
UNERASE (UnErase) C-20
UNFORMAT (UnFormat) C-20

Several components of the Norton Desktop can be run as separate utility programs. Of these, most can be run in two different ways: using the full-screen mode or using command-line switches (or, in some cases, a combination of these two). A few of these programs can be run only from the command line. Refer to the preceding chapters in this manual for a complete discussion about how to use each program.

You can run these programs from the DOS prompt (before loading the Norton Desktop), or you can run them in several fashions from the Norton Desktop:

- From the (long) File menu, choose RUN... to run a program.
- From the (long) Tools menu, choose DOS SESSION to start a DOS shell.
- From the (long) View menu, choose DOS BACKGROUND so that the DOS prompt is available on the Norton Desktop.
- From the Tools menu, choose SCHEDULER and specify a program to be run at a particular time.

The following table lists for each program the executable name, its popular name, and the menu (if any) in which it appears on the Norton Desktop. Those of you familiar with the Norton Utilities will find some old friends.

Executable Name	**Popular Name**	**Menu**
NDCALC	Calculator	Tools
DISKTOOL	Disk Tools	
IMAGE	Image	
NCACHE	Norton Cache	
ND	Norton Desktop	
NDD	Norton Disk Doctor	Tools
NMAIL	Norton Mail	Tools (long)
NMENU	Norton Menu	
NSCHED	Scheduler	Tools
SFORMAT	Safe Format	Disk/Format Diskette
SMARTCAN	SmartCan	

(continued)

(continued)

Executable Name	Popular Name	Menu
SPEEDISK	Speed Disk	Tools (long)
VIEW	Norton Viewer	File
SYSINFO	System Information	Tools (long)
UNERASE	UnErase	Tools
UNFORMAT	UnFormat	

This appendix briefly describes the command-line syntax for these programs. For each program you will find:

- The executable name of the program.
- A brief summary of what the program does.
- The command-line syntax.
- Definitions for each of the command-line parameters and switches.
- Important usage considerations.

SYNTAX DIAGRAM CONVENTIONS

In the descriptions in this appendix, a few simple conventions and keywords are used to show the command-line syntax for each program.

Conventions

UPPERCASE Words that must be entered as shown, such as command names and switches, are shown in uppercase. (You can, of course, enter them in uppercase or lowercase.)

lowercase Parameters that you replace with your own entry, such as the name of a file, are shown in lowercase.

[ ] Square brackets indicate an optional parameter or switch which may be omitted if desired. The brackets themselves are not entered.

| The vertical bar means use only one of the options presented in the group. For example, ON|OFF means use either ON or OFF, but not both.

Definitions

	...	The ellipsis means you can repeat the preceding option as many times as necessary. For example, IMAGE [drive:]... means you can enter more than one drive (IMAGE C: D:).
	space	A space is used to separate each of the elements on the command line.
	drive	The letter designating a hard disk or a floppy disk. In almost all cases, a colon (:) must follow the drive letter.
	path	The directory location (any legal DOS path). A single backslash (\) means the root directory, a single dot (.) means the current directory, and double dots (..) mean the parent directory.
	filename	The name of a file (including any filename extension). The wildcard characters (* and ?) can be used with most filenames.
	pathname	Drive, path and filename. For most programs and commands, if the drive is omitted, the default drive is assumed. If the directory is omitted, the current directory is assumed.
	parameter	Provides additional information to a command. Parameters that are replaced with your own information are shown in lowercase. Keyword parameters are shown in uppercase.
	string	A series of characters.
	/switch	A command-line control option. A switch begins with a forward slash and then the switch proper. The slash must be entered if it is indicated in the syntax diagram.

QUICK HELP

To display a summary help screen for any of the programs, type the program name followed by a forward slash and question mark.

```
program /?
```

GLOBAL SWITCHES

There are several switches which can be used with all of the programs that have a full-screen interface, including the Norton Desktop itself (ND.EXE). They are listed here, rather than repeating them each time. These switches are used primarily to set your display preferences.

```
program [/BW|/G0|/G1|/G2|/LCD] [/MULTITASK]
    [/NOZOOM]
```

program   One of the programs from the Norton Desktop.

/BW   For monochrome displays.

/LCD   For laptop LCD displays.

/G0   For EGA and VGA displays: disable graphic mouse and all graphic characters.

/G1   For EGA and VGA displays: disables graphic dialogs and graphic mouse.

/M0   Enable a non-graphical mouse cursor.

/M1   Enable a graphical mouse cursor.

/MULTITASK   Disable check for multitasking.

/NOZOOM   Disable dialog box zooming.

If you do not specify one of these switches, the default settings stored in the Norton Desktop configuration file, ND.INI, are used.

NDCALC (Calculator)

Calc is a simple, four-function calculator.

```
NDCALC
```

There are no command-line options.

DISKTOOL
(Disk Tools)

Disk Tools can be operated in full-screen mode only. Using the command-line switches lets you start the program with a preselected operation.

```
DISKTOOL [operation]
```

/DOSRECOVER	Recover from DOS's RECOVER.
/MAKEBOOT	Make a Disk Bootable.
/RESTORE	Restore from a Rescue Diskette.
/REVIVE	Revive a Defective Diskette.
/SAVERESCUE	Create Rescue Diskette.

IMAGE (Image)

Take a snapshot of your system area and save it to the IMAGE.DAT file for future disk and file recovery.

```
IMAGE [drive]... [/NOBACKUP]
```

drive	Save information for specified drive (if omitted, default drive).
/NOBACKUP	Overwrite the current IMAGE.DAT file. The backup file IMAGE.BAK is not created.

NCACHE
(Norton Cache)

NCACHE creates a memory buffer to speed up reading and writing from a disk.

To install the cache:

```
NCACHE [Install Switches] [[drive:] [Drive
    Switches]...]
```

or, in CONFIG.SYS:

```
DEVICE=NCACHE.EXE [Install Switches] [[drive:]
    [Drive Switches]...]
```

To reconfigure the cache:

```
NCACHE [Reconfigure Switches] [[drive:]
    [Drive Switches]...]
```

Install Switches

NCACHE without any parameters shows the current cache status.

Norton Cache must be installed from DOS, not from within Norton Desktop. You can, however, configure Norton Cache from within Norton Desktop.

The Norton Cache is usually installed or configured as part of the Norton Desktop installation program (NDCONFIG.EXE) with its default values stored in the file NCACHE.INI. You may choose, however, to install and configure the cache from either your AUTOEXEC.BAT or your CONFIG.SYS files (but not both).

You can also use the Drive Switches during installation.

If no unit of measure is specified in the following definitions, kilobytes are assumed. For example, specifying /EXT=1024 is the same as specifying /EXT=1024K.

/INSTALL — Installs cache with configuration stored in NCACHE.INI file (see /SAVE in "Reconfigure Switches"). If NCACHE.INI does not exist, the defaults are all extended memory and all expanded memory less 16K of extended memory (or 128K of conventional DOS memory if neither is available). This option must be specified unless a cache size is specified (/EXT, /EXP, or /DOS).

/DOS[=[-]n] — DOS memory to use for cache. If n (kilobytes) is omitted, the default is 128K. Optionally, a negative value is the amount of memory to reserve for applications; the remainder is used for the cache. /DOS cannot be used in combination with /EXP and /EXT.

/EXT[=[-]n[,m]]	Extended memory to use for cache. If n (kilobytes) is omitted, all extended memory less 16K is used for the cache. Optionally, a negative value is the amount of memory to reserve for applications; the remainder is used for the cache. m is the amount of extended memory to reserve for the cache when running Windows 3.x in the enhanced mode (defaults to 25% of n). If 25% of n is less than 256K, Norton Cache is disabled in Windows.

Norton Cache uses extended memory either in the traditional manner or by using the extended memory specification (XMS) implementation depending on the presence of an XMS memory manager such as HIMEM.SYS or QEMM386.EXE. |
| **/EXP[=[-]n[,m]]** | Expanded memory to use for cache. If n (kilobytes) is omitted, all expanded memory is used for the cache. Optionally, a negative value is the amount of memory to reserve for applications; the remainder is used for the cache. m is the minimum amount of expanded memory to reserve for the cache when running Windows 3.x in the enhanced mode (defaults to 25% of n). If 25% of n is less than 256K, Norton Cache is disabled in Windows. Note, however, use of /EXP in Windows is not recommended.

Norton Cache requires an expanded memory manager to be LIM EMS 4.0-compatible. |

	/OPTIMIZE=S ǀ E ǀ M	Optimize cache for Speed, Efficiency or Memory. See Chapter 29, "Using Norton Cache," for a discussion of these defaults.
	/READ=n	Maximum size for Read-Ahead buffer, from 8 to 64 kilobytes in 1K increments (default is 8). A value of 0 disables the Read-Ahead buffer.
	/WRITE=n	Maximum size for IntelliWrites buffer, from 8 to 64 kilobytes in 1K increments (default varies with /OPTIMIZE setting). A value of 0 disables the IntelliWrites buffer.
	/DELAY=ss.hh	Specify delay for IntelliWrites (ss seconds, hh hundredths).
		When writing data or copying files to a floppy disk with a delay value greater than 0 and IntelliWrites enabled (+I) for the target floppy, it is important to remember to wait for the actual disk writes to be completed before removing the diskette.
	/BLOCK=n	Cache block size (512, 1024, 2048, 4096, or 8192).
	/USEHIGH=ON ǀ OFF	Enable or disable use of high DOS memory to maximize available memory.
	/USEHMA=ON ǀ OFF	Enable or disable use of XMS HMA to maximize available DOS memory.
	/QUICK=ON ǀ OFF	Return the DOS prompt quickly after writes (default is ON). OFF means to wait until all deferred writes have been completed before returning the DOS prompt.

/MULTI=ON | OFF	Enables or disables the multitasking aspects of IntelliWrites (default is OFF). If you experience compatibility problems, such as unexpected machine lockups, try /MULTI=OFF.
/INI=pathname	Specify NCACHE initialization file. The file is created with the /SAVE option.
/REPORT[=ON | OFF]	Display complete NCACHE status information. Optionally, make it the default report.
/STATUS[=ON | OFF]	Display abbreviated NCACHE status information. Optionally, make it the default report.
/QUIET	Specify quiet mode. Only errors are reported.

Reconfigure Switches

Reconfiguration switches are used once Norton Cache has been installed. Use some of these switches to uninstall Norton Cache, as well as to flush the cache in memory.

When reconfiguring Norton Cache you can also use the /OPTIMIZE, /QUICK, /MULTI, /REPORT and /STATUS switches covered in the previous Installation Switches section, as well as the Drive Switches in the following section.

/RESET	Reset entire cache (cannot be used with a drive designator, see /F switch).
/DUMP	Forces all updated data waiting in cache buffers to be written to disk.
/UNINSTALL	UnInstall Norton Cache from memory. You cannot uninstall the cache if other TSRs were loaded after the cache. Also, you cannot uninstall if the cache was loaded from CONFIG.SYS.

	/SAVE	Save current cache configuration in the file specified with the /INI switch. If /INI was not specified, the configuration is saved in NCACHE.INI in the directory from which NCACHE was loaded.
	/DELAY=ss.hh	Specify delay for IntelliWrites (ss seconds, hh hundredths).
	/QUICK=ON|OFF	Return the DOS prompt quickly after writes. OFF means to wait until all deferred writes have been completed before returning the DOS prompt.

Drive Switches

The Drive Switches control the operation and performance of each cached drive. In general, these options are used to tune Norton Cache for optimum caching performance for each drive individually.

Any or all of these options can be made to affect a cached drive independently of other cached drives by preceding the option with a drive specifier. For example, /-A D:/A deactivates caching for all drives and then reactivates caching for the D: drive only.

The minus sign (-) deactivates each option.

Except for the /F switch, you can use these switches during installation or for reconfiguring Norton Cache. The /F switch can only be used after the cache is installed.

/[-]A	Activate or deactivate cache for specified drive(s).
/[-]C	Enable or disable Caching subsequent data for specified drive(s).
/[-]I	Enable or disable IntelliWrite support for specified drive(s).
	IntelliWrites are automatically disabled whenever /WRITE=0 has been specified at installation either directly or indirectly through the setting of the OPTIMIZE option (for example, OPTIMIZE=MEMORY).

Command-Line Reference **C-13**

/[-]W	Enable or disable cache Write-thru for specified drive(s).
/[-]P	Enable or disable write Protection for specified drive(s).
/R[=[D][n]]	Limit sector Read-ahead for specified drive(s). The D option enables read-ahead only for sequential disk reads. n is the amount of data to read specified in 1K increments.
/G=n	Limit caching of Group sector reads for specified drives (default is 128).
/F	Flush cache of data for specified drive(s). /F can only be specified as a reconfigure option.

ND (Norton Desktop)

The Norton Desktop program.

```
ND [/FORGET]
```

/FORGET Reset the Norton Desktop history file to its default state. The effect is that the following information is deleted:

- The RUN... command history.
- Filter specifications.
- The file specifications for opening a drive window for a compressed file.
- The file specifications for selecting and unselecting files.
- The drive and directory destination specification for copying or moving files.
- Drive window location, size, and pane settings.

See the section "Global Switches" in this appendix for other command-line options.

NDD (Norton Disk Doctor)

Diagnose and repair disks that are damaged or defective, or perform routine diagnostics and inspection to prevent such problems from developing.

```
NDD [drive:]... [/C | /Q | /DT]
    [/R[A]:pathname] [/X:drives]    [/SKIPHIGH]

NDD [drive:]... [/REBUILD] [/SKIPHIGH]

NDD [drive:]... [/UNDELETE] [/SKIPHIGH]
```

drive	Disk drive to diagnose or repair. More than one drive can be specified.
/C	Complete: perform all tests, including the surface test.
/Q	Quick: all tests except the surface test.
/DT	Disk Test: only perform the surface test.
/R[A]:pathname	Write (or Append) a report of all tests performed to the file specified with pathname.
/X:drives	Excludes drives from testing (for example, /X:def).
[/SKIPHIGH]	Skip using high memory.
/REBUILD	Rebuilds an entire disk that has been destroyed.
/UNDELETE	Undeletes a DOS partition that was previously skipped. (For example, NDD detected an old DOS partition and asked if you wanted to undelete it. If you responded "no," this switch allows you to go back and undelete it.)

When using NDD to diagnose and repair a problem disk, you will probably want to operate in full-screen mode. Use the command-line switches for routine maintenance, such as a diagnosis of your disk every time you start up your computer with the /Q switch.

NMAIL (Norton Mail)

Run Norton Mail to send and receive messages.

    NMAIL [/SEND] [/UNERASE] [/PURGE]

/SEND — Run an MCI communication send/receive session only.

/UNERASE — Undelete addressees that are marked as deleted. (Normally, addressees marked as deleted are not read by Norton Mail.)

/PURGE — Delete all addressees that are marked for deletion. This saves space in the address book.

NMENU (Norton Menu)

Create and run user menus.

    NMENU pathname [/EDIT] [/RUN]

/EDIT — Run and edit menus. This is the recommended mode for single-user menu systems.

/RUN — Run menus without the menu bar so that users can launch applications from menus but not edit the menus.

NSCHED (Norton Scheduler)

Automatically run applications and display reminders at specified times.

    NSCHED [/S=X | E | D] [/TSR] [/T=n | WAIT]
        [NOSAVER] [/SKIPHIGH]

    NSCHED [/D | /E | /U]

/S=X | E | D — Swapping:
- X Use XMS memory for swapping.
- E Use EMS memory for swapping.
- D Use disk space for swapping.

C-16   *Using Norton Desktop for DOS*

/TSR	Allow TSRs to be loaded after NSCHED (not recommended).
/T=n | WAIT	If no key is pressed within n minutes (0-1000) after the reminder appears, start the event (default is 1 minute). Specify /T=WAIT to always wait for confirmation to start the event.
/NOSAVER	Do not enable the screen saver.
/SKIPHIGH	Do not load NSCHED into high memory.
/D	Disable scheduler (remains in memory but is inactive).
/E	Enable scheduler (reactivate after disabling).
/U	Uninstall scheduler (remove from memory). You cannot uninstall if other TSRs have been loaded after NSCHED.

After Scheduler is installed, type NSCHED to display the current status.

The Scheduler must be configured from within Norton Desktop to determine which programs run at what times. See Chapter 23, "Using Scheduler," for information on how to configure Scheduler.

SFORMAT (Safe Format)

Safely and quickly format a disk.

```
SFORMAT [drive:] [/A] [/S | /B] [/V:label]
   [/Q | /D] [/1] [/4] [/8] [/N:n] [/T:n]
   [/size] [/F:size]
```

drive	Drive letter of disk to format.
/A	Automatic mode: The program does not pause during operation and returns to DOS when complete. (This is handy when Safe Format is run from a batch file or from a menu).
/S	Copy System files to the disk you are formatting.

/B	Leave space for system files on the disk.
/V:label	Place a Volume label on the disk.
/D	Use DOS Format mode (same as the DOS FORMAT command).
/Q	Use Quick format mode (reinitialize system area only).
/1	Format for single-sided use.
/4	Format a 360K diskette in a 1.2M drive.
/8	Format 8 sectors per track.
/N:n	Number of sectors per track (8, 9, 15, 18 or 36).
/T: n	Number of Tracks (40 or 80).
/size	Size of diskette (/360, /720, /1.2, /1.44, or /2.88). Same as /F:size.
/F:size	Format diskette a particular size (360, 720, 1.2, 1.44, or 2.88).

A default configuration for SFORMAT can be set in full-screen mode.

SMARTCAN (SmartCan)

SmartCan is a memory-resident program (TSR) that protects data by moving erased files to a "smartcan" (a hidden directory) for future recovery if needed.

```
SMARTCAN [/ON [/SKIPHIGH]]

SMARTCAN [/OFF | /UNINSTALL]

SMARTCAN [/STATUS]
```

/ON	Enable SmartCan.
/SKIPHIGH	Do not load into high memory.
/OFF	Uninstall SmartCan.
/UNINSTALL	Uninstall SmartCan (same as /OFF).
/STATUS	Display SmartCan status.

You must enter the full-screen mode to specify such things as how many days to keep files before overwriting them, how much disk space to allow for these files, and how often you wish to purge the smartcan.

SmartCan must be installed from DOS, not from within Norton Desktop. You can, however, configure SmartCan from within Norton Desktop.

SPEEDISK (Speed Disk)

Improve hard disk performance and speed up disk-access time by consolidating and unfragmenting the data on your disk.

```
SPEEDISK [drive:] [/F[D | F]] [/Sorder] [/V]
   [/B] [/SKIPHIGH]

SPEEDISK [drive:] [/Q | /U] [/V] [/B]
   [/SKIPHIGH]
```

drive	Disk drive to optimize.
/F	Full optimization.
/FD	Full optimization with directories first.
/FF	Full optimization with file reorder.
/Q	Unfragment free space (Quick compress optimization).
/U	Unfragment files only.
/S	Sort files in the specified order.
order	One of the following:
	N Name
	E Extension
	D Date and time
	S Size
	Add a minus (-) sign to the specified order to reverse the sort.

Command-Line Reference   C-19

/V	Verify sector read after writing data to disk.
/B	Reboot after optimization.
[/SKIPHIGH]	Skip loading data in high memory.

When using Speed Disk for the first time, you should use the full-screen mode to set and store the Speed Disk configuration. Then you can use the command-line switches to perform quick optimizations for routine maintenance.

VIEW (Norton Viewer)

View files on screen.

```
VIEW [pathname]
```

pathname   The file to view.

SYSINFO (System Information)

Display system configuration information and performance statistics.

```
SYSINFO [/AUTO:n] [/N] [/SOUND]

SYSINFO [drive:] [/DI] [/SUMMARY] [/TSR]

SYSINFO [/DEMO]
```

drive	Drive on which information is desired (if omitted, default drive).
/AUTO:n	Automatically cycle through all information screens, pausing n seconds between each screen.
/N	No memory scan: bypass the test that probes live memory.
/SOUND	Beep between CPU tests.
/DI	Drive Information: summary screen only.
/SUMMARY	System information: summary screen only.
/TSR	Display list of TSR programs.
/DEMO	Demo mode: cycle through the benchmark tests and summary screen only.

UNERASE
(UnErase)

Automatically recover erased (deleted) files.

```
UNERASE [pathname] [/IMAGE | /MIRROR]
    [/NOTRACK] [/SMARTCAN | /NOSMARTCAN]
    [/SKIPHIGH]
```

/IMAGE	Use image recovery information (excludes Mirror information).
/MIRROR	Use Mirror recovery information (excludes Image information).
/NOTRACK	Exclude delete tracking information.
/NOSMARTCAN	Exclude files saved by SmartCan.
/SKIPHIGH	Do not use high memory.
/SMARTCAN	Recover only those files saved by SmartCan.

UNFORMAT
(UnFormat)

For badly fragmented or partially overwritten files you must use Manual UnErase in the full-screen mode.

Recover a hard disk that has been accidentally formatted, corrupted by a power surge, or damaged by a virus.

```
UNFORMAT [drive:] [/IMAGE | /MIRROR]
```

drive	Drive letter of disk to unformat.
/IMAGE	Use image recovery information (excludes Mirror information).
/MIRROR	Use Mirror recovery information (excludes Image information).

A near-perfect recovery can be made if you have previously taken a snapshot of the disk using the IMAGE command.

Batch Enhancer Reference

This appendix describes how to use the Batch Enhancer—a collection of easy-to-use commands that enhance DOS batch files. With Batch Enhancer you can create batch files that let you choose options from custom menus, have conditional branching to other batch files and perform functions based on a date. You can also add sound and graphics to DOS batch files.

Contents

The Commands that DOS Forgot	D-4
Graphics	D-4
Screen	D-4
Keyboard Response	D-4
Sound	D-5
Execution	D-5
Date	D-5
Script File Commands	D-5
Syntax Diagram Conventions	D-5
Script Files	D-7
Getting Help	D-8
Exit Codes and Errorlevel	D-8
BE ASK	D-10
BE BEEP	D-13
BE BOX	D-17

BE CLS D-17
BE DELAY D-18
BE EXIT D-19
BE GOTO D-20
BE JUMP D-21
BE MONTHDAY D-22
BE PRINTCHAR D-23
BE REBOOT D-23
BE ROWCOL D-24
BE SA D-25
BE SHIFTSTATE D-28
BE TRIGGER D-29
BE WEEKDAY D-29
BE WINDOW D-30

Batch Enhancer gives power and flexibility to your DOS batch files. Batch files are powerful tools because they can automate many of the repetitive tasks you do every day, increasing your efficiency. Unfortunately, however, DOS does not provide the capability for you to control a batch file, based on input from you. That omission severely limits the situations in which you can use batch files. The Norton Batch Enhancer integrates this capability into the existing repertoire of batch file commands and in the process provides added speed and convenience in many other ways.

The Batch Enhancer program is a collection of easy-to-use commands. They can be used to accent any DOS batch file or special Batch Enhancer *script file*. By using Batch Enhancer you can add graphics and sound to your batch files. Batch Enhancer allows you to create batch files that let you choose options from custom menus, and even perform specific functions based on a particular date. Batch Enhancer also allows conditional branching to other batch files.

From DOS, use Batch Enhancer when you want to:

- Add flexibility to AUTOEXEC.BAT file tasks
- Automate commonly used command sequences
- Draw demonstration and sign-on screens

From the Norton Desktop, use Batch Enhancer commands for added flexibility when writing batch files called by Norton Menu and Scheduler.

NOTE: If you are unfamiliar with using batch files, please refer to your DOS documentation or another introductory text.

THE COMMANDS THAT DOS FORGOT

The 17 Batch Enhancer subcommands fall into a few distinct groups and are summarized here. Later in this chapter the commands are listed in alphabetical order and discussed in detail, with usage examples.

Graphics

These four subcommands may be used together to create interesting graphics for your batch programs. For example, you can draw a window, move the cursor to a location within the window, and write text to the screen within the window (or box). In this way, you can create your own alert and dialog boxes.

WINDOW	Draws a rectangle of a specified size at a particular location on the screen and clears existing text in the window.
BOX	Draws a rectangle of a specified size at a particular location on the screen without overwriting existing text.
PRINTCHAR	Displays a specified character a given number of times at the current cursor location.
ROWCOL	Positions the cursor at a particular row and column location on the screen, and, optionally, displays text.

Screen

You can use the Batch Enhancer subcommands to set screen colors and other text attributes.

CLS	Clears the screen, and, optionally, changes the screen colors.
SA	Controls the display of colors and other screen attributes.

Keyboard Response

These subcommands allow you to pause batch files and find out which key was pressed before continuing. Use these to create menus.

ASK	Displays text and waits for a response.
SHIFTSTATE	Reports the state of the left or right Shift keys, the Ctrl keys and the Alt key.

Sound

Use distinctive tones or tunes to signal events from your batch files or script files; for example, warnings when problems occur or reminders when a task is completed.

BEEP — Plays specified tone or tones through the computer's speaker.

Execution

Control your system from within batch files.

DELAY — Pauses execution of a batch file for a specified amount of time.

REBOOT — Performs a warm or cold boot of the computer.

TRIGGER — Pauses a batch file until a specified time.

Date

Control processing based on the day of the week or month.

MONTHDAY — Returns the day of the month to a batch file.

WEEKDAY — Returns the day of the week to a batch file.

Script File Commands

Control execution of Batch Enhancer script files. These three commands have no meaning if executed from DOS. Script file creation and usage is discussed in the section "Script Files," later in this chapter.

EXIT — Terminates execution of a script file.

GOTO — Controls the starting point of execution in a script file.

JUMP — Allows conditional branching within a script file.

SYNTAX DIAGRAM CONVENTIONS

Batch Enhancer commands are composed of three parts:

- The BE command
- A Batch Enhancer subcommand
- Any additional parameters to control the action of the command

In the descriptions that follow for each Batch Enhancer subcommand, a few simple conventions are used to show the syntax or grammar for each command. Consider the BOX subcommand:

```
BE BOX top left bottom right [SINGLE|DOUBLE]
   [color]
```

UPPERCASE	Words in uppercase (capital letters) are key words and must be entered exactly as shown, if used. You can, of course, enter them in uppercase or lowercase.
lowercase	Words in lowercase represent parameters that you replace with values appropriate to what you are doing. In the example of BOX, "top," "left," "bottom" and "right" are the screen coordinates for the box being drawn, while "color" is the color specification for the box.
/	The forward slash is used with some of the subcommand parameters. Often, the parameter is called a "switch." If the slash is indicated in the syntax diagram, it must be entered.
[ ]	Square brackets indicate an optional parameter which may be omitted, if desired. Do not, however, enter the brackets themselves.
|	The vertical bar means use only one of the parameters presented. In the example of BOX, either SINGLE or DOUBLE can be entered, but not both. (Note, too, that for BOX this is an optional parameter and can be omitted entirely which is indicated by the square brackets.)

Although you will usually use Batch Enhancer commands within a batch file or script file (see "Script Files" later in this chapter), you can also enter the commands directly at the DOS prompt, as shown in the following example.

SCRIPT FILES

To draw a red, single-line box, at the DOS prompt type:

```
be box 10 10 20 40 single red
```

While the Batch Enhancer commands can be used in regular DOS batch files, the real power of Batch Enhancer can best be seen when you use script files.

Script files contain a series of Batch Enhancer commands that would normally appear in a batch file. However, because the Batch Enhancer program can then execute the command directly, instead of through DOS, the speed of Batch Enhancer command processing is noticeably increased. The reason for this is that DOS executes batch files one line at a time and each time that BE is used, BE must be run separately. In a script file, BE need only be run once for all the Batch Enhancer commands.

The ability to create script files makes Batch Enhancer easier to use and much faster to operate. For example, complex screen setups will be drawn much faster if executed from a script file than if executed one command at a time in a regular DOS batch file.

Any Batch Enhancer command can be placed into a script file, but DOS commands will be ignored. Because Batch Enhancer is directly executing the commands found in the script files, the letters "BE" that normally begin a Batch Enhancer command line are optional in script files.

TIP: If you're using a script file for BE, then the command BE need not appear on every line within the file; that is, ASK is the same as BE ASK. You must use BE on each Batch Enhancer command within a DOS batch file, however.

Script files are DOS files that can be created with any text editor or word processor that creates ASCII text files. All that is necessary to execute a script file is to specify the filename on the command line. Batch Enhancer will search the PATH to try to locate the script file if it is in a different subdirectory.

The syntax for using a script file with Batch Enhancer is as follows:

```
BE scriptfile [[GOTO] label]
```

Script files can also be used with the BEEP command by using the following format:

```
BE BEEP scriptfile [/E]
```

See the entries for BE GOTO and BE BEEP for more information.

GETTING HELP

You can easily get on-line help about Batch Enhancer commands from the DOS prompt.

To get help about Batch Enhancer, enter:

```
be /?
```

For help on a particular Batch Enhancer subcommand, use the form

```
BE command /?
```

where "command" is the Batch Enhancer subcommand of interest.

To get help on the BOX subcommand, for example, enter:

```
be box /?
```

EXIT CODES AND ERRORLEVEL

The Batch Enhancer ASK, MONTHDAY, SHIFTSTATE, and WEEKDAY subcommands return a number as an "exit code" when they terminate or finish executing. In DOS parlance, this exit code is called the "errorlevel." For example, the WEEKDAY subcommand returns a number from 1 to 7, where 1 is Sunday, 2 is Monday, and so on through 7 for Saturday.

Although this number is not usually displayed on the screen, you can test for the value with the IF ERRORLEVEL command in DOS batch files and then act based upon the value. In Batch Enhancer script files, you can also jump to a particular label based upon the preceding exit code (see the JUMP subcommand later in this Appendix for more details).

In DOS batch files the exit code test takes the following form:

```
IF [NOT] ERRORLEVEL number command
```

The "number" is the exit code for which you wish to test. The "command" is the command to execute if the errorlevel condition is true. The "NOT" is an optional parameter should you wish to test for the reverse; that is, test if the errorlevel is *not* a particular value.

There are two important points to remember when using the DOS IF ERRORLEVEL command:

- The IF ERRORLEVEL command tests the exit codes in reverse order.
- If the exit code (or errorlevel) is greater than or equal to the "number" being compared, the condition will be true and the "command" will be executed.

The following DOS batch file uses the Batch Enhancer BE WEEKDAY command to demonstrate these two points (see the description for BE WEEKDAY later in this chapter). This batch file determines the day of the week when run and displays an appropriate message for the day.

```
echo off
be weekday
if errorlevel 7 goto sat
if errorlevel 2 goto weekday
if errorlevel 1 goto sun
:sat
     echo Ride your bicycle.
     goto end
:weekday
     echo Busy hands are happy hands.
     goto end
:sun
     echo Go back to sleep.
     goto end
:end
```

Using Norton Desktop for DOS

The first test is for Saturday. If the exit code from BE WEEKDAY is 7, the batch file continues executing at the ":sat" label. The second test is whether the exit code is 2 or greater, but less than 7. If so, the batch file continues executing at the ":weekday" label. In the third test, if the exit code is 1, the batch file continues executing at the ":sun" label.

BE ASK

Prompts you for a response to a question. This response allows you to determine how the batch file should proceed. The ASK command provides an easy way to create batch files that execute different commands based upon keyboard input.

Syntax

```
BE ASK "prompt" [key-list] [DEFAULT=key]
    [TIMEOUT=n] [ADJUST=n] [color] [/DEBUG]
```

Options

prompt
Text to display when the command runs. If the prompt text contains embedded spaces and/or commas, the entire text must be enclosed in quotes. Use two quotes together if you do not want to display a prompt.

key-list
An optional list of response keys (characters, symbols, or numbers).

DEFAULT=key
If no key is entered within the time-out period or if you press Enter, this key is returned.

TIMEOUT=n
Time in seconds before the default key is returned. If n is zero, or no TIMEOUT is specified, ASK will wait forever. Maximum value is 65,535.

ADJUST=n
Adds the returned value to this amount. This allows multi-layered menus to be tested in one pass. Maximum value is 254.

color
Optional Screen Attributes format color specification for the prompt text (see BE SA for information on specifying colors).

/DEBUG
Displays the exit code (errorlevel) returned.

Batch Enhancer Reference   D-11

Notes

When the ASK command is invoked, it displays the prompt text and then waits for a response. Generally, you use the prompt to list the keys you may type in response to the ASK command (any of the keys in the key-list) and explain the results of choosing each.

You respond to ASK by typing any one of the keys in the key-list. The key-list itself is not displayed on screen. The key-list is optional. When no key-list is given, you can press any key to continue.

A default key can be set if Enter is pressed and a default timeout period can be specified. The sequence number of the key in the key-list is returned as an exit code, which can also be adjusted with an offset.

A beep is generated if a key is pressed that is not in the designated key-list.

After you choose one of the keys in the key-list (or any key, if no key-list is specified), ASK returns control to the batch file. ASK passes the sequence number of the key that was pressed as an exit code which can be tested with the DOS IF ERRORLEVEL command. The first choice (key) in the key-list corresponds to errorlevel 1, the second to errorlevel 2, the third to 3, and so on. If no key-list is supplied, ASK returns the ASCII code of the key being pressed. The batch program can then branch to different labels in the batch file, in accordance with the errorlevel.

Examples

Because of the way batch file errorlevel codes work, you must list the "if errorlevel n goto label" statements in descending order of errorlevel. For example, if you wanted the following ASK command in your batch file:

```
BE ASK "Run the (E)ditor, (D)atabase, or
    (Q)uit?" edq
```

then you might create a batch file that looked like this:

```
@echo off
BE ASK "Run the (E)ditor, (D)atabase,
    or (Q)uit?" edq
if errorlevel 3 goto quit
if errorlevel 2 goto database
if errorlevel 1 goto editor
REM The previous line is not really
REM necessary, since the editor
REM commands follow immediately.
:editor
      edit
      goto quit
:database
      cd \progs\db
      db
      goto quit
REM The previous line is redundant.
:quit
```

Since there are three items in the key-list in this example, ASK returns one of three exit codes: 1, 2 or 3. Level 1 is returned if you press the first key in the key-list, e; level 2 is returned if you press the second key, d; and level 3 if you press q. The response is case-insensitive; uppercase Q and lowercase q, for example, have the same result.

Immediately following the ASK command are three statements that branch to different points in the batch program, according to the exit code returned by ASK. Note that the statements are arranged so that they check first to see if the highest errorlevel has been returned (errorlevel 3, corresponding to a Q response), then the next highest, and so on, so that errorlevel 1 is checked for last. Because an errorlevel code is true when it equals the number or is greater than the number, you must always arrange a sequence of statements that branch on errorlevels in descending order. Practically speaking, this means you should start listing "if errorlevel n goto label" statements starting with the rightmost key in the key-list, and proceed in order to the leftmost key. (See "Exit Codes and Errorlevel" earlier in this chapter for more information.)

Batch Enhancer Reference **D-13**

BE BEEP

Plays a tone or a series of tones through the computer's speaker. You can specify a single tone on the command line or a series of tones (or even music) in a script file.

Syntax

```
BE BEEP [/Dn] [/Fn] [/Rn] [/Wn]
BE BEEP [pathname [/E]]
```

Options

/Dn	Duration of the tone, in 1/18ths of a second.
/Fn	Frequency of the tone, where n is cycles per second (Hertz).
/Rn	Repeat the tone n times.
/Wn	Wait between tones n/18ths of a second.
pathname	The name of a script file containing BEEP tones.
/E	Echo the quoted text in comments.

Notes

BEEP uses the system speaker to create tones based on the specified frequency and duration. These tones can be used to create sounds that signal error conditions or the completion of a task.

If a script file is specified, BEEP will play the tones in the file as if they had been entered on the command line, one line at a time. This makes it easy and quite efficient to create music with BEEP. It is possible to include comments in the script files which BEEP will display as it plays the tones. This allows the lyrics of a song to be displayed on the screen as the song is playing (see the last example for BE BEEP).

The frequency of each tone is given by the /Fn switch, where n is cycles per second. The duration of each tone is indicated by the /Dn switch, where n is in 18ths of a second. To repeat a tone, use the /Rn switch, where n is the number of times the tone is to be repeated. The /Wn switch inserts a Wait between tones of n/18ths of a second.

Switches can be entered in any order.

The format of a script file is almost exactly the same as the command line. The only difference is that the forward slash (/) with the switches is optional. For instance, the command line

```
BE BEEP /F440 /D36 /R3 /W18
```

could appear in a script file as

```
F440 D36 R3 W18
```

Comments that appear in a script file must be preceded by a semicolon (;), and the parts of comments that BEEP will display if the /E (echo) switch is used must be enclosed in quotes.

The following table gives the frequency values for a five-octave range (middle C is 523 Hz):

Table D-1

C	65	131	262	523	1040	2093
C#/Db	69	139	277	554	1103	2217
D	73	147	294	587	1176	2349
D#/Eb	78	156	311	622	1241	2489
E	82	165	330	659	1311	2637
F	87	175	349	698	1391	2794
F#/Gb	93	185	370	740	1488	2960
G	98	196	392	784	1568	3136
G#/Ab	104	208	415	831	1662	3322
A	110	220	440	880	1760	3520
A#/Bb	117	233	466	932	1866	3729
B	123	248	494	988	1973	3951

Notes and Frequencies

Examples

To play a standard beep tone:

Use BEEP with no switches to generate the computer's standard tone.

    BE BEEP

To play a 440 Hz tone 3 times:

Use /Fn to specify the frequency and /Rn to specify the number of repetitions.

    BE BEEP/F440/R3

To play a ½-second, 660 Hz tone twice, pausing ½-second between repetitions:

/Dn and /Wn are given in units of ¹⁄₁₈ of a second, to allow you finer control.

    BE BEEP/F660/R2/D9/W9

To play a tune from a script file:

Beep can also play a tune listed in a script file. Enter the tones into the file as if you were entering them on the command line. For example:

    ;
    ;   A two-line tonefile
    ;
    /F330 /D36 /R3 /W18
    /F660 /D18
    ;   Put a semicolon before comments

This would repeat a two-second, 330 Hz tone three times, waiting one second between each repeat, and then immediately play a 660 Hz tone for one second. The "/" is optional when you're listing tones in a tonefile.

If these lines were stored in a file called TONEFILE, they could be played with the command:

    BE BEEP tonefile

You can enter comments into a tonefile by prefacing them with a semicolon; anything after a semicolon is ignored, with the following exception: If you use the /E switch, the parts of comments enclosed in quotes are printed on the screen while the tonefile is being played. Note that hyphens will not be displayed.

To play a tune and display text:

Beep can also display parts of comments from a tune listed in a script file.

```
;
;    A talking two-line tonefile
;
/F330 /D10 /R2 /W5 ;that's "mi"
/F440 /D10 /R3 /W5 ;this is "sol"
;    Put a semicolon before comments
```

If these lines were stored in a file called 2TONE, they could be played with the command:

```
BE BEEP 2tone /E
```

"mi" and "sol" will be displayed on the screen.

TIP: You can use BEEP within a batch file to signal the progress of commands, or to signal an unusual condition. You can place a beep with a distinctive tone at the end of a batch file or at intermediate points within the file to indicate what is happening. BEEP is particularly valuable in batch files that use the "if" command to vary their operation. Use BEEP in a batch file that dials your electronic mail service; you can use distinctive beeps to indicate whether or not you've received mail.

The SA command can be used in a similar way to provide a visual signal. See the later section on BE SA for more information.

BE BOX

Draw a rectangle at a specified location on the screen.

Syntax

```
BE BOX top left bottom right [SINGLE | DOUBLE]
   [color]
```

Options

top	Row for upper-left corner of box.
left	Column for upper-left corner of box.
bottom	Row for lower-right corner of box.
right	Column for lower-right corner of box.
SINGLE	Single-line border.
DOUBLE	Double-line border. This is the default.
color	Screen Attributes format color specification for the box (see BE SA for more information).

Notes

BE BOX draws boxes of various shapes, sizes and colors at a specified location on the screen. The boxes can have single-line or double-line borders. The boxes are not filled (unlike BE WINDOW), so any text within the confines of the box is not overwritten.

The row and column are zero-based. On a standard 25-line by 80-column display, valid rows are 0 to 24 and valid columns are 0 to 79.

Example

To draw a red box on a green background with a single-line border:

```
be box 10 10 20 40 single red on green
```

BE CLS

Clears the screen, optionally using the specified color attribute.

Syntax

```
BE CLS [color]
```

Options

color	Screen Attributes format color specification (see BE SA for more information).

Notes

BE CLS will clear the screen using either the color attribute at the current cursor location or the color attribute specified on the command line. One reason for clearing the screen with a certain color attribute is that Batch Enhancer commands like ROWCOL, ASK, and BOX (as well as others) use the existing screen attributes if no color is specified on their command line. By setting the screen to a certain color attribute ahead of time, other Batch Enhancer commands can be smaller and faster.

BE CLS is similar to the BE SA /CLS command. The SA command goes through the ANSI.SYS driver to clear the screen, while CLS uses a direct call to the BIOS clear screen function.

See Also

BE SA

Example

To clear the screen and change the colors to red on a blue background:

```
be cls red on blue
```

BE DELAY

Pauses execution of a batch file for a specified length of time.

Syntax

```
BE DELAY ticks
```

Options

ticks   Each clock tick is $1/18$ of a second.

Notes

BE DELAY pauses execution of a batch file for the specified number of clock ticks. The batch file resumes when the time has elapsed.

If Sleeper screen saver is enabled and the screen is in sleep state, BE DELAY won't time out until there is mouse or keyboard action.

Example

To pause execution of a batch file for one-half second:

```
be delay 9
```

BE EXIT

Terminates execution of a Batch Enhancer script file, before the end of the file is reached.

Syntax

BE EXIT

Options

None.

Notes

The BE EXIT command is used only in Batch Enhancer script files and has no meaning if executed directly from DOS.

The BE command word is not necessary because EXIT can be used only inside a script file.

While the GOTO command can provide variable entry points into script files, the script file would always execute from that point until the end of the file. The EXIT command immediately ends script file execution and returns to DOS, thus allowing selective execution of sections of a script file. Now, both the entry and exit points can be specified. This means you can set up several different scripts in one file and keep them independent from each other.

See Also

BE GOTO

Example

The following script file, COLOR.DAT, prompts for a numeric entry and then changes the screen colors according to the number pressed. EXIT is used to end the script file if the "onblack" label is selected.

Note that JUMP branches to a label in a script file based on the exit code of the previous command. See BE JUMP for details.

```
ask "1=White/Black, 2=White/Blue,
    3=Abort " 123 DEFAULT=3
jump onblack, onblue, nochange
:onblack
sa white on black
exit
:onblue
sa bright white on blue
:nochange
```

To execute the script, use:

```
be color.dat
```

BE GOTO

Specify where execution should begin in a Batch Enhancer script file.

Syntax

`BE pathname [[GOTO] label]`

Options

pathname A Batch Enhancer script file.

label A valid label that exists inside a script file.

Notes

The GOTO command provides the capability to control the starting point of execution in a Batch Enhancer script file. This means, for example, that for a batch file that uses a script file to display several menus, you can use GOTO to avoid having to display all the menus from the beginning if the desired conditions are met.

GOTO differs from the DOS batch file command GOTO in that it works only with Batch Enhancer script files.

The conventions used for labels are the same as in DOS: the label must start with a colon (:) and exist on its own line, starting in the first column of the script file.

The Batch Enhancer GOTO command should not be confused with the Batch Enhancer JUMP command, which allows conditional branching inside Batch Enhancer script files.

The GOTO keyword is optional as long as a label is defined after the name of the script file.

See Also

BE JUMP

Example

The following script file, COLOR.DAT, from the BE JUMP example prompts for a numeric entry and then changes the screen colors according to the number pressed.

Note that JUMP branches to a label in a script file based on the exit code of the previous command. See BE JUMP for details.

Batch Enhancer Reference   D-21

```
ask "1=White/Black, 2=White/Blue,
    3=Abort" 123 DEFAULT=3
jump onblack, onblue, nochange
:onblack
sa white on black
exit
:onblue
sa bright white on blue
exit
:nochange
```

To execute the script at the ":onblack" label, use:

```
be color.dat goto onblack
```

The GOTO token is optional. You could also enter:

```
be color.dat onblack
```

BE JUMP

Branches to a label in a Batch Enhancer script file based on the exit code (ERRORLEVEL) of the previous command.

Syntax

JUMP label1 [, label2 [, ..., labelN]]
    [/DEFAULT:label]

Options

label	A valid label that appears in the script file.
/DEFAULT:label	The label to branch to if the exit code is zero, or if the exit code is greater than the number of labels supplied.

Notes

Batch Enhancer script files can contain only Batch Enhancer commands. Any DOS or unrecognized commands are ignored, which means that without the JUMP command there is no way to control the path of execution inside a script file. The JUMP command allows conditional branching based on the exit code of the previous command.

The JUMP command allows you to specify a series of labels. The exit code is used as an offset into the series of labels, and execution continues at the appropriate label.

The first label will be selected if the exit code is 1, the second if it is 2, etc. If the exit code is zero or if no label exists for an exit code (that is, the exit code is 6 but there are only 5 labels), execution continues at the next line in the batch file (in other words, it falls through).

The BE JUMP command only appears in script files and has no meaning if executed directly from DOS.

BE JUMP is used for conditional branching within a script file, while BE GOTO is used for a conditional entry point into the script file.

See Also

BE GOTO, BE EXIT, BE ASK, BE WEEKDAY, BE MONTHDAY, and BE SHIFTSTATE.

Example

The following script file, COLOR.DAT, prompts for a numeric entry and then changes the screen colors according to the number pressed.

```
ask "1=White/Black, 2=White/Blue,
    3=Abort " 123 DEFAULT=3
jump onblack, onblue, nochange
:onblack
sa white on black
exit
:onblue
sa bright white on blue
exit
:nochange
```

To execute the script, use:

```
be color.dat
```

BE MONTHDAY

Returns the day of the month as an exit code.

Syntax

BE MONTHDAY [/DEBUG]

Options

/DEBUG   Display the exit code (ERRORLEVEL) returned.

Notes BE MONTHDAY determines the day of the month (1-31) and returns it to the batch file as an exit code. This code can then be tested with the DOS IF ERRORLEVEL command in a batch file or the BE JUMP command in a script file.

The MONTHDAY command is very similar to the Batch Enhancer WEEKDAY command. The difference is that WEEKDAY returns the day of the week while MONTHDAY returns the day of the month.

See Also BE WEEKDAY

Example **To display the day of the month on the screen:**

```
be monthday /debug
```

BE PRINTCHAR

Displays a character.

Syntax `BE PRINTCHAR character, count [color]`

Options
character	Character to display.
count	Number of times to display.
color	Screen Attributes format color specification for the character (see BE SA for more information).

Notes BE PRINTCHAR displays a specified character a given number of times at the current cursor location. The character can be repeated up to 80 times.

Example **To display the character "X" 30 times in blue with a red background:**

```
be printchar X,30 blue on red
```

BE REBOOT

Performs a warm or cold boot of the computer.

Syntax `BE REBOOT [/VERIFY] [/C]`

Options
/VERIFY	Prompt Y/N to confirm the reboot.
/C	Perform a cold boot.

Notes BE REBOOT provides the ability to restart the computer from a batch file. This is useful in the construction of batch files that affect system configuration.

/VERIFY is a fail-safe switch that allows prompting before rebooting.

/C reboots as if the computer had been turned off and then turned on again.

Note that some memory managers or TSRs may interfere with REBOOT.

Example

To warm boot the computer with a Y/N prompt:

```
be reboot /verify
```

BE ROWCOL

Positions the cursor at the specified row and column location, and, optionally, displays text.

Syntax

```
BE ROWCOL row col ["text"] [color]
```

Options

row	Row to move the cursor to.
col	Column to move the cursor to.
text	Optional line of text to display.
color	Screen Attributes format color specification for the text (see BE SA for more information).

Notes

BE ROWCOL provides control over the cursor position so that text can be written anywhere on the screen. After setting the cursor, the next command that displays text displays it at the current cursor location. BE ROWCOL can also save a step and display a line of text with an optional color specification.

Without a color specification, the current screen colors are used.

The row and column are zero-based. On a standard 25-line by 80-column display, valid rows are 0 to 24 and valid columns are 0 to 79.

Example

To display text near the top center of the screen:

```
be rowcol 1 27 "Kilroy was here!" blue
  on green
```

BE SA

Control the display of colors and attributes.

Syntax

```
BE SA NORMAL|UNDERLINE|REVERSE [/N]
BE SA [BRIGHT|BLINKING] foreground
   [ON background] [/N] [/CLS]
```

Options

UNDERLINE	Text is underlined.
REVERSE	Foreground and background colors are switched.
NORMAL	Undoes an UNDERLINE or REVERSE setting.
BRIGHT	High-intensity colors.
BLINKING	Text blinks.
foreground	Color selection for text.
background	Color selection for the background. Valid color choices for the foreground and background are the following: WHITE BLACK RED MAGENTA BLUE GREEN CYAN YELLOW
/N	Do not set the border color (defaults to same color as background).
/CLS	Clears the screen after setting the attributes.

Notes

BE SA (screen attributes) takes two forms:

- The first form sets the display to underline or reverse video. The UNDERLINE option is only available on monochrome monitors (it will be a blue foreground on a color monitor). The NORMAL option is used to undo an UNDERLINE or REVERSE setting.
- The second form of BE SA sets screen colors and high intensity or blinking.

The SA format color settings are also used with the BE ASK, BE BOX, BE CLS, BE PRINTCHAR, BE ROWCOL and BE WINDOW commands. However, the ANSI.SYS driver is not required with these BE commands (see the discussion of ANSI.SYS below).

BE SA instructs DOS as to which colors and attributes to use via an element of DOS known as the ANSI.SYS driver. To have your color choice in Screen Attributes remain in effect, you must first install the ANSI.SYS driver on your machine. ANSI.SYS is a special program file that comes on your DOS diskette.

ANSI.SYS must be loaded in your CONFIG.SYS file to use the BE SA command. Some versions of DOS automatically install the ANSI.SYS driver for you, but with most versions you have to install it yourself. You can easily test to see if the ANSI.SYS driver is installed in your machine by typing the following command:

```
BE SA NORMAL
```

If you see a message saying ANSI.SYS is needed, then it hasn't been properly installed.

To install ANSI.SYS, check if you have a file in your root directory called CONFIG.SYS. If you do, add the following line to it (if you don't, create a new file called CONFIG.SYS and put the following line in it):

```
DEVICE=C:\DOS\ANSI.SYS
```

This line assumes that the file ANSI.SYS is located in your C:\DOS directory. Make sure that the file exists in your DOS directory.

Now reboot the computer and the ANSI.SYS driver will be installed. As long as you leave the line in your CONFIG.SYS file, the driver is automatically installed each time you boot up.

> **TIP:** SA is useful in two ways. One is simply to set the color and attributes that you prefer to work with. The other is to call attention to special circumstances, particularly situations that may arise during the course of batch file execution. You can use distinctive settings, such as reverse, blinking, or a red background, to call your attention.

For example, you can use SA, together with the BEEP command, in a batch file that dials an electronic mail service. Distinctive screen attributes can tell you at a glance from across the room whether you've received any mail or not.

Examples

To bring special attention to the screen, try this command:

```
BE SA reverse
```

To set the display to high intensity blue on red:

```
BE SA bright blue on red
```

To use the most pleasing color combinations:

The best choice of colors and attributes depends on your personal taste and the characteristics of your display. For computers with full-color displays, many people find the following combinations attractive:

```
BE SA bright white on blue
BE SA bright yellow on blue
BE SA black on green
```

Because the results you get with SA vary from display to display, computer to computer, and program to program, you will probably want to experiment to see which combinations you prefer.

To restore screen colors after an ill-behaved program ends:

For ill-behaved programs that set their own attributes but do not reset the attributes to the way you set them before, you might want to consider using a simple batch file like this one:

```
program
BE SA bright white on blue
```

This way, the screen will be automatically set to white on blue, or whatever colors you prefer when the offending program terminates.

BE SHIFTSTATE

Reports the status of the Shift keys, the Alt key, and the Ctrl key.

Syntax

`BE SHIFTSTATE [/DEBUG]`

Options

/DEBUG   Displays the ERRORLEVEL value returned.

Notes

The BE SHIFTSTATE command returns an exit code (ERRORLEVEL) that defines the status of the Left Shift, Right Shift, Alt key and Ctrl key at the time it is run. SHIFTSTATE will return the following exit codes for the four keys, which can be added together for multiple keys:

1	Right Shift key
2	Left Shift key
4	Ctrl key (left or right)
8	Alt key (left or right)

Use BE SHIFTSTATE in your AUTOEXEC.BAT file if you want to branch to a different part of the file at certain times. For example, you may want to bypass a command that loads a shell or menu program.

Example

To act based on the shift state:

Your AUTOEXEC.BAT file may contain the following lines:

```
PATH = C:\BAT;\C:\DOS;C:\ND
PROMPT = $P$G
SET ND = C:\ND
    .
    .
    .
BE SHIFTSTATE
IF ERRORLEVEL 8 GOTO END
MENU
:END
```

If you hold down the Alt key when booting, the MENU command will not be executed. But don't press the key immediately after booting or you will generate a keyboard error. Wait until the Power On Self Test is completed.

Batch Enhancer Reference **D-29**

BE TRIGGER

Halts execution of a batch file until the time specified.

Syntax

BE TRIGGER hh:mm [AM|PM]

Options

hh:mm	Time in 24-hour format (0:00 to 23:59).
**AM	PM**	Optionally, specify time in 12-hour format.

Notes

BE TRIGGER allows a batch file to be paused until a specified time. The time, hh:mm, can be entered in 24-hour format or in 12-hour format with the AM or PM options.

12:00 am is same as midnight and 12:00 pm is the same as noon.

Press Ctrl-Break or Ctrl-C to cancel the trigger.

If Sleeper screen saver is enabled and the screen is in sleep state, BE TRIGGER won't time out until there is mouse or keyboard action.

Example

To pause execution of a batch file until 1:00 in the afternoon, place the following line in the batch file:

```
be trigger 1:00 pm
```

BE WEEKDAY

Return the day of the week to the batch file as an exit code (ERRORLEVEL).

Syntax

BE WEEKDAY [/DEBUG]

Options

/DEBUG	Display the ERRORLEVEL value returned.

Notes

BE WEEKDAY determines the day of the week (Sunday through Saturday) and returns it to the batch file as an exit code. Sunday is returned as 1 and Saturday is returned as 7. The exit code can be tested with the DOS IF ERRORLEVEL command or the BE JUMP command.

The WEEKDAY function is very similar to the Batch Enhancer MONTHDAY subcommand. The difference is that WEEKDAY returns the day of the week while MONTHDAY returns the day of the month.

Example

To display the number of the day of the week:

```
be weekday /debug
```

See also the example in the section "Exit Codes and Errorlevel" earlier in this Appendix.

BE WINDOW

Draw a solid rectangle, optionally using a drop shadow and a zoom effect.

Syntax

```
BE WINDOW top left bottom right [color]
    [ZOOM | EXPLODE] [SHADOW]
```

Options

top	Row for upper left-corner of box.
left	Column for upper-left corner of box.
bottom	Row for lower-right corner of box.
right	Column for lower-right corner of box.
color	Screen Attributes format color specification for the window (see BE SA for information).
ZOOM	Zooms the window while drawing it. EXPLODE is a synonym for ZOOM, use either.
SHADOW	Adds a see-through, drop shadow to the window.

Notes

BE WINDOW allows solid boxes of various sizes, shapes, and colors to be drawn on the screen. The windows can have either a single-line or double-line border, with the default being the double line. You can optionally use a drop shadow and a zooming effect when the window opens.

The boxes are solid filled, and the text within any box will be overwritten. This is the major difference between the WINDOW and BOX commands. Also, the BOX command does not offer zooming or drop shadows.

The row and column are zero-based. On a standard 25-line by 80-column display, valid rows are 0 to 24 and valid columns are 0 to 79.

See Also BE BOX and BE SA.

Example **To draw a shadow box on the screen:**

```
BE WINDOW 10 10 20 40 red on blue
   shadow
```

Norton Commander Reference

This appendix explains how you can change the Norton Desktop for DOS screen display to look like the Norton Commander screen display. It is primarily intended for users of Norton Commander.

Contents

Switching to Norton Commander Mode E-3
Using Norton Commander Mode E-4
    Changes in the Left and Right Panels E-4
    Changes in Dialog Boxes E-5
    Changes in Menus E-6

SWITCHING TO NORTON COMMANDER MODE

This appendix is for Norton Commander users who want their Norton Desktop screen to look like the familiar Norton Commander screen. This first version of Norton Desktop provides a Norton Commander Mode to help make the transition from Norton Commander to Norton Desktop an easy one.

> **NOTE:** This appendix assumes that you know how to use Norton Commander. What follows is an explanation of the *differences* between Norton Commander version 3.0 and the Norton Commander Mode in Norton Desktop, and is not intended to be a tutorial for learning how to use Norton Commander or Norton Desktop.
>
> If you are are not familiar with Norton Commander, you should probably skip this appendix.

To switch to Norton Commander Mode:

1   Choose PREFERENCES... from the (long) Configure menu.

    The Configure Preferences dialog box appears.

2   Select Norton Commander from the Style combination box in the Desktop group box.

3   Select OK.

    The Norton Desktop screen display changes to look like the Norton Commander screen display.

> **NOTE:** When you switch to Norton Commander Mode, all open windows in Norton Desktop are closed.

At any time, you can switch back to the Norton Desktop screen.

To switch back to the Norton Desktop screen display:

1. Choose CONFIGURATION... from the Options menu.

    The Configure Desktop dialog box appears.

2. Select Norton Desktop from the Desktop group box.

3. Select OK.

    The Norton Desktop screen display appears again.

USING NORTON COMMANDER MODE

The screen display in Norton Commander Mode looks very much like the screen display in the stand-alone product, The Norton Commander. The left and right panels contain the same kind of information (directory listings, file listings, etc.) you are accustom to seeing. The function key bar and DOS prompt display at the bottom of the screen, and the menu bar appears at the top of the screen. There are some differences, however, and these differences are explained below.

Changes in the Left and Right Panels

Panels in Norton Commander Mode are similar to panels in Norton Commander, with the following new features added (Figure E-1):

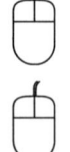

- A scroll bar so that you can scroll vertically through the panel using a mouse.

- A resize button so that you can resize the panel vertically using a mouse. (Panels can't be sized horizontally.)

- A Control menu so you can use menu commands to resize the panel, close the panel or switch to the other panel.

These new features are also features of drive windows in Norton Desktop. For details about how to use the new features, see the section "Windows" in Chapter 1, "Getting Started."

You will also notice that directories shown in full mode are not delimited with arrows.

Figure E-1

Control-menu box ── (top-left of window)

```
              C:\NU
Name          Name           Name
..            disktool exe   ncd      ico
DRAFT         ds       exe   nd       ext
FOLDERS       ep       exe   ndd      exe
IN            ep       ini   ndd      ico
MLLSTS        fa       exe   ndos     com
OUT           fd       exe   ndos     hlp
SENT          filefind exe   ndos     ico
aliases       filefind ico   ndos     ovl
be       exe  filefix  exe   ndos2e   com
calibrat exe  filefix  ico   nhelp    exe
chklist  cps  fl       exe   norton   cmd
compat   doc  fs       exe   norton   exe
descript ion  image    exe   norton   ico
diskedit exe  karen    ini   norton   ini
diskedit ico  keystack sys   norton   oin
diskmon  exe  lp       exe   norton   ovl
diskreet exe  ncache   exe   nu       hlp
diskreet ico  ncc      exe   nuconfig exe
diskreet sys  ncd      exe   nuconfig ovl
```

scroll bar (right side)
resize button (bottom-right)

Changes in Dialog Boxes

Dialog boxes in Norton Commander Mode are different from the dialog boxes you see in Norton Commander; most of them contain the same type of information, however. Figure E-2 shows the dialog box for the DELETE command from the Files menu. For general instructions on how to use Norton Desktop dialog boxes, see the section "Dialog Boxes" in Chapter 1, "Getting Started."

Figure E-2

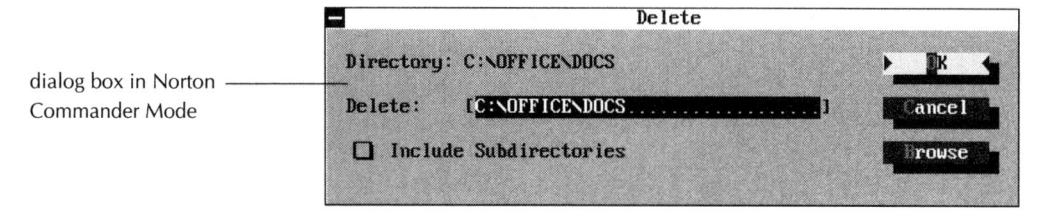

dialog box in Norton Commander Mode

```
                    Delete
Directory: C:\OFFICE\DOCS                    [  OK   ]
Delete:    [C:\OFFICE\DOCS..............]    [Cancel ]
[ ] Include Subdirectories                   [Browse ]
```

TIP: Learn how to use a Browse dialog box—it makes selecting a file easier.

Using Norton Desktop for DOS

Changes in Menus

The menu commands in Norton Commander Mode have the same functionality as the corresponding menu commands in Norton Commander. For example, QUICK VIEW from the Left/Right menus still displays the contents of a selected file, and FIND FILE from the Commands menu still does file searches. In addition, there are some new menu commands (including all of the commands in the Utilities menu) and a few menu-command name changes.

A change you will notice is that the dialog boxes that appear and the programs that run (as a result of choosing a menu command) correspond to programs and dialog boxes in Norton Desktop. To give you an example, FIND FILE in the Commands menu executes the Norton Desktop FIND... command found on the long Norton Desktop File menu.

The table that begins on the following page lists the Norton Commander Mode menu commands that are different in some way from the corresponding menu commands in Norton Commander. The far right column includes either a reference to a chapter in *Using Norton Desktop for DOS*, or a brief explanation of how to use the new or changed command. Menu commands that have not changed are not included in this table.

NOTE: Keep in mind that the references in the table to *Using Norton Desktop for DOS* are discussed in relation to the Norton Desktop menus. If you are using Norton Commander Mode while reading the procedures in this manual, you may find that you have to skip a few of the steps in the procedure to get to the information you want.

Table E-1

Menu	Menu Command	Description	Reference
Left and Right Menus	ENTIRE DRIVE	This is a new command for displaying a file listing for the entire drive.	For more information, see "Displaying Files from the Entire Drive" in Chapter 2, "Using Drive Windows."
	INFO	Displays information about your computer's memory and disk space. The Norton Desktop editor is used for editing the directory description.	For instructions on how to use the Norton Desktop Editor, see "Editing Text Files" in Chapter 4, "Managing Directories and Files."
	QUICK VIEW	Views the contents of a file in a panel.	For more information, see "Viewing Files in the View Pane" in Chapter 7, "Viewing Files."
	LINK	Links two PCs together so you can transfer files and share data. This feature corresponds to the Desktop Link feature in Norton Desktop. The Slave option sets up your computer as the server, and the Master option sets up your computer as the client.	For more information, see "Desktop Link" in Chapter 8, "Linking PCs." To configure the link, use the REMOTE LINK command in the Options menu.
	FILTER...	Filters a file listing.	For information on how to use the dialog box, see "Filtering the File Listing" in Chapter 2, "Using Drive Windows."

(continued)

E-8   Using Norton Desktop for DOS

Table E-1 (continued)

Menu	Menu Command	Description	Reference
Files Menu	HELP	Displays the Norton Desktop Help system.	For information on how to use the Help system, see "Getting Help" in Chapter 1, "Getting Started."
	USER MENU	Displays or creates a user menu with Norton Menu. If a user menu has already been created, the menu appears. If you do not yet have a menu, a dialog box asks if you want to create one manually or have the program build one automatically.	For information on how to use the menu, see Chapter 11, "Using the Menu." To create the menu manually, see "Creating the Menu Manually" in Chapter 11, "Using the Menu." To create the menu automatically, see "Creating the Menu Automatically" in Chapter 11, "Using the Menu."
	VIEW...	Views the contents of a file in full-screen, using the Norton Viewer.	For more information, see "Viewing a File in Norton Viewer" in Chapter 7, "Viewing Files."
	EDIT...	Allows editing of text files.	For more information, see "Editing Text Files" in Chapter 4, "Managing Directories and Files."
	COPY...	Copies files from one location to another.	For information on how to use the Copy dialog box, see "Copying Directories and Files" in Chapter 4, "Managing Directories and Files."

(continued)

Table E-1 *(continued)*

Menu	Menu Command	Description	Reference
Files Menu	RENAME OR MOVE...	Moves or renames files. The dialog box is similar to the one in Norton Commander for moving and/or renaming files.	**To rename or move a file:** 1 Type the name of the file you wish to move or rename in the Move/Rename text box. 2 Type one of the following in the To text box: • To rename the file, type the new filename. • To move the file, type the name of the directory you wish to move to, or select the Tree button to select a directory. • To move and rename the file at the same time, type the name of the directory to which you wish to move and the new filename. 3 Select OK.
	MAKE DIRECTORY...	Creates a directory.	For information on how to use this dialog box, see "Making Directories" in Chapter 4, "Managing Directories and Files."

(continued)

Table E-1 *(continued)*

Menu	Menu Command	Description	Reference
Files Menu	DELETE...	Deletes a file.	For information on how to use this dialog box, see "Using the DELETE... Command" in Chapter 4, "Managing Directories and Files."
	FIND FILE...	Finds a file.	For more information on how to use this dialog box, see Chapter 5, "Finding Files with SuperFind."
	PRINT...	Prints a file.	For more information on how to use this dialog box, see "Printing Files from Norton Desktop" in Chapter 4, "Managing Directories and Files."
	COMPRESS...	Compresses a file or group of files.	For more information on how to use this dialog box, see "Compressing Files" in Chapter 4, "Managing Directories and Files."
	FILE ATTRIBUTES...	Changes file attributes.	For information on how to use this dialog box, see "Changing File Attributes" in Chapter 4, "Managing Directories and Files."
	SEND FILES...	Starts Norton Mail and attaches the files you selected to your first message.	For more information, see "Creating a Message" in Chapter 21, "Using Norton Mail."

(continued)

Table E-1 *(continued)*

Menu	Menu Command	Description	Reference
Files Menu	SELECT	Selects a group of files using a file specification.	For information on how to use the Select Some dialog box, see "Using the SELECT Command" in Chapter 4, "Managing Directories and Files."
	DESELECT	Deselects a group of files using a file specification.	For information on how to use the Deselect Some dialog box, see "Using the DESELECT Command" in Chapter 4, "Managing Directories and Files."
	QUIT	Exits from Norton Desktop.	For more information, see "Exiting Norton Desktop" in Chapter 1, "Getting Started."
Commands Menu	NCD TREE...	Displays a directory tree. A new feature is the Prune button, which allows you to move directories.	For information on how to move directories within the directory tree, see "Using the PRUNE & GRAFT Command" in Chapter 4, "Managing Directories and Files."
	FIND FILE...	Searches for files on one or more drives.	For information on how to use the dialog box, see Chapter 5, "Finding Files with SuperFind."
	HISTORY...	Views and/or re-executes one of the previous 10 DOS commands you entered.	For information on how to use this dialog box, see "Launching Using the RUN... command" in Chapter 6, "Launching Files."

(continued)

Table E-1 *(continued)*

Menu	Menu Command	Description	Reference
Commands Menu	COPY DISKETTE...	Copies the contents of one disk to another.	For more information on how to use the dialog box, see "Copying a Floppy Disk" in Chapter 3, "Managing Disks."
	FORMAT DISKETTE...	Formats a disk.	This new feature is discussed in "Formatting a Diskette" in Chapter 3, "Managing Disks."
	MAKE DISK BOOTABLE...	Adds DOS system files to an existing disk which allows you to use the disk to boot your computer.	For more information on how to use the dialog box, see "Making a Disk Bootable" in Chapter 3, "Managing Disks."
	SEND/RECEIVE MAIL	Starts Norton Mail for the sole purpose of sending and receiving mail.	For more information, see "Sending and Receiving Messages" in Chapter 21, "Using Norton Mail."
	MAIL	Starts Norton Mail.	For more information, see Chapter 21, "Using Norton Mail."
	MENU EDIT...	Edits or creates a user menu. In Norton Commander, this menu command is called MENU FILE EDIT. If a user menu has been created, it appears on the screen for you to edit. If you do not yet have a menu, a dialog box asks if you want to create one manually.	For information on how to edit a menu, see Chapter 12, "Editing the Menu." For information on how to create a menu automatically, see "Creating the Menu Automatically" in Chapter 11, "Using the Menu."

(continued)

Table E-1 *(continued)*

Menu	Menu Command	Description	Reference
Commands Menu	ASSOCIATE...	Associates file extensions with applications so you can launch files from a file panel. In Norton Commander, this menu command is called EXTENSION FILE EDIT.	For more information, see "Associating a File" in Chapter 6, "Launching Files."
Options Menu	CONFIGURATION...	Selects configuration options. The Configure Desktop dialog box has most of the same options as the corresponding dialog box in Norton Commander.	You can set screen colors and mouse options using the VIDEO/MOUSE command in the Options menu. You can set Screen Blank Delay options by using the SCREEN SAVER... option in the Options menu. For information on how to use the 24 Hour Time option in the Other Options group box, see "Setting the Clock" in Chapter 9, "Configuring Norton Desktop."
	VIDEO/MOUSE...	This is a new command for selecting screen options (such as screen colors) and mouse options.	For more information, see "Setting Video and Mouse Options" in Chapter 9, "Configuring Norton Desktop."
	SCREEN SAVER...	This is a new command for configuring the Sleeper screen saver.	For information on how to use this dialog box, see Chapter 10, "Using the Screen Saver."

(continued)

Table E-1 *(continued)*

Menu	Menu Command	Description	Reference
Options Menu	SHUTDOWN...	This is a new command for configuring a shutdown routine.	For more information, see "Configuring Your Shutdown Routine" in Chapter 9, "Configuring Norton Desktop."
	PRINTER...	Customizes your printer configuration.	For information, see "Selecting Printer Options" in Chapter 9, "Configuring Norton Desktop."
	COMPRESS...	Configures your file compression options.	For more information, see "Selecting File Compression Options" in Chapter 9, "Configuring Norton Desktop."
	EDITOR...	Selects a default editor.	For information on how to use this dialog box, see "Selecting a Default Editor" in Chapter 9, "Configuring Norton Desktop."
	CONFIGURE LINK	This is a new command for configuring options for linking one computer to another for the purpose of sharing data.	For information on how to use this dialog box, see "Choosing the Desktop Link Options" in Chapter 9, "Configuring Norton Desktop."
			To use the cloning feature (via the Clone button), see "Cloning Norton Desktop" in Chapter 8, "Linking PCs."
			See also the LINK command in the Left/Right menus.

(continued)

Norton Commander Reference E-15

Table E-1 *(continued)*

Menu	Menu Command	Description	Reference
Options Menu	PATH PROMPT	Toggles the DOS command line prompt.	
		If PATH PROMPT is on and the PROMPT environment variable is set, Norton Desktop uses that setting; otherwise, the current drive and directory displays as the command-line prompt.	
Utilities Menu		The Utilities menu is new—it contains Utilities from Norton Desktop that are not in Norton Commander.	
	ADVISE	Helps you understand and solve common disk problems, DOS error messages and CHKDSK error messages.	This new feature is discussed in Chapter 24, "Using Advise."
	CALCULATOR	Performs basic mathematical operations using the Norton Desktop calculator.	This new feature is discussed in Chapter 13, "Using the Calculator."
	CALENDAR	Stores notes, to-do lists and appointments using the Calendar.	This new feature is discussed in Chapter 14, "Using the Calendar."
	NETWORK MESSAGE...	Sends messages over a network.	This new feature is discussed in Chapter 15, "Sending Network Messages."
	UNERASE	Recovers files that were erased or deleted by mistake.	This new feature is discussed in Chapter 16, "Using UnErase."

(continued)

Table E-1 *(continued)*

Menu	Menu Command	Description	Reference
Utilities Menu	SPEED DISK	Optimizes the layout of your disk so that data retrieval is faster.	This new feature is discussed in Chapter 17, "Using Speed Disk."
	NORTON DISK DOCTOR	Runs tests to determine if your disk has any problems, with the option to correct them.	This new feature is discussed in Chapter 18, "Using Norton Disk Doctor."
	NORTON BACKUP	Backs up files using Norton Backup.	This new feature is discussed in Chapter 19, "Using Norton Backup," and the manual *Using Norton Backup for DOS*.
	NORTON ANTIVIRUS	Protects your files from computer viruses and repairs or deletes infected files.	This new feature is discussed in Chapter 20, "Using Norton AntiVirus."
	SYSTEM INFORMATION	Reports on the operational status of your computer: the hardware, memory usage, network conditions, disk drives and benchmark comparisons to other computers.	This new feature is discussed in Chapter 22, "Using System Information."
	SCHEDULER	Automatically runs applications and displays reminders at specified times.	This new feature is discussed in Chapter 23, "Using Scheduler."

Menu Maps

This appendix provides a convenient display of the Norton Desktop for DOS menus—giving you an overview of the product. Both the short and long menus are shown so you can easily compare the two menu systems.

Contents

Menu Bar	F-3
Control Menu	F-3
File Menu	F-3
Disk Menu	F-4
View Menu	F-4
Configure Menu	F-5
Tools Menu	F-5
Window Menu	F-6
Help Menu	F-6
Button Bar	F-6

Menu Maps   F-3

NORTON DESKTOP FOR DOS

Menu Bar

```
- | Norton Desktop | 4.21▪
File Disk View Configure Tools Window Help
```

Control Menu

```
Restore
Move
Size
Maximize
Close      Ctrl+F4
Next       Ctrl+F6
```

File Menu

Short and Long

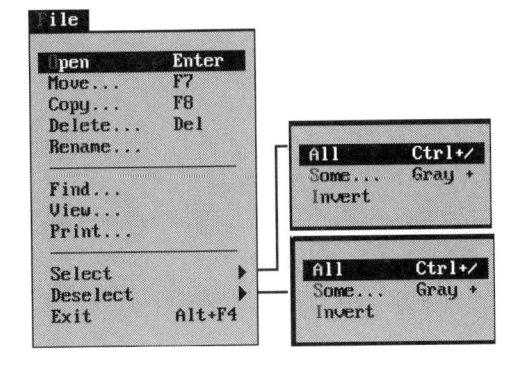

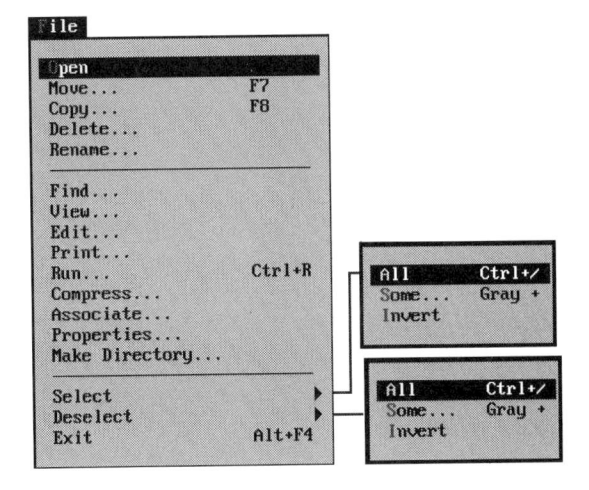

```
File
Open       Enter
Move...    F7
Copy...    F8
Delete...  Del
Rename...

Find...
View...
Print...

Select    ▶
Deselect  ▶
Exit       Alt+F4
```

```
All      Ctrl+/
Some...  Gray +
Invert
```

```
All      Ctrl+/
Some...  Gray +
Invert
```

```
File
Open
Move...    F7
Copy...    F8
Delete...
Rename...

Find...
View...
Edit...
Print...
Run...     Ctrl+R
Compress...
Associate...
Properties...
Make Directory...

Select    ▶
Deselect  ▶
Exit       Alt+F4
```

```
All      Ctrl+/
Some...  Gray +
Invert
```

```
All      Ctrl+/
Some...  Gray +
Invert
```

Disk Menu

Short and Long

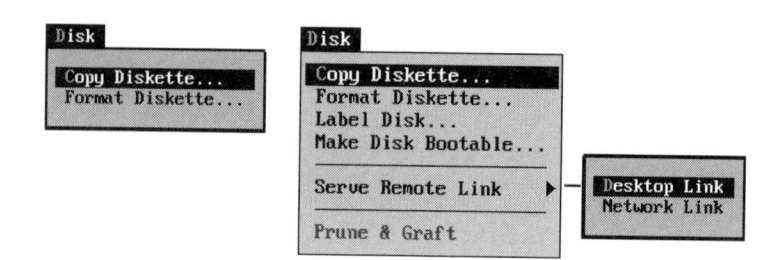

```
Disk
┌──────────────────┐
│ Copy Diskette... │
│ Format Diskette..│
└──────────────────┘
```

```
Disk
┌──────────────────────┐
│ Copy Diskette...     │
│ Format Diskette...   │
│ Label Disk...        │
│ Make Disk Bootable...│
│                      │
│ Serve Remote Link  ▶ │──┬──────────────┐
│                      │  │ Desktop Link │
│ Prune & Graft        │  │ Network Link │
└──────────────────────┘  └──────────────┘
```

View Menu

Short and Long

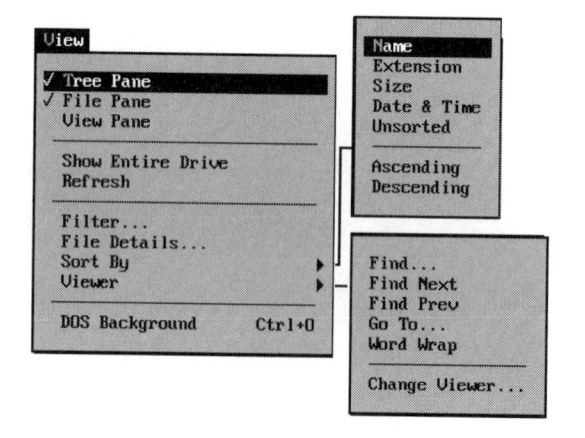

```
View
┌──────────────────┐
│ √ Tree Pane      │
│ √ File Pane      │
│   View Pane      │
│                  │
│   Refresh        │
│                  │
│   Filter...      │
│   Sort by Extension│
│   Sort by Name   │
└──────────────────┘
```

```
View
┌──────────────────────────┐
│ √ Tree Pane              │      ┌──────────────┐
│ √ File Pane              │      │ Name         │
│   View Pane              │      │ Extension    │
│                          │      │ Size         │
│   Show Entire Drive      │      │ Date & Time  │
│   Refresh                │      │ Unsorted     │
│                          │      │              │
│   Filter...              │      │ Ascending    │
│   File Details...        │      │ Descending   │
│   Sort By              ▶ │──────┘              │
│   Viewer               ▶ │──┐   ┌──────────────┐
│                          │  │   │ Find...      │
│   DOS Background  Ctrl+O │  └───│ Find Next    │
└──────────────────────────┘      │ Find Prev    │
                                  │ Go To...     │
                                  │ Word Wrap    │
                                  │              │
                                  │ Change Viewer...│
                                  └──────────────┘
```

Menu Maps   F-5

Configure Menu

Short and Long

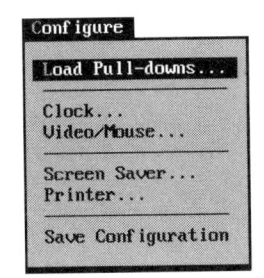

```
Configure
  Load Pull-downs...
  Clock...
  Video/Mouse...
  Screen Saver...
  Printer...
  Save Configuration
```

```
Configure
  Load Pull-downs...
  Edit Pull-downs...
  Password...
  Preferences...
  Button Bar...
  Confirmation...
  Clock...
  Video/Mouse...
  Editor...
  Screen Saver...
  Network...
  Printer...
  Compression...
  Desktop Link...
  Save Configuration
```

Tools Menu

Short and Long

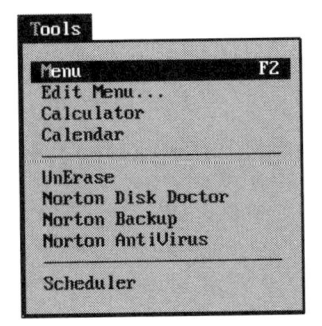

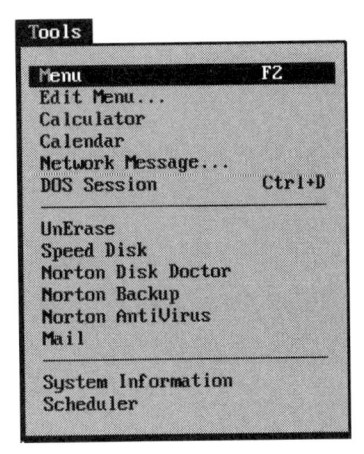

```
Tools
  Menu              F2
  Edit Menu...
  Calculator
  Calendar
  UnErase
  Norton Disk Doctor
  Norton Backup
  Norton AntiVirus
  Scheduler
```

```
Tools
  Menu              F2
  Edit Menu...
  Calculator
  Calendar
  Network Message...
  DOS Session      Ctrl+D
  UnErase
  Speed Disk
  Norton Disk Doctor
  Norton Backup
  Norton AntiVirus
  Mail
  System Information
  Scheduler
```

Window Menu

Short and Long

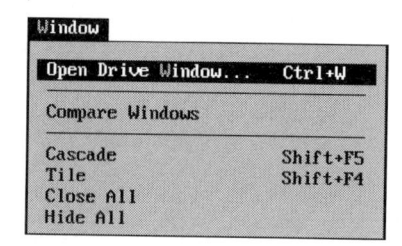

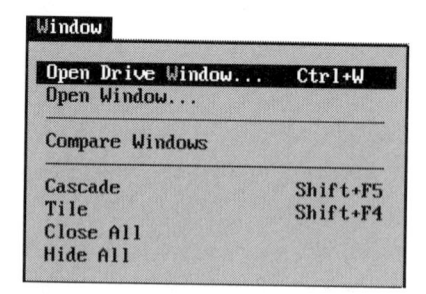

```
Window
┌─────────────────────────────┐
│ Open Drive Window...  Ctrl+W│
│ Compare Windows             │
│ Cascade              Shift+F5│
│ Tile                 Shift+F4│
│ Close All                   │
│ Hide All                    │
└─────────────────────────────┘
```

```
Window
┌─────────────────────────────┐
│ Open Drive Window...  Ctrl+W│
│ Open Window...              │
│ Compare Windows             │
│ Cascade              Shift+F5│
│ Tile                 Shift+F4│
│ Close All                   │
│ Hide All                    │
└─────────────────────────────┘
```

Help Menu

```
Help
┌──────────────┐
│ Advise       │
│ Index        │
│ Keyboard     │
│ Commands     │
│ Procedures   │
│ Using Help   │
│ Guided Tour..│
│ About...     │
└──────────────┘
```

Button Bar

`1Help  2Menu  3View  4Edit  5Find  6Print  7Move  8Copy  9Delete  10PullDn`

Glossary

active window — the currently selected window; always appears on top of any other window. The title bar in the active window is a different color or intensity than the title bar in an inactive window.

address book — a Norton Mail file that contains the addresses for the people to whom you send mail. You can add addresses to the address book either manually or automatically.

alphanumeric — comprising both characters and numbers. It is also used to mean any character you can type from the keyboard, including uppercase and lowercase letters, numbers, punctuation marks and keyboard symbols.

archive attribute — a code stored in a file's directory entry that indicates whether the file has been modified since the last backup.

ASCII — an acronym for American Standard Code for Information Interchange: a standardized set of 128 characters used by various types of data-processing equipment.

ASCII file — *see* ASCII text file.

ASCII text file — also called a text file or ASCII file. A document file that contains characters, spaces, punctuation, carriage returns, and sometimes tabs and an end-of-file marker. It does not contain formatting information, such as a word processing document would have.

attribute — a characteristic of a file: read-only, hidden, system, archive or directory (a directory is a special type of file).

AUTOEXEC.BAT — a batch file that is automatically executed when the computer is started. *See also* batch file.

batch file — a text file that contains a sequence of DOS commands. Batch files are used to save command sequences so that they can be re-executed at any time. Batch files typically have a .BAT extension.

baud rate — the speed at which a modem can transmit data; a baud is a measure of data-transmission speed. *See also* modem.

binary file	a file that contains 8-bit sequences of data or executable code. Binary files are in machine-readable format that humans cannot read. Contrast with ASCII text file.
bit	the smallest unit of storage in a computer's memory, enough to hold a 0 or 1 (a "binary digit").
bitmap file	a file containing a picture, which is stored as a set of colored dots called pixels, or picture elements.
block operation	an operation such as moving, copying or deleting that is performed on a marked block of information.
bootable disk	*see* boot disk.
boot disk	a disk that contains the disk operating system (DOS) necessary to start, or boot, the computer.
boot record	a sector at the beginning of each disk that identifies the disk's architecture (sector size, cluster size and so on). For a boot disk, it also contains the boot program.
boot-sector infection	a boot-sector infection is a virus that attacks the boot sector program which is responsible for loading DOS.
bootstrap file	a small program that implements file-transfer protocol and checks for data-transmission errors. When using the Norton Desktop Cloning feature the bootstrap file is used while transferring files to the receiving computer.
buffer	an area of computer memory set aside for temporary storage.
byte	eight contiguous bits of data (analogous to a single character in the English language). 1024 bytes are called a kilobyte, abbreviated as 1K.
cascading menu	a submenu that drops down from a menu item when that item is chosen. A menu item that leads to a cascading menu is identified by a right arrowhead that follows the menu item name.
check box	a dialog box component that acts like a switch, representing an option you can turn on or off. Sometimes a check box has three states: on (set), off (clear) and ignore (filled).
click	to press the primary mouse button once.

Glossary G-3

client — a computer that has been linked to a server so that it can access the server's files. Client computers access the server using either Network Link or Desktop Link.

clipboard — a buffer area in memory where data is stored when being transferred from one file to another.

cloning Norton Desktop — the process of copying Norton Desktop from one computer to another computer, when the two computers are joined by a serial cable.

cluster — the basic storage allocation unit for a disk (usually between 2K and 8K in size). Disk space is allocated to files in whole clusters.

CMOS — an acronym for Complimentary Metal Oxide Semiconductor: a battery-powered chip in 80286 (and more advanced) computers that preserves basic data about the system's hardware.

combination box — a dialog box component that combines the capabilities of a text box and a list box. Like a text box, you can enter information into the entry field; like a list box, it provides a roster of available choices.

command button — a rectangular button that carries out the action described by the text on the button. The two most common command buttons are OK (acknowledges a warning or message or performs an action) and Cancel (closes the dialog box without performing any pending action).

communication port — serial or parallel ports that allow you to connect your computer to devices such as printers, modems or another computer.

COM port — *see* serial port.

compressed file — a file that has gone through an encoding process to make it smaller; several files can be compressed together.

CONFIG.SYS — a text file containing commands that configure the system's hardware and load device drivers. It is automatically executed by DOS when the computer is started.

Control menu — a menu that allows you to move, size, close or switch to another window. The Control menu is revealed when you select the Control-menu box.

Control-menu box	a component of a window that is located in the upper-left corner of each window or dialog box. When the Control-menu box is selected, the Control menu drops down.
CPU	an acronym for Central Processing Unit that usually means the computer chip (for example, 8088 or 80486). Colloquially, CPU is used for the computer without the keyboard and monitor.
data area	the area on a disk where data files are located. This includes all of the disk except the system area.
desktop	the screen background for Norton Desktop on which windows, icons, dialog boxes and the Norton Desktop menu bar appear. It is analogous to the surface of a physical desk.
desktop link	to join two computers directly with a cable between either their serial ports or their parallel ports. Once the cable is in place, one computer acts as a server and the other computer, acting as a client, connects to the server and initiates file transfer, etc.
device driver	a program that allows DOS to communicate with a physical device for input and output, such as the console, a serial port or a printer. Some device drivers are used to manage memory or similar internal functions. A device driver is loaded into memory through a statement in the CONFIG.SYS file.
dial-in	to use a modem and communications software to call one computer from another.
dialog box	a special kind of window that either requests or provides information. Many dialog boxes obtain information Norton Desktop needs before it can complete a command. Other dialog boxes display warnings and other system messages.
dimmed	an option that is not available or selectable at the present time.
disk cache	a program that speeds up disk access by placing recently read data in a memory buffer. If the data is needed again, it can be read from the buffer rather than from the disk.
document	a data file that is created by or associated with an application.
DOS command line	a DOS prompt that appears at the bottom of the screen when DOS BACKGROUND in the View menu is on or when you're in DOS.

DOS prompt	the interface to the DOS operating system. It is a visual cue that prompts you for a command, usually displayed as A:> or C:>.
double-click	to press the primary mouse button twice in rapid succession.
download	copying files from a server to a client.
drag	to hold the primary mouse button down while moving the mouse in a given direction. Often used to move an object or select multiple items from a list.
drive icon	a pictorial representation of each drive available to you on your computer.
drive selector	a component of the drive window that displays the drive identifier and volume label of the currently selected drive, and allows you to change drives.
drive window	a window that displays the contents of a selected disk drive, including a directory listing, file listing, information summary and/or a view of a particular file's contents. Additionally, it displays disk information in the status bar.
drop-down list box	a special type of list box that reveals a list of choices when you press its prompt button.
edit mode	the Norton Menu mode of operation that lets you create, edit, run and test menus. It also lets you customize Norton Menu itself.
electronic mail service (EMS)	a service that transmits messages computer-to-computer over a communications network.
environment variable	the operating system keeps track of certain information it needs in an area of memory called the environment space. This area of memory contains the values of certain variables, such as the directories on your path, the location of the command processor (typically COMMAND.COM) and what to put in your DOS prompt. These values are called environment variables. Environment variables are generally set up in the AUTOEXEC.BAT and CONFIG.SYS files.
.EXE file	*see* executable file.
executable file	a file containing a program that can be run by DOS or Windows. Executable files generally have the following extensions: .COM, .EXE, .OVR, .OVL, .DRV, .BIN or .SYS.

extension	a three-letter suffix to a DOS filename; usually descriptive of the file's contents. For example, .EXE is an extension of a program's executable file; .TXT is often an extension of a text file.
file allocation table (FAT)	a table in the system area of each disk that identifies the use of each cluster as free, belonging to a file or bad (unusable).
file pane	a component of the drive window that displays a list of files within a selected directory, allowing you to select files for file operations such as copying or editing.
file server	a computer that provides network users access to shared applications and data files.
file set	the filenames or filename patterns of the files you want to locate using the FIND... command from the File menu. Typically, filename patterns are expressed as file specifications using DOS wildcard characters. For example, *.DOC specifies any file with a .DOC extension.
file specification	determines a file or set of files that is the target of some operation, such as copy, erase or find. A file specification may include DOS wildcard characters, as in *.EXE, or ????90.DOC. *See also* wildcard.
folders	subdirectories used by Norton Mail to store mail messages (files). Norton Mail folders include: In, used to store messages received through MCI Mail; Out, used to store messages that are waiting to be sent; Sent, used to store messages sent in previous mail sessions; and Draft, used to store incomplete messages. You can also create and name your own folders to organize your mail.
fragmentation	the condition that occurs when, over time and use (creating, copying and deleting), files are no longer stored on disk in contiguous clusters. This slows disk access time as disk head movement increases for read/write operations.
header information	a small block of data that precedes most non-ASCII files indicating the type of file, the version, the file's size and so on.
hexadecimal	the base-16 representation of a number.
hidden attribute	an attribute assigned to critical files to make them harder to access and more difficult to delete. *See* hidden files.

hidden files	files with file attributes set so the files do not appear in a directory listing, thus making the files more difficult to delete and copy.
history list	a compiled list of your previous entries in a text box. If you commonly make the same selections, the history list offers the convenience of being able to choose from a list and saves you from having to repeatedly type the same entries.
hotkey	the letter that appears in a contrasting attribute within a menu command, button or option. In Norton Menu, the hotkeys appear to the left of the menu item. Pressing the hotkey works the same as highlighting the item and pressing Enter.
implode	a method of compressing files. Imploding offers the greatest amount of compression, but at a slower speed.
infected file	a file that contains a virus.
inoculating with Virus Clinic	as Virus Clinic scans your disk for viruses, it can gather information about a file called inoculation data, which it stores in an inoculation file. From that point on every time you scan the disk with Virus Clinic the file is compared against the inoculation data; if there is a change in the file, it could signal the presence of a unknown virus. Using Virus Clinic is the fastest way to inoculate all files on a drive.
inoculating with Virus Intercept	Virus Intercept compares a file's characteristics to those recorded in an inoculation data file. The inoculation data file is usually created by scanning the disk using Virus Clinic. If the characteristics in the data file don't match the actual file, a Virus Alert box is displayed on the screen. If you have recently updated a file and know that it contains no viruses, you can update the inoculation file by choosing the Reinoc button in the Virus Intercept Alert box.
inoculation file	a file that contains inoculation data that is stored by Norton AntiVirus and is used in subsequent scans to verify the file's integrity. By examining the inoculation file, Norton AntiVirus can tell if the file has been altered in some way.
LAN	an abbreviation for Local Area Network. *See* Local Area Network.
launch	to start or run an application with or without a related document.

list box	a dialog box component that contains a roster of available choices.
load	to start or run an application. *See also* launch.
Local Area Network (LAN)	a group of computers linked together with cables that have access to a shared computer known as the server on which common programs and data files may reside.
location set	the drives and directories where the FIND... command searches for files matching the specified file set.
log files	shows the time a virus intercept occurred and records the response to the alert box.
long menus	Norton Desktop menus that have all of the available menu commands. *See also* short menus.
lost cluster	a cluster that contains current data but, because of errors in the FAT or in directories, the file that owns the cluster cannot be determined.
LPT port	*see* parallel port.
mail	*see* Norton Mail.
mail list	a Norton Mail file that contains a group of addressees. When you address a Norton Mail message to a mail list, each person in the group receives the message. Each individual mail list is a file stored in the MLISTS subdirectory. *See also* Norton Mail.
Maximize button	a component of a window that zooms a window to full-screen size.
MCI Mail	an electronic mail service owned by MCI Communications Corporation.
memory-resident program	a program that loads itself into random-access memory (RAM) the first time it runs and remains there until it is disabled or the computer is turned off or rebooted. Also called a TSR or terminate-and-stay-resident program.
menu bar	a component of the desktop that contains the available menus listed by menu name.
menu file	a binary file that contains a menu created by Norton Menu. It has the file extension .NMF.

modem	a communications device that enables a computer to transmit information over a standard telephone line. Communications software is required. Modems typically transmit data at speeds ranging from 300 baud to 9600 baud. *See also* baud rate.
.NAB file	a symbolic text file created by Norton Menu that is an exported "snapshot" of a menu. It contains a menu's items, passwords and hotkeys.
network link	a feature used by computers that share the same LAN (Novell or any LAN that supports the NetBIOS interface) and transfer files. One of the computers must be set up as a server and the other computer, acting as a client, connects to the server and initiates file transfer.
Norton Mail	a utility that allows you to send and receive electronic mail, as well as fax, telex and paper mail via MCI electronic mail service. Norton Mail can be accessed through the Norton Desktop Tools menu or run as a stand-alone program.
option button	a button in a dialog box that represents a set of choices that are mutually exclusive. This means that you may select only one option at any one time. Also called a radio button.
pane	a component of the drive window that displays the contents of a disk or file. *See also* tree pane, file pane and view pane.
Paper Mail	an MCI Mail option that lets you create and send paper mail via MCI using Norton Mail.
parallel port	Also known as LPT port. A connector passing data in and out of a parallel interface device. You can use parallel ports to transfer data between two computers using the Desktop Link feature.
partition table	a table in the system area of a disk that tells how the disk is set up, the size and location of the partitions, which operating system it uses, and whether the computer will try to boot from the disk.
partition-table virus	a virus that infects the small program in the partition table that locates the bootable partition. The virus loads into memory *before* DOS and Virus Intercept, taking control of your computer or preventing your computer from starting up at all from the infected hard disk.

paste	to insert text or graphics at a specified cursor position.
path	a list of directories where DOS automatically searches for files. A PATH= statement is typically placed at the beginning of an AUTOEXEC.BAT file. Programs listed in the PATH statement can be executed from any directory.
point	to position the mouse pointer over an object (a window or menu, for example).
prompt button	the small box to the right of a drop-down list or combination box, which, when pressed, reveals a list of choices in alphabetical order.
radio button	*see* option button.
read-only attribute	protects a file from being modified or deleted.
repair infected files	Virus Clinic may be able to repair a file that has been infected with a known virus; however, it is best to delete infected files and replace them with uninfected copies.
restore button	a component of a window that returns a window to its previous size—the size before it was maximized.
root directory	the directory DOS creates when you format a disk; the highest-level directory on your disk.
run mode	the Norton Menu mode of operation that runs a menu but does not let you edit it.
scan results	the list of infected files and files with unknown viruses created by Virus Clinic. The scan results appear in the Scan Results dialog box. You can select any file from the list for repair or deletion.
Scheduler	a Norton Desktop tool that lets you schedule a program execution and/or a message display at a specified time.
scroll bar	appears along the right side and/or bottom of a window when the window contains more data than can be displayed at one time.
scroll box	a small box that slides up and down in the scroll bar, indicating the relative position in a document or listing. Sometimes called a slider, elevator or thumb.

Glossary G-11

search set — the term applied to file sets and location sets used by the FIND... command in the File menu.

sector — the minimum number of bytes that are actually written to or read from disk in a single operation (usually 512 bytes). Four sectors commonly make up one cluster.

separator line — a horizontal line that divides a menu into logical groups of menu items.

serial port — also known as COM port. A connector for passing serial data in and out of a device. You can use serial ports to transfer data between two computers using the Desktop Link feature. You must use the serial ports to clone Norton Desktop to another computer.

server — a computer that allows other computers to access its files. *See also* network link and desktop link.

shell — an interface between you and DOS that makes managing your files easier. Norton Desktop is an interface that acts as a shell.

shrink — a method of compressing files. Shrinking offers less compression than imploding, but at a faster speed.

source floppy disk — the floppy disk from which you transfer information to a target floppy disk.

Speed Search box — appears as an appended component of the drive window when you begin typing letters while the tree or file pane is active. If the DOS command line is showing, press Alt+F1 to activate the Speed Search box. Using the Speed Search box is a convenient way to move to a particular directory or file within a pane.

status bar — a component of the drive window that displays information about the current drive, including the number of selected directories or files (when applicable), and the available space on the disk.

submenu — a menu that is called from a main menu.

switch — a command-line option that controls the operation of a program. Switches are used when a program is executed from the DOS prompt.

symbolic text file — a readable text file that is an exported "snapshot" of a menu. It contains a menu's items, passwords and hotkeys. It always has the file extension .NAB.

system area — the first sectors on disk where DOS stores the control information it needs to access the files on the disk. The system area includes the partition table, boot record, FAT and root directory.

system attribute — indicates a DOS or system-related file.

system disk — *see* bootable disk.

target floppy disk — the floppy disk that receives information transferred from a source floppy disk.

Telex — a worldwide telecommunications system that you can access using Norton Mail if you have an MCI account.

terminate-and-stay-resident (program) — a program that stays in your computer's random-access memory (RAM) so you can quickly access it with a keystroke, even if you are using another program or application. *See* memory-resident program, TSR.

text box — a rectangular box (usually one line) within a dialog box, into which you type the information needed to complete an action. A text box may be blank when it first appears or it may contain text.

text file — *see* ASCII text file.

time stamp — the date and time attached to a file, indicating when the file was last modified.

title bar — a component of a window or dialog box that shows either the name of the window or the name of the dialog box. The title bar in the currently selected, or active, window is a different color or intensity than the title bar in an inactive window.

toggle — *n.* an object that can be selected or deselected (or turned on or off) with the same action. *v.* to select or deselect an object (such as a check box or menu item) using the same control or action.

tracks	concentric rings encoded on a disk during a low-level format. Each track is made of sectors and defines a distinct data-storage area on the disk.
tree pane	a component of the drive window that displays a directory tree, making it easy to manage directories within the tree.
tree structure	the hierarchical organization of directory and subdirectory names.
TSR	an acronym for terminate-and-stay-resident (program). *See also* memory-resident program.
uninoculate	the UNINOCULATE... command on the Tools menu of Norton AntiVirus lets you remove the inoculation file from a disk.
unknown virus	a virus for which Norton AntiVirus does not contain a virus definition. Any change to an inoculated file could indicate the presence of an unknown virus. *See also* virus definition.
vector file	a file containing a drawing, stored as a series of commands that define lines, boxes, circles and other graphic primitives.
view pane	a component of the drive window that displays the contents of a selected document (such as a text, graphics or spreadsheet file) without launching the application that created it.
virus	a mischievous program that is spread from one computer to another either by booting from an infected diskette, by copying an infected file to a hard disk or by having an infected file transmitted to a computer through a network or over a modem line. Some viruses do annoying but relatively harmless things; others do destructive things, such as delete your files or reformat your hard disk.
Virus Clinic	a component of Norton AntiVirus that scans for viruses, deletes infected files or attempts to repair files.
virus definition	the data that includes a virus name, length, checksum and definition string for each known computer virus.
Virus Intercept	a component of Norton AntiVirus that is meant to be loaded into memory every time your computer boots. It works like a sentry in the background, alerting you when it detects an infected file.
volume label	an identifying name assigned to a disk.

wildcard a global filename character that represents all or part of a filename. The question mark (?) represents a single variable and an asterisk (*) represents a series of up to eight question marks.

write-protect to protect files from changes and erasure by setting the read-only attribute (see your DOS manual for details). Floppy disks can be write-protected with the write protect tab. Write-protected files and disks can be read but not written to. Program disks should be write-protected as a precaution against viruses and against accidental overwriting of their data.

Index

A

address book for Norton Mail
　about the address book, 21-8, 21-27
　backing up with mail lists, 21-36
　maintaining
　　adding an address, 21-29
　　automatically adding addresses,
　　　21-33
　　changing the type of address,
　　　21-10–21-11
　　copying an address, 21-11, 21-31
　　deleting an address, 21-32
　　editing an address, 21-30
　　opening the address book,
　　　21-27–21-29
　　restoring a deleted address, 21-32
　synchronizing with mail lists, 21-36
Advise
　choosing a problem group, 24-4
　choosing a topic, 24-4–24-5
　correcting a problem, 24-6
　defining a technical term, 24-5
　getting advice, 24-3
　how Advise works, 1-30, 24-3–24-7
　starting Advise, 1-31, 24-3–24-4
ADVISE... command, 24-3
alert dialog boxes, 1-27. *See also* system
　messages
　virus alerts, 20-42
application, starting
　launching a file, 6-3, 6-7–6-11
ASCII text file, viewing, 7-9
ASSOCIATE... command, 6-3

associating a file with a file extension
　about file extensions, 6-3, 6-5
　adding a new association, 6-5–6-6
　changing an association, 6-4
　deleting an association, 6-4
　specifying a custom startup command,
　　6-6
　viewing file associations, 6-3
autobuilding menus, 11-4
AUTOEXEC.BAT file
　editing. *See* editing text files
　Image program, 25-3
　Norton Cache, 29-3
　Norton Disk Doctor, 18-3, 18-7
　Norton Mail, 21-3
　Scheduler, 23-3
　SmartCan, 27-3
　viewing using Norton Viewer, 7-5–7-7
　viewing using System Information,
　　12-11

B

backing up your data. *See also Using the
　Norton Backup for DOS*
　creating a Rescue Diskette, 28-6–28-7
　taking a snapshot of your system
　　using Image program, 25-4
　using Norton Backup
　　about Norton Backup, 19-3–19-5
　　performing a backup, 19-4
　　scheduling a backup, 19-4–19-5
　　using the Backup Assistant,
　　　19-4–19-5

I-1

Backup
  See Norton Backup
Backup Assistant, 19-4–19-5
Batch Enhancer
  commands
    BE ASK command, D-10–D-12
    BE BEEP command, D-13–D-16
    BE BOX command, D-17
    BE CLS command, D-17–D-18
    BE DELAY command, D-18
    BE EXIT command, D-19
    BE GOTO command, D-20–D-21
    BE JUMP command, D-21–D-22
    BE MONTHDAY command, D-22–D-23
    BE PRINTCHAR command, D-23
    BE REBOOT command, D-23–D-24
    BE ROWCOL command, D-24
    BE SA command, D-25–D-27
    BE SHIFTSTATE command, D-28
    BE TRIGGER command, D-29
    BE WEEKDAY command, D-29–D-30
    BE WINDOW command, D-30–D-31
  ERRORLEVEL, D-8
  exit codes, D-8
  getting help, D-8
  how Batch Enhancer works, D-3
  script files, D-7
  syntax diagrams, D-5–D-7
  when to use Batch Enhancer, D-3
batch files. See also Batch Enhancer
  creating, 23-10
  editing, 23-10
  use with SuperFind
    creating from matching files, 5-13
    editing existing batch files, 5-15
    loading existing batch files, 5-15
BE ASK command, D-10–D-12
BE BEEP command, D-13–D-16
BE BOX command, D-17
BE CLS command, D-17–D-18
BE DELAY command, D-18

BE EXIT command, D-19
BE GOTO command, D-20–D-21
BE JUMP command, D-21–D-22
benchmarks, 22-10–22-11
BE MONTHDAY command, D-22–D-23
BE PRINTCHAR command, D-23
BE REBOOT command, D-23–D24
BE ROWCOL command, D-24
BE SA command, D-25–D-27
BE SHIFTSTATE command, D-28
BE TRIGGER command, D-29
BE WEEKDAY command, D-29–D-30
BE WINDOW command, D-30–D-31
bootable disk
  creating with Disk Tools, 28-3–28-4
  creating with MAKE DISK BOOTABLE... command, 3-10–3-11
boot record
  saving to Rescue Diskette, 28-6
  saving with Image program, 25-3
Boot Record Test, 18-4
boot-sector viruses. See Norton AntiVirus
browsing for files, 1-23, 1-25–1-26
button bar, 1-5, F-6
  configuring, 9-28–9-31
  using, 1-4, 1-5–1-7

C

cable pinout diagrams, 8-14–8-16
Calculator
  about the function keys, 13-3
  entering calculations, 13-4
  exiting the Calculator, 13-5
  how the Calculator works, 13-3–13-5
  starting the Calculator, 13-3
CALCULATOR command, 13-3
Calendar
  adding notes, 14-4–14-5
  changing the month display, 14-3–14-4
  changing the year display, 14-4
  command-line switches, C-6
  exiting the calendar, 14-5

Calendar *(continued)*
    how the calendar works, 14-3–14-5
    starting the calendar, 14-3
CALENDAR command, 14-3
CASCADE command, 2-19
cascading windows, 2-19–2-20
check box, 1-21
CHKDSK command
    comparing to Speed Disk, 17-8–17-9
    compared to Advise, 24-3
clock, setting, 9-31–9-32
CLOCK... command, 9-31
cloning Norton Desktop
    from one PC to another, 8-11
    how it works, 8-10–8-13
    port and cable requirements, 8-13–8-16
    system requirements, 8-3
CLOSE ALL command, 2-21
clusters
    how Speed Disk uses, 17-3, 17-4, 17-9
    lost, 18-4
CMOS
    Status report, 22-5
    values, 28-6
combination box, 1-23
command buttons, 1-22
command-line utilities
    getting help, C-6
    global switches, C-6
    how to access, 1-27, C-3
    program syntax and switches
        DISKTOOL (Disk Tools), C-7
        IMAGE (Image), C-7
        NCACHE (Norton Cache), C-7–C-13
        ND (Norton Desktop), C-13
        NDCALC (Calculator), C-6
        NDD (Norton Disk Doctor), C-14
        NMAIL (Norton Mail), C-15
        NMENU (Norton Menu), C-15
        NSCHED (Norton Scheduler), C-15
        SFORMAT (Safe Format), C-16–C-17
        SMARTCAN (SmartCan), C-17–C-18

command-line utilities *(continued)*
        SPEEDISK (Speed Disk), C-18–C-19
        VIEW (Norton Viewer), C-19
        SYSINFO (System Information), C-19
        UNERASE (UnErase), C-20
        UNFORMAT (UnFormat), C-20
    syntax diagrams, C-4–C-5
COMPARE WINDOWS command, 4-19
comparing directories, 4-19
compressing files
    how to compress a file, 4-22–4-24
    viewing a compressed file, 4-24
COMPRESS... command, 4-21
COMPRESSION... command, 9-44
CONFIG.SYS file
    editing. *See* editing text files
    viewing using Norton Viewer, 7-5–7-7
    viewing using System Information, 12-11
Configure menu, F-5
    BUTTON BAR... command, 9-28
    CLOCK... command, 9-31
    COMPRESSION... command, 9-44
    CONFIRMATION... command, 9-31
    DESKTOP LINK... command, 9-46
    EDIT... command, 4-26, 9-38
    EDIT PULL-DOWNS... command, 9-4
    LOAD PULL DOWNS... command, 1-10, 9-4, 9-18
    NETWORK... command, 9-39
    PASSWORD... command, 9-18
    PREFERENCES... command, 9-20
    PRINTER... command, 9-40
    SAVE CONFIGURATION... command, 9-49
    SCREEN SAVER... command, 9-39, 10-3
    VIDEO/MOUSE... command, 9-32
configuring Norton Desktop
    button bar
        changing button assignments, 9-30
        configuring, 9-28
        resetting default definitions, 9-30
        turning off and on, 9-29

configuring Norton Desktop *(continued)*
  confirmation options, 9-31
  Desktop Link, 9-46–9-49
  editor, changing default, 9-38–9-39
  file compression, selecting 9-44
  menus
    adding custom commands, 9-9–9-11
    adding a new menu, 9-7–9-8
    adding new menu items. *See* Norton Menu
    adding standard menu commands, 9-8–9-9
    corporate menus. *See* Norton Menu
    creating new menus. *See* Norton Menu
    creating a new menu set, 9-17
    creating pull-down menus, 9-5
    deleting menus and command, 9-15–9-16
    editing existing menu sets, 9-16
    editing menus and commands, 9-11–9-14
    long menus, 1-10, 9-4
    moving menus and commands, 9-14–9-15
    pull-down menus, 9-5–9-19
    restoring original menus and commands, 9-18
    short menus, 1-10, 9-4
    using a password, 9-18–9-19
  network options, configuring, 9-39–9-40
  overview, 9-3
  passwords, 9-18–9-19
  preferences, 9-20
    adding shadows, 9-24
    displaying drive icons, 9-27–9-28
    including directories, 9-25–9-26
    insert key for tagging files, 9-24
    keystroke preferences, 9-26–9-27
    options, 9-20
    scanning floppy drives with Norton AntiVirus, 9-24

configuring Norton Desktop *(continued)*
  selecting Norton Commander Mode, 9-26, E-3
  shutdown routine, 9-21–9-24
  Speed Search, 9-25
  printer options, 9-40–9-44
    configuration file, 9-41–9-44
    selecting, 9-40
  saving configuration settings, 9-49
  screen saver, configuring, 10-3–10-9
  setting the clock, 9-31
  shutdown routine, 9-21–9-24
  video and mouse options
    configuration display, 9-35–9-36
    confirming selections, 9-36
    customizing colors, 9-34–9-35
    selecting mouse options, 9-36–9-38
    setting screen colors, 9-33–9-35
CONFIRMATION... command, 9-31
connecting PCs
  cloning Norton Desktop, 8-10–8-13
  Desktop Link
    configuring options, 9-46
    using, 8-7–8-10
  Network Link, 8-3–8-7
Control menu, 1-13, F-3
COPY... command, 4-14
COPY DISKETTE... command, 3-3
copying a floppy disk
  about copying, 3-3–3-4
  floppy disk compatibility, 3-3
  source floppy disk, 3-3
  target floppy disk, 3-3
copying files, 4-14–4-16
copy-protected files and Speed Disk, 17-5
CPU Speed report, 22-10
creating a Rescue Diskette, 28-6
customizing Speed Disk
  saving configuration options, 17-15
  selecting an optimization method, 17-10
  selecting files to be accessed first, 17-13
  selecting hidden files to move, 17-14

customizing Speed Disk *(continued)*
  selecting sort criteria for files, 17-13
  selecting sort order of directories, 17-12–17-13
  specifying miscellaneous options, 17-15

D

DELETE... command, 4-17
Delete Tracking feature for DOS 5.0 and UnErase, 16-10
deleting files, 4-17–4-18
DESELECT command, 4-9
deselecting files, 4-8
desktop at a glance. *See* Norton Desktop
Desktop Link
  configuring options, 9-46
  connecting client to the server, 8-8–8-10
  ending the connection, 8-8
  how it works, 8-7–8-10
  port and baud rate requirements, 8-8
  port and cable requirements, 8-13–8-16
  setting up the server, 8-8
  system requirements, 8-3, 8-13–8-16
DESKTOP LINK... command, 8-4, 9-46
Device Drivers report, 22-10
dialog boxes
  about dialog boxes, 1-20–1-25
  alert dialog boxes, 1-27
  browsing for files, 1-23, 1-25–1-26
  components
    check box, 1-21
    combination box, 1-23
    command buttons, 1-22
    drop-down list box, 1-23
    group box, 1-20
    hotkey, 1-20
    list box, 1-22
    option buttons, 1-21
    prompt button, 1-22
    pull-down menus, 1-23
    text box, 1-22

dialog boxes *(continued)*
  navigating in, 1-23–1-25
  using wildcards, 1-26–1-27, 5-5
directories, managing
  about directory structures, 4-3
  comparing directories, 4-19
  copying directories, 4-14–4-16
  deleting directories, 4-17–4-18
  deselecting directories, 4-9–4-10
  making a directory, 4-3
  moving directories, 4-10–4-13
  naming a directory, 4-3
  renaming directories, 4-18–4-19
  selecting directories, 4-4–4-6
Directory Structure Test, 18-4
disks
  copying a floppy disk, 3-3–3-4
  creating a Rescue Diskette, 28-6–28-7
  Disk Characteristics report, 22-5
  floppy disk formatting, 3-4–3-11
    DOS format, 3-6
    Quick Format, 3-5
    Safe Format, 3-5
  hard disk formatting
    how to allow hard disk formatting, 3-8
    warning, 3-8
  labeling a disk
    adding a volume label, 3-7–3-10
    changing a volume label, 3-10
  making a bootable disk
    using Disk Tools, 28-3–28-4
    using the MAKE DISK BOOTABLE... command, 3-7, 3-11
  recovery
    determining number of floppy disks needed for backup, 19-3
    restoring from a Rescue Diskette, 28-7–28-8
    reviving a defective diskette, 28-5
    using Disk Doctor to repair defective disks, 18-7

disks *(continued)*
  selecting floppy disk drives, 3-9
  system messages, B-5–B-7
Disk Doctor. *See* Norton Disk Doctor
Disk menu, F-4
  COPY DISKETTE... command, 3-3
  FORMAT DISKETTE... command, 3-6
  LABEL DISK... command, 3-10
  MAKE DISK BOOTABLE... command, 3-11
  PRUNE & GRAFT command, 4-12
  SERVE REMOTE LINK... command, 8-8
disk problems. *See also* Norton Disk Doctor, problems, troubleshooting
  using Advise to solve, 24-3
Disk Summary report, 22-5
DISKTOOL (Disk Tools) command, C-7
Disk Tools
  command-line switches, C-7
  creating a Rescue Diskette, 28-6–28-7
  how Disk Tools works, 28-3–28-4
  invoking from the command line, C-7
  making a bootable disk, 28-3
  and Norton Disk Doctor, 28-4, 28-7
  recovering from DOS's RECOVER, 28-4–28-5
  restoring from a Rescue Diskette, 28-7–28-8
  reviving a defective diskette, 28-5
DOS
  command line. *See also* command-line utilities
    displaying, 6-9
    launching a file from, 6-10
    removing, 6-10
  Delete Tracking feature for DOS 5.0 and UnErase, 16-10
  error messages
    using Advise to solve, 24-3
  FASTOPEN
    compatibility with storage devices, 29-18

DOS *(continued)*
  Mirror feature for DOS 5.0
    and UnErase, 16-10
    and UnFormat, 26-9
  RECOVER
    using Disk Tools to recover, 28-4–28-5
  DOS session, 6-10–6-11
  DOS SESSION command, 6-10
drag and drop, 4-12–4-13, 4-16, 9-25–9-26
drive icon
  opening a drive window from, 2-5
drive selector, 2-5
drive windows
  arranging windows on the desktop, 2-19–2-20
  closing
    closing a single drive window, 1-16, 2-21
    closing all drive windows, 2-21
    when switching to Norton Commander Mode, E-3
  displaying file details, 2-13–2-14
  displaying files from the entire drive, 2-16–2-17
  displaying multiple drive windows
    cascading windows, 2-19–2-20
    hiding drive windows, 2-21
    selecting a drive window, 2-19
    tiling windows, 2-20
  filtering the file list
    by attribute, 2-13
    by type, 2-12
  finding directories and files, 2-7–2-9. *See also* SuperFind
  how drive windows work, 2-3
  navigating in, 1-16–1-19
  modifying the drive window
    enlarging to full screen, 2-18
    moving, 2-18
    resizing, 2-17–2-18

drive windows *(continued)*
　opening a drive window, 2-3
　panes
　　controlling, 2-9
　　file pane, 2-3, 2-10–2-11
　　tree pane, 2-3, 2-10
　　view pane, 2-3, 2-11
　sorting files, 2-14–2-16
　　by date and time, 2-15
　　by extension, 2-15
　　by name, 2-15
　　by size, 2-15
　　in ascending order, 2-16
　　in descending order, 2-16
　　unsorted, 2-15
　updating the drive window, 2-17
　selecting a drive, 2-5–2-7, 2-19
　Speed Search box, 2-6
　status bar, 2-5–2-6
　tagging files in, 9-24
drop-down list box, 1-22

E

EDIT… command, 4-26, 9-38
editing text files
　about Norton Desktop's editor, 4-25–4-26
　closing a file, 4-28, 4-29
　creating a new file, 4-28
　copying text, 4-34–4-35
　cutting text, 4-34–4-35
　default, 9-38–9-39
　deleting text, 4-34
　entering the editor, 4-25
　inserting text, 4-33–4-34
　inserting the contents of one file into another, 4-34
　insert mode, 4-34
　moving the cursor, 4-31–4-32
　navigating in the editor, 4-30–4-32
　opening an existing file, 4-28
　pasting text, 4-35

editing text files *(continued)*
　printing files, 4-40
　saving a file, 4-28, 4-29
　saving a file with a new name, 4-28, 4-29
　scrolling text, 4-30
　searching and replacing text, 4-35–4-38
　selecting text, 4-32–4-33
　starting the editor, 4-25
　switching from window to window, 4-27
　typeover mode, 4-34
　word wrap, 4-38
EDIT MENU… command, 12-3
EDITOR… command, 4-25, 9-38
EDIT PULL-DOWNS… command, 9-4
electronic mail system (EMS). *See also* Norton Mail
　other systems and Norton Mail, 21-45–21-46
EMS. *See* Norton Mail
error messages. *See* system messages
EXIT command, 1-3
exiting Norton Desktop, 1-3
Expanded Memory report, 22-7–22-8
Extended Memory report, 22-8–22-9

F

FAT Test, 18-4
fax, sending by Norton Mail, 21-45
File Allocation Table
　FAT Test, 18-4
　and Image program, 25-3
file associations
　about file extensions, 6-3, 6-5
　adding a new association, 6-5–6-6
　ASSOCIATE… command, 6-3
　changing an association, 6-4
　deleting an association, 6-4
　specifying a custom startup command, 6-6–6-7
　viewing file associations, 6-3

file attributes, assigning, 4-20, 4-21
file extensions, 6-3, 6-5
File menu, F-3
   ASSOCIATE... command, 6-3
   COMPRESS... command, 4-21
   COPY... command, 4-14
   DELETE... command, 4-17
   DESELECT command, 4-9
   EDIT... command, 4-26, 9-38
   EXIT command, 1-3
   FIND... command, 5-3
   MAKE DIRECTORY... command, 4-3
   MOVE... command, 4-10
   PRINT... command, 4-40
   PROPERTIES... command, 4-21
   SELECT command, 4-6
   RENAME... command, 4-18
   RUN... command, 6-8
   VIEW... command, 7-5
file pane
   launching files from, 6-7–6-8
   using in drive windows, 2-3, 2-10–2-11
file server, sending network messages, 15-3–15-5
File Structure Test, 18-4
files
   associations, 6-3–6-5
   displaying. *See* viewing files
   finding files with SuperFind
      customizing a file set, 5-7–5-9
      customizing location sets, 5-10–5-13
      defining your search, 5-9–5-13
      deleting file sets, 5-9
      deleting location sets, 5-13
      editing file sets, 5-8–5-9
      editing location sets, 5-12–5-13
      making searches case-sensitive, 5-13
      searching in multiple locations, 5-9–5-10
      selecting a directory, 5-11–5-12
      selecting drives, 5-10–5-11

files *(continued)*
   specifying files, 5-3–5-7
   specifying where to search, 5-9–5-13
   starting SuperFind, 5-3
   using wildcards, 5-6–5-7
   launching files, 6-3–6-10
   managing files
      assigning attributes to files, 4-20, 4-21
      compressing files, 4-22–4-24
      copying files, 4-14–4-16
      deleting files, 4-17–4-18
      deselecting files, 4-8–4-10
      editing text files, 4-25–4-40
      moving files, 4-10
      naming files, 4-3
      renaming files, 4-18–4-19
      selecting files, 4-3, 4-6
      sorting files, 2-24–2-26
      system messages, B-3–B-5
   recovering files. *See also Using the Norton Backup for DOS*
      copy-protected files and Speed Disk, 17-5–17-6
      fragmented files and Speed Disk, 17-4
      using UnErase to recover, 16-4–16-10
      using UnFormat, 26-5–26-8
   scanning files for viruses. *See* Norton AntiVirus
filtering the file list, 2-12–2-13
FIND... command, 5-3
finding files with SuperFind
   batch files
      creating from matching files, 5-14–5-15
      editing existing batch files, 5-16
      loading existing batch files, 5-16
   defining a search
      customizing file sets, 5-7–5-9
      customizing location sets, 5-10–5-13

finding files with SuperFind *(continued)*
    deleting file sets, 5-9
    deleting location sets, 5-13
    editing file sets, 5-8–5-9
    editing location sets, 5-12–5-13
    searching in multiple locations, 5-9–5-10
    selecting a directory, 5-11–5-12
    selecting drives, 5-10–5-11
    specifying files, 5-3–5-7
    specifying where to search, 5-9–5-13
    using wildcards, 5-5–5-7
  making searches case-sensitive, 5-13
  starting SuperFind, 5-3
folders for Norton Mail
  about the folder system, 21-5–21-6
  copying a message between folders, 21-22–21-23
  changing a folder's location, 21-37
  creating a folder, 21-5 , 21-24–21-25
  deleting a folder, 21-26
  moving a message between folders, 21-22
  opening a folder, 21-25
  renaming a folder, 21-26
  sorting messages, 21-26
FORMAT DISKETTE... command, 3-6
formatting
  floppy disks
    about formatting, 3-4
    DOS format, 3-5
    making a bootable disk, 3-7, 3-10–3-11
    Quick Format, 3-5
    Safe Format, 3-5
    saving Image information, 3-7
    specifying a volume label, 3-7, 3-10
  hard disk
    how to allow hard disk formatting, 3-8
    warning, 3-8
fragmented files
  how Speed Disk corrects, 17-4

G

general system messages, B-3–B-8
getting around in Norton Desktop. *See also* navigating in Norton Desktop
  using the button bar, 1-4, 1-5–1-7
  using hotkeys, 1-8, 1-20
  using shortcut keys, 1-9, 1-12
getting help
  Advise, 1-32
  commands, 1-31
  Guided Tour, 1-31
  Help menu, 1-31
  Help system, 1-32
  Help window, 1-32
  help index, 1-31
  keyboard, 1-32
  procedures, 1-31
getting started, 1-3–1-4
global switches for command-line utilities
  /BW, C-6
  /G0, C-6
  /G1, C-6
  /G2, C-6
  /LCD, C-6
  /MULTITASK, C-6
  /NOZOOM, C-6
group box, 1-21

H

hard disk drive
  backing up. *See* Norton Backup
  displaying contents, 2-16–2-17
  formatting a hard disk
    how to allow hard disk formatting, 3-8
    warning, 3-8
  optimizing using Speed Disk
    before using Speed Disk, 17-5
    comparing to CHKDSK, 17-8
    compatibility, 17-6
    customizing Speed Disk, 17-10–17-15
    generating reports, 17-7–17-9
    how Speed Disk works, 17-4

hard disk drive *(continued)*
  using Speed Disk, 17-6–17-7
  using the Walk Map, 17-9
  when to use Speed Disk, 17-3
  scanning for viruses. *See* Norton AntiVirus
  snapshot of system area, 25-4
Hard Disk Speed report, 22-10
Hardware Interrupts report, 22-4
Help menu, F-6
  ABOUT… command, 1-31
  ADVISE command, 1-31
  COMMANDS command, 1-31
  GUIDED TOUR command, 1-31
  INDEX command, 1-31
  KEYBOARD command, 1-31
  PROCEDURES command, 1-31
  USING HELP command, 1-31
Help window, using, 1-30–1-32. *See also* getting help
hidden files, 4-20, 17-14
HIDE ALL command, 2-21
hiding drive windows, 2-21

I

IMAGE command-line switches, C-7
IMAGE.BAK file, 25-4
IMAGE.DAT file, 3-7, 25-3, 25-4, 26-4
IMAGE.IDX file, 25-3, A-9
Image program
  how it works, 25-3
  questions and answers, A-9
  running Image, 25-4
  running Image automatically, 25-3
  taking snapshot of system area, 25-4
Insert Moves Down, 9-24

L

LABEL DISK… command, 3-10
labeling a disk
  adding a volume label, 3-9–3-10
  changing a volume label, 3-9–3-10

launching files
  about launching files, 6-3
  associating a file with a file extension
    about file extensions, 6-3, 6-5
    adding a new association, 6-5–6-6
    ASSOCIATE… command, 6-3
    changing an association, 6-4
    deleting an association, 6-4
    viewing file associations, 6-3
    specifying a custom startup command, 6-6
  from a DOS session, 6-10
  from the DOS command line, 6-9–6-10
  from the file pane, 6-7–6-8
  system messages about, B-3
  using the RUN… command, 6-8
linking PCs
  cloning Norton Desktop
    from one PC to another, 8-11
    how it works, 8-10–8-13
    port and cable requirements, 8-13–8-16
    system requirements, 8-3
  Desktop Link
    configuring, 9-46–9-49
    connecting client to the server, 8-8–8-10
    ending the connection, 8-8
    how it works, 8-7–8-10
    port and baud rate requirements, 8-8
    port and cable requirements, 8-13–8-16
    setting up the server, 8-8
    system requirements, 8-3, 8-13–8-16
  Network Link
    connecting client to the server, 8-5–8-7
    ending the connection, 8-5
    how it works, 8-3–8-7
    setting up the server, 8-3–8-5
    system requirements, 8-3, 8-13–8-16
list box, 1-22–1-23

LOAD PULL-DOWNS... command, 1-10, 9-4
long menus, selecting, 1-10, 9-4–9-5, 9-18
looking at files. *See* viewing files
Lost Cluster Test, 18-4

M

Mail. *See* Norton Mail
MAIL command, 21-3
mail lists for Norton Mail
   backing up with the address book, 21-36
   changing a mail list's location, 21-37
   maintaining
      creating, 21-34–21-35
      deleting, 21-36
      renaming, 21-35
      viewing contents, 21-35
   synchronizing with address book, 21-36
MAKE DIRECTORY... command, 4-3
MAKE DISK BOOTABLE... command, 3-11
managing directories
   about directory structures, 4-3
   comparing directories, 4-19
   copying directories, 4-14–4-16
   deleting directories, 4-17–4-18
   deselecting directories, 4-9–4-10
   making a directory, 4-3
   moving directories, 4-10, 4-13
   naming a directory, 4-3
   renaming directories, 4-18–4-19
   selecting directories, 4-4–4-6
   system messages, B-4
managing files
   compressing files
      how to compress a file, 4-22
      selecting compression options, 4-23
      viewing a compressed file, 4-24
   copying files, 4-14–4-16
   deleting files, 4-17–4-18
   deselecting files, 4-8–4-10
   editing text files, 4-25–4-40. *See also*
      EDIT... command, editing text files

managing files *(continued)*
   file attributes
      assigning to a file, 4-20
      assigning to multiple files, 4-21
   moving files, 4-10
   naming files, 4-3
   renaming files, 4-18–4-19
   selecting files, 4-3, 4-6–4-8
MCI accounts
   about MCI accounts, 21-37
   adding an account, 21-38–21-39
   deleting an account, 21-40
   editing account information, 21-40
   viewing an account, 21-39
MCI settings
   specifying modem settings, 21-42–21-43
   specifying telephone settings, 21-41–21-42
Memory Block List report, 22-9
Memory Usage Summary report, 22-7
menu bar, 1-7–1-8, F-3
MENU command, 11-3
menu maps, F-3–F-6
menus. *See also* Norton Menu
   administering, 31-3–31-12
      changing a password, 31-5
      removing a password, 31-6
      setting a password for a menu item, 31-3
      setting a system password, 31-3
   creating using Norton Menu, 30-4–30-10. *See also* Norton Menu
   creating using Tools menu
      about menus, 11-3
      autobuilding a menu, 11-4
      editing a menu
         adding a menu item, 11-5–11-7
         adding a similar item, 12-4
         changing the menu title, 12-5
         deleting a menu item, 12-4
         modifying a menu item, 12-3

menus *(continued)*
    moving a menu item, 12-4
    updating the menu automatically, 12-5
    exiting the menu, 12-6
    importing a menu to Norton Menu format, 11-8–11-9, 12-6
    prompting for arguments, 11-8
    starting the menu, 11-3
    testing the menu, 11-9
    using the menu
        choosing an item, 11-10
        moving from one submenu to another, 11-9
        returning to the main menu, 11-10
    using Norton Desktop default menus. *See also* long menus
        about menus, 1-7
        choosing a command, 1-8–1-9
        closing a menu, 1-9
        getting around in menus, 1-11
        selecting a menu, 1-8
        selecting long menus, 1-10, 9-4–9-5, 9-18
        selecting short menus, 1-10, 9-4, 9-18
messages
    creating in Norton Mail
        adding message handling, 21-14–21-16
        attaching files, 21-12–21-14
        copying a message between folders, 21-22–21-23
        correcting an error, 21-18–21-19
        creating a message, 21-6–21-8
        deleting a message, 21-23–21-24
        editing a message, 21-21–21-22
        forwarding a message, 21-21
        moving a message between folders, 21-22
        printing a message, 21-23
        reading a message, 21-19
        receiving a message, 21-16–21-18

messages *(continued)*
        replying to a message, 21-20–21-21
        sending a message, 21-16–21-18
    error messages. *See also* system messages
        using Advise to solve, 24-3
    sending network messages
        about network messages, 15-3
        answering a message, 15-5
        selecting names from a different file server, 15-4, 15-6
        sending a message, 15-3
        when a message cannot be sent, 15-3, 15-5
    system messages
        general, B-3
        launching files, B-3
        managing disks, B-5
        managing files, B-3
        network, B-8
        when system messages are displayed, B-3
    modifying the drive window
        enlarging to full screen, 2-18
        moving, 2-18
        resizing, 2-17–2-18
    MOVE... command, 4-10
    moving files, 4-10
    Mirror feature for DOS 5.0
        and UnErase, 16-10
        and Unformat, 26-9
    multiple drive windows
        cascading windows, 2-19–2-20
        hiding drive windows, 2-21
        selecting a drive window, 2-19
        tiling windows, 2-20

N

naming files, 4-3
navigating in Norton Desktop
    button bar, 1-4, 1-5–1-7
    dialog box, 1-23–1-25

navigating in Norton Desktop *(continued)*
  drive window, 1-16–1-19
  hotkeys, 1-8, 1-12, 1-20
  menu, 1-11
  shortcut keys, 1-9, 1-12
navigating in Norton Desktop Editor, 4-30–4-32
NCACHE (Norton Cache) command, C-7–C-13
ND (Norton Desktop) command, C-13
NDCALC (Calculator) command, C-6
NDD (Norton Disk Doctor) command, C-14
NDDUNDO.DAT (UnDo) file, 18-9
NETWORK... command, 9-39
Network Information report, 22-5
Network Link
  connecting client to the server, 8-5–8-7
  ending the connection, 8-5
  how it works, 8-3–8-7
  requirements, 8-13–8-16
  setting up the server, 8-3–8-5
NETWORK MESSAGE... command, 15-3
network messages
  about network messages, 15-3
  answering a message, 15-5
  selecting names from a different file server, 15-4, 15-6
  sending a message, 15-3
  system messages, B-8
  when a message cannot be sent, 15-3, 15-5
Network Performance Speed report, 22-10
network virus scanning, 20-44
NMAIL (Norton Mail) command, 21-3, C-15
NMENU (Norton Menu) command, 30-4, C-15
Norton AntiVirus
  alert boxes, 20-7–20-8
  network considerations, 20-44
  overview of Norton AntiVirus, 20-4–20-5

Norton AntiVirus *(continued)*
  questions and answers, A-16–A-24
  virus (defined), 20-3
  Virus Clinic
    boot-sector and partition-table infections, 20-22–20-26
    canceling a scan, 20-18
    configuring, 20-37–20-39
    executable infections, 20-20–20-22
    exiting Virus Clinic, 20-28
    recovering from boot-sector and partition-table infections, 20-23–20-26
      from Rescue Diskette, 20-24–20-26, A-17–A-19
      infected floppy disk, 20-25–20-26
      without Rescue Diskette, 20-25
    removing inoculation file, 20-16–20-17
    repairing infected files, 20-20–20-28
    scanning and inoculating files, directories and drives, 20-15–20-17
    scanning memory, 20-14–20-15
    setting passwords, 20-39
    starting Virus Clinic, 20-14
    system file and COMMAND.COM infections, 20-26–20-28
    understanding scan messages, 20-18–20-20
    working with scan results, 20-17–20-18
    when a file cannot be repaired, 20-22
  virus definitions
    adding definitions manually, 20-34
    deleting a definition, 20-35
    getting new definitions, 20-31–20-32
    loading, 20-33
    printing, 20-29–20-30
    updating, 20-30–20-36
    viewing, 20-29

Norton AntiVirus *(continued)*
  Virus Intercept
    Boot Sector alert box, 20-9
    command buttons,
      enabling/disabling, 20-41
    communication programs, 20-12
    configuration options, 20-41–20-42
    copying floppy disks and files, 20-12
    loading, 20-5–20-6
    and other programs, 20-11–20-13
    reinoculating files, 20-10–20-11
    responding to messages, 20-8–20-11
    versions, 20-7
    Virus Infection alert box, 20-11
NORTON ANTIVIRUS command, 20-14
Norton Backup. *See also Using the Norton Backup for DOS*
  about Norton Backup, 19-3–19-5
  questions and answers, A-10–A-16
  Quick Start backups
    before you start, 19-3
    performing a backup, 19-4
    using the Backup Assistant,
      19-4–19-5
NORTON BACKUP command, 19-4
Norton Cache
  about Norton Cache, 29-3
  advanced options 29-15–29-17
    buffering, 29-16
    optimize, 29-17
  AUTOEXEC.BAT and CONFIG.SYS files,
    29-13–29-14
  command-line switches, C-7–C-13
  configuring the cache, 29-8–29-17
    disable caching on floppy disks,
      29-11
    enable IntelliWrites, 29-11
    high memory, 29-11
    loading, 29-9
    memory usage, 29-11–29-12
    saving configuration, 29-13
  DOS FASTOPEN, 29-18

Norton Cache *(continued)*
  questions and answers, A-6–A-7
  SMARTDrive, 29-19
  system requirements, 29-3–29-4
  using Norton Cache
    cache reports, 29-4–29-6
    deactivating the cache, 29-6–29-7
    reloading the cache, 29-7
    removing the cache from memory,
      29-7–29-8
    resetting the cache, 29-6
  and Windows, 29-18
Norton Commander. *See* Norton
  Commander Mode
Norton Commander Mode
  differences between Norton
    Commander and Norton Commander
    Mode, E-4–E-16
    changes in dialog boxes, E-5
    changes in left and right panels,
      E-4–E-5
    changes in menus, E-6
  switching to Norton Commander Mode,
    9-26, E-3
  switching to Norton Desktop mode, E-4
  windows automatically closed
    note about, E-3
Norton Desktop
  command-line switches, C-13
  desktop at a glance
    button bar, 1-4, 1-5
    desktop, 1-4, 1-5
    dialog box, 1-4, 1-5
    icon, 1-4, 1-5
    menus, 1-4, 1-5
    windows, 1-4, 1-5
  dialog boxes
    about dialog boxes, 1-16
    alert dialog boxes, 1-26
    browsing for files, 1-23
    check box, 1-21
    combination box, 1-23

Norton Desktop *(continued)*
   command buttons, 1-21
   drop-down list box, 1-22
   group box, 1-20
   list box, 1-22
   navigating in a dialog box, 1-23
   option buttons, 1-21
   prompt button, 1-22
   pull-down menus, 1-23
   text box, 1-22
   using wildcards, 1-26
  drive windows
   about drive windows, 1-12
   closing a drive window, 1-16
   Control menu, 1-13
   drive icons, 1-14–1-15, 9-27
   Maximize/Restore button, 1-14
   navigating in a drive window, 1-17–1-19
   opening a drive window, 1-15
   panes, 1-13
   resize button, 1-12, 1-14
   scroll box, 1-12, 1-14
   selecting a drive window, 1-15–1-16
   status bar, 1-13, 2-6
   title bar, 1-13
  exiting Norton Desktop, 1-3–1-4
  getting Help, 1-30
  navigating in Norton Desktop
   using the button bar, 1-6–1-7
   using hotkeys, 1-6
   using shortcut keys, 1-6
  menus
   about menus, 1-7–1-11
   choosing a command, 1-8–1-9
   closing a menu, 1-9
   navigating in menus, 1-11
   selecting a menu, 1-8
   selecting long menus, 1-10
   selecting short menus, 1-10
  questions and answers, A-3–A-6
  starting Norton Desktop, 1-3

Norton Disk Doctor
  configuring Norton Disk Doctor
   adding a custom message, 18-9
   displaying options, 18-7
   modifying AUTOEXEC.BAT file, 18-3, 18-7
   skipping tests, 18-9
   surface test options, 18-8
  how Norton Disk Doctor works, 18-3
  Norton Disk Doctor tests, 18-3–18-5
  questions and answers, A-8
  using Norton Disk Doctor
   command-line switches, C-14
   diagnosing a disk, 18-5–18-7
   generating a report, 18-9–18-10
   performing a quick test, 18-7
   saving a report as a file, 18-10
   starting Norton Disk Doctor, 18-5
   UnDo (NDDUNDO.DAT) file, 18-9
   undoing changes, 18-5, 18-9
   when to use, 18-3
NORTON DISK DOCTOR command, 18-5
Norton Mail. *See also Installing Norton Desktop for DOS*
  address book
   about the address book, 21-8, 21-27
   backing up with mail lists, 21-36
   changing the type of address, 21-10–21-11
   maintaining
    adding an address, 21-29
    automatically adding addresses, 21-33
    copying an address, 21-11, 21-31
    deleting an address, 21-32
    editing an address, 21-30
    opening the address book, 21-27
    restoring a deleted address, 21-32
   synchronizing with mail lists, 21-36
  command-line switches, C-15
  exiting Norton Mail, 21-4

Norton Mail *(continued)*
  folders
    about the folder system, 21-5–21-6
    copying a message between folders, 21-22–21-23
    changing a folder's location, 21-37
    creating a folder, 21-5, 21-24–21-25
    deleting a folder, 21-26
    moving a message between folders, 21-22
    opening a folder, 21-25
    renaming a folder, 21-26
    sorting messages, 21-26
  how Norton Mail works, 21-3–21-6
  mail lists
    backing up with the address book, 21-36
    changing a mail list's location, 21-37
    maintaining
      creating, 21-34–21-35
      deleting, 21-36
      renaming, 21-35
      viewing contents, 21-35
    synchronizing with address book, 21-36
  MCI accounts
    about MCI accounts, 21-37
    adding an account, 21-38–21-39
    deleting an account, 21-40
    editing account information, 21-40
    viewing an account, 21-39
  MCI settings
    specifying modem settings, 21-42–21-43
    specifying telephone settings, 21-41–21-42
  messages
    adding message handling, 21-14–21-16
    attaching files, 21-12–21-14
    copying a message between folders, 21-22–21-23

Norton Mail *(continued)*
    correcting an error, 21-18–21-19
    creating a message, 21-6–21-8
    deleting a message, 21-23–21-24
    editing a message, 21-21–21-22
    forwarding a message, 21-21
    moving a message between folders, 21-22
    printing a message, 21-23
    reading a message, 21-19
    receiving a message, 21-16–21-18
    replying to a message, 21-20–21-21
    sending a message, 21-16–21-18
  and other electronic mail systems, 21-46
  sending faxes, 21-45
  sending paper mail, 21-46
  sending telex, 21-46
  setup options, 21-43. *See also Installing Norton Desktop for DOS*
  starting Norton Mail, 21-3
Norton Menu
  creating a basic menu
    adding menu items, 30-7–30-8
    selecting a menu, 30-5
    testing a menu, 30-9
  creating an advanced menu
    adding menu items, 30-10
    creating a batch menu item, 30-12–30-13
    creating a submenu, 30-12
    exiting to DOS, 30-15
    keeping messages on the screen, 30-11
    prompting for arguments, 30-11
    selecting a new menu, 30-5
  customizing Norton Menu
    assigning hotkeys automatically, 31-6–31-7
    displaying a confirmation box before deleting, 31-4
    saving your menus automatically, 31-5

Norton Menu *(continued)*
    sounding a security alert, 31-7
    distributing menus
        copying a menu file, 31-11
        exporting a menu, 31-10–31-11
        importing a menu, 31-12
        importing other menu formats, 31-10
        installing for several users, 31-8
        updating a menu automatically, 30-15–30-16, 31-12
        using menus on different computers, 31-8–31-9
    editing menus
        adding a menu item, 30-9, 30-13
        adding a similar menu item, 30-13
        autobuilding a menu, 30-15
        changing the menu title, 30-15
        copying a menu item, 30-13
        deleting a menu, 30-16
        deleting a menu item, 30-14–30-15
        modifying a menu item, 30-13–30-14
        moving a menu item, 30-14
    enabling screen saver, 31-7
    exiting Norton Menu, 30-4
    features, 30-3–30-4
    opening a menu, 30-5
    starting Norton Menu
        from the DOS prompt, 30-4
        using command-line options, 30-4, C-15
    using menus
        choosing an item, 30-17
        moving from one submenu to another, 30-17
        returning to the main menu, 30-17
    when to use Norton Menu, 30-2
Norton Viewer, 7-3–7-15
NSCHED
    Scheduler, 23-3, C-15
    screen saver, 10-3

O

OPEN DRIVE WINDOW... command, 2-3–2-4
OPEN WINDOW... command, 2-1, 8-5, 8-8
optimizing your disk
    using Norton Cache. *See also* Norton Cache
        about Norton Cache, 29-3
        advanced options, 29-15–29-17
        AUTOEXEC.BAT and CONFIG.SYS files, 29-13–29-14
        cache reports, 29-4–29-6
        configuring the cache, 29-17
        deactivating the cache, 29-6–29-7
        DOS FASTOPEN, 29-18
        questions and answers, A-1
        reloading the cache, 29-7
        removing the cache from memory, 29-7–29-8
        resetting the cache, 29-6
        SMARTDrive, 29-19
        system requirements, 29-3–29-4
        and Windows, 29-18
    using Speed Disk
        before using Speed Disk, 17-5
        comparing to CHKDSK, 17-8
        customizing Speed Disk, 17-10–17-15
        generating reports, 17-7–17-9
        how Speed Disk works, 17-4
        using Speed Disk, 17-6–17-7
        using the Walk Map, 17-9
        when to use Speed Disk, 17-3
option buttons, 1-20, 1-21
Overall Performance Index report, 22-10

P

panes
    controlling panes, 2-9
    file pane, 2-3, 2-10–2-11
    tree pane, 2-3, 2-10
    view pane, 2-3, 2-10–2-11

paper mail, 21-46
Partition Table Test, 18-3
partition tables
  displaying, 22-5
  report, 22-6
  saving to Rescue Diskette, 28-6
  virus infections in. *See* Norton AntiVirus
PASSWORD... command, 9-18
passwords
  configuring, 9-18–9-19
  menus, 9-18–9-21, 31-3, 31-5
  Norton AntiVirus, 20-39–20-41
  Norton Desktop, 9-18–9-19
  Sleeper, 10-7–10-8
performance benchmarks, 22-10–22-11
pinout diagrams, 8-14–8-16
PREFERENCES... command, 9-20
preferences, configuring
  adding shadows, 9-24
  displaying drive icons, 9-27–9-28
  including directories, 9-25–9-26
  insert key for tagging files, 9-24
  keystroke preferences, 9-26
  options, 9-20
  scanning floppy drives with Norton AntiVirus, 9-24
  selecting Norton Commander Mode, 9-26
  shutdown routine, 9-21–9-24
  Speed Search, 9-25
PRINT... command, 4-40
PRINTER... command, 9-40
printer options
  configuration file, 9-41–9-44
  selecting, 9-40
problems. *See also* troubleshooting
  questions and answers, A-1–A-24
  system messages, B-1–B-8
  using Disk Tools to correct, 28-3–28-8
  using Image to record system information, 25-4
  viruses. *See* Norton AntiVirus

prompt button, 1-23
PROPERTIES... command, 4-21
protecting your data
  overview of Norton Desktop's data protection features, 1-27–1-29
  using Disk Tools
    creating a Rescue Diskette, 28-6–28-7
    how Disk Tools work, 28-3–28-4
    making a bootable disk, 28-3
    recovering from DOS's Recover, 28-4–28-5
    restoring from a Rescue Diskette, 28-7–28-8
    reviving a defective diskette, 28-5
  using Image program
    how it works, 25-3
    running automatically, 25-3
    running Image, 25-4
    taking snapshot of system area, 25-4
  using Norton AntiVirus. *See also* Norton AntiVirus
    boot-sector infectors, 20-22–20-26
    partition-table infectors, 20-22–20-26
    scanning and inoculating drives, directories and files, 20-15–20-20
  using Norton Backup. *See also* Using the *Norton Backup for DOS*
    about Norton Backup, 19-3–19-5
    before you start, 19-3
    performing a backup, 19-4
    using the Backup Assistant, 19-4–19-5
  using Norton Disk Doctor
    configuring Norton Disk Doctor, 18-7–18-9
    diagnosing a disk, 18-5–18-7
    generating a report, 18-9–18-10
    how Norton Disk Doctor works, 18-3
    Norton Disk Doctor tests, 18-3–18-5
    performing a quick test, 18-7
    saving a report as a file, 18-10
    starting Norton Disk Doctor, 18-5

protecting your data *(continued)*
    undoing changes, 18-5, 18-9
    when to use, 18-3
  using SmartCan
    changing storage limits, 27-7
    default configuration, 27-3
    disabling, 27-4
    displaying options, 27-4
    enabling, 27-4
    excluding files from protection, 27-6
    getting a status report, 27-9
    how SmartCan works, 27-3
    protecting all files, 27-5
    protecting archived files, 27-6
    purging files, 27-7
    questions and answers, A-7–A-8
    RAM required, 27-3
    selecting files to protect, 27-5–27-6
    selecting other drives to protect,
      27-4–27-5
    turning SmartCan off and on, 27-8
PRUNE & GRAFT command, 4-12–4-14

Q
questions and answers, A-1–A-24

R
recovering data
  overview of Norton Desktop's recovery
    features, 1-27–1-29
  using Disk Tools
    creating a Rescue Diskette, 28-6–28-7
    how Disk Tools work, 28-3–28-4
    recovering from DOS's RECOVER,
      28-4
    restoring from a Rescue Diskette,
      28-7–28-8
    reviving a defective diskette, 28-5
  using Image program
    how it works, 25-3
    running automatically, 25-3
    running Image, 25-4

recovering data *(continued)*
    taking snapshot of system area, 25-4
  using Norton AntiVirus
    recovering from boot-sector and
      partition-table viruses, 20-22–20-26
    repairing infected files, 20-22–20-26
  using Norton Backup. *See Using the
    Norton Backup for DOS*
  using Norton Disk Doctor
    diagnosing a disk, 18-5–18-7
    how Norton Disk Doctor works, 18-3
    performing a quick test, 18-7
    starting Norton Disk Doctor, 18-5
    undoing changes, 18-5, 18-9
    when to use, 18-3
  using UnErase
    how UnErase works, 16-3
    manual UnErase, 16-7–16-10
    recovering erased files, 16-4–16-10
    starting UnErase, 16-4
  using UnFormat
    how UnFormat works, 26-3–26-4
    unformatting a disk without the
      Image file, 26-4, 26-8
    using UnFormat to recover a disk,
      26-5–26-9
    when to use UnFormat, 26-3
recovering from DOS's RECOVER, 28-4
REFRESH command, 7-9
RENAME... command, 4-17
renaming files, 4-17
reports
  Norton Disk Doctor reports, 18-9–18-10
  Speed Disk, 17-7
  system information reports, 22-3–22-11
Rescue Diskette
  creating, 28-6–28-7
  restoring from, 28-7–28-8
restoring from a Rescue Diskette,
  28-7–28-8
RUN... command
  using to launch files, 6-8–6-9

S

Safe Format, 3-7, C-16–C-17
SAVE CONFIGURATION... command, 9-49
Scheduler
   closing Scheduler, 23-12
   command-line switches, C-15
   how Scheduler works, 23-4–23-5
   starting Scheduler, 23-3
   using Scheduler
      adding an event, 23-6–23-9
      changing the month display, 23-4
      confirming events before running, 23-9–23-10
      creating a batch file, 23-10–23-11
      deleting events, 23-11
      editing a batch file, 23-10
      editing an event, 23-10
      exiting Scheduler without saving changes, 23-12
      scheduling backups. *See Using the Norton Backup for DOS*
      setting the frequency, 23-7
      setting viewing options, 23-5
      using Norton Utilities with Scheduler, 23-12
      viewing events, 23-5–23-6
SCHEDULER command, 23-3
screen options, configuring, 9-32–9-36
SCREEN SAVER... command, 9-39
screen saver, configuring, 10-3–10-9
searching for files with SuperFind
   batch files
      creating from matching files, 5-13
      editing existing batch files, 5-15
      loading existing batch files, 5-15
   defining a search
      customizing file sets, 5-7–5-9
      customizing location sets, 5-10–5-13
      deleting file sets, 5-9
      deleting location sets, 5-13
      editing file sets, 5-8–5-9
      editing location sets, 5-12–5-13

searching for files with SuperFind *(continued)*
   searching in multiple locations, 5-9–5-10
   selecting a directory, 5-11–5-12
   selecting drives, 5-10–5-11
   specifying files, 5-3–5-7
   specifying where to search, 5-9–5-13
   using wildcards, 5-6–5-7
   making searches case-sensitive, 5-13
   starting SuperFind, 5-3
SELECT command, 4-6–4-7
   ALL, 4-7
   SOME..., 4-7
   INVERT, 4-7
selecting a drive window, 2-5–2-7, 2-19
selecting files, 4-3, 4-6–4-8
sending mail messages. *See* Norton Mail
sending network messages. *See* network messages
SERVE REMOTE LINK... command, 8-4, 8-8
SFORMAT (Safe Format) command, 3-7, C-16–C-17
shadows, displaying, 9-24
short menus, selecting 1-10, 9-4, 9-18
Sleeper. *See* screen saver
SMARTCAN (SmartCan) command, C-16
SmartCan. *See also* UnErase
   command-line switches, C-17–C-18
   configuring SmartCan, 27-3–27-7
      changing storage limits, 27-7
      default configuration, 27-3
      disabling, 27-4
      displaying options, 27-4
      enabling, 27-4
      excluding files from protection, 27-6
      protecting all files, 27-5
      protecting archived files, 27-6
      selecting files to protect, 27-5–27-6
      selecting other drives to protect, 27-4–27-5
   getting a status report, 27-9

Index **I-21**

SmartCan *(continued)*
  how SmartCan works, 27-3
  purging files, 27-7–27-8
  questions and answers, A-7–A-8
  RAM required, 27-3
  turning SmartCan off and on, 27-8
SMARTDrive, 29-19
snapshot of your system, 25-4
Software Interrupts report, 22-5
sorting files, 2-14–2-16
source floppy disk, 3-3
Speed Disk
  before using Speed Disk, 17-5
  comparing to CHKDSK, 17-8
  customizing Speed Disk, 17-10
  generating reports, 17-7–17-9
  how Speed Disk works, 17-4
  questions and answers, A-9–A-10
  using Speed Disk, 17-6–17-7
  using the Walk Map, 17-9
  when to use Speed Disk, 17-3
SPEED DISK command, 17-6
SPEEDISK (Speed Disk) command, 17-6, C-18
Speed Search box, 2-6–2-9, 9-25
starting an application
  about launching files, 6-3
  launching a file
    at system startup, 6-6
    from a DOS session, 6-10
    from the DOS command line, 6-9
    from the file pane, 6-7–6-8
    using the RUN... command, 6-8
starting Norton Desktop, 1-3
status bar, 1-13, 2-6
SuperFind, using to find files
  batch files, 5-14–5-16
  defining a search
    customizing file sets, 5-7–5-9
    customizing location sets, 5-10–5-13
    deleting file sets, 5-9
    deleting location sets, 5-13

SuperFind *(continued)*
  editing file sets, 5-8–5-9
  editing location sets, 5-12–5-13
  searching in multiple locations, 5-9–5-10
  selecting a directory, 5-11–5-12
  selecting drives, 5-10–5-11
  specifying files, 5-3–5-7
  specifying where to search, 5-9–5-13
  using wildcards, 5-6–5-7
  making searches case-sensitive, 5-9–5-13
  starting SuperFind, 5-3
Surface Test, 18-4
syntax for command-line utilities, C-4–C-5
SYSINFO (System Information) command, C-19
System Information
  how system information works, 22-3
  printing reports, 22-11
  starting system information, 22-3, C-19
  System Information reports
    CMOS Status, 22-5
    CPU Speed, 22-10
    Device Drivers, 22-10
    Disk Characteristics, 22-5–22-6
    Disk Summary, 22-5
    Expanded Memory, 22-7–22-8
    Extended Memory, 22-8–22-9
    Hard Disk Speed, 22-10
    Hardware Interrupts, 22-4
    Memory Block List, 22-9
    Memory Usage Summary, 22-7
    Network Information, 22-5
    Network Performance Speed, 22-10
    Overall Performance Index, 22-10
    Partition Tables, 22-6
    Software Interrupts, 22-5
    System Summary, 22-4
    TSR Programs, 22-10
    Video Summary, 22-4

I-22 Using Norton Desktop for DOS

System Information *(continued)*
  viewing your CONFIG.SYS and AUTOEXEC.BAT files, 22-11
    See also editing text files, viewing files
SYSTEM INFORMATION command, 22-3
system messages
  general, B-3
  launching files, B-3
  managing disks, B-5–B-7
  managing files, B-3–B-5
  network, B-8
  when system messages are displayed, B-1
system snapshot, 25-4. *See also* Image
System Summary report, 22-4

T

taking a snapshot of system area
  using Image program, 25-4
target floppy disk, 3-3
telex
  sending by Norton Mail, 21-46
text box, 1-22
text files, editing, 4-25–4-40
TILE command, 2-20
tiling windows, 2-20
Tools menu, F-5
  CALCULATOR command, 13-3
  CALENDAR command, 14-3
  DOS SESSION command, 6-10–6-11
  EDIT MENU... command, 12-3
  MAIL command, 21-3
  MENU command, 11-3
  NETWORK MESSAGE... command, 15-3
  NORTON ANTIVIRUS command, 20-14
  NORTON BACKUP command, 19-4
  NORTON DISK DOCTOR command, 18-5
  SCHEDULER command, 23-3
  SPEED DISK command, 17-6, C-18
  SYSTEM INFORMATION command, 22-3
  UNERASE command, 16-4, C-20

tree pane
  using in a drive window, 2-3, 2-10
troubleshooting
  questions and answers, A-1–A-24
  using Disk Tools
    how Disk Tools work, 28-3–28-4
    making a bootable disk, 28-3
    recovering from DOS's RECOVER, 28-4–28-5
    restoring from a Rescue Diskette, 28-7–28-8
    reviving a defective diskette, 28-5
  using Image program
    how it works, 25-3
    running automatically, 25-3
    running Image, 25-4
    taking snapshot of system area, 25-4
  using Norton Disk Doctor
    configuring Norton Disk Doctor, 18-7–18-9
    diagnosing a disk, 18-5–18-7
    generating a report, 18-9–18-10
    how Norton Disk Doctor works, 18-3
    Norton Disk Doctor tests, 18-4
    performing a quick test, 18-7
    starting Disk Doctor, 18-5
    undoing changes, 18-5, 18-9
    when to use, 18-3
  using System Information
    how system information works, 22-3
    starting system information, 22-3
    system information reports, 22-5
    viewing your CONFIG.SYS and AUTOEXEC.BAT files, 22-11
    when to use system information, 22-3
  using UnErase
    how UnErase works, 16-3
    manual UnErase, 16-7–16-10
    recovering erased files, 16-4–16-10
    starting UnErase, 16-4
TSR Programs report, 22-10

U

UnDo (NDDUNDO.DAT) file, 18-9
UnErase
   and SmartCan, 16-3
   how UnErase works, 16-3
   manual UnErase, 16-7–16-10
      about manual UnErase, 16-7–16-8
      choosing clusters, 16-8–16-9
      saving your work, 16-10
      when to use, 16-7
   questions and answers, A-8
   recovering erased files, 16-4–16-10
      checking recovered files, 16-6
      more than one or all erased files in a directory, 16-6
      on network drive, A-8
      when directory cannot be recovered, 16-7
      when directory has been removed, 16-6
      when directory is unknown, 16-5
      when filename and directory are known, 16-4
      when filename is unknown, 16-7
   starting UnErase, 16-4
   UnErase and DOS 5.0, 16-10
UNERASE (UnErase) command, 16-4, C-20
UNERASE command, 16-4
UnFormat
   how UnFormat works, 26-3–26-4
   unformatting a disk without the Image file, 26-4, 26-8
   using Unformat to recover a disk, 26-5–26-9
   when to use UnFormat, 26-3
UNFORMAT (UnFormat) command, 26-5, C-20

V

VIDEO/MOUSE... command, 9-32
video and mouse options, configuring
   confirming selections, 9-36

video and mouse options, configuring *(continued)*
   customizing colors, 9-34–9-35
   customizing display, 9-35–9-36
   selecting mouse options, 9-36–9-38
   setting screen colors, 9-33–9-35
Video Summary report, 22-4
VIEW (Norton Viewer) command, C-19
VIEW... command, 7-4
VIEWER command, 7-9
viewing files
   changing viewers, 7-9
   compressed files, 4-24
   graphic files, 7-13–7-15
      flipping the image, 7-13
      inverting the image, 7-15
      refreshing the screen, 7-15
      rotating the image, 7-15
      scrolling the image, 7-13–7-14
      zooming the image, 7-14
   in Norton Viewer
      exiting Norton Viewer, 7-7
      opening Norton Viewer, 7-5
      selecting a file to view, 7-7
      viewing a database file, 7-7–7-8
   searching files for data, 7-11
   in the view pane, 7-3–7-5
   word wrapping text, 7-9
View menu, F-4
   DOS BACKGROUND command, 6-9
   FILE DETAILS... command, 2-11, 2-14
   FILE PANE command, 2-10
   FILTER command, 2-10, 2-12
   REFRESH command, 2-17
   SHOW ENTIRE DRIVE command, 2-11, 2-16
   SORT BY command, 2-11, 2-15, 2-16
   TREE PANE command, 2-10
   VIEWER, 7-9
view pane
   about the view pane, 2-3, 2-11
   closing, 7-5
   opening, 7-3
   viewing files in, 7-3–7-5

VIEW PANE command, 2-11, 7-3
Virus Clinic. *See also* Norton AntiVirus
  boot-sector and partition-table infections, 20-22–20-26
  executable infections, 20-20, 20-22
  exiting Virus Clinic, 20-28
  removing inoculation file, 20-16–20-17
  repairing infected files, 20-20–20-28
  restoring boot sector and partition table from Rescue Diskette, 20-24–20-26, A-17–A-19
  restoring boot sector of infected floppy disk, 20-25–20-26
  restoring boot sector without Rescue Diskette, 20-25
  restoring partition table without Rescue Diskette, 20-25
  scanning and inoculating files, directories and drives, 20-15–20-18
  scanning memory, 20-14–20-15
  scan results, 20-17–20-20
  starting Virus Clinic, 20-14
  system file and COMMAND.COM infections, 20-26
viruses. *See* Norton AntiVirus
Virus Intercept. *See also* Norton AntiVirus
  backup programs, 20-13

Virus Intercept *(continued)*
  Boot Sector alert box, 20-9
  communications programs, 20-12
  copying floppy disks and files, 20-12
  DOS format, 20-13
  file-compression programs, 20-12
  loading, 20-5
  and other programs, 20-11–20-13
  protecting itself, 20-11
  reinoculating files, 20-10–20-11
  responding to messages, 20-8
  versions, 20-7
  Virus Infection alert box, 20-8
volume label, 3-7, 3-10

W

Walk Map, using 17-9
wildcards, 5-6–5-7
Window menu
  CASCADE command, 2-19
  CLOSE ALL command, 2-21
  COMPARE WINDOWS command, 4-18
  HIDE ALL command, 2-21
  OPEN DRIVE WINDOW... command, 2-3
  OPEN WINDOW... command, 8-5, 8-8
  TILE command, 2-20
write-protection, 28-7

SYMANTEC CUSTOMER SERVICE PLAN (CSP)

Registration
To register your Symantec product, fill out the registration card included with it and drop the card in the mail.

Customer Service
Call Customer Service to:

- Register your Symantec product.
- Order an upgrade.
- Request product information or demonstration disks.
- Change your registration address.
- Obtain referrals to dealers and consultants.
- Request the replacement of missing or defective pieces (disks, manuals, etc.).
- Obtain general product information.

Customer Service handles all Symantec products. Contact Technical Support for specific questions about how to use software in the Norton product line.

If you are located outside the United States or Canada, please contact your local Symantec office or distributor for product support.

Replacing a Defective Disk
All Symantec products have a limited 90-day warranty. To replace a defective disk that is still under warranty, use the Disk Replacement Coupon enclosed in your software package.

Changing Your Registration Address
You can either mail, fax, or phone in your new address to Customer Service. Please mark your request to the attention of Customer Registration.

Technical Support

Contact Technical Support if you have a specific question about how to use software in the Norton product line. Refer to the following list for the appropriate telephone number. If you are located outside the United States or Canada, please contact your local Symantec office or distributor for technical support.

Before you call Technical Support, please fill out the Personal System Information form at the end of this section. Having this information on hand when you call will save you time and will allow us to better assist you.

Symantec BBS

You can get help or information electronically by accessing the Symantec Corporation bulletin board system (BBS). The Symantec BBS is available 24 hours a day; it provides a Customer Service forum, public-domain software, and product support forums for Symantec software.

Settings for Symantec bulletin board are: 8 data bits, 1 stop bit; no parity.

CompuServe

Symantec maintains the Symantec Forum on CompuServe, where you can exchange information and ideas with Symantec representatives and with other users of Symantec products. Check with CompuServe for data-communications settings to use.

If you don't have a CompuServe account, call (800) 848-8199, representative #124, to request a free introductory membership.

To access the Symantec Forum on CompuServe, type GO NORTON at any ! prompt. You can find the current Norton AntiVirus virus definitions file in the NORUTIL Forum, in the NAV-IBM Library Section.

Virus Definitions Update Disk Service

Symantec's virus definitions update disk service supplies floppy disks containing the most current virus definitions file available at the time your order is processed; updates are normally available quarterly.

To order, call (800) 343-4714, ext. 756.
Current fee: $12, excluding shipping, handling and applicable taxes.

CUSTOMER SERVICE AND TECHNICAL SUPPORT

Customer Service
Symantec Corp.
10201 Torre Ave.
Cupertino, CA 95014-9854

(800) 441-7234 United States and Canada only
(408) 255-3344 fax
Hours: 7:00 A.M.–5:00 P.M. Pacific Time (Mon.–Fri.)

Technical Support
Symantec Corp.
2500 Broadway Ave.
Suite 200
Santa Monica, CA 90404-3063

(310) 449-4900 DOS/Windows products
(310) 449-4990 Macintosh products
(310) 829-0247 fax
Hours: 7:00 A.M.–5:00 P.M. Pacific Time (Mon.–Fri.)

Symantec BBS
300-, 1200-, and 2400-baud modems
9600-baud modems only

(408) 973-9598 (24 hours)
(408) 973-9834 (24 hours)

Faxline
(virus definitions)

(310) 575-5018 from fax machine or touch-tone phone (have fax number ready)
(310) 477-2707 for assistance

International
United Kingdom

Symantec UK Limited
MKA House
36 King Street
Maidenhead
Berkshire
SL6 1EF
England

0628 776343 voice
0628 776775 fax

Europe
(all countries except UK)

Symantec Europe
Kanaalpark 145
Postbus 1143
2321 JV Leiden
Holland

31 71 353 111 voice
31 71 353 150 fax

Australia

Symantec Pty. Ltd.
Upper Level
408 Victoria Road
Gladesville, NSW 2111
Australia

61 2 879 6577 voice
61 2 879 6805 fax

All other countries

Symantec Corp.
10201 Torre Ave.
Cupertino, CA 95014
U.S.A.

(408) 252-3570 voice
(408) 253-4992 fax

PERSONAL SYSTEM INFORMATION

Symantec Software: Product Name _____

Version _____

Serial Number (if applicable) _____

Hardware: Computer _____

Model _____

RAM (random-access memory, in MB) _____

Operating System Software: ❏ MS-DOS Version _____

❏ Windows Version _____

❏ Macintosh System Version _____

Miscellaneous: *Include manufacturer name, product name, and model number for hardware, if known*

Hard Disk _____

Capacity (in MB) _____

Type: ❏ SCSI ❏ ESDI ❏ RLL ❏ MFM

❏ IDE ❏ Other _____

Video Board/Monitor _____

Printer/Plotter _____

RAM Expansion Board _____

Modem _____ Speed (in baud) _____

Other Hardware _____

TSRs/Device Drivers/Memory Managers/Other Software

_____